Services and Business Computing Solutions with XML:
Applications for Quality Management and Best Processes

Patrick C. K. Hung
University of Ontario Institute of Technology, Canada

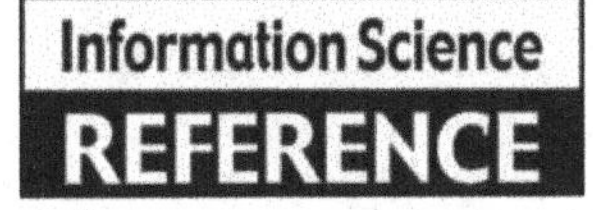

INFORMATION SCIENCE REFERENCE
Hershey · New York

Director of Editorial Content:	Kristin Klinger
Senior Managing Editor:	Jamie Snavely
Managing Editor:	Jeff Ash
Assistant Managing Editor:	Carole Coulson
Typesetter:	Jeff Ash
Cover Design:	Lisa Tosheff
Printed at:	Yurchak Printing Inc.

Published in the United States of America by
Information Science Reference (an imprint of IGI Global)
701 E. Chocolate Avenue
Hershey PA 17033
Tel: 717-533-8845
Fax: 717-533-8661
E-mail: cust@igi-global.com
Web site: http://www.igi-global.com/reference

and in the United Kingdom by
Information Science Reference (an imprint of IGI Global)
3 Henrietta Street
Covent Garden
London WC2E 8LU
Tel: 44 20 7240 0856
Fax: 44 20 7379 0609
Web site: http://www.eurospanbookstore.com

Copyright © 2009 by IGI Global. All rights reserved. No part of this publication may be reproduced, stored or distributed in any form or by any means, electronic or mechanical, including photocopying, without written permission from the publisher.

Product or company names used in this set are for identification purposes only. Inclusion of the names of the products or companies does not indicate a claim of ownership by IGI Global of the trademark or registered trademark.

Library of Congress Cataloging-in-Publication Data

Services and business computing solutions with XML : applications for quality management and best processes / Patrick C.K. Hung, editor.
p. cm.
Includes bibliographical references and index.

Summary: "This book collects the latest research that describe the use and synergy between data structure technologies"--Provided by publisher.

ISBN 978-1-60566-330-2 (hbk.) -- ISBN 978-1-60566-331-9 (ebook) 1. XML (Document markup language) 2. Web services. 3. Business--Data processing. I. Hung, Patrick C. K.

QA76.76.H94S2578 2009
006.7'4--dc22

2009005270

British Cataloguing in Publication Data
A Cataloguing in Publication record for this book is available from the British Library.

All work contributed to this book is new, previously-unpublished material. The views expressed in this book are those of the authors, but not necessarily of the publisher.

Editorial Advisory Board

Lalita Narupiyakul, *University of Ontario Institute of Technology, Canada*
Dickson K. W. Chiu, *Dickson Computer System, Hong Kong*
Chengfei Liu, *Swinburne University of Technology, Australia*
S.C. Cheung, *Hong Kong University of Science and Technology, Hong Kong*

Table of Contents

Detailed Table of Contents

Preface xiv

Chapter I
Extending XML Types Using Updates 1
Béatrice Bouchou, Université François Rabelais Tours, France
Denio Duarte, Universidade Comunitária Regional de Chapecó, Brazil
Mírian Halfeld Ferrari, Université François Rabelais Tours, France
Martin A. Musicante, Universidade Federal do Rio Grande do Norte, Brazil

The XML Messaging Protocol, a part of the Web service protocol stack, is responsible for encoding messages in a common XML format (or type), so that they can be understood at either end of a network connection. The evolution of an XML type may be required in order to reflect new communication needs, materialized by slightly different XML messages. For instance, due to a service evolution, it might be interesting to extend a type in order to allow the reception of more information, when it is available, instead of always disregarding it. The authors' proposal consists in a conservative XML schema evolution. The framework is as follows: administrators enter updates performed on a valid XML document in order to specify new documents expected to be valid, and our system computes new types accepting both such documents and previously valid ones. Changing the type is mainly changing regular expressions that define element content models. They present the algorithm that implements this approach, its properties and experimental results.

Chapter II
A Comparative Study of XML Change Detection Algorithms 22
Grégory Cobéna, INRIA, France
Talel Abdessalem, Telecom ParisTech, France

Change detection is an important part of version management for databases and document archives. The success of XML has recently renewed interest in change detection on trees and semi-structured data, and various algorithms have been proposed. We study different algorithms and representations of changes based on their formal definition and on experiments conducted over XML data from the Web. Our goal is to provide an evaluation of the quality of the results, the performance of the tools and, based on this, guide the users in choosing the appropriate solution for their applications.

Active XML (AXML) provides an elegant platform to integrate the power of XML, Web services and Peer to Peer (P2P) paradigms by allowing (active) Web service calls to be embedded within XML documents. In this chapter, the authors present some interesting aspects encountered while investigating a transactional framework for AXML systems. They present an integrated locking protocol for the scenario where the structure of both data and transactions are nested. They show how to construct the undo operations dynamically, and outline an algorithm to compute a correct optimum undo order in the presence of nesting and parallelism. Finally, to overcome the inherent problem of peer disconnection, the authors propose an innovative solution based on "chaining" the active peers for early detection and recovery from peer disconnection.

With the emergence of the World Wide Web, business' databases are increasingly being queried directly by customers. The customers may not be aware of the exact structure of the underlying data, and might have never learned a query language that enables them to issue structured queries. Some of the employees who query the databases may also not be aware of the structure of the data, but they are likely to be aware of some labels of elements containing the data. There is a need for a dual search engine that accommodates both business employees and customers. We propose in this chapter an XML search engine called SEEC, which accepts Keyword-Based queries (which can be used for answering customers' queries) and Loosely Structured queries (which can be used for answering employees' queries). We proposed previously a stand-alone Loosely Structured search engine called OOXSearch (Taha & Elmasri, 2007). SEEC integrates OOXSearch with a Keyword-Based search engine and uses novel search techniques. It is built on top of an XQuery search engine (Katz, 2005). SEEC was evaluated experimentally and compared with three recently proposed systems: XSEarch (Cohen & Mamou & Sagiv, 2003), Schema Free XQuery (Li & Yu & Jagadish, 2004), and XKSearch (Xu & Papakonstantinou, 2005). The results showed marked improvement.

More and more systems provide data through web service interfaces and these data have to be integrated with the legacy relational databases of the enterprise. The integration is usually done with enterprise

The tremendous growth of the Internet has introduced a number of interoperability problems for distributed multimedia applications. These problems are related to the heterogeneity of client devices, network connectivity, content formats, and user's preferences. The challenge is even bigger for multimedia content providers who are faced with the dilemma of finding the combination of different variants of a content to create, store, and send to their subscribers that maximize their satisfaction and hence entice them to come back. In this chapter, the authors will present a framework for trans-coding multimedia streams using an orchestration of Web-services. The framework takes into consideration the profile of communicating devices, network connectivity, exchanged content formats, context description, users' preferences, and available adaptation services to find a chain of adaptation services that should be applied to the content to make it more satisfactory to clients. The framework was implemented as a core component for an architecture that supports personal and service mobility.

In this chapter, the authors apply type-theoretic techniques to the service description and composition verification. A flexible type system is introduced for modeling instances and mappings of semi-structured data, and is demonstrated to be effective in modeling a wide range of data services, ranging from relational database queries to web services for XML. Type-theoretic analysis and verification are then reduced to the problem of type unification. Some (in)tractability results of the unification problem and the expressiveness of their proposed type system are presented in this chapter. Finally, the auhtors construct a complete unification algorithm which runs in EXP-TIME in the worst case, but runs in polynomial time for a large family of unification problems rising from practical type analysis of service compositions.

Compared to other middleware approaches like CORBA or Java RMI the protocol overhead of SOAP is very high. This fact is not only disadvantageous for several performance-critical applications, but especially in environments with limited network bandwidth or resource-constrained computing devices. Although recent research work concentrated on more compact, binary representations of XML data only very few approaches account for the special characteristics of SOAP communication. In this article we will discuss the most relevant state-of-the-art technologies for compressing XML data. Furthermore, we will present a novel solution for compacting SOAP messages. In order to achieve significantly better compression rates than current approaches, our compressor utilizes structure information from an XML Schema or WSDL document. With this additional knowledge on the "grammar" of the exchanged messages, our compressor generates a single custom pushdown automaton, which can be used as a highly efficient validating parser as well as a highly efficient compressor. The main idea is to tag the transitions of the automaton with short binary identifiers that are then used to encode the path trough the automaton during parsing. Our approach leads to extremely compact data representations and is also usable in environments with very limited CPU and memory resources.

Laura Irina Rusu, La Trobe University, Australia
Wenny Rahayu, La Trobe University, Australia
David Taniar, Monash University, Australia

This chapter presents some of the existing mining techniques for extracting association rules out of XML documents in the context of rapid changes in the Web knowledge discovery area. The initiative of this study was driven by the fast emergence of XML (eXtensible Markup Language) as a standard language for representing semistructured data and as a new standard of exchanging information between different applications. The data exchanged as XML documents become richer and richer every day, so the necessity to not only store these large volumes of XML data for later use, but to mine them as well to discover interesting information has became obvious. The hidden knowledge can be used in various ways, for example, to decide on a business issue or to make predictions about future e-customer behaviour in a Web application. One type of knowledge that can be discovered in a collection of XML documents relates to association rules between parts of the document, and this chapter presents some of the top techniques for extracting them.

Wan-Yeung Wong, The Chinese University of Hong Kong, Hong Kong, China
Tak-Pang Lau, The Chinese University of Hong Kong, Hong Kong, China
Irwin King, The Chinese University of Hong Kong, Hong Kong, China
Michael R. Lyu, The Chinese University of Hong Kong, Hong Kong, China

This chapter gives a tutorial on resource description framework (RDF), its XML representation, and Jena, a set of Java-based API designed and implemented to further simplify the manipulation of RDF documents. RDF is a W3C standard which provides a common framework for describing resources in the World Wide Web and other applications. Under this standard framework with the Jena, different resources can be manipulated and exchanged easily, which leads to cost reduction and better efficiency in business applications. In this tutorial, we present some basic concepts and applications of RDF and Jena. In particular, we use a television object to illustrate the usage of RDF in describing various resources being used, the XML syntax in representing the RDF, and the ways Jena manipulate various RDF documents. Furthermore, complete programming codes with detailed explanations are also presented to give readers a better understanding of Jena. References are given at the end for readers' further investigation.

Abbass Ghanbary, MethodScience.com & University of Western Sydney, Australia
Bhuvan Unhelkar, MethodScience.com & University of Western Sydney, Australia

Web Services (WS) technologies, generally built around the ubiquitous Extensible Markup Language (XML), have provided many opportunities for integrating enterprise applications. However, XML/Simple Object Access Protocol (SOAP), together with Web Services Definition Language (WSDL) and Universal Description Discovery and Integration (UDDI), form a comprehensive suite of WS technologies that have the potential to transcend beyond mere application integration within an organization, and to provide capabilities of integrating processes across multiple organizations. Currently, the WS paradigm is driven through parameters however; the paradigm shift that can result in true collaborative business requires us to consider the business paradigm in terms of policies-processes-standards. This chapter, based on experimental research carried out by the authors, demonstrates how the technologies of WS open up the doors to collaborative Enterprise Architecture Integration (EAI) and Service Oriented Architecture (SOA) resulting in Business Integration (BI). The chapter also provide a quantitative investigation based on organization's adaptation to mobile and Web Services technologies.

This chapter describes the application of MDA (model driven architecture) and UML for the modeling and specification of collaborative business processes, with the purpose of enabling enterprises to establish business-to-business collaborations. The proposed MDA approach provides the components and techniques required for the development of collaborative processes from their conceptual modeling to the specifications of these processes and the partners' interfaces in a B2B standard. As part of this MDA approach, a UML profile is provided that extends the semantics of UML2 to support the analysis and design of collaborative processes. This UML profile is based on the use of interaction protocols to model collaborative processes. The application of this UML profile in a case study is presented. Also, an overview is provided about the automatic generation of B2B specifications from conceptual models of collaborative processes. In particular, the generation of B2B specifications based on ebXML is described.

As a result of Hurricane Katrina, the destruction of property, assets, documentation, and human life in the Gulf Port has introduced a myriad of challenging issues. These issues involve human, social, government, and technological concerns. This chapter does not address the many immediate human and social concerns brought forth from a natural disaster or major terrorist attack (NDMTA); this chapter addresses a small but significant problem of re-establishing or laying the groundwork for an enterprise architecture for local government during the response phase of the disaster. Specifically, it addresses constructing a high-level data model and fundamental SOA, utilizing the remaining local assets, XML (extensible markup language), and Web services.

The eXtensible Business Reporting Language (XBRL) is an emerging XML-based standard which has the potential to significantly improve the efficiency and effectiveness of intra- and inter-organisational information supply chains in e-business. In this chapter, we present the case for using convergent interviews as an appropriate and efficient method for modelling factors impacting the adoption of emerging and under-researched innovations, such as XBRL. Using this method, we identify environmental, organisational, and innovation-related factors as they apply to XBRL adoption and diffusion. Contentious factors, such as the role of government organisations, XBRL education and training, and the readiness of XBRL as an innovation, and its supporting software solutions are also examined in detail. Taken together, these discussions constitute an important step towards theory development for emergent e-business innovations. Practical adoptions strategies and their implications are also discussed.

Preface

The Extensible Markup Language (XML) is used to represent fine-grained data that originates in repositories in machine readable format by providing structure and the possibility of adding type information, such as XML Schema. A Web service is a software system that supports interoperable application-to-application interaction over the Internet. Web services are based on a set of XML standards, such as Web Services Description Language (WSDL), Simple Object Access Protocol (SOAP), and Universal Description, Discovery and Integration (UDDI). Each service makes its functionality available through well-defined or standardized XML interfaces. The result of this approach is a Service-Oriented Architecture (SOA). XML is playing an important role in the data transport protocol for Web services. For example, SOAP messages are used both by service requestors to invoke Web services, and by Web services to answer requests. This book aims to explore and investigate various research issues of XML data and related applications that are encapsulated by Web services over the network. In particular, we call these networked services as XML services.

Many commercial systems built today are increasingly using these technologies together and it is important to understand the various research and practical issues. The goal of this book is to bring together academics and practitioners to describe the use and synergy between the above-mentioned technologies. This book is mainly intended for researchers and students working in computer science and engineering, and for industry technology providers, having particular interests in XML services as well as for users of Web service and grid computing technologies.

This book is structured as follows. Chapter I presents a XML technical framework for administrators to dynamically update a valid XML document without interfering with other documents in the XML database. Then Chapter II describes the mechanism of change detection on semi-structured XML data with various efficient algorithms for the XML databases. Next, Chapter III discusses an active XML transaction approach to support locking protocol, dynamic construction of undo operation and chaining the active peers. Based on the fundamental technologies for handling XML databases, Chapter IV proposes an XML search engine which accepts keyword-based queries and loosely structured queries.

Chapter V presents an enterprise information system which integrates different XML data sources by using Web services in the application domain of the digital libraries. Next, Chapter VI describes an integration technique that embeds a declarative data transformation technique based on Semantic data models. Chapter VII addresses an approach automatically generates the data access components. Further, Chapter VIII proposes a Web service-based framework for transcoding multimedia streams that supports personal and service mobility. Chapter IX applies type-theoretic techniques to the service description and composition verification. Applying the XML technologies into an illustrative example, Chapter X discusses the state-of-the-art technologies for compressing XML data and compacting SOAP messages.

On the other hand, Chapter XI presents some of the existing mining techniques for extracting association rules out of XML documents in the context of Web knowledge discovery area. For illustration,

Chapter XII gives a tutorial on resource description framework (RDF) and Jena for manipulating RDF documents. Chapter XIII demonstrates the support of Web service technologies in Enterprise Architecture Integration (EAI) and Business Integration (BI).

Chapter XIV describes the application of model-driven architecture (MDA) and UML for modeling business-to-business collaborations. Next, Chapter XV presents an enterprise SOA framework for government during the response phase of the disaster. Chapter XVI discusses the cases for using convergent interviews as an appropriate and efficient method for modelling factors impacting the adoption of emerging and under-researched innovations with XBRL.

Patrick C. K. Hung
University of Ontario Institute of Technology (UOIT), Canada

Chapter I
Extending XML Types Using Updates

Béatrice Bouchou
Université François Rabelais Tours, France

Denio Duarte
Universidade Comunitária Regional de Chapecó, Brazil

Mírian Halfeld Ferrari
Université François Rabelais Tours, France

Martin A. Musicante
Universidade Federal do Rio Grande do Norte, Brazil

ABSTRACT

The XML Messaging Protocol, a part of the Web service protocol stack, is responsible for encoding messages in a common XML format (or type), so that they can be understood at either end of a network connection. The evolution of an XML type may be required in order to reflect new communication needs, materialized by slightly different XML messages. For instance, due to a service evolution, it might be interesting to extend a type in order to allow the reception of more information, when it is available, instead of always disregarding it. The authors' proposal consists in a conservative XML schema evolution. The framework is as follows: administrators enter updates performed on a valid XML document in order to specify new documents expected to be valid, and the system computes new types accepting both such documents and previously valid ones. Changing the type is mainly changing regular expressions that define element content models. They present the algorithm that implements this approach, its properties and experimental results.

Copyright © 2009, IGI Global, distributing in print or electronic forms without written permission of IGI Global is prohibited.

INTRODUCTION

The main contribution of the World Wide Web is data exchange. The advent of web services has compelled researchers to investigate different problems concerning XML data when encapsulated, to be used over the network. Several technologies have been proposed in order to support service interactions. However, these technologies do not consider the significant problem of how to reconcile structural differences between types of XML documents supported by two different web services. Indeed, given two web services, they can be required to communicate by exchanging some XML documents. The type (schema) of the documents should be known by both parties. The successful composition of the services relays on this condition.

Sometimes, changes in the requirements of a service (or simple convenience of programming), promote modifications on the schema of documents used by the next version of a service (w.r.t. the ones produced by previous versions). This can affect the behaviour of the composed service, since the new documents produced or expected by the modified service do not match the agreed type. If the modifications are unavoidable, then the type of the documents, as expected by the other services, needs to be changed. As the new type is a modified version of the old one, we say that the new type is *an evolution* of the original one.

It would be interesting to achieve the evolution of this type in a validity-preserving way. More precisely, we would like to change our XML type in order to accept documents built on a slightly different format, without modifying the XML documents valid w.r.t. our original type. In other words, we would like to perform a *conservative* schema evolution.

Non-conservative schema evolution is problematic: documents valid for the original schema are no more guaranteed to meet the structural constraints described by the evolved schema. These documents should be revalidated against the new schema and, if they are not valid, they should be adapted to it. When documents to be revalidated are stored in different sites, not only their transfer cost should be considered (in addition to the whole revalidation cost) but also problems due to the access control should be faced. Several proposals consist in offering schema update primitives and, subsequently, in performing a transformation (with or without user interference) to the XML documents. Although some methods propose to revalidate only the parts of the documents involved in the schema updates, revalidation can still be considered as an expensive step of this schema evolution mechanism.

To achieve our goal, we foresee two important steps. The second one is the kernel of our work:

1. Compare two different XML documents *D* and *D'* in order to determine the structural differences between them. These structural differences can be expressed by means of the necessary update operations on *D* to obtain *D'*.
2. Given a set of updates on *D*, if the update is incompatible with the type of *D*, adapt the type in order to obtain a more general type that meets both the document structure produced by the update and the original document structure.

The first step has been treated in the area of tree matching (for instance, in (Wang, Zhang, Jeong & Shasha, 1994; Zhang, Statman, & Shasha, 1992)). The second step is, to our knowledge, much more unexplored, since other schema evolution approaches are not consistency preserving, i.e., they impose changes on documents which were valid w.r.t. to the original schema.

Different situations may require changing XML type in order to accept documents built on a slightly different format, without modifying the XML documents valid w.r.t. an original type. The following three points summarise our motivation on this domain.

- In web services that use XML-based message exchange, the problem of how to reconcile structural differences between types of XML documents supported by two different web services must be considered, as explained above.
- In XML applications (local or distributed ones), it is natural and unavoidable that both data and schemas continuously change for a multitude of reasons, including the expansion of the application scope over time or (to allow) the merging of several businesses into one.
- The increasing demand for tools specially designed for administrators not belonging to the computer science community, but capable of making decisions on the evolution of an application (Roddick et al., 2000). This kind of user needs a system that assures a consistent evolution of the schema in an incremental, interactive way.

In this paper, we consider an interactive data administration tool for XML databases. In this tool, changes on an XML type are activated by (special) updates that violate the validity of an XML document. Our approach offers the possibility of computing new schema options from the characteristics of both the schema and documents being updated. Different choices of schema are given to the administrator that decides which schema is to be adopted, based on his knowledge about the semantics of the documents.

Overview of our Method

An XML type (or schema) is a set of rules for defining the allowed sub-elements of any element in an XML document. In this paper, modifications on an XML type are changes on the regular expressions defined by the schema rules. Thus, our algorithm is based on the computation of new regular expressions to extend a given regular language in a conservative way, trying to foresee the needs of an application. Our problem can be formulated in terms of regular expression evolution, as follows:

- Given a regular expression E, suppose a *valid* word w (i.e., a word belonging to the language $L(E)$ defined by E). Let $w' \notin L(E)$ be an invalid word obtained by performing a sequence of updates on w.
- When this update sequence is performed by an advised user, changes on E are activated in order to propose several new regular expressions E' such that (*i*) $w' \in L(E')$, (*ii*) $L(E) \subseteq L(E')$, and (*iii*) E' has a structure as similar as possible to E.

We are neither interested in the trivial expression $E \mid w'$, that adds just w' to $L(E)$, nor in a too general expression allowing any kind of updates. We assume that the advised user is capable of choosing the candidate that fits best his/her application, based on its semantics.

In our method, changes on an XML schema are activated by (special) updates that violate the validity of an XML document. To deal with updates, we consider a word w and its positions (from 0 to $|w|$ - 1). We assume three kinds of update operations, namely, insertion, deletion and replacement. Each update operations is represented by a triple:

- The insertion *(pos, ins, a)* which adds the symbol a on position *pos* of w and shifts all its right siblings to the right. The resulting word has length $|w| + 1$.
- The deletion *(pos, del, null)* which removes the symbol at position *pos* of w and shifts all its right siblings to the left. The resulting word has length $|w|$ - 1.
- The replacement *(pos, rep, a)* which replaces the symbol at position *pos* of w by a. The resulting word has length $|w|$.

This chapter focuses on the insertion case (the most interesting one). Deletions can be solved by simply marking as optional those elements that were deleted. In this way, old documents will still match the new schema. Replacements can be treated as one deletion followed by one insertion.

Let $U = [u_1, \ldots, u_n]$ be a sequence of n updates over a word w. The resulting word w' is obtained by applying each single update u_i on w. Notice that each u_i refers to a position in the original word w. The following example illustrates our approach.

Example 1: Consider a hotel reservation system using XML messages. These messages have a schema. Suppose the following DTD for the Reservation element:

```
<!ELEMENT Reservation (Type (Date Hotel+)*) >
```

In this case, we will have that the children of a `Reservation` element are defined by a regular expression $E = Type\ (Date\ Hotel^{+})^{*}\ \#$. (We consider that the end of each expression and each message are marked by #. This is a realistic assumption since end markers are common in the implementation of computer data.)

In the following, we analyze two cases of a series of updates. The first one does not trigger the evolution of the schema. The second case will exemplify our schema evolution algorithm. Let $w = Type\ Date\ Hotel\ \#$ be a word in $L(E)$, where $w[0] = Type$, $w[1] = Date$, $w[2] = Hotel$ and $w[3] = \#$. Let $U = [u1, u2, u3]$ be a sequence of updates over w. The resulting word, $w' = Type\ Date\ Hotel\ Date\ Hotel\ Hotel\ \#$, is obtained by applying each single update as follows:

- If $u1 = (1, ins, Date)$ then w changes to a new word $w_1 = Type\ Date\ Date\ Hotel\ \#$.
- If $u2 = (1, ins, Hotel)$ then w_1 changes into $w_2 = Type\ Date\ Hotel\ Date\ Hotel\ \#$.
- If $u3 = (3, ins, Hotel)$ then w_2 changes into $w' = Type\ Date\ Hotel\ Date\ Hotel\ Hotel\ \#$ which represents the final result.

While intermediary words may not belong to $L(E)$, the resulting word $w' \in L(E)$. In this case, there is no need for schema evolution.

On the other hand, given the same word w as before, and given a set of updates $U = [(1, ins, Date), (1, ins, Hotel), (3, ins, Restaurant), (3, ins, Concert)]$, we have that the resulting word is $w' = Type\ Date\ Hotel\ Date\ Hotel\ Restaurant\ Concert\ \#$. Thus $w' \notin L(E)$. In this case, our evolution algorithm, called **GREC-e**, can be used (by an administrator) to compute new regular expressions. Here, **GREC-e** proposes candidates such as the following ones:

$E_1 = Type(Date\ Hotel^{+}\ Restaurant?\ Concert?)^{*}$,
$E_2 = Type(Date\ Hotel^{+}\ Restaurant?\ Concert^{*})^{*}$,
$E_3 = Type(Date\ Hotel^{+}\ Restaurant^{*}\ Concert?)^{*}$,
$E_4 = Type(Date\ Hotel^{+}\ Restaurant^{*}\ Concert^{*})^{*}$,
$E_5 = Type(Date(Hotel \mid Concert \mid Restaurant)^{+})^{*}$.

So, the possible solutions for the evolution of the schema, as proposed by our algorithm are:

```
<!ELEMENT Reservation (Type (Date Hotel+ Restaurant? Concert?)*) >
<!ELEMENT Reservation (Type (Date Hotel+ Restaurant? Concert*)*) >
<!ELEMENT Reservation (Type (Date Hotel+ Restaurant* Concert?)*) >
<!ELEMENT Reservation (Type (Date Hotel+ Restaurant* Concert*)*) >
<!ELEMENT Reservation (Type (Date(Hotel|Concert |Restaurant)+)*) >
```

These solutions are proposed to the data administrator, who will choose one of them, in accordance to his/her needs and to the semantics of the application.

Notice that the regular expressions E_1 to E_4, at the end of the example above are almost identical. Their only difference is in the operators affecting the symbols *Restaurant* and *Concert*. This condition is recurrent for the solutions proposed by our algorithm. In the rest of this paper, we will use the notation *a!* as an abbreviation for both *a?* and *a** in regular expressions.

THEORETICAL BACKGROUND

The transformation process proposed in (Caron & Ziadi, 2000) obtains a regular expression from a finite state automaton, by using a reduction process. In this process, the states of the (Glushkov) automaton are substituted by regular expressions. The algorithm of Glushkov, also given in (Caron & Ziadi, 2000) obtains a finite state automaton $M = (\Sigma, Q, \Delta, q_0, F)$, called a Glushkov automaton. Glushkov automata are *homogeneous*, this means that one always enters a given state by the same symbol. In a Glushkov automaton, each non initial state corresponds to a position in the regular expression, denoted by subscripts: for instance, given the regular expression $E = (a(b|c)^*)^*d$, the subscribed regular expression is $\underline{E} = (a_1(b_2|c_3)^*)^*d_4$. The corresponding *Glushkov graph* is the graph $G = (X, U)$ where X is the set of vertices (isomorphic to the set of states of the automaton) and U is the set of edges (corresponding to the transition relation). As we are dealing with homogeneous automata, we drop the superfluous labels on edges and work with an unlabelled directed graph (see Figure 1).

A graph is a *hammock* if either it has a unique node without loop, or it has two particular nodes r and s such that for any node v (*i*) there exists a path from r to s going through v, (*ii*) there is neither path from s to v nor from v to r. In this case, the graph has both a root (r) and an antiroot (s), with $r \neq s$. Thanks to the end mark (#), the Glushkov graphs used in this work are hammocks.

Given a Glushkov graph $G = (X, U)$, an *orbit* is a set $\Theta \subseteq X$ such that for all x and x' in Θ there exists a non-trivial path from x to x'. A *maximal orbit* Θ is an orbit such that for each node x of Θ and for each node x' not in Θ, there does not exist at the same time a path from x to x' and a path from x' to x. The *input* and *output nodes* of an orbit are respectively defined as follows: $In(\Theta) = \{x \in \Theta \mid \exists x' \in (X \setminus \Theta), (x', x) \in U\}$ and $Out(\Theta) = \{x \in \Theta \mid \exists x' \in (X \setminus \Theta), (x, x') \in U\}$. An orbit Θ is said to be *stable* if $\forall x \in Out(\Theta)$ and $\forall y \in In(\Theta)$, the edge (x, y) exists. An orbit Θ is *transverse* if $\forall x, y \in Out(\Theta), \forall z \in (X \setminus \Theta), (x, z) \in U \Rightarrow (y, z) \in U$ and if $\forall x, y \in In(\Theta), \forall z \in (X \setminus \Theta), (z, x) \in U \Rightarrow (z, y) \in U$.

An orbit Θ is *strongly stable* (resp. *strongly transverse*) if it is stable (resp. transverse) and if after deleting the edges in $Out(\Theta) \times In(\Theta)$ every sub-orbit is strongly stable (resp. strongly transverse). Given a Glushkov graph G, a graph without

Figure 1. (a) A FSA for $(a(b|c)^*)^*d$; (b) its Glushkov graph

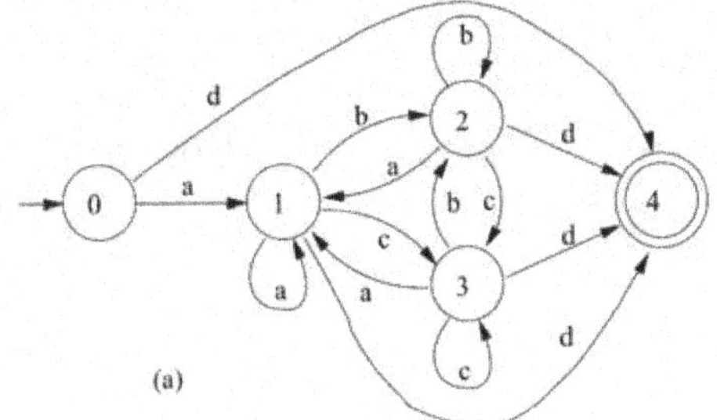

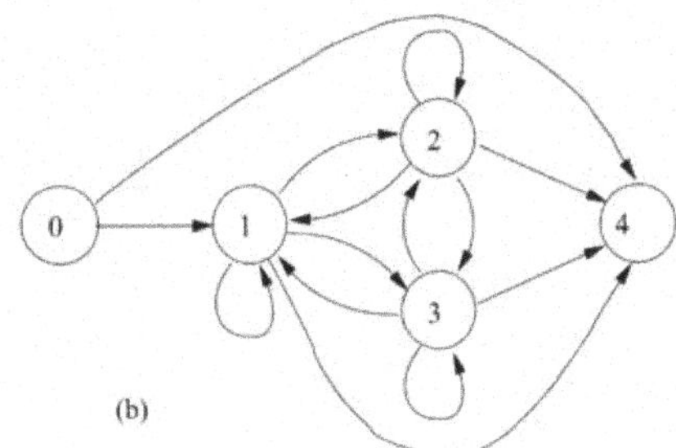

orbits G_{wo} is defined by recursively deleting, for each maximal orbit $\mathcal{O}$, all edges (x, y) such that $x \in Out(\mathcal{O})$ and $y \in In(\mathcal{O})$. The process ends when there are no more orbits.

Example 2: Figure 1(b) shows Glushkov graph *G* corresponding to the Glushkov automaton of Figure 1(a). Graph G has one maximal orbit: $\mathcal{O}_1 = \{1, 2, 3\}$ (with $In(\mathcal{O}_1) = \{1\}$ and $Out(\mathcal{O}_1) = \{1, 2, 3\}$). Orbit $\mathcal{O}_1$ is both transverse and stable. We can build a graph without orbit from *G* as follows: (*i*) Remove all the arcs in $Out(\mathcal{O}_1) \times In(\mathcal{O}_1)$ of *G*. (*ii*) The resulting graph *G'* also has one maximal orbit: $\mathcal{O}_2 = \{2, 3\}$ (with $In(\mathcal{O}_2) = Out(\mathcal{O}_2) = \{2, 3\}$). Delete the arcs in $Out(\mathcal{O}_2) \times In(\mathcal{O}_2)$ to obtain a new graph without orbits, such as the graph in Figure 3(a). Thus, both maximal orbits $\mathcal{O}_1$ and $\mathcal{O}_2$ are strongly stable and strongly transverse.

Given a graph without orbits G_{wo}, it is said to be reducible (Caron & Ziadi, 2000) if it is possible to reduce it to one state by successive applications of any of the three rules $\boldsymbol{R_1}$, $\boldsymbol{R_2}$ and $\boldsymbol{R_3}$ explained below (illustrated by Figure 2). Let *x* be a node in $G_{wo} = (X, U)$. We note $Q^-(x)$ the set of immediate predecessors of *x* and $Q^+(x)$ the set of immediate successors of *x*. The reduction rules are defined as follows (we denote *r(x)* the regular expression associated to node *x*, and *e* the resulting regular expression in each case):

Rule $\boldsymbol{R_1}$: If two nodes *x* and *y* are such that $Q^-(y) = \{x\}$ and $Q^+(x) = \{y\}$, i.e., node *x* is the only predecessor of node *y* and node *y* is the only successor of *x*, then concatenate *r(x)* and *r(y)* in *e*, assign *e* to *x*, and delete *y*.

Rule $\boldsymbol{R_2}$: If two nodes *x* and *y* are such that $Q^-(x) = Q^-(y)$ and $Q^+(x) = Q^+(y)$, i.e., the nodes *x* and *y* have the same predecessors and successors, then build *e* that corresponds to the union of *r(x)* and *r(y)*, assign *e* to *x*, and delete *y*.

Rule $\boldsymbol{R_3}$: If a node *x* is such that $y \in Q^-(x) \Rightarrow Q^+(x) \subseteq Q^+(y)$, i.e., each predecessor of node *x* is also a predecessor of any successor of node *x*, then delete the edges going from $Q^-(x)$ to $Q^+(x)$. In this case the new regular expression is built in the following way: if *r(x)* is of the form *E* (resp. E+) then *e* will be *E?* (resp. *E**). Recall that we use the notation *E!* to stand for either *E?* or *E+*.

During the construction of G_{wo}, the orbits are hierarchically ordered, according to the set inclusion relation. The reduction process starts at the lower level of the hierarchy of orbits and works bottom-up, from the smaller orbits to the maximal ones. The information concerning the orbits of the original graph is used to add the transitive closure operator ("+") to the regular expression being constructed. Thus, during the

Figure 2. Reduction rules

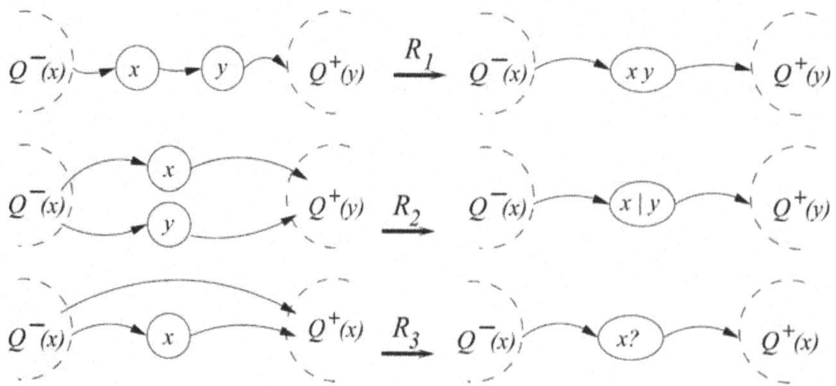

reduction process, when a single node representing a whole orbit is obtained, its content is decorated with a "+".

Example 3: Figure 3 illustrates the reduction process. Rule $\boldsymbol{R_2}$ is applied on Graph (a), giving Graph (b). Since the expression (2 | 3) represents orbit $\mathcal{O}_2$, the transitive closure symbol is added (Graph (c)). Then rule $\boldsymbol{R_3}$ transforms the graph into Graph (d), rule $\boldsymbol{R_1}$ gives Graph (e) and rule R3 leads to Graph (f). By applying twice rule $\boldsymbol{R_1}$, the expression 0(1(2|3)*)*4 is obtained.

Theorem 1. (Caron & Ziadi, 2000) Graph G = (X, U) is a Glushkov graph iff the following conditions are satisfied: (1) G is a hammock, (2) each maximal orbit in G is strongly stable and strongly transverse and (3) the graph without orbit of G is reducible.

We define now a very simple notion of distance between two regular expressions:

Definition 1. Let *E* and *E'* be regular expressions and $\underline{E}$ (resp. $\underline{E'}$) be the subscripted expression built from *E* (resp. *E'*). Let S_E (resp. $S_{E'}$) be the set of positions of $\underline{E}$ (resp. $\underline{E'}$). The distance between *E* and *E'*, denoted by *D(E, E')*, is $D(E, E') = |\,[S_E] - [S_{E'}]\,|$, where *[S]* represents the number of elements of the finite set *S*.

THE ALGORITHM GREC-E

Let *E* be a regular expression and *w* a word in *L(E)*. Let $M_E = (\Sigma, Q, \Delta, q_0, F)$ be the Glushkov automaton built as explained in the previous section (Caron & Ziadi, 2000). In M_E each state (but the initial one) corresponds to a position in the subscribed regular expression of *E*. The only final state of M_E is subscribed with the position of the end mark (#).

We consider now the execution of M_E over an updated word *w'*. We define the nearest left state (s_{nl}) as a state in M_E reached after reading the last valid symbol in *w'*. Similarly, we define the nearest right state (s_{nr}) as a state in M_E that succeeds s_{nl} discarding all symbols that do not have a valid transition from s_{nl}.

Without loss of generality, we assume that insertion operations always correspond to the insertion of new positions in *E*. Thus, to accept the new word, we should insert new states (s_{new}) in M_E and transitions from s_{nl} to s_{new}, while keeping the properties of a Glushkov graph. Such changes should be done for each new position inserted into *E*. As one insertion can be related to another one, we use two auxiliary structures, called *RTStates* and *STrans*. Relation *RTStates* informs where (and which) s_{new} is added to M_E. *RTStates* is built during the run of M_E on *w'* and contains triples (s_{nl}, s_{nr}, s_{new}) for each symbol to be inserted in *E*. When several insertions are performed on the same position of *E*, the order among the several states s_{new} should be considered. To this end, we introduce set *STrans* composed by pairs (*state, symbol*). Each pair indicates that, in the resulting automata, there must exist an outgoing transition from state *state* with label *symbol*.

The construction of *RTStates* and *STrans* is guided by a mapping from *w* to *w'*. A symbol *w[i]*

Figure 3. An example of a reduction

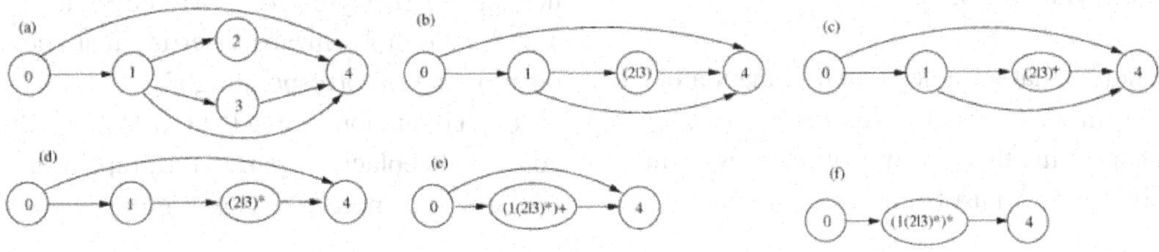

can be mapped to a symbol $w'[j]$ if $w[i] = w'[j]$. A symbol a in w not mapped into a symbol in w' indicates the deletion of a from w. A symbol a in w' that does not correspond to any symbol in w indicates the insertion of a in w'. For instance, for $w = abcd$ and $w' = aefbcd$ we have that symbols in positions 0, 1, 2, 3 in w are mapped to symbols in positions 0, 3, 4, 5 in w', respectively. New positions to be inserted are those corresponding to the symbols e and f. This mapping can be computed from the update operations.

To find s_{nl} and s_{nr}, we consider the subtrings defined by the mapping from w to w'. While the mapping is such that $w[i] = w'[j]$, the automaton M_E recognises the substring of w being considered and the value of s_{nl} is updated (it corresponds to the last common symbol found in a recognised substring). When symbols in w' (corresponding to insertions) are not recognised by M_E, our algorithms scan w' by going through the new symbols until finding a symbol a such that $\delta(s_{nl}, a)$ is defined in M_E. The state s_{nr} is the one given by transition $\delta(s_{nl}, a)$. Remark that both s_{nl} and s_{nr} exist and, when M_E is deterministic (so E is said to be unambiguous (Brüggeman-Klein & Wood, 1992)), they are unique.

Example 4: Let $E = ab^*cd$, $w = abcd$ and $w' = aefbcd$. Let M_E be an automaton where the state $s_{nl} = 1$ is the one reached after reading a in w'. The corresponding $s_{nr} = 2$ is given by $\delta(1, b)$ in M_E. Tuples $(1, 2, 5)$ and $(1, 2, 6)$ are added to *RTStates*, where 5 and 6 are new states corresponding to symbols e and f, respectively. To impose an order between these two states we add to *STrans* tuple $(5, f)$. This should avoid solutions such as $E' = af!e!b^*cd$ which contain the new required states but for which $w' \notin L(E')$.

We notice that for a deletion of a mandatory symbol s in E, tuples in *RTStates* are $(s_{nl}, s_{nr}, \text{NULL})$, meaning that new transition rules of the form $\delta(s_{nl}, s) = s_{nr}$ must be inserted into M_E.

The rest of this section details our XML type evolution method. Firstly we explain function **GREC-e** showing how new regular expressions are built and proposed as type candidates. Next we give some implementation details. We finish the section by considering some important properties of our approach and by presenting experimental results.

GREC-e and LookGraphAlternative Algorithms

In this section, we present the function **GREC-e**, responsible for generating new regular expressions from a Glushkov automaton and a set of updates. Figure 4 presents a high level algorithm for the function **GREC-e** (Generate Regular Expression Choices-extended).

GREC-e generates a list of regular expressions and it has four input parameters: a graph without orbits G_{wo}, a hierarchy of orbits H built from the original Glushkov graph and relations *RTStates* and *STrans*.

An important goal of our approach is to propose only new regular expressions E' such that $D(E, E') \leq n$, where n is the number of tuples in the relation *RTStates*. For a general regular expression E, the task of finding the places where the new symbol may be added is not trivial. There is a great variety of possible solutions and it is hard to find those ones that fit the best in a given context. We want candidates that respect the nesting of subexpressions of the original regular expression. The reduction process of (Caron & Ziadi, 2000) is well adapted to our goal of proposing solutions that preserve the general structure of the original regular expression E, since it follows the syntactic nesting of E using the orbits. Moreover, inserting a new state in M_E means inserting just one new position in the corresponding $\underline{E}$.

Each reduction step in (Caron & Ziadi, 2000) consists in replacing a part of the graph by a node containing a more complex regular expression

Figure 4. Algorithm to generate regular expressions from a Glushkov graph and updates

```
1.  function GREC-e (G_wo, H, RTStates, STrans) {
2.   if (RTStates is empty){
3.     return (setRegExp = Union(setRegExp, {GraphToRegExp(G_wo, H)}))
4.   } // setRegExp is a global variable
5.   if (G_wo has only one node) { return Empty-set }
6.   R_i := ChooseRule(G_wo, H)
7.   foreach (G_new, H_new, RTStates'):=
      LookGraphAlternative(G_wo, H, R_i,RTStates, STrans) do {
8.            setRegExp := Union(setRegExp, GREC-e(G_new, H_new, RTStates', STrans))}
9.   (G'_wo, H') := ApplyRule(R_i, G_wo, H)
10.  setRegExp := Union(setRegExp, GREC-e(G'_wo, H', RTStates, STrans))
11.  return setRegExp }
```

(as illustrated in Example 3). In **`GREC-e`** we do not only reduce a graph to a regular expression but we also generate new graphs (that we reduce to regular expressions too). This is the role of function **`LookGraphAlternative`**, which uses *RTStates* and *STrans*. More precisely, in line 6 of Figure 4, **`GREC-e`** chooses one reduction rule by using the information concerning orbits (Function **`ChooseRule`**). Then two different directions are taken:

Before applying the chosen rule, for each tuple $(s_{nl}, s_{nr}, s_{new})$ in *RTStates*, **`GREC-e`** checks whether nodes s_{nl} and s_{nr} satisfy some specified conditions. When it is the case, it modifies the graph to take into account the insertion of the corresponding node s_{new}. These modifications are driven by rules $\boldsymbol{R_1}$, $\boldsymbol{R_2}$ and $\boldsymbol{R_3}$ and by information concerning the orbits of the original graph. Each modification is performed by the iterator **`LookGraphAlternative`** (line 7), whose role is two-fold: (*i*) it verifies whether nodes s_{nl} and s_{nr} satisfy the conditions stated in $\boldsymbol{R_1}$, $\boldsymbol{R_2}$ or $\boldsymbol{R_3}$ and (*ii*) it generates new data (graph G_{new}, its hierarchy of orbits (H_{new}) and *RTStates'*, and updated version of *RTStates* without the tuple just used), over which Function **`GREC-e`** is recursively applied. When *RTStates* is empty (line 3), no more insertions have to be done, and Function **`GraphToRegExp`** computes a regular expression from a given graph.

Function **`ApplyRule`** in line 9, computes a new graph resulting from the application of the selected rule on the original graph G_{wo}. Function **`GREC-e`** is recursively applied over this new graph. The reduction process finishes only when G_{wo} is a single node.

Before presenting how **`LookGraphAlternative`** works, let us define two sets that help the construction of the candidates:

Definition 2. Given a graph $G = (X, U)$ and a node $x \in X$, the set of nodes that immediately follow a node x is defined as: $Foll(x) = \{y \in X \mid (x, y) \in U\}$. The set of nodes that immediately precede a node x is defined as: $Prev(x) = \{y \in X \mid (y, x) \in U\}$.

Note that the difference between *Foll(x)* (resp. *Prev(x)*) and $Q^+(x)$ (resp. $Q^-(x)$) is the graph used to define them. The sets *Foll(x)* and *Prev(x)* are defined over the Glushkov graph while the sets $Q^+(x)$ and $Q^-(x)$ are defined over the graph without orbits.

Figures 5 to 9 summarise the behaviour of **LookGraphAlternative**. They show the tests done (column **Condition**) as well as the modifications to be performed when the tested conditions are met (column **Result**).

Figure 5 shows how **LookGraphAlternative** builds new graphs when rule $\boldsymbol{R_1}$ is applied.

Conditions for the first case are: (*i*) the node x corresponds to s_{nl} and (*ii*) the node y corresponds to s_{nr}. In the first case, new graphs G^1, G^2 and G^3 are built by adding nodes s_{new} between s_{nl} and s_{nr} as follows: (*i*) G^1 adds the nodes s_{new} in a disjoint way (there can be several triples having the same s_{nl} and s_{nr}); (*ii*) G^2 adds a sequence of optional nodes s_{new} and (*iii*) G^3 has an optional sequence of nodes s_{new}. For example, let $w = abc$ be a valid word belonging to $E = abc$ and $w' = abxyc$ be w updated with two new symbols x and y; then, G^1, G^2 and G^3 represent $E^1 = ab(x|y)!c$, $E^2 = ab(x!y!)c$ and $E^3 = ab(xy)!c$, respectively.

Conditions for the second case are: (*i*) the node x corresponds to s_{nr} and (*ii*) the node y corresponds to s_{nl}. In this case, six new graphs are built by considering the insertion of s_{new} nodes in a disjoint way (G^1, G^2), in a sequence of optional nodes (G^3, G^4) and in an optional sequence of nodes (G^5, G^6). For example, let $w = ababc$ be a valid word belonging to $E = (ab)^+c$ and $w' = abxabyc$ be w updated with two new symbols x and y; then, G^1, G^2, G^3, G^4, G^5 and G^6 represent $E^1 = (ab(x|y)!)^+c$, $E^2 = ((x|y)!ab)^+c$, $E^3 = (abx!y!)^+c$, $E^4 = (x!y!ab)^+c$, $E^5 = (ab(xy)!)^+c$ and $E^6 = ((xy)!ab)^+c$, respectively.

Figure 5. Graph modifications and conditions for Rule $\boldsymbol{R_1}$

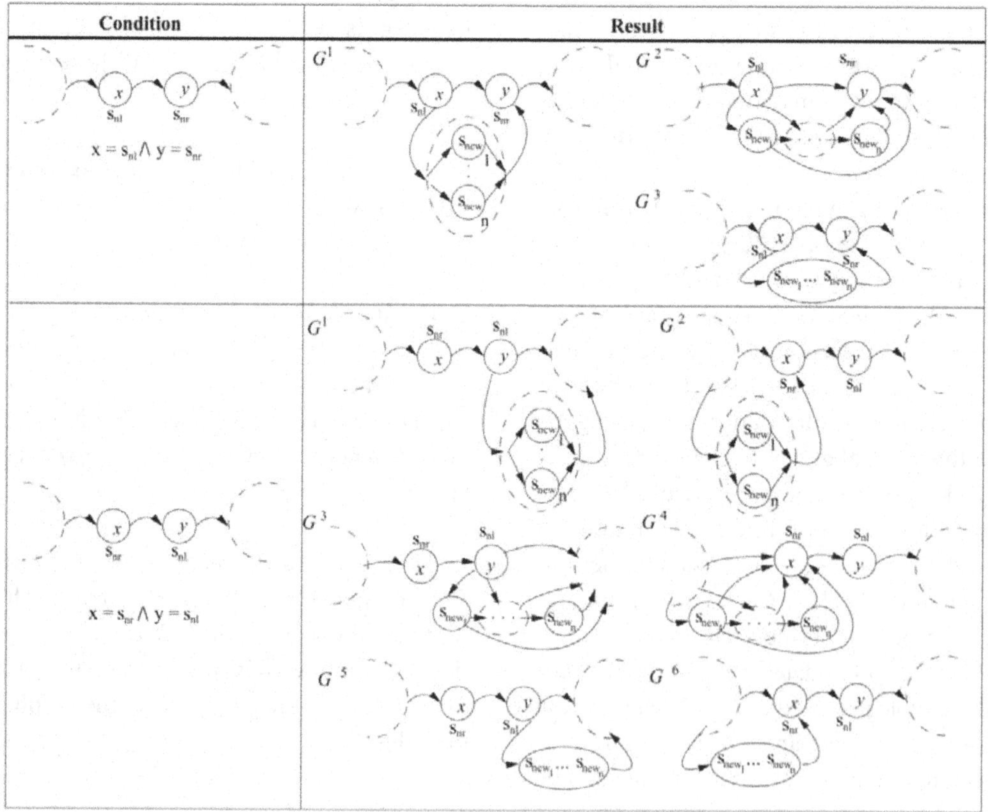

Figure 6 shows how **`LookGraphAlternative`** builds new graphs when rule $\boldsymbol{R_2}$ is applied. Three different cases are detected.

Conditions for the first case are: (*i*) the node x is s_{nl} and (*ii*) s_{nr} is a successor of x. Two graphs are built by inserting nodes s_{new} as successors of x; as choices *(G¹)* or as a sequence *(G²)*.

Conditions for the second case are: (*i*) the node x is s_{nr} and (*ii*) s_{nl} is an ancestor of x. Two graphs are built by inserting nodes s_{new} as predecessors of x.

Conditions for the third case are: (*i*) s_{nl} is a predecessor of x and (*ii*) s_{nr} is a successor of x. Two graphs are built by inserting nodes s_{new} as choices w.r.t. x and y. As an example, consider the regular expression $E = a(b|c)d$ and the words $w = abd$ and $w' = abxyd$. The candidates built by **`LookGraphAlternative`** with rule $\boldsymbol{R_2}$ (first case) are: $E^1 = a(b(x|y)!|c)d$, built from G^1 and $E^2 = a(bx!y!|c)d$ built from G^2. Figure 7 shows how **`LookGraphAlternative`** builds new graphs when rule $\boldsymbol{R_3}$ is applied. In this case, one of the following conditions holds: s_{nl} precedes x and s_{nr} is a successor of x. As an example, consider the regular expression $E = ab?c$ and the words $w{=}ac$ and $w' = axyc$. The candidates are (see Figure 7): $E^1 = a(x|y)!b?c$ from G^1, $E^2{=}ax!y!b?c$ from G^2, $E^3 = ab?(x|y)!c$ from G^3, $E^4 = ab?x!y!c$ from G^4, $E^5 = a(b|(x|y)!)c$ from G^5, and $E^6 = a(b?|x!y!)c$ from G^6.

Rules $\boldsymbol{R_1}$, $\boldsymbol{R_2}$ and $\boldsymbol{R_3}$ are first applied inside each orbit (Caron & Ziadi, 2000). During the reduction process, each orbit ʘ of the original graph is reduced to just one node containing a regular expression. This regular expression is then decorated by +. Before applying this decoration we have to consider the insertion of s_{new} in the orbit ʘ.

Figure 8 shows the conditions we have to check and the candidate graphs built according to them. Three cases are specified:

The first case is defined by the condition $s_{nl} \in In(ʘ)$ and $s_{nr} \in Out(ʘ)$. Graphs G^1, G^2, G^3, G^4, G^5 and G^6 are built as follows: G^1 has nodes s_{new} inserted as input nodes of the orbit in a disjoint way; G^2 is similar to G^1 but nodes s_{new} are in-

Figure 6. Graph modifications and conditions for Rule $\boldsymbol{R_2}$

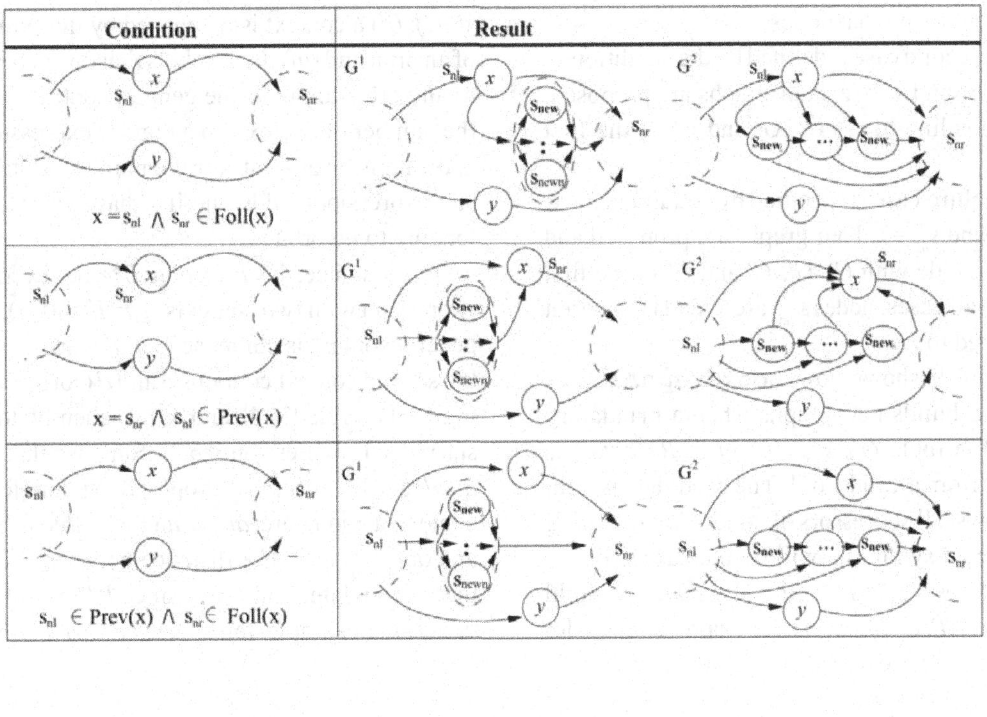

Condition	Result
$x = s_{nl} \wedge s_{nr} \in Foll(x)$	G^1 / G^2
$x = s_{nr} \wedge s_{nl} \in Prev(x)$	G^1 / G^2
$s_{nl} \in Prev(x) \wedge s_{nr} \in Foll(x)$	G^1 / G^2

Figure 7. Graph modifications and conditions for Rule $\boldsymbol{R_3}$

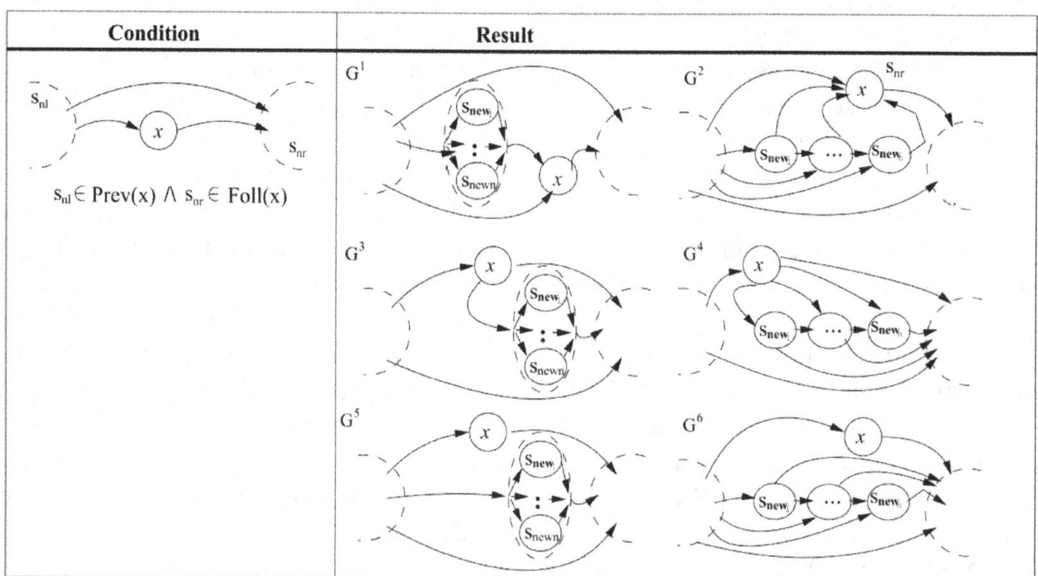

serted in a sequence of optional nodes; G^3 has nodes s_{new} inserted as output nodes of the orbit in a disjoint way; G^4 is the same as G^3 but nodes s_{new} are inserted in a sequence of optional nodes; G^5 has nodes s_{new} inserted in a disjoint way and they are disjoint in relation to the orbit, and G^6 is the same as G^5 but nodes s_{new} are inserted in a sequence of optional nodes.

The second case is defined by the condition $s_{nl} \in Prev(z)$ and $s_{nr} = z$. Four graphs are proposed, corresponding to G^1, G^2, G^5 and G^6 of the first case.

The third case is specified by conditions $s_{nr} \in Foll(z)$ and $s_{nl} = z$. Four graphs are proposed and they coincide with G^3, G^4, G^5 and G^6 of the first case. In all cases, nodes s_{new} are added to the orbit ⊝ reduced to z.

Figure 9 shows how **`LookGraphAlternative`** builds new graphs when a mandatory symbol (a tuple $(s_{nl}, s_{nr}, NULL)$ in *RTStates*) is deleted from a valid word. The candidate is built as follows: all successors of nodes n representing the deleted symbols s will be the successors of all predecessors of s, i.e., for all $p \notin Foll(n)$, build new arcs $(Prev(n), p)$. As an example, consider the regular expression $E = abc^+d$ and the words $w=abcd$ and $w' = ad$. The candidate is (see Figure 9) $E = ab?c^*d$.

Candidates proposed by **`GREC-e`** are easily classified according to the context of the insertion. It is straightforward to do it since: (*i*) for each maximal orbits in G there exists a starred sub-expression in E (Brüggeman-Klein & Wood, 1992); (*ii*) a context is composed by the symbols of an orbit and (*iii*) the symbols that do not belong to any orbit compose the general context. Thus, the number of contexts in a regular expression E is the number of orbits (or the number of starred sub-expressions) plus one if E has symbols belonging to no orbit.

For instance, let $E = ab(cd)^*e$ be a regular expression with two contexts ($\underline{E} = 12(34)^*5$). The general context is composed by a, b and e while the second context contains c and d (corresponding to the orbit {3, 4} and, consequently, to the starred sub-expression $(cd)^*$). Suppose that $w = abcde$ and $w' = abcduve$. Proposed solutions for the context of c and d are: *ab(cd(u|v)*)*e*, *ab(cdu!v!)*e* and *ab(u!v!cd)*e*. The distance between each of these candidates and E is 2 since *RTStates* has 2 tuples. For example, for $E_1 = ab(cd(u|v)^*)^*e$, $S_{E1} =$

Figure 8. Graph modifications performed after reducing an orbit

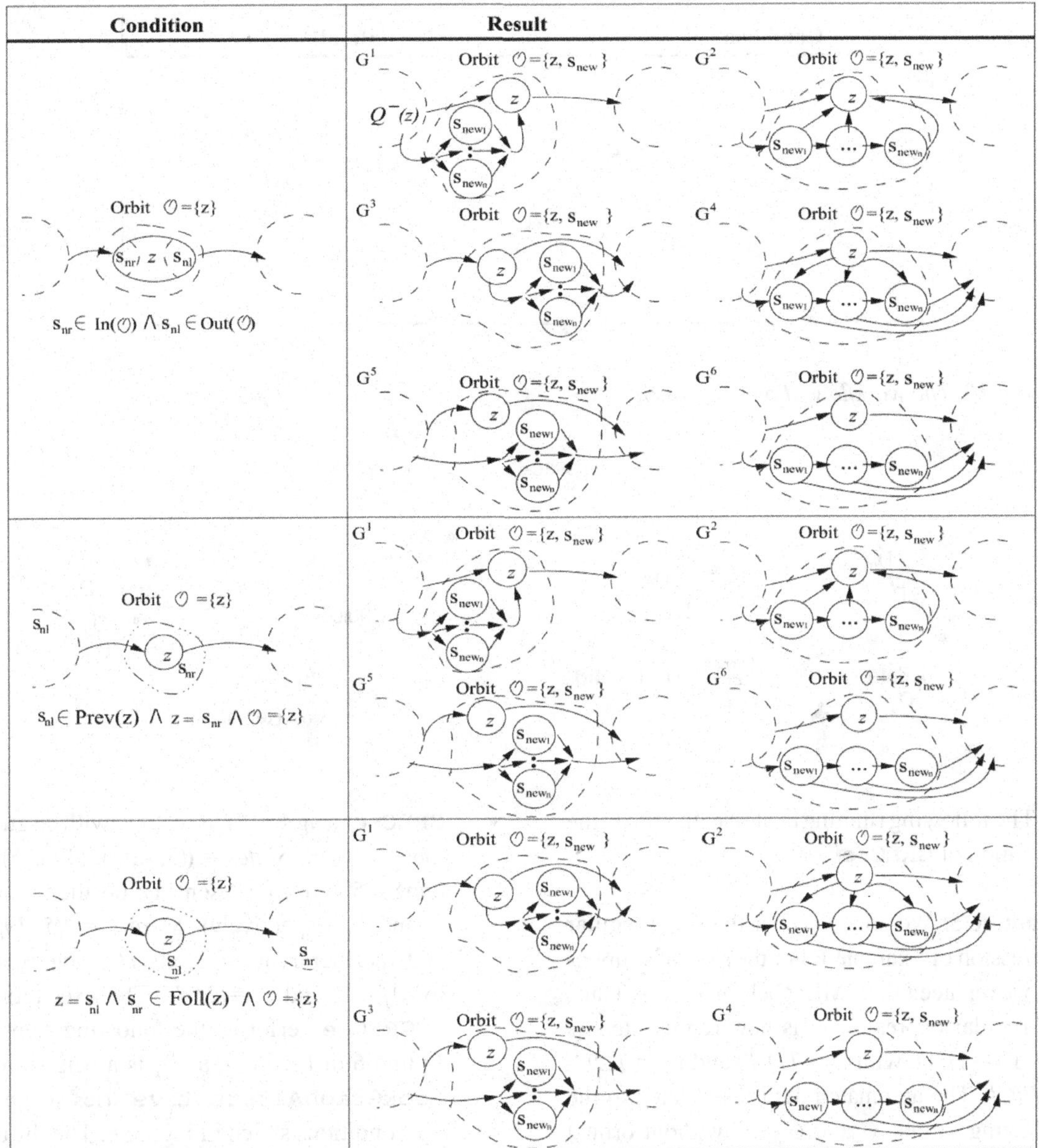

{1, 2, 3, 4, 5, 6, 7} and, as S_E = *{1, 2, 3, 4, 5}*, we have *D(E, E')* = |5 - 7| = *2*.

Implementation and Running Example

Figure 10 illustrates the use of our method. Updates on an XML document D_1 gives rise to a new document D'_1 which is not valid w.r.t. the existing schema (type) *S*. Function **GREC-e** is executed and proposes candidates to build a new schema which accepts D'_1 and a new class of XML documents. In Figure 10, **GREC-e** proposes candidates E_1, E_2..., E_n. An advised user chooses E_2 as the type to replace *S*. This new type describes not only D'_1 but also documents D_2..., D_m.

Figure 9. Graph modifications performed from a deletion of mandatory nodes

Condition	Result
S_{nl} $n_1 \cdots n_n$ S_{nr}	S_{nl} $n_1 \cdots n_n$ S_{nr}

Figure 10. The workflow of our approach

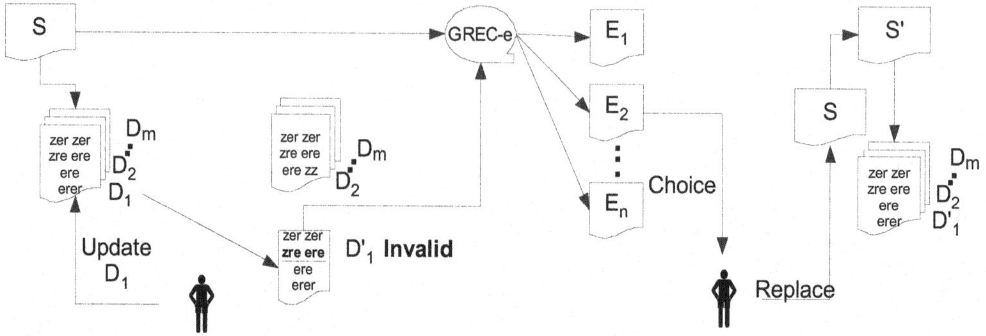

The following running example illustrates the execution of **GREC-e**.

Example 5: We now consider the same regular expression of Example 1. For the sake of simplicity, we replaced the XML labels by letters. Thus, the regular expression E is now represented as $E = T (D\ H^{+})\#$, with w = *TDH#* and w' = *TDH-DHRC#*. The automaton M_E is associated to the following graphs G and G_{wo} (G without orbits) (see Box 1).

- **GREC-e** (Figure 4) is called with arguments G_{wo}, *RTStates* = ((3, 4, 5), (3, 4, 6)) (where 5 and 6 represent the positions for C and P, respectively), *STrans* = *{(5, P)}* and the hierarchy of orbits H, composed by $\Theta_1=\{3\}$ and $\Theta_2=\{2, 3\}$. The execution of **GREC-e** performs the following steps: In line 6 of Figure 4, as Θ_1 is a singleton, **LookGraphAlternative** tries to apply conditions stated in Figure 8. The third condition of this figure is verified by both tuples in *RTStates*, and four new graphs are

Box 1.

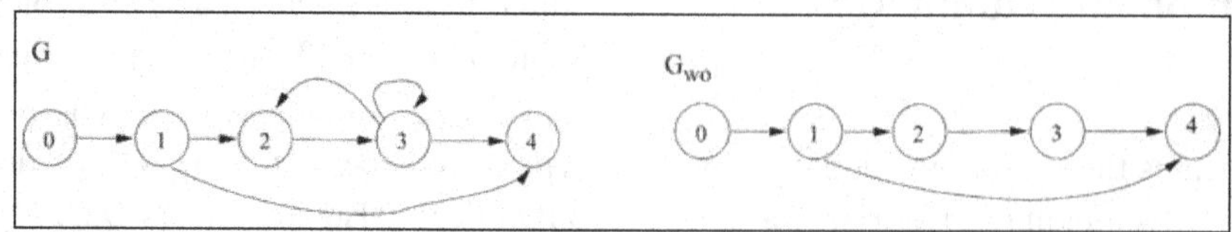

built. **GREC-e** is executed over each of these graphs (line 8) with an empty *RTStates*. The following regular expressions are added to **setRegExp** (line 3): T(D(H(R|C)*)$^+$)*# from G^1, T(D(HR!C!)$^+$)*# from G^2, T(D (H|R|C)$^+$)*# from G^3, T(D(H|R!C!)$^+$)*# from G^4.

- Following the reduction process of G_{wo} (the original graph), function **ApplyRule** (line 9) adds the operator "+" to the node that represents an orbit in *G*. Thus, this node corresponds to the regular expression H^+. **GREC-e** is recursively called at line 10 with G_{wo} and the new hierarchy of orbits (with only Θ_2).
- In this recursive call, Rule $\mathbf{R_1}$ is chosen at line 6, since it is the only one applicable over the nodes in Θ_2. As conditions from Figure 5 are not satisfied, **LookGraphAlternative** does not propose new graphs. In line 9, $\mathbf{R_1}$ is applied over nodes 2 and 3 from G_{wo}. **GREC-e** is recursively called with G_{wo} having nodes 2 and 3 replaced by one node labelled 2 3^+.
- In this new recursive call, the choice of Rule $\mathbf{R_3}$ gives no new graphs. However, as there exists a node that represents the entire orbit Θ_2, **LookGraphAlternative** builds four new graphs, since the third condition in Figure 8 holds. These candidates are: T(D H$^+$(R|C)*)*#, T(D H$^+$R!C!)*#, T(D H$^+$|(R|C)*)*#, and T(D H$^+$|R!C!)*#.
- The reduction process of the original input continues: Before applying $\mathbf{R_3}$, the procedure **ApplyRule** decorates node 2 3^+ with a "+" resulting in (2 3^+)$^+$. By application of $\mathbf{R_3}$, the node (2 3^+)$^+$ becomes (2 3^+)*.
- Next, $\mathbf{R_1}$ is chosen to be applied over nodes *0* and *1* resulting in a node labelled (0 1). Then, $\mathbf{R_1}$ is again chosen to be applied over nodes (0 1) and (2 3^+)*, resulting in a node labelled (0 1 (2 3^+)*).
- $\mathbf{R_1}$ is chosen again to reduce nodes (0 1 (2 3^+)*) and 4. In this case, the first condition of Figure 5 is satisfied and three new graphs are built. When **GREC-e** is called at line 9, the parameter *RTState* is empty and thus, this call results in adding candidates (line 5) T(D H$^+$)*(R|C)*#; T(D H$^+$)*R!C!# and T(D H$^+$)*(RC)!# to our result set.
- Finally, condition at line 5 holds and **GREC-e** terminates.

Our tool presents the candidate regular expressions according to the context of insertions:

- In the context of H (inside H$^+$) we have: T (D (H(R|C)*) $^+$)*, T (D (HR!C!) $^+$)*, T (D (H|R|C) $^+$)* and T (D (H|R!C!) $^+$)*.
- In the context of D (inside (D H$^+$)*) we have T (D (H) $^+$|(R|C)*)*, T (D H$^+$R!C!)*, T (D H$^+$|(R|C)*)* and T (D H$^+$|R!C!)*.
- Finally, in the context of *S* i.e., outside any starred sub-expression, we obtain T (D H$^+$)*(R|C)*, T (D H$^+$)*R!C! and T (D H$^+$)*(RC)! .

Our method was implemented in JAVA (Eclipse Platform 3.3.1.1 and JDK 5.0). Figure 11 shows how modules interact. The first step is to build a table *TMaps* that stores the mapping between the original word *w* and the updated word *w'* (Figure 11 (1)). In our implementation, Table *TMaps* is built based on *w* and the list of update operations that defines *w'*. Procedure Module *buildTable* inserts rows in Table *TMaps*. At the end of this procedure, Table *TMaps* contains information about the symbols that have been inserted into w, the symbols that have been deleted from w and the symbols that remained unchanged.

Table *TMaps* is used to build the relation *RTStates* and the set *STrans* used to compute candidates (step (2) in Figure 11). These two structures are defined using the Glushkov automaton M_E corresponding to the original regular expression (M_E accepts *w*). We recall that relation *RTStates* informs where (and which) s_{new} is added to M_E. It contains triples (s_{nl}, s_{nr}, s_{new}) for each symbol to

Figure 11. Approach's modules and their interaction

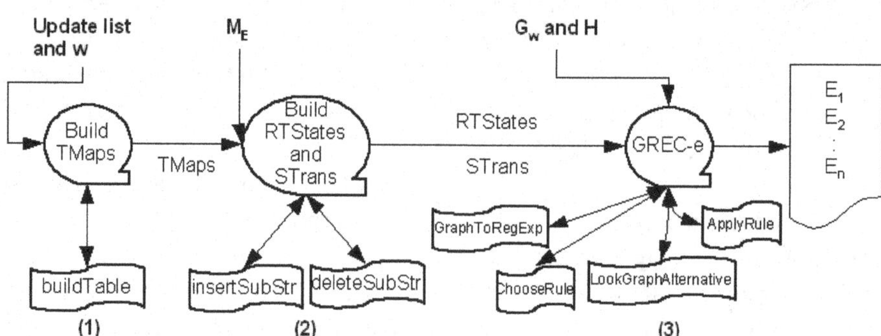

be inserted in *E*. The set STrans contains pairs (*state, symbol*) which indicate that, in the resulting automata, there must exist an outgoing transition from state *state* with label *symbol*. In other words *STrans* assures the order among several symbols (or states) inserted in the same position. Thus, in this step, Modules *insertSubStr* and *deleteSubStr* are called. On the first hand, Module *insertSubStr* adds into *RTStates* a tuple $(s_{nl}, s_{nr}, s_{new})$ that represents an insertion and, on the other hand, it adds (if necessary) a couple *(state, symbol)* into STrans. Module *deleteSubStr* adds into *RTStates* a tuple $(s_{nl}, s_{nr}, null)$ that represents a deletion.

RTStates and *STrans* are input parameters for **GREC-e**, together with the Glushkov graph without orbits G_w (built from M_E), and its hierarchy of orbits *H* (Figure 11 (3)). **GREC-e** calls functions *GraphToRegExp, ChooseRule, LookGraphAlternative* and *ApplyRule*. At the end of the whole process, candidates $E_1, E_2, ..., E_n$ are presented to the user for allowing him/her to choose one of them.

Properties and Experimental Results

Some properties of **GREC-e** can be stated. In particular, it can be proved that any given graph G_{new} built by **LookGraphAlternative(***G, H, R_p, RTStates, STrans***)** is reducible and that **GREC-e** finds correct solutions, as stated by theorem 2. As we focus on insertions, we have the following property: given *k* tuples $(s_{nl}, s_{nr}, s_{new})$ in *RTStates*, **GREC-e** returns, at least, one new regular expression *E'* different from the original *E* and *E'* has, at most, *k* new positions w.r.t. *E*, i.e., $D(E, E') < k + 1$. Moreover, the languages associated to the solutions proposed by **GREC-e** contain, at least, the original language as well as the new word.

Theorem 2: Let *E* be a regular expression and *L(E)* the regular language described by *E*. Given $w[0 : n] \in L(E)$ $(0 \leq n)$, let *w'* be a word resulting from a sequence of updates over positions *p* (with $0 \leq p \leq n$) of *w* such that $w' \notin L(E)$. Let M_E be a Glushkov automaton corresponding to *E* and *G* be a graph built from M_E. Let (G_{wo}, H) be a pair representing a graph without orbit obtained from *G* and the hierarchy of orbits obtained during the construction of G_{wo}, respectively. Let *RTStates* be a (nonempty) relation storing tuples $(s_{nl}, s_{nr}, s_{new})$ and *STrans* be a relation with tuples *(s, a)*, constraining the construction of candidates. Let *k* be the number of tuples $(s_{nl}, s_{nr}, s_{new})$ in *RTStates* such that $s_{new} \neq null$ (tuples having $s_{new} = null$ denote deletions). The execution of **GREC-e(***G_{wo}, H, RTStates, STrans***)** returns a finite, nonempty set of candidate regular expressions $\{E_1, \ldots, E_m\}$ such that, for each $E_i \in \{E_1, \ldots, E_m\}$, we have $L(E) \cup \{w'\} \subseteq L(E^i)$ and $D(E, E_i) \leq k$.

The number of candidates built by **GREC-e** depends on the number of orbits where the new symbols are inserted and the matched conditions described in Figures 5 to 8. Let us consider that

k is the number of new graphs G' proposed from a given graph G by applying once the modifications illustrated in Figures 5 to 8, according to the matching conditions. Notice that the maximum value for k is 6, which is the number of variations introduced at Case 4 of Figure 6 (considering the use of the operator "!"). For each graph found as a solution for one insertion, we build new graphs when taking into account other tuples of *RTStates*. Thus, if the number of such tuples is n, then **GREC-e** builds k^n candidate regular expressions in the worst case. Notice that all insertions at the same position are considered in only one step (one rule application), thus the maximum value n is reached only when all insertions are performed at different positions.

Given a candidate graph G with m nodes, the complexity of the reduction process that transforms G into a regular expression is $O(m^2)$ (proved in (Duarte, 2005)). As we have at most k^n graphs to be reduced, the worst case complexity of **GREC-e** is $O(k^n \times m^2)$.

Although the complexity of our method seems to be discouraging, our experimental results show that **GREC-e** can be reasonably used in the context of schema evolution, which is not an ordinary operation. Our implementation has been done in Java (JRE 1.5) running Window XP over an Intel Pentium M, 1.6 GHz machine with 512Mb of RAM, 80Gb of Disk.

We obtain the following statistical measures for 160 experiments considering 8 different regular expressions and 20 different kinds of updates: the median (the value separating the highest half from the lowest half of execution time) is 3.40 ms, the mode (the most frequent execution time) is 2.30 ms and mean execution time is 9.05 ms (with standard deviation 3.23 ms).

In terms of number of candidates, we have the following results: the median is 6.25, the mode is 8, and the mean is 14.10 (with standard deviation 6.30). The number of (embedded) starred sub-expressions has a strong impact on experimental results. In order to illustrate this aspect we show in Figure 10 execution time and number of candidates (a) for $E^o = a\ b(c|d)e(f\ g|h)\#$ ($\underline{E}^o = 1\ 2\ (3|4)\ 5\ (6\ 7|8)\ 9$), a regular expression with no starred sub-expressions; (b) for $E^* = a(b(c|d))^*e(fg|h)^*\#$ ($\underline{E}^* = 1(2(3|4))^*5(6\ 7|8)^*9$) with two non-nested starred sub-expressions, and (c) for $E^{**} = a(b(c|d)^*)^*e(f\ g|h)^*\#$ ($\underline{E}^{**} = 1(2(3|4)^*)^*5(6\ 7|8)^*9$) with nested starred sub-expressions.

The word $w = abdefg$, to be updated is the same in all three cases (it belongs to all $L(E^o)$, $L(E^*)$ and $L(E^{**})$. We assume seven insertion sequences over w giving rise to seven invalid words, namely, $w_1 = abdvefg$, $w_2 = abdvxefg$, $w_3 = abdvxyefg$, $w_4 = abdefvg$, $w_5 = abdefvxg$, $w_6 = abdefvxyg$ and $w_7 = avbxdeyfg$. The horizontal axes of graphics in Figure 10 are numbered by these seven cases.

*Figure 12. Execution of **GREC-e** for (a) E^o, (b) E^* and (c) E^{**}*

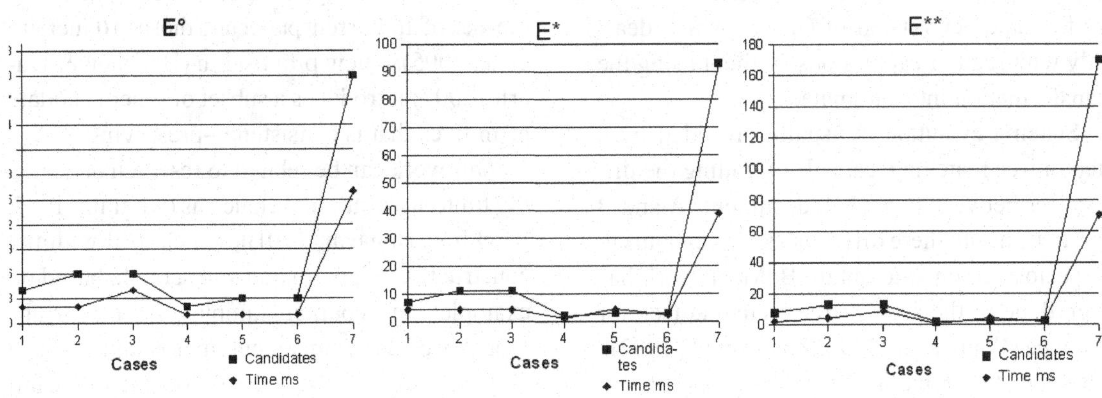

We count *a?* and *a** as two different solutions.

As it was concluded by our complexity analysis, results are better when the update position is the same for all insertions. In this case, *STrans* contains constraints that eliminate many candidates. Consider, for instance Figure 10(c). For w_7 and w_6, *RTStates* contains 3 tuples but w_7 provokes the construction of many candidates (less than 63), because it has each new symbol inserted into different positions (so *STrans* is empty). For w_6 **GREC-e** builds only 3 candidates thanks to *STrans* that contains two tuples. Our intuition is that the system could prune the combinatorial computation by asking the user to make intermediary choices limiting the number of solutions over which **GREC-e** continues to work.

RELATED WORK AND FUTURE TRENDS

The approach presented here is an extension of previous work by the same authors (Bouchou, Duarte, Halfeld Ferrari, Laurent, & Musicante, 2004). While our previous work deals with only one update at a time, our new algorithm **GREC-e**, proposed here, deals with a more complex scenario since it accepts any number of updates - a much more realistic situation. **GREC-e** is an automaton-based approach, inspired in the work of (Caron & Ziadi, 2000) that transforms regular expressions into finite state automata. In (da Luz, Halfeld Ferrari, & Musicante, 2007) we find another version of GREC, which deals only with regular expressions, without using the transformation into automata.

Schema evolution is usually preceded by a step of tree matching, capable of finding the differences between two XML documents A and B and to translate these differences into updates to be performed on A to obtain B. Much work has been done in the area of tree matching (see for instance (Wang et al., 1994; Zhang et al., 1992)). Although this topic is out of the scope of this chapter, we refer to (Su, Kuno, & Rundensteiner, 2001) as an approach where the cost model proposed in (Chawathe, Rajaraman, Garcia-Molina, & Widom, 1996) is refined in order to take into account XML characteristics, and to (Bouchou, Cheriat, Halfeld Ferrari, & Savary, 2006), which deals with (incremental) correction of XML documents, and whose proposal might be adapted to our context.

The goal of XML schema evolution research (Roddick et al., 2000; Costello & Schneider, 2000) is to allow schemas to change while maintaining access to the existing data. Most existing work, like (Kuikka, Leinonen, & Penttonen, 2000; Rougemont, 2003; Su, Kramer, Chen, Claypool, & Rundensteiner, 2001; Su, Kuno, & Rundensteiner, 2001), aim to change XML documents to conform to a given new schema (which can be the result of updating a schema with primitives such as the one proposed in (Al-Jadir & El-Moukaddem, 2003; Coox, 2003; Su et al., 2001)). In (Guerrini, Mesiti, & Rossi, 2005), a set of schema update primitives is proposed and the impact of schema updates over XML documents is analysed. The basic idea is to keep track of the updates made to the schema and to identify the portions of the schema that, because of the updates, require validation. The document portions affected by those updates are then revalidated (and changed, if necessary).

Our approach is the opposite of these methods. We intend to extend schemas in a conservative way, i.e. keeping the existing document validity without making any changes to them. Following the idea of the current paper and those in (Guerrini et al., 2005), a new proposal in (Bouchou & Duarte, 2007) introduces a subset of schema update primitives that is consistency-preserving.

Our work can be related to research on learning finite state automata (such as (Angluin, 1987; Parekh & Honavar, 2001)), which deal with the construction of automata from scratch, based on examples and counterexamples. As in our approach we start from an automaton and we have only one example (the updated document), we fall in the incremental learning automaton approach presented in (Dupont, 1996). However, as we do not have (and it is not necessary) the historical of the automaton construction, the incremental learning does not fit for our purpose. Moreover, the automata built from the finite learning automata approach may be non reducible.

We are studying the extension of our method in order to consider not only one regular expression but the entire XML type. Different directions can be taken into account. One approach might compare schema graphs and perform their evolution in a conservative way. Another approach might use logic programs to express the whole XML type and adapt the evolution of regular expressions to the evolution of the logic program. This direction is explored in (da Luz et al., 2007) by using Datalog programs.

Another perspective concerns the possibility of adapting our approach to schema constraints beyond regular (i.e., to consider XML trees respecting type constraints more powerful than those imposed by a regular tree grammar).

More important for our current researches, we plan also to investigate the use of **GREC-e** to perform the evolution of programs that describe or specify web service interfaces. Indeed, some languages for describing web service composition propose regular structures to define composed services. In this case, the evolution of a service interface can be seen as the evolution of an extended regular expression (one containing more operators than the usual ones) and **GREC-e** may be adapted to aid in the web service maintenance. This situation is more conspicuous in PEWS (Ba, Carrero, Halfeld Ferrari & Musicante 2005) but we believe it can also be explored in languages such as BPEL (Andrew et al., 2003). In a PEWS specification, each composed service interface defines a trace of operations or messages that can be seen as the language described by the program. Modifications to this language can trigger modifications on the program that describes the web service.

CONCLUSION

This paper presents **GREC-e**, an algorithm for conservative evolution of schemas for XML. The present work extends our previous algorithm (Bouchou, Duarte, Halfeld Ferrari, Laurent, & Musicante, 2004), in order to deal with multiple updates, to trigger the evolution of a schema. This extension deals with any number of updates over a word $w \in L(E)$ (resulting in $w' \notin L(E)$) in order to build new regular expressions E', such that:

- $w' \in L(E')$,
- $L(E) \subseteq L(E')$,
- E' still contains the starred sub-expressions of E and
- $D(E, E') \leq k$ (with k the number of insertions performed on w).

We start from the finite state automaton M_E corresponding to E and we proceed by computing information on changes performed on w, that we store in two structures, *RTStates* and *STrans*: the first one informs where (and which) states are to be added to M_E and specifies which transitions must appear in the new automaton; the second one is to avoid adding non accurate transitions. Then we perform the reduction process, generating new regular expressions that match modifications performed on w, while maintaining a strong syntactical relation to E. Although the complexity of our method is exponential in the number of updates (in the worst case), our experimental results show that **GREC-e** gives good results in most practical cases.

We have applied our algorithm to XML schema evolution: based on the update of one document, we allow an authoritative user to dynamically change the schema without interfering with other documents in the database. XML applications usually require that both the original and the derived regular expressions are unambiguous (i.e., corresponding automata are deterministic). If unambiguous expressions are required as a result, **GREC-e** can signal any ambiguity and equivalent unambiguous regular expressions can be computed along the lines of (Ahonen, 1997). Our method can be useful for web services if we consider the two different steps mentioned in Introduction: tree matching and validity-preserving type changing. This paper presents a solution for the second step. The first step can be solved by computing the distance from a new document to the language defined by the schema. We are currently considering different methods to perform this computation.

REFERENCES

Ahonen, H. (1997). Disambiguation of SGML Content Models. In C. Nicholas & D. Wood (Eds.), PODP 1996: *Proceedings of the workshop on principles of document processing* (pp. 27-37), Palo Alto, USA, Berlin: Springer-Verlag.

Al-Jadir, L., & El-Moukaddem, F. (2003). Once Upon a Time a DTD Evolved Into Another DTD. In Springer (Ed.), *Proceedings of the international conference on object-oriented information systems* (pp. 3-17), Geneva, Switzerland, proceedings. Berlin: Springer-Verlag.

Andrews, T., Curbera, F., Dholakia, H., Goland, Y., Klein, J., Leymann, F., Liu, K., Roller, D., Smith, D., Thatte, S., Trickovic, I., & Weerawarana, S. (2003). *Specification: Business Process Execution Language for Web Services, Version 1.1.* Available at http://www-106.ibm.com/developerworks/library/ws-bpel/.

Angluin, D. (1987). Learning Regular Sets From Queries and Counterexamples. *Information and Computation, 75*(2), 87-106.

Ba, C., Carrero, M., Halfeld Ferrari, M., & Musicante, M. (2005). PEWS: A New Language for Building Web Service Interfaces. *Journal of Universal Computer Science, 5*(11), 1215-1233.

Bouchou, B., Cheriat, A., Halfeld Ferrari, M., & Savary, A. (2006). XML document correction: Incremental approach activated by schema validation. In IDEAS 2006: *10th International Database Engineering and Applications Symposium* (pp. 228-238), Dehli, India, proceedings. Piscataway, USA: IEEE Computer Society.

Bouchou, B., & Duarte, D. (2007). Assisting XML schema evolution that preserves validity. In SBBD 2007: *XXII Brazilian Symposium on Databases* (pp. 270-284). João Pessoa, Brazil, proceedings. Porto Alegre: Brazilian Computer Society.

Bouchou, B., Duarte, D., Halfeld Ferrari, M., Laurent, D., & Musicante, M. A. (2004). Schema evolution for XML: A Consistency-Preserving Approach. In MFCS'04: *29th Mathematical Foundations of Computer Science* (pp. 876-888). Prague, Czech Republic, proceedings. Berlin: Springer-Verlag.

Brüggeman-Klein, A., & Wood, D. (1992). Deterministic Regular Languages. STACS 1992: *9th Annual Symposium on Theoretical Aspects of Computer Science*. Cachan, France, proceedings. Berlin: Springer-Verlag.

Caron, P., & Ziadi, D. (2000). Characterization of Glushkov Automata. *Theoretical Computer Science, 233*(1-2), 75-90.

Chawathe, S. S., Rajaraman, A., Garcia-Molina, H., & Widom, J. (1996). Change Detection in Hierarchically Structured Information. In *SIGMOD'96: ACM SIGMOD international conference on management of data* (pp. 493-504), Montreal, Canada, proceedings. New York: ACM Press.

Coox, S. V. (2003). Axiomatization of the Evolution of XML Database Schema. Programming and Computing Software, *29*(3), 140-146.

Costello, R., & Schneider, J. C. (2000). Challenge of XML Schemas - Schema Evolution. *The XML schemas: best practices.* Retrieved September,

2002, from http://www.xfront.org/Evolvable-Schemas.html

da Luz, R. da, Halfeld Ferrari, M., & Musicante, M. A. (2007). Regular Expression Transformations to Extend Regular languages (with Application to a Datalog XML Schema Validator). *Journal of algorithms, 62*(3-4), 148-167.

Duarte, D. (2005). *Une méthode pour l'évolution de schémas XML préservant la validité des documents.* Unpublished doctoral dissertation, University of Tours, Tours - France.

Dupont, P. (1996). Incremental Regular Inference. In ICGI 1998: *Third International Colloquium on Grammatical Inference* (pp. 222-237), Montpellier, France, proceedings. Berlin: Springer-Verlag.

Guerrini, G., Mesiti, M., & Rossi, D. (2005). Impact of XML Schema Evolution on Valid Documents. *In WIDM'05: 7th annual ACM international workshop on web information and data management,* (pp. 39-44), Bremen, Germany, proceedings. New York, USA: ACM Press.

Kuikka, E., Leinonen, P., & Penttonen, M. (2000). An Approach to Document Structure Transformations. In M.-C. G. Yulin Feng & D. Notkin (Eds.), *Conference on software: Theory and practice* (pp. 906-913), Beijin, China, proceedings. Dordrecht, Netherlands: Kluwer.

Parekh, R., & Honavar, V. (2001). Learning DFA From Simple Examples. *Machine learning, 44*(1-2), 9-35.

Roddick, J., Al-Jadir, L., Bertossi, L., Dumas, M., Estrella, F., Gregersen, H., et al. (2000). Evolution and Change in Data Management - Issues and Directions. *SIGMOD Record, 29*(1), 21-25.

Rougemont, M. d. (2003). The Correction of XML Data. In ISIP 2003: *The first franco-japanese workshop on information, search, integration and personalization* (pp. 1-17), Sapporo, Japan. Hokkaido, Japan: Hokkaido University Press.

Su, H., Kramer, D., Chen, L., Claypool, K. T., & Rundensteiner, E. A. (2001). XEM: Managing the Evolution of XML Documents. In RIDE 2001: *Eleventh International Workshop on Research Issues in Data Engineering: Document Management for Data Intensive Business and Scientific Applications* (pp. 103-110). Heidelberg, Germany, proceedings. Piscataway, USA: IEEE Computer Society.

Su, H., Kuno, H., & Rundensteiner, E. A. (2001). Automating the Transformation of XML Documents. *In WIDM'01: 3rd annual ACM international workshop on web information and data management,* (pp. 68-75), Atlanta, USA, proceedings. New York, USA: ACM Press.

Wang, J. T.-L., Zhang, K., Jeong, K., & Shasha, D. (1994). A System for Approximate Tree Matching. *Knowledge and data engineering, 6*(4), 559-571.

Zhang, K., Statman, R., & Shasha, D. (1992). On the Editing Distance Between Unordered Labelled Trees. *Information processing letters, 42*(3), 133-139.

Chapter II
A Comparative Study of XML Change Detection Algorithms

Grégory Cobéna
INRIA, France

Talel Abdessalem
Telecom ParisTech, France

ABSTRACT

Change detection is an important part of version management for databases and document archives. The success of XML has recently renewed interest in change detection on trees and semi-structured data, and various algorithms have been proposed. We study different algorithms and representations of changes based on their formal definition and on experiments conducted over XML data from the Web. Our goal is to provide an evaluation of the quality of the results, the performance of the tools and, based on this, guide the users in choosing the appropriate solution for their applications.

INTRODUCTION

The context for the present work is change detection in XML data warehouses. In such a warehouse, documents are collected periodically, for instance by crawling the Web. When a new version of an existing document arrives, we want to understand changes that occurred since the previous version. Considering that we have only the old and the new version for a document, and no other information on what happened between, a diff (i.e. the delta between the two versions) needs to be computed. A typical setting for the diff algorithm is as follows: the input consists in two files representing two versions of the same document; the output is a delta file representing the changes that occurred.

In this paper, we consider XML input documents and XML *delta* files to represent changes. The goal of this survey is to analyze the different

Copyright © 2009, IGI Global, distributing in print or electronic forms without written permission of IGI Global is prohibited.

existing solutions and, based on this, assist the users in choosing the appropriate tools for their applications. We study two dimensions of the problem: (i) the representation of changes (ii) the detection of changes.

Representing changes. To understand the important aspects of changes representation, we point out some possible applications:

- In Version management Chien et al. (2001), Marian et al. (2001), the representation should allow for effective *storage strategies* and efficient *reconstruction of versions* of the documents.
- In Temporal Applications Chawathe et al. (1999), Zhang et al. (2004), the support for a persistent identification of XML tree nodes is mandatory since one would like to identify (i.e. trace) a node through time.
- In Monitoring Applications Chen et al. (2000), Nguyen et al. (2001), Jacob et al. (2005), changes are used to detect events and trigger actions. The trigger mechanism involves queries on changes that need to be executed in real-time. For instance, in a catalog, finding the product whose type is "digital camera" and whose price has decreased.

As mentioned above, the deltas, that we consider here, are XML documents summarizing the changes. The choice of XML is motivated by the need to exchange, store and query these changes. XML allows supporting better quality services as in Chen et al. (2000) and Nguyen et al. (2001), in particular query languages (www.w3.org/TR/xquery), Aguiléra et al. (2000), and facilitates data integration (www.w3.org/rdf). Since XML is a flexible format, there are different possible ways of representing the changes on XML and semi-structured data Chawathe et al. (1998), La Fontaine (2001), Marian et al. (2001), XML Update Language (xmldb-org.sourceforge.net/xupdate), and build version management architectures Chien et al. (2001). In Section 3, we compare change representation models and we focus on recent proposals that have a formal definition, a framework to query changes and an available implementation, namely *DeltaXML* La Fontaine (2001), *XyDelta* Marian et al. (2001), *XUpdate* (xmldb-org.sourceforge.net/xupdate) and *Dommitt* (www.dommitt.com).

Change detection. In some applications (e.g. an XML document editor), the system knows exactly which changes have been made to a document, but in our context, the sequence of changes is unknown. Thus, the most critical component of change control is the *diff* module that detects changes between an old version of a document and the new version. The input of a *diff* program consists in these two documents, and possibly their DTD or XMLSchema. Its output is a *delta* document representing the changes between the two input documents. Important aspects are as follow:

- **Correctness:** We suppose that all diffs are "correct", in that they find a set of operations that is sufficient to transform the old version into the new version of the XML document. In other words, they miss no changes.
- **Minimality:** In some applications, the focus will be on the minimality of the result (e.g. number of operations, edit cost, file size) generated by the *diff*. This notion is explained in Section 2. Minimality of the result is important to save storage space and network bandwidth. Also, the effectiveness of version management depends both on minimality and on the representation of changes.
- **Semantics of the changes:** This is a challenging issue that can help users to understand "what happens" in the real world represented by the XML data. Some algorithms consider more than the tree structure of XML documents. For instance, they may consider keys (e.g. ID attributes defined in the DTD)

and match with priority two elements with the same tag if they have the same key. This may enable tracking the evolution of the identified elements. In Zhang et al. (2004), the tracked elements are identified using XPATH expressions. This needs that the information that identifies an element has to be conserved across changes to a document.

- **Performance and complexity:** With dynamic services and/or large amounts of data, good performance and low memory usage become mandatory. For example, some algorithms find a minimum edit script (given a cost model detailed in Section 2) in quadratic time and space.
- **"Move" Operations:** The capability to detect *move* operations (see Section 2) is only present in certain *diff* algorithms. The reason is that it has an impact on the complexity (and performance) of the *diff* and also on the minimality of the result and the semantics of changes.

To explain how the different criteria affect the choice of a *diff* program, let us consider the application of cooperative work on large XML documents. Large XML documents are replicated over the network. We want to permit concurrent work on these documents and efficiently update the modified parts. Thus, a *diff* between XML documents is computed. The support of ID attributes allows to divide the document into finer grain structures, and thus to efficiently handle concurrent transactions. Then, changes can be applied (propagated) to the files replicated over the network. When the level of replication is low, priority is given to performance when computing the *diff* instead of minimality of the result.

Experiment settings. Our analysis relies on experiments conducted over XML documents found on the web. *Xyleme* (www.xyleme.com) crawled more than five hundred millions web pages (HTML and XML) in order to find five hundred thousand XML documents. Because only part of them changed during the time of the experiment (several months), our measures are based roughly on hundred thousand XML documents. Most experiments were run on sixty thousand of them (because of the time it would take to run them on all the available data). It would also be interesting to run it on private data (e.g. financial data, press data). Such data is typically more regular. We intend to conduct such an experiment in the future.

Our work is intended to XML documents. But it can also be used for HTML documents, after closing properly the HTML tags. However, change management (detection+representation) for XML documents is semantically much more informative than for HTML. It includes pieces of information such as the insertion of particular subtrees with a precise semantics, e.g. a new product in a catalog.

The paper is organized as follows. First, we present the data operations and cost model in Section 2. Then, we compare change representations in Section 3. The next section is an in-depth state of the art in which we present change detection algorithms and their implementation programs. In Section 5, we present the results of our experiments, and the last section concludes the paper.

PRELIMINARIES

In this section, we introduce the notions that will be used along the paper. The data model we use for XML documents is labelled ordered trees as in Marian et al. (2001). We will alsobriefly consider some algorithms that support unordered trees.

Operations. The change model is based on editing operations as in Marian et al. (2001), namely *insert*, *delete*, *update* and *move*. There are various possible interpretations for these operations. For instance, in Kuo-Chung Tai's model Tai (1979), deleting a node means making its children become children of the node's parent.

But this model may not be appropriate for XML documents, since deleting a node changes its depth in the tree and may also invalidate the document structure according to its DTD.

Thus, for XML data, we consider Selkow's model Selkow (1977) in which operations are only applied to leaves or subtrees. For instance, when a node is deleted, the entire subtree rooted at the node is deleted. This is more appropriate for XML data, for instance removing a product from a catalog by deleting the corresponding subtree. Important aspects presented in Marian et al. (2001) include (i) management of positions in XML documents (e.g. the position of sibling nodes changes when some are deleted), and (ii) consistency of the sequence of operations depending on their order (e.g. a node can not be updated after one of its ancestors has been deleted).

Edit cost. The *edit cost* of a sequence of edit operations is defined by assigning a cost to each operation. Usually, this cost is 1 per node touched (inserted, deleted, updated or moved). If a subtree with *n* nodes is deleted (or inserted), for instance using a single *delete* operation applied to the subtree root, then the edit cost for this operation is *n*. Since most *diff* algorithms are based on this cost model, we use it in this study. The *edit distance* between document *A* and document *B* is defined by the minimal edit cost over all edit sequences transforming *A* in *B*. A *delta* is *minimal* if its edit cost is no more than the edit distance between the two documents.

One may want to consider different cost models. For instance, assigning the cost 1 for each edit operation, e.g. deleting or inserting an entire subtree. But in this case, a minimal edit script would often consist in the two following operations: (i) delete the first document with a single operation applied to the document's root (ii) insert the second document with a single operation. We briefly mention in Section 5.2 some results based on a cost model where the cost for *insert*, *delete* and *update* is 1 per node but the cost for *moving* an entire subtree is only 1.

The *move* operation. The aim of *move* is to identify nodes (or subtrees) even when their context (e.g. ancestor nodes) has changed. Some of the proposed algorithms are able to detect *move* operations between two documents, whereas others do not. We recall that most formulations of the change detection problem with *move* operations are NP-hard Zhang et al. (1995). So the drawback of detecting *moves* is that such algorithms will only approximate the minimum edit script. The improvement when using a *move* operation is that, in some applications, users will consider that a *move* operation is less costly than a *delete* and *insert* of the subtree. In temporal applications, *move* operations are important to detect from a semantic viewpoint because they allow to identify (i.e. trace) nodes through time better than *delete* and *insert* operations.

Mapping/matching. In this paper, we will also use the notion of "mapping" between two trees. Each node in *A* (or *B*) that is not deleted (or inserted) is "matched" to the corresponding node in *B* (or *A*). A *mapping* between two documents represents all matchings between nodes from the first and second documents. In some cases, a *delta* is said "minimal" if its edit cost is minimal for the restriction of editing sequences compatible with a given "mapping"[1].

The definition of the mapping and the creation of a corresponding edit sequence are part of the change detection. The change representation consists in a data model for representing the edit sequence.

COMPARISON OF THE CHANGE REPRESENTATION MODELS

XML has been widely adopted both in academia and in industry to store and exchange data. In Chawathe et al. (1999), the authors underline the necessity for querying semistructured temporal data. Recent Works Chawathe et al. (1999), La Fontaine (2001), Chien et al. (2001), Marian et al.

(2001), Zhang et al. (2004) study version management and temporal queries over XML documents. Although an important aspect of version management is the representation of changes, a standard is still missing.

In this section we recall the problematic of change representation for XML documents, and we present main recent proposals on the topic, namely *DeltaXML* La Fontaine (2001) and *XyDelta* Marian et al. (2001). Then we present some experiments conducted over Web data.

As previously mentioned, the main motivations for representing changes are: version management, temporal databases and monitoring data. Here, we analyse these applications in terms of (i) versions storage strategies and (ii) querying changes.

Versions storage strategies. In Chien et al. (2000), a comparative study of version management schemes for XML documents is conducted. For instance, two simple strategies are as follow: (i) storing only the latest version of the document and all the deltas for previous versions (ii) storing all versions of the documents, and computing deltas only when necessary. When only deltas are stored, their size (and edit cost) must be reduced. For instance, the delta is in some cases larger than the versioned document. We have analyzed the performance for reconstructing a document's version based on the delta. The time complexity is in all cases linear in the edit cost of the delta. The computation cost for such programs is close to the cost of manipulating the XML structure (reading, parsing and writing).

One may want to consider a flat text representation of changes that can be obtained for instance with the Unix diff tools. In most applications, it is efficient in terms of storage space and performance to reconstruct the documents. Its drawback is: (i) that it is not XML and can not be used for queries (ii) files must be serialized into flat text and this can not be used in native (or relational) XML repositories.

Querying changes. We recall here that support for both indexing and persistent identification is useful. On one hand, labeling nodes with both their prefix and postfix position in the tree allows to quickly compute ancestor/descendant tests and thus significantly improves querying Aguiléra et al. (2000). On the other hand, labeling nodes with a persistent identifier accelerates temporal queries and reduces the cost of updating an index. In principle, it would be nice to have one labeling scheme that contains both structure and persistence information. However, Cohen et al. (2002) shows that this requires longer labels and uses more space.

Also note that using *move* operations is often important to maintain persistent identifiers since using *delete* and *insert* does not lead to a persistent identification. Thus, the support of *move* operations improves the effectiveness of temporal queries.

Change Representation Models

We now present change representation models, and in particular *DeltaXML* La Fontaine (2001) and *XyDelta* Marian et al. (2001). In terms of features, the main difference between them is that only *XyDelta* supports *move* operations. Except for *move* operations, it is important to note that both representations are formally equivalent, in that simple algorithms can transform a *XyDelta* delta into a *DeltaXML* delta, and conversely.

DeltaXML: In La Fontaine (2001) (or similarly in Chawathe et al. (1999)), the delta information is stored in a "summary" of the original document by adding "change" attributes. It is easy to present and query changes on a single delta, but slightly more difficult to aggregate deltas or issue temporal queries on several deltas. The delta has the same look and feel as the original document, but it is not strictly validated by the DTD. The reason is that while most operations are described using attributes (with a *DeltaXML* namespace), a new type of tag is introduced to describe text nodes updates. More precisely, for obvious parsing reasons, the old and new values of a text node cannot be put side by side, and the tags <deltaxml:oldtext> and <deltaxml:newtext> are used to distinguish them.

There is some storage overhead when the change rate is low because: (i) position management is achieved by storing the root of unchanged subtrees (ii) change status is propagated to ancestor nodes. A typical example is shown in Box 1.

Note that it is also possible to store the whole document, including unchanged parts, along with changed data.

XyDelta: In Marian et al. (2001), every node in the original XML document is given a unique identifier, namely XID, according to some identification technique called *XidMap*. The *XidMap* gives the list of all persistent identifiers in the XML document in the prefix order of nodes. Then, the delta represents the corresponding operations: identifiers that are not found in the new (old) version of the document correspond to nodes that have been deleted (inserted)[2]. The previous example would generate a delta as follows. In this delta, nodes 15-17 (i.e. from 15 to 17) that have been deleted are removed from the *XidMap* of the second version *v2*. In a similar way, the persistent identifiers 31-33 of inserted nodes are now found between node 23 and node 24 (see Box 2).

XyDeltas have nice mathematical properties, e.g. they can be aggregated, inverted and stored without knowledge about the original document. Also the persistent identifiers and *move* operations are useful in temporal applications. The drawback is that the delta does not contain contexts (e.g. ancestor nodes or siblings of nodes that changed) which are sometimes necessary to understand the meaning of changes. Therefore, the context has to be obtained by processing the document.

XUpdate (xmldb-org.sourceforge.net/xupdate) provides means to update XML data, but it misses a more precise framework for version management or to query changes.

Dommitt (www.dommitt.com) representation of changes is in the spirit of *DeltaXML*. However, instead of using change attributes, new node types are created. For instance, when a *book* node is deleted, a *xmlDiffDeletebook* node is used. A drawback is that the delta DTD is significantly different from the document's DTD.

Remark. No existing change representation can be validated by (i) either a generic DTD (because of document's specific tags) (ii) or the versioned document's DTD (because of text nodes updates as mentioned previously). These issues will have to be considered in order to define a standard for representing changes of XML documents in XML.

Change Representation Experiments

Figure 1 shows the size of a *delta* represented using *DeltaXML* or *XyDelta* as function of the edit cost of the delta. The delta cost is defined according

Box 1.

```
<catalog deltaxml:delta='modified'>
    <product deltaxml:delta='unchanged' />
    <product deltaxml:delta='modified'>
        <status deltaxml:delta='deleted'>Unavailable</status>
        <name>Digital Camera</name>
        <description>...</description>
        <price deltaxml:delta='inserted'>$399</price>
    </product>
</catalog>
```

Box 2.

```
<xydelta
    v1 _ XidMap="(1-30)"
    v2 _ XidMap="(1-14;18-23;31-33;24-30)">
    <delete xid=(15-17) parent=6 position=1>
                <status>Not Available</status>
    </delete>
    <insert xid=(31-33) parent=6 position=4>
                <price>$399</price>
    </insert>
</xydelta>
```

to the "1 per node" cost model presented in Section 2. Each dot represents the average[3] delta file size for deltas with a given edit cost. It confirms clearly that *DeltaXML* is slightly larger for lower edit costs because it describes many unchanged elements. On the other hand, when the edit cost becomes larger, its size is comparable to *XyDelta*. The *deltas* in this figure are the results of more than twenty thousand XML diffs, roughly twenty percent of the changing XML that we found on the web.

STATE OF THE ART IN CHANGE DETECTION

In this section, we present an overview of the abundant previous work in this domain. The algorithms we describe are summarized in Figure 2.

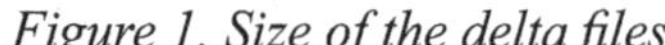

Figure 1. Size of the delta files

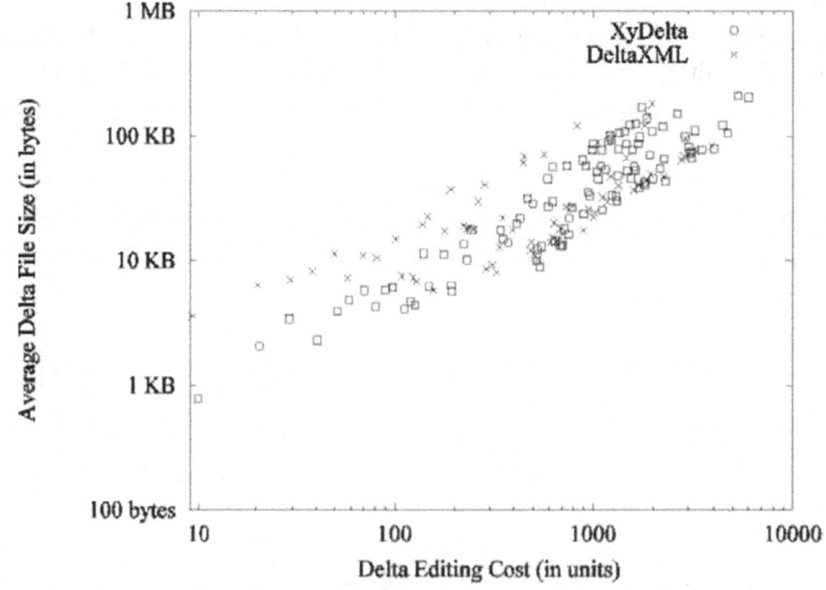

A *diff* algorithm consists in two parts: first it matches nodes between two documents, or two versions of a document. Second it generates a new document, namely a *delta*, representing a sequence of changes compatible with the matching.

For most XML *diff* tools, no complete formal description of their algorithms is available. Thus, our performance analysis is not based on formal proofs. We compared the formal upper bounds of the algorithms and we conducted experiments to test the average computation time. Also we give a formal analysis of the minimality of the *delta* results.

Following subsections are organized as follows. First, we introduce the String Edit Problem. Then, we consider optimal tree pattern matching algorithms that rely on the string edit problem to find the best matching. Finally we consider other approaches that first find a meaningful mapping between the two documents, and then generate a compatible representation of changes.

Introduction: The String Edit Problem

Longest Common Subsequence (LCS). In a standard way, the diff tries to find a minimum edit script between two strings. It is based on edit distances and the string edit problem Apostolico & Galil (1997), Levenshtein (1966), Sankoff & Kruskal (1983), Wagner & Fischer (1974). Insertion and deletion correspond to inserting and deleting a (single) symbol in a string. A cost (e.g. 1) is assigned to each operation. The string edit problem corresponds to finding an edit script of minimum cost that transforms a string x into a string y. A solution is obtained by considering the cost for transforming prefix substrings of x (up

*Figure 2. Quick summary of tested **diff** programs*

Program Name	Author	Time	Memory	Moves	Minimal Edit Cost	Notes
			Fully tested			
DeltaXML	DeltaXML.com	Linear	Linear	No	No	
MMDiff	Chawathe and al.	Quadratic	Quadratic	No	Yes	(tests with our implementation)
XMDiff	Chawathe and al.	Quadratic	Linear	No	Yes	Quadratic I/O cost (tests with our implementation)
GNU Diff	GNU Tools	Linear	Linear	No	-	No XML support (flat files)
XyDiff	INRIA	Linear	Linear	Yes	No	
			Not included in experiments			
LaDiff	Chawathe and al.	Linear	Linear	Yes	No	Criteria based mapping
XMLTreeDiff	IBM	Quadratic	Quadratic	No	No	
DiffMK	Sun	Quadratic	Quadratic	No	No	No tree structure
XML Diff	Dommitt.com					We were not allowed to discuss it
Constrained Diff	K. Zhang	Quadratic	Quadratic	No	Yes	-for unordered trees -constrained mapping
X-Diff	Y. Wang, D. DeWitt, Jin-Yi Cai (U. Wisconsin)	Quadratic	Quadratic	No	Yes	-for unordered trees -constrained mapping

to the i-th symbol) into prefix subtrings of y (up to the j-th symbol). On a matrix $[1..|x|]*[1..|y|]$, a directed acyclic graph (DAG) representing all operations and their edit cost is constructed. Each path ending on (i,j) represents an edit script to transform $x[1..i]$ into $y[1..j]$. The minimum edit cost $cost\ (x[1..i] \rightarrow y[1..j]$ is then given by the minimal cost of these three possibilities:

$cost(deleteCharSymbol(x[i]+cost(x[1..i-1]\rightarrow y[1..j])$

$cost(insertCharSymbol(y[j]))+cost(x[1..i]\rightarrow y[1..j-1])$

$cost(updateCharSymbol(x[i],y[j]))cost(x[1..i-1]\rightarrow y[1..j-1])$

The edit distance between x and y is given by $cost(x[1..|x|]\rightarrow y[1..|y|])$ and the minimum edit script by the corresponding path. Note that for example the cost for $updateCharSymbol(x[i],y[j])$ is zero when the two symbols are identical.

The sequence of nodes that are not modified by the edit script is a common subsequence of x and y. Thus, finding the edit distance is equivalent to finding the "Longest Common Subsequence" (LCS) between x and y. Note that each node in the common subsequence defines a matching pair between the two corresponding symbols in strings x and y.

The space and time complexity are $O(|x|*|y|)$. This algorithm has been improved by Masek and Paterson using the "four-russians" technique Masek & Paterson (1980) in $O\left(|x|*|y| / \log|x|\right)$ and $O\left(|x|*|y|*\log(\log|x|) / \log|x|\right)$ worst-case running time for finite and arbitrary alphabet sets respectively.

D-Band Algorithms. In Myers (1986), a $O(|x|*D)$ algorithm is exhibited, where D is the size of the minimum edit script. Such algorithms, namely *D-Band* algorithms, consist of computing cost values only close to the diagonal of the matrix $[1..|x|]*[1..|y|]$. A diagonal k is defined by (i,j) couples with the same difference $i-j=k$, e.g. for $k=0$ the diagonal contains (0,0),(1,1)(2,2),.... When using the usual "1 per node" cost model, diagonal areas of the matrix, e.g. all diagonals from $-K$ to K, contain all edit scripts Myers (1986) of cost lower than a given value K. Obviously, if a valid edit script of cost lower than K is found to be minimum inside the diagonal area, then it must be the minimum edit script. When k is zero, the area consists solely in the diagonal starting at (0,0). By increasing k, it is then possible to find the minimum edit script in $O(\max(|x|+|y|)*D)$ time. Using a more precise analysis of the number of deletions, Wu et al. (1990) improves significantly this algorithm performance when the two documents lengths differ substantially. This *D-Band* technique is used by the famous *GNU diff* (www.gnu.org/software/diffutils/diffutils.html) program for text files.

Optimal Tree Pattern Matching

Serialized XML documents can be considered as strings, and thus we could use a "string edit" algorithm to detect changes. This may be used as a raw storage and raw version management, and can indeed be implemented using *GNU diff* that only supports flat text files. However, in order to support better services, it is preferable to consider specific algorithms for tree data that we describe next. The complexity we mention for each algorithm is relative to the total number of nodes in both documents. Note that the number of nodes is linear in the document's file size.

Previous Tree Models. Kuo-Chung Tai, Tai (1979), gave a definition of the edit distance between ordered labeled trees and the first non-exponential algorithm to compute it. The time and space complexity is quasi-quadratic.

In Selkow's variant Selkow (1977), which is closer to XML, the LCS algorithm described previously is used on trees in a recursive algorithm. Considering two documents $D1$ and $D2$, the time complexity is $O(|D1|*|D2|)$. In the same spirit is Yang's algorithm, Yang (1991), to find the syntactic differences between two programs.

MMDiff and XMDiff. In Chawathe (1999), S. Chawathe presents an external memory algorithm *XMDiff* (based on main memory version *MMDiff*) for ordered trees in the spirit of Selkow's variant. Intuitively, the algorithm constructs a matrix in the spirit of the "string edit problem", but some edges are removed to enforce the fact that deleting (or inserting) a node will delete (or insert) the subtree rooted at this node. More precisely, (i) diagonal edges exists if and only if corresponding nodes have the same depth in the tree (ii) horizontal (resp. vertical) edges from (x,y) to $(x+1,y)$ exists unless the depth of node with prefix label $x+1$ in $D1$ is lower than the depth of node $y+1$ in $D2$. For *MMDiff*, the CPU and memory costs are quadratic $O(|D1|*|D2|)$. With *XMDiff*, memory usage is reduced but IO costs become quadratic.

Unordered Trees. In XML, we sometimes want to consider the tree as unordered. The general problem becomes NP-hard Zhang et al. (1992), but by constraining the possible mappings between the two documents, K. Zhang, Zhang (1996), proposed an algorithm in quasi quadratic time. In the same spirit is *X-Diff* Wang et al. (2003) from NiagaraCQ Chen et al. (2000). In these algorithms, for each pair of nodes from $D1$ and $D2$ (e.g. the root nodes), the distance between their respective subtrees is obtained by finding the minimum-cost mapping for matching children (by reduction to the minimum cost maximum flow problem Zhang (1996), Wang et al. (2003)). More precisely, the complexity is

$$O\begin{pmatrix}|D1|*|D2|*(\deg(D1)+\deg(D2)) \\ *\log(\deg(D1)+\deg(D2))\end{pmatrix},$$

where $deg(D)$ is the maximum outdegree (number of child nodes) of D. We do not consider these algorithms since we did not experiment on unordered XML trees. However, their characteristics are similar to *MMDiff* since both find a minimum edit script in quadratic time.

DeltaXML. One of the most featured products on the market is *DeltaXML* (www.deltaxml.com). It uses a similar technique based on longest common subsequence computations; more precisely it uses a *D-Band* algorithm Wu et al. (1990), Myers (1986), to run in quasi-linear time. The complexity is $O(|x|*D)$, where $|x|$ is the total size of both documents, and D is the edit distance between them. Because the algorithm is applied at each level separately, the result is not strictly minimal. The recent versions of *DeltaXML* support the addition of keys (either in the DTD or as attributes) that can be used to enforce correct matching (e.g. always match a *person* by its *name* attribute). *DeltaXML* also supports unordered XML trees.

Others. In a similar way, IBM developed XML Treediff (www.alphaworks.ibm.com/tech/xmltreediff) based on Curbera & Epstein (1999) and Shasha & Zhang (1990). A first phase is added which consists in pruning identical subtrees based on their hash signature, but it is not clear if the result obtained is still minimal. Sun also released an XML specific tool named *DiffMK* (www.sun.com/xml/developers/diffmk) that computes the difference between two XML documents. This tool is based on the Unix standard *diff* algorithm, and uses a *list* description of the XML document, thus losing the benefit of the tree structure in XML.

For both programs, we experienced difficulties in running the tools on a large set of files. Thus, these two programs were not included in our experiments.

We were surprised by the relatively weak offer in the area of XML diff tools since we are not aware of more featured XML diff products from important companies. We think that this may be due to a missing widely accepted XML change protocol. It may also be the case that some products are not publicly available. Fortunately, the algorithms we tested represent well the spirit of today's tools: quadratic minimum-script finding algorithm (*MMDiff*), linear-time approximation

(*DeltaXML*), and tree pattern matching with move operations described in the next section.

Tree Pattern Matching with a *Move* Operation

The main reason why few diff algorithms supporting *move* operations have been developed earlier is that most formulations of the tree diff problem are NP-hard Zhang et al. (1995), Chawathe & Garcia-Molina (1997) (by reduction from the "exact cover by three-sets"). One may want to convert a pair of *delete* and *insert* operations applied on a similar subtree into a single *move* operation. But the result obtained is in general not minimal, unless the cost of *move* operations is strictly identical to the total cost of deleting and inserting the subtree.

LaDiff. Recent work from S. Chawathe includes LaDiff Chawathe et al. (1996), Chawathe & Garcia-Molina (1997), designed for hierarchically structured information. It introduces matching criteria to compare nodes, and the overall matching between both versions of the document is decided on this base. A minimal edit script -according to the matching- is then constructed. Its cost is in $O(n * e + e^2)$ where n is the total number of leaf nodes, and e a weighted edit distance between the two trees. Intuitively, its cost is linear in the size of the documents, but quadratic in the number of changes between them. Note that when the change rate is maximized, the cost becomes quadratic in the size of the data. Since e^2we do not have an XML implementation of LaDiff, we could not include it in our experiments.

XyDiff. It has been proposed with one of the authors of the present paper in Cobena et al. (2002). *XyDiff* is a fast algorithm which supports *move* operations and XML features like the DTD ID attributes. Intuitively, it matches large identical subtrees found in both documents, and then propagates matchings. A first phase consists in matching nodes according to the key attributes. Then it tries to match the largest subtrees and considers smaller and smaller subtrees if matching fails. When matching succeeds, parents and descendants of identical nodes are also matched as long as the mappings are unambiguous (e.g. an unambiguous case is when two matched nodes have both a single child node with a given tag name). Its cost in time and space is quasi linear $O(n * \log(n))$ in the size n of the documents. It does not, in general, find the minimum edit script.

Summary of Tested *diff* Programs

As previously mentioned, the algorithms are summarized in Figure 2. The time cost given here (quadratic or linear) is a function of the data size, and corresponds to the case when there are few changes.

For GNU diff, we do not consider minimality since it does not support XML (or tree) editing operations. However, we mention in Section 5.2 some analysis of the result file size.

EXPERIMENTS

As previously mentioned our XML test data has been downloaded from the web. The files found on the web are on average small (a few kilobytes). To run tests on larger files, we composed large XML files from DBLP (dblp.uni-trier.de) data source. We used two versions of the DBLP source, downloaded at an interval of one year.

Speed and Memory Usage

The measures were conducted on a Linux system. Some of the XML diff tools are implemented in C++, whereas others are implemented in Java. Let us stress that this difference did not have an important impact on the obtained measures, in particular for large files. We ran tests that show that the same algorithm, compiled in Java (Just-In-Time compiler) or C++, run on average at the same speed.

Figure 3. Speed of different programs

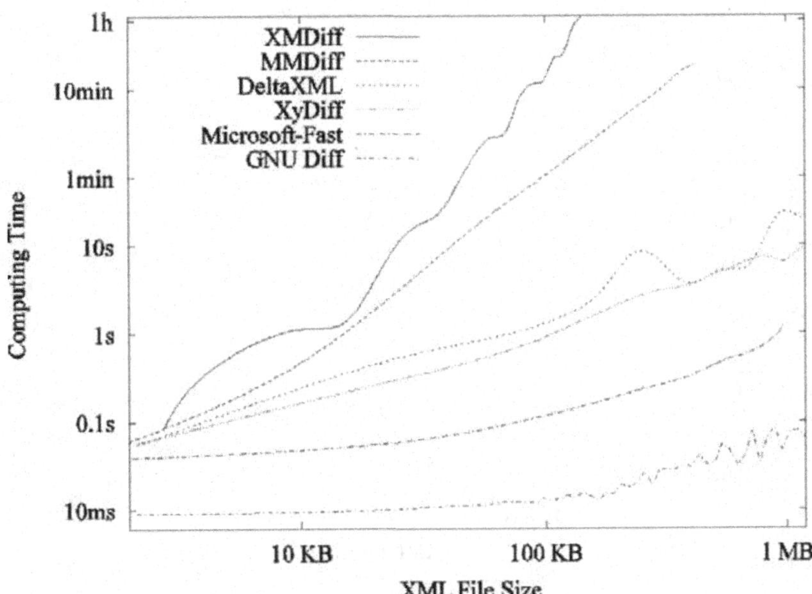

Let us analyze the behaviour of the time function plotted in Figure 3. It represents, for each diff program, the average computing time depending on the input file size. On the one hand, *XyDiff* and *DeltaXML* are perfectly linear, as well as *GNU Diff*. On the other hand, *MMDiff* increase rate corresponds to a quadratic time complexity. When handling medium files (e.g. hundred kilobytes), there are orders of magnitude between the running time of linear vs. quadratic algorithms.

For *MMDiff*, memory usage is the limiting factor since we used a 1Gb RAM PC to run it on files up to hundred kilobytes. For larger files, the computation time of *XMDiff* (the external-memory version of *MMDiff*) increases significantly when disk accesses become more and more intensive.

In terms of implementation, *GNU Diff* is much faster than others because it does not parse or handle XML. On the contrary, we know -for instance- that *XyDiff* spends ninety percent of the time in parsing the XML files. This makes *GNU Diff* very performant for simple text-based version management schemes.

A more precise analysis of *DeltaXML* results is depicted in Figure 4. It shows that although the average computation time is linear, the results for some documents are significantly different. Indeed, the computation time is almost quadratic for some files. We found that it corresponds to the worst case for D-Band algorithms: the edit distance *D* (i.e. the number of changes) between the two documents is close to the number of nodes N. For instance, in some documents, 40 percent of the nodes changed, whereas in other documents less than 3 percent of the nodes changed. This may be slight disadvantage for applications with strict time requirements, e.g. computing the diff over a flow of crawled documents as in NiagaraCQ, Chen et al. (2000), or *Xyleme*, Nguyen et al. (2001). On the contrary, for *MMDiff* and *XyDiff*, the variance of computation time for all the documents is small. This shows that their average complexity is equal to the upper bound.

Figure 4. Focus on ***DeltaXML*** *speed measures*

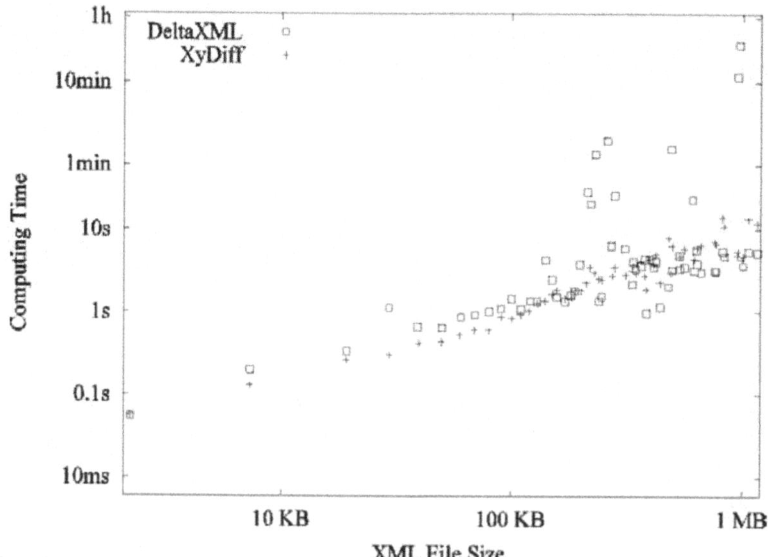

Quality of the Result

The "quality" study in our benchmark focuses on the minimality of the deltas, and consists in comparing the sequence of changes (deltas) generated by the different algorithms. We used the result of *MMDiff* and *XMDiff* as a reference because these algorithms find the minimum edit script. Thus, for each pair of documents, the quality for a diff tool (e.g. *DeltaXML*) is defined by the ratio:

$$r = \frac{C}{C_{ref}}$$

where C is the delta edit cost and C_{ref} is *MMDiff* delta's edit cost for the same pair of documents. A quality equals to one means that the result is minimum and is considered "perfect". When the ratio increases, the quality decreases. For instance, a ratio of 2 means that the delta is twice more costly than the minimum delta. In our first experiments, we didn't consider *move* operations. This was done by replacing for *XyDiff* each *move* operation by the corresponding pair of *insert* and *delete*. In this case, the cost of moving a subtree is identical to the cost of deleting and inserting it.

In Figure 5, we present an histogram of the results, i.e. the number of documents in some range of quality. *XMDiff* and *MMDiff* do not appear on the graph because they serve as reference, meaning that all documents have a quality strictly equal to one. *GNU Diff* do not appear on the graph because it doesn't construct XML (tree) edit sequences.

These results in Figure 5 show that:

- **DeltaXML.** For most of the documents, the quality of *DeltaXML* result is perfect (strictly equal to 1). For the others, the delta is on average thirty percent more costly than the minimum.
- **XyDiff.** For almost the half of the documents, the quality of *XyDiff* result does not exceed 2 (twice as costly as the minimum). For the other half, the delta is on average three times more costly than the minimum.
- **Result file size.** In terms of file sizes, we also compared the different delta documents, as

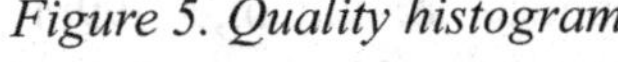

Figure 5. Quality histogram

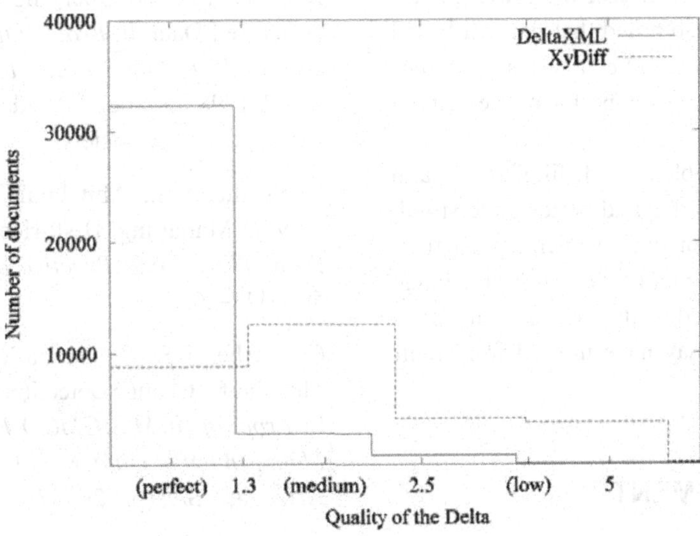

well as the flat text result of *GNU Diff.* The result *diff* files for *DeltaXML*, *GNU Diff* and *XyDiff* have on average the same size. The result files for *MMDiff* are on average twice smaller (using a *XyDelta* representation of changes).

- **Using "move".** We also conducted experiments by considering *move* operations and assigning them the cost 1. Intuitively this means that *move* is considered cheaper than deleting and inserting a subtree, e.g. moving files is cheaper than copying them and deleting the original copy. Only *XyDiff* detects *move* operations. On average, *XyDiff* performs a bit better, and it particular becomes better than *MMDiff* for five percent of the documents.

CONCLUSION

In this paper, we described existing works on the topic of change detection in XML documents. We first presented two recent proposals for change representation, and compared their features through analysis and experiments. Both support XML queries and version management, but the identification-based scheme (*XyDelta*) is slightly more compact for small deltas, whereas the delta-attributes based scheme (*DeltaXML*) is more easily integrated in simple applications. A key feature of *XyDelta* is the support of node identifiers and *move* operations that are used in temporal XML databases. More work is clearly needed in that direction to define a common standard for representing changes.

The second part of our study concerns change detection algorithms. We compared two main approaches; the first one consists in computation of minimal edit scripts, while the second approach relies on meaningfull mappings between documents. We underlined the need for semantical integration in the change detection process. The experiments presented show (i) a significant quality advantage for minimal-based algorithms (*DeltaXML*, *MMDiff*) (ii) a dramatic performance improvement with linear complexity algorithms (*GNU Diff*, *XyDiff* and *DeltaXML*).

On average, *DeltaXML* (www.deltaxml.com) seems the best choice because it runs extremely fast and its results are close to the minimum. It is a good trade-off between XMDiff (pure minimality of the result but high computation cost) and *XyDiff* (high performance but lower quality of the result). We also noted that flat text based version management (*GNU Diff*) still makes sense with XML data for performance critical applications.

Although the problem of "diffing" XML (and its complexity) is better and better understood, there is still room for improvement. In particular, *diff* algorithms could take better advantage of semantic knowledge that we may have on the documents or may have infered from their histories.

ACKNOWLEDGMENT

We would like to thank Yassine Hinnach for his precious collaboration. He helped us for the experiments conducted for this study. We also would like to thank Serge Abiteboul, Vincent Aguiléra, Robin La Fontaine, Amélie Marian, Tova Milo, Benjamin Nguyen and Bernd Amann for discussions on the topic.

REFERENCES

Aguiléra, V., Cluet, S., Veltri, P., Vodislav, D., & Wattez, F. (2000). Querying XML Documents in Xyleme. In *Proc. of the ACM-SIGIR 2000 Workshop on XML and Information Retrieval.* Athens, Greece.

Apostolico, A., & Galil, Z. (Eds.) (1997). *Pattern matching algorithms.* Oxford, UK: Oxford University Press.

Chawathe, S.S. (1999). Comparing Hierarchical Data in External Memory. In *Proc. of 25th Int. Conference on Very Large Data Bases (VLDB'99),* September 7-10, 1999, Edinburgh, Scotland, UK, (pp. 90–101). Morgan Kaufmann.

Chawathe, S.S., Abiteboul, S., & Widom, J. (1998). Representing and Querying Changes in Semistructured Data. In *Proc. of the 4th Int. Conference on Data Engineering (ICDE'98),* February 23-27, 1998, Orlando, Florida, USA, (pp. 4–13). IEEE Computer Society.

Chawathe, S.S., Abiteboul, S., & Widom, J. (1999). Managing Historical Semistructured Data. *Theory and Practice of Object Systems, 5*(3), 143–162.

Chawathe, S.S., & Garcia-Molina, H. (1997). Meaningful Change Detection in Structured Data. In *Proc. of ACM SIGMOD Int. Conference on Management of Data,* May 13-15, 1997, Tucson, Arizona, USA, (pp. 26–37). ACM Press.

Chawathe, S.S., Rajaraman, A., Garcia-Molina, H., & Widom, J. (1996). Change Detection in Hierarchically Structured Information. In *Proc. of the ACM SIGMOD Int. Conference on Management of Data,*. Montreal, Quebec, Canada, June 4-6, 1996, (pp. 493–504). ACM Press.

Chen, J., DeWitt, D.J., Tian, F., & Wang, Y. (2000). NiagaraCQ: A Scalable Continuous Query System for Internet Databases. In *Proc. of the ACM SIGMOD Int. Conference on Management of Data,* May 16-18, 2000, Dallas, Texas, USA, (pp. 379–390). ACM.

Chien, S.-Y., Tsotras, V.J., & Zaniolo, C. (2000). *A Comparative Study of Version Management Schemes for XML Documents.* Technical Report TR51, TimeCenter.

Chien, S.-Y., Tsotras, V.J., & Zaniolo, C. (2001). XML Document Versioning. *SIGMOD Record, 30*(3), 46–53.

Cobena, G., Abiteboul, S., & Marian, A. (2002). Detecting Changes in XML Documents. In *Proc. of the 18th Int. Conference on Data Engineering (ICDE'02),* 26 February - 1 March 2002, San Jose, CA, USA, (pp. 41–52). IEEE Computer Society.

Cohen, E., Kaplan, H., & Milo, T. (2002). Labeling Dynamic XML Trees. In *Proc. of the 21st ACM SIGACT-SIGMOD-SIGART Symposium on Principles of Database Systems*, June 3-5, Madison, Wisconsin, USA, (pp. 271–281). ACM.

Curbera, F., & Epstein, D.A. (1999). Fast difference and update of XML documents. In *XTech*. San Jose, CA, USA.

Jacob, J., Sachde, A., & Chakravarthy, S. (2005). CX-DIFF: a change detection algorithm for XML content and change visualization for WebVigiL. *Data & Knowledge Engineering, 52*(2), 209–230.

La Fontaine, R. (2001). A Delta Format for XML: Identifying changes in XML and representing the changes in XML. In *XML Europe*. Berlin, Germany.

Levenshtein, V. I. (1966). Binary codes capable of correcting deletions, insertions, and reversals. *Cybernetics and Control Theory 10*, (pp. 707–710).

Marian, A., Abiteboul, S., Cobena, G., & Mignet, L. (2001). Change-Centric Management of Versions in an XML Warehouse. In *Proc. of 27th Int. Conference on Very Large Data Bases (VLDB'01)*, September 11-14, 2001, Roma, Italy, (pp. 581–590). Morgan Kaufmann.

Masek, W.J., & Paterson, M. (1980). A Faster Algorithm Computing String Edit Distances. *Journal of Computer and System Sciences, 20*(1), 18–31.

Myers, E.W. (1986). An O(ND) Difference Algorithm and Its Variations. *Algorithmica, 1*(2), 251–266.

Nguyen, B., Abiteboul, S., Cobena, G., & Preda, M. (2001). Monitoring XML Data on the Web. In *SIGMOD Conference*. Santa Barbara, CA, USA.

Sankoff, D., & Kruskal, J. (1983). *Time warps, String Edits, and Macromolecules*. Addison-Wesley, Reading, Massachussets.

Selkow, S.M. (1977). The Tree-to-Tree Editing Problem. *Information Processing Letters, 6*(6), 184–186.

Shasha, D., & Zhang, K. (1990). Fast Algorithms for the Unit Cost Editing Distance Between Trees. *Journal of Algorithms, 11*(4), 581–621.

Tai, K. C. (1979). The Tree-to-Tree Correction Problem. *Journal of the ACM, 26*(3), 422–433.

Wagner, R.A., & Fischer, M.J. (1974). The String-to-String Correction Problem. *Journal of the ACM, 21*(1), 168–173.

Wang, Y., DeWitt, D.J., & Cai, J. (2003). X-Diff: An Effective Change Detection Algorithm for XML Documents. In *Proc. of the 19th Int. Conference on Data Engineering*, March 5-8, 2003, Bangalore, India, (pp. 519–530).

Wu, S., Manber, U., Myers, G., & Miller, W. (1990). An O(NP) Sequence Comparison Algorithm. *Information Processing Letters, 35*(6), 317–323.

Yang, W. (1991). Identifying Syntactic differences Between Two Programs. *Software - Practice and Experience, 21*(7), 739–755.

Zhang, K. (1996). A Constrained Edit Distance Between Unordered Labeled Trees. *Algorithmica, 15*(3), 205–222.

Zhang, K., Statman, R., & Shasha, D. (1992). On the Editing Distance Between Unordered Labeled Trees. *Information Proceedings Letters, 42*(3), 133–139.

Zhang, K., Wang, J.T.L., & Shasha, D. (1995). On the Editing Distance between Undirected Acyclic Graphs and Related Problems. In *Proc. of the 6th Annual Symposium on Combinatorial Pattern Matching*, (pp. 395–407).

Zhang, S., Dyreson, C.E., & Snodgrass, R.T. (2004). Schema-Less, Semantics-Based Change Detection for XML Documents. In *WISE 2004, Proc. of the 5th Int. Conference on Web Information Systems Engineering,* Brisbane, Australia, November 22-24, vol. 3306 of Lecture Notes in Computer Science, (pp. 279–290). Springer.

Chapter III
Active XML Transactions

Debmalya Biswas
SAP Research, Germany

Il-Gon Kim
Korea Information Security Agency, Korea

ABSTRACT

Active XML (AXML) provides an elegant platform to integrate the power of XML, Web services and Peer to Peer (P2P) paradigms by allowing (active) Web service calls to be embedded within XML documents. In this chapter, the authors present some interesting aspects encountered while investigating a transactional framework for AXML systems. They present an integrated locking protocol for the scenario where the structure of both data and transactions are nested. They show how to construct the undo operations dynamically, and outline an algorithm to compute a correct optimum undo order in the presence of nesting and parallelism. Finally, to overcome the inherent problem of peer disconnection, the authors propose an innovative solution based on "chaining" the active peers for early detection and recovery from peer disconnection.

1. INTRODUCTION

Active XML (AXML) (Abiteboul et. al., 2003) systems provide an elegant way to combine the power of XML, Web services and Peer to Peer (P2P) paradigms by allowing (active) Web service calls to be embedded within XML documents.

An AXML system consists of the following main components:

- **AXML documents:** XML documents with embedded AXML service calls (defined below). For example, the AXML snippet in Fig. 1 is an AXML document with the embed-

Copyright © 2009, IGI Global, distributing in print or electronic forms without written permission of IGI Global is prohibited.

ded service call 'getGrandSlamsWon'. The function of the service getGrandSlamsWon is basically to retrieve the Grand Slams won by a tennis player, and the abbreviations A, F, W and U correspond to the Australian, French, Wimbledon and US Grand Slams respectively.

- **AXML Services:** AXML services are basically Web services, defined as queries/ updates over local AXML documents. Note that while AXML services can be invoked remotely, the operations they encapsulate are local, that is, defined on AXML documents hosted on the same peer.
- Peers where both the AXML documents and services are hosted. AXML peers also provide a user interface to query/update the stored AXML documents locally.

An embedded service call may need to be *materialized*: 1) in response to a query on the AXML document (the materialization results are required to evaluate the query) or 2) periodically as specified by the 'frequency' attribute of the AXML service call tag <axml:sc>. We illustrate materialization with the following example: Let the AXML document D corresponding to Fig. 1 be hosted on peer AP_1, and the service getGrandSlamsWon hosted on another peer AP_2. Now, assuming the embedded service call getGrandSlamsWon needs to be materialized, the following sequence of steps takes place:

1. Fig. 2(a). AP_1 invokes the service getGrandSlamsWon of AP_2 with the parameter value children nodes of the service call getGrandSlamsWon node of D. Note that a service call's parameters may themselves be defined as service calls. Given such a scenario, AP_1 needs to first materialize the parameter service calls, and then invoke the service getGrandSlamsWon.
2. Fig. 2(b). On receiving the invocation results (an XML subtree), AP_1 does one of the following based on the 'mode' of the embedded service call getGrandSlamsWon. A service call can have the following modes: a) replace: the previous results are replaced by the current materialization results, or b) merge: the current results are appended as siblings of the previous results. The resulting AXML document, after a materialization of getGrandSlamsWon of D with parameter value "$year = 2004", is shown in Fig. 3. Analogous to parameter inputs, the invocation results may also be static XML or another service call. If the invocation results contain another service call, then AP_1 needs to materialize them first before inserting the results in D.

Transactions are a useful abstraction to provide fault-tolerance, reliability and robustness to distributed systems. A transaction (Bernstein et. al., 1987) can be considered as a group of operations encapsulated by the operations Begin and Commit/Abort having the following properties A (Atomicity), C (Consistency), I (Isolation), D (Durability). We assume prior knowledge of the basic transactional concepts, especially, lock based concurrency control protocols, undo/redo recovery and nested transactions. *In this work, we study a transactional framework for AXML systems.* Characteristics of an AXML system, important from a transactional point of view, are as follows:

- **Distributed:** The distributed aspect follows from: 1) the capability to invoke services hosted on remote peers, and 2) distributed storage of parts of an AXML document across multiple peers (Abiteboul et. al. 2003). In case of distributed storage, if a query Q on peer AP_1 requires part of an AXML document stored on peer AP_2, then there are two options: a) the query Q is decomposed and the relevant sub-query sent to peer AP_2 for evaluation, or b) AP_1 acquires

Figure 1. Sample AXML document with embedded service call getGrandSlamsWon

```
<?xml version = "1.0" encoding = "UTF-8"?>
<ATPList date = "18042005">
     <player rank = 1>
          <name>
               <firstname>Roger</firstname> <lastname>Federer</lastname>
          </name>
          <citizenship>Swiss</citizenship>
          <points>475</points>
          <axml:sc mode = "merge" serviceNameSpace = "getGrandSlamsWon"
serviceURL = "..." methodName = "getGrandSlamsWon">
               <axml:params>
                    <axml:param name = "name">
                    <axml:value>Roger Federer</axml:value>
                    <axml:param name = "year">
                    <axml:value>$year</axml:value>
               </axml:params>
               <grandslamswon year = "2003">A, W</grandslamswon>
          </axml:sc>
     </player>
...
</ATPList>
```

Figure 2. Materialization of the embedded service call getGrandSlamsWon

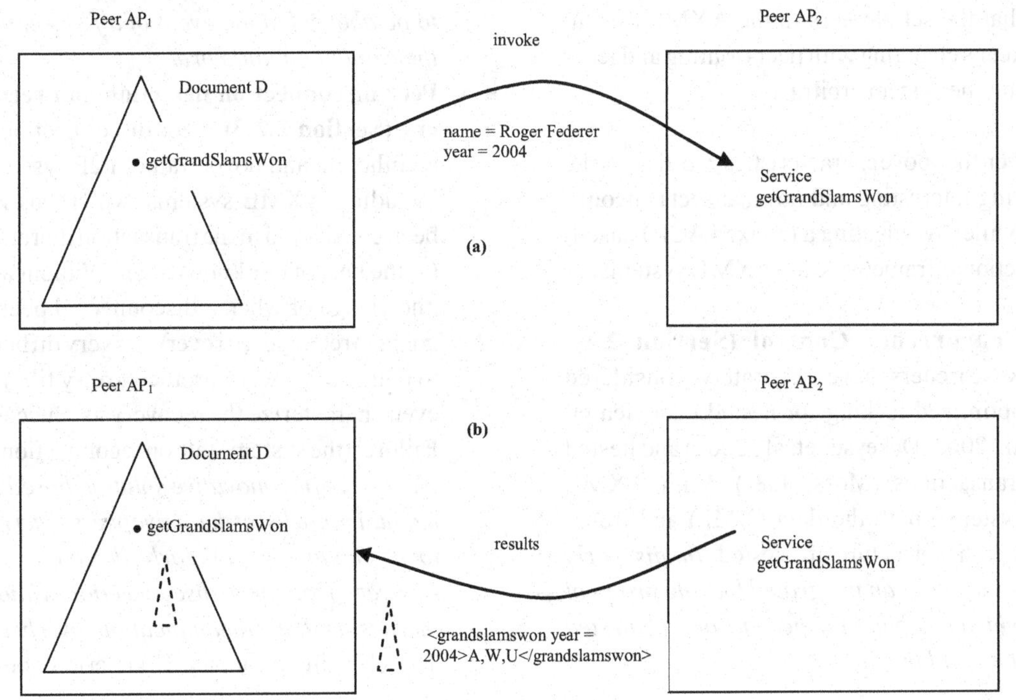

a copy of the required AXML document fragment and evaluates Q locally. Both the above options require invoking a service on the remote peer, and as such, are similar in functionality to (1).

- **Replication:** AXML documents (or fragments of the documents) and services may be replicated on multiple peers (Biswas, 2008).
- **Nested:** The nested aspect is mainly with respect to the nested (recursive) invocation of services. a) Local nesting: As a result of the possibility of service call parameters and invocation results themselves containing service calls. b) Distributed nesting: Invocation of a service S_X of peer AP_2, by peer AP_1, may require the peer AP_2 to invoke another service S_Y of peer AP_3, leading to a nested invocation of services across multiple peers. Note that a nested invocation of services may actually lead to a cycle, however we do not address that issue in this work and assume the invocations to be cycle-free.
- **Availability:** In true P2P style, we consider that the set of peers in the AXML system keeps changing with peers joining and leaving the system arbitrarily.

Given the above characteristics, we discuss the following interesting and novel aspects encountered while investigating a (relaxed ACID based) transactional framework for AXML systems:

- **Concurrency Control (Section 2.1):** Researchers have separately considered optimized locking for nested data (Jea et. al., 2002; Dekeyser et. al., 2004) and nested transactions (Moss, 1981). With AXML systems, both the data (XML) and transactional structure are nested. *In this work, we propose an integrated locking protocol which combines the benefits of both nested data and transactions.*
- **Undo operations (Section 2.2.1):** Current industry standards, e.g., Business Process Execution Language (BPEL, 2002) for Web services orchestrations, only allow static definition of the undo operations, that is, the undo/compensation handlers need to be defined at design time on the lines of exception handlers. However, static undo operation definition is neither feasible nor sufficient for AXML operations, especially, AXML query operations. *To overcome this limitation, we show how the undo operations (corresponding to AXML operations) can be constructed dynamically at run-time.*
- **Undo order (Section 2.2.2):** In general, the undo operations are executed sequentially in reverse order of their original execution order. We contend that the undo of operations executed in parallel originally, can also be executed in parallel to optimize performance. However, the presence of nesting leads to additional synchronization issues in such a scenario. *We present an algorithm to compute the subtransactions which need to be aborted in the event of a failure, and their optimum undo order.*
- **Peer disconnection detection and recovery (Section 2.2.3):** Peer disconnection is an inherent and novel trait of P2P systems, including AXML systems, which has not been considered in the transaction literature (to the best of our knowledge). Without any knowledge of when a disconnected peer is going to reconnect (if ever), it is very difficult to define a recovery protocol (retry till?) or even characterize the recovery as 'Success/Failure' (the system state on reconnection?). *We outline an innovative solution based on maintaining a list of the active peers, referred to as 'chaining', for early detection and recovery from peer disconnection without increasing the communication overhead.* The chaining approach is generic enough

Figure 3. Sample AXML document (after an invocation of the embedded service call getGrandSlamsWon)

```
<?xml version = "1.0" encoding = "UTF-8"?>
<ATPList date = "18042005">
     <player rank = 1>
          <name>
               <firstname>Roger</firstname> <lastname>Federer</lastname>
          </name>
          <citizenship>Swiss</citizenship>
          <points>475</points>
          <axml:sc mode = "merge" serviceNameSpace = "getGrandSlamsWon"
serviceURL = "..." methodName = "getGrandSlamsWon">
               <axml:params>
                    <axml:param name = "name">
                    <axml:value>Roger Federer</axml:value>
                    <axml:param name = "year">
                    <axml:value>$year</axml:value>
               </axml:params>
               <grandslamswon year = "2003">A, W</grandslamswon>
               <grandslamswon year = "2004">A, W,U</grandslamswon>
          </axml:sc>
     </player>
...
</ATPList>
```

to be applicable (for a nested application implemented) in any P2P setting. In addition, we show how AXML specific semantics can be exploited to reuse some of the work done before failure, during recovery (that is, there is no need to undo everything and start from scratch again in the event of a failure).

2. AXML TRANSACTIONS

The possible operations on AXML documents are queries, updates, inserts and deletes (update operations with action types 'replace', 'insert' and 'delete'). The operations as such are basically XML query and update operations, with the only exception being the query operation, which may involve invocation of relevant embedded service calls for evaluation. An operation can be submitted using the peer user interface or by invoking the corresponding service (encapsulating that operation). We do not differentiate between the two modes and use the terms operation and service interchangeably throughout the paper.

We consider a transactional unit as a batch of query/update operations (services).

2.1 Concurrency Control

In this section, we present a centralized lock based concurrency control protocol for AXML systems. We view an AXML (XML) document as an unranked, unordered tree, where each leaf node has a label, and the internal nodes (including the special <axml:sc> nodes for embedded service calls) have an identifier.

For a lock based protocol, we first need to determine the locking granularity. While locking at the node level allows maximum concurrency, it is very inefficient from the lock manager's point of view, that is, with respect to acquiring/releasing locks. Similarly, locking at the document (tree) level simplifies the task of the lock manager, but is very bad for concurrency. For nested data, we have another option which in general provides a nice balance between the two extremes: subtree level locking. As such, we choose subtree level locking and consider the following locking protocol (Gray, 1998): The protocol allows two modes of locking: L and I. Once a transaction T_A has locked a node N in mode L, the entire subtree rooted at N is considered to be locked in mode L by T_A. The other mode I, also referred to as the intention mode, is to 'tag' all ancestors of a node to be locked. These tags signal the fact that locking is being done at a lower level and thereby prevent any implicit or explicit locks on the ancestors. Given this, the locking protocol can be stated as follows:

Locking Protocol

- Locks are requested in root to leaf order.
- A transaction T_A is allowed to lock a node N in mode I if no other transaction holds a lock in mode L on N.
- A transaction T_A is allowed to lock a node N in mode L if (a) no other transaction holds a lock on N, and (b) T_A holds intention mode locks on all ancestors of N.
- Locks are released at commit in any order (usually, leaf to root).

In our case, there is further scope for optimization as the transactional structure is also nested. Given this, we extend the locking protocol presented above for nested transactions (integrate with Moss's nested transaction locking protocol (Moss, 1981)): Moss's concurrency control protocol for nested transactions is based on the concept of upward inheritance of locks. Besides holding a lock, a transaction can retain a lock. When a subtransaction commits, its parent transaction inherits its locks and then retains them. If a transaction holds a lock, it has the right to access the locked object. However, the same is not true for retained locks. A retained lock is only a place holder and indicates that transactions outside the hierarchy of the retainer cannot acquire the lock, but that descendants potentially can. As soon as a transaction becomes a retainer of a lock, it remains a retainer for that lock until it terminates.

Extended Locking Protocol with Nested Transaction Semantics

- Locks are requested in root to leaf order.
- A (sub)transaction T_A is allowed to lock a node N in mode I if (a) no other (sub)transaction holds a lock in mode L on N, and (b) all retainers of the I lock on N are superiors of T_A.
- A (sub)transaction T_A is allowed to lock a node N in mode L if (a) no other (sub) transaction holds a lock on N, (b) T_A holds intention mode locks on all ancestors of N, and (c) all retainers of the L lock on N are superiors of T_A.
- When a (sub)transaction commits, all its locks (held and retained of both modes) are inherited by its parent (if any). When a (sub) transaction aborts, all its locks are simply discarded.

The integrated protocol enjoys the advantages of both its constituent protocols, that is, the benefits due to the possibility of subtree level locking (nested data) and inheritance of locks (nested transactions). The correctness of the protocol also follows from its constituent protocols:

- 2PL serializability with respect to the top level subtransactions.
- The protocol provides implicit locking of an entire subtree rooted at node N by preventing a subtransaction from successfully locking the ancestors of N, while N is still being locked.

Finally, the proposed protocol, as with most lock based protocols, can lead to a deadlock. Deadlocks, especially distributed deadlocks, are difficult to prevent (even detect) in the absence of a global coordinator. We assume that the timeout mechanism is used to resolve deadlocks, that is, abort one of the waiting transactions after a timeout interval. We discuss how to handle aborts next.

2.2 Recovery

Here, we only consider recovery in the event of an abort, and not other types of failures, such as, 'stable' storage failure. Also, we would like to remind that, for a nested transaction, the subtransactions can be aborted after commit (only the effects of the root level subtransactions are durable on commit).

2.2.1 Dynamic Undo Construction

We consider compensation like undo operations and show how they can be constructed dynamically. A *compensating* operation (Biswas, 2004) is responsible for semantically undoing the effects of the original operation. For example, the compensation of 'Book Hotel' is 'Cancel Hotel Booking'. Usually, the compensation handlers for a service call are pre-defined statically on the lines of fault (exception) handlers. However, as mentioned earlier, static definition of undo operations is not feasible for AXML systems, especially, for AXML query operations. We consider this issue in detail in the sequel.

The compensation of an insert (AXML update operation with action type 'insert') is delete and vice versa. Similarly, the compensation for an update (AXML update with action type 'replace') is another update which reinstates the old data values. To illustrate, let us consider the AXML document ATPList.xml in Fig. 4.

Figure 4. Sample AXML document ATPList.xml

```
<?xml version = “1.0” encoding = “UTF-8”?>
<ATPList date = “18042005”>
      <player rank = 1>
            <name>
                  <firstname>Roger</firstname>
                  <lastname>Federer</lastname>
            </name>
            <citizenship>Swiss</citizenship>
            <axml:sc mode = “replace” serviceNameSpace = “getPoints”
serviceURL = “...” methodName = “getPoints”>
                   <axml:params>
                         <axml:param name = “name”>
                          <axml:value>Roger Federer</axml:value>
                   </axml:params>
                   <points>475</points>
             </axml:sc>
             <axml:sc mode = “merge” serviceNameSpace = “getGrandSlamsWonbyYear”
serviceURL = “...” methodName = “getGrandSlamsWonbyYear”>
                   <axml:params>
                         <axml:param name = “name”>
                   <axml:value>Roger Federer</axml:value>
                         <axml:param name = “year”>
                         <axml:value>$year (external value)</axml:value>
                   </axml:params>
                   <grandslamswon year = “2003”>A, W</grandslamswon>
                   <grandslamswon year = “2004”>A, U</grandslamswon>
             </axml:sc>
      </player>
...</ATPList>
```

AXML update operations, analogous to XQuery updates (Ghelli et. al., 2006), can be divided into two parts: 1) the <location> query to locate the target nodes, and 2) the actual update operations. The data (nodes) required for compensation cannot be predicted in advance, and would need to be read from the log at run-time. For example, let us consider an AXML delete operation and its compensation as shown in Fig. 5.

The <location> and <data> of the compensating insert operation are the parent (/..) of the deleted node and the result of the <location> query of the delete operation, respectively. Note that the above compensation does not preserve the original ordering of the deleted nodes. For ordered documents, the situation is slightly more complicated and formulation of the compensating operation would depend on the actual semantics of the insert operation. For example, the situation is simplified if the insert operation allows insertion 'before/after' a specific node (Ghelli et. al., 2006).

For AXML insert operations, we assume that the operation returns the (unique) ID of the inserted node. As such, the compensating operation (of the insert operation) is a delete operation to delete the node having the corresponding ID. An AXML replace operation is implemented as a combination of delete and insert operations, that is, delete the node to be replaced followed by insertion of a node having the updated value (at the same position). Compensation of a replace operation is shown in Fig. 6.

Finally, let us consider compensation of AXML query operations. Traditionally, query operations do not need to be compensated as they do not modify data. However, AXML query evaluation, due to the possibility of embedded service call materializations, is capable of modifying the AXML document, e.g. insertion of the invocation result nodes (and deletion of the previous result nodes in 'replace' mode). There are two possible modes for AXML query evaluation: lazy and eager. Of the two, lazy evaluation is the preferred mode, and implies that only those embedded service calls are materialized whose results are required for evaluating the query. As the actual set of embedded service calls materialized is determined only at run-time, the compensating operation for an AXML query cannot be pre-defined statically (has to be constructed dynamically). Given that the required insertion (deletion) of the result nodes are achieved using AXML Insert (Delete) operations, the compensating operation of an AXML query operation can be formulated as discussed earlier for the AXML update operations. The following couple of examples, query operations A and B in Figures 7 and 8 respectively, illustrate the above aspect.

Figure 5. An AXML delete and its compensating operations

```
Delete operation:
<action type = "delete">
<location>
Select p/citizenship from p in ATPList//player where p/name/lastname = Federer;
</location>
</action>

Compensating operation:
<action type = "insert">
     <data><citizenship>Swiss</citizenship></data>
<location>
Select p/citizenship/.. from p in ATPList//player where p/name/lastname = Federer;
</location>
</action>
```

Figure 6. An AXML replace operation, its decomposition and its compensating operation

```
Replace operation:
<action type = "replace">
<data><citizenship>USA</citizenship></data>
<location>
Select p/citizenship from p in ATPList//player where p/name/lastname = Nadal;
</location>
</action>

decomposes to:
<action type = "delete">
<location>
Select p/citizenship from p in ATPList//player where p/name/lastname = Nadal;
</location>
</action>
<action type = "insert">
<data> <citizenship>USA</citizenship></data>
<location>
Select p/citizenship/.. from p in ATPList//player where p/name/lastname = Nadal;
</location>
</action>

Compensating operation:
<action type = "delete">
<location>
Select p/citizenship from p in ATPList//player where p/name/lastname = Nadal;
</location>
</action>
<action type= "insert">
<data><citizenship>Swiss</citizenship></data>
<location>
Select p/citizenship/.. from p in ATPList//player where p/name/lastname = Nadal;
</location>
</action>
```

Lazy evaluation of query A results in materialization of the embedded service call getGrandSlamsWonbyYear (and not getPoints). As shown in Fig. 7, the only change in the AXML document, would be the addition of line 25 (lines 4-24 are the same as ATPList.xml). Thus, the compensation for query A is a delete operation to delete the node <grandslamswon year = "2005">A, F</grandslamswon>. Similarly, lazy evaluation of query B results in materialization of the embedded service call getPoints (and not getGrandSlamsWonbyYear), resulting in the modified ATPList.xml (line 14) as shown in Fig. 8. Thus, the compensation for query B would be a replace operation to change the value of the node <points>890</points> back to 475.

2.2.2 Undo Order

In the previous section, we discussed how to undo a service invocation. *Here, we determine the subtransactions (encompassing service invocations), which need to be aborted if a (sub)transaction is aborted, and the order in which to do so.*

We need some additional notations before presenting the protocol. The peer, at which a transaction T_A is originally submitted, is referred to as its origin peer. Peers, whose services are invoked

Figure 7. Query A, and the document ATPList.xml after A's evaluation

```
Query operation A:
<action type = "query">
<location>
Select p/citizenship, p/grandslamswon from p in
ATPList//player where p/name/lastname = Federer:
</location>
</action>

ATPList.xml (after Query A evaluation):
<?xml version = "1.0" encoding = "UTF-8"?>
<ATPList date = "18042005">
      <player rank = 1>
        ...
                   <grandslamswon year = "2005">A, F</grandslamswon>
              </axml:sc>
      </player>
...</ATPList>
```

while processing T_A (which process subtransactions of T_A), are referred to as the participant peers of T_A. On submission of a subtransaction of T_A at peer AP_1, the peer creates a transaction context TC_{A1}. We assume that at most one subtransaction of a transaction is submitted at any peer (no cyclic invocation of services). The transaction context, managed by the Transaction Manager, is a data structure which encapsulates the transaction ID with all the information required for concurrency control, commit and recovery of the corresponding transaction. In the sequel, we refer to a subtransaction by its subtransaction context identifier. Given this, for a pair of subtransactions TC_{A1} and TC_{A2}, if TC_{A2} was created (on peer AP_2) as a result of an invocation by TC_{A1} (on peer AP_1), then TC_{A1} (TC_{A2}) is referred to as the parent (a child) subtransaction of TC_{A2} (TC_{A1}), and its cor-

Figure 8. Query B, and the document ATPList.xml after B's evaluation

```
Query operation B:
<action type = "query">
<location>
Select p/citizenship, p/points from p in ATPList//player where
p/name/lastname = Federer;
</location>
</action>

ATPList.xml (after Query B evaluation):
            <axml:sc mode = "replace" serviceNameSpace = "getPoints"
serviceURL = "..." methodName = "getPoints">
                  <axml:params>
                      <axml:param name = "name">
                  <axml:value>Roger Federer</axml:value>
                  </axml:params>
                  <points>890</points>
             </axml:sc>
```

responding peer AP_1 (AP_2) is referred to as the parent (a child) peer of AP_2 (AP_1). The definitions of sibling, descendant and ancestor subtransactions (peers) follow analogously.

We outline the recovery protocol with the help of an example scenario as shown in Fig. 9. Fig. 9 shows a scenario where the peer AP_5 fails while processing the service S_5 (subtransaction TC_{A5}):

Nested recovery protocol

- AP_5 sends the 'Abort T_A' message to its parent peer (AP_2) to inform it about the failure of subtransaction TC_{A5}.
- The peer AP_2, on receiving the 'Abort T_A' message, aborts TC_{A2} and sends the 'Abort T_A' message to its parent (AP_1) and remaining children peers (AP_3).
- The peer AP_3, on receiving the 'Abort T_A' message, aborts TC_{A3} and sends the message to its children peers (AP_4).
- The processing of the peers AP_1 and AP_4, on receiving the 'Abort T_A' message, are analogous to that of AP_2 and AP_3, respectively.

Till now, we have conveniently sidelined the issue of the order in which the subtransactions need to be aborted. Analogous to the original invocation order, the *compensation* (undo) order is also important. For sequential invocations, we know that their corresponding aborts need to be performed in reverse order of their original execution order. *For parallel invocations, their aborts can also be performed in parallel to improve performance.*

Figure 9. Scenario to illustrate the nested recovery protocol

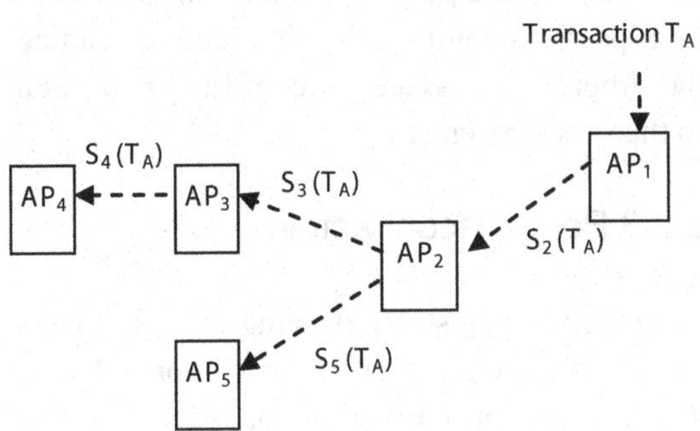

This aspect is often ignored by comparative systems, e.g., BPEL. In BPEL, compensation is associated with scopes which in turn act as containers for activities. A nested invocation in our scenario is analogous to a BPEL process with nested scopes. Although BPEL supports parallelism for forward activities (the flow operator), the default compensation behaviour of BPEL is *sequential* execution of the completed children scopes (in reverse order). While it is possible to override the default behaviour by specifying an explicit compensation handler of a scope in BPEL, our contention is that parallel compensation (of the completed children scopes which had executed in parallel originally) should be the *default* behaviour. And, any exceptions to this default behaviour should be specified using explicit compensation handlers.

However, allowing such parallelism, does lead to additional synchronization issues in a nested scenario. For example, let us consider the nested transaction in Fig.10. Now, let us assume that the peer AP_5 has failed while processing the service S_5. Given this, TC_{AX}, TC_{AY}, TC_{AZ}, TC_{A3} and TC_{A4}, all of them need to be aborted, but their ordering is important. Basically, TC_{AY} and TC_{AZ} can be aborted in parallel, but TC_{A3} needs to be aborted before either of them, and finally, all of them need to be aborted before (after) TC_{AX} (TC_{A4}) is aborted. We formalize the above discussion in the sequel.

The sequential and parallel invocation of subtransactions of a transaction T_A on peers AP_1 and AP_2, are denoted as [TC_{A1} => TC_{A2}] and [TC_{A1} || TC_{A2}], respectively. TC_{A1}^{-1} denotes the abort of subtransaction TC_{A1}, that is, the transaction encapsulating the (undo) operations needed to abort TC_{A1}. For a pair of subtransactions TC_{A1} and TC_{A1}, if both of them need to be aborted, then we need to adhere to the following rules:

Figure 10. Illustration for the abort (undo) order

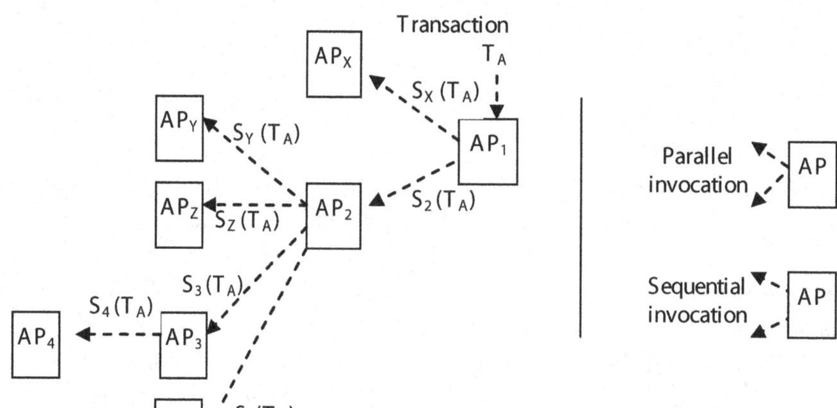

1. If they were invoked in sequence, that is, $TC_{A1} \Rightarrow TC_{A2}$, then $TC_{A2}^{-1} \Rightarrow TC_{A1}^{-1}$.
2. If they were invoked in parallel, that is, $TC_{A1} \parallel TC_{A2}$, then $TC_{A2}^{-1} \parallel TC_{A1}^{-1}$.
3. If TC_{A1} is the parent subtransaction of TC_{A2}, then TC_{A2}^{-1} should be executed before TC_{A1}^{-1}.

Nested recovery protocol with ordering semantics

- For a failure with respect to transaction T_A, the failed peer sends an 'Abort T_A' message to its parent peer.
- A peer AP_X, on receiving the 'Abort T_A' message from its *child* peer, does the following: (i) Wait for any currently executing siblings of the failed subtransaction to commit. While waiting, AP_X does not perform any new invocations with respect to T_A. (ii) For all its committed children subtransactions of T_A (if any), determine the abort order in accordance with Rules 1 and 2. Send 'Abort T_A' messages in the determined order, that is, for a pair of committed children subtransactions $[TC_{AY}^{-1} \Rightarrow TC_{AZ}^{-1}]$ ($[TC_{AY}^{-1} \parallel TC_{AZ}^{-1}]$), AP_X first sends the 'Abort T_A' message to AP_Y, and then to AP_Z, only after receiving the abort confirmation from AP_Y (AP_X sends the 'Abort T_A' message to both AP_Y and AP_Z in parallel). (iii) On receiving the abort confirmation from all its children peers, AP_X sends an 'Abort T_A' message to its parent peer (if any).
- A peer AP_X, on receiving the 'Abort T_A' message from its *parent* peer, determines the abort order for its children subtransactions of T_A (if any) in accordance with Rules 1 and 2. Note that all its children subtransactions (if any) have already committed. As before, the next step is to send 'Abort T_A' messages to its children peers in the specified abort order. On receiving the abort confirmation from all its children peers, AP_X sends an abort confirmation to its parent peer.

In the above protocol, Rule 3 implicitly holds as a result of the peers waiting for all their children peers to confirm abortion, before sending the 'Abort T_A' messages or confirming abortion to their own parents.

2.2.3 Peer Disconnection

Most P2P systems rely on ping (or keep-alive) messages to detect peer disconnection. Clearly, it is not an optimum solution, but provides a good trade-off against increased communication overhead. *Our objective is to further reduce loss of effort by detecting the disconnection as early as possible and reuse already performed work as much as possible.* The actual recovery steps to be executed vary, based on the peer which got disconnected and the peer which detected the disconnection. We illustrate the steps with the help of an example scenario as shown in Fig. 11.

Analogous to the invocation order of subtransactions, the sequential and parallel invocation of peers AP_Y and AP_Z's services by peer AP_X (to process parts of the same transaction), are denoted as $AP_X[AP_Y => AP_Z]$ and $AP_X[AP_Y || AP_Z]$, respectively. Super peers (peers which do not disconnect) are highlighted by an * following their identifiers (AP_X*). For a peer AP_X, at the time of invoking a service S of peer AP_Y as part of transaction T_A, the Active Peers List of T_A (APL_A) specifies the invocation order among the peers corresponding to (1) the committed descendant subtransactions of TC_{AX}, (2) the active (invoked, but not committed) sibling subtransactions of TC_{AX}, and (3) TC_{AX}'s ancestors. For example (Fig. 11), the APL_A passed to AP_8, at the time of its invocation by AP_6, would be AP_1*[$AP_2[AP_3[AP_4]] => [AP_5] || [AP_6]$], assuming AP_1 is a super peer. *Note that the creation and updation of such an APL does not require any additional message exchanges (communication overhead).* For a pair of parent-child peers AP_X and AP_Y, we assume that AP_X passes the latest APL to AP_Y during invocation, and AP_Y returns the APL to AP_X along with the invocation results after having updated it with information about its (committed) children.

a. *Leaf node disconnection* (AP_8 gets disconnected and the disconnection is detected by its parent AP_6): AP_6 follows the nested recovery protocol discussed earlier.
b. *Parent disconnection detected by child node* (peer AP_6 gets disconnected and the disconnection is detected by its child AP_8): We assume that AP_8 detects the disconnection of AP_6 while trying to return the invocation results of S_8 to AP_6. Traditional recovery would lead to AP_8 discarding its work, and actual recovery occurring only when the disconnection is detected by AP_6's parent (AP_2). A more efficient solution can be achieved if AP_6 passes the APL_A: AP_1*[$AP_2[AP_3[AP_4]] => [AP_5] || [AP_6]$] as well, while invoking the service S_8 of AP_8. Given this, as soon as AP_8 detects the disconnection of AP_6, it can send the results directly to AP_2 (informing AP_2 of the disconnection as well). Once AP_2 becomes aware of the disconnection, it follows the nested recovery protocol.

Figure 11. Illustration for peer disconnection detection and recovery

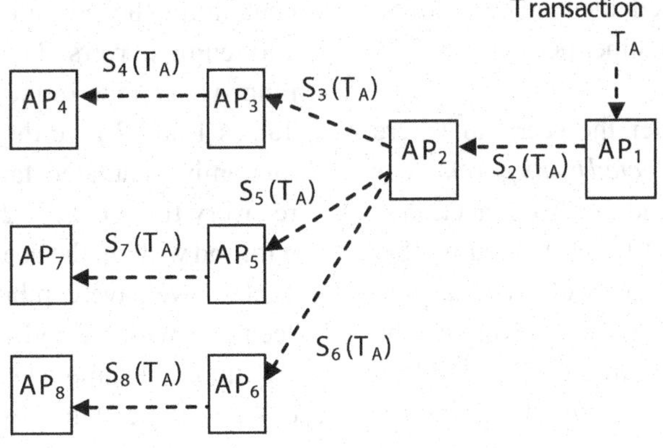

Furthermore, let us assume that AP_2 attempts forward recovery by invoking the service S_6 on a different peer (say, AP_X). In a general scenario, it might be very difficult to reuse the work already performed by AP_8. However, if we assume that S_8 was basically an invocation to materialize an input parameter of S_6 (recall that input parameters can also be defined as service calls), then it might be possible to reuse AP_8's work by passing the materialized results directly while invoking S_6 on AP_X. Finally, it is very likely that even AP_2 might have disconnected. Given this, AP_8 can try the next closest peer (AP_1) or the closest super peer (also, AP_1 in this case) in APL_A.

c. *Sibling disconnection* (AP_5 gets disconnected and the disconnection is detected by sibling AP_6): For data intensive applications, it is often the case that data is passed directly between siblings, especially, for concurrently executing siblings (invoked in parallel). In an AXML scenario, this is particularly relevant for subscription based continuous services (AXML User Guide) which are responsible for sending updated streams of data at regular intervals. Thus, a sibling would be aware of another sibling's disconnection if it didn't receive the expected data at the specified interval. Given such detection, AP_6 can use the APL_A: AP_1*[AP_2[AP_3[AP_4]] => [AP_5]] (passed to AP_6 by its parent AP_2) to notify AP_2 of the disconnection, and if AP_2 has also disconnected, then the next closest (still) active peer or super peer.

Finally, let us consider the scenario where *child disconnection is detected by its parent peer* (AP_6 gets disconnected and the disconnection is detected by its parent AP_2): Let us assume that AP_2 detects the disconnection of AP_6 via ping messages. Here, a more efficient recovery can be achieved if AP_2 is also aware of AP_6's children (AP_8). Given this, in addition to attempting recovery using the nested recovery protocol, AP_2 can use the information about the children peers (of AP_6) to see if any part of their work can be reused. Even if reuse is not possible, AP_2 can at least use the information to inform the descendants (AP_8) about the disconnection. This would prevent them from wasting effort (doing work which is anyway going to be discarded). However, this requires a more frequent update of the APL_A (which in turn implies, more message exchanges), that is, a peer (AP_6) would be required to send the updated APL_A to its parent (AP_2) after every child invocation (AP_8). Thus, the usefulness of APL in this scenario depends on the application semantics, unlike the previous scenarios where the use of APL always leads to a better performance (shown experimentally in the next section).

2.2.4 Implementation

We have developed a prototype implementation of the concepts proposed in this paper. The transactional framework builds on the AXML engine available at http://www.activexml.net. We simulated transactions leading to 30 AXML service invocations over 1-4 levels of nesting. The compensating operations for the invoked services were generated dynamically by the framework according to the logic presented in Section 2.2.1. Peer failure was simulated by a random shutdown of the peer server. The AXML operations corresponding to the service invocations were query and update operations over AXML documents containing the 'Grand Slams Won' history of 100 tennis players. The average operation time ranged from 15 to 180 seconds. For those timings, Tables 1 and 2 give the completion times (with randomly simulated failures and including the recovery time) over 1, 2 and 4 levels of nesting, with and without the use of APL respectively. For Table 1, we have combined the readings for the scenarios with 1, 2 and 4 levels of nesting, as they are almost the same. Clearly, the savings as a result of APL (Table 2) increase with an increase in the

Table 1. Completion time of the sample transaction T

Nesting Level	Average operation time (seconds) 15	180
1, 2, 4	5795	5838

Table 2. Completion time of the sample transaction T with APL

Nesting Level	Average operation time (seconds) 15	180
1	928	5861
2	869	5560
4	771	5105

number of nesting levels. Indeed, for a single level of nesting, the maintenance cost of APL seems to offset any potential benefits of APL.

3. RELATED WORKS

The notion of transactions has been evolving over the last 30 years. As such, it would be a vain effort to even try and mention all the related research here. Given this, we suffice to mention only the transactional models which have been proposed specifically for the XML, Web services and P2P paradigms.

Jea et. al. (2002) and Dekeyser et. al. (2003) discuss lock-based concurrency control protocols for XML repositories. While Dekeyser et. al. (2003) use 'path locks' to optimize locking, Jea et. al. (2002) use the fact that the nodes referred by the 'where' part of a select statement are only accessed for a short time (for testing) and introduce the 'P' lock to exploit it. The works are complementary to our approach, and can be integrated with the locking protocol presented in Section 2.1 to increase its efficiency.

Tartanoglu et. al. (2003) present a forward recovery based transactional model for Web services compositions. It introduces the concept of co-operative recovery (in the context of Web services). Pires et. al. (2003) propose a framework (WebTransact) for building reliable Web services compositions. Biswas (2004) stresses the importance of Cost of Compensation and end-user feedback while performing compensation for Web services compositions. Vidyasankar & Vossen (2004), Biswas & Vidyasankar (2005) discuss in detail the practical implications of recovery with respect to hierarchical Web Services Compositions.

From a P2P perspective, transactions haven't received much attention till now as their commercial use has been mostly restricted to file (or resource) sharing systems where failure resilience equates to maintaining sufficient information (by the P2P client) so that the file download can be resumed (from the original or a different peer). However, the trend is slowly changing with a steady rise in the use of P2P systems for collaborative work, e.g., AXML and the Grid (Tucker et. al., 2005). In this paper, we consider the issue of peer disconnection from a transactional perspective.

4. CONCLUSION

In this work, we discussed a transactional framework for AXML systems. AXML systems integrate XML, Web Services and P2P platforms, leading to some novel challenges which are not addressed by transactional models specific to any of the above. We started with an integrated locking protocol when the structure of both data and transactions are nested. With respect to recovery, we showed how to construct the undo operations dynamically at run-time, and presented an algorithm to compute an optimum undo order which takes advantage of the inherent parallelism. To overcome the issue of peer disconnection, we outlined a solution based on chaining the active peers for early detection and recovery from peer disconnection.

5. FUTURE PERSPECTIVES

With more and more data stored as XML documents, transaction management is becoming increasingly important for XML data management. However, unlike database management systems, we see XML data systems evolving more in conjunction with Web services and P2P systems, rather than as stand-alone systems. As such, the transactional guarantees would also need to be provided at the Web services or P2P middleware level (and it will not be sufficient to provide such guarantees at the XML query/ update operations level). Given this, any proposed transactional middleware should be able accommodate the unique and inherent aspects of Web services and P2P systems. We discuss some such aspects below which we believe are still missing from a successful implementation of a transactional framework for Web services and P2P based XML systems:

- **Long running:** Given the long running nature of some Web services compositions, locking may not always be feasible. An alternative here would be to explore optimistic concurrency control protocols (Kung & Robinson, 1981). Optimistic protocols tend to perform well in scenarios with a lot of query operations, that is, fewer conflicts. However, (as discussed earlier) even AXML queries are capable of updating the AXML document. Thus, it would be interesting to see how optimistic protocols perform against pessimistic ones in an AXML scenario, as well as in a general Web services-XML context.
- **Logging:** The usual way of recording execution history is via logging. From a XML perspective, data logging is expensive as it is usually necessary to log the whole node rather than just the updated values, to preserve the ordering (with respect to the parent node) or to preserve the details of the children nodes (which are also deleted with the deletion of a parent node). From a Web services perspective, the log may be distributed across the component provider sites of a composite service. As such, it may not always be feasible to access the whole log due to heterogeneity and security issues. Given this, the intuition would be to minimize logging as much as possible. We already have some interesting results in this regard for providing atomicity guarantees in a Web services context (Biswas & Genest, 2008; Biswas et. al., 2008), and it would be interesting to carry them forward to AXML systems in the future.
- **Dynamicity:** P2P systems are characterized by their high dynamicity with peers connecting and disconnecting at random. With AXML systems, we are still in a collaborative mode where it is possible to impose some restrictions on the behaviors of the peers. In a general P2P setting, the situation is much more chaotic and it may not be practical to assume that the peers will follow any specified protocol. Given this, the emphasis should be on studying relaxed transactional properties that can be guaranteed in such a setting, e.g. allowing deviation from a transactional property up to a bounded limit (Pu & Leff, 1992).

NOTES

This work was done while both the authors were affiliated to IRISA/INRIA, France. Also, this work is an extended version of (or a preliminary version of the chapter appeared in) Biswas, D., & Kim, I.-G (2007). Atomicity for P2P based XML Repositories. In International Workshop on Services Engineering (pp. 363-370). IEEE CS Press.

ACKNOWLEDGMENT

We would like to thank Ashwin Jiwane who was mainly responsible for developing the AXML Transactions prototype. Thanks are also due to Krishnamurhty Vidyasankar, Blaise Genest and the reviewers for their useful comments. This work is supported by the ANR DOCFLOW and CREATE ACTIVEDOC projects.

REFERENCES

Abiteboul, S., Bonifati , A., Cobena , G., Manolescu , I., & Milo, T. (2003). Dynamic XML Documents with Distribution and Replication. In *ACM SIGMOD International Conference on Management of Data* (pp. 527-538). ACM Press.

Biswas, D. (2008). Active XML Replication and Recovery. In *International Conference on Complex, Intelligent and Software Intensive Systems* (pp. 263-269). IEEE CS Press.

Biswas, D. (2004). Compensation in the World of Web Services Composition. In *International Workshop on Semantic Web Services and Web Process Composition* (pp. 69-80). Lecture Notes in Computer Science, vol. 3387, Springer-Verlag.

Jea, K.-F, Chen, S.-Y, & Wang, S.-H (2002). Concurrency Control in XML Document Databases: XPath Locking Protocol. In *International Conference on Parallel and Distributed Systems* (pp. 551-556). IEEE CS Press.

Dekeyser, S., Hidders, J., and Paredaens, J. (2003). A Transactional Model for XML Databases. *World Wide Web, 7*(1), 29-57. Kluwer Academic.

Andrews, T., Curbera, F., Dholakia, H., Goland, Y., Klein, J., Leymann, F., Liu, K., Roller, D., Smith, D., Thatte, S., Trickovic, I., & Weerawarana, S. (2002). *Specification: Business Process Execution Language for Web Services (BPEL)*. Retrieved October, 2006, from http://www-106.ibm.com/developerworks/library/ws-bpel/

Ghelli, G., Re, C., & Simeon, J. (2006). XQuery!: An XML query language with side effects. In *International Workshop on Database Technologies for Handling XML Information on the Web* (pp. 178-191). Lecture Notes in Computer Science, vol. 4254, Springer-Verlag.

Bernstein, P. A., Hadzilacos, V., & Goodman, N. (1987). *Concurrency Control and Recovery in Database Systems*. Addison-Wesley.

Moss, T.E.B. (1981). *Nested Transactions: An Approach to Reliable Distributed Computing*. Unpublished doctoral dissertation, MIT Laboratory for Computer Science, USA.

Tartanoglu, F., Issarny, V., Romanovsky, A., & Levy, N. (2003). Coordinated Forward Error Recovery for Composite Web Services. In *22nd Symposium on Reliable Distributed Systems* (pp. 167-176). IEEE CS Press.

Pires, P.F., Mattoso, M.L.Q., and Benevides, M.R.F. (2003). Building Reliable Web Services Compositions. In *Web, Web-Services, and Database Systems* (pp. 59-72). Lecture Notes in Computer Science, vol. 2593, Springer-Verlag.

Vidyasankar, K., & Vossen, G. (2004). Multi-level Model for Web Service Composition. In *International Conference on Web Services* (pp. 462-471). IEEE CS Press.

Biswas, D., & Vidyasankar, K. (2005). Spheres of Visibility. In *European Conference on Web Services* (pp. 2-13). IEEE CS Press.

Turker, C., Haller, K., Schuler, C., & Schek, H.-J (2005). How can we support Grid Transactions? Towards Peer-to-Peer Transaction Processing. In *Biennial Conference on Innovative Data Systems Research* (pp. 174 -185).

Biswas, D., & Genest, B. (2008). Minimal Observability for Transactional Hierarchical Services. In *International Conference on Software Engineering and Knowledge Engineering* (pp. 531-536).

Biswas, D., Gazagnaire, T., & Genest, B. (2008). Small Logs for Transactional Services: Distinction is much more accurate than (Positive) Discrimination. In *High Assurance Systems Engineering Symposium* (pp. 97-106). IEEE CS Press.

Gray, J.N. (1998). *Notes on Database Operating Systems* (RJ 2188). IBM Research Lab, California, USA.

Kung, H.T., and Robinson, J.T. (1981). On Optimistic Methods for Concurrency Control. *Transactions on Database Systems, 6*(2), 213-226. ACM Press.

Pu, C., & Leff, A. (1992). Autonomous Transaction Execution with Epsilon-serializability. In *RIDE Workshop on Transaction and Query Processing* (pp. 2 -11).

Chapter IV
SEEC:
A Dual Search Engine for Business Employees and Customers

Kamal Taha
University of Texas at Arlington, USA

Ramez Elmasri
University of Texas at Arlington, USA

With the emergence of the World Wide Web, business' databases are increasingly being queried directly by customers. The customers may not be aware of the exact structure of the underlying data, and might have never learned a query language that enables them to issue structured queries. Some of the employees who query the databases may also not be aware of the structure of the data, but they are likely to be aware of some labels of elements containing the data. There is a need for a dual search engine that accommodates both business employees and customers. We propose in this chapter an XML search engine called SEEC, which accepts Keyword-Based queries (which can be used for answering customers' queries) and Loosely Structured queries (which can be used for answering employees' queries). We proposed previously a stand-alone Loosely Structured search engine called OOXSearch (Taha & Elmasri, 2007). SEEC integrates OOXSearch with a Keyword-Based search engine and uses novel search techniques. It is built on top of an XQuery search engine (Katz, 2005). SEEC was evaluated experimentally and compared with three recently proposed systems: XSEarch (Cohen & Mamou & Sagiv, 2003), Schema Free XQuery (Li & Yu & Jagadish, 2004), and XKSearch (Xu & Papakonstantinou, 2005). The results showed marked improvement.

INTRODUCTION

XML has had significant boost with the emergence of the World Wide Web, online businesses, and the concept of ubiquitous computing. The majority of current web services are based on XML. In a corporate environment, XML has been used to import/export data as well as in internal documentation. The popularity of XML is due, in part, to the following:

Copyright © 2009, IGI Global, distributing in print or electronic forms without written permission of IGI Global is prohibited.

- XML defines the type of information contained in a document, which helps in restricting the search and makes it easier to return the most relevant results. Consider for example a university professor, who is participating in many activities. When using HTML to search for courses that the professor plans to teach, the results are likely to contain information outside the context of courses. When using XML, on the other hand, the search could be restricted to information contained in the appropriate element type (e.g. <courses>).
- XML implementations make electronic data interchange more accessible for e-businesses, as they are easily processed by automated programs.
- XML can be customized to suit the need of any institution or business.
- XML is URL-addressable resource that can programmatically return information to clients.

With the increasing interest in XML databases, there has been extensive research in XML querying. Some work model the XML data as a rooted tree (Cohen & Mamou & Sagiv, 2003; Li & Yu & Jagadish, 2004; Xu & Papakonstantinou, 2005), while others model it as a graph (Balmin & Hristidis & Papakonstantinon, 2003; Balmin & Hristidis & Papakonstantinon, 2004; Botev & Shao & Guo, 2003; Cohen & Kanza, 2005). However, most of these work targets either naïve users (such as business customers) by proposing Keyword-Based search engines or sophisticated users by proposing fully structured query search engines. We believe there is a need for an XML search engine that answers each user based on his/her *degree of knowledge* of the underlying data and its structure. Business customers are most likely not to be aware of the underlying data and its structure. On the other hand, business employees are likely to be aware of some data elements' labels (elements containing data), but they are unlikely to be aware of the structure of the data. We propose in this chapter an XML dual search engine called SEEC (Search Engine for Employees and Customers), which meets the needs of both customers and employees. It accepts XML Keyword-Based queries (e.g. for answering customers' queries), and XML Loosely Structured queries (e.g. for answering employees' queries). Consider that a user wants to know the data D, which is contained in an element labeled E. If the user knows ONLY the keywords k_1, k_2, .., k_n, which are relevant to D, the user can submit a Keyword-Based query in the form: Q ("k_1", "k_2", .., "k_n"). If, however, the user knows the label E and the labels (which belong to the elements containing the keywords k_1, k_2, .., k_n respectively), but is unaware of the structure of the data, this user can submit a loosely structured query in the form: Q *(= "k_1",..., = "k_n", E?).* We proposed previously a stand-alone Loosely Structured search engine called OOXSearch (Taha & Elmasri, 2007). SEEC integrates OOXSearch with a Keyword-Based search engine and uses novel search techniques. It is built on top of an XQuery search engine (Katz, 2005).

Few researchers (Cohen & Mamou & Sagiv, 2003; Li & Yu & Jagadish, 2004) propose XML search engines that answer both Keyword-Based and Loosely Structured queries. Computing the Lowest Common Ancestor (LCA) of elements containing keywords is the common denominator among these engines. Despite their success, however, they suffer *recall* and *precision* limitations. As we will show in the coming sections, the reason for these limitations stems from the fact that these engines employ mechanisms for building relationships between data elements based solely on their labels and proximity to one another while overlooking the *contexts* of these elements. The context of a data element is determined by its parent, because a data element is generally a characteristic (or a property) of its parent. If for example a data element is labeled "title", we cannot determine whether it refers to a book title or a job title without referring to its parent. Consider as another example that an XML document containing two elements labeled "name", one of which refers to the name of a student, while the other refers to the student's school name. Building a relationship between these two "name" elements without consideration of their parents may lead to the incorrect conclusion that the two elements belong to the same type. Building relationships between data elements while overlooking their contexts may lead to relationships that are semantically disconnected. Consequently, the results generated by non context-driven systems are susceptible to errors, especially if the XML document contains more than one element having the same label but representing different types of information or having different labels but representing the same type of information. SEEC avoids the pitfalls cited above of non context-driven search engines by employing context-driven search techniques. The context of an element is determined by its parent, since a data element is generally a characteristic of its parent.

XML documents are modeled as rooted and labeled trees in the framework of SEEC. A node in a tree represents an element in an XML document. The framework considers each parent-children set of elements as one unified entity, called a *Canonical Tree*. We propose novel context-driven search techniques for establishing relationships between different Canonical Trees. A Canonical Tree is the simplest semantically meaningful entity. A data node by itself is an entity that is semantically meaningless. Consider again the example stated above of the XML document that contains two nodes having the same label "name" where one of them refers to the name of a student, while the other to the student's school name. Each of the two nodes alone is semantically meaningless and does not convey meaningful information, such as whether or not the node refers to a student's name or a school's name. However, when considering each of the two nodes with its parent, we can then determine that one of them refers to a student's name, while the other refers to the student's school name. Therefore, SEEC's framework treats the set of nodes that consists of the student "name" node along with its siblings and parent as one entity (Canonical Tree); the same thing applies to the school "name" node. Consider for example Figure 1. The parent node customer (1) along with its child data node name (2) constitute a Canonical Tree. Also, the parent node address (3) along with its children data nodes street (4) and city (5) constitute a Canonical Tree.

A data model is a metaphor of real-world entities. Two real-world entities may have different names but belong to the same type of information (e.g. a paper and an article belong to the same publication type), or may have the same names but refer to two different types (e.g. a "name" of a student and a "name" of a school). To overcome this kind of labeling **ambiguity**, we observe that if we cluster Canonical Trees based on the reduced essential characteristics and cognitive qualities of the parent nodes, we will identify a number of *clusters*. Each cluster contains Canonical Trees whose parent nodes components belong to the same ontological concept. In Figure 1 for example we can have a cluster that contains the Canonical Tree whose parent node component is node 10 "book" and another Canonical Tree whose parent component is node 35 "magazine", since both "book" and "magazine" fall under the same "publication" cluster (type). On the other hand, the Canonical Tree, whose parent node component is node 1 "customer" falls under the "person" cluster. Thus, we would be able to determine that the two nodes labeled "name" in the example presented previously are not semantically identical; rather, they refer to two different types of entities, since the student's "name" node will be contained in a Canonical Tree falling under the "person" cluster, while the student's school "name" will be contained in a Canonical Tree falling under the "institution" cluster. The result of fragmenting the XML tree shown in Figure 1 into Canonical Trees is shown in Figure 2. If we consider the *ontology label* of each cluster as a supertype and the label of each parent node component in a Canonical Tree falling under that cluster as a subtype, then any characteristic that describes the supertype can also describe all its subtypes. For instance, the "publication" supertype could be characterized by "title" and "year" of publication, and likewise its subtypes "book" and "article".

Figure 1. XML tree representing customer publication order

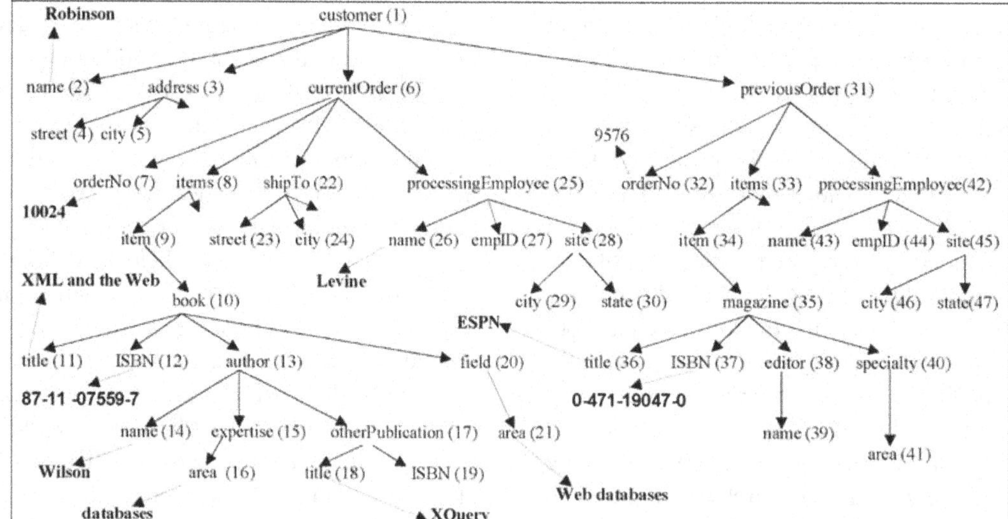

Note: The customer (node 1) ordered a book (node 10) and had previously ordered a magazine (node 35) .The author (node 13) authored the book (node 10) as well as another publication (node 17). Note that the XML tree is exaggerated for the purpose of demonstrating all the concepts proposed in this paper.

A Canonical Trees graph (e.g. Figure 2) is a hierarchical representation depicting the relationships between the Canonical Trees in the graph. The relationships between Canonical Trees are determined based on their degree of associability and relativity to one another and not on their proximity to one another. There are two types of relationships, *immediate* and *extended.* The *Immediate Relatives* of a Canonical Tree T_i are Canonical Trees that have strong and close relationships with T_i, while its *extended relatives* have weak relationships with it. We call the immediate relatives of Canonical Tree T_i the *Related Canonical Trees of* T_i (denoted by RCT_{T_i}). For each Canonical Tree T_i, we need to determine its RCT_{T_i} because if T_i contains a query's keyword(s), the user is most likely looking for data contained in RCT_{T_i}. We propose in this chapter semantic mechanisms for determining RCT_{T_i}.

The process of answering Keyword-Based and Loosely Structured queries goes through four phases. In the first phase, we locate the Canonical Trees containing the query's keyword(s). In the second phase, we select subsets from these Canonical Trees, where the Canonical Trees in each subset are semantically related to one another and contain at least one occurrence of each keyword. In the third phase, we either determine the Canonical Trees containing the answer return element nodes of the query (if it is a Loosely Structured query), or the Canonical Trees comprising the answer subtree for the query (if it is a Keyword-Based query).

We make the following technical contributions in this chapter:

- We propose novel mechanisms for determining for each Canonical Tree T_i, its RCT_{T_i}.
- We propose mechanisms for determining the answer return element nodes of a Loosely Structured query and mechanisms for constructing the answer subtrees of a Keyword-Based query. These mechanisms avoid returning results with low *recall* and *precision,* which is one of the pitfalls of non context-driven search systems.
- We experimentally evaluate the quality and efficiency of SEEC and compare it with three non context-driven search systems:

XKSearch (Xu & Papakonstantinou, 2005), Schema-Free XQuery (Li & Yu & Jagadish, 2004), and XSEarch (Cohen & Mamou & Sagiv, 2003).

The rest of this chapter is organized as follows. In the section titled "background", we discuss the topic of keyword search and present the views of others in the topic. In the section titled "context-driven search", we present the problems of non context-driven search engines caused by overlooking nodes' contexts, and then introduce SEEC and the techniques it employs and show how it overcomes these problems. In the section titled "future trend", we discuss our future research in XML querying. We present our conclusions in the section titled "conclusion".

BACKGROUND

Keyword-Based querying in Relational Databases has been studied extensively (Agrawal & Chaudhuri & Das, 2002; Aditya & Bhalotia & Sudarshan, 2002; Hristidis & Papakonstantinou, 2002). These researches model the database as a graph, where tuples are regarded as the graph's nodes and the relationships between tuples are regarded as the graph's edges. Then, a keyword query is answered by returning a subgraph that satisfies the query's search terms. A number of studies (Balmin & Hristidis & Papakonstantinon, 2003; Balmin & Hristidis & Papakonstantinon, 2004; Botev & Shao & Guo, 2003; Cohen & Kanza, 2005) propose modeling XML documents as graphs, and keyword queries are answered by processing the graphs based on given schemas. Some studies (Balmin & Hristidis & Papakonstantinon, 2003; Balmin & Hristidis & Papakonstantinon, 2004; Botev & Shao & Guo, 2003) propose techniques for ranking results of XML keyword queries based on importance and relevance. Other studies (Amer-Yahia & Cartmola & Deutsch, 2006) evaluate full-text XML queries in terms of keyword patterns matches.

A number of recent studies (Cohen & Mamou & Sagiv, 2003; Li & Yu & Jagadish, 2004; Xu & Papakonstantinou, 2005) model XML documents as rooted trees and propose semantic search techniques, which make them the closest to our work. Despite their success, however, they suffer *recall* and *precision* limitations as a result of basing their techniques on building relationships between data nodes based solely on their labels and proximity to one another while overlooking their contexts. As a result, the proposed search engines may return faulty answers especially if the XML doc contains more than one node having the same label but representing different types, or having different labels but belonging to the same type. We compared three of these proposed search techniques experimentally with SEEC (see the experimental results section). The following is an overview of each of these three systems:

In XSEarch (Cohen & Mamou & Sagiv, 2003), if the *relationship tree* of nodes a and b (the path connecting the two nodes) contains two or more nodes with the same label, then the two nodes are *unrelated*; otherwise, they are *related*. Consider for example Figure 1 and the relationship tree that connects nodes 10 (book) and 35 (magazine). This relationship tree contains nodes 10, 9, 8, 6, 1, 31, 33, 34, and 35. Since the relationship tree contains more than one node having the same label (nodes 34 and 9 and also nodes 33 and 8), then nodes 35 and 10 are not related.

In Schema Free XQuery (Li & Yu & Jagadish, 2004), nodes "a" and "b" are NOT *meaningfully related* if their Lowest Common Ancestor (LCA), node 'c' is an ancestor of some node "d", which is a LCA of node "b" and another node that has the same label as "a". Consider for example nodes 2, 14, and 18 in Figure 1. Node 18 (title) and node 2 (name) are not related, because their LCA (node 1) is an ancestor of node 13, which is the LCA of nodes 18 and 14, and node 14 has the same label as node 2. Therefore, node 18 is related to node 14 and not to node 2. Node 13 is called the *Meaningful Lowest Common Ancestor* (MLCA) of nodes 18 and 14.

XKSearch (Xu & Papakonstantinou, 2005) returns a subtree rooted at a node called the Smallest Lowest Common Ancestor (SLCA), where the nodes of the subtree contain all the query's keywords and have no descendant node(s) that also contain all the keywords. Consider for example Fig. 1 and that node 18 contains the keyword "XML and the Web". Thus, nodes 18 and 11 are both now containing the same title "XML and the Web". Now consider the query Q("XML and the Web", "Wilson"). The answer subtree will be the one rooted at node 13, which contains nodes 18 and 14, and not the one rooted at node 10, which contains nodes 11 and 14.

CONTEXT-DRIVEN SEARCH

We present below the problems of non context-driven search engines caused by overlooking nodes' contexts, and demonstrate these problems by using sample of queries selected from the ones used in the experiments. We then introduce SEEC, the techniques it employs, and show how it solves and overcomes the problems of non context-driven search engines.

The customer (node 1) ordered a book (node 10) and had previously ordered a magazine (node 35) .The author (node 13) authored the book (node 10) as well as another publication (node 17). Note that the XML tree is exaggerated for the purpose of demonstrating all the concepts proposed in this paper.

PROBLEMS OF NON CONTEXT-DRIVEN SEARCH ENGINES

Non context-driven search engines, such as XSEarch (Cohen & Mamou & Sagiv, 2003), Schema Free XQuery (Li & Yu & Jagadish, 2004), and XKSearch (Xu & Papakonstantinou, 2005) build relationships between data elements without consideration of their contexts (parents), which may result in faulty answers specially if the XML document contains more than one element having the same label but representing different types, or having different labels but representing the same type. We are going to take XSEarch, Schema Free XQuery, and XKSearch as samples of non context-driven search engines and show how they may return faulty answers as a result of overlooking nodes' contexts. We present below query samples selected from the ones used in the experiments and show how each one caused one of the three systems to return faulty answer. These query samples are selected from the ones we ran against the XML document generated from the XML tree shown in Figure 1. First, recall the techniques used by each of the three systems in the previous section titled "background".

Consider Figure 1 and the query (who is the author of the publication titled "XML and the Web"). The correct answer is node 14, but Schema Free XQuery will return null. The reason is that the LCA of nodes 11 (which contains the keyword "XML and the Web") and 14 is node 10, and node 10 is an ancestor of node 13, which is the LCA of nodes 14 and 18 (which has the same label as node 11). Therefore, Schema Free XQuery considers node 14 is related to node 18 and not to node 11.

Consider if we prune node 12 (ISBN) from Figure 1 and we have the query (what is the ISBN of the publication titled "XML and the Web"). Instead of returning null, Schema Free XQuery will return node 19.

Consider Figure 1 and the query "what is the title of the publication that was ordered in order number is 10024". Instead of returning node 11 only, Schema Free XQuery will return also node 18, which is irrelevant.

Consider Figure 1 and the query "what is the ISBN of the publication that had been ordered by a customer, who also ordered a publication with ISBN "87-11-07559-7". Instead of returning node 37, Schema Free XQuery will return node 19, because the LCA of nodes 37 and 12 is node 1, and node 1 is an ancestor of node 10, which is the LCA of nodes 12 and 19, and the label of node 19 is the same as the label of node 37. Therefore,

Schema Free XQuery considers node 19 is related to node 12, while node 37 is not.

Consider Figure 1 and the query "what is the title of the publication that was ordered in order number 10024". Instead of returning node 11 only, XSEarch will return also nodes 36 and 18, because the relationship tree of nodes 36 and 7 and the relationship tree of nodes 18 and 7 do not contain two or more nodes having the same label. If XSEarch employs the ontological concepts we are proposing, it would have discovered that the first relationship tree contains nodes 31 (previousOrder) and 16 (currentOrder) which belong to the same type, and the second relationship tree contains nodes 10 (book) and 17 (otherPublication) which also belong to the same type (publication).

On the flip side, consider Figure 1 and the query "what is the ISBN of the publication that had been ordered by the same customer, who ordered a publication with ISBN 87-11-07559-7". Instead of returning node 37, XSEarch will return node 19, because the relationship tree of nodes 37 and 12 contains more than one node having the same label (nodes 33 and 8 and also nodes 34 and 9). And, the relationship tree of nodes 19 and 12 does not contain more than one node having the same label.

Consider if, we prune node 11 (title) from Figure 1 and we have the query "what is the title of the publication, whose ISBN is 87-11-07559-7". Instead of returning null, XKSearch will return the subtree rooted at node 10 and contains nodes 12 and 18, because XKSearch will incorrectly consider node 18 containing the title of the publication, whose ISBN is 87-11-07559-7.

SEEC SOLUTION

Preliminaries

In this section we present definitions of key notations and basic concepts used in the chapter. We model XML documents as rooted and labeled trees. A node in a tree represents an element in an XML document. Nodes are numbered for easy reference. SEEC accepts the following two query forms. The first is Q("k_1", "k_2", .., "k_n"), which is a Keyword-Based query form, where k_i denotes a keyword. The second is Q(l_{k_1} = "k_1",..., l_{kn} = "k_n", E_1?,..., E_n?), which is a Loosely Structured query form, where k_i denotes a keyword, l_{k_i} denotes the label of the element containing the keyword k_i, and E_i denotes the label of the element containing the data that the user is looking for. We call each label-keyword pair a search term, and we call each "label?" a return element node or an answer return element node. Consider for example Figure 1 and that the user wants to know the title of the book, whose ISBN is 87-11-07559-7 (node 12). The user could issue the following Loosely Structured query: Q (ISBN = "87-11-07559-7", title?).

Definition: Ontology Label (OL) and Ontology Label Abbreviation (OLA)

If we cluster parent nodes (interior nodes) in an XML document based on their reduced characteristics and cognitive qualities, the label of each of these clusters is an Ontology Label (OL). Table 1 shows the Ontology Labels and clusters of parent nodes in the XML tree in Figure 1. A Dewey ID (see the definition of Dewey ID) is a series of OLs. For the sake of compacting Dewey IDs, we abbreviate each OL to a letter called an Ontology Label Abbreviation (OLA). Table 1 shows also the OLA of each OL in the table.

Definition: Canonical Tree

If we fragment an XML tree to the simplest semantically meaningful fragments, each fragment is called a Canonical Tree and it consists of a parent node and its leaf children data nodes. That is, if a parent node has leaf child/children data nodes, the parent node along with its leaf children data nodes constitute a Canonical Tree. In Figure 1 for example, the parent node "customer" (node 1) and its leaf child data node "name" (node 2) constitute a Canonical Tree, whose ID is T_1 (see Figure 2).

Figure 2. Canonical Trees graph of the XML tree presented in Figure 1

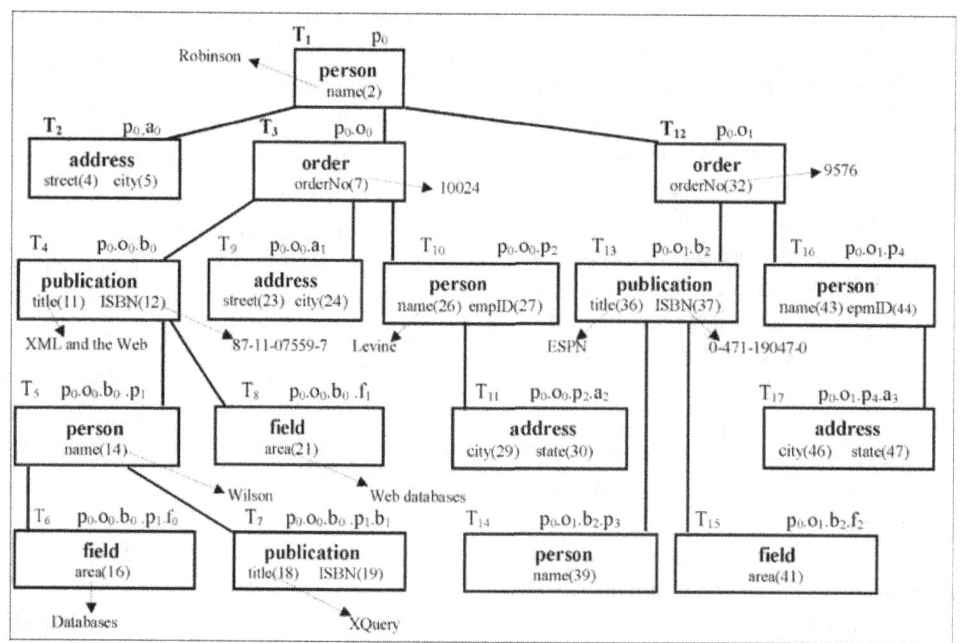

Similarly, the parent node "address" (node 3) and its children data nodes "street" (4) and "city" (5) constitute a Canonical Tree, whose ID is T_2 (see Figure 2). Leaf children data nodes represent the characteristics of their parents. The Ontology Label of a Canonical Tree is the Ontology Label of the parent node component in this Canonical Tree. For example, the Ontology Label of Canonical Tree T_1 in Figure 2 is the Ontology Label of the parent node component customer (1), which is "person". Each Canonical Tree is labeled with three labels as the Figure below shows. The label inside the rectangle is the Ontology Label of the Canonical Tree. The label on top of the rectangle and located in the left side, which has the form T_i represents the numeric ID of the Canonical Tree, where $1 \leq i \leq |T|$. The label on top of the rectangle and located in the right side is called a Dewey ID (see the Dewey ID definition). Figure 2 shows the *Canonical Trees graph* representing the XML tree in Figure 1. For example, the Ontology Label of the root Canonical Tree is "person", its numeric ID is T_1, and its Dewey ID is p_0. We sometimes use the abbreviation "CT" to denote "Canonical Tree".

Table 1. Ontology labels (OL) and ontology labels abbreviation (OLA) of parents in Fig. 1

Parent nodes (with their IDs)	*OL*	*OLA*
customer (1), author (13), editor (38), processingEmployee (25, 42)	person	p
book (10), magazine (35), otherPublication (17)	publication	b
expertise (15), field (20), specialty (40)	field	f
address (3), shipTo (22), site (28, 45)	address	a
currentOrder (6), previousOrder (31)	order	o

Numeric ID Dewey ID

Ontology Label data node(s)

Definition: Dewey ID

Each Canonical Tree is labeled with a Dewey number-like label called a Dewey ID. A Dewey ID of a Canonical Tree T_i is a series of components, each has the form OLA_x where OLA is an Ontology Label Abbreviation and x denotes a subscript digit. Each OLA represents the Ontology Label of an ancestor canonical Tree T_j of T_i and the digit x represents the number of Canonical Trees preceding T_j in the graph using Depth First Search, whose Ontology Labels are the same as the Otology Label of T_j. When the series of components OLA_x in the Dewey ID of CT T_i are read from left to right, they reveal the chain of ancestors of T_i and their Ontology Labels, starting from the root CT and the last component reveals the Ontology Label of T_i itself. Consider for example Canonical Tree T_4 in Figure 2. Its Dewey ID $p_0.o_0.b_0$ reveals that the Dewey ID of the root Canonical Tree is p_0 and its Ontology Label is "person". It also reveals that the Dewey ID of the parent of T_4 is $p_0.o_0$ and its Ontology Label is "order". The last component b_0 reveals the Ontology Label of T_4, which is "publication", and the subscript 0 attached to "b" indicates that there are zero Canonical Trees preceding T_4 in the graph (using Depth First Search) whose Ontology Labels is "publication".

Definition: Keyword Context (KC)

KC is a Canonical Tree containing a keyword(s) of a Keyword-Based query, or containing a search term's keyword(s) of a Loosely Structured query. Consider for example that "Robinson" is a keyword of a query. Since this keyword is contained in Canonical Tree T_1 (recall Figure 2), T_1 is considered a KC.

Definition: Intended Answer Node (IAN)

When a user submits a query, he is usually looking for data that is relevant to the query's keywords. Each one of the data nodes containing this data is called an Intended Answer Node (IAN). Consider for example Figure 1 and that the user submitted the query Q("10024", "Levine"). As the semantics of the query implies, the user wants to know information about the order, whose number is "10024" and processed by the employee "Levine". One of the nodes containing this information is node 11. Node 11 is called an IAN. In the case of a Loosely Structured query, each return element node in the query is an IAN.

Definition: Canonical Trees graph

When we fragment an XML tree to Canonical Trees, the resulting graph is called a Canonical Trees graph. For example, Figure 2 is the Canonical Trees graph representing the XML tree in Figure 1. A Canonical Trees graph is undirected. The edges connecting Canonical Trees in a Canonical Trees graph are determined as follows. Let n and be the parent nodes components of Canonical Trees and respectively. If is a descendant of n, and there is no interior node in the path between them that has a child data node, then Canonical Tree is considered a child of Canonical Tree . Consider for example Figure 1. Since node "address" (3) is a descendant of node "customer" (1) and there is no interior node in the path connecting them that has a child data node, Canonical Tree T_2 is considered a child of Canonical Tree T_1 (recall Figure 2).

Determining Related Canonical Trees

Each Canonical Tree represents a real-world entity. A Canonical Trees graph (e.g. Figure 2) depicts the hierarchical relationships between the entities represented by the Canonical Trees. A relationship between two Canonical Trees could be described as either immediate or extended. The immediate relatives of Canonical Tree T_i are Canonical Trees that have strong and close relationships with T_i, while its extended relatives have weak relationships with it. We call the immediate relatives of Canonical Tree T_i the Related Canonical Trees of T_i.

Definition: Related Canonical Tree (RCT)
A Canonical Tree *T* is considered a RCT of Canonical Tree *T′*, if it is closely related to *T′*.

Notation: RCT_T
RCT_T denotes the set of Canonical Trees that are considered RCT of Canonical Tree T.

Notation: OL_T
OL_T denotes the Ontology Label of Canonical Tree T. In Figure 2 for example OL_{T_1} is "person".

Let k be a keyword contained in either a Keyword-Based query or the search term of a Loosely Structured query. If k is contained in a Canonical Tree T, then the IAN should be contained in either T itself or in IR_T. If a query's keywords k_1 and k_2 are contained in Canonical Trees T_1 and T_2 respectively, the IAN should be contained in T_1, T_2, and/or the intersect $IR_{T1} \cap IR_{T2}$. Therefore, for each Canonical Tree T_i, we need to determine its Related Canonical Trees (RCT_{T_i}). Determining RCT_{T_i} could be done using the combination of intuition and logics that govern relationships between real-world entities. Consider for example the Keyword-Based query Q("XQuery") (recall Figures 1 and 2). It is intuitive that the IAN to be data nodes 14, 16, and/or 19 but it is not intuitive to be, for instance, node 2 since "Robinson" (node 2) has nothing to do with the publication "XQuery". Since "XQuery" is contained in Canonical Tree T_7, we can conclude that each of the Canonical Trees containing nodes 14, 16, and 19 $\in RCT_{T7}$ while the Canonical Tree containing node 2 $\notin RCT_{T7}$. We present below three lemmas that help in determining RCT_{T_i}. Their proofs are based on intuition and logics that govern relationships between real-world entities. We are going to sketch the proofs. We can determine RCT_{T_i} by pruning all the Extended Relatives of T_i from the Canonical Trees graph and the remaining ones would be RCT_{T_i}. We present three properties that regulate the pruning process and they are inferred from the conclusions of the three lemmas.

Lemma 1:
In order for the answer of a query to be intuitive and meaningful, the IAN should never be contained in a Canonical Tree whose Ontology Label is the same as the Ontology Label of the KC (the Canonical Tree containing the keyword). It could be contained in either the KC itself or in a Canonical Tree whose Ontology Label is different than the Ontology Label of the KC. Therefore, the Related Canonical Trees of the KC (RCT_{KC}) should have different Ontology Labels than the Ontology Label of the KC. That is, the Related Canonical Trees of any CT *T* (RCT_T) always have different Ontology Labels than the Ontology Label of *T*.

Proof (sketch): Consider Figure 3, which shows a "paper" and an "article" Canonical Trees. They both have the same Ontology Label "publication". The two Canonical Trees contain nodes "title" and "year", which are characteristics of the "publication" supertype. However, each of them has its own specific node: "conference" in the "paper" and "journal" in the "article" Canonical Tree. Consider that the "paper" Canonical Tree is a KC and let N_k denote a node containing a keyword. Below are all possible query scenarios that involve the two CTs:

Scenario 1: N_k is "title": If the IAN is "year", then intuitively this year is the one contained in the KC and not the one contained in the "article" Canonical Tree. If IAN is "conference", then obviously it is the "conference" node contained in the KC.

Scenario 2 N_k is "year": Similar to scenario 1

Scenario 3: N_k is "conference": If the IAN is "title" or "year", then intuitively they are the ones contained in the KC and not the ones contained in the "article" Canonical Tree. If, however, the IAN is "journal", then obviously, the query is meaningless and unintuitive, since the user wants to know a journal's name by providing a conference's name. The query would be unintuitive even if both the "paper" and the "article" are authored by the same author.

As the example scenarios above show, the IAN cannot be contained in the "article" Canonical Tree if the KC is the "paper" Canonical Tree. That is, if the IAN of an intuitive and meaningful query is contained in a Canonical Tree T, then either $OL_T \neq OL_{KC}$ or T is itself the KC. In other words, the RCT of a KC have different Ontology Labels than the Ontology Label of the KC. The reason is that Canonical Trees, whose Ontology Labels are the same have common entity characteristics (because they capture information about real-word entities sharing the same type) and therefore they act as rivals and do not participate with each other in immediate relative relationships: one of them cannot be among the RCT of another one. They can, however, participate with each other in a relationship by being RCT to another Canonical Tree, whose Ontology Label is different than theirs. As an example, Canonical Trees T_4 and T_7 in Figure 2 have the same Ontology Label "publication" and they are both RCT of Canonical Tree T_5 (the author contained in T_5 authored the publications contained in T_4 and T_7). Therefore, the answer for the query Q("Wilson"), where T_5 is the KC, should include both T_4 and T_7 in the answer subtree for the query.

Property 1:
This property is based on lemma 1. When computing RCT_{KC}, we prune from the Canonical Trees graph any Canonical Tree, whose Ontology Label is the same as the Ontology Label of the KC.

Lemma 2:
Related Canonical Trees of a KC (RCT_{KC}) that are located in the same path should have distinct Ontology Labels. That is, if Canonical Trees T and T' are both $\in RCT_{KC}$ and if they are located in the same path from the KC, then $OL_T \neq OL_{T'}$.

Proof (sketch): Consider that Canonical Trees T, T', and T'' are located in the same path and that T' is a descendant of T while T'' is a descendant of both T' and T. In order for T'' to be a RCT of T, T'' has to be a RCT of T', because T' relates (connects) T'' with T. If T' and T'' have the same Ontology Label, then $T'' \notin RCT_{T'}$ (according to lemma 1), and therefore $T'' \notin RCT_T$. As an example, consider Figure 4, which shows Canonical Trees located in the same path from the KC. The letter on top of each Canonical Tree is an OLA (recall Table 1) and represents the Ontology Label of the CT. In order for T_3 to be a RCT of the KC, it has to be a RCT of both T_2 and T_1 because they are the ones that connect and relate it with the KC. CTs T_3 and T_1 have the same Ontology Label, therefore CT $T_3 \notin RCT_{T1}$ (according to lemma 1). Consequently, $T_3 \notin RCT_{KC}$, while $T_1, T_2 \in RCT_{KC}$. Consider as another example Figure 2 and that the KC is CT T_3. In the path: $T_3 \rightarrow T_4 \rightarrow T_5 \rightarrow T_7$, Canonical Trees T_4 and T_7 have the same Ontology Label. Therefore, CT $T_7 \notin RCT_{T3}$, while $T_4 \in RCT_{T3}$.

Property 2:
This property is based on lemma 2. When computing, we prune from the Canonical Trees graph any CT if there is another CT whose Ontology Label is the same as the Ontology Label ofand it is located between and the KC

Lemma 3:
If a Canonical Tree $T \notin RCT_{KC}$, and if another Canonical Tree T' is related (connected) to the KC through T, then $T' \notin RCT_{KC}$.

Figure 3. A "paper" and an "article" CTs

paper title, year, conference	article title, year, journal

Figure 4. CTs located in the same path

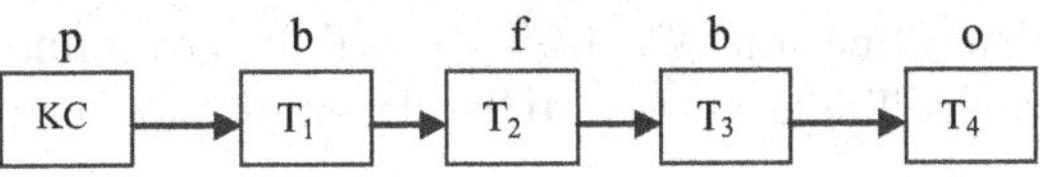

Proof (sketch): Every Canonical Tree T has a domain of influence. This domain covers Canonical Trees, whose *degree of relativity* to T is strong. Actually, these Canonical Trees are the RCT of T. If by applying property 1 or 2 we have determined that a Canonical Tree $T' \notin RCT_T$, then the degree of relativity between T' and T is weak. Intuitively, the degree of relativity between any other CT T'' and T is even weaker if T'' relates (connected) to T through T', due to the proximity factor. Consider for example Figure 2 and that CT T_1 is a KC. By applying property 1, $T_5 \notin RCT_{T1}$ because T_5 has the same Ontology Label as T_1. Canonical Trees T_6 and T_7 are connected and related to T_1 through T_5. As can be seen, the degree of relativity between each of these CTs and T_1 is even weaker than the one between T_5 and T_1. Therefore, each of them $\notin RCT_{T1}$.

Property 3:
This property is based on lemma 3. When computing RCT_{KC}, we prune from the Canonical Trees graph any Canonical Tree that is related (connected) to the KC through a Canonical Tree T, if $T \notin RCT_{KC}$.

Computing RCT_T online is expensive. Therefore, for each Canonical Tree T in a Canonical Trees graph we compute its RCT_T offline and store the information in a hash table called RCT_TBL for future references. The naïve approach for computing RCT_T is to apply the three properties to EACH other CT in the Canonical Trees graph. The time complexity of this approach for computing the RCT of all CTs in the graph is $O(|T|^2)$. We constructed an alternative and efficient algorithm for computing RCT_T called ComputeRCTs (see Figure 5), which takes advantage of property 3 as follows. To compute RCT_T, instead of examining each Canonical Tree in the graph for determining if it satisfies one of the three properties, we ONLY examine the Canonical Trees that are *adjacent* to any Canonical Tree $T' \in RCT_T$. If the algorithm determines that $T' \in RCT_T$, it will then examine each CT adjacent to T'. If the algorithm, however, determines that $T' \notin RCT_T$, it will not examine ALL Canonical Trees that are connected to T through T', because they are known $\notin RCT_T$ (according to property 3). Subroutine ComputeRCT (recall Figure 5) works as follows. Set $S_{KC}^{T'}$ (line 4) stores the Ontology Label of each CT located between CT T' and the KC. In line 2, if the Ontology Label of T' is not the same as that of the KC (which indicates that T' is not satisfying property 1) or if it is not included in set $S_{KC}^{T'}$ (which indicates that T' is not satisfying property 2), then $T' \in RCT_T$ (line 3), and we recursively examine the CTs that are adjacent to T' (line 5). Otherwise, if $T' \notin RCT_T$, all CTs connected to T through T' will not be examined. The time complexity of the algorithm is

$$O\left(\sum_{i=1}^{|T|} |RCT_{T_i}|\right)$$

Answering Loosely Structured Queries

The following examples show how a Loosely Structured query is answered using the pruning schemes of the three properties described previously. The examples are based on Figures 1 and 2.

Example 1:
Q (ISBN="0-471-19047-0", name?). Sine "0-471-19047-0" is the ISBN of the magazine that was ordered by customer "Robinson" prior to his current order (which is a book), the answer for the query should be the "name" elements involving the magazine order ONLY. That is, it should not include the "name" element nodes 14 and 26. Since the keyword "0-471-19047-0" is contained in CT T_{13}, the "name" answer return element nodes should be contained in Canonical Trees $\in RCT_{T13}$. Let's now determine RCT_{T13} using the three properties described previously. By applying property 2, CT T_3 is pruned from the Canonical Trees graph, because it is located in the path $T_{13} \rightarrow T_{12} \rightarrow T_1 \rightarrow T_3$ and its Ontology Label is

Figure 5. Algorithm ComputeRCTs

```
ComputeRCTs {
  for each Canonical Tree T
    KC ← T                          /* Canonical Tree T is the KC */
    S^T_KC ← null
    RCT_KC ← null                   /*Set contains the RCT of a KC */
    ComputeRCT(KC) }                /*Call subroutine ComputeRCT*/
ComputeRCT(T) {        /*Compute Immediate Relatives of T */
  for each Canonical Tree T' ∈ Adj [T] /* T' is adj. to T*/
    if OL_T' ≠ OL_KC && OL_T' ∉ S^T'_KC
        /* If true, then T' doesn't satisfy properties 1 and 2*/
        then { RCT_KC = RCT_KC + OL_T'      /* OL_T' ∈ RCT_KC*/
               S^T'_KC ← S^T_KC + OL_T'     /*add OL_T' to set S^T'_KC */
               ComputeRCT(OL_T') }  }
```

the same as the Ontology Label of T_{12}, which is closer to T_{13}. By applying property 3, CTs T_4, T_5, T_6, T_7, T_8, T_9, T_{10}, and T_{11} are pruned, because they are related to T_{13} through the pruned T_3. The remaining CTs in the Canonical Trees graph are RCT_{T13} (see Figure 6). The answer for the query is nodes 2, 43, and 39 contained in CTs T_1, T_{16}, and T_{14} respectively.

Example 2:

Consider the following two queries:
Q_1 (orderNo = "10024", title?).
Q_2 (name = "Robinson", title?).

The answer for Q_1 should be a "title" node(s) associated with order number 10024. Since the keyword "10024" is contained in T_3, node 11 should be contained in a Canonical Tree ∈ RCT_{T3}. Therefore, the answer should be node 11 ONLY. On the other hand, the answer for Q_2 should be the "title" nodes associated with customer "Robinson". Since the keyword "Robinson" is contained in T_1, the "title" nodes should be contained in Canonical Trees ∈ RCT_1. These nodes are nodes 11 and 36 (the title of the book in the current order and the title of the magazine in the previous order). Let's determine RCT_{T3} for Q_1. By applying property 1, T_{12} is pruned, because its Ontology Label is the same as the Ontology Label of T_3. By applying property 3, T_{13}, T_{14}, T_{15}, T_{16}, and T_{17} are pruned because they are related to T_3 through the pruned T_{12}. By applying property 2, T_7 is pruned, because it is located in the path $T_3 \rightarrow T_4 \rightarrow T_5 \rightarrow T_7$ and its Ontology Label is the same as the Ontology Label of T_4, which is closer to T_3. The remaining CTs in the Canonical Trees graph are RCT_{T3} (see Figure 7). Therefore, the answer for Q_1 is node 11 contained in T_4. Let's now determine RCT_{T1} for Q_2. By applying property 1, T_5, T_{10}, T_{14}, and T_{16} are pruned, because their Ontology Labels are the same as the Ontology Label of T_1. By applying property 3, T_6, T_7, T_{11}, and T_{17} are pruned because they are related to T_1 through either T_5, T_{10}, or T_{16}. The remaining CTs in the CTs graph are RCT_{T1} (see Figure 8). Therefore, the answer for Q_2 is nodes 11 and 36 contained in CTs T_4 and T_{13} respectively.

Example 3:

Consider the following two queries:
Q_1 (area = "databases", title?).
Q_2 (area = "web databases", title?).

Figure 6. RCT_{T13} *Figure 7. RCT_{T3}*

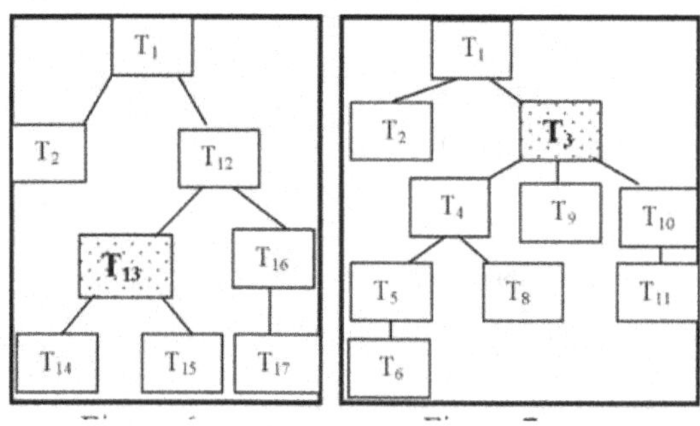

Q_1 asks for the title of publications that were authored by an author, whose area of expertise is "databases". The keyword "databases" is contained in T_6. The answer for this query should be contained in Canonical Trees $\in RCT_{T6}$ (see Figure 9). The answer is nodes 11 and 18 contained in CTs T_4 and T_7 respectively. Q_2 on the other hand asks for the book's title, whose field area is "web databases" (node 21). The keyword "web databases" is contained in T_8. Therefore, the answer for Q_2 should be contained in a CT $\in RCT_{T8}$ (see Figure 10). The answer is node 11.

Example 4:

Q (title = "XML and the Web", orderNo?). The keyword "XML and the Web" is contained in T_4. Therefore, node orderNo should be contained in a Canonical Tree $\in RCT_{T4}$ (see Figure 11).

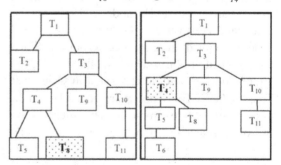

Figure 8. RCT_{T1} *Figure 9. RCT_{T6}*

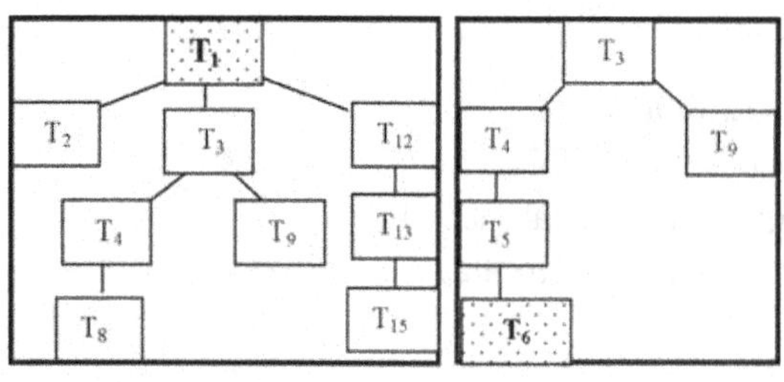

Computing RCT for a Loosely Structured Query Whose Search Terms are Contained in More than One Canonical Tree

Definition: Canonical Relationship Tree

The Canonical Relationship Tree of Canonical Trees T, T', and T'' is the set of Canonical Trees that connects the three Canonical Trees. For example, the Canonical Relationship Tree of CTs T_1 and T_{17} in Figure 2 is the set $\{T_1, T_{12}, T_{16}, T_{17}\}$.

Let $T_i...T_j$ be the set of Canonical Trees that contain the search terms of a Loosely Structured query. Let $ST_i...T_j$ denote the Canonical Relationship Tree of $T_i...T_j$.

If there are no two or more Canonical Trees in set $ST_i...T_j$ whose Ontology Labels are the same, the Canonical Trees in set $ST_i...T_j$ collectively constitute the KC of the query. Consider for example Figures 1 and 2 and consider that node 43 contains the keyword "Wilson". Thus, nodes 43 and 14 are both now containing this keyword. Now, consider a query, whose search terms are (name = "Wilson") and (orderNo = "10024"). The search term (name = "Wilson") is contained in CTs T_5 and T_{16} while the search term (orderNo = "10024") is contained in Canonical Tree T_3. There are two sets of Canonical Relationship Trees. The first set connects T_3 with T_5. Let ST_3,T_5 denote this set. The second set connects T_3 with T_{16}. Let ST_3,T_{16} denote this set. Set $ST_3,T_5 = \{T_3, T_4, T_5\}$ and set $ST_3,T_{16} = \{T_3, T_1, T_{12}, T_{16}\}$. Set ST_3,T_{16}

Figure 10. RCT_{T8} *Figure 11. RCT_{T4}*

contains Canonical Trees T_1 and T_{16}, whose Ontology Labels are the same; therefore, this set is not a valid KC. Since set ST_3,T_5 does not contain more than one Canonical Tree, whose Ontology Labels are the same, the Canonical Trees in the set collectively constitute a valid KC. That is, T_3,T_4, T_5 collectively constitute the KC of the query. The intuition behind that is as follows. Consider that a Canonical Tree T_b is located in the Canonical Relationship Tree of Canonical Trees T_a and T_c. Canonical Tree T_b is related to both T_a and T_c and it semantically relates T_a to T_c. Thus, without T_b, the relationship between T_a and T_c is semantically disconnected. Therefore, if T_a and T_c satisfy the search terms of a query, the KC of the query should also include T_b. So, the KC will consist of T_a, T_b, and T_c.

The answer for a query is computed as follows. Let *S* be a set containing the Canonical Trees that contain the search terms of a query. Let us store in a set called *S'* each Canonical Tree T that is a RCT of EACH Canonical Tree in set *S*. The answer for the query should be contained in a Canonical Tree(s) $\in S'$. That is, the answer for the query should be contained in the intersect $\bigcap_{T_i \in S'} RCT_{T_i}$.

Example 5:

Consider Figures 1 and 2 and the query: Q (ISBN = "0-471-19047-0", ISBN ="87-11-07559-7", name?). The query asks for the "name" of the customer, who ordered two publications, whose ISBNs are "0-471-19047-0" and "87-11-07559-7". The keyword "0-471-19047-0" is contained in CT T_{13} and the keyword "87-11-07559-7" is contained in CT T_4. See Figure 6 for RCT_{T13} and Figure 11 for RCT_{T4}. The intersect $RCT_4 \cap RCT_{T13} = \{T_1, T_2\}$. The answer for the query is node 2, which is contained in Canonical Tree T_1.

Answering Keyword-Based Queries

The answer of a Keyword-Based query is a subtree rooted at a Canonical Tree called the *Lowest Meaningful Common Ancestor (LMCA)*. The leaves of the subtree are the Canonical Trees containing the keywords (the KCs). Canonical Trees that are located in a path between a Keyword Context KC_i and the LMCA are called *Related Ancestor Canonical Trees of* KC_i, and are denoted by $RACT_{KC_i}$.

Definition: Related Ancestor Canonical Tree (RACT):

Let $A^T_{KC_i}$ denote Canonical Tree *T* is an ancestor of a Keyword Context KC_i. If $A^T_{KC_i}$ and $T \in RACT_{KC_i}$, then *T* is called a Related Ancestor Canonical Tree (RACT) of KC_i. That is, if a Canonical Tree *T* is both an ancestor and a RCT of KC_i, then it is considered a RACT of KC_i.

Notation $RACT_{KC_i}$:

$RACT_{KC_i}$ denotes the set of Canonical Trees that are RACT of KC_i

We constructed an efficient algorithm for computing RACTs, called computeRACT (see Figure 12). The algorithm uses the Dewey IDs of KCs (recall the definition of Dewey ID) and applies the pruning schemes of properties 1, 2, and 3 described previously. Function getComps (line 1) is input the Dewey ID of a Keyword Context (KC_i) and it returns the components comprising this Dewey ID. The returned components are assigns to set comps. For example, if the function is input the Dewey ID $OLA_i.OLA_j....OLA_k$, it would return the components OLA_i, OLA_j, ..., and OLA_k. Function scan_next_comp (lines 2 and 7) read the right-most component (OLA_x) in set comps. The function scans the components in the set from right to left. That is, every time the function is called, it reads the current right-most component. A currently scanned component will be stored in a set called S (lines 4 and 11). If function OLAin (line 8) is input a component OLA_x, it extracts and returns the subcomponent OLA, by stripping the subscript digit x. And, if the function is input a set S, it extracts the subcomponent OLA from each component OLA_x in the set and returns them. Line 8 checks properties 1 and 2 as follows. If the set of OLAs subcomponents

Figure 12. Algorithm computeRACT

```
ComputeRACT {
1. comps ← getComps(KC_i)
 /* Read the right-most component OLA_x in set compst */
2. cur_comp = scan_next_comp(comps)
3. S ← null
4. S← S + cur_comp
5. RACT_KC_i ← nul /*It is a set containing all RACTs of KC_i */
6. while set comps is not empty {
        /*Scan from right to left and read next component */
7.      cur_comp = scan_next_comp(comps)
8.      if (OLAin (cur_comp) ∉ OLAin (S) {
            /*if true, then properties 1 and 2 are not satisfied*/
9.          CTcomps ← comps \ S /*set difference operation*/
            /*Canonical Tree T_CTcomps ∈ RACT_KC_i */
10.         RACT_KC_i ← RACT_KC_i + T_CTcomps
11.         S← S + cur_comp
12.         }
13.     else return RACT_KC_i
14. }
15. }

OLAin(y) {
If y is a Dewey ID component OLA_x, extract and return the
subcomponent OLA (by stripping the subscript digit x). If y is
a set containing Dewey ID components, extract the
subcomponent OLA from each component OLA_x in the set,
and return them. }
```

that were extracted from set S does not contain a matching subcomponent to the one extracted from cur_comp, then neither property 1 nor property 2 is satisfied. If this is the case, then line 9 will compute a set difference operation between sets comps and S, and assigns the result to CTcomps. The Canonical Tree, whose Dewey ID has the same components as the ones in CTcomps is considered a RACT of the KC (line 10). If neither property 1 nor property 2 is satisfied, line 13 will return set $RACT_{KC_i}$.

Example 6:
Let's determine $RACT_{T5}$ (the set of CTs that are RACT of T_5) using algorithm computeRACT (recall Figure 2).

Line 1: comps = $\{p_0, o_0, b_0, p_1\}$.
Line 2: cur_comp = p_1. Line 4: S= $\{p_1\}$.

1st while iteration:
Line 7: cur_comp = b_0. Line 8: b $\notin$ {p}. Line 9: CTcomps = $\{p_0, o_0, b_0, p_1\}\backslash\{p_1\} = \{p_0, o_0, b_0\}$. Line 10: $RACT_{T5} = \{T_4\}$. Line 11: S= $\{p_1, b_0\}$.

2nd while iteration:
Line 7: cur_comp = o_0. Line 8: o $\notin$ {p, b}.
Line 9: CTcomps = $\{p_0, o_0, b_0, p_1\}\backslash \{p_1, b_0\} = \{p_0, o_0\}$. Line 10: $RACT_{T5} = \{T_4, T_3\}$.
Line 11: S= $\{p_1, b_0, o_0\}$.

3rd *while iteration:*
Line 7: cur_comp = p_0. Line 8: p $\in$ {p, b, o}.
Line 13: return set $RACT_{T5} = \{T_4, T_3\}$. See Figure 13-a.

Example 8:
Figure 13 parts b, c, d, e, and f show $RACT_{T3}$,

$RACT_{T4}$, $RACT_{T6}$, $RACT_{T8}$, and $RACT_{T13}$respectively.

Computing the Root of an Answer Subtree

As described previously, the answer of a Keyword-Based query is a subtree rooted at a Canonical Tree called the Lowest Meaningful Common Ancestor (LMCA). Consider a Keyword-Based query consisting of n keywords, and each of them is contained in a different KC: KC_1,KC_2,...,KC_n. Let $RACT_{KC1}$, $RACT_{KC2}$,..., $RACT_{KCn}$ be the RACTs of the n KCs. Let S be a set containing Canonical Trees that have the following property. Each one of them is contained in EACH one of the n RACTs. That is, if a Canonical Tree $T \in$ S, then $T \in RACT_{KCi}$, where i = 1 → n. The Canonical Tree in set S, whose hierarchical level is the lowest, is considered the LMCA (considering the hierarchical level in the Canonical Trees graph increases in the direction bottom-up). Consider for example Figure 14 (part a), which shows three KCs along with their RACTs. In the Figure, each an ancestor Canonical Tree $T_j \in RACT_{KCz}$ (where z = 1 → 3) is denoted by $T_j^{l_i}$, where l_i is the hierarchical level of T_j. As can be seen, Canonical Trees $T_y^{l_4}$ and $T_x^{l_5}$ are shared by the three RACTs. Since the hierarchical level of $T_y^{l_4}$ is lower than that of $T_x^{l_5}$, it is considered the LMCA. Figure 14 (part b) shows the answer subtree rooted at the LMCA.

Constructing the Answer Subtree

We constructed algorithm ComputeAnsSubTree (see Figure 15), for computing answer subtrees. The algorithm works as follows. It is input the RACT of each KC and a table called level_TBL, which stores for each Canonical Tree its hierarchical level in the Canonical Trees graph. In line 1, the algorithm determines the common Canonical Trees that are shared by all the RACTs by computing their intersect. From among these Canonical Trees, the one whose hierarchical level in the Canonical Trees graph is the lowest is considered the LMCA (line 2). Note that the algorithm considers the hierarchical level in the Canonical Trees graph increases from bottom to up. Lines 4 – 7: a Canonical Tree T_j is considered part of the answer subtree if $T_j \in RACT_{KCi}$ (line 5), and if its hierarchical level is lower than the level of the LMCA (line 6). Set AnsT contains the Canonical Trees comprising the answer subtree. It contains the KCs and the LMCA (line 3) in addition to the Canonical Trees that satisfy the condition in line 6 (see line 7).

ComputeAnsSubTree ($RACT_{Tx}$, ..., $RACT_{Ty}$, *level_TBL)* {

/* Compute the intersect of all RACTs */

1. Set P ← $RACT_{Tx} \cap ... \cap RACT_{Ty}$
2. LMCA ← T whose hierarchical level is the lowest in set P

Figure 13. (a) $RACT_{T5}$; (b) $RACT_{T3}$; (c) $RACT_{T4}$; (d) $RACT_{T6}$; (e) $RACT_{T8}$; (f) $RACT_{T13}$

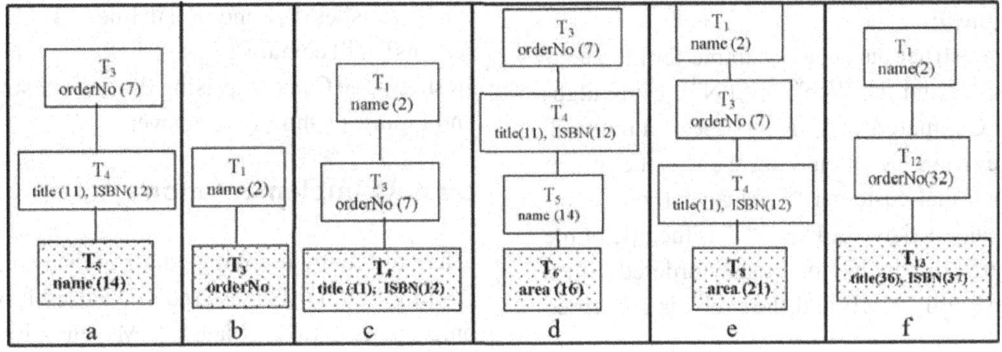

Figure 14. (a) Three KCs with their RACTs; (b) The answer subtree rooted at the LMCA

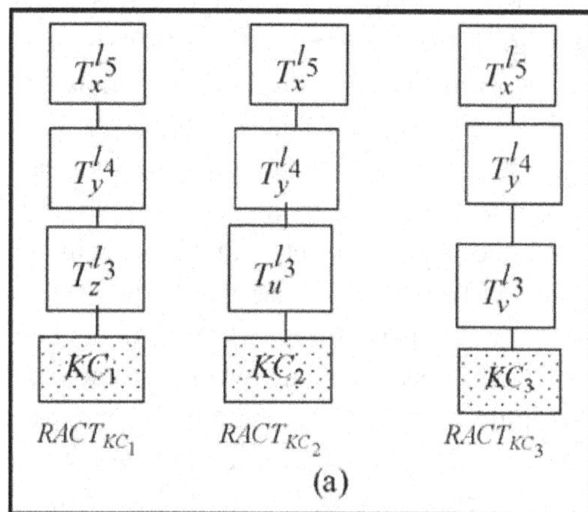

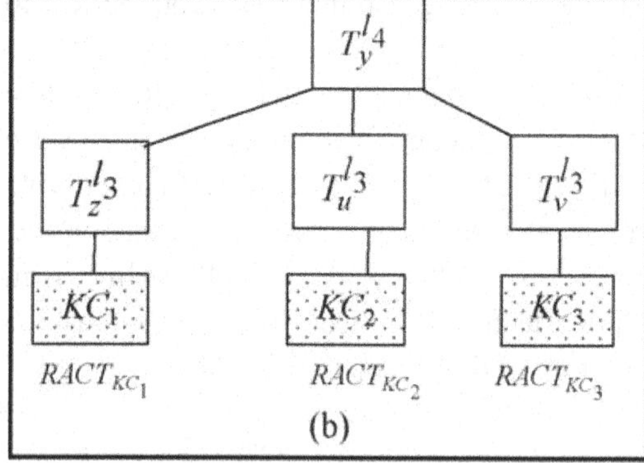

3. AnsT ← KCs + LMCA
4. for each Keyword Context KC_i
5. for each CT $T_j \in RACT_{KCi}$
6. If (level(T_j) < level(LMCA)
7. AnsT = AnsT + T_j
}

Example 9:

Let's construct the answer subtree for the query Q ("XML and the Web", "ESPN"), using algorithm ComputeAnsSubTree. Recall Figure 2. The keyword "XML and the Web" is the title of the book that customer "Robinson" (node 2) ordered and the keyword "ESPN" is the title of the magazine that he had previously ordered. Since the keyword "XML and the Web" is contained in Canonical Tree T_4 and the keyword "ESPN" is contained in Canonical Tree T_{13}, $RACT_{T4}$ and $RACT_{T13}$ are input to the algorithm (recall Figure 13-C for $RACT_{T4}$ and Figure 13-f for $RACT_{T13}$). The algorithm proceeds as follows. line 2: LMCA = T_1. Line 4 will iterate twice, one for $KC_i = T_4$ and the other for $KC_i = T_{13}$. When $KC_i = T_4$, the only Canonical Tree that satisfies the condition in line 6 is Canonical Tree T_3. When $KC_i = T_{13}$, only CT T_{12} satisfies the condition in line 6. At the end, set AnsT will contain {T_4, T_{13}, T_1, T_3, T_{12}}. Figure 16 shows the CTs comprising the answer subtree and Figure 17 shows the answer.

Figure 15. Algorithm ComputeAnsSubTree

```
ComputeAnsSubTree (RACT_Tx, ..., RACT_Ty, level_TBL)
{
   /* Compute the intersect of all RACTs */
1. Set P ← RACT_Tx ∩ ... ∩ RACT_Ty
2. LMCA ← T whose hierarchical level is the
          lowest in set P
3. AnsT ← KCs + LMCA
4. for each Keyword Context KC_i
5.     for each CT T_j ∈ RACT_KCi
6.         If ( level(T_j) < level(LMCA)
7.             AnsT = AnsT + T_j
}
```

Figure 16. The Canonical Trees comprising the answer subtree of the query in Example 9

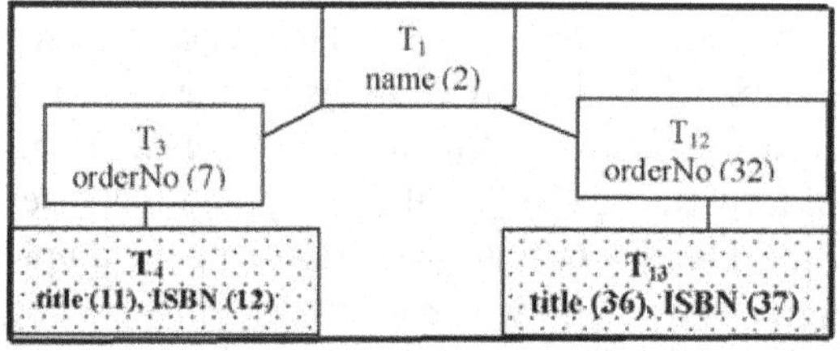

System Implementation

There are many ontology editor tools available. (Denny, 2002) lists these tools. We used Protégé ontology editor (Knublauch & Musen & Rector,

Figure 17. The answer for the query in Example 9

```
<customer>
    <name> Robinson </name>
    <currentOrder>
        <orderNo> 10024 </orderNo>
        <items>
            <item>
                <book>
                    <title> XML and the Web </title>
                    <ISBN> 87-11-07559-7 </ISBN>
                </book>
            </item>
        </items>
    </currentOrder>
    <previousOrder>
        <orderNo> 9576 </orderNo>
        <items>
            <item>
                <magazine>
                    <title> ESPN </title>
                    <ISBN> 0-471-19047-0 </ISBN>
                </magazine>
            </item>
        </items>
    </previousOrder>
</customer>
```

2002) in the implementation of SEEC for determining the Ontology Labels of nodes. Protégé is an open source ontology editor. It allows a system administrator to build taxonomies of concepts and relations and to add constraints onto domains of relations. Web pages are one of several ways to create instances of the concepts in an ontology and they are a good source of instance information. In the implementation of SEEC, the population of ontologies was semi-automated.

Figure 18 shows the system architecture. The OntologyBuilder uses an ontology editor tool to create ontologies and populates them with instances. The XML schema describing the structure of the XML document is input to the OntologyBuilder, which outputs to the GraphBuilder the list of Ontology Labels corresponding to the interior nodes in the XML schema. Using the input XML schema and the list of Ontology Labels, the GraphBuilder creates a Canonical Trees graph. Using the input XML document and the Canonical Trees Graph, the IndexBuilder stores in a table called K_TBL for each keyword the CTs containing it. This table is saved in a disk. Module ComputeRCT uses algorithm ComputeRCTs (recall Figure 5) to compute for each Canonical Tree T its RCT_T and saves this information in a hash table called RCT_TBL. Module ComputeRACT computes the LMCA for an answer subtree upon a request from the Query Engine. SEEC's Query Engine is built on top of XQuery engine. After determining the elements that contain the answer data, SEEC's Query Engine uses XQuery engine to extract this data.

Figure 18. System architecture

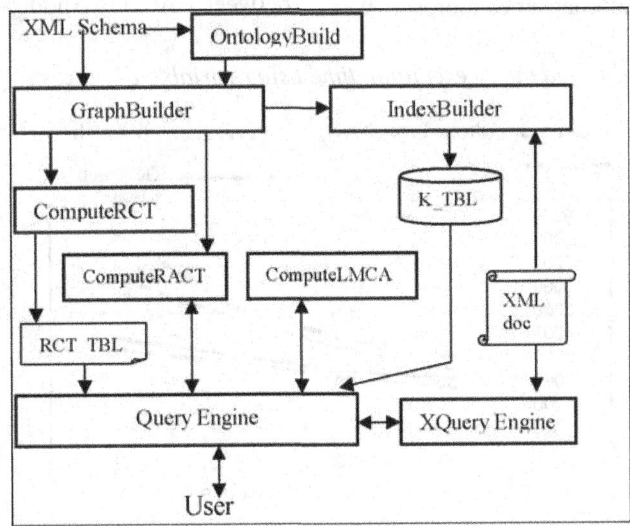

EXPERIMENTAL RESULTS

The experiments were carried out on a AMD Athlon XP 1800+ processor, with a CPU of 1.53 GHz and 736 MB of RAM, running the Windows XP operating system. We implemented SEEC using Java. We evaluated the recall, precision, and search performance of SEEC and compared it with three systems: XSEarch (Cohen & Mamou & Sagiv, 2003), Schema Free XQuery (Li & Yu & Jagadish, 2004), and XKSearch (Xu & Papakonstantinou, 2005). The implementation of Schema Free Xquery has been released as part of the TIMBER project (Jagadish & Patel, 2006). We used TIMBER for the evaluation of Schema Free XQuery. As for XSEarch and XKSearch, we implemented their entire proposed systems from scratch. We used test data from four different sources. The first is XMark Benchmark (Schmidt & Waas & Kersten & Florescu & Manolescu & Carey & Busse, 2002). XMark provides 20 queries written in schema aware XQuery and accompanied by a 100 MB XML document. The second is XML Validation Benchmark from Sarvega (Juneja, 2005). From the XML documents provided by the XML Validation Benchmark, we selected 25 that are suitable for testing Keyword-Based and Loosely Structured-based systems. The third is XML Query Use Cases provided by W3C (Chamberlin & Fankhauser & Florescu & Robie, 2006). Each use case query is accompanied by a DTD and sample data. The fourth test data is INEX test collection (INEX, 2004). The fifth test data is an XML document generated from the XML tree presented in Figure 1 using ToXgene (Barbosa & Mendelzon & Keenleyside & Lyons, 2002). We constructed 30 queries based on this document.

Search Performance Evaluation

To evaluate the query execution times of SEEC under different document sizes, we ran queries against XMark, Use Cases, and XML Validation Benchmark documents of sizes 150, 200, 250, and 300 MB. For each of the four document sizes, we ran 20 random Keyword-Based queries and computed the average query execution time of SEEC, XSEarch, Schema Free XQuery, and XKSearch. Figure 19 shows the results. Also, for each of the four document sizes, we ran 20 random Loosely Structured queries and computed the average query execution time of the four systems. Figure 20 shows the results. As Figures 19 and 20 show, the average query execution time of SEEC is less than those of XSEarch, Schema Free XQuery, and XKSearch. The reason for the expensive running times of XSEarch and Schema Free XQuery stems from the fact that they build a relationship between EACH two nodes containing keywords,

Figure 19. Avg. keyword-based query execution time using variable doc sizes

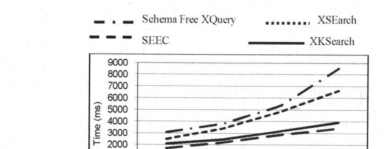

Figure 20. Avg. loosely structured query execution time using variable doc sizes merge algorithm, whose overhead augments its running time

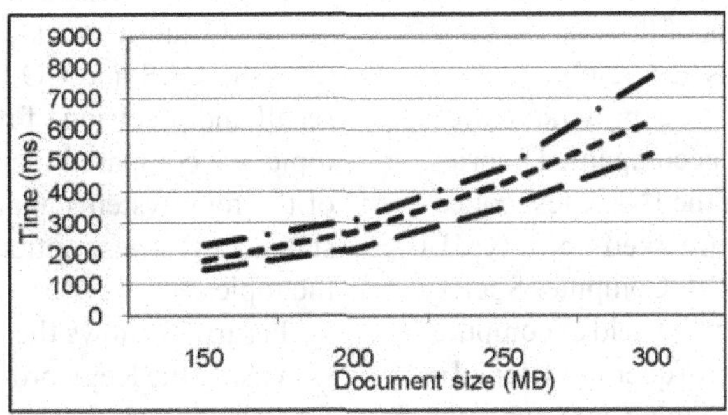

and THEN filter results according to the search terms. As a result the time complexity of Schema Free XQuery is

$$O(h \sum_{i=1}^{m} n_i + \prod_{i=1}^{m} n_i)$$

where h denotes the height of an XML tree, m the number of input elements, and the expression n_i denotes the number of nodes that have the same label as the input element number i $(1 \leq i \leq m)$. And, the reason that the average query execution time of SEEC is less than that of XKSearch is because XKSearch employs stack based sort-merge algorithm, whose overhead augments its running time.

Recall and Precision Evaluation

Recall is the ratio of the number of relevant records retrieved to the total number of relevant records in the database. Precision is the ratio of the number of relevant records retrieved to the total number of irrelevant and relevant records retrieved. Using the test data of XMark, XQuery Use Cases, XML Validation Benchmark, INEX, and the XML document generated from the XML tree in Figure 1, we measured the recall and precision of SEEC and compared them with those of XSEarch, Schema Free XQuery, and XKSearch. While the queries of INEX and Schema Free XQuery are accompanied by answers (expected results), the others are not. We describe below the process we followed for computing the results of the queries of XMark, XML Validation Benchmark, and the XML document generated from Figure 1, and then describe the mechanisms we adopted for computing recall and precision.

We computed the answers for the queries accompanied the test data of XMark, XML Validation Benchmark, and the XML document generated from Figure 1 using (Katz, 2005) and recorded the results. The recorded results represent the correct answers, which would be compared later with the results returned by each of the four systems. We converted each of the schema-aware queries of the test data into an equivalent keyword-based and loosely structured query accepted by each of the four systems. We simply extracted the keywords from the search terms of the schema-aware queries and plugged them in the query forms of the four systems. Let Q_s denote a schema-aware query and Q_k denote the same query after being converted into keyword-based. Let y denote the set of result records of query Q_S. Let x denote the set of result records of query Q_k (records containing the query's keywords are not included). The recall and precision are measured as follows: recall = $\frac{|x \cap y|}{|y|}$, and precision = $\frac{|x \cap y|}{|x|}$. While this recall measure is a good indicative of the actual recall of a system, the precision measure may not reflect the actual precision of the system, because the number of result records of query Q_k is usually more than the number of result records of query Q_s. This precision measure, however, can accurately compares the precision of different keyword-based systems: it may not reflect the actual precisions of the four systems, but it ranks their precisions accurately.

INEX and XQuery Use Cases provide answers (expected results) for their accompanied queries. Some of the documents in the INEX test collection are scientific articles (marked up in XML) from publications of the IEEE Computer Society covering a range of topics in the field of computer science. There are two types of queries included in the INEX test collection, *Content-and-structure (CAS)* queries and *Content-only (CO)* queries. All topics contain the same three fields as traditional IR topics: title, description, and narrative. The title is the actual query submitted to the retrieval system. The description and narrative describe the information need in natural language. The described information need is used to judge the relevancy of the answers retrieved by a system. The difference between the CO and CAS topics lies in the topic title. In the case of the CO topics, the title describes the information need as a small list of keywords. In the case of CAS topics, the title describes the information need using descendant axis (//), the Boolean *and/or*, and *about* statement (it is the IR counterpart of **contains** function in XPath). CAS queries are loosely structured queries while CO queries are keyword-based queries. We used the CAS and CO topics for measuring the recall and precision of the four systems. In each topic, we compared the results returned by each of the four systems against the expected results stated in the description and narrative fields of the topic.

Figure 21 shows the average recall and precision using the Keyword-Based queries of the test data, and Figure 22 shows the average recall and precision using the Loosely Structured queries of the test data. As the Figures show, SEEC outperforms the other three systems and Schema Free XQuery outperforms XSEarch and XKSearch. On the other hand, XSEarch performs poorly. The recall and precision performance of SEEC is attributed to its context-driven search techniques inferred from the three properties presented previously, and to the fact that the other three systems build relationships between data nodes based solely on their labels and proximity to one another, while overlooking the contexts of the nodes. And, the reason that Schema Free XQuery outperforms

Figure 21. Average recall and precision using keyword-based queries

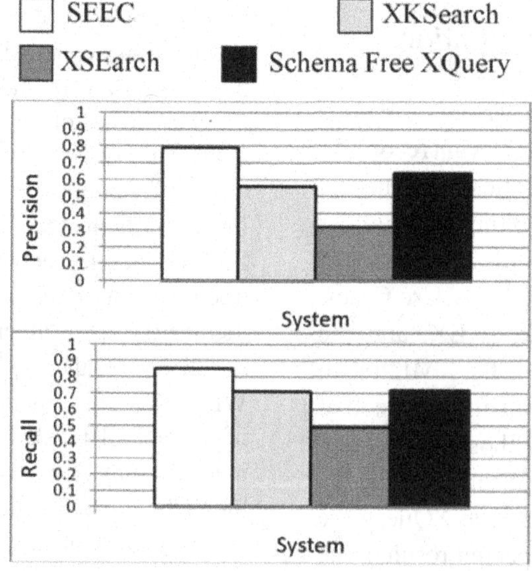

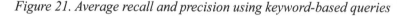

Figure 22. Average recall and precision using loosely structured queries

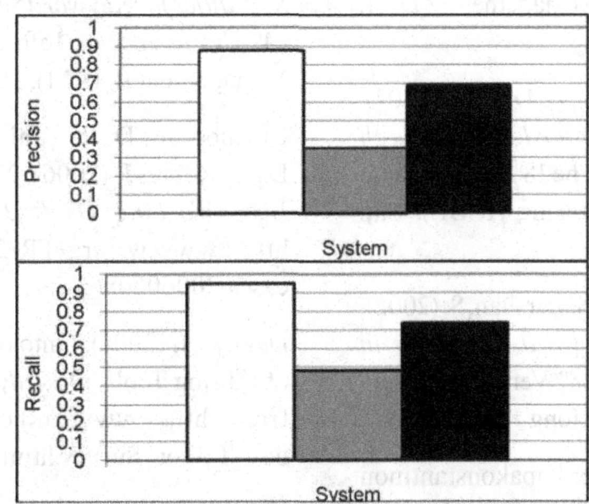

XSEarch and XKSearch is because the technique it uses for building relationships between nodes is based on the hierarchical relationships (ancestor-descendant relationships) between the nodes, which alleviate node-labeling conflicts.

CONCLUSION AND FUTURE TRENDS

We proposed in this chapter an XML search engine called SEEC, which answers XML Loosely Structured queries as well as Keyword-Based queries. We proposed previously a stand-alone Loosely Structured search engine called OOX-Search (Taha & Elmasri, 2007). SEEC integrates OOXSearch with a Keyword-Based search engine and uses novel search techniques. It is built on top of XQuery search engine.

SEEC is a context-driven search engine. The context of an element is determined by its parent element, since a data element is generally a characteristic of its parent. Non context-driven search engines build relationships between data elements based solely on their labels and proximity to one another, while overlooking the contexts of the elements, which may lead to relationships that are semantically disconnected. Consequently, the results generated by non context-driven systems are susceptible to errors, especially if the XML document contains more than one element having the same label but representing different types or having different labels but representing the same type. We experimentally evaluated the quality and efficiency of SEEC and compared it with three non context-driven search systems: XSEarch (Cohen & Mamou & Sagiv, 2003), Schema Free XQuery (Li & Yu & Jagadish, 2004), and XKSearch (Xu & Papakonstantinou, 2005). The experimental results showed that the recall and precision of SEEC outperform those of the other three systems, and its average query execution time is less than those of the three systems.

Future directions for our research include expanding SEEC by incorporating a fully-structured query search engine so that it becomes a comprehensive XML search engine. The prospective search engine will answer each user based on his/her degree of knowledge of the underlying data and its structure. We also intend to investigate other techniques that improve the search performance.

REFERENCES

Amer-Yahia, S., & Cartmola E., & Deutsch, A. (2006). *Flexible and Efficient XML Search with*

Complex Full-Text Predicates. ACM SIGMOD International Conference on Management of Data, Chicago, Illinois.

Agrawal, S., & Chaudhuri S., & Das, G. (2002). *DBXplorer: a System for Keyword-Based Search Over Relational Databases.* The 18th International Conference on Data Engineering (ICDE), San Jose, California

Aditya, B., & Bhalotia, G., & Sudarshan, S. (2002). *BANKS: Browsing and Keyword Searching in Relational Databases.* The 28th Very Large Data Bases (VLDB) conference, Hong Kong, China.

Balmin, A., & Hristidis, V., & Papakonstantinon Y., & Koudas, N. (2003). *A System for Keyword Proximity Search on XML Databases.* The 29th Very Large Data Bases (VLDB) conference, Berlin, Germany.

Balmin, A., & Hristidis, V., & Papakonstantinon, Y. (2003). *Keyword Proximity Search on XML Graphs.* The 19th International Conference on Data Engineering (ICDE), Bangalore, India.

Balmin, A., & Hristidis, V., & Papakonstantinon Y. (2004). *ObjectRank: Authority-Based Keyword Search in Databases.* The 30th Very Large Data Bases (VLDB) conference, Toronto, Canada.

Botev, C., & Shao, F., & Guo, L. (2003). *XRANK: Ranked Keyword Search over XML Documents.* GMOD International Conference on Management of Data, San Diego, California.

Barbosa, D., & Mendelzon, A., & Keenleyside, J., & Lyons, K. (2002). *ToXgene: a template-based data generator for XML.* The Fifth International Workshop on the Web and Databases (WebDB), Madison, Wisconsin. The code downloaded from: http://www.cs.toronto.edu/tox/toxgene/downloads.html

Cohen, S., & Mamou, J., & Sagiv, Y. (2003). *XSEarch: A Semantic Search Engine for XML.* The 29th Very Large Data Bases (VLDB) conference, Berlin, Germany.

Cohen, S., & Kanza, Y. (2005). *Interconnection Semantics for Keyword Search in XML.* The ACM 14th Conference on Information and Knowledge Management (CIKM), Bremen, Germany.

Chamberlin, D., & Fankhauser, P., & Florescu, D., & Robie, J. (2006). XML Query Use Cases. *W3C Working Draft 2006.* Retrieved from: http://www.w3.org/TR/2006/WD-xquery-use-cases-20060608/

Denny M. (2002). Ontology Building: A Survey of Editing Tools. *O'Reilly XML.COM.* Retrieved from: http://www.xml.com/2002/11/06/Ontology_Editor_Survey.html

Hristidis, V., & Papakonstantinou, Y. (2002). *DISCOVER: Keyword search in Relational Databases.* The 28th Very Large Data Bases (VLDB) conference, Hong Kong, China.

INEX (2004). *Initiative for the Evaluation of XML Retrieval.* Retrieved from: http://inex.is.informatik.uni-duisburg.de:2004/

Jagadish, H. V., & Patel, J. M. (2006). TIMBER. *University of Michigan.* Retrieved from: http://www.eecs.umich.edu/db/timber/

Juneja, G. (2005). XML Validation Benchmark. *Sarvega.* Retrieved from: http://www.sarvega.com

Knublauch, H., & Musen, M., & Rector, A. (2002). *Editing Description Logic Ontologies with the Protégé OWL Plugin.* Technical discussion for logicians, Stanford University, CA.

Katz, H. (2005). XQEngine version 0.69. *Fatdog Software.* Retrieved from http://www.fatdog.com/. The engine downloaded from: http://sourceforge.net/projects/xqengine

Li, Y., & Yu, C., & Jagadish, H. (2004). *Schema-Free XQuery.* The 30th Very Large Data Bases (VLDB) conference, Toronto, Canada.

Schmidt, A. R., & Waas, F., & Kersten, M. L., & Florescu, D., & Manolescu, I., & Carey, M. J., &

Busse, R. (2002). The XML Benchmark Project. *Technical Report INS-R0103, CWI.* Retrieved from: http://www.xml-benchmark.org/. The benchmark downloaded from http://monetdb.cwi.nl/xml/downloads.html

Taha, K., & Elmasri, R. (2007). *OOXSearch: A Search Engine for Answering Loosely Structured XML Queries Using OO Programming.* The 24th British National Conference on Databases (BNCOD), Glasgow, Scotland.

Xu, X., & Papakonstantinou, Y. (2005). *Efficient Keyword Search for Smallest LCAs in XML Databases.* SIGMOD International Conference on Management of Data, Baltimore, Maryland.

Chapter V
Web Services as XML Data Sources in Enterprise Information Integration

Ákos Hajnal
Computer and Automation Research Institute, Hungary

Tamás Kifor
Computer and Automation Research Institute, Hungary

Gergely Lukácsy
Budapest University of Technology and Economics, Hungary

László Z. Varga
Computer and Automation Research Institute, Hungary

ABSTRACT

More and more systems provide data through web service interfaces and these data have to be integrated with the legacy relational databases of the enterprise. The integration is usually done with enterprise information integration systems which provide a uniform query language to all information sources, therefore the XML data sources of Web services having a procedural access interface have to be matched with relational data sources having a database interface. In this chapter the authors provide a solution to this problem by describing the Web service wrapper component of the SINTAGMA Enterprise Information Integration system. They demonstrate Web services as XML data sources in enterprise information integration by showing how the web service wrapper component integrates XML data of Web services in the application domain of digital libraries.

Copyright © 2009, IGI Global, distributing in print or electronic forms without written permission of IGI Global is prohibited.

INTRODUCTION

Traditional Enterprise Information Integration focuses mainly on the integration of different relational data sources, however recent enterprise information systems follow the service oriented architecture pattern and are based on web services technology[1]. In addition, more and more information and service providers on the internet provide web service interface to their system. The integration of these new information sources requires that the Enterprise Information Integration system has an interface towards web services.

This chapter describes a solution to this problem using the SINTAGMA Enterprise Information Integration System[2] and extending this system with a *Web Service Wrapper* component (which is the main contribution of this chapter). SINTAGMA is a data centric, monolithic information integration system supporting semi-automatic integration of relational sources using tools and methods based on logic and logic programming (see Benkő et al. 2003) based on the SILK tool-set which is the result of the SILK (System Integration via Logic & Knowledge) EU project.

In order to prepare for the challenge of integrating XML data provided by web services, we extended the original SINTAGMA system in two directions. First, the architecture of the SINTAGMA system was changed significantly to be made up of loosely coupled components rather than a monolithic structure. Second, the functionality has become richer as, among others, the system now deals with Web Services as information sources. The component responsible for this is the Web Service Wrapper which is the main contribution of this chapter.

Mixing relational data sources and web services during an information integration scenario can be very useful as demonstrated by a use case by Lukácsy et al. 2007 and poses the challenge of representing procedural information as relational data.

This chapter is structured as follows. First we put the problem in the context of related work, then we describe the main ideas behind the SINTAGMA system in a nutshell, then we provide an overview of the basic web service concepts and the modelling language of SINTAGMA, then we present how we model and query web services, with samples. Finally, we demonstrate web service integration in a digital library application and summarize our application experiences and conclusions.

RELATED WORK

There are several completed and ongoing research projects in using logic-based approaches for Enterprise Application Integration (EAI) and Enterprise Information Integration (EII) as well.

The generic EAI research stresses the importance of the Service Oriented Architecture, and the provision of new capabilities within the framework of Semantic Web Services. Examples for such research projects include DIP (see Vasiliu et al. 2004) and INFRAWEBS (see Grigorova 2006). We have also approached the EAI issue from the agent technology point of view (see Varga et al. 2005 and Varga et al. 2004). These attempts aim at the semantic integration of Web Services, in most cases using Description Logic based ontologies, agent and Semantic Web technologies. The goal of these projects is to support the whole range of EAI capabilities like service discovery, security and high reliability.

Most of the logic-based EII tools use description logics and take a similar approach as we did in SINTAGMA, that is, they create a description logic model as a view over the information sources to be integrated. The basic framework of this solution is described e.g. by Calvanese et al. 1998. The disadvantage is that these types of applications deal with relational sources only and are therefore not applicable to process modeling.

This chapter unifies the procedural EAI approach and the relational EII approach by integrating relational and functional XML information sources within the SINTAGMA system. The advantage of this approach is that the integration team does not have to implement web service interface to relational databases nor relational database interface to web services, because the SINTAGMA system automatically integrates the different sources. In addition to the integration, the SINTAGMA system includes several optimizations when answering queries on the integrated system.

The integration of web services with the relational data sources includes two important tasks: modeling the web services in the SINTAGMA system and querying the XML data returned by the web service.

Modeling web services in SINTAGMA is a reverse engineering task that seems to be straightforward, however it is necessary. Most tools available for modeling web services represent the opposite approach: they create WSDL from UML. Although there exist tools for modeling WSDL in UML (e.g. http://wsdl2xmi.tigris.org/) or modeling XSD in UML (e.g. supported by an XML editor), we did not find a tool that combines the two in the appropriate way from our point of view. WSDL modeling tools focus on the structure of the WSDL, but do not provide the model of the message schema contained (or imported) within the WSDL. XSD modeling tools do not provide information about WSDL specific information such as SOAP protocols and network locations. Another problem is that, although models in SINTAGMA are similar to UML, models generated by the available tools cannot be used directly because SINTAGMA has an own modeling language (called SILan) and not all UML components/features are supported by SINTAGMA. These are the reasons why the new modeling procedure (described in this chapter) is needed.

There are tools for querying XML, the most well-known tools are XPATH and XQUERY. We studied the possibility of transforming SQL-like queries supported by SINTAGMA to XQUERY statements. However we found that the SQL-like query language and XQUERY are essentially different. XQUERY is based on the XML instance, and not on the schema: it is possible to query XML fragments in the XML instance given by XPATH expressions, but not XML fragments corresponding to specific complex type definition (class instances in our terms). The problem is that, if the schema is recursive, to query the instances of a complex type would require (theoretically) infinite number of XPATH expressions. Another problem was that the results provided by XQUERY require further transformation before it is returned to SINTAGMA. For these reasons we decided to implement a query engine as described in this chapter.

THE SINTAGMA APPROACH

The main idea of our approach is to collect and manage meta-information on the sources to be *integrated.* These pieces of information are stored in the *model warehouse* of the system in a form of UML-like models, constraints and mappings. This way we can represent structural as well as non-structural information, such as class invariants, implications, etc. All of our modeling constructs have well defined semantics.

The process of querying these models is called *mediation.* Mediation decomposes complex integrated queries to simple queries answerable by individual information sources and, having obtained data from these, composes the results into an integrated form. For mediation, we need mappings between the separate sources and the integrated model. These mappings are called *abstractions* because often they provide a more abstract view of the notions present in the lower level models.

We handle models of different kinds. From one point of view we can speak of unified models and local models. Unified models are created from other ones in the process of integration, while the local models represent particular information sources. More importantly, we distinguish between application and conceptual models. The application models represent the structure of an existing or potential system and because of this they are fairly elaborate and precise. Conceptual models, however, represent mental models of user groups, therefore they are more vague than application models.

Access to heterogeneous information sources is supported by *wrappers*. Wrappers hide the syntactic differences between the sources of different kind (e.g. RDBMS, XML, Web services, etc.) by presenting them to upper layers uniformly as UML models. Wrappers also support queries over these models as they are capable of directly accessing the types of data sources they are responsible for.

WEB SERVICE INTEGRATION

In the following we briefly overview the most important concepts of web services and introduce the modeling language of SINTAGMA called SILan. Then we describe in detail how different web services can be represented by models and queried in the system. Finally, we discuss sample web service models.

Web Services

Web services aim to provide some document or procedure-oriented functionality over the network that can be accessed in a standardized way, typically using SOAP (Simple Object Access Protocol[3]) message exchange over HTTP.

SOAP is an XML based protocol for exchanging structured and typed information between peers. SOAP messages consist of an `<Envelope>` element followed by child element `<Body>`. Body entries will be referred to as the message content throughout this chapter.

The interface of a web service is described in WSDL (Web Services Description Language[4]), which is based on XML. In WSDL, a set of operations with input and output messages are described abstractly to define a network endpoint. These endpoints are then bound to concrete protocol and message serialization format. A web service is defined as a collection of ports that are bound to the network endpoints defined previously. The location of ports and protocol bindings are specified by SOAP extensibility elements in the WSDL. Messages are defined using the XSD (XML Schema Definition[5]) type system.

WSDL is structured as follows. Within the root `<definitions>` element, child element `<types>` encapsulates the XSD definitions (XSD schema) of different data types and structures used in message contents. It is followed by a series of `<message>` declarations that refer (in the `<part>` elements) to the types defined previously. `<portType>` element(s) wrap a sequence of `<operation>` elements representing abstract operations, each having `<input>` and `<output>` (and optional `<fault>`) elements that refer to the defined messages. `<binding>` element(s) specify the transport protocol and message formats for the set of operations listed in `<portType>`. Finally, the `<service>` element contains one or more `<port>` elements, each linked to a `<binding>`, and a network location in the `<soap:address>` child element. (We use the soap namespace prefix to indicate elements belonging to the SOAP URI. WSDL namespace prefixes are omitted. XSD elements will be prefixed by `xs`.)

In this chapter, we consider web services conforming to Basic Profile Version 1.1 of Web Service Interoperability Organization[6]. For simplicity, we assume document-literal style messaging protocol, one targetNamespace in the XSD type definition, and one service in the WSDL with one port and (potentially) several operations. In document-literal style, message contents are entirely defined by the XSD schema within the WSDL. We note that none of the above constraints are theoretical limitations of our approach, and are typically met by web services in practice.

Modeling in SINTAGMA

Different data sources are modeled uniformly in SINTAGMA using the modeling language of the system called SILan. This language is based on UML (Unified Modeling Language, see Fowler & Scott 1998) and Description Logics (see Horrocks 2002), and the syntax resembles IDL[7], the Interface Description Language of CORBA.

The main constructs are classes and associations, since these are the carriers of information. A class denotes a set of entities called the instances of the class. Similarly, an `n`-ary association denotes a set of `n`-ary tuples of class instances called links. In a binary association one of the connections can be declared composite, which means that the instance at the composite end is part of the instance at the other end (and is not part of any other instance). Composition associations are also referred to as compositions for short. Connections of associations can be declared as input, which means that the association can only be queried if all the input ends are available. Associations also have multiplicity that is used to define cardinality constraints, e.g. one-to-one, one-to-many relations. Classes and associations have unique name within a model.

Classes can have attributes which are defined as functions mapping the class to a subset of values allowed by the type of the attribute. Attributes have unique names within a class and are one of the SINTAGMA supported types.

Invariants can be specified for classes and associations. Invariants give statements about instances of classes (and links of associations) that hold for each of them. Invariants are based on the language OCL (Object Constraint Language, see Clark & Warmer 2002.).

Modeling Web Services

Modeling web services in SINTAGMA basically means the construction of a SILan representation of data structures and data types used in communication with the web service. The schemes of different web service messages are defined by an XSD language description in the `<schema>` element in the WSDL (or imported here).

The schema typically consists of a set of element declarations, simple and complex type definitions. Element declarations declare named XML elements with type corresponding to a built-in XML type (e.g. `int`, `string`), simple or complex type definition. Simple type definitions restrict built-in XML types (or other simple types) by giving enumerations, minimum, maximum values, etc. Complex type definitions combine a set of element declarations, or declare XML attributes, respectively. To each element declaration cardinality can be assigned to specify optional or multiple occurrences for the element. Simple and complex type definitions can also be extended, restricted by other type definitions. We note that there are many features of XSD omitted here for clarity considerations.

The SINTAGMA model is obtained by transforming the XSD description to a SILan representation. A unique SILan class is assigned to each complex type with unique name. Simple type element declarations (having a built-in XML type or simple type definition) within a complex type are added as SILan attributes of the class. The name of the attribute is given the name attribute of the element declaration, and the SILan type is derived from the built-in XML type according to a predefined mapping. Complex type element declarations within a complex type are represented by composition associations between classes assigned to different complex types.

Compositions are named uniquely, connection end aliases are given by the name attribute of the element declarations (used at navigation), and occurrence indicators (`minOccurs`, `maxOccurs`) are converted to the appropriate multiplicity of the composition (e.g. 1..1, 1..*). Simple type element declarations with multiple occurrences cannot be represented as simple class attributes in SILan. Therefore separate classes are created wrapping simple types that are then connected to the original container class by composition association with the appropriate multiplicity. Optional attributes cannot be expressed in SILan. Their values are simply set to null at query (see next section) if they are absent, instead of creating compositions with optional multiplicity. The default `String` type is assigned to XML types that cannot be represented precisely in SILan (e.g. `date`). These types will hold the string content of the related XML element. Simple type restrictions are added as attribute invariants, complex type extensions are indicated by inheritance relations between the corresponding classes.

Message schemes modeled above are then associated with web service operations: an association is created between classes representing input and output messages for each operation in the WSDL. Associations are named uniquely, and end connections corresponding to input messages are labeled as `<<input>>` in SILan (angle quotes notation corresponds to UML's stereotype notation). Connection aliases of associations are given the element names wrapping input and output XML messages of the operation (referred in `<part>` element in WSDL).

An example WSDL fragment of a simple *add* web service is shown in Figure 1 together with the created SILan model and the corresponding UML class diagram.

The constructed model contains every single data that can be passed to or returned by the web service in terms of classes, compositions and attributes, as well as the different web service operations which are represented by associations. Web service invocation, however, requires

Figure 1. An example WSDL fragment of a simple add web service together with the created SILan model and the corresponding UML class diagram (© 2008 Á. Hajnal, T. Kifor, Luckácsy, L.Z. Varga, Used with Permission)

```
...
<types>
  <xs:schema targetNamespace="http://add.com">
    <xs:element name="AddOperation">
      <xs:complexType>
        <xs:element name="op1" type="int"/>
        <xs:element name="op2" type="int"/>
      </xs:complexType>
    </xs:element>
    <xs:element name="AddResponse">
      <xs:complexType>
        <xs:element name="result" type="int"/>
        <xs:element name="Details"/>
          <xs:complexType>
            <xs:element name="time"
                        type="string"/>
          </xs:complexType>
        </xs:element>
      </xs:complexType>
    </xs:element>
  </xs:schema>
</types>
<message name="addRequestMsg">
<part name="body" element="tns:AddOperation">
</message>
<message name="addResponseMsg">
<part name="body" element="tns:AddResponse">
</message>
<portType name="addWebServicePortType">
  <operation name="addOperation">
    <input message="tns:addRequestMsg"/>
    <output message="tns:addResponseMsg"/>
  </operation>
</portType>
...
```

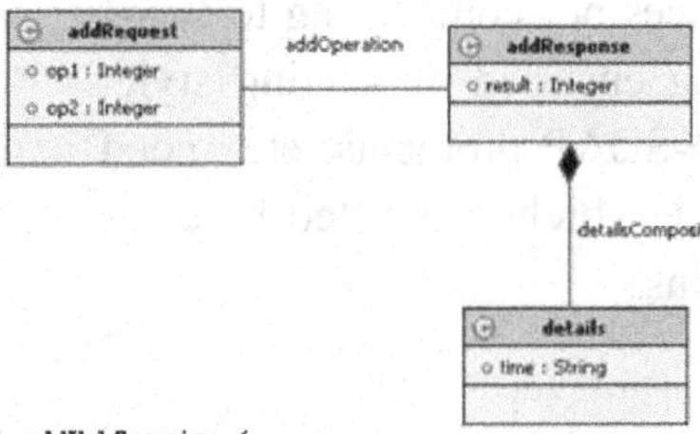

```
Model addWebService {
    association addOperation {
        <<input>> connection addRequest as AddOperation;
        connection addResponse [1..1] as AddResponse navigable;
    };
    class addRequest {
        attribute Integer op1;
        attribute Integer op2;
    };
    class addResponse {
        attribute Integer result;
    };
    association detailsComposition {
        connection addResponse composite [1..1];
        connection details [1..1] as Details navigable;
    };
    class details {
        attribute String time;
    };
};
```

additional details of the WSDL that are stored as metadata in the model (used by the Web Service Wrapper component). One is the network location of the web service that is obtained from the `<soap:address>` element of the port. The other is the namespace of the XML messages used in the communication with the web service that is given by the `tartgetNamespace` attribute of the `<schema>` element.

In practice, web services can be more complicated. It may occur that a web service uses several schemes and namespaces that require introducing namespace metadata into different classes instead of using a single, global namespace in the model. A WSDL can declare several ports combining web service operations at different network locations. In this case, the network location(s) need to be assigned to the associations representing operations instead of the model.

When a web service uses *rpc* protocol (`<soap:binding>`), `<part>` elements that are declared at input and output messages are wrapped first in input and output classes, which are then connected by the operation association. In the case of *document* style binding no such problem occurs, since these classes are already created at processing the schema. A single `<part>` element is allowed in message definitions that refer to them. Web services not conforming to WS-I Basic Profile, using encoded messaging style, WSDL arrays, non-SOAP protocols, etc., need further workaround, which is omitted here for clarity considerations.

Querying Web Services through SINTAGMA

SILan query language is an object oriented query language designed to formulate queries over SINTAGMA models. The syntax is similar to SQL used at relational databases: a SILan query is composed of `SELECT`, `FROM`, `WHERE` parts. The `SELECT` keyword is followed by a comma separated list of class attributes (columns) of interest, `FROM` part enumerates classes (tables) whose instances (rows) we search among, and `WHERE` part specifies constraints that must be satisfied by all the instances in the result. On the other hand, SILan is an object oriented language that relies on UML modeling, and SILan also supports OCL expressions in queries by which we can specify navigations through objects.

In contrast to relational databases functional data sources require input to populate the "database" with data before the query can actually be executed. In the case of web services, input includes the name of the web service operation and the input parameters of the operation.

When models representing web services are queried in SINTAGMA, the web service operation must be given in the `FROM` part as the association representing the operation. For example, the web service operation called *addOperation* of the example in Figure 1 is queried by the construct below (relevant parts are highlighted in boldface characters) (see Box 1).

Box 1.

```
SELECT     addOperation.AddResponse.result,
           addOperation.AddResponse.Details.time
FROM       addOperation
WHERE      addOperation.AddOperation.op1=1 AND
           addOperation.AddOperation.op2=2
```

Operation's input parameters are given by constraints in the `WHERE` part of the query. Constraints use the '=' operator, in the form of `Class.field=value`, which have value assignment semantics with respect to the input parameters. The '.' operator is used to refer to a class attribute in SILan, but it is also used to navigate along associations or compositions. For example, `Class1.association1.field1` denotes attribute `field1` in the class referred by `association1` in `Class1`. Navigation is used to assign values to input parameters starting from the association representing the operation. In the case of several input parameters, the list of assignments is separated by the `AND` logical operator. This way, arbitrary complex web service inputs can be formulated. For example, input parameters *op1*, *op2* of *addOperation* are given values by the query shown in Box 2.

Queries for models representing web services are executed by the Web Service Wrapper component. The passed query is parsed first, then the appropriate SOAP message is constructed and sent to the web service provider. Starting from the association in the query and collecting all the constraints for the input side (navigations towards the input end) an XML tree is constructed that combines all the web service inputs. Navigations are represented by wrapper XML elements, and attribute constraints are represented by simple XML elements with content corresponding to the constant value. Navigations and constraints that refer to the same instance are unified in the XML tree. The namespace of the XML fragment is set accordingly to the namespace metadata in the model (targetNamespace of the schema) that is then wrapped in an appropriate SOAP envelope. The input SOAP message composed for the query of the *addOperation* is shown below:

```
<SOAP-ENV:Envelope ...>
  <SOAP-ENV:Body>
    <AddOperation xmlns="http://add.com">
      <op1>1</op1>
      <op2>2</op2>
    </AddOperation>
  <SOAP-ENV:Body>
</SOAP-ENV:Envelope>
```

When the SOAP message is sent to the internet location of the web service (stored as metadata in the model), the requested operation will be executed by the web service provider. Results are sent back to the Web Service Wrapper component as another SOAP message, and, unless SOAP fault (e.g. missing input parameters) or no response errors occur, a temporary internal "database" is populated with data.

The internal database is set up by mapping the content of the answer SOAP message to the model. First, the XML document root is added as instance to the class representing operation's output, then child nodes are processed recursively considering the model schema: XML sub-elements are added as attributes of the current instance, if they are simple, or added as new instances in the corresponding classes, respectively, if they are complex. Intuitively, it means that a new row is created for the root element in the table of operation output, and field values are obtained by iterating through

Box 2.

```
SELECT      addOperation.AddResponse.result,
            addOperation.AddResponse.Details.time
FROM        addOperation
WHERE       addOperation.AddOperation.op1=1 AND
            addOperation.AddOperation.op2=2
```

all child elements. If the name of the child element corresponds to a class attribute (simple type), the value of the field is given by the content of the XML element. If the child element corresponds to a composition (complex type), the child node is processed recursively (considering the referred class), and a relation is created from the current row to the new row in another table representing the child node. Class attributes for which no appropriate child element can be found are set to null. The textual content of XML elements are converted to the proper attribute type at filling field values. The input SOAP message content sent to the web service provider previously is also loaded into the internal database in the same way. An example answer SOAP message and the associated classes, attributes are shown in Box 3.

The query specifies the set of classes and attributes of interest in the `FROM` and `SELECT` parts. Note that in SILan it is allowed to query associations as well as compositions in the `FROM` part, and give navigations to attributes in the `SELECT` part. The `WHERE` part declares constraints for the instances by constant constraints, where class attributes are compared to constant values using relational operators, or by association constraints that must hold between instances.

The Web Service Wrapper component, in the knowledge of the temporary internal database, can execute the query similarly to an SQL engine. Basically, the result is constructed by taking the Cartesian product of the instances of the relevant classes (listed in the `FROM` part). Constraints in the `WHERE` part are checked for each *n*-tuple of instances, and if all of them are satisfied, the selected attributes (`SELECT` part) are added to the result. The result of the query for the add web service operation contains a single row with field *result* containing integer value 3, and field *time* containing the string representing the execution time of the operation, e.g. 0.01s.

Sample Web Service Models in SINTAGMA

We have implemented the Web Service Wrapper component for SINTAGMA and applied it to several web services ranging from simple ones (such as Google SOAP Search API providing three operations) to complex ones (such as Amazon E-Commerce Service providing over 30 operations with transactions).

After entering the URL of the WSDL the model of the web service is built automatically. It can be viewed, browsed in a graphical user interface, and queries can be composed for the model. SILan abstractions can be created by which web services can participate in integration scenarios. Namely, the web service model can be connected to other models representing different

Box 3.

```
<SOAP-ENV:Envelope ...>
<SOAP-ENV:Body>
  <AddResponse>              ◄ instance in class addResponse
      <result>3</result>    ◄ attribute result of the addResponse instance
      <Details>              ◄ instance in class details
        <time>0.01s</time> ◄ attribute time of the details instance
      </Details>
    </AddResponse>
<SOAP-ENV:Body>
</SOAP-ENV:Envelope>
```

data sources, for example other web services or relational databases.

Queries for the model are executed transparently by the wrapper that communicates with the web service using SOAP. Necessary inputs are obtained from the query, the appropriate request message is constructed, and sent to the web service provider automatically. Result data are extracted from the answer message, and returned to SINTAGMA.

An example screenshot of the SINTAGMA system is shown in Figure 2, where Amazon's web service is queried.

DIGITAL LIBRARY DEMONSTRATION APPLICATION

In the previous section we have seen how a single web service can be modeled and queried in SINTAGMA. In this section we show a digital library application that demonstrates the integration of web services with the help of SINTAGMA. The digital library application is an OpenURL resolver application developed in the SINTAGMA project. OpenURL[8] is a NISO standard[9] for identifying documents with different types of metadata (for example author, title, ISBN, ISSN) using the URL format. The following is a sample OpenURL: http://viola.oszk.hu:8080/sokk/OpenURL_Servlet?sid=OSZK:LibriVision&genre=book&aufirst=Jeno&aulast=Rejto&isbn=963-13-5374-5&title=Quarantine%20in%20the%20Grand%20Hotel&date=2005

The first part of the URL is a link resolver, in the above example `viola.oszk.hu:8080/sokk/OpenURL_Servlet`. The other part contains the metadata of the documents, in the above example parameters like the first and last name of the author, the ISBN code and the title of the book. The same OpenURL can be created by several sources (for example in articles containing citations from the identified document or in a document meta database like The European Library[10]). In our demonstration application the query OpenURL is created by a web based user

Figure 2. Amazon's web service is queried in SINTAGMA (© 2008 Á. Hajnal, T. Kifor, Luckácsy, L.Z. Varga, Used with Permission)

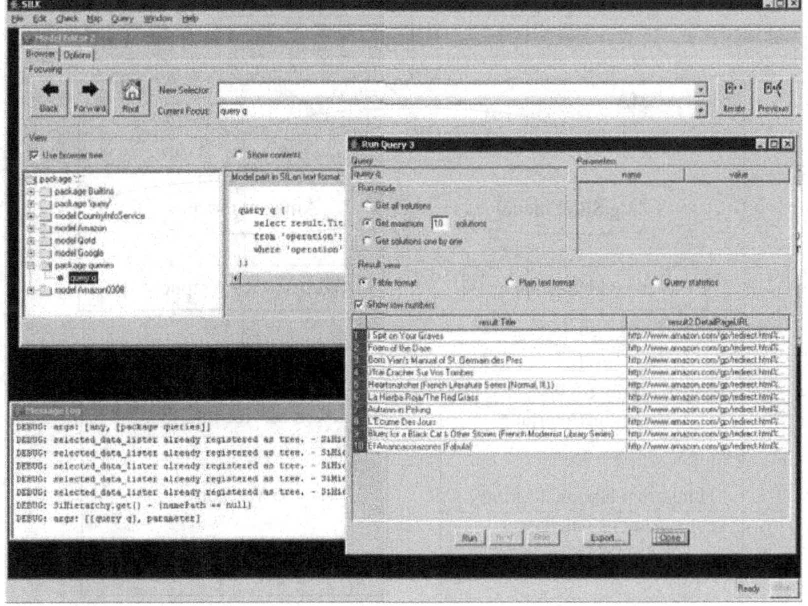

interface as shown on Figure 3. The document identified by the OpenURL can be located in several target places. In our demonstration application, as shown on Figure 3, the target places are the Amazon book store, which is a web service information source providing XML data services, and the Hungarian National Library, which contains a relational database.

The OpenURL resolver has to search in several places using different protocols and different data model for the different possible targets of the document, therefore our OpenURL resolver application uses the different wrappers of SINTAGMA to integrate the different data models of the different protocols.

SINTAGMA executes the queries for the targets and collects the result into a single unified model. The OpenURL resolver queries this unified model only and does not need to know the details of the lower level protocols and data models. As long as the OpenURL model remains the same, the OpenURL resolver does not need to be changed even if the protocol or the lower level data model changes.

We have created an OpenURL unified conceptual model in SINTAGMA (upper model) manually and the local application models (lower models) for the targets (in our case for Amazon and for the Hungarian National Library) using the wrappers. Then we have created abstractions (relations) between the upper model and the lower models (one for each data source). The OpenURL resolver application queries the upper model and sees it as one single target.

If there is a new target we only have to generate a new lower model using the SINTAGMA wrapper and create an abstraction between the new model and the upper model. If the protocol

Figure 3. Digital library demonstration application architecture (© 2008 Á. Hajnal, T. Kifor, Luckácsy, L.Z. Varga, Used with Permission)

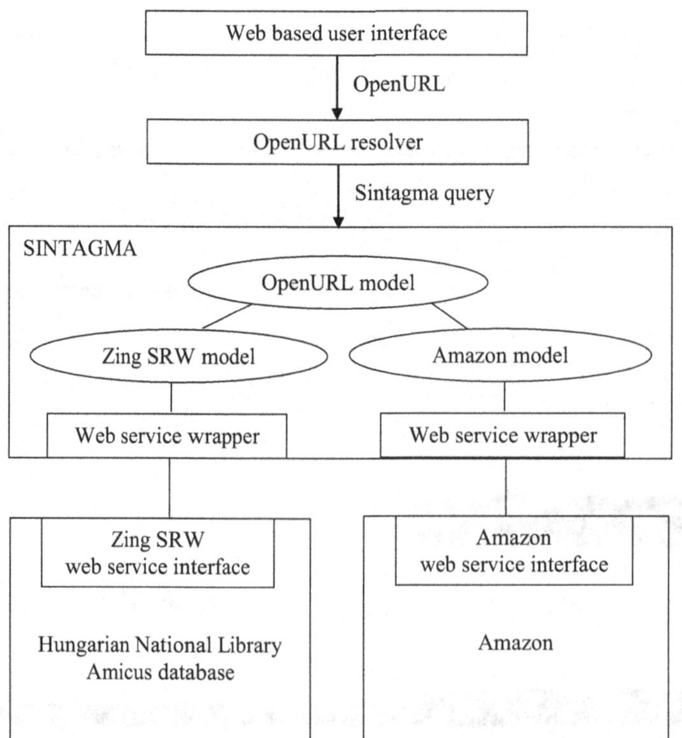

or the data model of the target changes we only have to regenerate the lower model and modify the old mapping (or create a new one) between the lower and the upper model. We do not have to modify, recompile and redeploy the source code of the client application.

First we created the following upper (conceptual) model of the openURL resolver in SILAN (see Box 4).

This model is simple because it contains an OpenURLDescription, which contains the parameters of the query OpenURL, a SearchResult, which contains the parameters of the search result, and an AnswerOfQuestion, which connects the OpenURL query with the search result. The resolver queries this model only and does not know about the different data models below this model.

Then we generated the lower model of Amazon and Hungarian National Library. We only had to pass the WSDL of the applications to the SINTAGMA wrapper and it created the models automatically. These models are very complex and not shown here, because the data models of the Amazon and the Zing SRW (the web service used by Hungarian National Library) web services are complex.

The next step was to create two abstractions. The first abstraction is between the application model of Amazon and the conceptual model of OpenURL. This abstraction connects the corresponding elements in the Amazon model and the OpenURL, because there are direct connections between the elements, except the author name, where the Amazon author name is the concatena-

Box 4.

```
model OpenURLModel {
  class OpenURL {
        attribute Integer id;
  };
  class OpenURLDescription {
        attribute Integer id;
                 attribute Integer openURL;
                 attribute String auFirst;
                 attribute String auLast;
                 attribute String title;
                 attribute String issn;
                 attribute String isbn;
                 attribute String pubDate;
  };
  class SearchResult {
        attribute Integer id;
                 attribute Integer openURLDescription;
                 attribute String source;
                 attribute String author;
                 attribute String title;
                 attribute Integer stock;
                 attribute String link;
                 attribute String price;
  };
 association AnswerOfQuestion {
     connection ::OpenURLModel::OpenURLDescription as inp;
     connection ::OpenURLModel::SearchResult [1..1]  as outp navigable ;
 };
};
```

Box 5.

```
map bundle Amazon_OpenURLModel between Amazon and OpenURLModel {
  abstraction nev3 (isop: Amazon::ItemSearch_OPERATION,
              isr: Amazon::ItemSearchRequest,
       items: Amazon::Items,
       item: Amazon::Item ->
              ourl: OpenURLModel::OpenURL) {
  constraint
 isop.itemSearch.Request = isr and
 isop.ItemSearch.Items = items and
 items.Item = item and
 isop.itemSearch.SubscriptionId = "0W2KPT35SFFX0RVEK002" and
 isr.ResponseGroup = "Small" and
 isr.SearchIndex = "Books"
  implies
 isr.Author = ourl.auLast.concat(" ".concat(ourl.auFirst)) and
 ourl.result_isbn = item.ASIN and
 ourl.origin = "Amazon";
  };
```

tion of the first and last name of the author in the OpenURL model (see Box 5).

The second abstraction is between the application model of the Zing SRW service of the Hungarian National Library and the conceptual model of OpenURL. This abstraction is again a direct mapping between the corresponding elements (see Box 6).

The last step was to query the conceptual model of OpenURL from our Open URL resolver. We used the Java library of the distributed SINTAGMA system to create the SINTAGMA query. The following is the SINTAGMA query of the sample OpenURL mentioned at the beginning of this section (see Box 7).

Creating models and mappings between the models do not need a programmer, only a knowledge engineer who knows the business area (library system in our case). This is possible because SINTAGMA raised the problem to a higher

Box 6.

```
map bundle Zing_OpenURLModel between Zing and OpenURLModel {
  abstraction nev1 (op: Zing::SearchRetrieveOperation_OPERATION,
              in0: Zing::searchRetrieveRequestType ->
              out:  OpenURLModel::OpenURL) {
  constraint
 op.searchRetrieveRequestType = in0 and
 in0.maximumRecords = "10" and
 in0.version = "1.1" and
 in0.recordSchema = "dc"
  implies
 let d = op.SearchRetrieveOperation.records.record.recordData.toMap in
        out.result_title   = (String)d.get("title") AND
 in0.query = out.query;
  };
};
```

Box 7.

```
select
openURLquery.outp.source, openURLquery.outp.author,
openURLquery.outp.title, openURLquery.outp.stock,
openURLquery.outp.link, openURLquery.outp.price
from
openURLquery: OpenURLModel:: AnswerOfQuestion
where
openURLquery.inp.auFirst.contains(\"Jeno\") and
openURLquery.inp.auLast.contains(\"Rejto\") and
openURLquery.inp.title.contains(\"Quarantine%20in%20the%20Grand%
20Hotel\") and openURLquery.inp.isbn.contains(\"963-13-5374-5\")
and openURLquery.inp.puDate.contains(\"2005\")
```

abstraction level and the OpenURL resolver can use always the SINTAGMA query to resolve the OpenURL expression to any target.

CONCLUSION

This chapter presented how XML data provided by web services and relational data can be integrated. The main tool to integrate web services with relational data is the Web Service Wrapper component of the SINTAGMA Enterprise Information Integration system. This component makes easy the integration of XML data services with relational databases, because the data model of web services is automatically created by the Web Service Wrapper of the SINTAGMA system. Based on these application level data models a knowledge engineer can create a unified conceptual model of all data sources, as well as abstract mapping between the unified conceptual model and the application level models. Then the conceptual model can be queried from the SINTAGMA system which hides the diversity of different data sources. The set of data sources can be extended easily by generating the application level data model for the new data source and creating an abstraction between the new application model and the existing conceptual model. The source code of the querying program does not have to be changed. Creating the models and mappings between the models does not need a programmer but a knowledge engineer who can focus on the business area and logic.

ACKNOWLEDGMENT

The authors acknowledge the support of the Hungarian NKFP programme of the SINTAGMA project under grant number 2/052/2004. We also would like to thank all the people participating in this project.

REFERENCES

Benkő, T., Lukácsy, G., Fokt, A., Szeredi, P., Kilián, I., & Krauth, P. (2003). Information Integration through Reasoning on Meta-data. *Proceeding of the workshop, AI moves to IA", IJCAI 2003*, Acapulco, Mexico, (pp. 65-77).

Calvanese, D., De Giacomo, G., Lenzerini, M., Nardi, D., & Rosati, R. (1998). *Description Logic Framework for Information Integration, Principles of Knowledge Representation and Reasoning*, (pp. 2-13).

Clark, T., & Warmer, J. (2002). *Object Modeling with the OCL: The rationale behind the Object Constraint Language*. Springer.

Fowler, M., & Scott, K. (1998). *UML Distilled: Applying the Standrad Object Modeling Language*. Addison-Wesley.

Grigorova, V. (2006). Semantic Description of Web Services and Possibilities of BPEL4WS. *Information Theories and Application, 13*, 183-187.

Horrocks, I. (2002). Reasoning with Expressive Description Logics: Theory and Practice. In *Proceeding of the 18th International Conference on Automated Deduction (CADE 2002)* (pp. 1-15).

Lukácsy, G., Benkő, T., & Szeredi, P. (2007). Towards Automatic Semantic integration. In *3rd International Conference of Interoperability for Enterprise Software and Applications (I-ESA 2007).*

Vasiliu, L., Harand, S., & Cimpian, E. (2004). The DIP Project: Enabling Systems & Solutions For Processing Digital Content With Semantic Web Services. *EWIMT 2004 European Workshop on the Integration of Knowledge, Semantics and Digital Media Technology.*

Varga, L.Z., Hajnal, A., & Werner, Z. (2004). An Agent Based Approach for Migrating Web Services to Semantic Web Services. *Lecture Notes in Computer Science Vol. 3192*, Springer-Verlag GmbH, Heidelberg, Germany. In C. Bussler & D. Fensel (Eds.), *Artificial Intelligence: Methodology, Systems, and Applications 11th International Conference, AIMSA 2004*, Varna, Bulgaria, September 2-4, 2004, Proceedings, (pp. 371-380). ISBN-3-540-22959-0.

Varga, L.Z., Hajnal, Á., & Werner, Z. (2005). The WSDL2Agent Tool. In R. Unland, M. Klusch, & M. Calisti (Eds.), Software Agent-Based Applications, Platforms and Development Kits. Whitestein Series in Software Agent Technologies, (pp. 197-223). Viaduktstrasse 42, CH-4051 Basel, Switzerland, Springer Group, ISBN 3-7643-7347-4, 2005.

ADDITIONAL READING

Apps, A., & MacIntyre, R. (2006). Why OpenURL? *D-Lib Magazine 12*(5).

Baader, F., Calvanese, D., McGuinness, D., Nardi, D., & Patel-Schneider, P. (2003). *The Description Logic Handbook, Theory, Implementation and Applications*. Cambridge University Press.

Booch, G., Jacobson, I., & Rumbaugh, J. (1999). *The Unified Modeling Language User Guide*. Addison-Wesley.

Cerami, E. (2002). *Web Services Essentials*. O'Reilly & Associates.

Chawathe, S., Garcia-molina, H., Hammer, J., Irel, K., Papakonstantinou, Y., Ullman, J., & Widom, J. (1994). The Tsimmis Project: Integration of Heterogeneous Information Sources. *Proceedings of IPSJ Conference*. (pp. 7-18).

Hepp, M., Leymann, F., Domingue, J., Wahler, A., & Fensel, D. (2005). Semantic Business Process Management: A Vision Towards Using Semantic Web Services for Business Process Management. *Proceedings of the IEEE International Conference on e-Business Engineering (ICEBE 2005)*, (pp. 535-540). IEEE Computer Society.

Hodgson, C. (2005). Understanding the OpenURL Framework. *NISO Information Standards Quarterly, 17*(3), 1-4.

Kline, K., & Kline, D. (2001). *SQL in a Nutshell*. O'Reilly & Associates.

Lukácsy, G., & Szeredi, P. (2008). Combining Description Logics and Object Oriented Models in an Information Framework. *Periodica Polytechnica.*

Polleres, A., Pearce, D., Heymans, S., & Ruckhaus, E. (2007). Proceedings of the 2nd International Workshop on Applications of Logic Programming to the Web, Semantic Web and Semantic Web Services (ALPSWS2007). *CEUR Workshop Proceedings*, Vol. 287, http://ceur-ws.org/Vol-287.

Ricardo, J.G., Müller, J.P., Mertins, K., Zelm, M. (2007). *Enterprise Interoperability II: New Challenges and Approaches, Proceedings of the 3rd International Conference on Interoperability for Enterprise Software and Applications (IESA-07)*. Springer Verlag.

St. Laurent, S., Johnston, J., & Dumbill, E. (2001). *Programming Web Services with XML-RPC*. O'Reilly & Associates.

Studer, R., Grimm, S., & Abecker, A. (Eds.) (2007). *Semantic Web Services*. Springer.

T. Ray, E. (2001). *Learning XML*. O'Reilly & Associates.

Van der Vlist, E. (2002). *XML Schema*. O'Reilly & Associates.

Walmsley, P. (2007). *XQuery*. O'Reilly Media.

Walsh, A.E. (2002). UDDI, SOAP, and WSDL: The *web services specification reference book*. Pearson Education.

ENDNOTES

1. Web Services Architecture, W3C Working Group Note 11 February 2004. http://www.w3.org/TR/2004/NOTE-ws-arch-20040211
2. SINTAGMA Enterprise Information Integration System was developed under the Hungarian NKFP programme of the SINTAGMA project. Web page: http://www.sintagma.hu (available in Hungarian language only)
3. Simple Object Access Protocol. http://www.w3.org/TR/2000/NOTE-SOAP-20000508
4. Web Services Description Language. http://www.w3.org/TR/2001/NOTE-wsdl-20010315
5. XML Schema. http://www.w3.org/XML/Schema.
6. Web Services Interoperability Organization. http://www.ws-i.org
7. Object Management Group: The Common Object Request Broker: Architecture and Specification, revision 2, July 1995.
8. http://alcme.oclc.org/openurl/docs/pdf/openurl-01.pdf
9. http://www.niso.org/standards/standard_detail.cfm?std_id=783
10. http://www.theeuropeanlibrary.org

Chapter VI
Consistency and Modularity in Mediated Service-Based Data Integration Solutions

Yaoling Zhu
Dublin City University, Ireland

Claus Pahl
Dublin City University, Ireland

ABSTRACT

A major aim of the Web service platform is the integration of existing software and information systems. Data integration is a central aspect in this context. Traditional techniques for information and data transformation are, however, not sufficient to provide flexible and automatable data integration solutions for Web service-enabled information systems. The difficulties arise from a high degree of complexity in data structures in many applications and from the additional problem of heterogeneity of data representation in applications that often cross organisational boundaries. The authors present an integration technique that embeds a declarative data transformation technique based on semantic data models as a mediator service into a Web service-oriented information system architecture. Automation through consistency-oriented semantic data models and flexibility through modular declarative data transformations are the key enablers of the approach.

INTRODUCTION

A major aim of the Web service platform is the integration of existing software and information systems (Alonso et al., 2004). Information and data integration is a central aspect in this context. Traditional techniques based on XML for data representation and XSLT for transformations between XML documents are not sufficient to provide a flexible and automatable data integra-

Copyright © 2009, IGI Global, distributing in print or electronic forms without written permission of IGI Global is prohibited.

tion solution for Web service-enabled information systems. Difficulties arise from the high degree of complexity in data structures in many business and technology applications and from the problem of heterogeneity of data representation in applications that cross organisational boundaries.

The emergence of the Web services platform and service-oriented architecture (SOA) as an architecture paradigm has provided a unified way to expose the data and functionality of an information system (Stal, 2002). The Web services platform has the potential to solve the problems in the data integration domain such as heterogeneity and interoperability (Orriens, Yang and Papazoglou, 2003; Haller, Cimpian, Mocan, Oren and Bussler, 2005; Zhu et al., 2004). Our contribution is an integration technology framework for Web-enabled information systems comprising of

- Firstly, a data integration technique based on semantic, ontology-based data models and the declarative specification of transformation rules and
- Secondly, a mediator architecture based on information services and the construction of connectors that handle the transformations to implement the integration process.

A data integration technique in the form of a mediator service can dynamically perform transformations based on a unified semantic data model built on top of individual data models in heterogeneous environments (Wiederhold, 1992). Abstraction has been used successfully to address flexibility problems in data processing (Rouvellou, Degenaro, Rasmus, Ehnebuske and McKee, 2000). With recent advances in abstract, declarative XML-based data query and transformation languages (Zhu et al., 2004) and Semantic Web and ontology technology (Daconta, Obrst and Smith, 2003), the respective results are ready to be utilised in the Web application context. The combination of declarative and semantic specification and automated support of architecture implementations provides the necessary flexibility and modularity to deal with complexity and consistency problems. Two central questions to the data integration problem and its automation shall be addressed in this investigation:

- How to construct data model transformation rules and how to express these rules in a formal, but also accessible and maintainable way is central.
- How integration can be facilitated through service composition to enable interoperability through connector and relationship modelling.

We show how ontology-based semantic data models and a specific declarative data query and transformation language called Xcerpt (Bry and Schaffert, 2002) and its execution environment can be combined in order to allow dynamic data transformation and integration. We focus on technical solutions to semantically enhance data modelling and adapt Xcerpt and its support environment so that it can facilitate the dynamic generation of Xcerpt query programs (in response to user requests) from abstract transformation rules.

BACKGROUND

Information integration is the problem of combining heterogeneous data residing at different sources in order to provide the user with a unified view (Lenzerini, 2002). This view is central in any attempt to adapt services and their underlying data sources to specific client and provider needs. One of the main tasks in information integration is to define the mappings between the individual data sources and the unified view of these sources and vice versa to enable this required adaptation. Fig.1 shows two sample schemas, which might represent the views of client and provider on a collection of customers, that require integration. The integration itself can be defined using transformation languages.

Information integration has the objective of bringing together different types of data from different sources in order for this data to be accessed, queried, processed and analysed in a uniform manner. Recently, service-based platforms are being used to provide integration solutions. In the Web services context, data in XML representation, which is retrieved from individual Web-based data services, needs to be merged and transformed to meet the integration requirements. Data schema integration cannot be fully automated on a syntactic level since the syntactic representation of schemas and data does not convey the semantics of different data sources. For instance, a customer can be identified in the configuration management repository by a unique customer identifier; or, the same customer may be identified in the problem management repository by a combination of a service support identifier and its geographical location, see Fig. 1. Ontology-based semantic data models can rectify this problem by providing an agreed vocabulary of concepts with associated properties.

XSLT is the most widely used XML data integration language, but suffers from some limitations within our context due its is syntactical focus and operational language.

- **Semantics:** Only the syntactical integration of query and construction part of a XSLT transformation program is specified, but consistency in terms of the semantics can not be guaranteed.
- **Modularity:** XSLT does not support a join or composition operator on XML documents that allows several source XML documents to merged into one before being transformed.
- **Maintainability:** XSLT transformations are difficult to write, maintain, and reuse for large-scale information integration. It is difficult to separate the source and target

Figure 1. Two schema diagrams of the global data model that need to be integrated (© 2008, Claus Pahl. Used with permission).

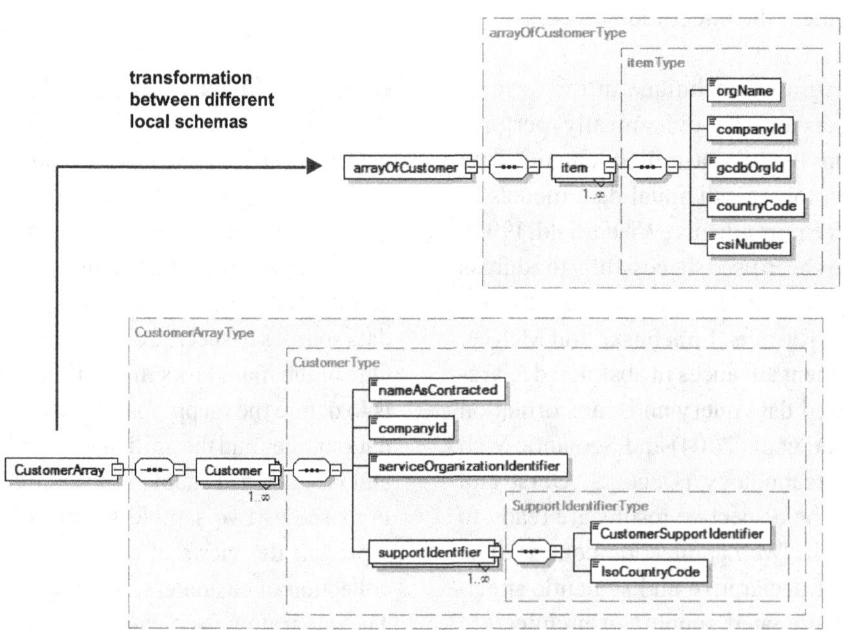

parts of transformation rules as well as the filtering constraints due to its operational character without a separation of query and construction concerns.

Due to these drawbacks, we propose semantic data models and a declarative query and transformation approach providing more expressive power and the ability to automatically generate query and transformation programs as connectors for services-based data integration in Web-enabled information systems. A range of characteristics of XML query and transformation languages beyond XSLT, which have been studied and compared (Jhingran, Mattos and Pirahesh, 2002; Lenzerini, 2002; Peltier, Bezivin, and Guillaume, 2002), led us to choose the fully declarative language Xcerpt (Bry and Schaffert, 2002) as our transformation platform (Zhu, 2007).

DATA TRANSFORMATION AND CONNECTOR ARCHITECTURE

Mappings between data schemas of different participants might or might not represent the same semantical information. The Semantic Web and in particular ontology-based data domain and service models (Daconta et al., 2003) can provide input for improvements of current integration approaches in terms of data modelling and transformation validation by providing a notion of consistency, based on which an automated transformation approach can become reliable (Reynaud, Sirot and Vodislav, 2001, Haller et al., 2005). We define consistency here as the preservation of semantics in transformations.

Information Architecture

Ontologies are knowledge representation frameworks that represent knowledge about a domain in terms of concepts and properties of these concepts. We use a description logic notation here, which is the formal foundation of many ontology languages such as OWL (Daconta et al., 2003). Description logic provides us with a concise notation here to express a semantic data model. The elements of the XML data models of each of the participants are represented as concepts in the ontology. The concept `Customer` is defined in terms of its properties – data type-like properties such as a name or an identifier and also object type properties such as a collection of services used by a customer. Three concept descriptions, using the existential quantifier "∃" here, express that a customer is linked to an identification through a `supportID` property, to a name using the `custName` property, and to services using `Services`. In some cases, these properties refer to other composite concepts, sometimes they refer to atomic concepts that act as type names here. Technically, the existential quantification means that there exits for instance a name that is a customer name.

```
Customer =
∃ supportID . Identification ∧
∃ custName . Name            ∧
∃ usedServices . Service

Service =
∃ custID . ID          ∧
∃ servSystem . System

System =
∃ hasPart . Machine
```

The ontology represents syntactical and semantical properties of a common overarching data model, which is agreed upon by all participants such as service (or data) provider and consumer. This model is actually a domain ontology, capturing central concepts of a domain and defining them semantically. This means that all individual XML data models can be mapped onto this common semantic model. These mappings can then be used to automatically generate transformations between different concrete participant data models. The overall information architecture is summarised in Fig. 2.

Although there is a standardised OWL-based equivalent for our description logic ontology, for practical reasons a corresponding semantically equivalent XML representation is needed. The corresponding global XML schema representation for the customer element is:

```
<!ELEMENT Customer ( Service, System ) >
<!ATTLIST Customer
      supportID  ID
      custName   Name >
```

Here, the principle of this mapping becomes clear: ontology concepts are mapped to XML elements and specific predefined atomic concepts serve to represent simple properties that are mapped to XML attributes. We have focused on the core elements of ontologies and XML data here to highlight the principles. Description elements of XML such as different types of attributes or option and iteration in element definition can also be captured through a refined property language. In particular the Web Ontology Language OWL provides such constructs (W3C, 2004).

Transformation Rule Construction

The ontology provides a semantically defined global data model from which transformations between different participant data representations can be derived. This construction needs to address a number of specific objectives regarding the transformation rules:

- Modularity of transformation rules is needed for the flexible generation and configuration of transformation rules by allowing these rules to be specific to particular data elements,
- Consistency needs to be addressed for the reliable generation and configuration of transformation rules by allowing semantics-

Figure 2. Information architecture overview (© 2008, Claus Pahl. Used with permission)

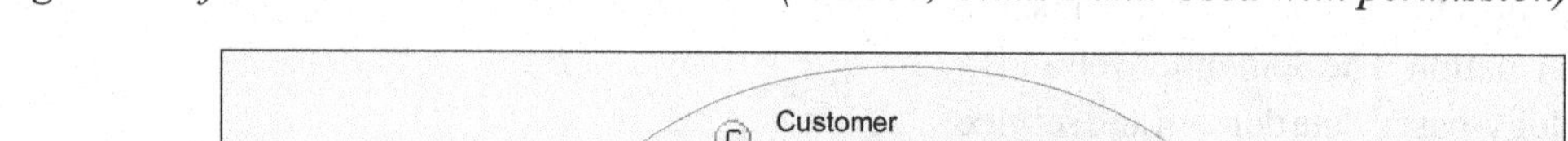

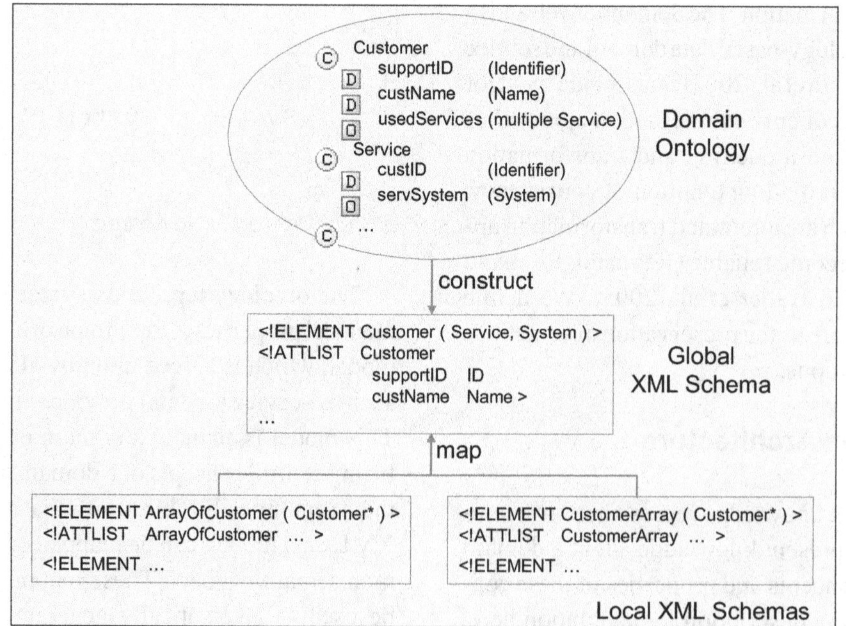

preserving rules to be constructed automatically.

Based on a data-oriented domain ontology and two given local data models (source and target, expressed as XML schemas) that are mapped onto the ontology, the rule construction process is based on three steps:

1. Define one transformation rule per concept in the ontology that is represented in the target data model.
2. Identify semantically equivalent concepts of the selected concepts in the source data model.
3. For each identified concept:
    a. determine required attributes – these are end nodes of the ontological structure,
    b. copy semantically equivalent counterparts from the source model.

A necessary prerequisite is that all concepts of the source model are actually supported by the target data model. Otherwise, the transformation definition cannot be completed.

The transformation rules based on the sample ontology for the given customer example will be presented later on once the transformation language is introduced. These could be formulated such that data integration problem depicted in Fig. 1 is formally defined. The mappings between participant data models and the data ontology define semantically equivalent representation of common agreed ontology elements in the data models. Consequently, the presented rule construction process is consistent in that it preserves the semantics in transformations.

The concrete target of this construction is the chosen declarative transformation language Xcerpt. The construction process has been expressed here in abstract terms – a complete specification in terms of transformation languages such as QVT or even Xcerpt itself would have been too verbose for this context. Declarativeness and modularity provide the required flexibility for our solution, in addition to consistency that has been addressed through the semantic ontology-based data models. The construction of transformation rules is actually only the first step in the provision of XML data integration. These transformations can be constructed prior to the customer query construction and stored in rule repositories.

Xcerpt Background

We describe Xcerpt principles and the rationale for choosing it and demonstrate how such a declarative language and its environment need to be adapted for their deployment in a dynamic, mediated service context. Xcerpt is a query language designed for querying and transforming traditional XML and HTML data, as well as Semantic Web data in the form of RDF and OWL. One of the design principles is to strictly separate the matching part and the construction part in a transformation specification, see Fig. 3. Xcerpt follows a pattern-based approach to querying XML data.

Fig. 3 shows a transformation example for a customer array based on Fig. 1. The structure of this specification is based on a construction part (CONSTRUCT) and a source query part (FROM). An output customer in `CustomerArray` is constructed based on the elements of an item in an `arrayOfCustomer` by using a pattern matching approach, identifying relevant attributes in the source and referring to them in the constructed output through variables such as `Name` or `CompanyID`. During transformation, these hold the concrete values of the selected (matched) elements.

Xcerpt distinguishes two types of specifications:

- Goal-based query programs, identified by the keyword GOAL, are executable query programs that refer to input and output

Figure 3. Declarative query and transformation specification of a customer array element in Xcerpt (© 2008, Claus Pahl. Used with permission)

```
CONSTRUCT
    CustomerArray [
        all Customer[
            nameAsContracted[var Name],
            companyId[var CompanyId],
            serviceOrganizationIdentifier[var OrgId],
            all supportidentifier[
                CustomerSupportIdentifier [var Code],
                ISOCountryCode [var CSI]
            ]
        ]
    ]
FROM
    arrayOfCustomer[[
        item [[
            orgName[var Name],
            companyId[var CompanyId],
            gcdbOrgId [var OrgId],
            countryCode[var Code],
            csiNumber[var CSI]
        ]]
    ]]
```

resources and that describe data extraction and construction.

- Abstract transformation rules, identified by the keyword CONSTRUCT as in Fig. 3, are function-like transformation specifications with no output resource associated.

Xcerpt extends the pattern-based approach, which is also used in other query and transformation languages, in following ways:

- Firstly, query patterns can be formulated as incomplete specifications in three dimensions. Incomplete query specifications can be represented in depth, which allows XML data to be selected at any arbitrary depth; in breadth, which allows querying neighbouring nodes by using wildcards, and in order. Incomplete query specifications allow patterns to be specified more flexibly without losing accuracy.
- Secondly, the simulation unification computes answer substitutions for the variables in the query pattern against underlying XML terms.

Xcerpt provides a runtime environment with an execution engine at its core (Schaffert, 2004). The central problem is to embed this type of environment, which can also be found for other query and transformation languages, into a dynamic, mediated service setting.

Connector Construction and Query Composition

We have adapted Xcerpt to support the construction of service connectors, i.e. executable query and transformation programs that integrate different data services:

- In order to promote modularity and code reuse, individual integration rules should not be designed to perform complex transformation tasks – rather a composition of individual rules is preferable. The composition of rules through rule chaining demand the query part of a service connector to be built ahead of the construction part.

- The data representation of the global data model changes as element names change or elements are being removed – these should not affect the query and integration part of the rules. Only an additional construction part is needed to enable versioning of the global data model.

Modularity and incomplete query specifications turn out to be essential features that are required from a query and transformation language in our context. In order to achieve the compositionality of modular rules, a layered approach shall be taken:

- Ground rules are responsible for populating XML data in the form of Xcerpt data terms by reading XML documents from individual service providers. These ground rules are tightly coupled to individual data Web services. These rules instruct the connector where to retrieve elements of data objects.
- The Xcerpt data terms are consumed subsequently by non-ground queries based on intermediate composite rules. These rules are responsible for integrating ground rules to render data types in the global XML schema. However, these rules still do not produce output.
- Finally, the composite rules are responsible for rendering the data objects defined in the interfaces of the mediator Web services based on customer requests. The composite rules are views on top of ground and intermediate representations according to the global schema. Therefore, the exported data from a mediator Web service is the goal of the corresponding connector (a query program).

Xcerpt is a document-centric language, designed to query and transform XML documents. Therefore, ground rules, which read individual data elements from the resources, are associated to at least one resource identifier. This is a bottom-up approach in terms of data population because data is assigned from the bottom level of the rules upward until it reaches the ultimate goal of a hierarchically structured rule. These rules are defined through an integration goal (the top-level query program) and structured into sub-rules down to ground rules.

These layered rules are saved in a repository. When needed, a rule will be picked and a backward rule chaining technique for rule composition enables data objects to be populated to answer transformation requests. Rule chaining means that resulting variable bindings from a transformation rule that is used within a query program are chained with those of the query program itself. Rule chaining is used to build recursive query programs. Consistent connectors can then be constructed on the fly based on input data such as the data services and the layered rules.

We apply backward goal-based rule chaining to execute complex queries based on composite rules. Fig. 4 shows an example of this pattern matching approach that separates a possibly partial query into resource and construction parts. The transformation rule maps the `supportIdentifier` element of the customer example from Fig. 1. Fig. 4 is a composite rule based on the `SupportIdentifier` construction rule at a lower level. Fig. 5 demonstrates the transformation that produces the resulting XML data for the `Customer` service. The output from the `Customer` mediator represents a customer as identified in a servicing system. In the example, rule `CustomerArray` is a composite rule, based on the `Customer` and `Service` rules, that could be used to answer a user query directly. The resource identifiers in form of variables and the interfaces for the data representation will be supplied to the connector generator. Rule mappings in the connector generator determine which queries are constructed from the repository for execution.

Figure 4. Transformation specification in Xcerpt based on goal chaining with one goal-based query program and two supporting transformation rules (© 2008, Claus Pahl. Used with permission)

```
GOAL
   Out { Resource {"file:SupportIdentifier_Customer.xml"},
         SupportIdentifier [ All var SupportIdentifier ] }
FROM
   Var SupportIdentifier -> SupportIdentifier {{}}
END
CONSTRUCT
   SupportIdentifier [var Code, optional Var Cname, Var Code]
FROM
in { Resource {"file:customer1.xml"},
     ArrayOfCustomer [[
         customer [[ optional countryName [var CName],
                     couuntryCode [var Code]
                     csiNumber [var CSI]  ]]  }
END
CONSTRUCT
   SupportIdentifier [var Code, Var Cname, optional Var Code]
FROM
in { Resource {"file:customer2.xml"},
     Customers [[ customer [[
                     countryName [var CName],
                     optional couuntryCode [var Code]
                     csiNumber [var CSI]  ]] }
END
```

THE MEDIATED SERVICE INTEGRATION ARCHITECTURE

We propose a mediated service-based architecture for the integration of XML data in Web service-based information systems. The major aims of the proposed mediated software architecture for the integration and mediation of XML data in the context of Web services are threefold: improved modifiability through declarative rule-based query programs, improved reusability of declarative integration rules through automated connector construction, and improved flexibility through dynamic generation of consistent, i.e. semantics-preserving connectors.

Service-Based Mediator Architectures

A declarative, rule-based approach can be applied to the data transformation problem (Orriens et al., 2003, Peltier et al., 2002). The difficulty lies in embedding a declarative transformation approach into a service-based architecture in which clients, mediators, and data provider services are composed (Garcia-Molina et al., 1997). A data integration engine can be built in the Web service business process execution language WS-BPEL. In (Rosenberg and Dustdar, 2005), a business rule engine-based approach is introduced to separate the business logic from the executable WS-BPEL process, which demonstrates that one of our objectives can be achieved (Rouvellou et al., 2000). These rules, stored in a repository, can be used to dynamically create executable query and transformation programs using a consistency-guaranteeing connector or integration service as the mediator. These integration services are the cornerstones of a mediator architecture that processes composite client queries that possibly involve different data sources provided by different Web services (Wiederhold, 1992). Mediators

Figure 5. The composite rules for customer transformation in Xcerpt (© 2008, Claus Pahl. Used with permission)

Rule 1: This rule produces the CustomerArray by grouping and reconstructing.

```
CONSTRUCT
   CustomerArray [[
      all var customer,
      all var supportidentifier,
      all var services [[
         var customerName,
         all var system [[ var systemId,  all var machine ]]
      ]]
   ]]
FROM
   Customer [[ var customer, var supportidentifier ]]
AND
   Service [[var services [[ var system [[ var machine]] ]] ]]
```

Rule 2a: This rule gets Customer data terms according to the global data model.

```
CONSTRUCT
   Customer[[ var customer, all var supportidentifier ]]
FROM
   arrayOfCustomer[[ var customer, var supportidentifier ]]
```

Rule 2b: This rule gets Service data terms according to the global data model.

```
CONSTRUCT
   Service [[ var service [[ var system [[ var machine]] ]] ]]
FROM
   arrayOfService [[
      var service [[ var system[[ var systemId ]] ]]
   ]]
AND
   Machine [[ var machine, var systemId ]];
```

Rule 3: This construct rule gets Machine data terms.

```
CONSTRUCT
   Machines [[
      all machine-of-system [[var machine]],
      var systemId
   ]]
FROM
   machineItem [[ var machine, var systemId ]]
```

in an architecture harmonise and present the information available in heterogeneous data sources (Stern and Davies, 2003). This harmonisation comes in the form of an identification of semantic similarities in data while masking their syntactic differences. Figs. 1 and 2 have illustrated an example whose foundations we have defined in terms of an ontology in order to guarantee consistency for transformations.

Zhu et al. (2004) and Widom (1995) argue that traditional data integration approaches such as federated schema systems and data warehouses fail to meet the requirements of constantly changing and adaptive environments. With the support of Web service technology, however, it is possible to encapsulate integration logic in a separate component as a mediator Web service between heterogeneous data service providers and consumers. Therefore, we build a connector construction component as a separate integration service, based on (Szyperski, 2002; Haller et al. 2005, Zhu et al., 2004, Rosenberg and Dustdar 2005). We develop an architecture where broker or mediator functionality is provided by a connector generator and a transformation engine:

- The connector construction is responsible for providing connectors based on transformation rules to integrate and mediate XML documents. The connector construction generates, based on schema information and transformation rules, an executable service process that gathers information from the required resources and generates a query/ transformation program that compiles and translates the incoming data into the required output format.
- The process execution engine is responsible for the integration of XML data and mediation between clients, data providers and the connector component. The execution engine is implemented in WS-BPEL and shall access the Xcerpt runtime engine, which executes the generated query/transformation program.

The connector construction component is responsible for converting the client query, dynamically create a transformation program based on stored declarative transformation rules, and to pass all XML data and programs to the execution engine. The system architecture is explained in Fig. 6 with a few sample information services from an application service provider scenario – Customer Data, E-business System, and Request Analysis Service.

Exposing data sources as services is only the first step towards building a SOA solution. Without a service integrator, the data user needs to understand each of the data models and relationships of service providers. The mediator architecture has the following components:

- **Query service.** The query service is responsible for handling inbound requests from the application consumer side and transferring outbound results back. The WS-BPEL process engine handles the internal

Figure 6. Component view of a mediator Web service with interactions (© 2008, Claus Pahl. Used with permission)

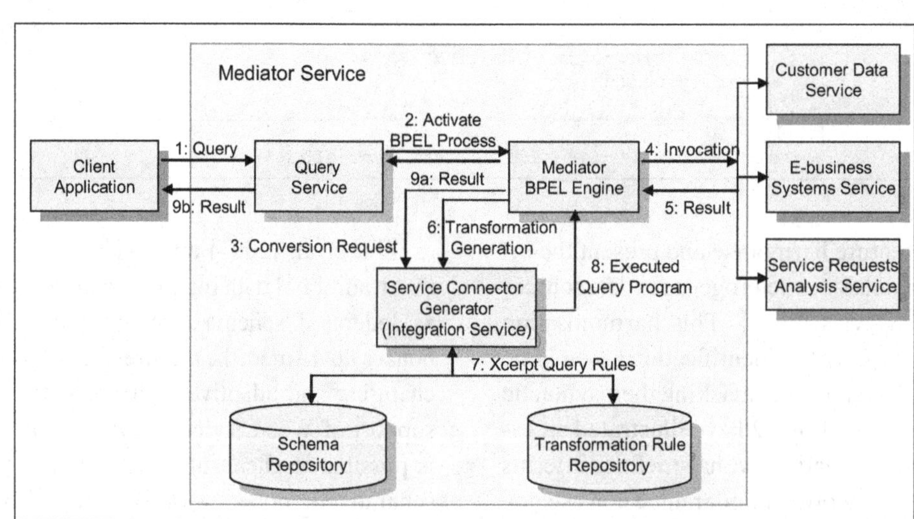

messaging of the architecture. The query service decomposes input messages into a set of pre-defined WS-BPEL processes.

- **Mediator (BPEL) engine.** A mediator engine is itself a WS-BPEL process. Mediators deliver data according to a global schema. The schema may consist of various data entities for large enterprise integration solutions.
- **Connector generation service.** This component is responsible for generating connectors for transforming messages both entering the WS-BPEL engine from service clients and leaving the WS-BPEL engine from data provider services according to the global data model.

The active components, provided as information services, are complemented by two repositories:

- **Transformation rule repository.** The repository allows the reuse of rules and can support multiple versions of service providers and mediator services.
- **Schema repository.** The repository stores the WSDL metadata and the XML schema information for the Web service providers and the mediator Web service. The schema information is used to validate the XML documents at runtime before they are integrated and returned to the client applications.

Connector Generation

The construction of a service connector means to generate an executable Xcerpt query program by composing each Xcerpt query with the corresponding transformation rules. In an Xcerpt query program, there is only one goal query, which will be processed first. The goal query is made up of composite transformations rules that in turn are made up of ground rules that read XML data from external resources. The process begins by expanding each composite query according to the definitional data mappings that are stored in a rule repository. The rule chaining mechanism in Xcerpt needs the goal query and all supporting queries in one query program at runtime.

The Xcerpt runtime engine reads XML-based resources and populates them into data terms before the query terms can start to evaluate them. The drawback is that all resources identifiers have to be specified inside a query program rather than be passed into a query program as parameters. Consequently, we adapted the Xcerpt approach to processing transformation requests in an information integration solution. The resource identifiers are not hard-coded in ground rules in our setting in order to achieve the desired loose coupling to achieve flexibility and reusability. These resource identifiers are invisible to the connector construction service. Xcerpt does not support automatic query program construction by default, although it provides the necessary backward rule chaining technique to evaluate a chain of queries.

We have developed a wrapper mechanism to pass the resource identifiers from the goal level down to the ground rules. Therefore, as an extension to the original Xcerpt approach, a mediator-based data integration architecture is needed where the rules are decoupled from the resources and the only the generated Xcerpt-based connectors are integrated with the client and provider Web services. WS-BPEL code that coordinates the mediation and transformation process is generated by a connector generator for transformations within the mediator service.

FUTURE TRENDS

Integration has currently been investigated from a static perspective looking at existing systems integration. We discuss emerging needs to address this as part of software evolution and legacy systems integration. Another current trend is the increasing utilisation of semantic enhancements, such as ontologies and reasoning frameworks, to support integration. We address briefly attempts of using service ontologies, which would complement the presented ontology-based information architecture.

Re-engineering and the integration of legacy systems is an aspect that goes beyond the integration context we described – although the application service provider (ASP) context is a typical example of a field where ASPs currently convert their systems into service-based architectures (Seltsikas and Currie, 2002). The introduction of data transformation techniques for re-engineering activities can improve the process of re-engineering legacy systems and adopting service-oriented architecture to manage the information technology services (Zhang and Yang, 2004). Business rules often change rapidly – requiring the integration of legacy systems to deliver a new service. How to handle the information integration in the context of service management has not yet been explored in sufficient detail in the context of transformation and re-engineering.

The utilisation of the semantic knowledge that is available to represent the services that make up the mediator architecture is another promising direction that would increase flexibility in terms of dynamic composition. The functionality and quality attributes of Web services can be in terms of one of the widely known service ontologies such as OWL-S or WSMO (Payne and Lassila, 2004). Abstract service descriptions can be derived from the semantic properties of the data they provide, process, or consume. Some progress has been made with respect to semantics-based service discovery and composition; the interplay between semantic data integeration and semantic service integration needs a deeper investigation. Karastoyanova et al. (2007), for instance, discuss a middleware architecture to support semantic data mediation based on semantically annotated services. Their investigation demonstrates how your semantic data mediation can be incorporated into a service-based middleware architecture that supports SOA-based development. However, the need to have an overarching semantic information architecture also becomes apparent, which supports our results.

CONCLUSION

The benefit of information systems on demand must be supported by corresponding information management services. Many application service providers are currently modifying their technical infrastructures to manage and integrate information using a Web services-based approach. However, the question of handling information integration in a flexible and modifiable way in the context of service-based information systems has not yet been fully explored.

The presented framework utilises semantic information integration technologies for XML data in service-oriented software architectures. The crucial solutions for the information integration problem are drawn from mediated architectures and data model transformation, allowing the XML data from local schemas to be consistently transformed, merged and adapted according to declarative, rule-based integration schemas for dynamic and heterogeneous environments. We have proposed a declarative style of transformation based on a semantic, ontology-based data model, with implicit source model traversal and target object creation. The development of a flexible mediator service is crucial for the success of the service-based information systems architecture from the deployment point of view. Our solution based on the query and transformation language Xcerpt is meant to provide a template for other similar languages. One of our central objectives was to introduce an integration solution from a technical perspective.

A number of extensions of our approach would strongly benefit its flexibility. Essentially, we plan to address the trends outlined in the previous section. Systems evolution and legacy system integration shall be addressed through a more transformation systems-oriented perspective on integration. We are also working on an integration of service ontologies and general data-oriented domain ontologies for service-oriented architectures.

REFERENCES

Alonso, G., Casati, F., Kuno, H., & Machiraju, V. (2004). *Web Services – Concepts, Architectures and Applications*. Berlin, Germany: Springer Verlag.

Bry, F., & Schaffert, S. (2002). Towards a Declarative Query and Transformation Language for XML and Semistructured Data: Simulation Unification. *In Proceedings Intl. Conference on Logic Programming. LNCS 2401*, (pp. 255-270). Heidelberg, Gerrnany: Springer-Verlag.

Daconta, M.C., Obrst, L.J., & Smith, K.T. (2003). *The Semantic Web – a Guide to the Future of XML, Web Services, and Knowledge Management*. Indianapolis, USA: Wiley & Sons.

Garcia-Molina, H., Papakonstantinou, Y., Quass, D., Rajaraman, A., Sagiv, Y., Ullman, Y. D., Vassalos, V., & Widom, J. (1997). The TSIMMIS approach to mediation: Data models and languages. *Journal of Intelligent Information Systems, 8(2)*, 117-132.

Haller, A., Cimpian, E., Mocan, A., Oren, E., & Bussler, C. (2005). WSMX - a semantic service-oriented architecture. *In Proceedings Intl. Conference on Web Services ICWS 200 5*, (pp. 321-328).

Jhingran, A.D., Mattos, D., & Pirahesh, N.H. (2002). Information Integration: A research agenda. *IBM System Journal*, 41(4) , 55-62.

Karastoyanova, D., Wetzstein, B., van Lessen, T., Wutke, D., Nitzsche, J., & Leymann, F. (2007). Semantic Service Bus: Architecture and Implementation of a Next Generation Middleware. *In Proceedings of the Second International Workshop on Service Engineering SEIW 2007*, (pp. 347-354).

Lenzerini, M. (2002). Data integration: A theoretical perspective. *In Proceedings Principles of Database Systems Conference PODS'02*, (pp. 233-246).

Orriens, B., Yang, J., & Papazoglou, M. (2003). A Framework for Business Rule Driven Web Service Composition. Jeusfeld, M.A. & Pastor, O. (Eds.), *In Proceedings ER'2003 Workshops, LNCS 2814*, (pp. 52-64). Heidelberg, Germany: Springer-Verlag.

Payne, T. and Lassila, O. (2004). Semantic Web Services. *IEEE Intelligent Systems*, 19(4), 14-15.

Peltier, M., Bezivin, J, & Guillaume, G. (2001). MTRANS: A general framework, based on XSLT, for model transformations. *In Proceedings of the Workshop on Transformations in UML WTUML'01*. Retrieved 21 July 2008 from: http://citeseer.ist.psu.edu/581336.html

Reynaud, C., Sirot, J.P., & Vodislav, D. (2001). Semantic Integration of XML Heterogeneous Data Sources. *In Proceedings IDEAS Conference 2001*, (pp. 199–208).

Rosenberg, F., & Dustdar, S. (2005). Business Rules Integration in BPEL - A Service-Oriented Approach. *In Proceedings 7th International IEEE Conference on E-Commerce Technology*, (pp. 476- 479).

Rouvellou, I., Degenaro, L., Rasmus, K., Ehnebuske, D., & McKee, B. (2000). Extending business objects with business rules. *In Proceedings 33rd Intl. Conference on Technology of Object-Oriented Languages*, (pp. 238-249).

Schaffert, S. (2004). *Xcerpt: A Rule-Based Query and Transformation Language for the Web*. PhD Thesis, University of Munich.

Seltsikas, P., & Currie, W.L. (2002). Evaluating the application service provider (ASP) business model: the challenge of integration. *In Proceedings 35th Annual Hawaii International Conference 2002.* 2801 – 2809.

Stal, M. (2002). Web Services: Beyond Component-based Computing. *Communications of the ACM, 45(10)*, 71-76.

Stern, A., & Davis, J. (2004). Extending the Web services model to IT services. *In Proceedings IEEE International Conference on Web Services*, (pp. 824-825).

Szyperski, C. (2002). *Component Software: Beyond Object-Oriented Programming – 2nd Ed.* New York, USA: Addison-Wesley.

W3C – the World Wide Web Consortium. (2004). *The Semantic Web Initiative.* Retrieved March 9, 2008 from http://www.w3.org/2001/sw.

Widom, J. (1995). Research problems in data warehousing. *In Proceedings of 4th International Conference on Information and Knowledge Management,* (pp. 25-30).

Wiederhold, G. (1992). Mediators in the architecture of future information systems. *IEEE Computer, 25*, 38-49.

Zhang, Z., & Yang, H. (2004). Incubating Services in Legacy Systems for Architectural Migration. *In Proceedings 11th Asia-Pacific Software Engineering Conference APSEC'04*, (pp. 196-203).

Zhu, Y. (2007). *Declarative Rule-based Integration and Mediation for XML Data in Web Service-based Software Architectures.* M.Sc. Thesis. Dublin City University.

Zhu, F., Turner, M., Kotsiopoulos, I., Bennett, K., Russell, M., Budgen, D., Brereton, P., Keane, J., Layzell, P., Rigby, M., & Xu, J. (2004). Dynamic Data Integration Using Web Services. *In Proceedings 2nd International Conference on Web Services ICWS'2004*, (pp. 262-269).

ADDITIONAL READING

Textbooks:

Bass, L. Clements, & P. Kazman, R. (2003). *Software Architecture in Practice.* 2nd Edition. Boston, USA: Addison-Wesley.

Krafzig, D., Banke, K., & Slama, D. (2004). *Enterprise SOA: Service-Oriented Architecture Best Practices.* Upper Saddle River, USA: Prentice Hall.

Mahmoud, Q.H. (2004). *Middleware for Communications: Concepts, Designs and Case Studies.* Indianapolis, USA: John Wiley and Sons.

Articles:

Abiteboul, S., Benjelloun, O., & Milo, T. (2002). Web services and data integration. *In Proceedings of the Third International Conference on Web Information Systems Engineering,*. (pp. 3-6).

Bengtsson, P., Lassing, N. , Bosch, J., & Vliet, H. (2004): Architecture-Level Modifiability Analysis (ALMA). *Journal of Systems and Software, 69(1)*, 129-147.

Bing Q., Hongji, Y., Chu, W.C., & Xu, B. (2003): Bridging legacy systems to model driven architecture. *In Proceedings 27th Annual International Computer Software and Applications Conference COMPSAC 2003.* (pp. 304- 309).

Bolzer, M. (2005). *Towards Data-Integration on the Semantic Web: Querying RDF with Xcerpt.* Master Thesis. University of Munich.

Calvanese, D., Giacomo, G, Lenzerini, M., & Nardi. D. (2001). Data Integration in Data Warehousing. *International Journal of Cooperative Information Systems. 10(3)*, 237-271.

Djuric, D. (2004). MDA-based Ontology Infrastructure. *Computer Science and Information Systems, 1(1)*, 91–116.

Hasselbring, W. (2000). Information System Integration. *Communications of the ACM, 43(6)*, 32-36.

Hasselbring, W. (2002). Web data integration for e-commerce applications. *IEEE Multimedia, 9(1)*, 16-25.

Lehti, P., & Fankhauser, P. (2004). XML data integration with OWL: experiences and challenges. *In Proceedings 2004 International Symposium on Applications and the Internet.* (pp. 160-167).

Levy, A. (1998). The information manifold approach to data integration. *IEEE Intelligent Systems, 13*, 12-16.

Li, S.-H., Huang, S.-M., Yen, D.C., & Chang, C.-C. (2007). Migrating Legacy Information Systems to Web Services Architecture. *Journal of Database Management, 18(4)*, 1-25.

Milanovic, N., & Malek, M. (2004). Current solutions for Web service composition. *IEEE Internet Computing, 8(6)*, 51-59.

Milo, T., & Zohar, S. (1998). Using Schema Matching to simplify heterogeneous Data Translation. Proceeding of the Int'l VLDB Conference. (pp. 122-133).

Oquendo, F. (2006). π-Method: a model-driven formal method for architecture-centric software engineering. SIGSOFT Software Engineering Notes, 31(3), *1-13.*

Pahl, C. (2007). An Ontology for Software Component Description and Matching. *International Journal on Software Tools for Technology Transfer, 9(2)*, 169-178.

Pahl, C. (2007). Semantic Model-Driven Architecting of Service-based Software Systems. *Information and Software Technology. 49(8)*, 838-850.

Rahm, E., & Bernstein, A. (2001). A Survey of Approaches to Automatic Schema Matching. *VLDB Journal, 10 (4)*, 334-350.

Selic, B. (2003). The Pragmatics of Model-Driven Development. *IEEE Software, 20(5)*, 19-25.

Sheth A. P., & Larson A. (1990). Federated database systems for managing distributed, heterogeneous, and autonomous databases. *ACM Computing Surveys, 22(3)*, 183-236.

Velegrakis, Y., Miller, R., & Mylopoulos, J. (2005). Representing and Querying Data Transformations. *In Proceedings of the 21st International Conference on Data Engineering ICDE'05.* (pp. 81-92).

Willcocks, P., & Lacify, C. (1998). The sourcing and outsourcing of IS: Shock of the New? P. Willcocks and C. Lacity (Eds.), *Strategic Sourcing of Information Technology: Perspective and Practices.* Chichester, UK : Wiley.

Yang, Y., Peng, X., & Zhao, W. (2007). An Automatic Connector Generation Method for Dynamic Architecture. *In Proceedings International Computer Software and Applications Conference COMPSAC 2007.* (pp. 409-414).

Standards:

Object Management Group (2003). *Model-Driven Architecture MDA Guide V1.0.1.* OMG.

Chapter VII
Facilitating Design of Efficient Components by Bridging Gaps Between Data Model and Business Process via Analysis of Service Traits of Data

Ning Chen
Xi'an Polytechnic University, China

ABSTRACT

In many large-scale enterprise information system solutions, process design, data modeling and software component design are performed relatively independently by different people using various tools and methodologies. This usually leads to gaps among business process modeling, component design and data modeling. Currently, these functional or non-functional disconnections are fixed manually, which increases the complexity and decrease the efficiency and quality of development. In this chapter, a pattern-based approach is proposed to bridge the gaps with automatically generated data access components. Data access rules and patterns are applied to optimize these data access components. In addition, the authors present the design of a toolkit that automatically applies these patterns to bridge the gaps to ensure reduced development time, and higher solution quality.

INTRODUCTION

With the development of information technology, enterprise information becomes more complex and tends to change more frequently; consequently enterprise should adjust its business according to market, which requires enterprise IT system to be flexible and agile enough to response to the changes. Now, business process modeling consists of service modeling, data modeling and

Copyright © 2009, IGI Global, distributing in print or electronic forms without written permission of IGI Global is prohibited.

component modeling, which are the three main threads in enterprise IT system solution design (Ivica, 2002; Mei, 2003). They are usually performed relatively independently, for different roles employ different methodologies. The result is in a gap among process model, data model and components, which requires significant amount of efforts to fill in the gap. Enterprise information system is an application with dense data (Martin, 2002) and mass data access. Both functional and non-functional aspects, such as system response time and data throughput etc., are satisfied in system integration in order to provide efficient data access within process execution. Meeting these requirements is a challenge presented to the solution designed, which will greatly affect the efficiency of system development. Therefore, how to build the relationship model between business process and data model, and how to use the orchestration model to automatically generate data access components are two questions that have great impact to software development.

RELATION WORKS

The existing enterprise modeling approaches are focused on two domains including peer-to-peer enterprise system and multilayer Enterprise Modeling.

David (2004) presents a loosely coupled service-composition paradigm. This paradigm employs a distributed data flow that differs markedly from centralized information flow adopted by current service integration frameworks, such as CORBA, J2EE and SOAP. Distributed data flows support direct data transmission to avoid many performance bottlenecks of centralized processing. In addition, active mediation is used in applications employing multiple web services that are not fully compatible in terms of data formats and contents.

Martin Fowler and Clifton Nock summarize customary patterns of enterprise application architecture to accelerate development of enterprise modeling (Martin, 2002; Clifton, 2003).

However, the existing enterprise modeling methods remain largely unharnessed due to the following shortages: (1) They lack the automation of analysis mechanism which makes the enterprise unresponsive to the enterprise changes and increases the maintaining overhead of the evolution of these models; (2) Some enterprise models are just conceptual models and should be analyzed by hand. Others employ the complex mathematical models for analysis, which are hard for the business users to comprehend and manipulate. (3) The knowledge reuse is difficult for the business users due to the heterogeneity of the enterprise models.

In order to tackle the above problems, through deep analysis of business process modeling and data modeling, we extract process data mapping and data access flow to build data access components for bridging business process and data model. Furthermore, a pattern is automatically applied to data access component for facilitating an efficient service.

PROCESS/DATA RELATIONSHIP MODEL

In present environment for software development, different tools are used by separate roles in business process modeling, data modeling, software component designing and coding. These tasks are so independent that the whole software development becomes rather complex. Take the IBM develop studio as an example, we need to use modeling and programming tools such as WBI-Modeler, Rational Software Architect and WSAD-IE (Osamu, 2003). The development procedure contains the following steps:

- The analyst will analyze requirement to design the use case using UML.

- By analyzing the relationship between enterprise entities, the data model designer will design the data model, and create the database on the basis of UML.
- The process analyst will design the abstract business process using WBI Modeler.
- The software engineer will design the functions and APIs for components using RSA.
- The developer will implement the software components and access the database using RSA.
- The process developer will develop the executable process based on the abstract process model, and assemble the software components as web services using WSAD-IE.
- The system deployer will run the developed business model (EAR file) on WBI-SF.

Obviously, a good command of process orchestration, OOD and UML is a prerequisite for a designer to complete the solution design. The Figure 1 presents the relationships among design flows of business process, software components, and database.

DATA ACCESS COMPONENT

Identification of Frequent Activity

Business process provided much global information on the whole. Not only can these information be used for developer to generate the data access component, but also these information can be used for developer to analyze the process and data relationship model, and consequently for developer to optimize data access activity, produce approximate index for data model, create views and apply data access patterns (Clifton, 2003), which can enhance the data access performance (Fig.1).

A business process usually contains some sub processes, and a sub process usually contains some activities, where activity is operation on data.

Let $\{P_1, P_2, P_3, \ldots P_r, \ldots\}$ be a process set in process model.

Definition 1: <Frequency of process > Let a set ***PS*** contain some sub-processes, which are processes directly or indirectly invoked by a business process *P*, as denoted by $PS = \{P_r\}_{r\in I}$, where I is index set. P_r is invoked in process *P* N_r times, the frequency of process P_r is defined as $N_r / \sum_{r\in I} N_r$.

Figure 1. Map relationships between process service and data service

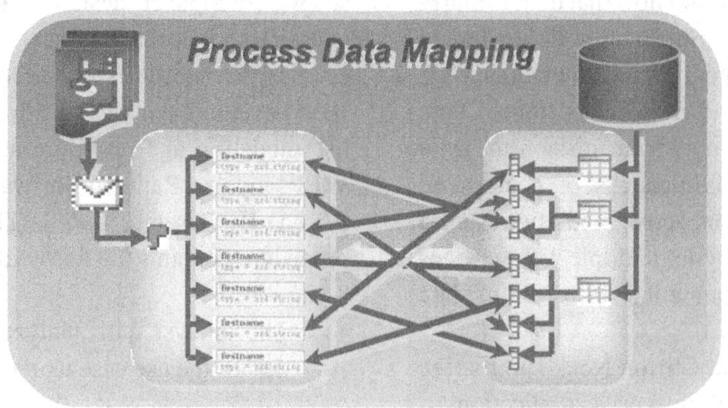

Definition 2: <Activity frequency of sub-process > If the kth data-access-activity in sub process P_r is invoked $n_{r,k}$ times, the activity frequency of sub-process P_r is defined by $n_{r,k} / \sum_{k \in I} n_{r,k}$, where I is index set.

Definition 3: <Frequency of activity > The frequency of activity $a_{r,k}$ is defined as the ratio of times of data access to the total access, i.e. $n_{r,k} / \sum_{P_r \in PS} \sum_{k \in I} n_{r,k}$.

Definition 4: <Frequent querying activity> Defined as activity with frequency of activity greater than frequent-querying-activity threshold $MAXSearch_{AF}$.

Definition 5: <Frequent updating activity> Defined as activity with frequency of activity greater than frequent-updating-activity threshold $MAXUpdate_{AF}$.

Frequency of activities can be computed by traversing data access flow, and frequent querying activity and frequent updating activity can be identified based on rules.

Automatic Application of Cache Pattern

We can represent the optimization with rules. According to the customized threshold, frequent data access activities can be selected, and then rule-analyzing system can use rules to recommend approximate data access patterns. The performance index and user preference can be added to identify cache pattern. The following is a strategy of configuration of data access:

Algorithm: Application strategy of cache pattern
Input: data access flow
Output: cache pattern of data access

Step 1: Analyze the data access flow, then find all frequent querying activity, which form the activity set T;
Step 2: For all activity a∈T, given the corresponding data model D by user interface, if the activation of D is 0, static cache pattern is applied; otherwise, if the activation of D is not equal to 0($0<active\leq 1$), timing update cache pattern is applied, the period of updating is $\frac{K_{active}}{active}$, where K_{active} is a constant representing ratio of activation;
Step 3: The developer can adjust the collection strategy of cache by user interface;
Step 4: Generate cache pattern code according to cache updating strategy and collect strategy.

Knowledge base of cache pattern strategy stores the criterion how to apply cache patterns, and recommends corresponding configuration of cache pattern and cache parameters according to activation information and different querying condition capacity provided by user. The rules for selection of proper cache pattern and configuration of cache parameter are as follows:

Cache pattern rules:
RULE1: IF ActivityEstimate = static AND VolumeEstimate <= Pre-Fetching Threshold
THEN latest least replace strategy
RULE2: IF ActivityEstimate = active AND VolumeEstimate <= Pre-Fetching Threshold
THEN non-active expiration strategy
RULE3: IF ActivityEstimate = veryactive AND VolumeEstimate <= Pre-Fetching Threshold
THEN fix-time expiration strategy
RULE4: IF ActivityEstimate = static AND VolumeEstimate > Pre-Fetching Threshold
THEN latest least replace strategy
RULE5: IF ActivityEstimate = active AND VolumeEstimate > Pre-Fetching Threshold
THEN non-active expiration strategy with limited queue
RULE6: IF ActivityEstimate = veryactive AND VolumeEstimate > Pre-Fetching Threshold

THEN fix-time expiration strategy with limited queue

Rules for determining cache pattern parameters:
Cache collection period

$$T_{collector} = \frac{T_{ontime}}{T_{response}} \bullet \eta_{collector} + T_{ontime},$$

where T_{ontime} denotes the change period of data items, $T_{response}$ denotes response time of querying operation, $\eta_{collector}$ is a constant ratio.
Cache queue capacity
$Q_{queue} = \max\{Q_{\max}, Volume\}$, where Q_{max} denote the maximum queue, *Volume* denotes different query condition volume.

TOOLKIT AND RESULT ANALYSIS

Based on Eclipse3.0 IDE and JSDK1.5, we developed a pattern-based tool-box to facilitating efficient service, including process/data relation analyzer, data access component builder and data access optimizer, which can run alone or cooperate with other modeling tool as Eclipse plugin, as shown in Fig.2.

Figure 2. Toolkit

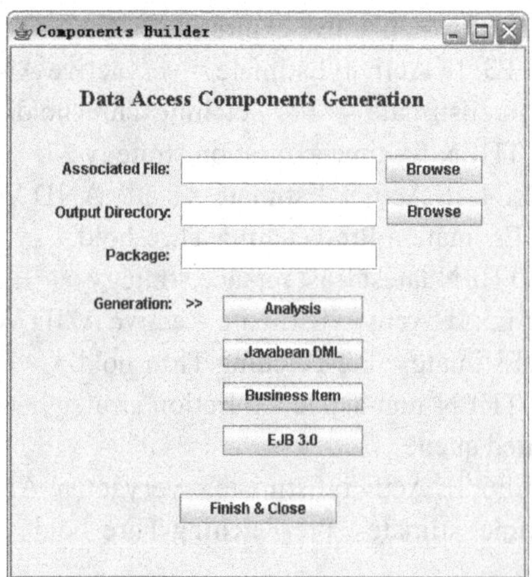

Through an analysis of process model file and data model file, process/data relation analyzer can construct map relation files between processes in process model and tables in data model; then on the basis of map relation files, data access component builder can generate data access components, for example JavaBeans or EJB code; finally cache pattern builder integrates cache pattern with generated data access components (Fig.3).

Figure 3. Automatic generation of code

```
Flight.java

package edu.xjtu.ctec.par;

import javax.persistence.*;
import java.util.*;

@SuppressWarnings("serial")
@Entity
@Table(name="FLIGHT")
public class Flight  implements java.io.Serializable {

    // Fields

     private Integer fno;
     private String cityfrom;
     private String cityto;
     private Date datetimedeparture;
     private Date datetimereturn;
     private java.math.BigDecimal flightprice;
     private java.util.Set<edu.xjtu.ctec.par.Reservation> reservations;

    // Constructors

    /** default constructor */
    public Flight() {
    }

    /** constructor with id */
```

(a) Generation of class representing data

```
FlightQuery.java

package ctec.javabean;
import java.sql.*;
import com.ibm.db.beans.*;

/**
 * This class sets the DBSelect property values. It also provides
 * methods that execute your SQL statement, return
 * a DBSelect reference, and return an array of objects
 * representing the rows in the result set.
 * Generated: 2005-11-29 20:45:55
 */

public class FlightQuery {
        private DBSelect select;

        /**
         * Constructor for a DBSelect class.
         */
        public FlightQuery() {
                super();
                initializer();
        }

        /**
         * Creates a DBSelect instance and initializes its properties.
         */
        protected void initializer() {
                select = new DBSelect();
                try {
                        select.setDriverName("COM.ibm.db2.jdbc.app.DB2Driver");
                        select.setUrl("[illegible]");
```

(b) Generation of class representing EJB

Figure 4. Cache pattern performance

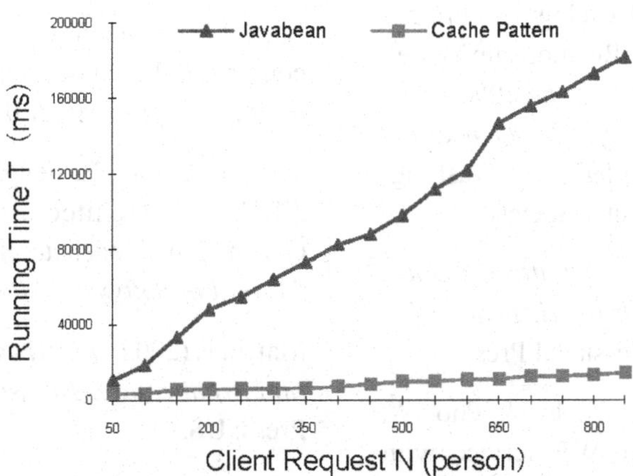

In order to show effect of cache pattern component on optimizing data access, we simulate N client inquiring transaction time of JavaBeans component and cache pattern component, as shown in Fig.4. The experimental result shows that consumption time of data access components with cache is less than consumption time of JavaBeans component for big transaction. However, information queried by data access components varies frequently, cost of cache data validation will rise, due to renewing or substituting cache items of cache queue in small interval, thus decreasing performance of data access component. In different scenario, effect of parameter-selection of cache pattern on performance will be discussed in future study.

CONCLUSION

In this chapter, a pattern-based approach to facilitate an efficient service is developed to automate the analysis of large-scale enterprise information system. The approach will effectively reduce the number of system development problems by automatic bridging of the gaps between development team and system analyst efficiently and effectively. In addition, automatically generated approach, flexible data access components can provide data access services, hiding the access complexity and satisfying system's functional requirements. The result is an approach for producing a pattern-based application, which completely improve on data access and minimizes the amount of code development required (Chen, 2008).

Further effort in this area is required in enhancing the flexibility to deal with the increasing complexities of business process design, and improving the performance with cluster analysis adjusting the granularity of components.

ACKNOWLEDGMENT

Our thanks to the IBM China Research Laboratory (CRL) in Beijing for helping us investigate the challenge. We specially owe thanks to investigation participants for their ideas and efforts, including Guanqun Zhang (IBM). This work is supported by IBM University Joint Research Project (Process/Data Orchestrated Solution Design), 2005.

REFERENCES

Chen, N. (2008). A Quick Development Framework Based on Process/Data Relationship Model. In J. Zhou (Ed.), *Proceedings of the 2008 International Conference on Computer Science and Information Technology.* (pp. 597-600). Washington, DC, USA: IEEE Computer Society.

Clifton, N. (2003). *Data Access Patterns: Database Interactions in Object-Oriented Applications.* USA: Addison-Wesley Professional Press.

David, L., Jun, P., Kincho, H. L., & Gio, W. (2004). Efficient Integration of Web Services with Distributed Data Flow and Active Mediation. In M. Janssen (Ed.), *ACM International Conference Proceeding Series: Vol. 60. Proceedings of the 6th international conference on Electronic commerce.* (pp. 11-20). New York, NY: ACM.

Ivica, C., & Magnus, L. (2002). Challenges of component-based development. *Journal of Systems and Software, 61(3),* 201-212.

Mei, H., Cheng, F., Feng, Y., & Yang, J. (2003). ABC: An Architecture Based, Component Oriented Approach to Software Development. *Journal of Software, 14(4),* 721-732.

Martin F. (2002). *Patterns of Enterprise Application Architecture.* Addison-Wesley Professional Press: USA.

Osamu, T. (Ed.). (2003). *Exploring WebSphere Studio Application Developer Integration Edition V5, IBM RedBook SG24-6200-00.* USA: IBM.

Chapter VIII
On the Use of Web Services in Content Adaptation

Khalil El-Khatib
University of Ontario Institute of Technology, Canada

Gregor v. Bochmann
University of Ottawa, Canada

Abdulmotaleb El- Saddik
University of Ottawa, Canada

ABSTRACT

The tremendous growth of the Internet has introduced a number of interoperability problems for distributed multimedia applications. These problems are related to the heterogeneity of client devices, network connectivity, content formats, and user's preferences. The challenge is even bigger for multimedia content providers who are faced with the dilemma of finding the combination of different variants of a content to create, store, and send to their subscribers that maximize their satisfaction and hence entice them to come back. In this chapter, the authors will present a framework for trans-coding multimedia streams using an orchestration of Web-services. The framework takes into consideration the profile of communicating devices, network connectivity, exchanged content formats, context description, users' preferences, and available adaptation services to find a chain of adaptation services that should be applied to the content to make it more satisfactory to clients. The framework was implemented as a core component for an architecture that supports personal and service mobility.

Copyright © 2009, IGI Global, distributing in print or electronic forms without written permission of IGI Global is prohibited.

1. INTRODUCTION

The tremendous growth of the Internet has introduced a number of interoperability problems for distributed multimedia applications. These problems are related to the heterogeneity of client devices, network connectivity, content formats, and user's preferences. The diversity of client devices, network connectivity, content formats, and user's preferences posed also some challenges in aligning and customizing the exchanged data between different users with different preferences. The challenge is even bigger for multimedia content providers who are faced with the dilemma of finding the combination of different variants of a content to create, store, and send to their subscribers that maximize their satisfaction and hence entice them to come back. Most content providers have taken the costly approach of creating different versions of content for different access devices and networks.

Content adaptation is an effective and attractive solution to the problem of mismatch in content format, device capability, network access and user's preferences. Using content adaptation, a number of adaptations is applied to the original content to make it satisfy the device constrains of the receiving device and the preferences of its user. Most currently available content adaptation modules are designed to make the Web easier to use. Examples of such adaptations modules include conversion of HTML pages to Wireless Markup Language (WML, 2001) pages, enlarging text size, reducing the size of an image, changing text and background colors for better contrast, removal of redundant information, audio to text conversion, video to key frame or video to text conversion, content extraction to list a few. These adaptation modules do not have though the same requirements and challenges of real-time multimedia content adaptations. Real-time multimedia applications involve large volumes of data making trans-coding a computationally very expensive task (Chandra & Ellis , 1999, Han et al.,1998). To address this challenge, some trans-coding services have been implemented in hardware and deployed on intermediate network nodes or proxies. The disadvantage of this approach is that there are always new types of clients that cannot be supported by the deployed hardware. A more suitable approach to address the computational challenge of multimedia trans-coding is based on the observation that the general trans-coding process can be defined as a combinatorial process (Mohan, Smith, & Li, 1999), and that multiple trans-coding services can be chained effectively together to perform a complex trans-coding task. So, instead of having all trans-coding done by one single trans-coding service, a number of trans-coding services can collaborate to achieve a composite adaptation task. For instance, trans-coding a 256-color depth *jpeg* image to a 2-color depth *gif* image can be carried out in two stages: the first stage covers converting 256-color to 2-color depth, and the second stage converts *jpeg* format to *gif* format. Using the software approach, transcoders can then be built more easily in software, and deployed and advertised more quickly to meet the needs of the users. Software-based trans-coding are also more reliable since its components can be simpler and they can also be replicated across the network. Moreover, transcoders can be modularized and re-used in different situations and contexts.

Given a composite adaptation task that can be carried out in a number of stages, and given that there could be a number of possible configurations to adapt the sender's content to make it presentable at the receiver's device, the challenge is to find the appropriate chain of available trans-coding services that best fits the capabilities of the device, and at the same time, maximizes the user's satisfaction with the final delivered content. In this chapter, we will discuss a Quality of Service (QoS) selection algorithm for providing personalized content through web-service composition. The function of the algorithm is to find the most appropriate chain of available trans-coding services between the sender and the receiver, and also to select the values for the configuration parameters for each trans-coding service. The proposed algorithm uses the user's satisfaction with the quality of the trans-coded content as the optimization metric for the path selection algorithm.

The rest of the chapter is organized as follows: In Section 2, we will introduce content adaptation and present the existing different models used in content adaptation. Section 3 lists all the required elements for providing customized content adaptation. In Section 4 we present our methodology for using the required element from Section 3 to construct a graph of trans-coding services; the algorithm for selecting the chain of trans-coding services is then presented. The selection criterion for the algorithm as well as its characteristics is also presented in Section 4, and finally, we end Section 4 with an example that shows step-by-step the results of the algorithm. Our conclusion is presented in Section 5.

2. CONTENT ADAPTATION

In today's Internet, there is a wide range of client devices in terms of both hardware and software capabilities. Device capabilities vary in different dimensions, including processing power, storage space, display resolution and color depth, media type handling, and much more. This variety on device capabilities makes it extremely difficult for the content providers to produce a content that is acceptable and appreciated by all the client devices (Fox, Gribble, & Chawathe, 1998), making application-level adaptation a necessity to cover the wide variety of clients.

There are three main approaches for handling this diversity in content formats: a static content adaptation, a dynamic content adaptation, and a hybrid of the static and dynamic approaches (Chang & Chen, 2002, Lum & Lau, 2002). The first two approaches differ in the time when the different content variants are created (Lei & Georganas, 2001) to match the requested format. In static adaptation, the content creator generates and stores different variants of the same content on a content server, with each variant formatted for a certain device or class of devices. Hafid and Bochmann (1996) presented an architecture for news-on-demand using this scheme. Static adaptation has three main advantages: (1) it is highly customized to specific classes of client devices, and (2) it does not require any runtime processing, so no delay is incurred, and (3) the content creator has the full control on how the content is formatted and delivered to the client. On the other hand, static adaptation has a number of disadvantages, mainly related to the management and maintenance of different variants of the same content (Lum & Lau, 2002): (1) different content formats need to be created for each sort of device or class of devices, and needs to be re-done when new devices are introduced, and (2) it requires large storage space to keep all variants of the same content.

With dynamic content adaptation, the content is trans-coded from one format to the other only when it is requested. Depending on the location where the trans-coding takes place, dynamic content adaptation technologies can be classified into three categories: server-based, client-based, and proxy-based. In the server-based approach (Mohan, Smith, & Li, 1999), the content server is responsible for performing the trans-coding; the content provider has all the control on how the content is trans-coded and presented to the user. Additionally, it allows the content to be trans-coded before it is encrypted, making it secure against malicious attacks. On the other hand, server-based adaptation does not scale properly for a large number of users and requires high-end content and delivery server to handle all requests.

As for the client-based approach (Björk et a., 1999, Fisher et al., 1997), the client does the trans-coding when it receives the content. The advantage of this approach is that the content can be adapted to match exactly to the characteristics of the client. But at the same time, client-based adaptation can be highly expensive in terms of bandwidth and computation power, especially for small devices with small computational power and slow network connectivity, with large volume of data might be wastefully delivered to the device to be dropped during trans-coding.

The third adaptation approach is the proxy-based approach (Chandra & Ellis, 1999, Chandra, Ellis, & Vahdat, 2000, Floyd & Housel, 1998, Fox, A., Gribble, Chawathe, Brewer, & Gauthier, 1997), where an intermediary computational entity can carry out content adaptation on the fly, on behalf of the server or client. Proxy adaptation has a number of benefits including leveraging the installed infrastructure and scaling properly with the number of clients. It also provides a clear separation between content creation and content adaptation. On the other hand, some content provider may argue that they prefer to have full control on how their content is presented to the user. Also, using proxies for adaptation does not allow the use of end-to-end security solutions.

3. CHARACTERIZATION AND REQUIREMENTS FOR CONTENT ADAPTATION

Advances in computing technology have led to a wide variety of computing devices, which made interoperability very difficult. Added to this problem is the diversity of user preferences when it comes to multimedia communications. This diversity in devices and user preferences has made content personalization an important requirement in order to achieve results that satisfy the user. The flexibility of any system to provide content personalization depends mainly on the amount of information available on a number of aspects involved in the delivery of the content to the user. The more information about these aspects is made available to the system, the more the content can be delivered in a format that is highly satisfactory to the user. These relevant aspects are: user preferences, media content profile, network profile, context profile, device profile, and the profile of intermediaries (or proxies) along the path of data delivery. We will briefly describe here each of these aspects; interested readers might refer to (El-Khatib & Bochmann, 2003) for more details.

User Profile: The user's profile captures the personal properties and preferences of the user, such as the preferred audio and video receiving/sending qualities (frame rate, resolution, audio quality...). Other preferences can also be related to the quality of each media types for communication with a particular person or group of persons. For instance, a customer service representative should be able to specify in his profile his/her preference to use high-resolution video and CD audio quality when talking to a client, and to use telephony quality audio and low-resolution video when communicating with a colleague at work. The user's profile may also hold the user's policies for application adaptations, such as the preference of the user to drop the audio quality of a sport-clip before degrading the video quality when resources are limited. The MPEG-21 standard (MPEG-21, 2001) is the most notable standards on user profiles.

Content Profile: Multimedia content might enclose different media types, such as audio, video, text, and each type can have different formats (Lei & Georganas, 2001). Each type has its format characteristics and parameters that can be used to describe the media. Such information about the content may include storage features, variants, author and production, usage, and many other metadata. The MPEG-7 standard (MPEG-7, 2000), formally named "Multimedia Content Description Interface", offers a comprehensive set of standardized description tools to describe multimedia content.

Context Profile: A context profile would include any dynamic information that is part of the context or current status of the user. Context information may include physical (e.g. location, weather, temperature), social (e.g. sitting for dinner), or organizational information (e.g. acting senior manager). The MPEG-21 standard includes tools for describing the natural environment characteristics of the user, including location and time, as well as the audio and illumination characteristics of the user's environment. Resource adaptation engines can use these elements to deliver the best experience to the user.

Device Profile: To ensure that a requested content can be properly rendered on the user's device, it is essential to include the capabilities and characteristics of the device into the content adaptation process. Information about the rendering device may include the hardware characteristics of the device, such as the device type, processor speed, processor load, screen resolution, color depth, available memory, number of speakers, the display size, and the input and output capabilities. The software characteristics such as the operating system (vendor and version), audio and video codecs supported by the device should also be included in the device profile. The User Agent Profile (UAProf) created by the Wireless Application Forum (WAP) and the MPEG-21 standard, both include description tools for describing device capabilities.

Network Profile: Streaming multimedia content over a network poses a number of technical challenges due to the strict QoS requirements of multimedia contents, such as low delay, low jitter, and high throughput (Ng, Tan, & Cheng, 2001). Failing to meet these requirements may lead to a bad experience of the user (Katchabaw, Lutfiyya, & Bauer, , 1998, Poellabauer, Abbasi, & Schwan, 2002). With a large variety of transport networks, it is necessary to include the network characteristics into content personalization and to dynamically adapt the multimedia content to the fluctuating network resources (Wu, Hou, Zhang, 2001). Achieving this requires collecting information about the available resources in the network, such as the maximum delay, error rate, and available throughput on every link over the content delivery path. A description tool for network capabilities, including utilization, delay and error characteristics are included in the MPEG 21 standard.

Profile of Intermediaries: When the content is delivered to the user across the network, it usually travels over a number of intermediaries. These intermediaries have been traditionally used to apply some added-value services, including on-the-fly content adaptations services (Chandra, Ellis, & Vahdat, 2000, Fox, Gribble, Chawathe, Brewer, & Gauthier, 1997). For the purpose of content adaptation, the profile of an intermediary would usually include a description of all the adaptation services that an intermediary can provide. These services can be described using any service description language such as the JINI network technology (JINI, 1998), the Service Location Protocol(Guttman, Perkins, Veizades, & Day, 1999), or the Web Service Description Language (WSDL, 2002). A description of an adaptation service would include, for instance, the possible input and output format to the service, the required processing and computation power of the service, and maybe the cost for using the service. The intermediary profile would also include information about the available resources at the intermediary (such as CPU cycles, memory) to carry out the services.

4. QOS SELECTION ALGORITHM

In this section, we will describe the overall QoS selection algorithm that finds the most appropriate chain of trans-coding services between the sender and the receiver, and also selects the configuration for each trans-coding service. We will first start by defining the user's satisfaction as the selection criterion for the algorithm, and then show how to construct the directed graph for adaptation, using the sender's content profile, receiver's device profile, and the list of available trans-coding services. After constructing the graph, we will show how to apply some optimization techniques on the graph to remove the extra edges in the graph, and finally present the actual QoS path and parameter selection algorithm.

4.1. User's Satisfaction as Selection Criteria

Most Internet users are indifferent about the underlying technologies such as protocols, codecs, or resource reservation mechanisms that enable their communication session. They are also indifferent about network level QoS characteristics, such as bandwidth, delay, or throughput. All what is important for these users in the end is making the communication session work in a satisfactory way: for instance, hearing without jitter and seeing without irregularity.

As we mentioned earlier, the user's preferences expressed in the user's profile can be classified as application layer QoS parameters. In order to compute the user's satisfaction with all values of the application layer configuration parameters, we have used the approach presented by Richards, Rogers, Witana, & Antoniades (1998), where each application level QoS parameter is represented by a variable x_i over the set of all possible values for that QoS parameter. The satisfaction or appreciation of a user with each quality value is expressed as a satisfaction function $S_i(x_i)$. All satisfaction functions have a range of [0..1], which corresponds to the minimum acceptable (M) and ideal (I) value of x_i. The satisfaction function $S_i(x_i)$ can take any shape, with the condition that it must increase monotonically over the domain. Figure 1 shows a possible satisfaction function for the frame rate variable.

In the case when there are more than one application parameter (frame rate, resolution, color depth, audio quality,...), Richards *et. al.* proposed using a combination function f_{comb} that computes the total satisfaction S_{tot} from the satisfactions s_i for the individual parameters (Equa. 1).

$$S_{tot} = f_{comb}(s_1, s_2, s_3 \ldots, s_n) = \frac{n}{\sum_{i=1}^{n} \frac{1}{s_i}} \qquad (1)$$

4.2 Extending User's Satisfaction to Support Weighted Combination and Multi-User Conference Sessions

We think that the approach described above is a major step towards a simple user-friendly interface for user level QoS specification, however, further considerations could be taken into account as described below. A first improvement results from the observation that users in telecommunication session might find some media types more important than others. For instance, a user of a news-on-demand service might prefer to receive high quality audio with low quality video as compared to average quality audio and average quality video. In the case of a user watching a sport event the situation may be the opposite (if the user does not care about the audio of the commenter).

This preference to individual media can play a factor when it comes to the calculation of the total satisfaction S_{tot}. By assigning different weights w_i to the different parameters x_i, S_{tot} will reflect the user preference for different media types. The combination function for the total user satisfaction can be redefined as follows:

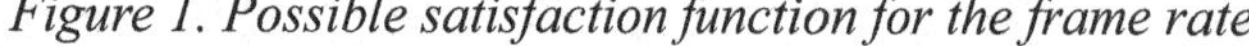
Figure 1. Possible satisfaction function for the frame rate

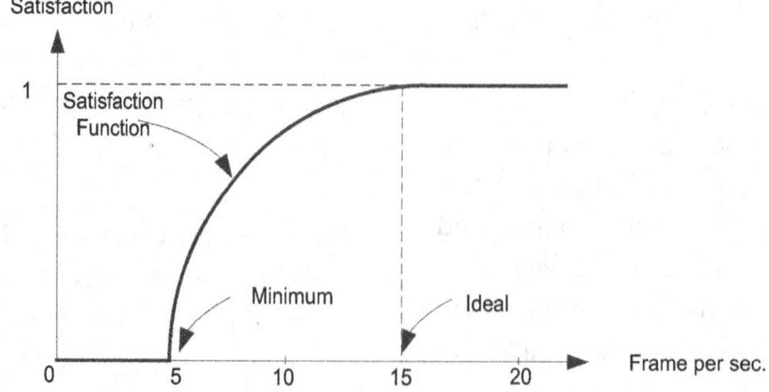

$$s_{tot}^{user} = f_{comb}(s_1, s_2, s_3 \ldots, s_n, w_1, w_2, w_3 \ldots, w_n) = \frac{n\overline{w}}{\sum_{i=1}^{n} \frac{w_i}{s_i}} \quad (2)$$

where is the weight for the individual satisfaction and . Equa. 2 have similar properties as Equa. 1, which is to:

Prop. 1. One individual low satisfaction is enough to bring the total satisfaction to a low value.
Prop. 2. The total satisfaction of equal individual satisfactions s_i with equal weight is equal to the satisfactions s_i.

These constants weight factors (AudioWeightFactor, VideoWeightFactor,..) can be selected by the user, and stored in the user profile. The selection of these weights depends on the type of service the user is willing to receive when using a specific service or communicating with a given callee.

Additionally, we have so far considered only the QoS preferences of a single user. But all conversational multimedia applications involve several users. It is therefore important to determine how the possibly conflicting preferences of the different users are reconciled in order to come up with QoS parameters that are suitable for all participating users.

In certain circumstances, some given parameters may be determined simply based on the preferences of a single user. This may be the case in a two-way teleconference between two users A and B, where the parameters of the video visible by User A would be determined based on the preferences of User A alone, and the video in the opposite direction based on the preferences of User B. However, the situation may be more complex if the cost of the communication is paid by User A and the selection of the video received by User B has an impact on the communication cost.

In other circumstances, as for instance in the case of the joint viewing of a video clip by several participants in a teleconference, the selected quality parameters should be determined based on the preferences of all participating users. In such circumstances, we propose to use the same combination function for user satisfaction considered above and (optionally) introduce a weight for each of the participating users, called the *QoS selection weight*, which determines how much the preferences of the user influences overall QoS parameter selection. The total satisfaction (computed for all users) is then given by

$$S_{tot} = f_{comb}(s_{tot}^{usr_1}, s_{tot}^{usr_2} \ldots, s_{tot}^{usr_m}, a_1, a_2 \ldots, a_m) = \frac{m\overline{a}}{\sum_{i=1}^{m} \frac{a_i}{s_{tot}^{usr_i}}} \quad (3)$$

where is the total satisfaction for user *i,* and is the *QoS selection weight* for user *i*. In the case that the weight of a given user is zero, the preferences of this user are not taken into account for the selection of the QoS parameters.

4.3. Constructing a Directed Graph of Trans-Coding Services

Now that we have decided on the selection criteria, the first step of the QoS selection algorithm would be to construct a directed acyclic graph for adaptation, using the content profile, device profile, and the list of available trans-coding services. Using this graph, the route selection algorithm would then determine the best path through the graph, from the sender to the receiver, which maximizes the user's satisfaction with the final received adapted content. The elements of the directed graph are the following:

1. Vertices in the graph represent trans-coding services. Each vertex of the graph has a number of properties, including the computation and memory requirements of the corresponding trans-coding service. Each vertex has a number of input and output links. The input links to the vertex represent the possible input formats to the trans-coding service. The output links are the output formats of the trans-coding service. Figure

2 shows a trans-coding service T1, with two input formats, F5 and F6, and four possible output formats, F10, F11, F12 and F13. The sender node is a special case vertex, with only output links, while the receiver node is another special vertex with only input links.

To find the input and output links of each vertex, we rely on the information in different profiles. The output links of the sender are defined in the content profile, which includes as we mentioned earlier, meta-data information (including type and format) of all the possible variants of the content. Each output link of the sender vertex corresponds to one variant with a certain format. The input links of the receiver are exactly the possible decoders available at the receiver's device. This information is available through the description of the receiver's device in the device profile. The input and output links of intermediate vertices are described in the service description part of the intermediaries profile. Each intermediary profile includes the list of available trans-coding services, each with the list of possible input and output formats. Each possible input format is represented as an input link into the vertex, and the output format is represented as an output link.

2. Edges in the graph represent the network connecting two vertices, where the input link of one vertex matches the output link of another vertex.

To construct the adaptation graph, we start with the sender node, and then connect the outgoing edges of the sender with all the input edges of all other vertices that have the same format. The same process is repeated for all vertices. To make sure that the graph is acyclic, the algorithm continuously verifies that all the formats along any path are distinct.

Figure 3 shows an example of an adaptation graph, constructed with one sender, one receiver, and seven intermediate vertices, each representing a trans-coding service. As we can see from the graph, the sender node is connected to the trans-coding service T1 along the edge labeled F5. This means that the sender S can deliver the content in format F5, and trans-coding service T1 can convert this format into format F10, F11, F12, or F13.

Figure 2. Trans-coding service with multiple input and output links

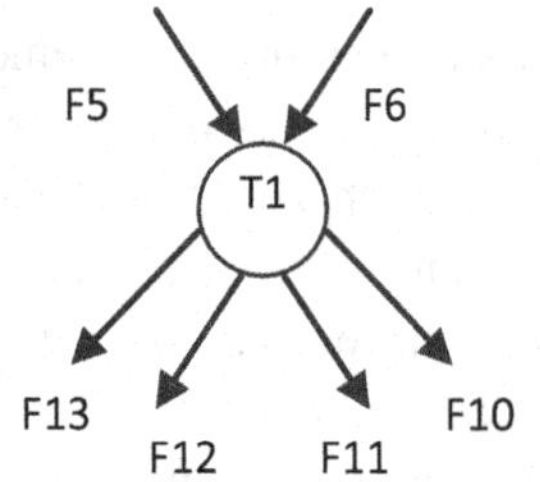

4.4. Adding Constraints to the Graph

As we have discussed earlier, the optimization criterion we have selected for the QoS selection

Figure 3. Directed trans-coding graph

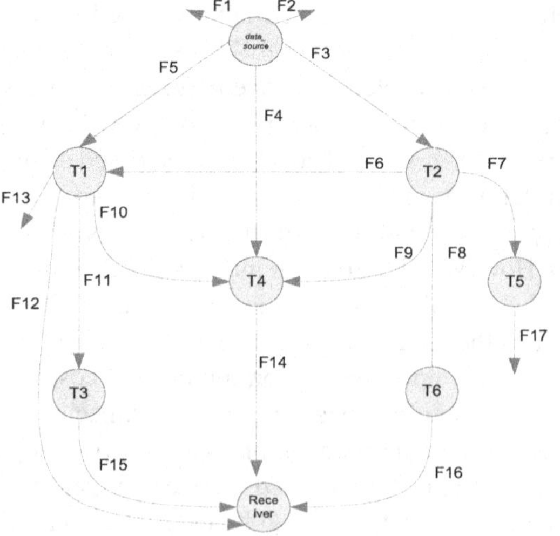

algorithm is the user's satisfaction computed using the function f_{comb} presented in Section 4.2. The maximum satisfaction achieved by using a trans-coding service T_i depends actually on a number of factors.

The first factor is the bandwidth available for the data generated by the trans-coding service T_i. The more bandwidth is available to the trans-coding service, the more likely the trans-coding service will be able to generate trans-coded content that is more appreciated by the receiver. The available bandwidth between two trans-coding services is restricted by the amount of bandwidth available between the intermediate servers where the trans-coding service T_i is running and the intermediate server where the next trans-coding service or receiver is running. We can assume that connected trans-coding services that run on the same intermediate server have an unlimited amount of bandwidth between them.

Other factors that can affect the user's satisfaction are the required amount of memory and computing power to carry out the trans-coding operation. Each of these two factors is a function of the amount of input data to the trans-coding service.

4.5. Graph Optimization

By looking at the graph in Figure 3, we can see that there are some edges like F1, F2 or F17 that are connected only to one trans-coder. These edges cannot be a part of any path from the sender to the receiver. The same principle also applies to trans-coders other than the sender and receiver that are not on any path from the sender to the receiver. T5 is an example of a trans-coder that cannot be used to send data through it on the way from the sender to the receiver. Removing these edges and vertices help reduce the computational time of the algorithm, since it helps pruning dead-ends from the graph. Applying optimization for the graph in Figure 3 would result in the graph shown in Figure 5. The pseudo-code for the graph optimization is shows in Figure 4.

4.6. QoS Selection Algorithm

Once the directed acyclic adaptation graph has been constructed, the next step is to perform the QoS selection algorithm to find a chain of trans-coding services, starting from the sender node and ending with the receiver node, which generates the maximum satisfaction of the receiver. Finding such as path can be similar to the problem of finding the shortest path in a directed weighted graph with similar complexity, except that the optimization criterion is the user's satisfaction, and not the available bandwidth or the number of hops.

Our proposed algorithm uses two variables representing two sets of trans-coding services, the set of already considered trans-coding services, called VT, and the set of candidate trans-coding services, called CS, which can be added next on

Figure 4. Pseudo-code for the graph optimization

```
graph_optimization(Transcoder t){
if t ≠ receiver then {
        for all ne ∈ neighbor(t)
                graph_optimization(ne);
        if is_empty(neighbor(ne)) then
                delete(ne);
                }
}
```

Figure 5. Optimized directed trans-coding graph

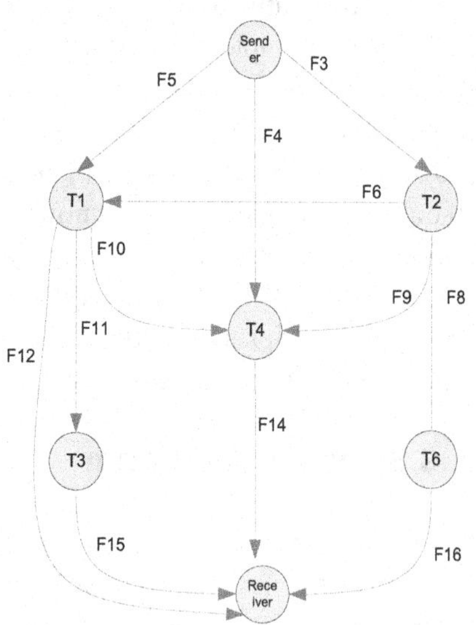

the partially selected path. The candidate trans-coding services set contains the trans-coding services that have input edges coming from any trans-coding service in the set VT. At the beginning of the algorithm, the set VT contains only the *sender* node, and CS contains all the other trans-coding services in the graph that are connected to *sender*, and also the *receiver*. In each iteration, the algorithm selects the trans-coding service T_i that, when using it, generates the highest user satisfaction. The user satisfaction is computed as an optimization function of the audio and video parameters for the output format for T_i, subject to the constraint of available bandwidth between T_i and its ancestor trans-coding service, and also subject to the remaining user's budget. T_i is then added to VT. The CS set is then updated with all the neighbor trans-coding services of T_i. The algorithm stops when the CS set is empty, or when the *Receiver* node is selected to be added to VT. The complete description of the algorithm is given in Figure 6.

As indicated in Step 2 and Step 8, the algorithm selects from CS the transcoder T_i that can generate the highest satisfaction value for the receiver. To compute the satisfaction value for each transcoder T_i in CS, the algorithm selects the QoS parameter values x_i that optimize the satisfaction function in Equa. 2, subject only to the constraint remaining user's budget and the bandwidth availability that connects T_i to T_{prev} in VT. i.e.

$$bandwith\_requirement(x_1..x_n) \leq Bandwidth\_AvailableBetween(T_i, T_{prev}). \quad (4)$$

Since each trans-coding service can only reduce the quality of the content, when the algorithm terminates, the algorithm would have computed the best path of trans-coding services from the *sender* to the *receiver*, and the user's satisfaction value computed on the last edge to the receiver node is the maximum value the user can achieve. To show this, assume that the selected path is the path $\{T_{11}, \ldots T_{1n}\}$ in Figure 7. If the path $\{T_{21}, \ldots T_{2m}\}$ is a better path, then T_{2m} should have converted the content into variant that is more appreciated by the user than the variant generated by T_{1n}. Since transcoders can only reduce the quality of content, all transcoders along the path $\{T_{21}, \ldots T_{2m}\}$, should have also produced a content with higher satisfaction function than the variant produce by T_{1n}, and hence all these transcoders should have been selected before T_{1n}, which contradicts with the assumption.

4.7. Example

In this section, we will present an example to show how the QoS path selection algorithm works. We will assume that the graph construction algorithm has generated the graph shown in Figure 8. The graph also shows the selected path with and without trans-coding service T_7 as part of the graph. The selected trans-coding services, user satisfaction, as well as the best current path produced by the algorithm are also shown in Table 1. Each row in the table shows the results for one iteration of the algorithm.

Figure 6. QoS selection algorithm

```
Step 1: // Let VT be the set of all considered trans-coding services.
        VT = {sender};
// Let CS be the set of all direct neighbor transcoders of all transcoders in VT
    CS = neighbor(sender);
        // Let user_budget be the amount of money the user is willing to pay
Step 2: // Each trans-coding service keeps a track of its parent trans-coding service. Let T_prev be the trans-coding services in CS connected to
        // T_i; Compute the perceived user's satisfaction for using all the trans-coding services in CS, subject to two constraints: the remaining
        // user budget and the available bandwidth between T_i and T_prev.
        For ∀ T_i ∈ CS
          Optimize( user_profile, input_format, output_format, Sat_T[i],
                    user_budget,cost,available_bandwith)
Step 3: // If there are no more transcoders to consider and the receivers can
        // not be reached from the sender through any transcoding path.
        if is_empty(CS) then
          TERMINATE(FAILURE)
Step 4: Select the trans-coding service T_i that has the highest satisfaction
        value Sat_T[i], for the user.
        CS = CS – { T_i };
Step 5: VT = VT + { T_i };
Step 6: Let T_i. previous_selected_transcoder = T_prev;
        T_i.accumulated_cost = T_i.previous.accumulated_cost + transcoding_and_transmission_cost [i];
Step 7: if T_i = receiver , then GOTO Step 10
Step 8: // compute the satisfaction for using all the neighboring transcoders of T_i and add them to CS
        For ∀ T_j ∈ neighbors( T_i );
          Optimize( user_profile, input_format, output_format, Sat_T[i], user_budget,cost[i],available_bandiwth)
          CS = CS ∪ {T_j };
Step 9: GOTO Step 3
Step 10:   Print the reverse path from the Receiver to the Sender by following the link "previous" of all transcoders, starting from the Receiver.
```

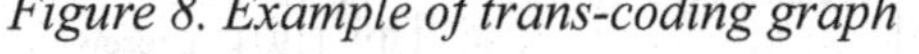

Figure 7. Graph selection

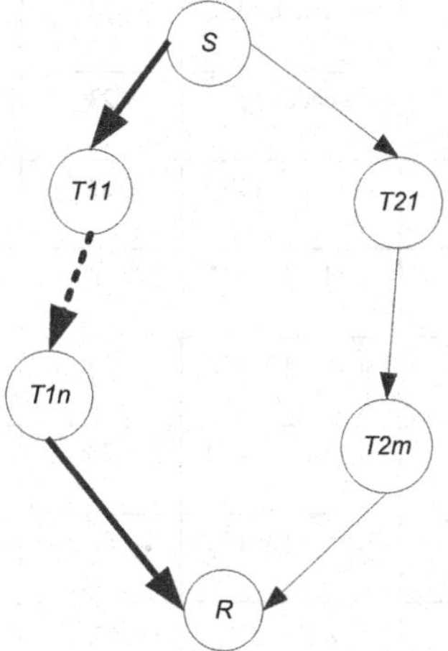

Figure 8. Example of trans-coding graph

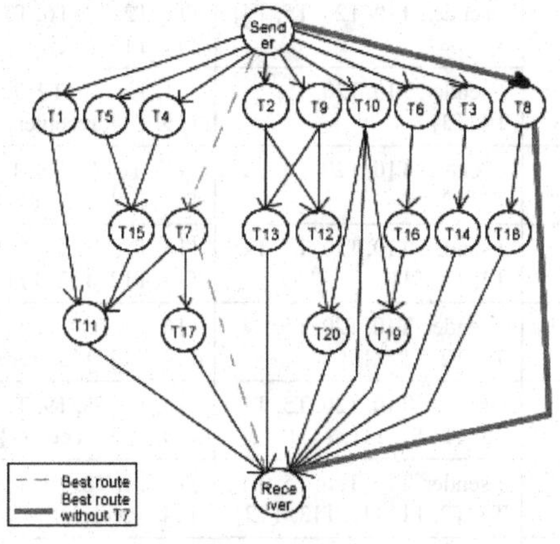

FUTURE RESEARCH DIRECTION

In this section, we will outline some potential directions for future research works.

In this chapter, we have not addressed the issues regarding autonomic service management of real-time multimedia services. One of the challenges is the efficient, autonomous management of these real-time content adaptation services in future generation networks. The autonomous service management is crucial for the self-management of real-time multimedia services. According to Ganek and Corbi of IBM (Ganek and Corbi, 2003), the autonomous or self-management aspects include self-optimizing, self-healing, self-configuring, and self-protecting. The existing approach and framework contributes towards a system that is not fully autonomic in all four management aspects.

Current, we are looking at nature-inspired automatic service management solution that is inspired from the Bee colony metaphor. The allegory comprises how bee agents mimic functional services related to multimedia applications, in order to autonomously monitor and configure multimedia services. The objective of this research is to ensure complete autonomic behaviour of the four main management activities (configuration, repair, optimization and protection) of an autonomous system. Such direction could enable customization of the service for the current and future generation network conditions.

Table 1. Results for each step of the path selection algorithm

Round	Considered Set (VT)	Candidate set (CS)	Selected trans-coding service	Selected Path	Delivered Frame Rate	User satisfaction
1	{ *sender* }	{T1, T2, T3, T4, T5, T6, T7, T8, T9, T10}	T10	*sender*,T10	30	1.00
2	{ *sender*, T10}	{T1, T2, T3, T4, T5, T6, T7, T8, T9, T19, T20, *receiver*}	T20	*sender*,T10,T20	30	1.00
3	{ *sender*, T10, T20}	{T1, T2, T3, T4, T5, T6, T7, T8, T9, T19, *receiver*}	T5	*sender*,T5	27	0.90
4	{ sender, T10, T20, T5}	{T1, T2, T3, T4, T6, T7, T8, T9, T19, T15, receiver}	T4	sender,T4	27	0.90
5	{ sender, T10, T20, T5, T4}	{T1, T2, T3, T6, T7, T8, T9, T19, T15, receiver}	T3	sender,T3	23	0.76
6	{ sender, T10, T20, T5, T4, T3}	{T1, T2, T6, T7, T8, T9, T19, T15, T14, receiver}	T2	sender,T2	23	0.76
7	{ sender, T10, T20, T5, T4, T3, T2}	{T1, T6, T7, T8, T9, T19, T15, T14, T12, T13, receiver}	T1	sender,T1	23	0.76
8	{ sender, T10, T20, T5, T4, T3, T2, T1}	{T6, T7, T8, T9, T19, T15, T14, T12, T13, T11, receiver}	T11	sender,T1, T11	23	0.76
9	{ sender, T10, T20, T5, T4, T3, T2, T1, T11}	{T6, T7, T8, T9, T19, T15, T14, T12, T13, receiver}	T13	sender,T2, T13	23	0.76
10	{ sender, T10, T20, T5, T4, T3, T2, T1, T11, T13}	{T6, T7, T8, T9, T19, T15, T14, T12, receiver}	T12	sender,T2, T12	23	0.76
11	{ sender, T10, T20, T5, T4, T3, T2, T1, T11, T13, T12}	{T6, T7, T8, T9, T19, T15, T14, receiver}	T14	sender,T3, T14	23	0.76
12	{ sender, T10, T20, T5, T4, T3, T2, T1, T11, T13, T12, T14}	{T6, T7, T8, T9, T19, T15, receiver}	T8	sender, T8	20	0.66
13	{ sender, T10, T20, T5, T4, T3, T2, T1, T11, T13, T12, T14, T8}	{T6, T7, T9, T19, T15, receiver}	T7	sender, T7	20	0.66
14	{ sender, T10, T20, T5, T4, T3, T2, T1, T11, T13, T12, T14, T8, T7}	{T6, T9, T19, T15, receiver}	T6	sender, T6	20	0.66
15	{ sender, T10, T20, T5, T4, T3, T2, T1, T11, T13, T12, T14, T8, T7, T6}	{T9, T19, T15, receiver}	receiver	sender, T7, receiver	20	0.66

5. CONCLUSION

Content adaptation is a natural solution to address the problem of heterogeneity of Internet clients and users. In this chapter, we have presented a solution to the problem of heterogeneity which takes into consideration the capabilities of the client devices, network connectivity, content format, and users' preferences. An important part of the framework is the QoS path selection algorithm that decides on the chain of adaptation services to add and the configuration parameters for each service. The decision is based on the profile of communicating devices, network connectivity, exchanged content formats, context description, and available adaptation services.

6. REFERENCES

Björk, S., Holmquist, L.E., Redström, J., Bretan, I., Danielsson, R., Karlgren, J., & Franzén, K., (1999). WEST: a Web browser for small terminals. *Proceedings of the 12th annual ACM symposium on User interface software and technology* (pp.187-196). Asheville, North Carolina, United States.

Chandra, S., & Ellis, C.S. (1999). JPEG Compression Metric as a Quality Aware Image Transcoding. *Second Usenix Symposium on Internet Technologies and Systems* (USITS '99). (pp. 81–92) Boulder, CO.

Chandra, S., Ellis, C., & Vahdat, A. (2000). Application-Level Differentiated Multimedia Web Services Using Quality Aware Transcoding, *IEEE Journal on Selected Areas in Communications*, *18*(12), 2265–2544.

Chang, C.Y., & Chen, M.S. (2002). Exploring Aggregate Effect with Weighted Transcoding Graphs for Efficient Cache Replacement in Transcoding Proxies. *Proceedings of the 18th IEEE International Conference on Data Engineering (ICDE-O)* (pp. 383—392). San Jose, CA, USA.

El-Khatib, K., & Bochmann, G. v. (2003, December). *Profiles in Content Adaptation.* Technical report. University of Ottawa, Canada.

El-Khatib, K., Zhang, Z. E., Hadibi, N. & Bochmann, G. v. (2004). Personal and Service Mobility in Ubiquitous Computing Environments. *Journal of Wireless communications and Mobile Computing, 4*(6), 595-607.

Fisher, B., Agelidis, G., Dill, J., Tan, P., Collaud, G., & Jones, C. (1997). CZWeb: Fish-Eye Views for Visualizing the World-Wide Web. In *Proceeding of the 7th Int. Conf. on Human-Computer Interaction (HCI International '97)* (pp. 719-722). Elsevier, Amsterdam.

Floyd, R., & Housel, B. (1998). Mobile Web Access Using eNetwork Web Express. *IEEE Personal Communications, 5*(5), 47–52.

Fox, A., Gribble, S.D., Chawathe, Y., Brewer, E.A., & Gauthier, P. (1997). Cluster-Based Scalable Network Services. In *Proceeding of the 16th ACM Symp. On Operating Systems Principles* (pp. 78–91). Saint-Malo, France.

Fox, A., Gribble, S.D., & Chawathe, Y. (1998). Adapting to Network and Client Variation Using Infrastructural Proxies: Lessons and Perspectives. (1998). *IEEE Personal Communications, 5*(4) 10–19. Springer Berlin/Heidelberg.

Ganek, A. G., & Corbi, T. A. (2003). The dawning of the autonomic computing era. *IBM Systems J., 42*(1), 5-18.

Guttman, E., Perkins, C., Veizades, J., & Day, M. (1999). Service Location Protocol. Version 2. http://ietf.org/rfc/rfc2608.txt.

Hafid, A., & Bochmann, G.v., (1996). Quality of Service Negotiation in News-on-Demand Systems: an Implementation. In *Proceedings of the Third International Workshop on Protocols for Multimedia Systems* (pp. 299-315). Springer Berlin/Heidelberg.

Han, R., Bhagwat, P., LaMaire, R., Mummert, T., Perret, V., & Rubas, J. (1998). Dynamic adaptation in an image trans-coding proxy for mobile WWW browsing. *IEEE Personal Communication, 5*(6).

JINI network technology (TM) (1998). Http: // java.sun.com/product/JINI

Katchabaw, M., Lutfiyya, H., & Bauer, M. (1998). *Driving resource management with application-level quality of service specifications,* (pp. 83-91) ACM Press.

Lei Z., & Georganas N.D. (2001). Context-based Media Adaptation in Pervasive Computing. On *Proceeding Can.Conf. on Electr. and Comp. Engg.* (pp. 913-918). Toronto, Canada.

Lum, W.Y., & Lau, F.C.M. (2002) On Balancing Between Trans-coding Overhead and Spatial Consumption in Content Adaptation. *Mobicom 2002,* (pp. 239 - 250). Atlanta, USA.

Mohan, R., Smith, J.R., & Li, C.S. (1999). Adapting Multimedia Internet Content for Universal Access. *IEEE Trans. on Multimedia, 1*(1), 104-114.

MPEG-7. http://www.chiariglione.org/mpeg/standards/ mpeg-7/mpeg-7.htm. Accessed on Jan 10, 2007.

MPEG-21 (2001): International Standards Organisation. Information technology – multimedia framework (MPEG-21) – part 1: Vision, technologies and strategy. ISO/IEC 21000-1. Accessed on Jan 10, 2007.

Ng, C.W., Tan, P.Y., & Cheng, H. (2001). *Quality of Service Extension to IRML.* IETF INTERNET-DRAFT, 'draft-ng-opes-irmlqos-00.txt'.

Poellabauer, C., Abbasi, H., & Schwan, K. (2002). Cooperative run-time management of adaptive applications and distributed resources. In *Proceeding of the Tenth ACM International conference on Multimedia,* (pp. 402-411) ACM Press.

Richards, A., Rogers, G., Witana, V., & Antoniades, M. (1998). Mapping user level QoS from a single parameter. In *Second IFIP/IEEE International Conference on Management of Multimedia Networks and Services.* (pp. 14-20). Versailles, France.

Smith, J. R., Mohan, R., & Li, C.-S. (1999). Scalable Multimedia Delivery for Pervasive Computing. *ACM Multimedia,* (pp. 131 – 140). Orlando, Florida, United States.

WML: Wireless Markup Language (2001). *Wireless Markup Language (WML) 2.0 Document Type Definition.*

WSDL: Web Service Description Language (2002). http://www.w3.org/TR/wsdl.

Wu, D., Hou, Y.T., & Zhang, Y. (2001). Scalable Video Coding and Transport over Broad-band Wireless Networks. *Proceeding of the IEEE, 89*(1), 6-20.

ADDITIONAL READING

Ahmed, I., Wei, X., Sun, Y., & Zhang, Y. Q. (2005). Video transcoding: an overview of various techniques and research issues. IEEE Trans. Multimedia, *7*(5), 793-804.

Ardon S., et al. (n.d.). MARCH: a distributed content adaptation architecture. *Intl. J. Commun. Syst., 16*, 97-115.

Dey, A. K. (2001). Understanding and Using Context. *Springer Personal and Ubiquitous Computing, 5*(1), 4-7.

El Saddik, & Hossain, M. S. (2007). Multimedia Streaming for wireless communication. In B. Furht (Ed.), *Encyclopedia of Wireless and Mobile Communications.* CRC Press, Taylor & Francis Group.

El Saddik, A., & Hossain, M. S. (2006). Multimedia content repurposing. In B. Furht, (Ed.),

Encyclopedia of Multimedia. Berlin, Germany: Springer Verlag.

Han, J. R. et al.(1998, December). Dynamic adaptation in an image transcoding proxy for mobile WWW browsing. *IEEE Personal Commun., 5*(6).

Han, R., & Smith, J. R. (1999). Internet Transcoding for Universal Access. In J. Gibson (Ed.), *Multimedia Communications Handbook*.

Hossain, M. S., & El Saddik, A. (2008). A Biologically Inspired Multimedia Content Repurposing System in Heterogeneous Network Environments. *ACM/Springer Multimedia Systems J., 14*(3), 135-144.

Hossain, M. S., Alamri, A., & El Saddik, A. (2007). A framework for qos-aware multimedia service selection for wireless clients. In *Proc. the 3rd ACM Workshop on Wireless Multimedia Networking and Performance Modeling (WMuNeP 07)*, Chania, Crete Island, Greece, October 22 - 22.

Liang, Y., Chebil, F., & Islam, A. (2006). Compressed domain transcoding solutions for MPEG-4 visual simple profile and H.263 baseline videos in 3GPP services and applications. *IEEE Trans. Consum. Electron., 52*(2), 507-515.

Lum, W. Y., & Lau, F. C. M. (2002). On Balancing between Transcoding Overhead and Spatial Consumption in Content Adaptation. In *Proc. MobiCom'02*, Atlanta, Georgia, USA, Sep. 23-26. (pp. 239-250).

Maheshwari, A., Sharma, A., Ramamritham, K., & Shenoy, P. (2002). TransSquid:Transcoding and caching proxy for heterogeneous e-commerce environments. In *Proc. 12th IEEE Int. Workshop Research Issues in Data Engg*, San Jose, California, USA, 26 Feb. - 1 March, 2002, (pp. 50-59).

Mao, M., So, H. W., Kang, B., & Katz, R. H. (2001). Network support for mobile multimedia. In *Proc. 11th Intl. Workshop on Network and Operating System Support for Digital Audio and Video (NOSSDAV-2001)*, New York, USA.

Nahrstedt, K., & Balke, W. T. (2004). A taxonomy for multimedia service composition. In *Proc. 12th ACM Conf. Multimedia (ACMMM04)*, New York, NY, USA, 10–16 October 2004, (pp. 88-95).

Nahrstedt, K., & Balke, W. T. (2005). Towards building large scale multimedia systems and applications: Challenges and status. In *Proc. the First ACM Intl.Workshop Multimedia Service Composition*, Hilton, Singapore, (pp. 3-10).

Nguyen, V. A., & Tan, Y. P. (2005). Efficient video transcoding between H.263 and H.264/AVC standards. In *Proc. IEEE Intl. Symposium on Circuits and Systems (ISCAS'05)*, Kobe, Japan, May 23-26.

Richards, A., Rogers, G., Witana, V., & Antoniades, M. (1998, November). Mapping user level QoS from a single parameter. IIn *2nd IFIP/IEEE Intl. Conf. Manage. Multimedia Networks and Services*, Versailles.

Shin I., & Koh, K. (2004). Hybrid Transcoding for QoS Adaptive Video-on-Demand Services. *IEEE Trans.Consumer Electronics, 50*(2).

Smith, J. R., Mohan, R., & Li, C. S. (1999). Scalable Multimedia Delivery for Pervasive Computing. In *Proc. ACM Multimedia' 99*, Orlando, FL, USA, Oct.30 - Nov.5.

Vetro, A., Xin, J., & Sun, H. (2005). Error resillence video transcoding for wireless communications. *IEEE Wirel. Commun, 12*(4), 14-21.

Vukovic, M., & Robinson, P. (2004). Application Modeling for Context Awareness. Building and Evaluating Ubiquitous System Software. IEEE Pervasive Computing Mag., 3(3), pp. 59-59.

Chapter IX
Analysis of Service Compatibility:
Complexity and Computation

Ken Q. Pu
University of Ontario Institute of Technology, Canada

ABSTRACT

In this chapter, the authors apply type-theoretic techniques to the service description and composition verification. A flexible type system is introduced for modeling instances and mappings of semi-structured data, and is demonstrated to be effective in modeling a wide range of data services, ranging from relational database queries to web services for XML. Type-theoretic analysis and verification are then reduced to the problem of type unification. Some (in)tractability results of the unification problem and the expressiveness of their proposed type system are presented in this chapter. Finally, the auhtors construct a complete unification algorithm which runs in EXP-TIME in the worst case, but runs in polynomial time for a large family of unification problems rising from practical type analysis of service compositions.

INTRODUCTION

Service engineering has been of great interest for both researchers as well as practitioners. As part of the Web 2.0 movement of reforming the World Wide Web, service-oriented computing is a fundamental platform to support novel features such as web services (e.g. Curbera et al. (2005)), messaging services (e.g. Maheshwari et al.(2004)), multimedia distribution (e.g Chawathe (2003),) and dynamic content management and database integration (e.g. Deutsch et al. (2004)). A common approach to the problem of service description and service integration is through functional modeling of the underlying data model and the input/output characteristics of the available services, as discussed by Narayanan & McIlraith (2002); Pu et al. (2006). For the purpose of verification and au-

Copyright © 2009, IGI Global, distributing in print or electronic forms without written permission of IGI Global is prohibited.

tomatically discovering relevant and composable services, it becomes necessary to reason about the services both semantically and syntactically.

In this chapter, we present a type-theoretic approach to model the type information of data instances and service functions using a flexible type system. Unlike existing description frameworks such as description logic presented by Baader et al. (2003), and RDF defined by RDF Core Working Group, our proposed type system is used to express structural information of the data instances and the service functions. By extending existing nested record type systems from the programming language community, our type system can be used to for a wide range of data models:

- Semi-structured documents such as XML,
- Structured data such as relational and multidimensional data warehouses.

Furthermore, with the help of a rich set of type variables, we are able to express a wide range of data services:

- Web services
- Query services such as queries in SQL
- Analytical services such as aggregation queries

It is important to incorporate traditional databases and their query languages, such as legacy relational database management systems (RDBMS), in the SOA framework because today's services still rely heavily on relational back-ends. Since our proposed type system is expressive enough to describe structured data and structured query constructs, it can be used to reason about the composibility between services and relational data sources.

A type system for service-oriented architectures (SOA) brings exciting possibilities of applying static analysis techniques from programming languages. For instance, type checking is the verification of input/output compatibility between composed services before runtime. Type checking is now a standard feature of all modern compilers. However, in order to apply type checking to compositions of web services, database queries and other services, one must first have a type system capable of expressing the type information of all the service providers. Another well-known type analysis is type inference. Services can often handle data of different structures – this is known as polymorphism. When using polymorphic services, one is required to instantiate the polymorphic input type signature to the actual input data. Type inference is a static procedure which automatically infers the necessary instantiation so that the resulting service invocation is free of type errors. As we will demonstrate, type inference can be applied to the problem of service discovery and automatic service composition. Of course, due to syntactic and semantic ambiguity, service composition cannot be inferred uniquely, however the type inference algorithm, as we will demonstrate in this chapter, offers the following salient features:

- Assist the user with top admissible compositions – a feature similar to method completion in modern integrated development environment (IDE).
- Verify the correctness of existing interoperability of multiple services and backend data sources.
- Complete partially formulated compositions. Services typically have complex input/output structures. User can assist the composition inference process by partially specifying the correspondence between the input and output types, and the type inference algorithm can complete the rest whenever it is possible.

In this chapter, we formally present the proposed type system for SOA, and demonstrate how it can be used to modeling various services. We also present a number of theoretical results on the expressiveness of our type system, and the computational complexity of the static type analysis including type checking and type inference.

Outline of chapter

In Section *The Type System*, we formally define the type expressions in our type system. Type expressions describe nested record structures with collection types. In addition, user can use type variables in the expressions to represent unspecified parts of the expression. Those type variables are used extensively for polymorphic services. We formally define type substitutions and functional symbols which are used to model web services and data query languages. In Section *Types and Functions in SOA*, we show by example how the formalism is applied to model both the data as well as services found in the service-oriented architecture. We show how data ranging from XML to relational tables and multidimensional cubes can be properly typed by our type system. In Section *Type Checking, Inference and Unification*, we discuss type analysis procedures of type checking and type inference, and show how both problems can be reduced to solving systems of equations of type expressions, which is commonly referred to as unification. Section *Computational Complexity of Unification* states the computational complexity of the general unification problem for our type system. We also present the theoretical results on a number of restricted unification problems, ranging from NP-complete to polynomial time. The computational issues are discussed in Section A, Algorithm for Type Matching by Unification where we present a complete unification algorithm and its run-time analysis.

BACKGROUND

Type analysis originated from research of programming languages. While web services and semi-structured data bring new challenges, it is important for us to survey some important work in type analysis of programming languages that are most relevant to the type system presented in this chapter.

Much work R′emy(1989,1994); Cardelli & Mitchell (1991) has been done to include integrating polymorphic record types into functional programming languages such as ML. However, the main interest there was to study extensible records and inheritance of record objects. So those record type systems and their type inference algorithms are not suitable for the purpose of typing services.

The heart of our type inference algorithm is the unification algorithm presented in previous section. Unification algorithms have received much attention by researchers Paterson & Wegman (1978); Kapur & Narendran (1992); Carpenter (1992); Dantsin & Voronkov (1999) from different areas. Unfortunately due to the distinct requirements we have on the unifiers, the unification algorithms in existing literature do not directly apply. For instance, syntactic unification Paterson & Wegman (1978); Martelli & Montanari (1982) can only match two type expression with only field variables exactly, and they do not take into account of the order invariance of the attributes, nor supports attribute and row variables. Associative-Commutative (AC) unification Kapur & Narendran (1992) can be used to take into account of the order invariance nature of the attributes. One can also encode row variables as term variables in AC unification. However, it does not take into account of the syntactic requirements of type expression for SOA, such as distinct attribute names in a record, etc. On a related issue, it has been shown that there can be double-exponentially many AC unifiers, so any complete AC unification algorithm is double-exponential in the worst case, whereas, for our unification algorithm, there exists at most single exponentially many unifiers. Finally, we note that Dantsin & Voronkov (1999) studied unification of trees with sets and bags in the context of logical programming. They allow trees with set or bag terms. However, their unification algorithm also has several limitations which make it not directly applicable. Though they support row variables, there is nothing similar to attribute variables, and more importantly they do not support union of two row variables.

THE TYPE SYSTEM

The type system we use to describe data is based on record type systems proposed by Wand (1987); R'emy (1989,1994); Cardelli & Mitchell(1991) from programming languages with suitable adaptation to meet the needs of typing database query languages. A type expression, or simply a type, is a record structure characterized by a set of attributes, each of which is typed by some other type expression. These type expressions form the functional signatures (namely the input-output characteristics) of query constructs. In order to capture the polymorphic nature of the query constructs, we allow partially specified type expressions with type variables of various kinds.

Type Expressions

We allow four types of variables:

- $\mathbf{V}^{attr} = \{u_1, u_2, ...\}$ are the attribute variables which represent unspecified attribute names.
- $\mathbf{V}^{row} = \{\mathbf{x}^1, \mathbf{x}^2, ...\}$ are the row variables which represent general unspecified types.
- $\mathbf{V}^{fld} = \{y_1, y_2, ...\}$ are the field variables which represent unspecified field of a record.
- $\mathbf{V}^{coll} = \{\underline{coll}_1, \underline{coll}_2, ...\}$ are the collection variables representing unspecified collection types.

By definition, the four families of variables are pair wise disjoint. Collectively, we refer to these variables as type variables, denoted by $\mathbf{V}^{type} = \mathbf{V}^{attr} \cup \mathbf{V}^{row} \cup \mathbf{V}^{fld} \cup \mathbf{V}^{coll}$. We also assume that at our disposal, there are constant attribute names $\mathbf{A}_0$ and primitive types $\mathbf{T}_0$ = {numeric, string, date,...}. We allow three types of collections, **Coll** = {Set, Bag, List}. The type expressions are built in the following way.

Definition 1 (Type Expressions).

$$T^{rec} ::= [(T^{fld}|V^{row})^*]$$

$$T^{fld} ::= (A_0|V^{attr}) : (T^0|T^{coll}|T^{rec})$$

$$\text{coll} ::= (\text{COLL}|V^{coll})$$

$$T ::= T^{rec}|T^{fld}|T^{coll}$$

Given a field type $f \in \mathbf{T}^{fld}$ in the form of $(\boldsymbol{a}:\boldsymbol{t})$, we refer to $\boldsymbol{a}$ the attribute of f, written $\mathbf{A}(f)$ and $\boldsymbol{t}$ the type of f, written $\mathbf{T}(f)$. For a type $t \in \mathbf{T}^{rec}$ in the form of $(f_1, f_2, ..., f_n, \mathbf{x}_1, ..., \mathbf{x}_k)$, the set of fields of t is defined as $\mathbf{Fields}(t) = \{f_1, f_2, ..., f_n\}$, and the row variables of t as $\mathbf{V}^{row}(t) = \{\mathbf{x}_1, ..., \mathbf{x}_k\}$. We require that for all types $t \in \mathbf{T}^{rec}$, attribute names of fields of t must be distinct. The unique type that does not contain fields or variables is denoted by unit. A type is polymorphic if it makes use of type variables, and concrete otherwise.

Variables in polymorphic type expressions represent unspecified parts which can be instantiated in the future. Attribute variables $\mathbf{V}^{attr}$ represent anonymous attributes – they can only be instantiated to other attribute variables or attribute names. Row variables $\mathbf{V}^{row}$ can be instantiated into zero or more fields or primitive types. Finally collection variables $\mathbf{V}^{coll}$ correspond to unknown kinds of collection. How type variables can be instantiated will be formalized in Definition 2 below. First, we demonstrate the expressiveness of the type system by example.

Example 1. Consider the following type expressions in $\mathbf{T}^{rec}$. They are shown vertically as trees (see Box 1).

The type $\mathbf{s}_0$ is a concrete type that describes a flat record with three fields and their types. The type $\mathbf{s}_1$ expresses the type of a relational table (set of records) with the table name **T1** and at least three columns *Name*, *Income* and *Expense*. According to the type $\mathbf{s}_1$, the table can be extended with additional columns. The type $\mathbf{s}_2$ describes

Box 1.

$$s_0 = \begin{bmatrix} \text{NAME}: \textit{string} \\ \text{INCOME}: \textit{numeric} \\ \text{EXPENSE}: \textit{numeric} \end{bmatrix} \qquad s_1 = \text{T1}:\text{SET}\begin{bmatrix} \text{NAME}: \textit{string} \\ \text{INCOME}: \textit{numeric} \\ \text{EXPENSE}: \textit{numeric} \\ x^{other} \end{bmatrix}$$

$$s2 = \text{T2:SET}\begin{bmatrix} \text{NAME:string} \\ \text{INCOME}: x^1 \\ \text{EXPENSE}: x^1 \\ u^{\text{other}}: \textit{string} \end{bmatrix} \qquad s_3 = u^1 \;\; \text{SET}\begin{bmatrix} \text{NAME}: \textit{string} \\ \text{INCOME}: \textit{numeric} \\ \text{EXPENSES}: \text{SET}\begin{bmatrix} \text{ACCOUNT}: \textit{string} \\ \text{AMOUNT}: \textit{numeric} \end{bmatrix} \end{bmatrix}$$

a table **T2** with exactly four columns. The first three columns are named *Name, Income* and *Expense*, and the last is an anonymous column represented by the attribute variable u^{other} which is of type string. Note also, the types of column *Income* and *Expense* are unspecified, but they must be of the same type because a common row variable $\mathbf{x}^1$ is used as the type of both fields. Finally the last type $\mathbf{s}_3$ describes an anonymous nested relation.

The order of the fields and row variables of a type does not matter, so two types $\mathbf{t}_1$ and $\mathbf{t}_2$ are equal if they only differ by permutation of the fields or variables.

Functional Symbols

Functional symbols represent mappings which transform one or more input data structures described by some type expression to an output data structure. Higher-order functions can take other functions as inputs and return a function as an output.

A first order functional symbol is of the form: $f: s \rightarrow t$ where s and $t \in \mathbf{T}^{\text{rec}}$. We refer to s and t as the domain and codomain of f respectively. The semantics is that f is the name of a function whose input value must be of the type s and output value is of the type t. A second-order functional symbol g with arity n is of the form:

$$g: (s_1 \rightarrow t_1), (s_2 \rightarrow t_2), \ldots, (s_n \rightarrow t_n) \rightarrow (s_0 \rightarrow t_0)$$

The semantics is that g is a mapping from a tuple $(f_1, f_2, \ldots, f_n)$ of first order functions to a first order function $g(f_1, f_2, \ldots, f_n)$. The input functions f_i need to be of the type $s_i \rightarrow t_i$ for all $1 \leq i \leq n$, and the output function is of the type $s_0 \rightarrow t_0$.

A functional symbol is polymorphic if its signature contains type variables, and concrete otherwise. A first order function is a constant if its domain is the type unit. An functional alphabet Σ is simply a collection of typed functional symbols.

Type Substitutions

Definition 2 (Type Substitutions).

A type substitution is a partial mapping

$\theta: \mathbf{V}^{\text{type}} \rightarrow (\mathbf{V}^{\text{attr}} \cup \mathbf{A}_0) \cup (\mathbf{T}_0 \cup \mathbf{T}) \cup (\text{COLL} \cup \mathbf{V}^{\text{coll}})$

such that
for all $u \in \text{V}^{\text{attr}}$, if $\theta(u)$ is defined, then $\theta(u) \in \mathbf{V}^{\text{attr}} \cup \mathbf{A}_0$,
for all $x \in \text{V}^{\text{row}}$, if $\theta(x)$ is defined, then $\theta(x) \in \mathbf{T}_0 \cup \mathbf{T}^{\text{coll}} \cup \mathbf{T}^{\text{rec}}$, and
for all $c \in \text{V}^{\text{coll}}$, if $\theta(c)$ is defined, then $\theta(c) \in \mathbf{Coll} \cup \mathbf{V}^{\text{coll}}$.

The domain dom(θ) is the set of type variables for which θ is defined. Given a type substitution θ, we define a partial mapping θ* on T as:

- For $t \in \mathbf{T}^{rec}$, $\theta^*(t) = \{\theta^*(f) : f \in \mathbf{Fields}(t)\} \cup \{\theta(\mathbf{x}) : \mathbf{x} \in \mathbf{V}^{row}(t)\}$,

$$\theta^*(f) = \begin{cases} \theta(a) : \theta^*(t) & \text{if } a \in V^{attr} \\ a : \theta^*(t) & \text{otherwise} \end{cases}$$

- For field $f = a: t \in \mathbf{T}^{fld}$,
- Finally, for a collection type coll(t), $\theta^*(\text{coll}(t)) = \text{coll}(\theta^*(t))$.

We say that a type substitution θ is valid with respect to a type expression $t \in \mathbf{T}^{rec}$ if $\theta^*(t) \in \mathbf{T}^{rec}$. Unless otherwise specified, we simply write θ^* as θ for brevity.

Definition 3 (Instances of Polymorphic Types).

Let $t \in \mathbf{T}^{rec}$ be a polymorphic type. An instance of t is a type $t' \in \mathbf{T}^{rec}$ such that there exists some type substitution θ that is valid with respect to t and $\theta(t) = t'$. An instance is polymorphic if it contains type variables, and concrete otherwise.

Example 2. Consider the type expression ***t*** and a substitution θ as follows. The instance $\theta(\boldsymbol{t})$ is shown below.

$$t = a : \begin{bmatrix} b : x^1 \\ x^1 \end{bmatrix} \quad \theta_1 = \left\{ x^1 \mapsto \begin{bmatrix} a : string \\ c : numeric \end{bmatrix} \right. \quad \theta_1(t) = a : \begin{bmatrix} b : \begin{bmatrix} a : string \\ c : numeric \end{bmatrix} \\ a : string \\ c : numeric \end{bmatrix}$$

Since $\theta_1(t) \in \mathbf{T}^{rec}$, the substitution θ_1 is valid with respect to ***t***, and $\theta_1(t)$ is an instance of ***t***. Now consider the substitution: $\theta_2 = \{\mathbf{x}_1 \rightarrow \text{string}\}$, and $\theta_3 = \{\mathbf{x}_1 \rightarrow [\text{b: string}]\}$.

Then

$$\theta_2(t) = a : \begin{bmatrix} b : string \\ string \end{bmatrix} \quad \theta_3(t) = a : \begin{bmatrix} b : [b : string \\ b : string \end{bmatrix}$$

Since neither $\theta_2(t)$ nor $\theta_3(t)$ are not valid type expression in $\mathbf{T}^{rec}$, θ_2 and θ_3 are not valid substitutions with respect to ***t***.

Type substitutions can be composed in a natural way. Given two substitutions θ_1 and θ_2, the composition $\theta_2 \circ \theta_1$ is defined as a substitution as:

$$dom(\theta_2 \circ \theta_1) = dom(\theta_2) \cup dom(\theta_1)$$

$$(\theta_2 \circ \theta_1)(x) = \begin{cases} \theta_1(x) & \text{if } x \in dom(\theta_1) - dom(\theta_2) \\ \theta_2(\theta_1(x)) & \text{if } x \in dom(\theta_1) \cap dom(\theta_2) \\ \theta_2(x) & \text{if } x \in dom(\theta_2) - dom(\theta_1) \end{cases}$$

Type substitutions are also ordered by a preorder: $\theta_1 \leq \theta_2$ if there exists some third substitution θ_3 such that $\theta_2 = \theta_3 \circ \theta_1$, in which case, we say that θ_1 is more general than θ_2.

TYPES AND FUNCTIONS IN SOA

In the service-oriented architecture, data comes in various forms: some are semi-structured, some are relational, and some are multidimensional. Available services are also as diverse as the data: web services transform semi-structured data, the structured query language (SQL) processes relational data, and OLAP analytic aggregations process multidimensional data. In this section, we demonstrate how our proposed type system can be used to model both data as well as functional services in a SOA setting.

Modeling Non-Recursive Semi-Structured Data

In this section, we describe how our type system can be used to express structures of non-recursive semi-structured data such as XML documents described by non-recursive Document Type Definition (DTD). By non-recursiveness, we mean that nodes of the XML document do not refer to itself as a descendant. It is well-known from studies by Barbosa et al.(2005) that nearly all DTD and XML documents found on the Internet are non-recursive. Consider a sample DTD shown in figure. It is not difficult to see that the DTD can be abstracted in our type system by the type expression shown in Figure 1.

Remarks:

We have not included DTD attributes in our example because they can always be thought of as special children nodes – in fact, they are special children nodes in the Document Object Model (DOM). We used the collection type **List** to model list of nodes which all have identical structure, e.g. the type of the body field is a list of paragraphs, **para**. The field **para**, in turn, is a primitive type: *string*. The semantics is that **List** includes the empty list, corresponding to the regular expression **para***. If one is to enforce non-empty lists, the DTD will use **para**$^+$, which can then be rewritten as **para,para***. The latter regular expression **para,para*** can be expressed in our type system.

The semantics of our type system is that the ordering of the fields do not matter, but in the case of XML, the ordering of fields do matter (even though, in practice, they don't). So at first glance, one may suggest that the proposed type system needs to be augmented with additional constructs to specify ordering, but this is not the case. In later section, we will show how the proposed type system is sufficient to express ordered tuples without additional constructs.

Modeling Web Services

Web services can be seen as collections of mappings of XML documents. They may have internal states (such as database-update services), but all web services can be abstracted by functional symbols with specific input/output types. Consider a web service function which takes books as input and returns the online bookstore with the lowest price. It can be modeled as:

$$\text{bargin}: \begin{bmatrix} \text{TITLE}: \textit{string} \\ \text{ISBN}: \textit{string} \\ x^{\text{other}} \end{bmatrix} \rightarrow \begin{bmatrix} \text{BOOKSTORE}: \textit{string} \\ \text{PRICE}: \textit{numeric} \\ \text{URL}: \textit{string} \end{bmatrix}$$

Observe that bargain service is polymorphic because it can be applied to different types of inputs – any XML fragment with the title and ISBN field will suffice.

One may have noticed that there are important standard features in modern type systems which we have not included: tuples, enumeration and union. Those features are included as first-class

Figure 1. Mapping XML DTD to a type expression

```
<!ELEMENT note (to, from, heading, body)>
<!ELEMENT from (name)>
<!ELEMENT to (name)>
<!ELEMENT heading (#PCDATA)>
<!ELEMENT body (para*)>
<!ELEMENT para (#PCDATA)>
<!ELEMENT name (lastname, firstname)>
```

$$\begin{bmatrix} \text{from}: \begin{bmatrix} \text{lastname}: \textit{string} \\ \text{firstname}: \textit{string} \end{bmatrix} \\ \text{to}: \begin{bmatrix} \text{lastname}: \textit{string} \\ \text{firstname}: \textit{string} \end{bmatrix} \\ \text{heading}: \textit{string} \\ \text{body}: \text{List}(\text{para}: \textit{string}) \end{bmatrix}$$

type constructs in XML Schema. Fortunately, we do not need to augment our type system with additional constructions to express these two features. In this section, we demonstrate how the existing type system is sufficient to express tuples, enumerations and unions.

Expressing Tuples

Similar to record types, tuple types can be seen as a collection of type expressions: $<\mathbf{e}_1,\mathbf{e}_2,\ldots,\mathbf{e}_n>$. In records, individual type expressions $\mathbf{e}_i$ are named by the attribute name ATTR_i, whereas, in tuple types, the type expressions $\{\mathbf{e}_i\}$ are simply ordered from left to right. In our framework, we do not directly support ordering among fields of a record. However, using distinct attribute names, we can simulate tuple types. Given a tuple type:

$$\left(\begin{bmatrix}\mathrm{TITLE}:\textit{string}\\ \mathrm{ISBN}:\textit{string}\end{bmatrix},\mathrm{NAME}:\textit{string}\right),$$

we can construct the following record:

$$\begin{bmatrix}1:\begin{bmatrix}\mathrm{TITLE}:\textit{string}\\ \mathrm{ISBN}:\textit{string}\end{bmatrix}\\ 2:[\mathrm{NAME}:\textit{string}\end{bmatrix}$$

The ordering information is saved in the distinct attribute names: 1,2.

Expressing Enumeration

Enumeration is a special type which states that data value can only be one of many values. For instance, in the Java programming language, one can declare an enumeration type by

enum Choices {candy, coffee, chocolate};

Enumeration is also useful for polymorphic attribute names of certain fields. For instance, one may want to state that a book record must have at least an attribute with the name *title* or *ISBN*. This can be done by enumeration on the attribute:

$$BOOK:\begin{bmatrix}u^{\mathrm{name}}:\textit{string}\\ x^{\mathrm{other}}\end{bmatrix}$$

where $u^{\mathrm{name}}\in\{\mathrm{title,ISBN}\}$. We do not need any directly support for restrictions on the values of the attribute variable u^{name}, because by using system of equations of type expressions (which we support through unification), we can express the constraint $u^{\mathrm{name}}\in\{\mathrm{title,ISBN}\}$. We introduce the following equation additional to any other equations that arise from type analysis:

$$\begin{bmatrix}u^{\mathrm{name}}:\textit{string}\\ x\end{bmatrix}\simeq\begin{bmatrix}\textit{title}:\textit{string}\\ \textit{ISBN}:\textit{string}\end{bmatrix}$$

The above equation holds if and only if u^{name} is substituted to a value in the set {title, ISBN}, as required.

Expressing Unions

If the type of a piece of data is the union of two type expressions $\mathbf{e}_1$, $\mathbf{e}_2$, written $(\mathbf{e}_1 \mid \mathbf{e}_2)$, then the semantics is that the data is either of type $\mathbf{e}_1$ or of type $\mathbf{e}_2$. Though we do not directly support union constructs, similar to the case of enumerations, we specify the union construct in form of equations of type expressions. Consider the following union type:

$$x=\left(\begin{bmatrix}\textit{NAME}:\textit{string}\\ \textit{AGE}:\textit{string}\end{bmatrix}\middle|\begin{bmatrix}\textit{NAME}:\textit{string}\\ \textit{ADDRESS}:\textit{string}\end{bmatrix}\right)$$

which specifies that the row variables $\mathbf{x}$ must be a record which either contains name and age, or name and address. We can specify the constraint on $\mathbf{x}$ using the following equation:

$$\begin{bmatrix}u:x\\ z\end{bmatrix}\simeq\begin{bmatrix}A:\begin{bmatrix}\textit{NAME}:\textit{string}\\ \textit{AGE}:\textit{string}\end{bmatrix}\\ B:\begin{bmatrix}\textit{NAME}:\textit{string}\\ \textit{ADDRESS}:\textit{string}\end{bmatrix}\end{bmatrix}$$

where the attribute variable u and the row variable $\mathbf{z}$ do not appear anywhere else. The above equation is satisfied if and only if x is instantiated to either one of the following types:

$$\begin{bmatrix} NAME : string \\ AGE : string \end{bmatrix} \text{ and } \begin{bmatrix} NAME : string \\ ADDRESS : string \end{bmatrix}$$

as required by the semantics of union types.

TYPE CHECKING, INFERENCE AND UNIFICATION

In Section *Types and Functions in SOA*, we illustrated how the type system in conjunction with functional symbols can be used to model individual services and query constructs. Collectively, we denote all available functional symbols as Σ. Based on symbols in Σ, one can construct infinitely many different functions using the standard functional compositions in programming languages such as ML (see Ullman(1997)) and Lisp (see Graham(1995)). We denote all the functional compositions using symbols by Σ as an infinite set **Q**(Σ). Functional compositions in **Q**(Σ) can be formed by:

- Concatenation
- Product
- Projection

The procedure of type checking is to detect type errors in a functional composition. Namely, it checks if the output of one function is, in fact, compatible with the expected input of another function. Type variables substantially complicate the problem because if the input/output type expresses are polymorphic, then the type checking procedure needs to check for possible substitutions of the type variables. There is a type error only if it is such that no type substitutions can match the input/output types.

Consider the following example of a simple functional composition. Given two services, the first is the web service which locates the best online source to purchase a given book, and the second is a service which locates the text book used for a given course (see Box 2).

One can combine the two into a new service which finds the best online store to purchase the text book for a given course. The composition uses functional catenation: (bargain)∘(textbook).

Type Checking

Type checking needs to verify that there is a type substitution θ such that the output, cod(textbook), can match the input, dom(bargain). Formally, we need to solve the equation:

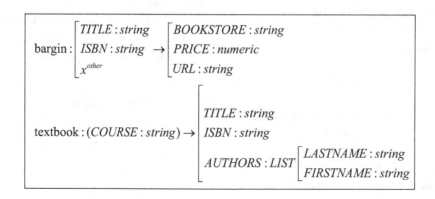

dom(bargain))≃cod(textbook)

Box 2.

$$\text{bargin} : \begin{bmatrix} TITLE : string \\ ISBN : string \\ x^{other} \end{bmatrix} \rightarrow \begin{bmatrix} BOOKSTORE : string \\ PRICE : numeric \\ URL : string \end{bmatrix}$$

$$\text{textbook} : (COURSE : string) \rightarrow \begin{bmatrix} TITLE : string \\ ISBN : string \\ AUTHORS : LIST \begin{bmatrix} LASTNAME : string \\ FIRSTNAME : string \end{bmatrix} \end{bmatrix}$$

which can graphically be stated as:

$$\begin{bmatrix} TITLE : string \\ ISBN : string \\ x^{other} \end{bmatrix} \simeq \begin{bmatrix} TITLE : string \\ ISBN : string \\ AUTHORS : LIST \begin{bmatrix} LASTNAME : string \\ FIRSTNAME : string \end{bmatrix} \end{bmatrix}$$

In this case, the solution is trivial:

{$\mathbf{x}^{other}$ →authors : List[LASTNAME:string, FIRSTNAME:string]}.

Type checking for general functional compositions is far from trivial. The complexity of type checking is discussed in later sections.

Type Inference

Type inference is to infer the necessary substitutions of the type variables and the type signature of the functional composition. For the functional concatenation, (bargain)∘(textbook), we can infer that the final type signature is:

$$(\text{bargin} \circ \text{ textbook}) : (COURSE : string) \rightarrow \begin{bmatrix} BOOKSTORE : string \\ PRICE : numeric \\ URL : string \end{bmatrix}$$

Unification

Both type checking and type inference involve solving a system of equations. In the context of type analysis, solving a system of equations of type expressions is known as unification. Unification has been studied and applied to type analysis of various type systems. Simple unification of records with only field variables is known to have linear-time complexity (see Carpenter (1992)). However, in our case, the presence of row variables and attribute variables make unification significantly more complex. We present the computational complexity of the unification problem for our type system in Section *Computational Complexity of Unification*. The unification algorithm is presented in Section *An Algorithm for Type Matching by Unification.*

COMPUTATIONAL COMPLEXITY OF UNIFICATION

Our type system is distinct to the well-studied type systems Rémy (1994); Wand (1987) in that we allow different types of type variables (row, field, attribute and collection variables) in order to capture the polymorphisms that exist in modern services. The added flexibility of the type systems comes with the cost of intractability. The general unification problem is NP-hard. In fact, many restricted cases of unification problems are also NP-hard. However, we have defined a particular restricted case which we refer to as the unambiguous unification which can be solved in polynomial time.

In this section, we present a series of complexity results of unification. Those complexity results also apply to type checking and type inference of composition of services.

Intractability Results

Definition 4. Let **U** be the set of decision problems defined as:

Instance: A system of equations of the form $\{e_k^{left}, e_k^{right}\}_{k<n}$ where $e_k^{left}, e_k^{right} \in \mathbf{T}^{rec}$ for all k.

Question: Does there exist a substitution θ on variables that appear in the equations such that

$$\forall k < n,\ \theta(e_k^{left}) \simeq \theta(e_k^{right})$$

Theorem 1. The decision problem **U** is NP-hard.

Definition 5. Let $\mathbf{U}^{attr}$ be a restricted unification problem in which the expressions e_k^{left}, e_k^{right} only contain attribute variables. Let $\mathbf{U}^{row}$ be a restricted unification problem in which expressions only contain row variables.

Theorem 2. All restrictions $\mathbf{U}^{attr}$, $\mathbf{U}^{row}$ are NP-hard.

Proof of Theorem 1 and Theorem 2.

First we reduce the 3-SAT problem, see Garey & Johnson (1979), to unification of type equations involving only attribute variables. Given an instance of the 3-SAT problem where $\{C_i\}$ are the clauses. For each Boolean variable x, introduce a type equation:

$[u_x{:}A, u'_x{:}A] \approx [\mathrm{TRUE} : A, \mathrm{FALSE} : A]$

where A is any primitive type. For each clause $C_i = \{t_{i1}, t_{i2}, t_{i3}\}$, introduce an equation:

$$\begin{bmatrix} ATTR_1 : \begin{bmatrix} u_{i1} : A \\ u_{i2} : A \end{bmatrix} \\ ATTR_2 : \begin{bmatrix} u_{i3} : A \\ FALSE : A \end{bmatrix} \end{bmatrix} = \begin{bmatrix} v_1 : \begin{bmatrix} TRUE : A \\ v_3 : A \end{bmatrix} \\ v_2 : \begin{bmatrix} v_4 : A \\ v_5 : A \end{bmatrix} \end{bmatrix}$$

where the attribute variables v_j are fresh, and variables u_{ij} are defined as:

$$u_{ij} = \begin{cases} u_x & \text{if } t_{ij} = x \\ u'_x & \text{if } t_{ij} = \overline{x} \end{cases}$$

It is easy to check that if the equations are unifiable, then there is an assignment to the boolean variables that satisfies all $\{C_i\}$, and conversely, if $\{C_i\}$ is satisfiable, then there exists a valid substitution that unifies the equations.

Next we show that any monotone one-in-three 3SAT can be reduced to a matching problem involving only row variables. The proof is similar to the proof of NP-hardness for AC-unification by Kapur & Narendran (1992). For each boolean variable x_i, we introduce an equation:

$[x_i, x'_i] \approx \mathrm{TRUE} : \mathrm{A}$

For each monotone clause $C_j = \{x_{j1}, x_{j2}, x_{j3}\}$, we introduce an equation:

$[x_{j1}, x_{j2}, x_{j3}] \approx [\mathrm{TRUE} : \mathrm{A}]$

It follows that the equations are unifiable if and only if for each clause C_j, exactly one boolean variable x_{jk} is assigned true.

A Tractable Restriction

In this section, we present a tractable unification problem which we call *unambiguous unification*. We believe that unambiguous unification arises frequently from type analysis in practice, making it a very practical and reasonable restriction of the general unification.

Definition 6. Two type variables **x**, **y** are siblings in an expression e if there exists some sub-record e' of e such that $\{\mathbf{x},\mathbf{y}\} \in \mathbf{V}^{type}(e)$; namely, both variables **x** and **y** appear as fields of the same record in e'. A type expression e is *unambiguous* if it does not contain two sibling type variables. Let $\mathbf{U}^{unambi}$ be the unification problems involving only unambiguous type expressions.

Example 3. Consider the following expressions.

$$\mathrm{t}_1 = \begin{bmatrix} A_1 : \begin{bmatrix} x^1 \\ u^1 : string \end{bmatrix} \\ u^2 : numeric \end{bmatrix} \qquad \mathrm{t}_2 = \begin{bmatrix} A_1 : \begin{bmatrix} x^1 \\ A_2 : string \end{bmatrix} \\ u^2 : numeric \end{bmatrix}$$

$$\mathrm{t}_3 = \begin{bmatrix} u^1 : \begin{bmatrix} x^1 \\ A_2 : string \end{bmatrix} \\ u^2 : numeric \end{bmatrix} \qquad \mathrm{t}_4 = \begin{bmatrix} u^1 : x^1 \\ A_2 : numeric \end{bmatrix}$$

Type $\mathbf{t}_1$ is not unambiguous because the two variables: $\mathbf{x}^1$ and u^1 are siblings. Type $\mathbf{t}_2$ is unambiguous. Type $\mathbf{t}_3$ is not unambiguous because the two variables: u^1 and u^2 are siblings. Type $\mathbf{t}_4$ is unambiguous. Note the two row variables $\mathbf{x}^1$ and $\mathbf{x}^2$ are not siblings in $\mathbf{t}_4$.

Theorem 3. The decision problem $\mathbf{U}^{unambi}$ can be solved in polynomial time.

Theorem 3 will be proven in Section *An Algorithm for Type Matching by Unification,* where we construct a polynomial time algorithm for $\mathbf{U}^{unambi}$.

Composition Verification and Discovery via Unification

It is straight-forward to apply unification to the problem of verification of service composition correctness – a composition of multiple polymorphic services is type-correct if and only if there exists a type substitution such that the input-output types match. Equivalently, the composition is type-correct if and only if the input-output types are unifiable. Unification can also be used for discovery of potential compositions. Given a collection of functions, by means of unification, one can identify compatible pairs (or triples etc.) whose input-output types are unifiable.

AN ALGORITHM FOR TYPE MATCHING BY UNIFICATION

In this section, we present a complete unification algorithm which can be used for type matching in SOA. The algorithm is complete in the sense that it identifies all variable instantiations that match of two given polymorphic types. Similar to syntactic unification, our

algorithm represents the polymorphic types as a single directed acyclic graph (DAG), and iteratively builds a node equivalence relation which represents the variable instantiation. Unlike existing unification algorithms, our algorithm also performs node expansion on certain variable nodes.

Graphical Representation of a Unification Problem

Similar to the approach of efficient syntactic unification algorithms Paterson & Wegman (1978); Martelli & Montanari (1982), given a unification problem, we first construct a directed acyclic graph (DAG) from it in a straight forward fashion. Without loss of generality, we assume that the unification problem consists of only one equation $s \sim t$.

It is easy to see how a type expression $t \in \mathbf{T}^{rec}$ can be viewed as a labeled tree **Tree**(t) with a distinguished root node **root**(t) labeled by a fresh constant $\bot_t$. For each field f and row/field variables **x** of t, we have a unique node $\mathbf{n}_f$ labeled by the attribute $\mathbf{A}(f) \cup \mathbf{A}_0 \cup \mathbf{V}_{attr}$ or the variable $\mathbf{x} \cup \mathbf{V}^{fld} \cup \mathbf{V}^{row}$ respectively. Recursively, we extend the tree at $\mathbf{n}_f$ by the tree encoding of $\mathbf{T}(f)$. Given an equation $s \sim t$, we construct the tree representations **Tree**(s) and **Tree**(t), and then merge all isomorphic subtrees of both **Tree**(s) and **Tree**(t), and thus reduce Tree(s) $\cup$ Tree(t) into a single DAG representation **Dag**(s ~ t) with two distinguished root nodes **root**(s) and **root**(t). Denote DAG as **D**, the nodes of the DAG is written as $\mathbf{N}_\mathbf{D}$ and the labeling function as

$$\ell_\mathbf{D} : \mathbf{N}_\mathbf{D} \rightarrow \text{coll} \cup \text{A0} \cup \text{T0} \cup \text{Vtype}.$$

When the DAG **D** is understood, we may safely omit the subscript and refer to the labeling function simply as ℓ. The children of a node **n** is written as **children(n)**. For convenience, we use the notation **children(n,n′)= children(n)** $\cup$ **children(n′)**. Furthermore, we define

$$\mathbf{V}^{fld}(\mathbf{D}) = \ell^{-1}(\mathbf{V}^{fld}), \text{ and } \mathbf{V}^{row}(\mathbf{D}) = \ell^{-1}(\mathbf{V}^{row}).$$

Remark: Nodes labeled by $V^{fld} \cup V^{row}$ are necessarily leaf nodes in DAG, and since the DAG is fully reduced, for each $x \cup V^{fld} \cup V^{row}$, there can be at most one node $n \in N$ with $\ell_D(n) =$ **x**. Therefore, without ambiguity, we sometimes refer to **x** both as a type variable or the DAG node labeled by **x**.

Example 4. Consider the type expressions

$$t = \begin{bmatrix} a : \begin{bmatrix} c : \begin{bmatrix} x_3 \\ x_4 \end{bmatrix} \end{bmatrix} \\ b : \begin{bmatrix} c : \begin{bmatrix} x_3 \\ x_4 \end{bmatrix} \\ b : SET(x_1) \end{bmatrix} \end{bmatrix} \qquad t' = \begin{bmatrix} b : [b : SET(x_1)] \\ b : \begin{bmatrix} c : SET(x_1) \\ x_2 \end{bmatrix} \end{bmatrix}$$

The tree presentation of type t′ is given by Tree(t′), shown in Figure 2A. The DAG representation of the type equation t ~ t′ are shown in Figure 2B.

Figure 2. Tree representation of t and the directed acyclic graph (DAG) representing the equation t ~ t'

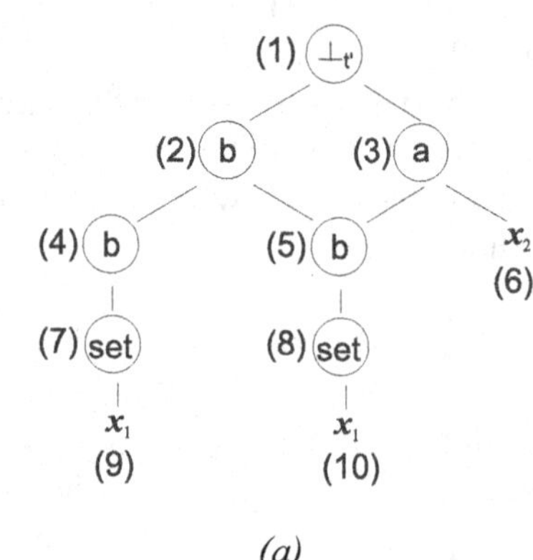

(a)

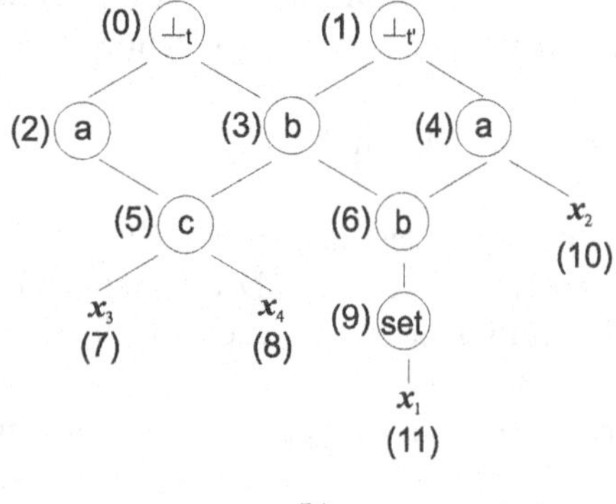

(b)

Unification Relation

In this section, we define unification relations which are equivalent relations. They are the graph-theoretic analog of unifiers. We view a equivalence relation $\boldsymbol{E}$ as a partition of nodes, $\boldsymbol{E} \subseteq \mathbf{Pwr}(\mathbf{N}_D)$ where $\mathbf{N}_D$ is the nodes of the DAG **D**. The binary relation corresponding to $\boldsymbol{E}$ is denoted by $\equiv_E$.

A set of nodes $\mathbf{N} \subseteq \mathbf{N}_D$ of a DAG **D** is homogeneous if no two nodes $n, n' \in \mathbf{N}$ are labeled by distinct "constant" labels in $\mathbf{T}_0 \cup \mathbf{A}_0$ (primitive types and attribute names). More precisely, **N** is homogeneous if and only if $|\ell_D(\mathbf{N}) \cap (\mathbf{T}_0 \cup \mathbf{A}_0)| \leq 1$.

Definition 7 (Unification Relation). A unification relation of a DAG is an equivalence relation $\boldsymbol{E}$ on the nodes $\mathbf{N}_D - \mathbf{V}^{row}(\mathbf{D})$ satisfying the following conditions:

- ***Homogeneity:*** For every node $n \in \mathrm{dom}(\boldsymbol{E})$, $[n]_E$ is homogeneous. For each $u \in \mathbf{V}^{attr}$, $\ell^{-1}(n)$ is homogeneous.
- Distinct-Sibling: if n,n' are siblings, then $\ell([n]_E) \neq \ell([n']_E)$.
- ***Congruence:*** For all $n,n' \in \mathbf{N}_D - \mathbf{V}^{fld}(\mathbf{D})$, $n \equiv_E n'$ implies that $\mathbf{children}_D(n)/\boldsymbol{E} = \mathbf{children}_D(n')/\boldsymbol{E}$.
- ***Acyclicity:*** If n is an ancestor of n', then $[n]_E \neq [n']_E$.

A unification relation $\boldsymbol{E}$ is complete at the pair of nodes (n,n') where $n,n' \in \mathbf{N}_D - \mathbf{V}^{fld}(\mathbf{D})$ if $\forall m \in \mathbf{children}(n)$, $\exists m' \in \mathbf{children}(n')$ such that $m \equiv_E m'$. The unification relation $\boldsymbol{E}$ is a complete unification relation if it is complete at for all node pairs n,n' where $n \equiv_E n'$.

Unification relations can be compared as equivalence relations:

$\boldsymbol{E} \leq \boldsymbol{E}'$ if $\mathrm{dom}(\boldsymbol{E}') \subseteq \mathrm{dom}(\boldsymbol{E})$ and $n \equiv_{E'} n'$ implies $n \equiv_E n'$.

Definition 8 (Node expansion). A node expansion of a DAG **D** is a partial mapping $\mu : \mathbf{V}^{row} \rightarrow$ **Pwr**($\mathbf{V}^{fld} \cup \mathbf{V}^{row}$) such that for each $\mathbf{x} \in dom(\mu)$, either $\mu(\mathbf{x}) = V$ or $\mu(\mathbf{x}) = V \cup \{\mathbf{x}\}$ where V is a set of fresh nodes labeled uniquely by fresh field variables. The expanded DAG $\mu(\mathbf{D})$ is defined to be the DAG obtained by replacing $\mathbf{x} \in dom(\mu)$ with the nodes $\mu(\mathbf{x})$.

Node expansions can be compared: $\mu \leq \mu'$ if there exists μ'' such that $\mu'(\mathbf{D}) = \mu''(\mu(\mathbf{D}))$.

Theorem 4. Given an equation $s \sim t$, let $\mathbf{D} = \mathbf{Dag}(s \sim t)$. The equation $s \sim t$ is unifiable if and only if there exists some node expansion of **D** such that the expanded DAG $\mu(\mathbf{D})$ has a complete unification relation E such that $\mathbf{root}(s) \equiv_E \mathbf{root}(t)$.

Proof. Given a unifier θ of $s \sim t$, we define a pair (μ, E) as follows.

For each row variable **x**, define $\mu(\mathbf{x}) = \{y_f : f \in \theta(\mathbf{x})\}$. Namely, for each field f in $\theta(\mathbf{x})$, we create a fresh field variable y_f. If $\theta(\mathbf{x})$ is a primitive type, then we consider it as a single field.

Extend the type substitution θ to map $\mathbf{V}^{fld} \rightarrow$ **T** as follows. For each $y \in \mathbf{V}^{fld}(\mathbf{D})$, by definition of μ, $y = y_f$, so we can safely define $\theta(y) = f$.

This way, each node $n \in \mathbf{N}_D$ is mapped to a type expression by $\varphi : \mathbf{N}_D \rightarrow \mathrm{T}$, where $\varphi(n) = \theta(\mathbf{T}(\mathbf{D}|n))$. Finally, we define the equivalence relation $E = \ker(\varphi)$. One can verify that (μ, E) is a unification relation such that $\mathbf{root}(s) \equiv_E \mathbf{root}(t)$.

The converse uses the standard construction of variable substitution from node equivalence relations, similar to Paterson & Wegman (1978); Martelli & Montanari (1982) in the context of syntactic unification.

Therefore, in order to solve the unification of a type equation, we aim to find a complete unification relation of an expanded version of $\mathbf{Dag}(s \sim t)$.

Definition 9 (Solutions). Let **D** be the the DAG Dag(s~t), a solution of D is a pair (μ,E) where is a node expansion of D and E a unification relation of μ(D) such that root(s)≡E root(t). We say that the solution (μ,E)is complete if E is a complete unification relation, otherwise the solution is partial.

The solutions are ordered by: $(\mu, E) < (\mu', E')$ if and only if ($\mu < \mu'$ and $E < E'$). Define S(D) the minimal complete solutions of D.

Proposition 1. Every minimal unifier $\theta \in \min U(s \sim t)$ can be constructed in polynomial time from a minimal solution $(\mu, E) \in S(Dag(s \sim t))$.

By Proposition1, in order to compute the complete set of minimal unifiers, it suffices to compute the set minimal solutions S(Dag(s ~ t)).

Computing Minimal Solutions

Proposition 2. If (μ,E) is a minimal complete solution, then

$$\forall \dot{y} \in V^{fld}(\mu(D)), [\dot{y}]_E \cap (N_0 \cup N^{attr})(D) \neq \varnothing$$

Therefore,

$$\forall x \in Vrow(D), \ |\mu(x)| \leq |D|$$

Proof. If y is not equivalent to any nodes in $\mathbf{N}_0 \cup \mathbf{N}^{attr}$, then it can only be equivalent to other field variables, thus, its equivalent class can be completely deleted. This contradicts with the fact that the solution is minimal.

Proposition 2 places a upper bound on the size of minimal complete solutions (μ, E) that is polynomial to the size of the initial unification problem. Therefore, along with Theorem 1, we have the following important corollary.

Corollary 1. Unification of type expressions in NP, thus is NP-complete.

Definition 10 (Extensions and Local Extensions). Let (μ, E) and (μ', E') be two (possibly partial) solutions of Dag(s ~ t). We say that (μ', E')

is an extension of $(\mu,\boldsymbol{E})$ if $(\mu,\boldsymbol{E}) < (\mu',\boldsymbol{E}')$. Furthermore, (μ',E') is a local-extension of $(\mu,\boldsymbol{E})$ at some nodes (n,n') if $dom(\mu')-dom(\mu) \subseteq children_{\mathbf{D}}(n,n')$ and $dom(\boldsymbol{E}')-dom(\boldsymbol{E}) \subseteq children_{\mu'D}(n,n')$. We may refer to $(\mu',\boldsymbol{E}')$ as a (n,n')-extension of $(\mu,\boldsymbol{E})$.

Namely, a (n,n')-extension of a partial solution $(\mu,\boldsymbol{E})$ is obtained by further expanding row variables that are children of *n* and *n'* and match nodes among the expanded children of *n* and *n'*.

Lemma 1. Let $\mathbf{D} = Dag(s \sim t)$. Define $\mu_0 = \emptyset$, and $\boldsymbol{E}_0 = \{ \{root(s),root(t)\} \}$. Then, for any minimal complete solution $(\mu,\boldsymbol{E}) \in \mathbf{S}(\boldsymbol{D})$, there exists a finite chain of length at most $k \le |D|^4$: $(\mu_0,E_0),(\mu_1,E_1), \ldots ,(\mu_k,E_k)$ such that $(\mu_k, E_k)=(\mu,E)$, and for all $1 \le i \le k$, $(\mu_i,\boldsymbol{E}_i)$ is a local-extension of $(\mu_{i-1},\boldsymbol{E}_{i-1})$.

Lemma 1 provides a recipe for a way to compute the set S(D) of all minimal solutions to the unification problem. That is, we start with an initial partial solution (μ_0,E_0) as defined in Lemma 1, and explore all of its local extensions until a complete solution is found.

A local-extension (μ',E') of a partial solution (μ,E) is completely characterized by

- A pair of nodes (n,n') in $\mathbf{N}(\mu\boldsymbol{D})$,
- An incremental node expansion $\Delta\mu$ such that $\mu'=\Delta\mu \circ \mu$,
- A binary matching relation $\Delta R \subseteq children_{\mu'D}(n) \times children_{\mu'D}(n')$ such that $\equiv_{E'} = (\equiv_E \cup \Delta R)^*$, where $(\equiv_E \cup \Delta R)^*$ is the transitive, reflexive and symmetric closure of the relation $\equiv_E \cup \Delta R$.

We use the notation shown in Figure 3 to denote that $(\mu',E') = (\Delta\mu\circ\mu, (E\cup\Delta R)^*)$.

One can easily verify that the orders of local-extensions do not matter. Namely, local-extensions commute as illustrated in Figure 4.

By the commutatively, we don't have to explore all chains of the local extensions, but rather only all of the (n_1,n_2)-local extensions at some pair (n, n') of nodes where the current partial solution is incomplete. Suppose we have a procedure Local-Ext(μ,E,D,n1,n2) that computes all minimal(n1,n2)-extensions of the solution (μ,E) that are complete at (n1,n2), then one can easily construct a procedure COMPLETE_SOLUTION(s ~ t) that computes the set S(Dag(s ~ t)). The two procedures are shown in Figure 5 and Figure 6.

Figure 3. Graphical notation for extension

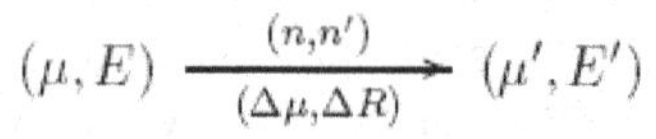

$$(\mu, E) \xrightarrow[(\Delta\mu,\Delta R)]{(n,n')} (\mu', E')$$

Figure 4. Commutativity of local extensions

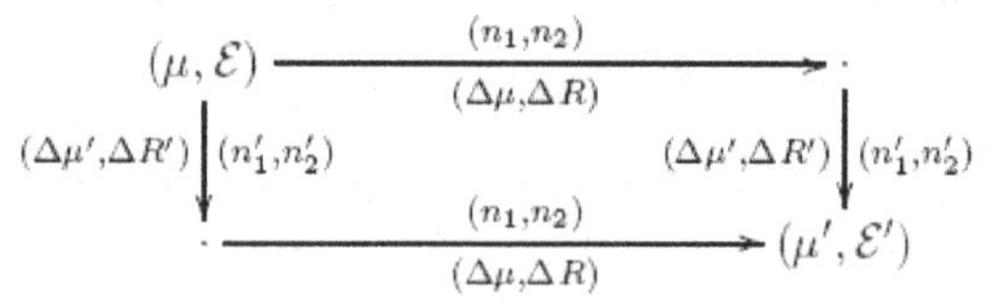

$$\begin{array}{ccc} (\mu,\mathcal{E}) & \xrightarrow[(\Delta\mu,\Delta R)]{(n_1,n_2)} & \cdot \\ {\scriptstyle(\Delta\mu',\Delta R')}\downarrow{\scriptstyle(n_1',n_2')} & & {\scriptstyle(\Delta\mu',\Delta R')}\downarrow{\scriptstyle(n_1',n_2')} \\ \cdot & \xrightarrow[(\Delta\mu,\Delta R)]{(n_1,n_2)} & (\mu',\mathcal{E}') \end{array}$$

Enumerating Minimal Local Extensions

We present a simple way to enumerate the minimal local extensions of a partial solution (μ,E) at two given nodes (n,n'). The outline of our enumeration method is:

- Enumerate potential matches between children of *n* and children of *n'*.
- For each potential match, construct a candidate minimal extension.
- Verify that the extension gives rise to a valid partial solution.

Given an arbitrary binary relation R, we make the following definitions: given a node m,

$R(m) = \{m' = (m,m') \in R\}$
$R^{-1}(m) = \{m': (m',m) \in R \}$

and $deg_R(m) = |R(m) \cup R^{-1}(m)|$.

Figure 5. The algorithm for COMPLETE_SOLUTIONS

```
COMPLETE_SOLUTIONS(s ≈ t)
s, t are type expressions
      LET D = DAG(s ≈ t)
      LET n1 = root(s)
      LET n2 = root(t)
      LET μ = EMPTY
      LET E = {{n1, n2}}
      IF (μ,E) is complete
            RETURN {(μ,E)}
      LET SOLpart = {(μ,E)}
      LET SOLcomplete = EMPTY
      WHILE SOLpart ≠ EMPTY
            FOR EACH (μ,E) IN SOLpart
Pick (m1, m2) in μ(D) at which E is incomplete
                  LET ext = LOCAL_EXT(μ, E, D, m1, m2)
                  REMOVE (μ,E) from SOLpart
                  ADD complete solutions in ext to SOLcomplete
                  ADD partial solutions in ext to SOLpart.
      RETURN SOLcomplete
```

Figure 6. The algorithm for performing local extension

```
LOCAL_EXT( D, μ, E, n, n')
Returns the set of minimal local extensions
LET MLE = EMPTY
FOR EACH potential match R
      (Δμ, ΔR) = extension constructed from R
      LET (μ', E') = (Δμ·μ, transitive closure of
(E∪ΔR))
      IF (μ', E') is a partial solution
            Add {(μ', E')} to MLE
RETURN MLE
```

By a potential match, we mean a binary relation R relating children of *n* to children of *n'* satisfying the following conditions:

- *R*⊆(children(*n*)-children(*n'*))×(children(*n'*)-children(*n*)) i.e., *R* does not mach common children nodes
- For all $m \in$ children(*n*) ∪ children(*n'*) - V^{row}, we require $deg_R(m) = 1$. i.e., nodes that are not row variables are matched to exactly one other node. Row variables can be matched to zero or more other nodes.
- No two row variables are related by *R*.

Given a potential match *R*, we construct an extension (Δμ, Δ*R*) as follows.

- dom(Δμ) = $V^{row} \cap$ dom(*R*),
- For each $x \in dom(\Delta\mu)$, $\Delta\mu(x) = \{y: 1 \leq i \leq deg_R(x)\}$ where are y fresh field vaiables
- $dom(\Delta R) = dom(R) - V^{row} \cup \bigcup_{x \in dom(\Delta\mu)} \Delta\mu(x)$
- The relation Δ*R* is defined as

$$\Delta R = \{(m, m') \in R : m \notin V^{row} \text{ and } m' \notin V^{row}\}$$
$$\cup \bigcup_{x \in \pi_{\text{left}}(R) \cap V^{row}} \{(\dot{y}_i, m_i) : \dot{y}_i \in \Delta\mu(x), m_i \in R(x)\}$$
$$\cup \bigcup_{x \in \pi_{\text{right}}(R) \cap V^{row}} \{(m_i, \dot{y}_i) : \dot{y}_i \in \Delta\mu(x), m_i \in R^{-1}(x)\}$$

Proposition 3. The time complexity of COMPLETE_SOLUTION(s ≈ t) is $O((2^N)^4)$ where **N** is the number of nodes of DAG(s ≈ t). Therefore COMPLETE_SOLUTION is in EXPTIME.

Tractable Unification

Definition 11. A DAG, *D*, is unambiguous if

$$\forall n \in N_D, \ \left|\text{children}_D(n) \cap \ell^{-1}(V^{\text{type}})\right| \leq 1$$

A type unification problem s ≈ t is unambiguous if DAG(s ≈ t) is unambiguous.

Intuitively, a DAG is unambiguous if no two siblings are labeled by type variables.

Theorem 5. If a unification problem s ≈ t is unambiguous, then it can be solved in PTIME. In particular, COMPLETE_SOLUTION(s ≈ t) terminates polynomial time.

Thus, unambiguous unification problems can be solved in polynomial time. Furthermore, it has the additional property that it is either un-unifiable or it has a unique most general unifier as formally stated in the following proposition.

Proposition 4. If s ≈ t is unambiguous, then |min U(s ≈ t)| ≤ 1.

Since one only needs to check for the existence of sibling variable nodes in the graph Dag(s ~ t) to decide if the unification problem is ambiguous or not, the following result follows immediately.

Lemma 2. Given a unification problem s ≈ t, one can decide if it is unambiguous in linear time.

Application of Unambiguous Unification

When a user leaves certain type variables of query operators unspecified when forming a service composition, the type inference algorithm can either infer the necessary instantiation or suggest the admissible instantiations. The complete unification algorithm allows the system to perform type inference, however, its runtime can be exponential in the worst case. Unambiguous unification is a good compromise to save the user to fully instantiate all type variables. The user is required to instantiate enough type variables until the unification problem is unambiguous. Testing if a composition problem is sufficiently instantiated is tractable by Lemma 2, and solving the resulting unification problem is also tractable by Theorem 5. In our experience, most reasonably formed queries lead to unambiguous unification problems.

FUTURE TRENDS

One of many challenges in SOA is the management and utilization of a vast collection of services. We argue that an expressive type system that is amendable to automatic analysis is a crucial element of SOA. The type system and its unification algorithm discussed in this chapter can be applied to areas such as verification of service composition and automatic discovery of composable services. With the proliferation of the services available on the web, future integrated development environments (IDE) can extract the type signatures from the known services, and enforce that all compositions must be type error free. Furthermore, developers can query which services are candidates for a composition if the develop is to specify the data available and the desired data type. Both tasks can be performed by solving a set of type equations using the unification as shown in the chapter.

CONCLUSION

In this chapter, we have presented a formalism to model data sources and services in SOA from a type-theoretic approach. The benefit of our framework is that we are able to statically analyze the type correctness of complex service compositions involving services and data queries. The central technique used for type analysis is unification. The computational complexity results of several different kinds of unification are shown: ranging from restricted but tractable cases to the most general but intractable cases. A unification algorithm was proposed. Its correctness and time complexity has been studied.

REFERENCES

Baader, F., Calvanese, D., McGuinness, D.L., Nardi, D., & Patel-Schneider, P.F.(Eds.). (2003). *The description logic handbook*. Cambridge University Press.

Barbosa, D., Mignet, L., & Veltri, P. (2005). Studying the XML web: Gathering statistics from an XML sample. In *Proceeding of World Wide Web Conference 2005*, (pp. 413-438).

Cardelli, L., & Mitchell, J.C. (1991). Operations on records. *Mathematical Structures in Computer Science, 1*, 3–48.

Carpenter, B. (1992). *The logic of typed feature structures*. Cambridge University Press.

Chawathe, Y. (2003). Scattercast: an adaptable broadcast distribution framework. *Journal Multimedia Systems, 9*(1), 104-118.

Curbera, F., Ferguson, D.F., Nally, M., & Stockton, M.L. (2005). Toward a programming model for service-oriented computing. In *Proceedings of International Conference on Service Oriented Computing*, (pp. 33-47).

Dantsin, E., & Voronkov, A. (1999). A nondeterministic polynomial-time unification algorithm for bags, sets and trees. In Proceedings of *the Second International Conference on Foundations of Software Science and Computation Structure 1999*, (pp. 180-196).

Deutsch, A., Sui, L., & Vianu, V. (2004). Specification and verification of data-driven web services. In *Proceedings of Symposium in Principles of Database 2004*, (pp. 71–82).

Garcia-Molina, H.,Ullman, J.D., & Widom, J.D. (2005). *Database systems: the complete book*. Prentice-Hall.

Garey, M.R., & Johnson, D.S. (1979). *Computers and intractability*. San Francisco: W.H. Freeman.

Graham, P. (1995). *ANSI common LISP*. Prentice-Hall.

Kapur, D., & Narendran, P. (1992). Complexity of unification problems with associative-commutative operators. *Journal of Automatic Reasoning, 9*(2), 122-140.

Li, S-H., Huang, S-M., Yen, D. C., & Chang, C-C. (2006). Migrating Legacy Information Systems to Web Services Architecture. *Journal of Database Management, 18*(4), 1-25.

Maheshwari, P., Tang, H., & Liang, R. (2004). Enhancing web services with message-oriented middleware. In *Proceedings of IEEE International Conference on Web Services 2004*, (pp. 524–531).

Martelli, A., & Montanari, U.(1982). An efficient unification algorithm. *ACM Transactions on Programming Languages, 4*(2), 258– 282.

Narayanan, S., & McIlraith, S.A. (2002). Simulation, verification and automated composition of web services. In *Proceedings of World Wide Web Conference 2002*, (pp. 77–88).

Paterson, M.S., & Wegman, M.N.(1978). Linear unification. *Journal of Computer and System Sciences, 16*(1), 181-186.

Pu, K.Q., Hristidis,V., & Koudas, N.(2006). Syntactic rule based approach to web service composition. In Proceedings of *International Conference on Data Engineering 2006*, (pp. 31–43).

RDF Core Working Group. *Resource description framework.* Available at http://www.w3.org/RDF

R'emy, D. (1989). Type checking records and variants in a natural extension of ML. In *Proceedings of Symposium on Principles of Programming Languages 1989*, (pp. 77–88).

R'emy, D. (1994). Type inference for records in a natural extension of ML. In Proceedings of *Theoretical Aspects of Computer Software 1994*, (pp. 67-95).

Ullman, J. (1997). *Elements of ML programming.* Prentice-Hall.

W3C. Document type definition. Available (http://www.w3.org/TR/html4/sgml/dtd.html)

Wand, M. (1987). Complete type inference for simple objects. In Proceedings of *IEEE Symposium on Logic in Computer Science 1987,* (pp. 37–44).

ADDITIONAL READINGS

This chapter applies methods from type checking and programming languages to web service composition. In addition to the references, below are some reading material in areas of programming languages, semantic web and web service composition.

Programming Languages and Type Systems

Hosoya, H., & Pierce, B.C. 2003. XDuce: A statically typed XML processing language. *ACM Trans. Interet Technol., 3*(2),117-148.

Pierce B.C. (2002). *Types and Programming Languages.* MIT Press.

Seibel, P., & Margolin, B. (2005). *Practical Common Lisp Apress.*

Thompson, S. (2002), *Haskell: The Craft of Functional Programming,* 2nd Edition. Addison Wesley.

Ullman, J.D. (1994). *Elements of ML Programming.* Prentice Hall.

Vansummeren, S. 2006. Type inference for unique pattern matching. *ACM Trans. Program. Lang. Syst., 28*(3), 389-428.

Semantic Web

Acuña, C.J., & Marcos, E. 2006. Modeling semantic web services: a case study. In *Proceedings of the 6th international Conference on Web Engineering* (pp. 32-39).

Antoniou, G., & Van Harmelen, F. (2004). *A Semantic Web Primer.* MIT Press.

Brambilla, M., Ceri, S., Facca, F.M., Celino, I., Cerizza, D., & Valle, E. D. 2007. Model-driven design and development of semantic Web service applications. *ACM Trans. Interet Technol., 8*(1), 3.

Dahanayake, A., & Gerhardt, W. (2003). *Web-enabled Systems Integration: Practices and Challenges.* IGI Global.

Elgedawy, I., Tari, Z., & Thom, J.A. (2008). Correctness-aware high-level functional matching approaches for semantic Web services. *ACM Trans. Web, 2*(2),1-40.

Fensel, D., Hendler, J.A., Lieberman, H., & Wahlster, W. 2005 *Spinning the Semantic Web: Bringing the World Wide Web to its Full Potential.* The MIT Press.

Horrocks, I. (2008). Ontologies and the semantic web. *Commun. ACM, 51*(12), 58-67.

McCormack, D.A. (2002). *Web 2.0. Aspatore Books.*

Wu, X., Zhang, L., & Yu, Y. 2006. Exploring social annotations for the semantic web. In *Proceedings of the 15th international Conference on World Wide Web.* (pp. 417-426).

Web Services and Composition

Benatallah, B., Sheng, Q. Z., & Dumas, M. (2003). The Self-Serv Environment for Web Services Composition. *IEEE Internet Computing, 7*(1), 40-48.

Chun, S.A., Atluri, V., & Adam, N.R. (2005). Using Semantics for Policy-Based Web Service Composition. *Distrib. Parallel Databases, 18*(1), 37-64.

Hamadi, R., & Benatallah, B. (2003). A Petri net-based model for web service composition. In *Proceedings of the 14th Australasian Database Conference - Volume 17.* (pp. 191-200).

Ko, J.M., Kim, C.O., & Kwon, I. (2008). Quality-of-service oriented web service composition algorithm and planning architecture. *J. Syst. Softw., 81*(11), 2079-2090.

Krafzig, D., Banke, K., & Slama, D. (2005). *Enterprise SOA: Service-oriented Architecture Best Practices.* Prentice Hall.

Maamar, Z., Benslimane, D., & Narendra, N. C. (2006, December). What can context do for web services? *Commun. ACM,* 49(12), 98-103

Narayanan, S. & McIlraith, S.A. (2002). Simulation, verification and automated composition of web services. In *Proceedings of the 11th international Conference on World Wide Web,* (pp. 77-88).

Weerawarana, S., Curbera, F., Leymann, F., Storey, T., & Ferguson, D.F. (2005). *Web Services Platform Architecture: SOAP, WSDL, WS-Policy, WS-Addressing, WS-BPEL, WS-Reliable Messaging, and More.* Prentice Hall.

Yu, Q., Liu, X., Bouguettaya, A., & Medjahed, B. (2008, May). Deploying and managing Web services: issues, solutions, and directions. *The VLDB Journal, 17*(3), 537-572.

Zeng, L., Benatallah, B., Dumas, M., Kalagnanam, J., & Sheng, Q. Z. (2003). Quality driven web services composition. In Proceedings of the 12th international Conference on World Wide, (pp. 411-421).

Chapter X
XML Compression for Web Services on Resource-Constrained Devices[1]

Christian Werner
University of Lübeck, Germany

Carsten Buschmann
University of Lübeck, Germany

Ylva Brandt
University of Lübeck, Germany

Stefan Fischer
University of Lübeck, Germany

ABSTRACT

Compared to other middleware approaches like CORBA or Java RMI the protocol overhead of SOAP is very high. This fact is not only disadvantageous for several performance-critical applications, but especially in environments with limited network bandwidth or resource-constrained computing devices. Although recent research work concentrated on more compact, binary representations of XML data only very few approaches account for the special characteristics of SOAP communication. In this article we will discuss the most relevant state-of-the-art technologies for compressing XML data. Furthermore, we will present a novel solution for compacting SOAP messages. In order to achieve significantly better compression rates than current approaches, our compressor utilizes structure information from an XML Schema or WSDL document. With this additional knowledge on the "grammar" of the exchanged messages, our compressor generates a single custom pushdown automaton, which can be used as a highly efficient validating parser as well as a highly efficient compressor. The main idea is to tag the transitions of the automaton with short binary identifiers that are then used to encode the path trough the automaton during parsing. Our approach leads to extremely compact data representations and is also usable in environments with very limited CPU and memory resources.

Copyright © 2009, IGI Global, distributing in print or electronic forms without written permission of IGI Global is prohibited.

INTRODUCTION

The text-oriented data encoding of XML (extensible markup language) is the reason for SOAP messages causing significantly more overhead than the binary message formats of Java RMI (Remote Method Invocation) and CORBA (common object request broker architecture). In an earlier work, we compared different approaches for realizing remote procedure calls (RPCs) and showed that SOAP over HTTP (hypertext transfer protocol) causes significantly more traffic than similar technologies. Using SOAP, the data volume is about three times higher than with Java RMI or CORBA (Werner, Buschmann, & Fischer, 2005).

Fortunately, most of today's wired networks are fast enough to provide sufficient bandwidth for all applications. However, there are still some application domains with tight bandwidth limits: For example, in cellular phone networks, it is still common to charge the customer according to the transmitted data volumes. Another very common example is a dial-up connection over older technologies like modem or ISDN (integrated services digital network) links. Although their bandwidth is very limited, they are still in use in many enterprise networks. Additional limitations are imposed by foreseen application domains of Web services such as ubiquitous computing. In such energy-constrained environments, the radio interface is usually a main power consumer and therefore tight restrictions apply to the transmitted data volumes on mobile devices.

In order to address the problem of excessive XML message sizes in these domains, a lot of research effort went into the development of binary (and therefore more compact) representations of XML data.

In order to preserve the universal compatibility of binary-encoded XML, standardization is a very important issue: The World Wide Web Consortium (W3C) founded the W3C XML Binary Characterization Working Group in March 2004. Its members analyzed various application scenarios and created a survey of the existing approaches in this field (W3C, 2005b). Furthermore, this working group has specified a set of requirements that are important for binary XML representations. The most requested features are compactness, the possibility of directly reading and writing the binary format, independence of certain transport mechanisms, and processing efficiency.

Another major outcome of this working group was a set of 18 typical use cases for binary XML representations with a detailed analysis of their individual requirements. In all use cases, the property *compactness*, which is in the focus of this article, was of major importance or was rated as a nice-to-have feature. In 10 of 18 cases, it was even rated as mandatory.

The W3C XML Binary Characterization Working Group has finished its work, and its successor, the Efficient XML Interchange Working Group (W3C, 2005a), took up the work in December 2005. It focuses on interoperability aspects of binary XML and published a first working draft of the efficient XML interchange (EXI) format (W3C, 2007) in December 2007. Although not in the focus of this article, we are currently working on an implementation of this data format. To the knowledge of the authors, there are no other implementations of the EXI format available up to now.

In this article, we elaborate on how to encode SOAP messages efficiently with an approach that has been developed independently of EXI. It exploits the fact that Web service messages are described by an XML grammar that is known to both the sender and the receiver (usually in the form of a WSDL [Web services definition language] file). A large part of the information contained in a message can be inferred from this grammar. This a priori known part can therefore be omitted during transmission; this leads to very promising compression results.

Although the idea of creating Web-service-specific compressors from WSDL descriptions is not new and has already been presented by the authors in a previous publication in this journal (Werner et al., 2005), considerable advances are presented here. The original idea was to create a set of empty Web service messages, called skeletons, containing all XML constructs that reoccur in subsequent service calls. When a service is called, only the differences between the message and the corresponding skeleton are transmitted over the network. We could show that this differential encoding leads to very promising results in terms of message size. However, calculating the difference between two XML documents is a task with high computational complexity. This slows down Web service communication and degrades the applicability of this approach in practice. In the following, we will present a novel encoding technique that is extremely efficient and, as we will show, can be implemented even on devices with very limited resources. With this technique, it is possible to implement SOAP-based Web services on tiny embedded systems.

Please note that XML message compression is not an all-embracing solution to the problem of Web services overhead. Furthermore, the used transport binding may introduce a significant amount of additional overhead. Therefore, it is advisable to combine message compression with an optimized transport binding in order to get the best results in real-world environments. We have comprehensively studied the influence of transport binding in a previous contribution (Werner, Buschmann, Jäcker, & Fischer, 2006).

The remainder of this article is structured as follows. First, we conduct a survey on state-of-the-art compression methods for SOAP and XML. We focus on techniques that make use of the availability of grammar descriptions. We then present the results of an extensive evaluation measuring the compression effectiveness of the different algorithms. After this, we present our new approach to SOAP compression and evaluate its effectiveness. In the subsequent section, we show an exemplary implementation of our approach on an embedded device. Finally, we draw a conclusion and give an outlook on promising topics for future work.

RELATED WORK

Because XML documents are usually represented as text, the approach of applying well-known general-purpose text compressors such as gzip is obvious. Unfortunately, typical Web service messages are rather small, and this fact heavily degrades the compression effectiveness of such compressors (Werner et al., 2005). Therefore, the subsequent section takes into account only approaches that specialize in XML data.

Overview

In the past years, many XML-aware concepts have been invented. A very common approach is to separate the markup from the character data and compress both independently with different algorithms. XMill (Liefke & Suciu, 2000) and XMLPPM (Cheney, 2001) are two compressors that are based on this technique.

Another promising idea is to exploit the XML syntax rules: When compressing well-formed documents, the name of any end tag can be inferred from the name of the corresponding opening tag. Hence, the name of an end tag does not have to be encoded. The Fast Infoset (Sandoz, Triglia, & Pericas-Geertsen, 2004) compressor uses this technique and produces a binary serialization that is optimized for high-speed XML processing. A recent approach in the field of XML compression that does not rely on schema information is Exalt (Toman, 2004). It analyzes typical tag sequences in the input data and stores this information by generating a set of finite-state automata (FSA). Using these, Exalt predicts the next tag at a certain stage of compression and encodes only the difference between the read value and the prediction.

A different way of efficiently compacting XML data is to build a compressor that is custom tailored to a certain XML language. If the vocabulary and the grammar of an XML language is known in advance, specialized compressors can be built that map the markup structures of this particular language to shorter binary tokens. A very common approach for implementing this is to use fixed coding tables that are integrated into the compression engine. WBXML (http://wbxmllib.sourceforge.net/) and Millau (Girardot & Sundaresan, 2000) are two examples of such compressors. Both support various languages in the field of mobile devices like WML (wireless markup language) or SyncML (synchronization markup language). A similar technique is used by the Binary Format for MPEG-7 Metadata (BiM) compressor (Niedermeier, Heuer, Hutter, Stechele, & Kaup, 2002), which specializes in processing MPEG-7 metadata.

While these highly optimized schema-based XML compressors feature very impressive compression results (Werner et al., 2005), their practical value is limited. Their main disadvantage is that they do not support the extensibility XML has been designed for. The SOAP format is a typical example: The SOAP body can carry arbitrary application-specific data; hence, a compression algorithm that relies on fixed coding tables is obviously not optimal in this case.

XML Compressors Supporting Dynamic Schema Processing

The idea of combining the high compression performance of language-specific compressors with the flexibility of general-purpose compressors was the driver for developing compressors with dynamic schema support, that is, compression algorithms that can be customized to application-specific XML grammars at run time.

Information on the document structure, typically available through an XML grammar description like XML schema or DTD, enables two new compression strategies. The first is to infer optimized binary content encodings from the data type definitions in the XML grammar. Thus, numeric values in the XML document can be represented as binary-encoded integer numbers instead of strings, which is the default representation. Second, improvements of the compression effectiveness are possible because the XML grammar provides information on how valid instance documents are structured. Therefore, large parts of the structure information are redundant and can be omitted in the compressed document. Of course, the reconstruction of the original document during decompression also requires the schema information to be present in order to avoid information loss.

An example of a compressor that can dynamically process schema information is XGrind (Tolani & Haritsa, 2002). It employs a so-called context-free compression strategy; that is, it generates a data format that is capable of processing XML queries efficiently without decompressing the whole content. Therefore, XGrind can neither omit tags that can be inferred from the grammar nor use efficient binary encodings for numeric content like xsd:int. Instead, it represents the text values of tag and attribute names by mapping them to shorter identifiers, using the grammar (in DTD format) to identify all possible tag names, which are then assigned to compact 8-bit identifiers in the binary format. Additionally, XGrind omits the names of closing tags because these can be inferred from the name of the corresponding opening tag in well-formed XML documents. Furthermore, XGrind represents the values of enumeration types using binary block codes. The remaining XML content is Huffman encoded. In order to minimize the code-word lengths, a separate Huffman table is maintained for each tag name in the document. With these techniques, XGrind is able to generate quite compact data representations even under the constraint of context-free compression.

Another compressor that supports dynamic grammar processing is Xebu (Kangasharju,

Tarkoma, & Lindholm, 2005). It uses a general-purpose SAX (simple application programming interface for XML) parser to prepare the input data and encodes the resulting sequence of events in a compact binary fashion: During compression, all tag names are indexed on their first appearance, and on repetition, only the index ID (a byte value) is encoded. Unlike XGrind, the Xebu encoder also detects numeric data and encodes them in an efficient binary format. These two compression features are always available even if no grammar is present.

To further improve the effectiveness of the Xebu compressor, so-called omission automata can be generated from a Relax NG grammar (Clark & Murata, 2001). The basic idea here is to omit the encoding of SAX events that can be inferred from the grammar. For example, if the grammar prescribes a sequence of elements with each element occurring exactly once, we do not have to encode any structure information because there is only one correct tag sequence, which can be unambiguously inferred from the grammar. Unfortunately, the work on this topic (Clark & Murata) does not provide an algorithm for constructing these omission automata.

Another feature of Xebu is called precaching. The idea is to prefill the index ID tables with initial values extracted from the schema. This is possible because the XML grammar usually contains detailed information on the possible element and attribute names in the document. Precaching leads to significantly better compression results, especially on short input files, because strings in the document can be replaced by shorter IDs throughout the whole document and not only on repetition.

XML Xpress (http://www.ictcompress.com/products_xmlxpress.html) is another compressor with dynamic schema-processing capabilities. It is based on a two-step processing algorithm. First, a so-called schema-model file is generated from an XML schema document and a set of sample XML files that represent typical data the compressor will be exposed to later on. In Step 2, the actual compression takes pace. The compressor reads in the schema-model file and the XML source file and generates a binary XML representation from both. The decompressor also relies on the schema-model file while decoding the compressed representation. Unfortunately, no details about the conversion processes are publicly available because XML Xpress is a commercial product. Furthermore, it remains unclear whether the generation of the schema-model file is a fully automatic process or requires manual intervention.

The differential encoding approach (Werner et al., 2005) targets the special requirements of SOAP communication and also belongs to the category of compressors with dynamic-schema support. The authors apply the well-known method of differential encoding to generate more compact SOAP message representations. The compression process works as follows: Instead of transmitting the whole SOAP message, only the difference between the message and a so-called skeleton message is sent over the network. Skeletons can be automatically generated from WSDL service descriptions. The difference information can be expressed using various data formats. Practical experiments showed that the document update language (DUL) in combination with the XMLPPM compressor performs very well. This approach yields very high compression rates (even with files smaller than 10 Kb, which is typical for SOAP communication). Unfortunately, the differential encoding approach is afflicted with very high algorithmic complexity due to the problem of calculating the differences between two XML documents. Hence, on devices with limited memory and CPU (central processing unit) resources, this approach can only be used with small input documents.

Evaluation Setup

In order to compare the compression performance of the different schemes, we generated a consistent test bed that was used to evaluate all available compressors.

To obtain representative results, we chose to use two different benchmark Web services that are typical for current SOA (service-oriented architecture) applications. These were used to evaluate the compression efficiency of the aforementioned schemes.

The first service represents a class of applications transmitting only little payload. A stock-quote service may serve as an example for this kind of Web service. Its request might contain a short string that identifies the stock of interest, the so-called ticker symbol. The service answers with a response containing nothing but the current stock price encoded as an integer value. It is rather difficult to compress such messages because any static overhead imposed by the compressor (such as coding tables) quickly becomes as big as or even bigger than the original message. As a result, not all schemes that yield promising compression ratios on long messages work equally well on small messages. An additional characteristic of such services is that the XML schema that describes the message format is usually very restraining. This means that little or no message structure variation is possible.

To represent this kind of service, we constructed a benchmark Web service implementing a calculator. It features four different operations that exchange messages with different payload lengths. While void doNothing() does not respond with anything, int increment(int i1) replies with a message that contains the call parameter plus 1. Both int add(int i1, int i1) and int add6ints(int i1, int i2, int i3, int i4, int i5, int i6) return the sum of their input parameters. The calculator was implemented as a literal-style Web service using the Microsoft .NET framework. We then called the different operations with random values and saved the resulting SOAP requests and responses into files. These where then fed into the different compressors for evaluating their compression performance.

The second class of services transmits significantly more data, particularly string data, resulting in large messages. Here, the amount of payload clearly dominates the enveloping SOAP protocol overhead. The Amazon e-commerce service (http://webservices.amazon.com/AWSECommerceService/AWSECommerceService.wsdl) is an example of this type. Its message format is defined by a complex XML schema that makes heavy use of attributes for content structuring.

This service was used for our performance evaluation as the second benchmark. The underlying SOA provides an ItemSearch operation with a ResponseGroup parameter that controls the response message verbosity. We started three calls with the search keyword *Web service*. While we set the ResponseGroup parameter to *small* for the first call, we chose *medium* and *large* for the other two requests. The request and response messages were again saved into files. For analytical reasons, we recorded the fraction of xsd:string data in the response messages: 47% (small), 35% (medium), and 37% (large).

For evaluating XML-schema-aware compressors, we needed to obtain the schemas for both benchmark Web services. These consist of an application-specific part (that can be extracted from the corresponding WSDL file) and an application-independent part for the enveloping SOAP 1.1 markup (available at http://schemas.xmlsoap.org/soap/envelope). In order to be able to include Xebu into our evaluation, we had to convert the schemas to the Relax NG language because Xebu does not support XML schema. We used the tools Sun Relax NG Converter (http://www.xml.com/pub/r/1265) and Trang (http://www.thaiopensource.com/relaxng/trang.html) for this conversion.

Compression Performance

We used the SOAP data generated by the previously described benchmark Web services to evaluate the compression effectiveness of the different approaches. We applied all compressors in their default settings; that is, we did not use any additional command-line parameters. Because Xebu is not a ready-to-use command-line tool but a set of Java classes providing an API (application programming interface), we implemented a minimal wrapper application that uses omission automata as well as precaching.

For the results achieved by the different compressors, we state not only the resulting file sizes S but also λ, the so-called compression ratio which is the quotient $S_{compressed}/S_{uncompressed}$. Besides the values for every single operation request and response, we also state the sum of all file sizes $\sum$. The results are shown in Table 1.

For the sake of readability, we omitted the individual values of λ. Instead, we specify only the best, worst, and average values here. Since the average compression value is not weighted by file size, it differs from $\sum_{compressed}/\sum_{uncompressed}$.

Because WBXML, Millau, and BiM cannot be applied to SOAP data, we could not include them into our evaluation. We also excluded XML Xpress because there is no publicly available implementation. Unfortunately, the implementation of XGrind from July 19, 2002 (which is available online at http://sourceforge.net/projects/xgrind), did not work properly. When decompressing, XGrind yielded invalid SOAP messages and thus was excluded from our evaluation, too. Because Xebu failed to process the Relax NG translation of the Amazon Web service grammar, we omitted the corresponding test cases for this compressor.

Even though these problems show that some implementations are not yet ready for everyday use, the performance of the schema-aware com-

Table 1. Compression results for the SOAP data from both Web services (all file sizes are specified in bytes)

	Uncompr.	gzip	XMill	XMLPPM	Fast Infoset	Xebu	Diff. Enc.
doNothing (Request)	336	224	338	167	210	103	21
doNothing (Response)	344	229	352	173	210	103	21
increment (Request)	381	236	334	177	246	127	52
increment (Response)	425	249	351	187	246	127	52
add (Request)	401	239	360	181	269	135	106
add (Response)	401	238	361	180	246	127	95
add6ints (Request)	559	307	436	242	397	217	155
add6ints (Response)	429	255	378	195	254	135	104
Amazon *small* (Request)	680	371	519	319	455	-	255
Amazon *small* (Response)	9,144	1,625	2,072	1,576	7,446	-	2,366
Amazon *medium* (Request)	681	373	518	321	456	-	257
Amazon *medium* (Resp.)	60,319	8,795	8,298	7,190	46,283	-	16,096
Amazon *large* (Request)	680	371	520	319	455	-	255
Amazon *large* (Response)	229,619	31,977	31,977	32,171	236,349	-	88,103
$\sum$	374,399	59,353	46,814	43,398	293,522	-	107,938
λ_{best}	1.00	0.15	0.11	0.11	0.58	0.30	0.06
λ_{worst}	1.00	0.67	1.02	0.50	0.81	0.39	0.38
$\lambda_{average}$	1.00	0.50	0.71	0.39	0.67	0.32	0.24

pressors is quite promising. The best average compression ratios are achieved by differential encoding and Xebu. They perform especially well with the small messages originating from the calculator Web service. These can hardly be compressed by gzip and XMill because they have to embed extra encoding rules in addition to the actual data. The compressor XMLPPM shows the best performance out of the approaches that are not schema aware. Fast Infoset achieves its best performance for small files, but the best compression ratio is only 0.58.

The situation is different for the large messages of the Amazon Web service. Here, differential encoding is clearly outperformed by gzip, XMill, and XMLPPM for medium and large responses. The reason is the large fraction of hardly predictable tag sequences containing large amounts of string data: Differential encoding cannot compact these effectively and thus does not yield files of competitive size. Again, Fast Infoset achieves only poor compression ratios.

While none of the available compressors achieved good compression ratios for all kinds of files and file sizes, it becomes obvious that schema-aware compression seems to be the most promising way to arrive at compact SOAP message encodings.

PUSHDOWN AUTOMATA APPROACH

XML compression tools with dynamic-schema support are either using very expensive computations (differential encoding) or dynamically growing data structures like coding tables (Xebu). Both strategies are disadvantageous, especially in the domain of resource-constrained devices. For this reason, it was our major concern to develop an approach with excellent compression ratios that features low computational complexity and requires only small amounts of memory.

Existing XML compressors like Exalt, BiM, and Xebu suggest that using automata for representing structure information of XML data is a promising way to achieve these goals. However, since the languages described by a DTD or XML schema do not necessarily belong to the class of regular languages, a plain FSA as used by Exalt, BiM, and Xebu is not sufficient to represent the described grammars. Therefore, only parts of the XML tree, like the direct children of a node, can be processed by a single FSA. Segoufin and Vianu (2002) discuss this problem in detail. Consequently, BiM and Exalt have to employ multiple automata and an additional mechanism that organizes the compression process by deciding when to use which of them. In Xebu, the implemented FSA does not fully represent the Relax NG grammar, either. Instead, it only extends the compression algorithm in order to improve the compression results.

Hence, more powerful automata concepts like tree or pushdown automata (PDA) are required for expressing XML grammars entirely (Murata, Lee, & Mani, 2001).

Architecture

The commonly available WSDL description of a Web service provides an XML schema definition. Our approach is based on a single deterministic PDA that is derived from this specific grammar. Both the sender and the receiver generate this PDA as a first step. Before sending a SOAP message, the sender traverses the PDA according to the message structure. The markup structure of the message is thus represented by the path taken through the automaton. The states passed (markup) as well as the values of the leaf elements (simple types) are encoded and sent to the receiver. Finally, the receiver reconstructs the original document following the encoded path through the automaton.

For DTD grammars, Segoufin and Vianu (2002) show that improvement in the speed of parsing can be achieved by using deterministic pushdown automata. Since DTD grammars are outdated, we adopted the concept of using PDAs for XML processing and extended it for use with XML schema.

In the following, we introduce an algorithm that constructs a single PDA representing an entire XML schema. It is due to the nature of this approach that the PDA provides two important features. On the one hand, it is a highly efficient parser and on the other hand it can also be used for data compression, as we will show.

The input of our algorithm is an arbitrary XML schema document that defines the structure of the documents to be exchanged. Figure 1 shows an example that will be used to demonstrate our approach. Common SOAP applications use more complex schema documents, of course, and import other XML schema documents for processing different name spaces.

First of all, the XML schema document has to be converted into a regular tree grammar (RTG) G. An RTG is defined as a four-tuple consisting of a set of nonterminal symbols N, a set of terminal symbols T, a set of production rules P, and a set of start symbols $S \subseteq N$. Murata et al. (2001) describe the conversion of an XML schema document into an RTG in detail. The RTG for our example is as follows.

$$G = (N, T, P, S) = (\{A, B, C, \text{xsd:int}\}, \{a, b, c\}, P, \{A\})$$

with

$$P = \{$$
$$A \rightarrow a\,(B + \varepsilon),$$
$$B \rightarrow b\,(AA + C),$$
$$C \rightarrow c\,(\text{xsd:int})$$
$$\}$$

Every simple and complex data type used is converted into a nonterminal symbol (written in capital letters or prefixed with *xsd:*). Element names result in terminal symbols (small letters). Each nonterminal symbol that represents an element that is declared on the top level of the XML schema document belongs to the set of start symbols.

The structure of valid documents is defined by the production rules. The nonterminal symbols on the left-hand side are subsequently replaced by the terminal symbol and the regular expression on the right-hand side. The regular expression describes the content model of the terminal symbol. Since the nonterminal symbols of the content model will also be replaced by terminal symbols matching the rules, the content model defines which child elements an XML element may have. The rules in this example can be read as follows: An element a contains an element b or (+) nothing (ε), while b contains either two a elements or a c element, which contains an integer value. Therefore, G is equivalent to the schema in Figure 1.

In a second step, an FSA is constructed for each content model, that is, for each regular expression (see Figure 2). Aho, Sethi, and Ullman (1988) describe the underlying conversion algorithm in detail. For each element of the grammar, the FSAs define the sequences of direct child elements that are allowed to follow.

Finally, the PDA is constructed. It accepts input words by emptying the stack. Thus, it stops when a special start symbol Z that is initially put on the stack is popped and not pushed again immediately. The states of the PDA consist of a special start state, one state for each simple type (like xsd:int, xsd:string, etc.), and two states for each complex type (an opening one and a closing one).

Creating the transitions of the PDA comes next. Each transition consists of a three-tuple (read, pop, push), where *read* represents the tag to be read from the input. The value *pop* indicates the top-stack symbol. Both have to be matched by the current input stream and stack for the transition to be executed. The *push* value announces the symbols that will be written onto the stack. It can consist of zero, one, or more symbols. Note that *push* values consisting of multiple symbols are specified in inverse order.

Figure 1. Recursive XML schema description

```
<xsd:schema xmlns:xsd="http://www.w3.org/2001/XMLSchema">
  <xsd:element name="a" type="A"/>
  <xsd:complexType name="A">
    <xsd:choice>
      <xsd:element name="b" minOccurs="0">
        <xsd:complexType>
          <xsd:choice>
            <xsd:element ref="a" minOccurs="2" maxOccurs="2"/>
            <xsd:element name="c" type="xsd:int"/>
          </xsd:choice>
        </xsd:complexType>
      </xsd:element>
    </xsd:choice>
  </xsd:complexType>
</xsd:schema>
```

Figure 2. Set of finite-state automata generated from the regular tree grammar

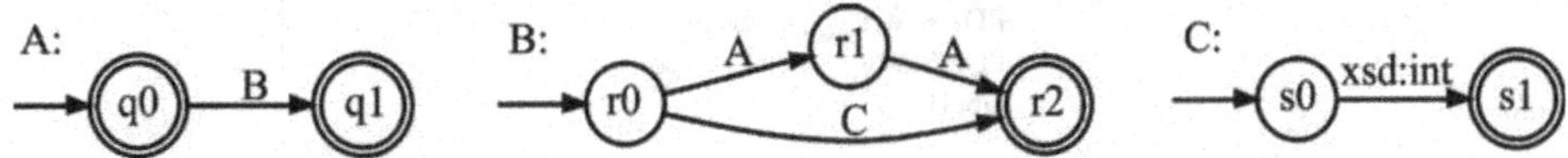

There need to be transitions from the start state to each opening state of a nonterminal symbol n_i that belongs to the set of start symbols ($n_i \in S$). Each transition consists of the opening tag that belongs to the destination state (read), the stack start symbol Z (pop) that will be pushed onto the stack again, and is followed by the start state of the FSA belonging to the destination state type (push). Matching transitions from all closing states that belong to $n_i \in S$ and to themselves are added. They read an empty string (#) from the input stream and pop Z from the stack. Thus, the PDA terminates. Figure 3 shows the algorithm that describes how to create all other transitions.

A graphical representation of the resulting PDA is given in Figure 4. The basic idea behind this type of automaton is to simulate the processing of the FSAs by stack operations. In this way, the PDA checks if the number and sequence of child elements is correct for each element.

At this stage, the automaton is ready for parsing. Finally, we augment the PDA with the core feature that additionally allows data compression: Each transition that originates in a state with more than one outgoing path is tagged with a unique binary identifier (depicted as circled values in Figure 4).

The basic idea of our compression method is to represent a document by the sequence of transitions that were passed when processing the document with the PDA. It is an essential premise, of course, to ensure an unambiguous decoding of the code words used for tagging the transitions. A suitable and beneficial algorithm for generating such codes is the Huffman algorithm (Huffman, 1952). Our implementation creates a Huffman table for every state that maps code words to outgoing transitions. Currently, we apply equal probabilities for each transition. In future implementations, one could, however, deduce appropriate heuristics about transition traversal probabilities from the schema.

While the Huffman algorithm is used to encode the path through the PDA, that is, the markup of the document, another method is needed to encode the simple type values efficiently. Our compressor provides the functionality of encoding, decoding, and validating for all simple types considered

Figure 3. Constructing the PDA transitions from a set of FSAs

```
for all fsa ∈ FSAs do
    for all state ∈ fsa.states do

        for all t_in ∈ state.transitions_incoming do
            for all t_out ∈ state.transitions_outgoing do
                label = (
                    t_out.type.tag_open,
                    state,
                    (FSAs.getFSA(t_out.type).startState, t_out.destState));
                createPDATransition(
                    PDAStates_close.get(t_in.type),
                    PDAStates_open.get(t_out.type),
                    label);
            end for
        end for

         if state ∈ fsa.finalStates then
            for all t ∈ state.transitions_incoming do
                label = (fsa.type.tag_close, state, null);
                createPDATransition(
                    PDAStates_close.get(t.type),
                    PDAStates_close.get(fsa.type),
                    label);
            end for
        end if

        if state = fsa.startState then
            for all t ∈ state.outgoingTransitions do
                label = (
                    t.type.tag_open,
                    state,
                    (FSAs.getFSA(t.type).startState, t.destState));
                createPDATransition(
                    PDAStates_open.get(fsa.type),
                    PDAStates_open.get(t.type),
                    label);
            end for
        end if

        if state ∈ ({fsa.startState} ∩ fsa.finalStates) then
            label = (fsa.type.tag_close, state, null);
            createPDATransition(
                PDAStates_open.get(fsa.type),
                PDAStates_close.get(fsa.type),
                label);
        end if

    end for
end for
```

by XML schema. For each simple type, an appropriate binary encoding is used, for example, a 32-bit integer value for xsd:int. Whenever the PDA executes a transition labeled with a simple type, it appends the binary-encoded value to the output bit stream. Since this data format does not require any data to be buffered during compression or decompression, it is ideal for XML streaming. This is a principal advantage compared to container-based approaches like XMill.

Figure 5 illustrates the encoding generated by the automaton in Figure 4 for an exemplary document matching the grammar in Figure 1. The markup is encoded as the path of transitions

Figure 4. Pushdown automaton constructed form the XML grammar

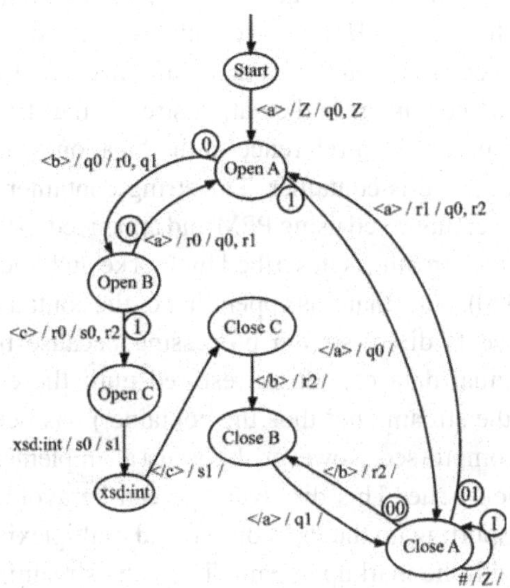

through the PDA (using zero bits for unambiguous transitions). Compact binary representations are used to encode the simple types in line.

The decompression process works vice versa; the receiver seeks the path through the instance of the PDA according to the instructions of the bit stream generated during compression. Whenever a transition is executed, the matching XML tag is written into the output document. Transitions labeled with simple types are processed as follows: Either the PDA reads a fixed number of bits from the bit stream (e.g., 32 bits for xsd:int) or it reads an arbitrary number of bytes until it encounters a stop byte sequence (this is done for all character-encoded data types like xsd:string).

In order to keep our example simple and compact, it does not provide any information about the handling of attributes and name spaces. Both features are supported, though. Attributes are

Figure 5. Example XML document before and after compression

```
<?xml version="1.0" encoding="ISO-8859-1"?>
  <a>
    <b>
      <a>
      </a>
      <a>
        <b>
          <c>64382739</c>
        </b>
      </a>
    </b>
  </a>
```

(a) Text encoding using 119 bytes

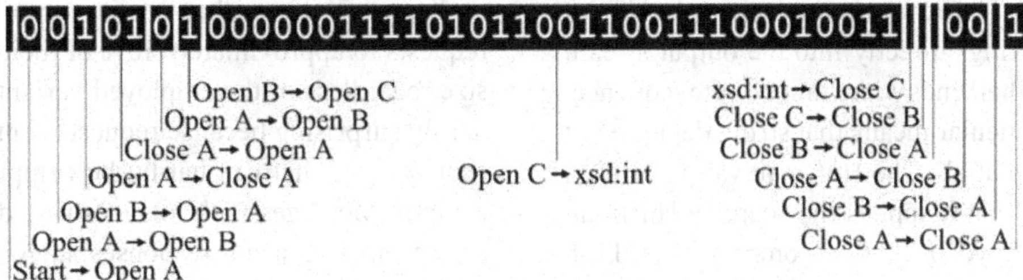

(b) Binary encoding using 42 bits ≈ 6 bytes

handled in the same way as elements. However, they are marked with a special flag to avoid naming ambiguities. For instance, <a b="c">d</a> is treated like <a><b$_{att}$>c</b$_{att}$>d</a>. All of the name-space information provided by an XML schema document is also adopted and incorporated into the PDA; that is, each transition label holds information about the name space of the tag to be processed. Since the name-space prefixes of the input document are not encoded, this information is lost during compression. Therefore, the decompression step includes the generation of new generic name-space prefixes.

Our approach addresses the main requirements annunciated by W3C. If an application uses an API like SAX and interacts with the automaton instead of working with the XML text representation, the binary representation can be written (or read) directly. Furthermore, the generated encoding is independent of transport mechanisms in any case and can be processed very efficiently. In the following section, we will evaluate the compactness achieved by our approach.

Performance Comparison

As the first step to evaluation, we implemented our approach in Java. The resulting program, called Xenia, was used to compress the recorded messages of the two benchmark Web services described in the above section during the evaluation setup.

Three different settings for string encoding were tested. The *none* encoding places the UTF-8 encoded strings directly into the output stream and marks their ends with a unique byte sequence. This in particular means that string data are not compressed at all. The Huffman variant differs in the way that it applies the adaptive Huffman algorithm (Sayood, 2000) to compress the UTF-8 encoding string. The third encoding applies the prediction-by-partial-match (PPM) algorithm instead, which is known to be one of the best schemes for string compression. However, single strings are rather short, and PPM needs a few hundred bytes of data to achieve its maximum performance. Hence, we gathered all string data occurring in the input stream in a so-called string container. In the output stream, the string is replaced by a reference to the location of the string in this container. The string container is then compressed using PPM and appended to the output stream, as described by Liefke and Suciu (2000). Note that this appending of the container prevents direct stream processing because the original data cannot be restored until the end of the stream (and thus the container) has been decompressed. However, this is just an implementation issue. This disadvantage can be avoided by splitting up the PPM output and multiplexing it with the markup stream. Thus, the streaming option is preserved (Cheney, 2001).

Compression results for the messages yielded by the calculator Web service are shown in Figure 6. Because no strings are exchanged here, all three Xenia variants produce the same results. Hence, variants are not differentiated. Xenia outperforms all other compressors clearly in this benchmark.

The results for the messages of the Amazon Web service are depicted in Figure 7. We chose to show the compression ratio λ instead of file sizes. The reason is that the size of the uncompressed files varies between 680 and 229.619 bytes. Hence, file size depiction would have rendered small byte values nearly invisible.

Figure 7 shows that Xenia compresses all requests to approximately 10% of their original size regardless of the employed variant. This is hardly surprising because requests contain only short strings that can hardly be compressed in general. Messages with lots of string data such as the three Amazon responses show far more differentiated results for the three string compression variants of Xenia. The *none* encoding achieves compression ratios of 48% (small), 37%

Figure 6. Compression results for the calculator Web service

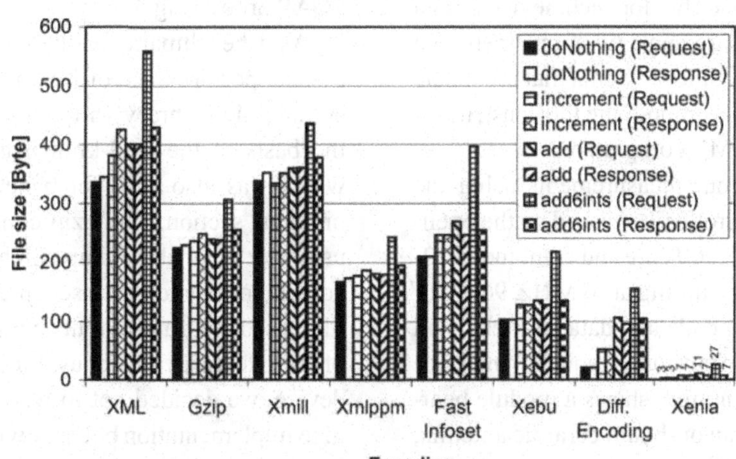

Figure 7. Compression results for the Amazon Web service

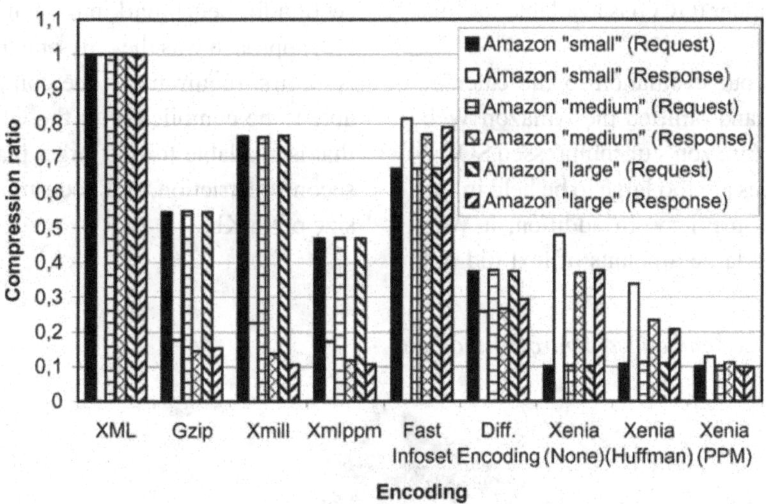

(medium), and 38% (large) for the three responses. Note that this implies that the markup is nearly compressed to zero as the fraction of text that remains uncompressed here was 47%, 35%, and 37% (cf. the section titled "Evaluation Setup" previously). If the string compression variants of Xenia are employed, the compression ratio for the large response improves to approximately 20% (Huffman) and 10% (PPM).

IMPLEMENTATION ON RESOURCE-CONSTRAINED DEVICES

In the introduction, we pointed out that a very important application domain of SOAP compression is the field of mobile and embedded computing. The devices predominating here are typically battery powered. Furthermore, they have only limited computing power and memory resources at their disposal. We evaluated our approach with regard to code size and processing time in order to show that our solution is viable for such devices. As a basis for our measurements, we implemented a code generation module for Xenia that is capable of outputting C code embodying the constructed schema-specific XML compressor.

We conducted our measurements using the Jennic JN5121 controller. It is based on the open-source OpenRISC 1000 core and combines a 32-bit microcontroller running at 16 MHz, 96 Kb of shared memory for code and data, as well as an IEEE 802.15.4 compliant radio frequency interface on a single chip. Figure 8 shows a module bearing the controller, an on-board ceramic antenna, a crystal, and a nonvolatile memory chip. All that is needed to make such a stamp-sized board operational is a battery. An adapted version of the GNU C Compiler (GCC) is available for this platform.

We confined our evaluation to the calculator Web service and omitted the Amazon Web service because Amazon's uncompressed SOAP response messages are too large to be held in the microcontroller's memory. In addition, a Web service returning large amounts of text did not appear to be a typical use case for embedded SOAP processing.

As a benchmark for the code size and processing performance of Xenia, we used the zlib compression library (http://www.zlib.net). It is the basis of the well-known gzip compressor, which was also used for benchmarking in the previous section. The gzip compressor directly uses the algorithms implemented in zlib and adds a command-line user interface as well as file-based input and output operations. Since both of these features are not useful on our embedded device, we decided not to work with the whole gzip implementation but only with zlib as its core component.

We originally planned to also include the other compressors that were used in the previous section for benchmarking, but unfortunately the zlib approach was the only one that was feasible. As a first requirement, the compressor must be able to be compiled with the GNU C Compiler that is available for the target platform and, as a second restriction, the code must not exceed a size of 96 Kb.

Figure 8. Coin-sized embedded controller module

Since the differential encoding approach has been implemented in Java and Python instead of C, it was not usable on our target platform. The same holds for the Fast Infoset implementation, which is written in Java. XMill and XMLPPM are written in C++, which is generally supposed to compile. Unfortunately, both projects exceeded the available memory size, which made the linking process fail. It is impossible to name the exact code sizes for our target platform because these are determined by the linking process. However, in order to roughly estimate the sizes of their memory footprints, we compiled and linked both projects successfully on an Intel 32-bit system. This resulted in the following code size for the statically linked binaries: 829.404 bytes (XMill compressor), 828.508 bytes (XMill decompressor), 643.416 bytes (XMLPPM compressor), and 647.512 bytes (XMLPPM decompressor). Although these code sizes are generally not transferable to our target device (because they where measured for a different architecture), these values show clearly that it is certainly impossible to build these projects with a memory limit of 96 Kb. Therefore, we use zlib as the only benchmark for Xenia in this section.

One difficulty in conducting run-time measurements is to isolate different sources of execution time and memory demand from each other. In order to consider the compression step only, we parsed the XML input files off line and then fed the resulting sequences of SAX events into the Xenia compression engine running on the microcontroller. In a real application scenario, these SAX events would have been generated by the application. For zlib we used the plain XML strings since this is the most natural way of using a general-purpose compressor. In order to eliminate input and output times as far as possible, we included all input data into our binaries instead of using the serial port or radio interface of our device. In consequence, we could continuously measure in-memory compression and decompression performance.

The Xenia pushdown automaton for compressing the SOAP messages of the calculator Web service has 59 states and 83 transitions. In the generated C file, it is implemented through a number of cascaded switch-case statements for transiting the automaton from the current state to the next one. This stepping is triggered by the reception of a SAX event for the compression case or the reception of the corresponding bit sequence for the decompression case.

In order to use zlib on our device, we had to isolate all relevant parts for doing gzip-compatible compression and decompression because the full-featured zlib library was too big to fit into the device memory. Then we implemented a short wrapper program (minimal in-memory gzip/gunzip) for invoking these routines in their default settings.

Table 2 gives an overview of the resulting code sizes for the calculator Web service. The values in the Xenia row include the code sizes of the automaton, the stack, and a number of helper functions. The zlib row shows the code sizes of all functionalities needed for executing gzip-compatible compression and decompression. We have listed the code sizes for compression and decompression separately as well as for the case where both functions are included. For Xenia,

Table 2. Code sizes for compressing and decompressing calculator Web service messages using Xenia and the general-purpose compression library zlib

	Compression	Decompression	Both
Code size for Xenia (bytes)	22,328	20,228	39,556
Code size for zlib (bytes)	39,420	39,504	51,608

the code for compression is slightly bigger than for decompression. This mainly results from the fact that the compression PDA contains a number of string constants that incoming SAX tokens must be compared to. In addition, the stack is not required for decompression and can thus be omitted there. If both automata are included, the resulting code is slightly smaller than the sum of compression and decompression because they share a certain amount of functionality that is not duplicated. Even though the PDAs for compression and decompression are basically the same—except for switching input and output—we currently generate two stand-alone automata for the sake of simplicity. However, if both functionalities are required, a shared automaton could be realized that is hardly bigger than one of the two separate ones. Like this, even smaller implementations are possible. The results clearly show that Xenia has a significantly smaller memory footprint than the general-purpose compression and decompression routines of zlib. This is true for compression, decompression, and the combination of both.

It is important to stress that the measured code sizes of Xenia do not include code for transforming the string representation of a SOAP message into a sequence of SAX events. If this functionality is required, an additional SAX token creator must be implemented on the device. A suitable solution is available from Unicoi Systems, Inc., which roughly adds 15 Kb of code (http://www.unicoi.com/fusion_web/fusion_xml_sax_microparser.htm). Most applications in this field will fire these events directly, bypassing the string representation of SOAP messages.

To measure the execution time, we subtracted the time when the first piece of input data was fed into the (de)compressor from the time when the last output piece left it. The measurement resolution (the so-called tick time) was 0.25 ms. This means that if, for example, an execution time of 3 ms was measured, the execution actually took between 3.0 and 3.25 ms. In order to compensate for this systematic error, we added the average underestimation of 0.125 ms (half a tick time) to the measured time intervals. Table 3 shows the resulting execution times of compression and decompression for the eight different SOAP messages. As a benchmark, the performance of the zlib routines is also shown in the table. We repeated the experiment 10 times but did not notice any differences in execution time.

The performance result of Xenia can be interpreted as follows. It is notable that in most cases decompression works faster than compression. We found two reasons for this. One is that the strings attached to the transitions must be compared with those in the SAX events in order to

Table 3. Execution time of compression and decompression for different messages of the calculator Web service

	Xenia		zlib	
	Compression (ms)	Decompression (ms)	Compression (ms)	Decompression (ms)
doNothing (Request)	1.875	0.875	27.125	14.375
doNothing (Response)	1.875	0.875	27.875	14.625
increment (Request)	2.875	1.875	29.125	15.375
increment (Response)	2.875	2.125	30.625	16.625
add (Request)	3.375	3.125	31.125	16.375
add (Response)	2.875	2.125	30.875	16.375
add6ints (Request)	6.625	11.125	42.625	24.375
add6ints (Response)	3.125	2.875	32.625	17.625

trigger the automaton for the compression case. This inherently slow operation is not required for decompression. The other reason is that the stack of the pushdown automaton does not have to be considered during decompression. Despite this, the decompression of the add6ints request is slower than the corresponding compression. This is due to an implementation issue: The conversion of numeric values into strings is currently implemented rather inefficiently. This becomes especially noticeable for this request because it contains six integer values. Comparing the processing times of the different SOAP documents shows that the duration of both compression and decompression correlates with the number of XML elements contained in the input files. This is hardly surprising because each element causes a number of state transitions in the PDA that in turn dominate the execution time. As the binary Xenia encodings of the SOAP messages hold the contained information in a very compact fashion, the execution time correlates closely with the size of the binary encodings of the corresponding messages (cf. the rightmost column of Figure 6).

The zlib compression and decompression routines work significantly slower than Xenia, with factors ranging between 2 and 15. Unlike Xenia, the execution time obviously does not correlate linearly with the input data sizes. Comparing the results in the different rows, we can clearly see a temporal offset: roughly 20 ms for compression and 10 ms for decompression. This traces back to certain initialization tasks that have to be executed each time before starting a new compression or decompression task. Similar to Xenia, the zlib decompression works nearly two times faster than the zlib compression. This effect is caused by the run-time profile of the Lempel-Ziv-Storer-Szymanski algorithm (Storer & Szymanski, 1982), which has to carry out a text pattern search for compression. Decompression, on the other hand, is basically done by performing an index lookup, which is a significantly faster operation.

All in all, these results show that Xenia achieves very promising compression results with respect to compression effectiveness, code size, and run-time performance. Although the current Xenia implementation in C definitely leaves room for further performance optimizations, it already outperforms the general-purpose compression routines of zlib in terms of speed and memory efficiency.

CONCLUSION AND FUTURE WORK

The verbose nature of XML text representation has bred several efforts in research and standardization groups aiming at more compact serializations. In this article, we contribute a schema-aware XML binary encoding algorithm that complies with the recommendations of the W3C Binary XML Working Group.

We outlined how a pushdown automaton can be derived from an XML schema document. In addition to XML parsing and validation, such an automaton can be used for XML compression. This is done by encoding the path through the automaton while parsing the input document instead of encoding the document directly. Most simple types can inherently be serialized very efficiently with their optimal binary representations because the PDA also incorporates type information. In addition, three different encodings for string data were proposed and evaluated.

We conducted an extensive performance analysis that compared our PDA compressor implementation, called Xenia, with other XML compression approaches. We showed that Xenia compresses markup nearly to zero. Even XML files containing extensive string passages can be serialized efficiently if PPM string encoding is chosen. All in all, Xenia compacted all XML files down to sizes between 1 and 15%.

Our current implementation does not yet support all features of XML schema such as constraint checking for the ID/IDREF tags. Although it is already capable of compressing most SOAP documents, we are currently completing our Java implementation.

A key advantage of our compression approach is that it economizes on resources. Hence, it is predestinated for SOAP processing on embedded devices. We implemented a code generator module for Xenia that is capable of exporting a schema-specific (de)compressor in C. In our evaluation, we showed that this approach leads to encoders that are fast and memory saving at the same time. We will extend the idea of exporting source code from our Java implementation to application-specific XML compression hardware: To reach this goal, future work might include code generation for hardware description languages like VHDL or Verilog.

While Web service technology promised to overcome heterogeneity problems in distributed systems, it so far failed to penetrate the field of ubiquitous computing, which is considered to be one of the major developments in recent years. From our perspective, one of the key inhibitors for XML gaining ground here is its resource-demanding nature. Thus, the rise of techniques for efficient XML handling will boost the coalescence of two of the most exciting fields in computer science.

REFERENCES

Aho, A. V., Sethi, R., & Ullman, J. D. (1988). *Compilers: Principles, techniques and tools.* New York: Addison-Wesley.

Cheney, J. (2001). Compressing XML with multiplexed hierarchical PPM models. In *Data Compression Conference*, Snowbird (pp. 163-172).

Clark, J., & Murata, M. (2001). *Definitive specification for RELAX NG using the XML syntax.* Retrieved December 20, 2006, from http://www.relaxng.org/spec-20011203.html

Girardot, M., & Sundaresan, N. (2000, May). Millau: An encoding format for efficient representation and exchange of XML over the Web. In *Ninth International World Wide Web Conference*, Amsterdam (pp. 747-765).

Huffman, D. A. (1952). A method for the construction of minimum-redundancy codes. *Proceedings of the Institute of Radio Engineers, 40*(9), 1098-1101.

Kangasharju, J., Tarkoma, S., & Lindholm, T. (2005, November). Xebu: A binary format with schema-based optimizations for XML data. In *Proceedings of the International Conference on Web Information Systems Engineering*, New York (pp. 528-535).

Liefke, H., & Suciu, D. (2000). XMill: An efficient compressor for XML data. In *Proceedings of the 2000 ACM SIGMOD International Conference on Management of Data*, Dallas, TX (pp. 153-164).

Murata, M., Lee, D., & Mani, M. (2001, August). Taxonomy of XML schema languages using formal language theory. In *Proceedings of Extreme Markup Languages*, Montreal, Canada (pp. 153-166).

Niedermeier, U., Heuer, J., Hutter, A., Stechele, W., & Kaup, A. (2002, August). An MPEG-7 tool for compression and streaming of XML data. In *Proceedings of the IEEE International Conference on Multimedia and Expo*, Lausanne, Switzerland (pp. 521-524).

Sandoz, P., Triglia, A., & Pericas-Geertsen, S. (2004). *Fast infoset.* Retrieved December 20, 2006, from http://java.sun.com/developer/technicalArticles/xml/fastinfoset

Sayood, K. (2000). *Introduction to data compression* (2nd ed.). San Francisco: Morgan Kaufmann Publishers.

Segoufin, L., & Vianu, V. (2002). Validating streaming XML documents. In *Proceedings of the 21st ACM SIGMOD-SIGACT-SIGART Sym-*

posium on Principles of Database Systems, New York (pp. 53-64).

Storer, J., & Szymanski, T. (1982). Data compression via textural substitution. *Journal of the ACM, 29*(4), 928-951.

Tolani, P., & Haritsa, J. R. (2002, February). XGRIND: A query-friendly XML compressor. In *Proceedings of the International Conference on Data Engineering*, San Jose, CA (pp. 225-234).

Toman, V. (2004, June). Syntactical compression of XML data. In *Proceedings of the International Conference on Advanced Information Systems Engineering*, Riga, Latvia.

Werner, C., Buschmann, C., & Fischer, S. (2005). WSDL-driven SOAP compression. *International Journal of Web Services Research, 2*(1), 18-35.

Werner, C., Buschmann, C., Jäcker, T., & Fischer, S. (2006). Bandwidth and latency considerations for efficient SOAP messaging. *International Journal of Web Services Research, 3*(1), 49-67.

World Wide Web Consortium (W3C). (2005a). *Charter of the efficient XML interchange working group.* Retrieved December 20, 2006, from http://www.w3.org/2005/09/exi-charter-final.html

World Wide Web Consortium (W3C). (2005b). *Working group note: XML binary characterization.* Retrieved December 20, 2006, from http://www.w3.org/TR/xbc-characterization

World Wide Web Consortium (W3C). (2007). *Working draft: Efficient XML interchange (EXI) format 1.0.* Retrieved January 22, 2008, from http://www.w3.org/TR/2007/WD-exi-20071219

ENDNOTE

1 This article is based on the paper "Compressing SOAP Messages by Using Pushdown Automata" by C. Werner, C. Buschmann, Y. Brandt, and S. Fischer, which appeared in the Proceedings of the IEEE International Conference on Web Services (September 18-22, 2006, Chicago, IL, USA). © 2006 IEEE.

This work was previously published in International Journal of Web Services Research, Vol. 5, Issue 3, edited by L. Zhang, pp. 44-63, copyright 2008 by IGI Publishing (an imprint of IGI Global).

Chapter XI
Mining Association Rules from XML Documents

Laura Irina Rusu
La Trobe University, Australia

Wenny Rahayu
La Trobe University, Australia

David Taniar
Monash University, Australia

ABSTRACT

This chapter presents some of the existing mining techniques for extracting association rules out of XML documents in the context of rapid changes in the Web knowledge discovery area. The initiative of this study was driven by the fast emergence of XML (eXtensible Markup Language) as a standard language for representing semistructured data and as a new standard of exchanging information between different applications. The data exchanged as XML documents become richer and richer every day, so the necessity to not only store these large volumes of XML data for later use, but to mine them as well to discover interesting information has became obvious. The hidden knowledge can be used in various ways, for example, to decide on a business issue or to make predictions about future e-customer behaviour in a Web application. One type of knowledge that can be discovered in a collection of XML documents relates to association rules between parts of the document, and this chapter presents some of the top techniques for extracting them.

INTRODUCTION

The amount of data stored in XML (eXtensible Markup Language) format or changed between fferent types of applications has been growing during the last few years, and more companies are considering XML now as a possible solution for their data-storage and data-exchange needs (Laurent, Denilson, & Pierangelo, 2003). The first immediate problem for the researchers was how to represent the data contained in the old relational databases using this new format, so

Copyright © 2009, IGI Global, distributing in print or electronic forms without written permission of IGI Global is prohibited.

various techniques and methodologies have been developed to solve this problem. Next, the users realised that they not only required storing the data in a different way, which made it much easier to exchange data between various applications, but they required getting interesting knowledge out of the entire volume of XML data stored as well. The acquired knowledge might be successfully used in the decisional process to improve business outcomes. As a result, the need for developing new languages, tools, and algorithms to effectively manage and mine collections of XML documents became imperative.

A large volume of work has been developed, and research is still pursued to get solutions that are as effective as possible. The general idea and goal for researchers is to discover more powerful XML mining algorithms that are able to find representative patterns in the data, achieve higher accuracy, and be more scalable on large sets of documents. The privacy issue in knowledge discovery is also a subject of great interest (Ashrafi, Taniar, & Smith, 2004a).

XML mining includes both the mining of structures as well as the mining of content from XML documents (Nayak, 2005; Nayak, Witt, & Tonev, 2002). The mining of structure is seen as essentially mining the XML schema, and it includes intrastructure mining (concerned with mining the structure inside an XML document, where tasks of classification, clustering, or association rule discovering could be applied) and interstructure mining (concerned with mining the structures between XML documents, where the applicable tasks could be clustering schemas and defining hierarchies of schemas on the Web, and classification is applied with name spaces and URIs [uniform resource identifiers]). The mining of content consists of content analysis and structure clarification. While content analysis is concerned with analysing texts within the XML document, structural clarification is concerned with determining similar documents based on their content (Nayak, 2005; Nayak et al., 2002).

Discovering association rules is looking for those interesting relationships between elements appearing together in the XML document, which can be used to predict future behaviour of the document. To our knowledge, this chapter is the first work that aims to put together and study the existing techniques to perform the mining of association rules out from XML documents.

BACKGROUND

The starting point in developing algorithms and methodologies for mining XML documents was, naturally, the existing work done in the relational database mining area (Agrawal, Imielinski, & Swami, 1993; Agrawal & Srikant, 1998; Ashrafi, Taniar, & Smith, 2005; Ashrafi, 2004; Daly & Taniar, 2004; Tjioe & Taniar, 2005). In their attempt to apply various relational mining algorithms to the XML documents, researchers discovered that the approach could be a useful solution for mining small and not very complex XML documents, but not an efficient approach for mining large and complex documents with many levels of nesting.

The XML format comes with the acclaimed extensibility that allows the change of structure, that is, adding, removing, and renaming nodes in the document according to the information necessary to be encoded in. Furthermore, using the XML representation, there are a lot of possibilities to express the same information (see Figure 1 for an example) not only between different XML documents, but inside the same document as well (Rusu, Rahayu, & Taniar, 2005a).

In a relational database, it is not efficient to have multiple tables to represent the same data with different field names, types, and relationships as the constraints and table structures are defined at the design time. In an opposite manner, a new XML document can be added to a collec-

Figure 1. Different formats to express the same information using the XML structure

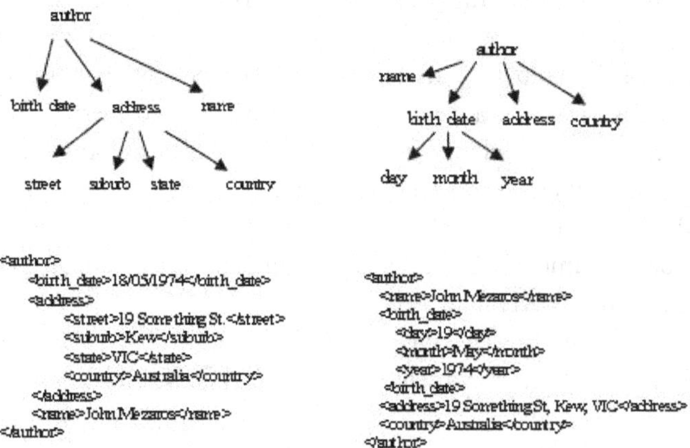

tion of existing XML documents even though it represents the same type of data using a totally different structure and element names, that is, a different XML schema. As a result, researchers concluded that the logic of the relational mining techniques could be maintained, but they needed to assure that the steps of the existing algorithms were looking to the specific characteristics of the XML documents.

Among other XML mining methods, association rule discovery, and the classification and clustering of XML documents have been the most studied as they have a high degree of usability in common user tasks or in Web applications. In this chapter, we present a number of techniques for mining association rules out of XML documents. We chose to analyse this particular type of mining because (a) it is, in our opinion, the most useful for general types of applications in which the user just wants to find interesting relationships in his or her data and wants help to make better business decisions, and (b) the techniques used are easy to understand, replicate, and apply for the common user who does not have a high degree of knowledge of mathematics or statistics, often required by some techniques for performing classification or clustering.

Overview of the Generic Association Rule Concepts

The concept of association rules was first introduced by Agrawal (1993) for relational-database data to determine interesting rules that could be extracted from some data in a market basket analysis. The algorithm is known as the Apriori algorithm, and an example of an association rule extracted could be "If the user buys the product A, he or she will buy the product B as well, and this happens in more than 80% of transactions." The generic terms and concepts related to the Apriori algorithm are as follows. If I represents the set of distinct items that need to be mined, let D be the set of transactions, where each transaction T from D is a set of distinct items $T \subseteq I$. An association rule R is an implication $X \rightarrow Y$, where $X, Y \subset I$ and $X \cap Y = \emptyset$. The rule R has the support s in D if s% of transactions in D contain both X and Y, and the confidence c if c% of transactions in D that contain X also contain Y. If we use a freq(X,D) function to calculate the percentage of transactions in D that contain X, the support and confidence for the association rule R could be written as the following formulas:

Support (X→Y) = freq (XUY, D) and Confidence (X→Y) = freq (XUY, D) / freq (X, D).

The minimum support and minimum confidence are set at the beginning of the mining process, and it is compulsory that they are observed by the determined rules. In the Apriori algorithm, all the large *k*-itemsets are determined, starting from *k*=1 (itemsets with only one item) and looping through *D* (the set of all transactions) to calculate its support and the confidence. If they are not validated against the minimum required, the *k*-itemset is considered to be not large and is pruned. The algorithm assumes that any subset of items that is not large determines its parent (i.e., the itemset that contains it) to not be large, and this improves the speed of the process a lot. At the end, when all the large itemsets are found, association rules are determined from the set of large itemsets.

Overview of XML Association Rules

For the XML documents, finding association rules means finding relationships between simple or complex elements in the document: in other words, finding relationships between substructures of the XML document. For example, in an XML document containing details of the staff members and students in a computer-science university department, including details of their research publications, an association rule could be "Those staff members who publish their papers with X publisher received an award, and this happens in 75% of cases." Later in the chapter (see the section on Apriori-based approaches), we give some examples of how the generic concepts of *transaction* and *item* are perceived by the XML association rules. We will also show how the concepts of *support* and *confidence* are used by the presented approaches as they need to be correct with regard to the total number of XML transactions that need to be mined.

Our analysis is split in two subsections based on the type of XML documents mined, that is, (a) static XML documents and (b) dynamic XML documents. Static XML documents contain data gathered for a specific period of time that do not change their content (for example, details about purchases in a store for March 2005 and June 2005 might come as two separate static XML documents if the business process stores the data at the end of each month). Dynamic XML documents contain data that are continuously changing in time (an online bookstore, for example, will change its content, represented as an XML document, from one day to another, or even multiple times during the same day depending on the e-customers' behaviour).

Most of the work done in the area of mining association rules from static XML documents use classical algorithms based on the Apriori algorithm, described before in the overview section, while a number of non-Apriori-based approaches have been developed as well. In this chapter we will analyse at least one of each type of algorithms.

In case of dynamic XML documents, the focus is on mining association rules out of historic versions of the documents or out of the effective set of changes extracted between two successive versions. The difference between two versions of the same XML document is named delta, and it can be (a) structural delta, when the difference between versions is done at the schema level, or (b) content delta, when the difference is calculated at the content level (Chen, Browmick, & Chia, 2004).

DISCOVERING ASSOCIATION RULES FROM STATIC XML DOCUMENTS

As specified in the background section, some of the XML association rule mining techniques use the Apriori general algorithm (Agrawal et al., 1993; Agrawal & Srikant, 1998) as a starting point for developing new methodologies specific to the XML document format and extensibility, while completely different techniques have been developed as well. The following analysis is split in two subsections depending on the type of mining algorithm used, that is, (a) Apriori-based approaches and (b) non-Apriori-based approaches.

Apriori-Based Approaches

A first thing to do is to see how the generic concepts related to the association rules (mentioned in the previous section), that is, transactions and items, are mapped to the particular XML format. Even though most of the papers detailed further in the chapter (Braga, Campi, & Ceri, 2003; Braga, Campi, Klemettinen, & Lanzi, 2002; Braga, Campi, Ceri et al., 2002; Wan & Dobbie, 2003, 2004) do not give certain definitions for these concepts, we can determine their view on the matter by analysing the algorithms. If an XML document is seen as a tree (see the example in Figure 3), the set of transactions *D* will be a list of complex nodes formed by querying the XML document for a specific path, a single complex node will form a transaction, and the children of the transaction node will be the items. The main difference from the generic concepts is that, while a generic transaction contains only a limited number of items and is easier to quantify, one XML tree transaction can have a different number of items depending on the level of nesting of the document. A similar definition is given in Ding, Ricords, and Lumpkin (2003), but at a more general level; that is, all the nesting depths (paths) in an XML document are considered to be records starting with the root, so for any node in the document, each child is viewed as a record relative to the other records at the same depth or with similar tags.

A simple and direct method to mine association rules from an XML document by using XQuery (*XQuery*, 2005) was proposed by Wan and Dobbie (2003, 2004). Based on the fact that XQuery was introduced by W3C (World Wide Web Consortium) to enable XML data extraction and manipulation, the algorithm is actually an implementation of the Apriori algorithm's phases using the XQuery Language. In Figure 2, we exemplify the algorithm on an XML document containing information about items purchased in a number of transactions in a store (Figure 2a). The algorithm loops through the XML document, generates the large itemsets in the "large.xml" document (Figure 2b), and then builds the association rule document (Figure 2c). For details on the XQuery code implementation of the *apriori* function and the other functions involved, we

Figure 2. Example of a direct association-rule mining algorithm using XQuery (Wan & Dobbie, 2003, 2004)

```
<transactions>
  <transaction id='1'>
    <items>
      <item>a</item>
      <item>d</item>
      <item>e></item>
    </items>
  </transaction>
  <transaction id='2'>
    <items>
      <item>b</item>
      <item>c</item>
      <item>d</item>
    </items>
  </transaction>
    ..........
</transactions>
```

(a)

```
let $src:=document("transactions.xml")//items
let $minsup:=0.4
let $total:=count($src)*1.00
let $C:=distinct-values($src/*)
let $l:=(for $itemset in $C
        let $items:=(for $item in $src/*
                where $itemset=$item
                return $item)
        let $sup:=(count($items)*1.00) div $total
          where $sup>=$minsup
          return <largeItemset>
             <items>{$itemset}</items>
             <support>{$sup}</support>
          </largeItemset>)
let $L:=$l
return <largeItemsets> {apriori($l, $L, $minsup, $
$src)}
        </largeItemsets>
```

(b)

```
let $minconf:=1.00
let $src:=document("large.xml")//largeItemset
for $itemset1 in $src
let $items1:=$itemset1/items/*
  for $itemset2 in $src
  let $items2:=$itemset2/items/*
  where count(items1)>count(items2) and
          count(commonIts($items1,$items2))=
          count($items2) and $itemset1/support div
            $itemset2/support>=$minconf
  return <rule support="{$itemset1/support}"
             confidence="{(itemset1/support *1.0) div
                        ($itemset2/support *1.0)}">
             <antecedent>{$items2}</antecedent>

<consequent>{removeItms($items1,$items2)}
             </consequent>
          </rule>
```

(c)

refer the reader to the original papers (Wan & Dobbie, 2003, 2004).

The significance of this approach is that the authors demonstrated for the first time that XML data can be mined directly without the necessity of preprocessing the document (for example, mapping it to another format, such as a relational table, which would be easier to mine). The algorithm could work very well in case of XML documents with a very simple structure (as in our example in Figure 2), but it is not very efficient for complex documents. Also, a major drawback, assumed by the authors, is that in the XQuery implementation, the first part of the algorithm, that is, discovering large itemsets (Figure 2b), is more expensive regarding time and processor performance than in other language implementations (e.g., in C++). This drawback is explained by the lack of update operations in XQuery: a large number of loops through the document is required in order to calculate the large itemsets. However, the algorithms promise a high speed when the update operations are finally implemented in XQuery.

Other methodologies for discovering association rules from XML documents are proposed by Braga et al. (2003) and Braga, Campi, Ceri et al. (2002); they are also based on the Apriori algorithm as a starting point and mine the association rules in three major steps, that is, (a) preprocessing data, (b) extracting association rules, and (c) postprocessing association rules. In our opinion, due to the specific XML format, when many levels of nesting could appear inside of a document, simple loops and counts (as in Figure 2) are no longer possible, so the three-step approach seems to be more appropriate for mining various types of XML documents.

Preprocessing Phase

At this stage, a lot of operations are done to prepare the XML document for extracting association rules. In the following, we discuss some important terms and concepts appearing during this step, noting that this phase is the most extended one because a proper identification of all the aspects involved in mining preparation will significantly reduce the amount of work during the other two phases (extracting and postprocessing rules).

The concept of the *context* of the association rules refers to the part(s) of the XML documents that will be mined (similar to the generic concept of a set of transactions). Sometimes, we do not want to mine all of the information contained in an XML document, but only a part of it. For example, in an XML document containing university staff and student information (see Figure 3), we may want to find association rules among people appearing as coauthors. In this case, the *identified context* includes the multitude of nodes relating to publications, no matter if they belong to PhD students or professors. This means the algorithm will not consider the <PhD_courses> nodes or <Personal_info> nodes as they are not relevant to the proposed rules to discover.

Context selection refers to the user's opportunity to define constraints on the set of transactions *D* relevant to the mining problem (Braga, Campi, Ceri et al., 2002). Referring again to our example (Figure 3), we may want to look for association rules considering all the authors in the document, but only for publications after the year 2000, so a constraint needs to be defined on the "year" attribute of each publication element (not visible in the graph, but existing in the original XML document).

If we talk about an association rule as an implication $X \rightarrow Y$, X is the *body* of the rule and Y is the *head* of the association rule. The body and head are always defined with respect to the context of the rule as the support and the confidence will be calculated and relevant only with respect to the established context. In the XML association rule case, the body and the head will be, in fact, two different lists of nodes, that is, substructures of the context list of nodes; only nodes from these two lists will be considered to compose valid XML association rules.

We exemplify the above described concepts, that is, context identification, context selection, and the head and body of the rules, by using the XMINE RULE operator (Braga et al., 2003) on the working example in Figure 3, that is, the "research.xml" document.

We visually identify the mentioned concepts in Figure 4, which details the algorithm proposed by Braga et al. (2003) and Braga, Campi, Ceri, et al. (2002).

The working document is defined in the first line, then the *context*, *body*, and *head* areas are defined together with the *minimum support* and *minimum confidence* required for the rules. The WHERE clause allows constraint specification; in this example, only publications after 2000 will be included in the context of the operator.

The XMINE RULE operator brings some improvements, which could not be solved by the direct association rule mining algorithm in one step which uses XQuery, described at the beginning of the section, as follows:

- The context, body, and head of the operator can be as wide as necessary by specifying multiple areas of interest for them as parts of the XML document or even from different XML documents.
- When specifying the context, body, and head segments, a variable can be added to take some specific values that enhance the context selection facility.

Figure 3. Example of an XML document presented as a tree (research.xml) with the identified context, body, and head

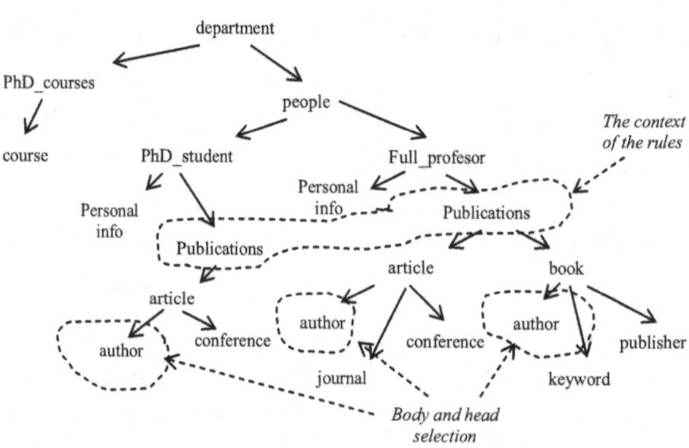

Figure 4. Mining association rules from an XML document using the XMINE RULE syntax

```
XMINE RULE
IN document ("research.xml")
FOR ROOT IN //People/*/Publications/*   <-------- Context identification
LET BODY:=ROOT/author,   }<---- Body & Head
    HEAD:=ROOT/author    }
WHERE ROOT//@year>2000   <-------- Context selection
EXTRACTING RULES WITH
    SUPPORT = 0.1 AND CONFIDENCE =0.2
RETURN
    <Rule support={SUPPORT}
        confidence={CONFIDENCE}>
      <BODY>{ FOR $item IN BODY
            RETURN <Item>{$item}</Item>}
     </BODY>
      <HEAD>{ FOR $item IN HEAD
            RETURN <Item>{$item} </Item>}
      </HEAD>
```

- A GROUP clause can be added to allow the restructuring of the source data.

We exemplify how the first feature can be implemented using the same working example, that is, the "research.xml" document. Suppose we now want to determine rules between publishers and keywords, that is, to find which publishing companies are focusing on specific areas of research. See Figure 5 for a visual representation of the new body and head selections.

The main difference from the one-step mining approach (Wan & Dobbie, 2003, 2004) is that the three-step algorithm (Braga et al., 2003; Braga, Campi, Ceri et al., 2002; Braga, Campi, Klemettinen et al., Klemettinen, 2002) does not work directly on the XML document all the way down to the phase of extracting the association rules; instead, the first phase, that is, preprocessing, has as a final output a relational binary table (R). The table is built as follows (the authors suggest the use of the Xalan, 2005, as an XPath interpreter in the actual implementation): (a) The fragments of the XML document specified in the context, body, and head are extracted and filtered by applying the constraints in the WHERE clause (in case one exists), (b) the XML fragments obtained by filtering the body and head will become columns in the relational table R, (c) the XML fragments obtained by filtering the context will become rows in the table R, and (d) by applying a *contains* function (which, for a given XML fragment *x* and an XML fragment *y*, returns 1 if *x* contains *y*, and 0 otherwise), the binary relational table R is obtained, which will be used during the rule-extraction step to determine binary association rules applicable to the XML document.

The selection done during the preprocessing phase, by specifying the context, the body, and the head of the association rules, is considered by some researchers not generic enough (Ding et al., 2003) because it limits from the beginning the possibility to find and extract other rules (involving other parts of the documents).

Extracting Association Rules

For the one-step mining approach, Figure 2 exemplifies the XQuery implementation of the generic Apriori algorithm. It mainly performs the following steps. Starting from the 1-itemsets (i.e., itemsets with one single item), a *k*-itemset (*k*>1) is built by extending the (*k*-1)-itemset with a new item. For each itemset, the support is calculated as a percentage of the total number of transactions that contain all the items of the itemset. If the itemset is not frequent (large) enough (i.e., its support is less than the minimum support required), it will be removed (pruned), and the algorithm continues with the next itemset until all the large itemsets are determined. Before the calculation of an itemset's support to decide on

Figure 5. The syntax of the XMINE RULE operator introduced by Braga et al. (2003)

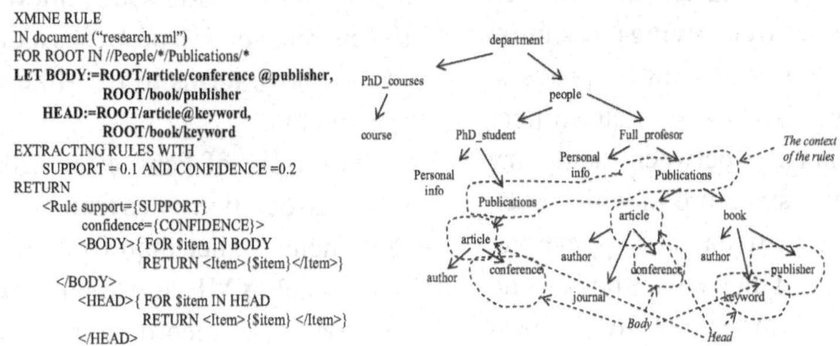

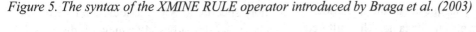

pruning or keeping it, the itemset is considered to be a candidate itemset (i.e., possibly large) if all its sub sets are large (i.e., observe the minimum support required). The association rules are determined from the largest itemsets extracted, and for each of them a confidence is calculated as follows: For a rule X→Y, its confidence is equal to the percentage of transactions containing X that also contain Y.

In the three-step approaches presented in the previous subsection, after obtaining the binary table R in the preprocessing phase, any relational association rule algorithm can be applied (e.g., generic a priori) to get the relationship between the binary values in the table, which represent the existence of an XML fragment inside another XML fragment. The steps of the generic Apriori algorithm have been detailed in the previous paragraph. In the particular case of the binary matrix R, the rows of the matrix will be transactions to be mined by the algorithm. The binary knowledge extracted at this step will signify the simultaneous presence of fragments from the body or head in the selected context.

Postprocessing Phase

After the extraction of the binary association rules from the relational table during the second step, they will be transformed back into XML-specific representations of the discovered rules. We remember from the preprocessing step that the filtered XML fragments obtained by applying the body and head path queries on the XML document became columns in the table, while filtered XML fragments obtained by applying the context path queries became rows. Reversing the process, together with the new knowledge determined, that is, the association rules between the binary values, we get an XML structure in which each <rule> element has two attributes, support and confidence, and two child elements, <body> and <head>, where the fragments of the body and head participating in the rule are listed. An example of the result of applying the XMINE algorithm is presented in Figure 6, in which the following rules are given: "Author A → Author H has 85% support and 20% confidence" and "Author H and Author B → Author A has 70% support and 22% confidence."

Figure 6. Example of XML association rules obtained by applying the XMINE RULE algorithm

```
<RULE support='0.85' confidence='0.20'?
  <BODY>
    <Item><Author>Author A</Author></Item>
  </BODY>
  <HEAD>
    <Item><Author>Author H</Author></Item>
  </HEAD>
</RULE>
<RULE support='0.70' confidence='0.22'?
  <BODY>
    <Item><Author>Author H</Author></Item>
    <Item><Author>Author B</Author></Item>
  </BODY>
  <HEAD>
    <Item><Author>Author A</Author></Item>
  </HEAD>
</RULE>
```

Non-Apriori-Based Approach

In this section, we present one framework for discovering association rules that is different from the earlier described approaches, which were based on the Apriori algorithm sequence. The main feature is that this framework (Feng, Dillon, Wiegand, & Chang, 2003) considers in more detail the specific format of the XML documents, that is, their possible representation as trees. We recall that at the beginning of the section on Apriori-based approaches, we proposed a translation of the terms *transaction* and *item* into some concepts more specific to XML association rule mining. The non-Apriori-based framework discussed in the current section proposes a different mapping of the above terms to tree-like structured XML documents.

The work of Feng et al. (2003) aims to discover association rules from a collection of XML documents rather than from a single document, hence each XML document or tree corresponds to a database record (transaction), where each XML fragment (subtree) corresponds to an item in the transaction. In this context, the framework proposed intends to discover association rules among trees in XML documents rather than among simple-structured items. Each tree is named a *tree-structured item* and is a rooted, ordered tree having its nodes classified into (a) basic nodes with no edges emanating from them and (b) complex nodes, which are internal nodes with one or more edges emanating from them. In Figure 7 we present some of the concepts introduced to define the framework for mining XML association rules.

In Figure 7, there are two tree-structured items, the <PERSON> and <ITEM> elements, extracted from the order.xml example document (Feng et al., 2003), in which the nodes $n_{1,1}$, $n_{2,1}$, $n_{2,2}$, and $n_{2,3}$ are complex, while $n_{1,2}$, $n_{1,3}$, $n_{1,4}$, $n_{2,4}$, $n_{2,5}$, and $n_{2,6}$ are basic. The edges inside the trees are labeled depending on the type of relationship between the nodes. There are two types of labels attached to edges: *ad* (ancestor-descendant) and *ea* (element-attribute). In Figure 7, the edge that connects the PERSON with the Profession node is labeled *ea* because Profession is an attribute of the PERSON in the XML document. All the other edges are labeled *ad* as they represent connections between a parent node and a child node.

There are three types of constraints that can be imposed on nodes and edges, as follows.

1. Level constraints: If *e* is an *ad* relationship $n_{source} \rightarrow n_{target}$, Level (e)=m (m integer) means that n_{target} is the *m*th descendant of the n_{source}.
2. Adhesion constraints: If *e* is an *ea* relationship $n_{source} \rightarrow n_{target}$, Adhesion(e)=strong means that n_{target} is a compulsory attribute of n_{source}, while Adhesion(e)=weak means that n_{target} is an optional attribute of the n_{source}.
3. Position constraints: They refer to the actual contextual position of the node among all the nodes sharing the same parent. For example, in Figure 7, Posi($n_{2,4}$)=last() means the Title node with the Star War Game content is the title of the last ordered CD.

In this framework, a well-formed tree is a tree that observes three conditions: (a) It has a unique root node, (b) for any chosen edge in the tree, if it is labelled *ad*, it will link a complex node with a basic node, while if it is labeled *ea*, the source node needs to be a complex node, and (c) all the constraints are correctly applied, that is, a level constraint can be applied only on an *ad* edge, while an adhesion constraint can be applied only on an

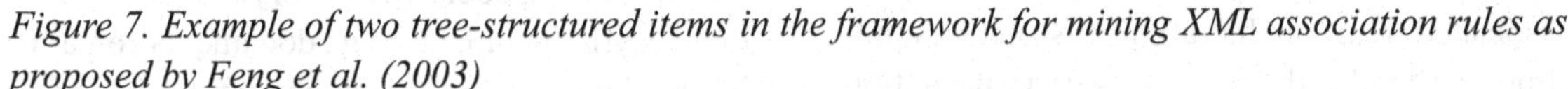

Figure 7. Example of two tree-structured items in the framework for mining XML association rules as proposed by Feng et al. (2003)

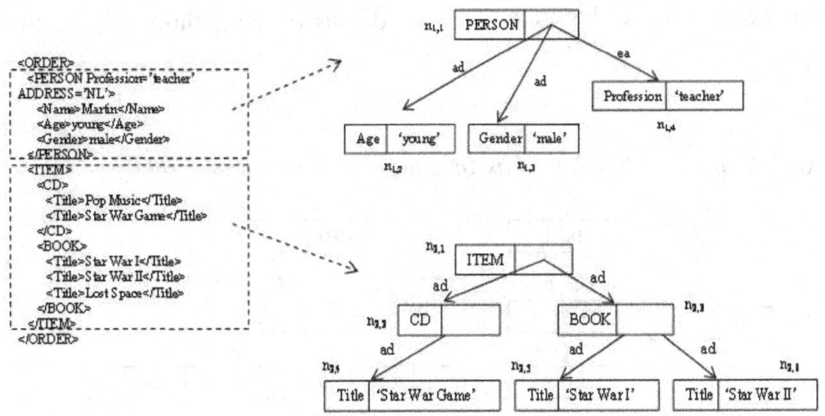

ea edge. Using the above described concepts, the subtree concept (subitem) is defined based on the definition of the subtree relationship. A tree T with root r is a subtree of the tree T' with root r' (noted $T \leq_{tree} T'$) if and only if there is a node n' in T' such that r is a part of n' (noted $r \leq_{node} n'$). We refer the reader to the original paper (Feng et al., 2003) for more details and explanations on these concepts.

Finally, the association rule is defined as an implication $T_1 \rightarrow T_2$ that satisfies two conditions.

1. $X \subset T$, $Y \subset T$ and $X \cap Y = \varnothing$, where T is the set of tree-structured items and
2. For any T_m and $T_n \in (X \cup Y)$, there is no tree T_p that can satisfy the conditions $T_p \leq_{tree} T_m$ and $T_p \leq_{tree} T_n$.

An example of the association rule in terms of tree-structured items (named XML-enabled association rules by the authors) is presented in Figure 8.

The rule exemplified in Figure 8 tells that if a male person orders a CD with the title Star War Game, he will also order two books, that is, *Star War I* and *Star War II*, in this order. Though an algorithm to implement the above described framework is still under development, the obtained association rules are powerful as they address the specific format of the XML documents; the associated items are hierarchical structures, not simple nodes. Furthermore, they carry the notion of order, as exemplified by rule in Figure 8.

Summary of Association Rule Mining Techniques for Static XML Documents

To conclude this section, we make some comments on the major differences between the above discussed XML association rule techniques and the degree of the possible generalization of them, considering both the number of XML documents mined at once and the structure of these documents, together with some experimental results of the authors.

The main difference between the Apriori-based approaches and the non-Apriori-based framework presented in this chapter consists of the way they perceive the notion of *item*, which they consider in their mining algorithms. While the former ones extract the items to be mined as a list of nodes by querying the XML document for a specific path, for the last one, each subtree (substructure) in the XML document tree representation is an item and the framework actually looks to discover association rules between the substructures of the document.

Another significant difference resides in the number of XML documents allowed by the algorithms and the degree of the complexity of the documents (levels of nesting). Sometimes we may want to find association rules from a single XML document (e.g., books in a library) or from two or more XML documents (e.g., documents containing books in a library, one containing personal details of the authors and the third containing

Figure 8. An example of the XML-enabled association rule (Feng et al., 2003)

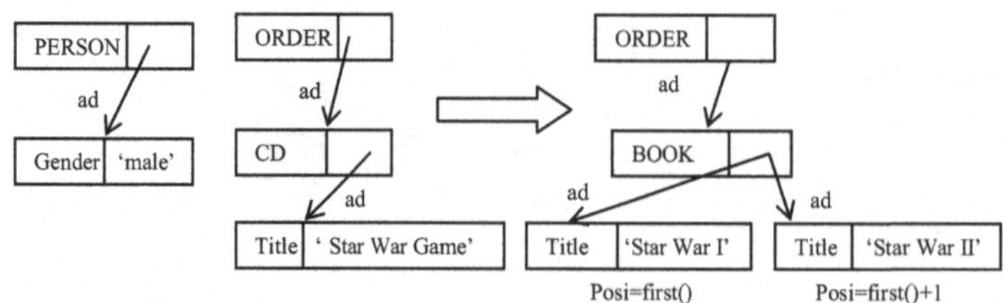

sales of the books for a period of time). If we have a collection of XML documents, it is probable that we will get more interesting information by analysing all the documents together instead of one at a time.

The simple (one-step) XML association rule mining techniques (Wan & Dobbie, 2003, 2004) are considering one single document, with a simple structure (see Figure 2a), for example, an XML document containing transactions in a superstore, with the corresponding purchased items. The authors state that their proposed algorithm "works with any XML document, as long as the structure of it is known in advance" (p. 94), but they consider that applying their algorithm to an XML document with a more complex structure is still an open issue from the performance point of view.

The three-step approaches (Braga et al., 2003; Braga, Campi, Ceri et al., 2002; Braga, Campi, Klemettinen et al., 2002) are designed to work with more complex-structured XML documents (see the example in Figure 3 with five levels of nesting). Still, the structure of the document needs to be known in advance as the context, body, and head of the association rules should be defined at the beginning of the algorithm. The authors acknowledge that, even if the experiments were done without considering efficiency as a main concern, the results proved excellent performance when using the Xalan (2005). Also, the experimental results showed that only a small percentage of time was spent for preprocessing and postprocessing the XML document, while the actual mining was the slowest phase. The authors reckon that any future step in the XQuery development to allow more complex conditions in filtering XML documents will determine a substantial improvement of the mining step's efficiency and speed.

DISCOVERING ASSOCIATION RULES FROM DYNAMIC XML DOCUMENTS

As specified in the background section, this section details some of the work done for dynamic XML document versioning and mining. A dynamic XML document is one that is continually changing its content and/or structure in time depending on the data requested to be stored at a certain moment. An example could be the content of an online bookstore, where any change in the number of existing books, their prices, and/or availability will affect the content of the XML document that stores this information. The possible user (e.g., the online store manager) might decide to store each new version of the XML document, which results after each change, so he or she would be able to refer to the history of the store's content at any time in the future for business purposes. In this case, a high degree of redundancy might appear, and the user will end up with a large collection of XML documents in which a large amount of information is repeated.

The issue for researchers was how to efficiently store all these versions so the user will be able to get a historic version of the document with as less redundancy of information as possible. Moreover, a new question was raised about what kind of knowledge can be discovered from the multiple versions of an XML document; the goal in the case of mining dynamic XML documents would be to find a different type of knowledge than can be obtained from snapshots of data. For example, some parts of the XML document representing the online store could change more often, and some other parts could change together; for instance, deletions could appear more often than updates, and so on. All this information could be usefully utilised by the end user in making business decisions related to the online store's content.

In this section, we will first refer to the work done for versioning XML documents, that is, methodologies that efficiently store the changing XML documents in a way that allows the fast retrieval of the historic versions. They will include our own proposed solution to the issue of versioning dynamic XML documents to collect all the changes between versions in a single XML document, named consolidated delta. Finally, we will describe our proposed solution for mining association rules from changes supported by the dynamic XML documents.

Most of the methodologies addressing the issue of versioning XML documents are based on the concept of the *delta* document (Cobena, Abiteboul, & Marian, 2005; Marian, Abiteboul, Cobena, & Mignet, 2001). This is calculated and built by comparing two consecutive versions of the XML document and recording the changes that have been taking place.

XML versioning techniques come to solve two main issues (Zhao, 2004), as follows:

1. The querying time can be improved by limiting the amount of data that need to be queried if the result of the same query in the previous state of the document is already known.
2. Storing historical structural deltas (the actual changes) of the XML documents can help to find knowledge (e.g., association rules) not just for snapshot data (as in mining static XML documents), but also considering their evolution in time.

For a better understanding of the differences between the XML versioning techniques, we will exemplify them on two versions of an XML document (catalog.xml), which contains data about some products in an online store (Figure 9).

A change-centric management of versions in an XML warehouse was first introduced by Marian et al. (2001). They consider a sequence of snapshots of XML documents and, for each pair of consecutive versions, the algorithm calculates a delta document as the difference between them.

Figure 9. Two consecutive versions of the same XML document, catalog.xml, with corresponding IDs, in both XML document format and trees

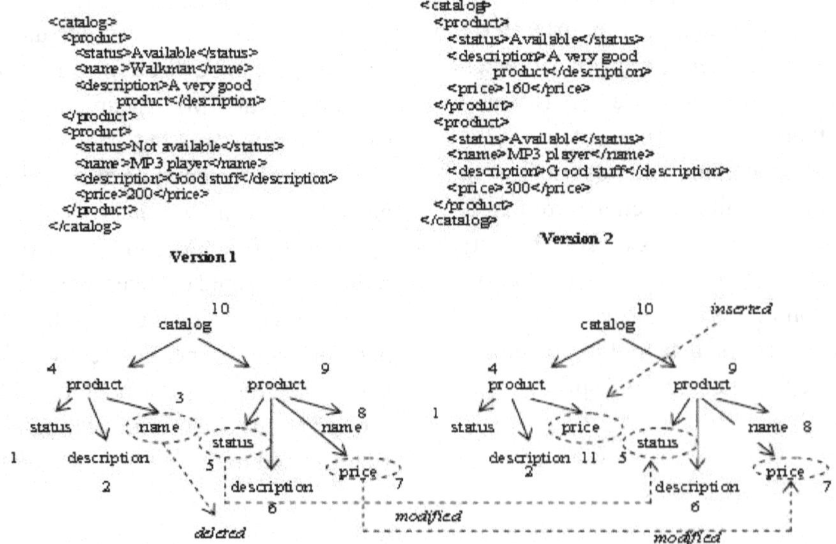

Figure 10. Examples of forward, backward, and completed deltas

Forward delta:	Backward delta:	Completed delta:
Delete (3)	Insert (4,3, T_2)	Delete (4,3,T_2)
Update (5,"Available"	Update (5, "Not available")	Update (5, "Available", "Not available")
Update (7,300)	Update (7, 200)	Update (7,300,200)
Insert (4,3, T_1)	Delete (11)	Insert (4,3,T_1)

Delta Δ_i is a sequence of *update, delete,* and *insert* operations capable to transform the initial version of the document (D_i) into the final version (D_{i+1}). Furthermore, based on the observation that the delta Δ_i is not enough to transform D_{i+1} back into D_i, the authors introduce the notion of *completed delta*. This is a delta that contains more information and works both forward and backward, being able to obtain D_i or D_{i+1} when the other version is available.

In our working example (Figure 9), the forward, backward, and completed deltas are shown in Figure 10.

In the example in Figure 10, T_1 is the tree rooted at node 11, that is, the <price> node, while T_2 is the tree rooted at node 3, the <name> node. These two trees will be included in the completed delta XML document. In the delete and insert sequences, the first parameters are the parent node, the second parameters are the affected node positions, and the third parameters are the trees rooted at the affected nodes. In the update sequences, the first parameters are the affected nodes, the second ones are the new values, while the third parameters are the old values.

In this approach (Marian et al., 2001), a presumptive XML warehouse will need to store the initial version of an XML document together with all the completed deltas calculated in time so the model will be able to successfully solve different versioning requests. At the same time, the authors acknowledge that one of the most important issues in their approach is the storage of the redundant information (e.g., both the old version and new version of elements consecutively updated will be stored in the completed deltas).

Another change detection algorithm, X-Diff, was proposed by Wang, DeWitt, and Cai (2003), focusing on unordered XML document trees (where the left-to-right order among siblings is not important). They argue that an unordered tree model is more appropriate for most applications than the ordered model (where both the ancestor-descendant and the left-to-right order among siblings are important) and propose a methodology that detects changes in XML documents by integrating specific XML structure characteristics with standard tree-to-tree correction techniques. We do not detail here the X-Diff algorithm, but mainly, it performs the followings steps to determine the minimum-cost edit sequence that is able to transform document D_1 into document D_2. (a) It parses the D_1 and D_2 documents and builds the associated T_1 and T_2 trees while at the same time, it computes an XHash value for every node used to represent the entire subtree rooted at the node. (b) It compares the XHash values for the roots and decides if the trees are equivalent (when the XHash values are equal); otherwise, it calculates $\min(T_1, T_2)$ as a minimum-cost matching between trees. (c) It determines the generated minimum-cost edit script E based on the min (T_1,T_2) found at step b.

For our working example, the minimum edit script generated by X-Diff would be:

E= {delete (3), update (5, "Available"), update (7,300), insert (4, (Price, 160)}.

As it can be noticed, the insert operation does not include the position of the new inserted node because the X-Diff technique is focused on the unordered XML trees, and the position of the node is not considered important for the algorithm.

A novel way of storing changes in time with less overhead was proposed by Rusu, Rahayu, and Taniar (2005b). In this approach, earlier versions of the documents can be easily queried and the degree of redundancy is very small. Our algorithm replaces the way of storing differences between two versions of an XML document in deltas and keeping all the deltas in the warehouse with a new concept of *consolidated delta*, in which changes between versions are recorded in a new XML document, modified any time a new version appears. The main idea is to build a single (consolidated) XML delta document containing all the changes supported by the versioned XML document in the T_1–T_n period of time by introducing a new temporal element (namely, <stamp>) to store the changes at each time stamp for each altered element. Each <stamp> element has two attributes: *time* to store the time stamp and *delta* to store the type of change (delta can take one of the values inserted, modified, or deleted).

To exemplify the consolidated delta approach, Figure 11 shows another set of changes that have been applied to the document in Figure 9. The changes between Version 1 and Version 2 are recorded in the first consolidated delta (left), which is built starting from the initial version (Version 1), adding the <stamp> elements as explained before. Similarly, after another set of changes happen at time T_3 (Version 3), new <stamp> elements are added and the consolidated delta is updated to reflect these (right). Every time the consolidated delta is modified to reflect new changes, there are rules to be observed in order to increase the efficiency of the algorithm and eliminate the redundancy as much as possible; we list them here, as follows. (a) If all the children are unchanged, the parent is unchanged. If a parent is unchanged at the time *Ti*, its children are not marked (stamped) for that particular time stamp; they will be easily

Figure 11. Example of the consolidated delta after two series of changes applied to the initial XML document catalog.xml

rebuilt from the existing previous versions of their parents. (b) If any of the children are modified, deleted, or inserted, the parent is modified. If a parent is modified at the time *Ti*, all its children will be stamped, each with their own status, that is, modified, inserted, deleted, or unchanged. (c) If a parent is deleted at the time *Ti*, all its children will be deleted so they will not appear in the consolidated delta for that particular time stamp or for any time stamp after that.

To get a high speed in building the consolidated delta, we assign unique identifiers to elements in the initial XML document and store the maximum ID value. When new elements are inserted in a following version, they will receive IDs based on the existing maximum ID so at any time, one element will be uniquely identified and we will be able to track its changes.

The two big advantages of the consolidated approach are the following: (a) There is a very small degree of redundancy of the stored data as unchanged data between versions will not be repeated, and (b) it is enough for the user to store the calculated consolidated delta to be able to get an earlier version of the document at any time. We have tested the algorithm of building the consolidated delta and it has excellent results for various dimensions of XML documents.

Versioning Dynamic XML Documents Using the Consolidated Delta Approach

The consolidated delta is a very efficient tool when the user wants to retrieve an old version of the document. Suppose the latest version of the document is at the moment T_n in time (see Figure 12), and the user wants to determine the effective look (structure and content) for the XML document at a moment *Ti*, where i<n (i=3 in the example in Figure 12). Using the consolidated delta, he or she does not need to re-create the entire set of intermediate documents from T_n to T_i ($T_n \rightarrow T_{n-1}$, $T_{n-1} \rightarrow T_{n-2} \ldots T_{i+1} \rightarrow T_i$). Instead, the consolidated delta can be directly queried to get the elements that have <stamp> elements with a T_i value of the time attribute. This query will not return at once the entire structure and content of the XML document at the moment T_i— this would be an ideal output. We still have to query backward in the history of certain elements, but only for a limited number, that is, the unchanged ones as the modified or inserted elements will contain the actual values at the time T_i.

When an earlier version is required, the consolidated delta document is scanned starting from the root, and for each element, the algorithm determines if the delta attribute has one of the *modified*, *deleted*, *added*, or *unchanged* values, building, at the same time, the required D_i version of the document as follows. (a) When the delta has the *modified* value, if the element is a complex one (it has children), we analyse the changes for each of its children elements; they may have a *modified*, *deleted*, *added*, or *unchanged* value as well. If the element is not a complex one, we take its value. (b) When the delta has the *inserted* value, if it is a complex element, all its children were inserted, too; so, we take their values as they are returned for the T_i time stamp. If the element is not a complex one, we take its value. (c) When the delta has the *deleted* value, if the parent element was deleted (together with its children) at the time T_i, the consolidated delta will contain the

Figure 12. Using consolidated delta to get an earlier version of an XML document

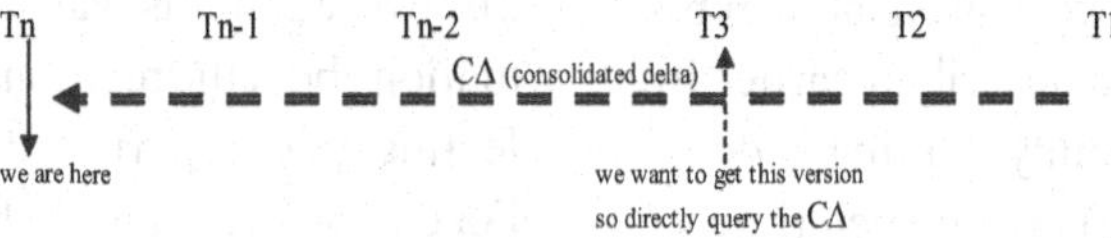

deleted value for the delta and no children details; consequently, the element will not appear in the built version document. (d) When the delta has the *unchanged* value, we know a complex unchanged element does not include its unchanged children; so if we find an unchanged element, we will query backward for each of the T_{i-1}, T_{i-2}, and so forth, and earlier time-stamp changes until we get to a version without an unchanged delta attribute or until we get to the initial D_1 version of the document (included in the consolidated delta as a starting point).

Mining the Changes Extracted from Dynamic XML Documents

In our view, there are two different ways to approach the task of mining dynamic XML documents. Supposing there is a collection of versions of *n* dynamic XML documents stored in an XML data warehouse, composed by using one of the above presented methods, the user might be interested in discovering either of the following:

a. Interesting knowledge (in our case, association rules) that can be found in the collection of historic versions of the document(s)
b. Association rules extracted from the actual changes between versions, that is, from the differences recorded in delta documents

There was some work done to discover frequently changing structures in versions of XML documents (Chen et al., 2004; Zhao, Bhowmick, Mohania, & Kambayashi, 2004; Zhao, Bhowmick, & Mandria, 2004) applicable more to discovering the first type of knowledge (Case a above). We do not detail them here; instead, we will propose a novel method of mining changes extracted from dynamic XML documents (applicable for the second type of knowledge, Case b above) by using the consolidated delta described earlier in the previous subsection. Mainly, mining is done by extracting the set of changes for each time T_i ($2<i<n$, where n is the total number of versions and T_i is the time of each set of changes) as a set of transactions. After that, we mine them applying one of the classic algorithms for discovering association rules, for example, the a priori one (Agrawal et al., 1993). Because the implementation of the actual algorithm is still under review, we will give only a general description of the technique using an example.

We consider again the consolidated delta example in Figure 10. If we extract only the changes from the consolidated delta for each of the times T_2 and T_3, we get the following two transactions:

At time T2 → <catalog> modified & <product> modified & <name> deleted & <price> inserted value="160" & <status> modified value="Available" & <price> modified value=300;

At time T3 → <catalog> modified & <product> modified & <description> modified value="A new stuff" & <price> modified value="150" & <price> modified value="400" & <product> inserted & <status> inserted value="Not available" & <description> inserted value="good book" & <price> inserted value="25";

In a generalized Apriori-based algorithm, the set of items *I* will be the list of all distinct elements from the initial XML document. In our example, *I* = {<catalog>, <product>, <status>, <name>, <description>, <price>}. The extracted changes will form the set of transactions *D*, where each transaction *T* from *D* is a set of items from *I* represented by one set of changes extracted for one time stamp T_i, $2<i<n$. A possible association rule will be an implication $X \rightarrow Y$ where $X, Y \subset I$ and $X \cap Y = \varnothing$. The rule's support and confidence will be calculated with regard to the total number of changes extracted. Dynamic association rules discovered in this way could give precious information about the relationship between changes affecting specific parts of the initial XML document. For example, it could be found that the insertion of

new products determine a fall in the availability of certain products. We are currently working on implementing and proving the efficacy of this mining algorithm.

Summary of Association Rule Mining Techniques for Dynamic XML Documents

In this section, we have presented some of the state-of-the-art work in the area of recording changes between versions of dynamic XML documents, detailing more on the consolidated delta approach, which is an effective way to store successive changes of the documents in a single document. Then, we have presented an algorithm for extracting a historic version of the document at any time where its versions are stored by using the consolidated delta approach. Finally, we presented our view on mining the set of changes extracted for a given period of time.

The methods presented for storing the changes between versions of the XML documents are all using the concept of *delta* as a difference between two consecutive versions of the XML document, but each approach comes with its own definition and implementation as the target is to find the most efficient representation that is easy to interrogate and mine later on. While the work of Marian et al. (2001) proposes building a consolidated delta as a set of instructions able to reverse the initial version of the document to the final one and vice versa for ordered XML documents, the technique introduced by Wang et al. (2003) is similar but focuses on unordered XML documents. A different approach is given by Rusu, Rahayu, and Taniar (2005), in which the proposal is to record the historic changes in one single document, named consolidated delta, that is easy to be queried when the user needs to extract an old version of the document. The same consolidated delta approach can be used to perform the mining of association rules out of the set of changes applied to the initial document, returning possible interesting information about the relationships between changes and their influences on the XML document's behaviour in the future.

FUTURE TRENDS

In this section, we present our view on the future trends in the area of mining XML documents, considering how the existing work answers possible user needs.

- **Mining association rules from static XML documents** (i.e., documents that are not changing their content in time): In this area, the majority of the research work has been focused not so much on determining generic association rules (what type of knowledge can be extracted from a certain XML document or from a collection of XML documents), but more on seeking a confirmation of possible association rules between elements or parts of the document. For example, the majority of the presented algorithms for mining static XML documents need to know from the beginning which are the specific areas they need to look at to find either the antecedent or the consequent of the association rule. In this context, future work is needed to improve the existing methodologies in terms of generalization (Buchner, Baumgarten, Mulvenna, Bohm, & Anand, 2000; Garofalakis, Rastogi, Seshadri, & Shim, 1999). Finding algorithms with a high degree of generalization is imperative as scalability is a priority for the current and future XML-driven applications.
- **Mining association rules from dynamic XML documents** (i.e., documents that change their content in time to allow different formats of data): Dynamic mining is still a very young area in which a lot of research has been undertaken. From our perspective,

intense activity in this field will be noticed soon as Web applications are used on a large scale and manipulate dynamic data. Besides association rules, researchers are looking to find other types of patterns in dynamic XML documents, that is, structural changes from an XML document version to another, and content changes. Our next research work is to implement and evaluate a mining algorithm able to discover association rules and other types of knowledge from the sequence of actual changes of dynamic XML documents. The outcome of this work will be very useful in finding not only what the patterns are in the changing documents, but also how they relate to one another and how they could affect the future behaviour of the initial XML document.

CONCLUSION

This chapter is a systematic analysis of some of the existing techniques for mining association rules out of XML documents in the context of rapid changes and discoveries in the Web knowledge area. The XML format is more and more used to store data that now exist in the traditional relational-database format, and also to exchange them between various applications over the Internet.

In this context, we presented the latest discoveries in the area of mining association rules from XML documents, both static and dynamic, in a well-structured manner, with examples and explanations so the reader will be able to easily identify the appropriate technique for his or her needs and replicate the algorithm in a development environment. At the same time, we have included in this chapter only the research work with a high level of usability in which concepts and models are easy to be applied in real situations without imposing knowledge of any high-level mathematics concepts.

The overall conclusion is that this chapter is a well-structured tool very useful for understanding the concepts behind discovering association rules out of collections of XML documents. It is addressed not only to the students and other academics studying the mining area, but to the real end users as a guide in creating powerful XML mining applications.

REFERENCES

Agrawal, R., Imielinski, T., & Swami, A. N. (1993). Mining association rules between sets of items in large databases. *Proceedings of the ACM International Conference on Management of Data (SIGMOD 1993)* (pp. 207-216).

Agrawal, R., & Srikant, R. (1998). Fast algorithms for mining association rules. In *Readings in database systems* (3rd ed., pp. 580-592). San Francisco: Morgan Kaufmann Publishers Inc.

Ashrafi, M. Z., Taniar, D., & Smith, K. A. (2004a). A new approach of eliminating redundant association rules. In *Database and expert systems applications* (LNCS 3180, pp. 465-474). Heidelberg, Germany: Springer-Verlag.

Ashrafi, M. Z., Taniar, D. & Smith, K. A. (2004b). ODAM: An optimized distributed association rule mining algorithm. *IEEE Distributed Systems Online, 5*(3).

Ashrafi, M. Z., Taniar, D., & Smith, K. (2005). An efficient compression technique for frequent itemset generation in association rule mining. In *Proceedings of International Conference in Advances in Knowledge Discovery and Data Mining (PAKDD 2005)* (LNCS 3518, pp. 125-135). Heidelberg, Germany: Springer-Verlag.

Braga, D., Campi, A., & Ceri, S. (2003). Discovering interesting information in XML with association rules. *Proceedings of 2003 ACM Symposium on Applied Computing (SAC'03)* (pp. 450-454).

Braga, D., Campi, A., Ceri, S., Klemettinen, M., & Lanzi, P. L. (2002). A tool for extracting XML association rules. *Proceedings of the 14th International Conference on Tools with Artificial Intelligence (ICTAI '02)* (p. 57).

Braga, D., Campi, A., Klemettinen, M., & Lanzi, P. L. (2002). Mining association rules from XML data. In *Proceedings of International Conference on Data Warehousing and Knowledge Discovery (DaWak 2002)* (LNCS 2454, pp. 21-30). Heidelberg, Germany: Springer-Verlag.

Buchner, A. G., Baumgarten, M., Mulvenna, M. D., Bohm, R., & Anand, S. S. (2000). Data mining and XML: Current and future issues. *Proceedings of 1st International Conference on Web Information System Engineering (WISE 2000)* (pp. 127-131).

Chen, L., Browmick, S. S., & Chia, L. T. (2004). Mining association rules from structural deltas of historical XML documents. In *Proceedings of International Conference in Advances in Knowledge Discovery and Data Mining (PAKDD 2004)* (LNCS 3056, pp. 452-457). Heidelberg, Germany: Springer-Verlag.

Cobena, G., Abiteboul, S., & Marian, A. (2005). *XyDiff tools: Detecting changes in XML documents.* Retrieved February 2006, from http://www.rocq.inria.fr/gemo

Daly, O., & Taniar, D. (2004). Exception rules mining based on negative association rules. In *Computational science and applications* (LNCS 3046, pp. 543-552). Heidelberg, Germany: Springer-Verlag.

Ding, O., Ricords, K., & Lumpkin, J. (2003). Deriving general association rules from XML data. *Proceedings of the ACIS 4th International Conference on Software Engineering, Artificial Intelligence, Networking and Parallel/Distributed Computing (SNPD'03)* (pp. 348-352).

Feng, L., Dillon, T., Wiegand, H., & Chang, E. (2003). An XML-enabled association rules framework. In *Proceedings of International Conference on Database and Expert Systems Applications (DEXA 2003)* (LNCS 2736, pp. 88-97). Heidelberg, Germany: Springer-Verlag.

Garofalakis, M. N., Rastogi, R., Seshadri, S., & Shim, K. (1999). Data mining and the Web: Past, present and future. *Proceedings of the 2nd Workshop on Web Information and Data Management (WIDM 1999)* (pp. 43-47).

Laurent, M., Denilson, B., & Pierangelo, V. (2003). The XML Web: A first study. *Proceedings of the International WWW Conference* (pp. 500-510).

Marian, A., Abiteboul, S., Cobena, G., & Mignet, L. (2001). Change-centric management of versions in an XML warehouse. *VLDB Journal*, 581-590.

Nayak, R. (2005). Discovering knowledge from XML documents. In J. Wong (Ed.), *Encyclopedia of data warehousing and mining* (pp. 372-376). Hershey, PA: Idea Group Reference.

Nayak, R., Witt, R., & Tonev, A. (2002). Data mining and XML documents. *Proceedings of the 2002 International Conference on Internet Computing* (pp. 660-666).

Rusu, L. I., Rahayu, W., & Taniar, D. (2005a). Maintaining versions of dynamic XML documents. In *Proceedings of the 6th International Conference on Web Information System Engineering (WISE 2005)* (LNCS 3806, pp. 536-543). Heidelberg, Germany: Springer-Verlag.

Rusu, L. I., Rahayu, W., & Taniar, D. (2005b). A methodology for building XML data warehouses. *International Journal of Data Warehousing and Mining, 1*(2), 67-92.

Tjioe, H. C., & Taniar, D. (2005). Mining association rules in data warehouses. *International Journal of Data Warehousing and Mining, 1*(3), 28-62.

Wan, J. W., & Dobbie, G. (2003). Extracting association rules from XML documents using XQuery. *Proceedings of the 5th ACM International Workshop on Web Information and Data Management (WIDM'03)* (pp. 94-97).

Wan, J. W., & Dobbie, G. (2004). Mining association rules from XML data using XQuery. *Proceedings of International Conference on Research and Practice in Information Technology (CRPIT 2004)* (pp. 169-174).

Wang, Y., DeWitt, D. J., & Cai, J. Y. (2003). X-Diff: An effective change detection algorithm for XML documents. *Proceedings of the 19th International Conference on Data Engineering (ICDE 2003)* (pp. 519-530).

World Wide Web Consortium (W3C). (n.d.). Retrieved February 2006, from http://www.w3c.org

Xalan. (2005). *The Apache Software Foundation: Apache XML project.* Retrieved December 2005, from http://xml.apache.org/xalan-j/

XQuery. (2005). Retrieved February 2006, from http://www.w3.org/TR/2005/WD-xquery-20050915/

Zhao, Q., Bhowmick, S. S., & Mandria, S. (2004). Discovering pattern-based dynamic structures from versions of unordered XML documents. In *Proceedings of International Conference on Data Warehousing and Knowledge Discovery (DaWaK 2004)* (LNCS 3181, pp. 77-86). Heidelberg, Germany: Springer-Verlag.

Zhao, Q., Bhowmick, S. S., Mohania, M., & Kambayashi, Y. (2004). Discovering frequently changing structures from historical structural deltas of unordered XML. *Proceedings of ACM International Conference on Information and Knowledge Management (CIKM'04)* (pp. 188-197). Heidelberg, Germany: Springer Berlin.

This work was previously published in Web Data Management Practices: Emerging Techniques and Technologies, edited by A. Vakali and G. Pallis, pp. 79-103, copyright 2007 by IGI Publishing (an imprint of IGI Global).

Chapter XII
A Tutorial on RDF with Jena

Wan-Yeung Wong
The Chinese University of Hong Kong, Hong Kong, China

Tak-Pang Lau
The Chinese University of Hong Kong, Hong Kong, China

Irwin King
The Chinese University of Hong Kong, Hong Kong, China

Michael R. Lyu
The Chinese University of Hong Kong, Hong Kong, China

ABSTRACT

This chapter gives a tutorial on resource description framework (RDF), its XML representation, and Jena, a set of Java-based API designed and implemented to further simplify the manipulation of RDF documents. RDF is a W3C standard which provides a common framework for describing resources in the World Wide Web and other applications. Under this standard framework with the Jena, different resources can be manipulated and exchanged easily, which leads to cost reduction and better efficiency in business applications. In this tutorial, we present some basic concepts and applications of RDF and Jena. In particular, we use a television object to illustrate the usage of RDF in describing various resources being used, the XML syntax in representing the RDF, and the ways Jena manipulate various RDF documents. Furthermore, complete programming codes with detailed explanations are also presented to give readers a better understanding of Jena. References are given at the end for readers' further investigation.

Copyright © 2009, IGI Global, distributing in print or electronic forms without written permission of IGI Global is prohibited.

INTRODUCTION

The resource description framework (RDF) (W3C, 2004a) is a W3C (W3C, 2005b) standard which is commonly used to describe resources for any application. For business applications, a resource may be a product, a service, or a person. Since having a standard framework to manipulate different resources often leads to cost reduction and better efficiency, RDF is widely used in business applications. In this chapter, we give a simple tutorial on RDF, the language (RDF/XML) used by RDF, and a Java API (Jena) for manipulating RDF/XML. We assume that readers should have some background knowledge on URI, XML, and Java. Readers may refer to Wu (2004) for more information about programming in Java.

We mention that RDF is used to describe resources such as products, services, or people. It provides the data model and XML (W3C, 2005a) syntax so that RDF documents can be easily exchanged by different applications. The XML language used by RDF is called RDF/XML. Moreover, the use of RDF/XML makes RDF documents to be both human readable and computer readable. There are some examples for using RDF such as RDF Site Summary (RSS) (RSS-DEV Working Group, 2000) and Friend of a Friend (FOAF) (Brickley, 2005). The former one is designed for the Web syndication, while the latter one is designed to describe people, interests, and interconnections.

The first work on RDF was started by R. V. Guha when he was with Apple Computer and later with Netscape. In 1999, the specification of RDF data model and XML syntax was published in W3C. The work continued and a new specification of RDF was published in 2004, completely replacing the old specification rather than being assigned a new version number.

In this tutorial, we first use a television product as a resource example. In RDF, we use a *URI* to uniquely identify a *resource* (The Internet Society, 2005). The URI of a television resource may consist of the company information (e.g., `www.kingstv.com`), category (e.g., `plasma`), and model number (e.g. `PSM2000`) like "`http://www.kingstv.com/plasma/PSM2000`". Unlike the URL of a Web site, the URI of a resource is not necessary to be Internet accessible. For example, the aforementioned URI that begins with "`http`" does not necessarily have to represent that the television resource is accessible via HTTP. Such URI only denotes the abstract notion of world peace.

After defining the television resource, we can describe the resource by its *properties* and *property values*. A property is a resource that has a name, while a property value is the value of the property. For a television resource, the properties may be its model number, detail description, and price. Similar to the resource identification, we use a URI to uniquely identify a property. For example, the URI of the model number property may be "`http://www.kingstv.com/tv_property/model`" and its property value may be "`PSM2000`". In addition, a property value can be another resource. We may have a user property which value is a resource for describing a person who uses that television.

The whole scenario can be represented by a labeled, directed graph called *RDF graph* (see Figure 1). Inside an RDF graph, we use an *ellipse* to represent a resource, an *arrow* to represent a property, and a *rectangle* to represent a non-resource property value (literal). For a literal (rectangle), further properties are not allowed. On the other hand, further properties are allowed for a resource (ellipse). In this example, the user resource has no further property although further properties are allowed. Besides the RDF graph, the whole scenario can be represented by a list of RDF statements. An RDF statement is a *triple* that contains a subject (resource), a predicate (property), and an object (property value). Table 1 shows a list of RDF triples, which is equivalent to the RDF graph in Figure 1.

Figure 2 shows a more complicated example of an RDF graph. The television resource contains two properties "`model`" and "`accessories`". The

Figure 1. An RDF graph representing a television resource

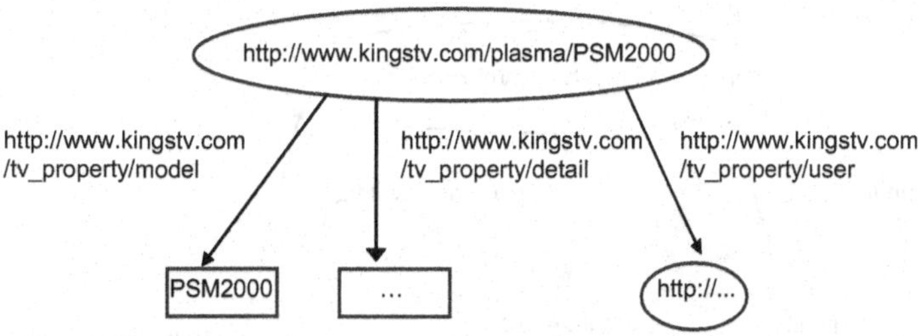

Table 1. RDF triples representing a television resource

Subject	Predicate	Object
http://www.kingstv.com/plasma /PSM2000	http://www.kingstv.com /tv_property/model	PSM2000
http://www.kingstv.com/plasma /PSM2000	http://www.kingstv.com /tv_property/detail	...
http://www.kingstv.com/plasma /PSM2000	http://www.kingstv.com /tv_property/user	http://...

"model" property specifies the model number of the television which is similar to the previous example. The "accessories" property refers to an intermediate node without URI reference which contains two accessories user manual and remote controller (http://.../rc). Since the intermediate node does not represent an actual resource, it does not have a URI and we generate an arbitrary ID (A123) to represent it. Furthermore, the "accessory2" property refers to a remote controller resource of the television which has a "belong_to" property. This property refers back to the television resource that forms a loop in the graph. Table 2 shows the corresponding RDF triples.

SYNTAX OF RDF/XML

So far, we explain how to use graphs and triples to describe resources in RDF. Besides graphs and triples, we can use XML to describe resources. The XML language used by RDF is called RDF/XML. By using RDF/XML, plain text RDF data can be easily stored in computers. We can also easily edit the data which is human readable. In this section, we give a simple tutorial on RDF/XML.

Consider the example in Figure 1, Listing 1 shows the corresponding RDF/XML.

Line 1 is the XML declaration which specifies the XML version of the document. In line 2 and 3, we specify the root <rdf:RDF> element of the RDF document. The URI of the "rdf" namespace for all predefined RDF elements and attributes must be "http://www.w3.org/1999/02/22-rdf-syntax-ns#". In line 3, we defined our "tv" namespace which is the URI prefix of all television resource properties. Starting from line 4, we describe our resources. For each resource, we use the <rdf:Description> element to enclose the resource description. Inside the <rdf:Description> element, we use the "rdf:about" attribute to specify the resource URI. The "rdf:about" attribute can be omitted if the resource does not have a URI. In that case, the

Figure 2. An RDF graph containing an intermediate node and a loop

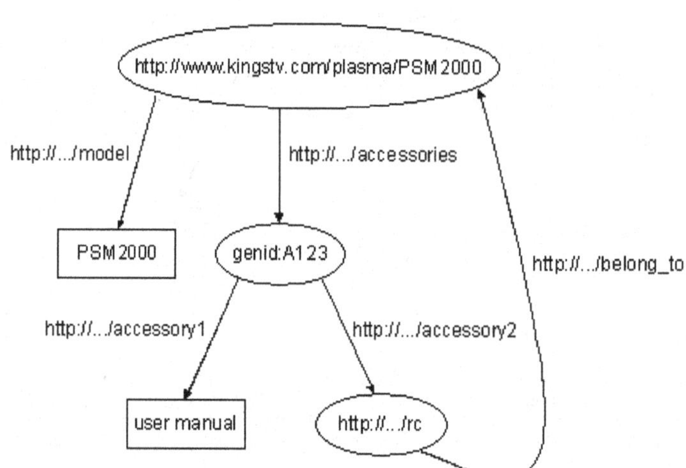

Table 2. The corresponding RDF triples

Subject	Predicate	Object
http://www.kingstv.com /plasma/PSM2000	http://.../model	PSM2000
http://www.kingstv.com /plasma/PSM2000	http://.../accessories	genid:A123
genid:A123	http://.../accessory1	user manual
genid:A123	http://.../accessory2	http://.../rc
http://.../rc	http://.../belong_to	http://www.kingstv.com /plasma/PSM2000

Listing 1.

```
<?xml version="1.0"?>
<rdf:RDF xmlns:rdf="http://www.w3.org/1999/02/22-rdf-syntax-ns#"
  xmlns:tv="http://www.kingstv.com/tv_property/">
  <rdf:Description rdf:about="http://www.kingstv.com/plasma/PSM2000">
    <tv:model>PSM2000</tv:model>
    <tv:detail>This is a plasma TV.</tv:detail>
    <tv:user rdf:resource="http://www.kingstv.com/user/1"/>
  </rdf:Description>
</rdf:RDF>
```

application should automatically generate an arbitrary ID to represent that resource. In line 5 and 6, we specify two properties "model" and "detail" by using our defined elements <tv:model> and <tv:detail> which values are literal. Since "tv" is our defined namespace which URI is "http://www.kingstv.com/tv_property/", the URI of "model" property is concatenated and becomes "http://www.kingstv.com/tv_property/model". Similarly, the URI of "detail" property is concatenated and becomes "http://www.kingstv.com/tv_property/detail". In line 7, we specify the "user" property by using our defined <tv:user> element. However, its property refers to another resource with URI "http://www.kingstv.com/user/1" which is specified by the "rdf:resource" attribute. Since the user resource has no further property, we need not further describe the user resource by using the <rdf:Description> element. Finally, line 8 and 9 are the closing tags for line 4 and 2 respectively.

Currently, W3C provides a useful online RDF validation service in W3C (2004b) (see Figure 3). After inputting the RDF document, the validation engine parses the RDF document and checks its validity. If it is valid, a list of RDF triples (see Figure 4) and the RDF graph (see Figure 5) will be displayed.

Consider the more complicated example in Figure 2, Listing 2 shows the corresponding RDF/XML.

There are two main resources which are described in line 4 and 14. The former one describes the television resource, while the latter one describes its remote controller resource. As shown in Figure 2, the "accessories" property refers to the intermediate node, which does not represent an actual resource. Therefore, under the <tv:accessories> element in line 6, we use the <rdf:Description> element in line 7 to represent the intermediate node without URI which ID should be automatically generated by the application. Then we describe two accessories from line 8 to 10. The "accessory2" property in line 9 refers to the remote controller resource which is further

Figure 3. An online RDF validation service provided by W3C

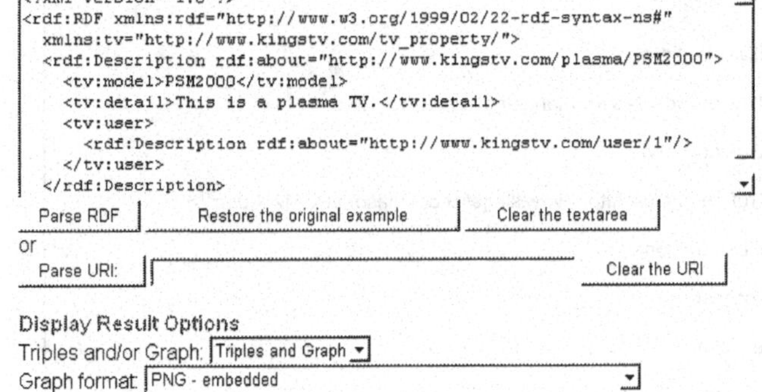

Figure 4. Results displayed by triples

Triples of the Data Model

Number	Subject	Predicate	Object
1	http://www.kingstv.com/plasma/PSM2000	http://www.kingstv.com/tv_property/model	"PSM2000"
2	http://www.kingstv.com/plasma/PSM2000	http://www.kingstv.com/tv_property/detail	"This is a plasma TV."
3	http://www.kingstv.com/plasma/PSM2000	http://www.kingstv.com/tv_property/user	http://www.kingstv.com/user/1

Figure 5. Results displayed by a graph

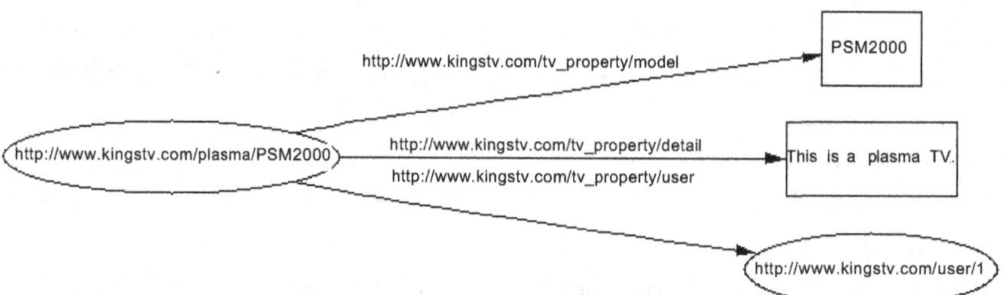

described in line 14. Similarly, the "belong_to" property of the remote controller resource in line 16 refers to the television resource which is already described in line 4.

The use of intermediate nodes represented by <rdf:Description> elements makes the RDF document nested. Although the document in the previous example is still easy to read, it is hard to read if there are too many nested <rdf:Description> elements. A better solution is to take out the descriptions of all intermediate nodes to the same level as the actual resources. Listing 3 shows another RDF/XML, which is equivalent to the example in Figure 2.

The main difference between the current and previous examples is in line 6. As shown in Figure 2, the "accessories" property refers to the intermediate node which ID is "A123". Therefore, we use

Listing 2.

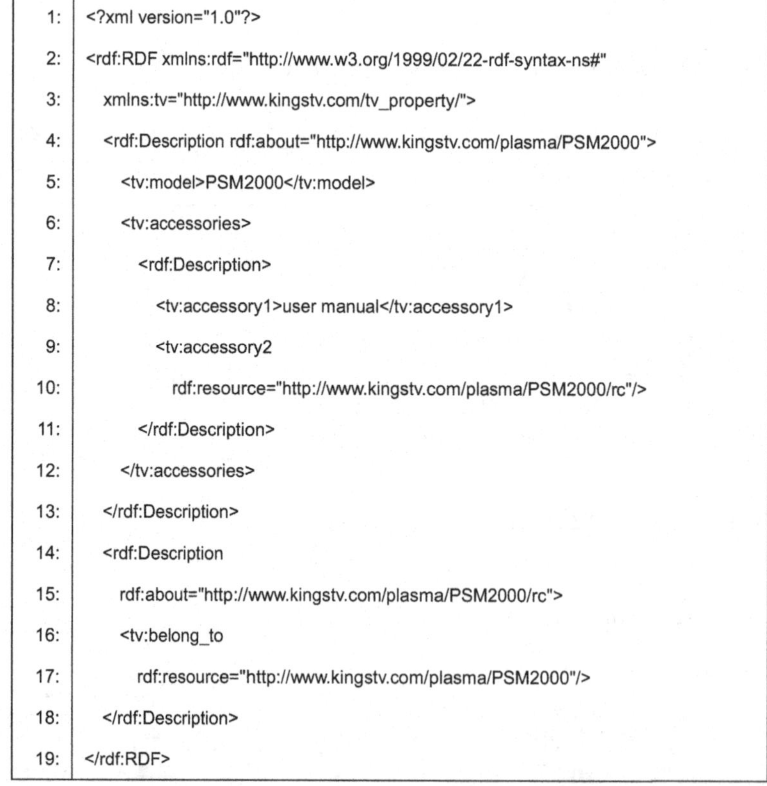

```
1:  <?xml version="1.0"?>
2:  <rdf:RDF xmlns:rdf="http://www.w3.org/1999/02/22-rdf-syntax-ns#"
3:    xmlns:tv="http://www.kingstv.com/tv_property/">
4:    <rdf:Description rdf:about="http://www.kingstv.com/plasma/PSM2000">
5:      <tv:model>PSM2000</tv:model>
6:      <tv:accessories>
7:        <rdf:Description>
8:          <tv:accessory1>user manual</tv:accessory1>
9:          <tv:accessory2
10:           rdf:resource="http://www.kingstv.com/plasma/PSM2000/rc"/>
11:       </rdf:Description>
12:     </tv:accessories>
13:   </rdf:Description>
14:   <rdf:Description
15:     rdf:about="http://www.kingstv.com/plasma/PSM2000/rc">
16:     <tv:belong_to
17:       rdf:resource="http://www.kingstv.com/plasma/PSM2000"/>
18:   </rdf:Description>
19: </rdf:RDF>
```

the "rdf:nodeID" attribute in line 6 to refer to the intermediate node which description is taken out to the same level as the actual resources (see line 8 to 12). The value of the "rdf:nodeID" attribute must be an alphanumeric string and begin with an alphabet. When we compare line 4 with line 8, we use the "rdf:about" attribute to indicate that the current resource is an actual resource, whereas we use the "rdf:nodeID" attribute to indicate that the current resource is an intermediate node. By taken out the descriptions of all intermediate nodes, the RDF document is less nested and easier to read.

In the previous example, the television resource contains multiple accessories. If we add more accessories, we may need to add more <tv:accessory*N*> elements where *N* is an integer. However, using such method to represent multiple items of a property is inextensible because we need to increase *N* manually and modify our application to process those new <tv:accessory*N*> elements. In RDF/XML, we can use the container element to describe a list of items and Listing 4 shows an example which is functionally equivalent to the previous example.

In this example, we no longer use our defined intermediate node to represent the multiple items of the "accessories" property. Instead, we use the <rdf:Bag> element in line 7 to represent the unordered list of accessories. For each item in the list, we use the <rdf:li> element to describe its value (see line 8 to 10). Figure 6 shows the corresponding RDF graph. The "accessories" property refers to the intermediate node which is generated by the <rdf:Bag> element. The ID (A123) of the intermediate node is automatically generated too. Unlike Figure 2, the intermediate node has an extra "type" property with URI "http://www.w3.org/1999/02/22-rdf-syntax-ns#type" which refers to the "Bag" container resource with URI "http://www.w3.org/1999/02/22-rdf-syntax-

Listing 3.

```
1:  <?xml version="1.0"?>
2:  <rdf:RDF xmlns:rdf="http://www.w3.org/1999/02/22-rdf-syntax-ns#"
3:    xmlns:tv="http://www.kingstv.com/tv_property/">
4:    <rdf:Description rdf:about="http://www.kingstv.com/plasma/PSM2000">
5:      <tv:model>PSM2000</tv:model>
6:      <tv:accessories rdf:nodeID="A123"/>
7:    </rdf:Description>
8:    <rdf:Description rdf:nodeID="A123">
9:      <tv:accessory1>user manual</tv:accessory1>
10:     <tv:accessory2
11:       rdf:resource="http://www.kingstv.com/plasma/PSM2000/rc"/>
12:   </rdf:Description>
13:   <rdf:Description
14:     rdf:about="http://www.kingstv.com/plasma/PSM2000/rc">
15:     <tv:belong_to
16:       rdf:resource="http://www.kingstv.com/plasma/PSM2000"/>
17:   </rdf:Description>
18: </rdf:RDF>
```

Listing 4.

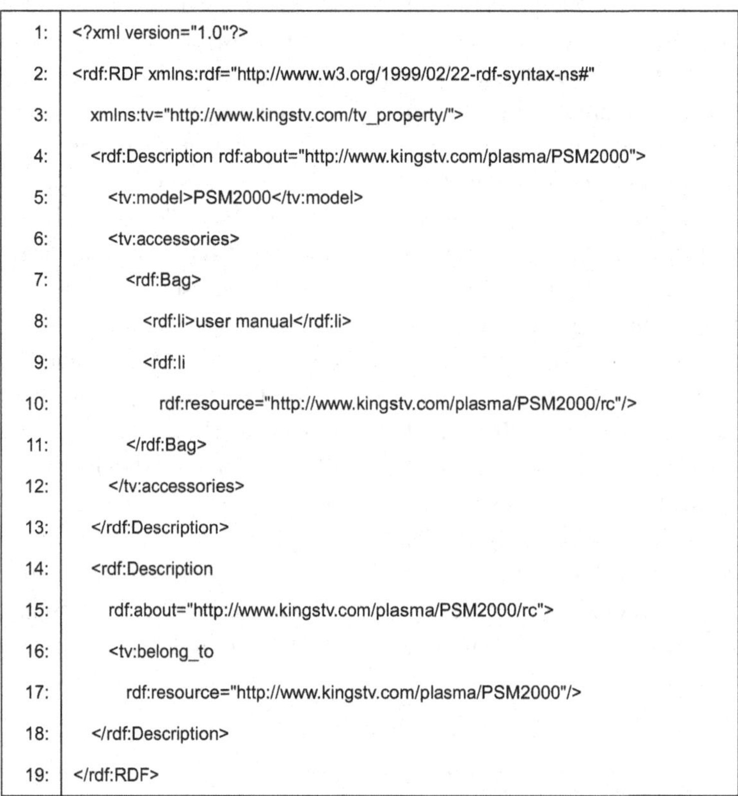

```
<?xml version="1.0"?>
<rdf:RDF xmlns:rdf="http://www.w3.org/1999/02/22-rdf-syntax-ns#"
   xmlns:tv="http://www.kingstv.com/tv_property/">
   <rdf:Description rdf:about="http://www.kingstv.com/plasma/PSM2000">
      <tv:model>PSM2000</tv:model>
      <tv:accessories>
         <rdf:Bag>
            <rdf:li>user manual</rdf:li>
            <rdf:li
               rdf:resource="http://www.kingstv.com/plasma/PSM2000/rc"/>
         </rdf:Bag>
      </tv:accessories>
   </rdf:Description>
   <rdf:Description
      rdf:about="http://www.kingstv.com/plasma/PSM2000/rc">
      <tv:belong_to
         rdf:resource="http://www.kingstv.com/plasma/PSM2000"/>
   </rdf:Description>
</rdf:RDF>
```

Figure 6. An RDF graph with a property containing multiple items

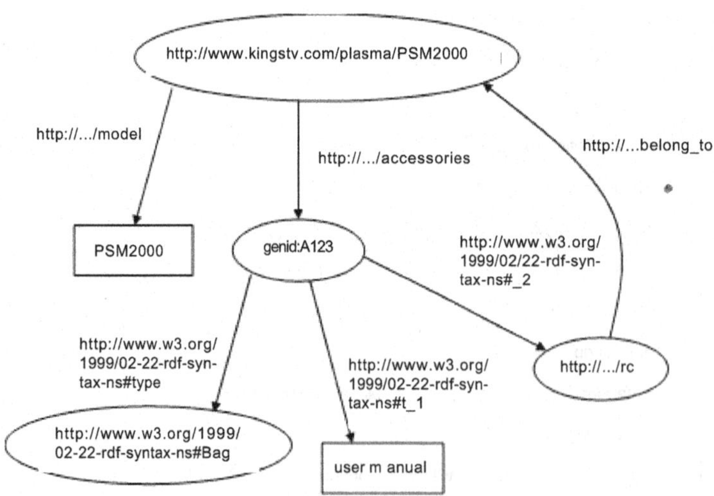

ns#Bag". The "Bag" container resource specifies the property value of the "accessories" property to be an unordered list. Each item in the list is referred by the auto-numbered property with URI "http://www.w3.org/1999/02/22-rdf-syntax-ns#_*N*" where *N* is an integer. Beside the <rdf:Bag> element, the <rdf:Seq> and <rdf:Alt> elements can also be used. The <rdf:Seq> element represents an ordered list of items, while the <rdf:Alt> element represents a list of alternative items. All <rdf:Bag>, <rdf:Seq>, and <rdf:Alt> elements may contain duplicate items. To use the <rdf:Seq> or <rdf:Alt> element in this example, we only need to replace "Bag" in both line 7 and 11 by "Seq" or "Alt". For the RDF graph, the URI of the "Seq" resource is "http://www.w3.org/1999/02/22-rdf-syntax-ns#Seq", while the URI of the "Alt" resource is "http://www.w3.org/1999/02/22-rdf-syntax-ns#Alt". Other values remain unchanged.

SYNTAX OF JENA

In the previous section, we describe how to write the RDF/XML code manually. However, we may need to integrate RDF with our own applications. It is time consuming if we write our own code to compose and parse RDF documents even if we use some general purpose XML libraries. Therefore, using specific purpose libraries like Jena (Hewlett-Packard Development Company, 2005; McBride, 2001) helps us to process RDF documents more easily. Jena is a Java framework for building semantic Web applications which provides a programmatic environment for RDF and other related technologies. In addition, Jena is open source and grown out of work with the HP Labs Semantic Web Program. The official Web site of Jena is "http://jena.sourceforge.net". Currently, Jena 2.2 is the latest version. Hence, we give a simple tutorial on Jena 2.2 in this section.

Before using Jena, we need to download "Jena-2.2.zip" via the official Web site and extract the ZIP file. To install Jena, we need to copy all ".jar" files from "Jena-2.2/lib/" to "$JAVA_HOME/jre/lib/ext/" directory where "$JAVA_HOME" is the JDK (Sun Microsystems, Inc. 2005) home path. For a Linux platform, JDK is usually installed under the "/usr/java/" directory. For a Windows platform, JDK is usually installed under the "C:\" or "C:\Program Files\Java\" directory. To test Jena, we may create "Test.java" with the following code which composes an empty RDF document without any resource. Then we compile and run "Test.java" (Listing 5) so that the output should be the same as Figure 7.

We begin the Jena tutorial by showing how to compose a simple RDF document which is equiva-

Listing 5.

```
import com.hp.hpl.jena.rdf.model.*;

public class Test
{
  public static void main(String[] args)
  {
    Model model = ModelFactory.createDefaultModel();
   m odel.write(System.out);
  }
}
```

lent to the example in Figure 1. "Example1.java" (Listing 6) outputs the RDF file "example1.rdf" which can be viewed by any plain text editor.

In line 1 and 2, we import two packages "java.io" and "com.hp.hpl.jena.rdf.model". The former one contains classes for writing files, while the latter one contains classes for composing RDF documents. Then we declare the public class called "Example1" in line 4 and declare the main method in line 6. There are six steps to compose the RDF document.

Step 1. First, we use the "createDefaultModel" method to create an empty RDF document

Listing 6.

```
1:  import java.io.*;
2:  import com.hp.hpl.jena.rdf.model.*;
3:
4:  public class Example1
5:  {
6:    public static void main(String[] args) throws Exception
7:    {
8:      Model model = ModelFactory.createDefaultModel();
9:
10:     String tvNS = "http://www.kingstv.com/tv_property/";
11:    m  odel.setNsPrefix("tv", tvNS);
12:
13:     Resource psm2000 = model.createResource(
14:       "http://www.kingstv.com/plasma/PSM2000");
15:     Resource user1 = model.createResource(
16:       "http://www.kingstv.com/user/1");
17:
18:     Property tvModel = model.createProperty(tvNS, "model");
19:     Property tvDetail = model.createProperty(tvNS, "detail");
20:     Property tvUser = model.createProperty(tvNS, "user");
21:
22:    m  odel.add(psm2000, tvModel, "PSM2000");
23:    m  odel.add(psm2000, tvDetail, "This is a plasma TV.");
24:    m  odel.add(psm2000, tvUser, user1);
25:
26:     FileOutputStream fileOut = new FileOutputStream("example1.rdf");
27:    m  odel.write(fileOut);
28:     fileOut.close();
29:   }
30: }
```

Figure 7. Output of Test.java

```
<rdf:RDF
    xmlns:rdf="http://www.w3.org/1999/02/22-rdf-syntax-ns#" >
</rdf:RDF>
```

which is represented by the "model" object in line 8.

Step 2. After creating the "model" object, we define the namespace in line 10 for the television properties and we use the "setNsPrefix" method to assign the namespace to the "model" object in line 11. The first parameter of the "setNsPrefix" method is the namespace and the second parameter is the corresponding URI.

Step 3. We use the "createResource" method to define two resources with their own URI from line 13 to 16. The television resource is represented by the "psm2000" object, while the user resource is represented by the "user1" object.

Step 4. We use the "createProperty" method to define all properties from line 18 to 20. The first parameter of the method is the namespace of the property and the second parameter is the name of the property.

Step 5. After defining the resources and properties, we use the "add" method to add the relationships between them to the "model" object in terms of RDF triples from line 22 to 24. The first parameter of the "add" method is the subject (resource), the second parameter is the predicate (property), and the third parameter is the object (literal or resource).

Step 6. Finally, the "model" object contains the composed RDF document and we use the "write" method to write the document to the "example1.rdf" file from line 26 to 28. The parameter of the "write" method can be any "OutputStream" object.

Consider the more complicated example in Figure 2, "Example2.java" (Listing 7) outputs the corresponding RDF file "example2.rdf".

Although Figure 2 is more complicated than Figure 1, their programs "Example2.java" and "Example1.java" are more or less the same. The extra feature of the current example is the presence of the intermediate node. To define the intermediate node, we do not pass the URI to the "createResource" method in line 14. The way for adding the relationships involved the intermediate node is the same as those actual resources (see line 22 to 26). In the previous section, we mention that the use of intermediate nodes represented by <rdf:Description> elements makes the RDF document nested and hard to read. Fortunately, Jena automatically takes out the descriptions of all intermediate nodes to the same level as the actual resources. We can see the effect by viewing the generated "example2.rdf" file.

Consider the example in Figure 6 which uses the "Bag" container, Listing 8, "Example3.java", outputs the corresponding RDF file "example3.rdf".

The main difference between the current and previous examples is that the current example creates a "Bag" container, which is represented by the "accessories" object in line 18, to replace the intermediate node in the previous example. Then we add the literal or resource to the container by using the "add" method in line 19 and 20. The way for adding the relationships involved the container is the same as those actual resources (see line 26 to 28). Besides the "Bag" container, we can use the "Seq" and "Alt" containers. To use them in this example, we only need to replace "Bag" in

Listing 7.

```
import java.io.*;
import com.hp.hpl.jena.rdf.model.*;

public class Example2
{
  public static void main(String[] args) throws Exception
  {
    Model model = ModelFactory.createDefaultModel();

    String tvNS = "http://www.kingstv.com/tv_property/";
   model.setNsPrefix("tv", tvNS);

    Resource psm2000 = model.createResource(
      "http://www.kingstv.com/plasma/PSM2000");
    Resource rc = model.createResource(
      "http://www.kingstv.com/plasma/PSM2000/rc");
    Resource node = model.createResource();

    Property tvModel = model.createProperty(tvNS, "model");
    Property tvAccessories = model.createProperty(tvNS, "accessories");
    Property tvAccessory1 = model.createProperty(tvNS, "accessory1");
    Property tvAccessory2 = model.createProperty(tvNS, "accessory2");
    Property tvBelongTo = model.createProperty(tvNS, "belong_to");

   model.add(psm2000, tvModel, "PSM2000");
   model.add(psm2000, tvAccessories, node);
   model.add(node, tvAccessory1, "user manual");
   model.add(node, tvAccessory2, rc);
   model.add(rc, tvBelongTo, psm2000);

 FileOutputStream fileOut = new FileOutputStream("example2.rdf");
    model.write(fileOut);
    fileOut.close();
  }
}
```

Listing 8.

```
import java.io.*;
import com.hp.hpl.jena.rdf.model.*;

public class Example3
{
   public static void main(String[] args) throws Exception
   {
      Model model = ModelFactory.createDefaultModel();

      String tvNS = "http://www.kingstv.com/tv_property/";
      model.setNsPrefix("tv", tvNS);

      Resource psm2000 = model.createResource(
         "http://www.kingstv.com/plasma/PSM2000");
      Resource rc = model.createResource(
         "http://www.kingstv.com/plasma/PSM2000/rc");

      Bag accessories = model.createBag();
      accessories.add("user manual");
      accessories.add(rc);

        Property tvModel = model.createProperty(tvNS, "model");
        Property tvAccessories = model.createProperty(tvNS, "accessories");
        Property tvBelongTo = model.createProperty(tvNS, "belong_to");

      model.add(psm2000, tvModel, "PSM2000");
      model.add(psm2000, tvAccessories, accessories);
      model.add(rc, tvBelongTo, psm2000);

        FileOutputStream fileOut = new FileOutputStream("example3.rdf");
      model.write(fileOut);
        fileOut.close();
   }
}
```

line 18 by "Seq" or "Alt", and replace "createBag" by "createSeq" or "createAlt".

So far, we describe how to use Jena to compose RDF documents. It is time to describe how to use Jena to read and query in RDF documents. We demonstrate this by using a long example "Example4.java" as shown in Listing 9.

In this example, we read the RDF file "example3.rdf" which is generated by the previous "Example3.java". The corresponding RDF graph is shown in Figure 6. In line 6, we declare the "model" object which represents the RDF document to be read. There are two methods "main" and "query" which are declared in line 8 and 50 respectively. The former one is the entry point of the program, while the latter one performs the query according to three input parameters and then prints the result on the screen. The program starts in line 10 which creates an empty RDF document by using the "createDefaultModel" method. Then we use the "read" method to read the RDF file "example3.rdf" and store it to the "model" object from line 12 to 14. The first parameter of the "read" method can be any "InputStream" object and the second parameter specifies the base to use when converting the relative URI to absolute URI. Starting from line 16, there are six queries.

Query 1. First, we want to query all namespaces which are used in this document. Therefore, we use the "listNameSpaces" method in line 17 to obtain a list of namespaces which are stored in the "nsIterator" object. Then in line 18, we use the "hasNext" method to check if the next namespace exists. Finally, we use the "nextNs" method in line 19 to get each namespace as a "String" object.

Query 2. In this query, we want to list out all RDF statements (triples) in this document. Therefore, we use our defined "query" method in line 24 which jumps to line 50. Inside the "query" method, we use the "listStatements" method in line 52 to obtain a list of statements which are stored in the "stmtIterator" object. The parameters "s", "p", and "o" of the "listStatements" method are null which means that we do not require matching the statement with the specific subject, predicate, and object respectively. Then we use the "hasNext" method in line 53 to check if the next statement exists and we use the "nextStatement" method in line 54 to get each "statement" object. Finally, we use the methods "getSubject", "getPredicate", and "getObject" to get the subject (resource), predicate (property), and object (literal or resource) respectively (see line 55 to 57). Please note that Jena automatically generates an ID (66c7f061:104e5c9bff0:-8000) for the node referred by the "accessories" property.

Query 3. In this query, we want to list out all RDF statements (triples) in this document which has the remote controller resource with URI "http://www.kingstv.com/plasma/PSM2000/rc". Therefore, we use our defined "query" method in line 27 and 28 which first parameter is our target resource. Before passing the first parameter to the "query" method, we need to use the "createResource" method to create the corresponding "Resource" object.

Query 4. In this query, we want to list out all RDF statements (triples) in this document which has the "model" property. Therefore, we use our defined "query" method in line 31 and 32 which second parameter is our target property. Before passing the second parameter to the "query" method, we need to use the "createProperty" method to create the corresponding "Property" object. Moreover, the first parameter of the "createProperty" method is the namespace of the property which URI can be obtained by using the "getNsPrefixURI" method.

Query 5. In this query, we want to list out all RDF statements (triples) in this document which property value is "user manual". Therefore,

Listing 9.

```
import java.io.*;
import com.hp.hpl.jena.rdf.model.*;

public class Example4
{
  private static Model model = null;

  public static void main(String[] args) throws Exception
  {
    model = ModelFactory.createDefaultModel();

    FileInputStream fileIn = new FileInputStream("example3.rdf");
    model.read(fileIn, "");
    fileIn.close();

    System.out.println("Query 1:");
    NsIterator nsIterator = model.listNameSpaces();
    while (nsIterator.hasNext()){
      System.out.println(nsIterator.nextNs()+";");
    }
    System.out.println();

    System.out.println("Query 2:");
    query(null, null, null);

    System.out.println("Query 3:");
    query(model.createResource(
      "http://www.kingstv.com/plasma/PSM2000/rc"), null, null);

    System.out.println("Query 4:");
    query(null,
      model.createProperty(model.getNsPrefixURI("tv"), "model"), null);

    System.out.println("Query 5:");
    query(null, null, model.createLiteral("user manual"));

    System.out.println("Query 6:");
    StmtIterator stmtIterator = model.listStatements(
      model.createResource("http://www.kingstv.com/plasma/PSM2000"),
```

continued on following page

Listing 9. continued

```
40:         model.createProperty(model.getNsPrefixURI("tv"), "accessories"),
41:         (RDFNode)null);
42:       Statement statement = stmtIterator.nextStatement();
43:       Bag bag = statement.getBag();
44:       NodeIterator nodeIterator = bag.iterator();
45:       while (nodeIterator.hasNext()){
46:         System.out.println(nodeIterator.next()+";");
47:       }
48:     }
49:
50:     private static void query(Resource s, Property p, RDFNode o)
51:     {
52:       StmtIterator stmtIterator = model.listStatements(s, p, o);
53:       while (stmtIterator.hasNext()){
54:         Statement statement = stmtIterator.nextStatement();
55:         System.out.println("("+statement.getSubject()+",");
56:         System.out.println(" "+statement.getPredicate()+",");
57:         System.out.println(" "+statement.getObject()+");");
58:       }
59:       System.out.println();
60:     }
61:   }
```

we use our defined "query" method in line 35 which third parameter is our target property value. Before passing the third parameter to the "query" method, we need to use the "createLiteral" method to create the corresponding "Literal" object which is typecast to the "RDFNode" object when passing to the "query" method.

Query 6. In the last query, we want to list out all accessories of the television resource which URI is "http://www.kingstv.com/plasma/PSM2000". Therefore, we use the "listStatements" method from line 38 to 41 and we use the "nextStatement" method in line 42 to get the target statement. Then we use the "getBag" method in line 43 and the "iterator" method in line 44 to get the list of items which is represented by the "nodeIterator" object. Furthermore, we use the "hasNext" method in line 45 to check if the next item exists. Finally, we use the "next" method in line 46 to get each item.

In addition to the query operation, Jena provides three useful operations for manipulating RDF documents as a whole. These are the common set operations of *union*, *intersection*, and *difference*. The union operation creates a new RDF document containing all triples in this

Query 1:

http://www.w3.org/1999/02/22-rdf-syntax-ns#;

http://www.kingstv.com/tv_property/;

Query 2:

(66c7f061:104e5c9bff0:-8000,

h ttp://www.w3.org/1999/02/22-rdf-syntax-ns#type,

h ttp://www.w3.org/1999/02/22-rdf-syntax-ns#Bag);

(66c7f061:104e5c9bff0:-8000,

h ttp://www.w3.org/1999/02/22-rdf-syntax-ns#_1,

u ser manual);

(66c7f061:104e5c9bff0:-8000,

h ttp://www.w3.org/1999/02/22-rdf-syntax-ns#_2,

h ttp://www.kingstv.com/plasma/PSM2000/rc);

(http://www.kingstv.com/plasma/PSM2000,

h ttp://www.kingstv.com/tv_property/accessories,

6 6c7f061:104e5c9bff0:-8000);

(http://www.kingstv.com/plasma/PSM2000,

h ttp://www.kingstv.com/tv_property/model,

P SM2000);

(http://www.kingstv.com/plasma/PSM2000/rc,

h ttp://www.kingstv.com/tv_property/belong_to,

h ttp://www.kingstv.com/plasma/PSM2000);

Query 3:

(http://www.kingstv.com/plasma/PSM2000/rc,

h ttp://www.kingstv.com/tv_property/belong_to,

h ttp://www.kingstv.com/plasma/PSM2000);

Query 4:

(http://www.kingstv.com/plasma/PSM2000,

h ttp://www.kingstv.com/tv_property/model,

P SM2000);

Query 5:

(66c7f061:104e5c9bff0:-8000,

h ttp://www.w3.org/1999/02/22-rdf-syntax-ns#_1,

u ser manual);

Query 6:

user manual;

http://www.kingstv.com/plasma/PSM2000/rc;

document together with all of those in another given document. Moreover, the intersection operation creates a new RDF document containing all triples which are in both this document and another. Since RDF documents are sets of triples, a triple contained in both documents only appears once in the resulting document. Finally, the difference operation creates a new RDF document containing all triples in this document which are not in another. We demonstrate the union of the examples in Figure 1 and Figure 2 in Listing 10, "Example5.java".

Using the union operation in Jena is simple as shown in this example. First, we use the "createDefaultModel" in line 8 and 9 to create two RDF documents. Second, we use the "read" method to read the RDF documents so that the "model1" object represents the "example1.rdf" file and the "model2" object represents the "example2.rdf" file (see line 11 to 17). Third, we use the "union" method in line 19 to perform the union operation and the "model" object represents the resulting RDF document. Finally, we use the "write" method to write the resulting document to the "example5.rdf" file from line 21 to 23. To use the intersection or difference operation in this example, we only need to replace "union" in line 19 by "intersection" or "difference". Figure 8 shows the corresponding RDF graph after the union.

CONCLUSION

In this chapter, we give a simple tutorial on RDF, RDF/XML, and Jena. The tutorial is summarized as follows.

For RDF, it is a W3C standard which is commonly used to describe resources for any application. We use RDF graphs to describe resources.

Listing 10. Example5.java

```
import java.io.*;
import com.hp.hpl.jena.rdf.model.*;

public class Example5
{
  public static void main(String[] args) throws Exception
  {
    Model model1 = ModelFactory.createDefaultModel();
    Model model2 = ModelFactory.createDefaultModel();

    FileInputStream fileIn = new FileInputStream("example1.rdf");
   m odel1.read(fileIn, "");
    fileIn.close();

    fileIn = new FileInputStream("example2.rdf");
   m odel2.read(fileIn, "");
    fileIn.close();

    Model model = model1.union(model2);

    FileOutputStream fileOut = new FileOutputStream("example5.rdf");
   m odel.write(fileOut);
    fileOut.close();
  }
}
```

Figure 8. An RDF graph after the union

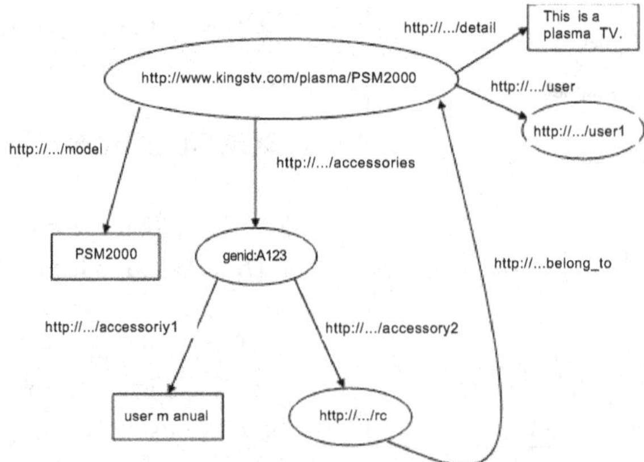

An RDF graph contains resources, properties, and property values which are connected together. Resources are represented by ellipses, properties are represented by arrows, and literals are represented by rectangles. In addition, a list of RDF triples can also be used to describe resources. An RDF triple contains a subject, a predicate, and an object. The subject is the resource, the predicate is the property, and the object is the property value.

For RDF/XML, it is the XML language used by RDF. A resource is described by the `<rdf:Description>` element and its URI is specified by the "`rdf:about`" attribute. A property is described by our defined element under the `<rdf:Description>` element of a resource. A property value is enclosed by a property element. A list of items can be contained by using the "`Bag`", "`Seq`", or "`Alt`" container. The "`Bag`" container contains an unordered list of items, the "`Seq`" container contains an ordered list of items, and the "`Alt`" container contains a list of alternative items.

For Jena, it is a Java framework for building semantic Web applications which provides a programmatic environment for RDF and other related technologies. To compose an RDF document, there are six steps, which are (1) empty RDF document creation, (2) property namespace assignment, (3) resource creation, (4) property creation, (5) RDF triple creation, and (6) RDF file composition. Besides RDF document composition, Jena also provides API for reading and querying in RDF documents. Finally, Jena provides three useful operations for manipulating RDF documents as a whole. These are the common set operations of union, intersection, and difference.

Readers may refer to the resources listed in References section for further investigation. W3Schools (n.d.a), and W3Schools (n.d.b) provide good online tutorials on XML and RDF respectively. Antoniou and Harmelen (2004), Hjelm (2001), Klein (2001), Oberle (2005), Passin (2004), and Powers (2003) provide complete discussions on developing applications using RDF and the related Internet technologies.

REFERENCES

Antoniou, G., & Harmelen, F. V. (2004). *A semantic web primer.* Cambridge, UK: The MIT Press.

Brickley, D. (2005). The Friend of a Friend (FOAF) Project Web site. Retrieved from http://www.foaf-project.org/

Hewlett-Packard Development Company (2005). Jena Semantic Web Framework Web site. Retrieve from http://jena.sourceforge.net/

Hjelm, J. (2001). *Creating the semantic web with RDF: Professional developer's guide.* New York: Wiley.

The Internet Society (2005). Uniform Resource Identifier (URI) Generic Syntax. Retrieved from http://www.gbiv.com/protocols/uri/rfc/rfc3986.html

Klein, M. (2001). XML, RDF, and relatives. *IEEE Intelligent Systems, 16*(2), 26-28.

McBride, B. (2001). Jena: Implementing the RDF Model and Syntax Specification. In *Proceedings of the 2nd International Workshop on the Semantic Web*, Hong Kong, China.

Oberle, D., Staab, S., Studer, R., & Volz, R. (2005). Supporting application development in the semantic web. *ACM Transactions on Internet Technology, 5*(2), 328-358.

Passin, T. B. (2004). *Explorer's guide to the semantic web.* Greenwich, CT: Manning Publications.

Powers, S. (2003). *Practical RDF.* Sebastopol, CA: O'Reilly.

RSS-DEV Working Group (2000). Resource Description Framework Site Summary (RSS)

1.0 Web site. Retrieved from http://web.resource.org/rss/1.0/

Sun Microsystems, Inc. (2005). Java 2 Platform, Standard Edition (J2SE) Web site. Retrieved from URL http://java.sun.com/j2se/

W3Schools (n.d.a). Extensible Markup Language (XML) Tutorial Web site. Retrieved from http://www.w3schools.com/xml/

W3Schools (n.d.b). Resource Description Framework (RDF) Tutorial Web site. Retrieved from http://www.w3schools.com/rdf/

World Wide Web Consortium (W3C) (2004a). Resource Description Framework (RDF) Official Web site. Retrieved from URL http://www.w3.org/RDF/

World Wide Web Consortium (W3C) (2004b). Resource Description Framework (RDF) Validation Service. Retrieved from http://www.w3.org/RDF/Validator/

World Wide Web Consortium (W3C) (2005a). Extensible Markup Language (XML) Official Web site. Retrieved from http://www.w3.org/XML/

World Wide Web Consortium (W3C) (2005b). World Wide Web Consortium (W3C). Retrieved from http://www.w3.org/

Wu, C. T. (2004). *An introduction to object-oriented programming with Java* (3rd ed.). New York: McGraw-Hill.

This work was previously published in Advances in Electronic Business, Vol. 2, edited by E. Li and T. Du, pp. 116-140, copyright 2007 by Information Science Publishing (an imprint of IGI Global).

Chapter XIII
Extending Enterprise Application Integration (EAI) With Mobile and Web Services Technologies

Abbass Ghanbary
MethodScience.com & University of Western Sydney, Australia

Bhuvan Unhelkar
MethodScience.com & University of Western Sydney, Australia

ABSTRACT

Web Services (WS) technologies, generally built around the ubiquitous Extensible Markup Language (XML), have provided many opportunities for integrating enterprise applications. However, XML/Simple Object Access Protocol (SOAP), together with Web Services Definition Language (WSDL) and Universal Description Discovery and Integration (UDDI), form a comprehensive suite of WS technologies that have the potential to transcend beyond mere application integration within an organization, and to provide capabilities of integrating processes across multiple organizations. Currently, the WS paradigm is driven through parameters however; the paradigm shift that can result in true collaborative business requires us to consider the business paradigm in terms of policies-processes-standards. This chapter, based on experimental research carried out by the authors, demonstrates how the technologies of WS open up the doors to collaborative Enterprise Architecture Integration (EAI) and Service Oriented Architecture (SOA) resulting in Business Integration (BI). The chapter also provide a quantitative investigation based on organization's adaptation to mobile and Web Services technologies.

Copyright © 2009, IGI Global, distributing in print or electronic forms without written permission of IGI Global is prohibited.

INTRODUCTION

This chapter describes how WS can be used in order to align and integrate business processes of organizations (internal and external processes) to satisfy the needs of Enterprise Architecture (EA). Thus far, the concept of Business Integration (BI) has been mainly focused on integrating the business processes internal to an organization; however this chapter is an investigation to identify how the organizations can extend this integration with those business processes belonging to other enterprises and how they adapt mobile and Web Services technologies in order to integrate with those business processes.

According to Finkelsteing (2006) Enterprise Architecture (EA) builds on business knowledge and allows business specialist experts to apply their respective knowledge to determine the most effective technology and process solutions for the business.

Information and Communication Technology (ICT) architectures have not paid enough attention to integration of the services in the past. Service Oriented Architecture (SOA) is an architecture that makes the services of a system to interact and perform a task supporting a request. SOA is classified as sub-architecture of Enterprise Architecture.

Based on Barry (2003), a Service Oriented Architecture (SOA) is a part of an EA and can be viewed as "sub-architecture" of an Enterprise Architecture. SOA existed before the advent of Web Services. Technologies such as Common Object Request Broker (CORBA) and Distributed Component Object Model (DCOM) afforded the opportunity to create SOA. Web Services is ideal technology for developing sophisticated architecture.

The Open Group Architecture Framework (TOGAF) is a critical architecture for the effective and safe construction of business and information systems. TOGAF provides the TOGAF Architecture Development Method (ADM). TOGAF ADM is a comprehensive, detailed, industry standard method for developing Enterprise Architectures Integration (EAI), and related information, application, and technology architectures that address the needs of business, technology, and data systems (http://www.integrationconsortium.org).

Based on Chase (2006), originally designed as a way to develop the technology architecture for an organization, TOGAF has evolved into a methodology for analysing the overall business architecture. The first part of TOGAF is a methodology for developing the architecture design, which is called the Architecture Development Method (ADM). It has the following nine basic phases:

- **Preliminary phase: Framework and principles.** Get everyone on board with the plan.
- **Phase A: Architecture vision.** Define your scope and vision and map your overall strategy.
- **Phase B: Business architecture.** Describe your current and target business architectures and determine the gap between them.
- **Phase C: Information system architectures.** Develop target architectures for your data and applications.
- **Phase D: Technology architecture.** Create the overall target architecture that you will implement in future phases.
- **Phase E: Opportunities and solutions.** Develop the overall strategy, determining what you will buy, build or reuse, and how you will implement the architecture described in phase D.
- **Phase F: Migration planning.** Prioritize projects and develop the migration plan.
- **Phase G: Implementation governance.** Determine how you will provide oversight to the implementation.
- **Phase H: Architecture change management.** Monitor the running system for

necessary changes and determine whether to start a new cycle, looping back to the preliminary phase.

These phases provide a standardised way of analysing the enterprise and planning and managing the actual implementation. The Service Oriented Architecture is considered in **Phase D: Technology architecture** where the TOGAF defines the services and their relationship with each other and define how the services could be invoked by different requesters.

Service Oriented Architecture (SOA) describes how the service could be invoked and how the service attributes are implemented. The concepts of SOA and TOGAF relate to each other when Technology Architecture is invoked by different requesters. TOGAF contains two reference models that can be used in this way: a platform-centric Technical Reference Model that focuses on the services and structure of the underlying platform necessary to support the use and reuse of applications, and an Integrated Information Infrastructure Reference Model that focuses on the applications space, and addresses the need for interoperability, and for enabling secure flow of information where and when it is needed (http://www.ebizq.net).

The highly competitive nature of the current business environment creates tremendous pressure for organizations to collaborate. It is essential for companies to understand rapidly changing business circumstances. The rapidly changing environment encourages the enterprises to integrate their business functions into a system that efficiently utilises ICT.

The chapter proposes a theoretical model as the recommended implementation of the integration that requires a substantial amount of time and financial commitment. The supplemental technologies of SOA, EAI and TOGAF automate the integration process with the collaborative environment of the business processes of multiple organizations.

LITRATURE REVIEW

The increase in the demand of the management of the Information and Communication Technology (ICT) has caused the research to focus their efforts on integrating of business processes and data. The term Enterprise Integration (or System Integration) reflects the capability to integrate a variety of different system functionalities.

Traditionally, information systems were implemented to support specific functional areas. However, the advancement of information technology enables new forms of organizations and facilitates their business processes to collaborate even when these organizations are not necessarily known to each other. As organizations become more complex and diverse in the collaborative context, it becomes nearly impossible for them to implement their collaborative business concepts without enterprise integration.

New technology seems to suggest that mobile services will be the greatest opportunity for businesses to develop richer and more profitable relationships with individual customers by giving them what they actually want (Falcone and Garito, 2006)

According to Jostad, et al, (2005) the demand for flexible, efficient and user-friendly collaborative services is becoming more and more urgent as competition in the current market oriented arena is becoming more intense. Enterprises have to be more dynamic in terms of collaboration with partners and even competitors. The Service Oriented Architecture is a promising computing paradigm offering solutions that are extendible, flexible and compatible with legacy systems. This chapter proposes and investigates the use of SOA in the construction of collaborations across multiple organizations.

Harrison and Taylor (2005) define an SOA that builds on the concept of a service. It is a collection of services capable of interacting in three ways, commonly referred to as 'publish, find and bind'. In other words, a service must be able to make its interface available to other services (publish), other services must be capable of discovering the interface (find), and finally services must be able to connect to one another to exchange messages (bind). The loose coupling of an SOA is achieved firstly through the separation of data exchange from the software agents involved in the exchange, and secondly through the discrete nature of the service.

The biggest challenge may be the behaviour of the users to adapt to the developed system. According to Chen, et al, (2006) the consumer of a service is not required to have a detailed knowledge of implementation, implementation language, or execution platform of the service. The only concern of the consumer is how a service can be invoked according to the service interface.

Change management and transformation of an organization can be very difficult and sensitive issues. Conversely, it can be argued that behavioural integration is critical to the success of enterprise integration. The technical integration can be a success but if the organization is not going to internalise the enterprise system, the entire project is a failure. As such, to achieve the maximum benefit and impact from enterprise integration, we need to have both successful technical and behavioural integration (http://delivery.acm.org).

The successful architecture confirms that business requirements and information technology design are captured in models. The modelling technique of abstraction to separate business concerns from technology concerns (what the business system needs to do, versus its underlying computing platform) is also an important aspect of the success of the architecture.

The following issues also could be classified as the critical factor for the success of the Service Oriented and Enterprise Architecture:

- To capture business requirements.
- Platform-Independent Model (PIM) by promoting designing a business solution prior to selecting how it will be deployed.
- The Platform-Specific Model (PSM) adds to the PIM the details of a specific computing platform on which the business solution will be deployed.
- Transformations (mappings) are performed on these models to progress from a higher level of abstraction to a lower level of abstraction.
- All of this activity is based on internationally accepted standards.

Businesses that aim to support mobile workers and enhance process effectiveness will need to consider extending their process and systems beyond the workplace (Alag, 2006). According to Godbole, (2006) Mobile Commerce is best suited where the consumer is driven by a "sense of urgency" when they need to have their goods and services immediately for upcoming functions and events.

Every organization on the planet consisting of more than one person has already realised that their information technology infrastructure is effectively a distributed computing system. To integrate information assets and use information effectively, it must be accessible across the department, across the company, across the world and more importantly across the service- or supply-chain from the supplier, to one's own organization, to one's customers. This means that CPUs must be intimately linked to the networks of the world and be capable of freely passing and receiving information, not hidden behind glass and cooling ducts or the complexities of the software that drives them. www.omg.org/docs/omg/03-06-01.pdf

UNDERSTANDING SOA AND WEB SERVICES

Service-Oriented Architecture is architecture based on internal and external processes of an organization. Web Services technology is the most appropriate technology to develop SOA.

Curbera, et al, (2003) states that Web Services provide generic coordination mechanisms that can be extended for specific protocols and Ghanbary (2006) extends this expression by stating that WS represent the applications that organizations publish/locate on unknown and disparate platforms. According to Unhelkar & Deshpande (2004), Web Services based technologies enable applications to "talk" with one another even across organizational firewalls, resulting in an opportunity for a cluster or group of organizations to simultaneously transition to Web-based entities.

Barry (2003) clearly states that the use of Web Services appears to be the missing puzzle piece in creating a complete picture of a service oriented architecture work. The statement given by Barry (2003) identifies the importance of universal adoption of Web Services by software vendors.

Figure 1 illustrates the importance of the adoption of the Web Service by internal as well as the external architecture. The following is the explanation of the functionality of the Web Services that could create successful service oriented architecture.

XML/SOAP AND SOA

Extensible Mark-up Language (XML) is a simple, very flexible text format derived from SGML (ISO 8879). Originally designed to meet the challenges of large-scale electronic publishing, XML is also playing an increasingly important role in the exchange of a wide variety of data on the Web and elsewhere (http://www.w3.org/XML/).

XML schemas associated with SOAP message payloads often need to be designed with some of the more advanced features of the XML Schema Definition Language. Specifically, the use of extensible or redefined schemas may be required when building documents that represent multiple data contexts. See Exhibit A.

WSDL AND SOA

WSDL is an XML format for describing network services as a set of endpoints operating on messages containing either document-oriented or procedure-oriented information. The operations and messages are described abstractly, and then bound to a concrete network protocol and

Figure 1. Internal and external impacts of WS

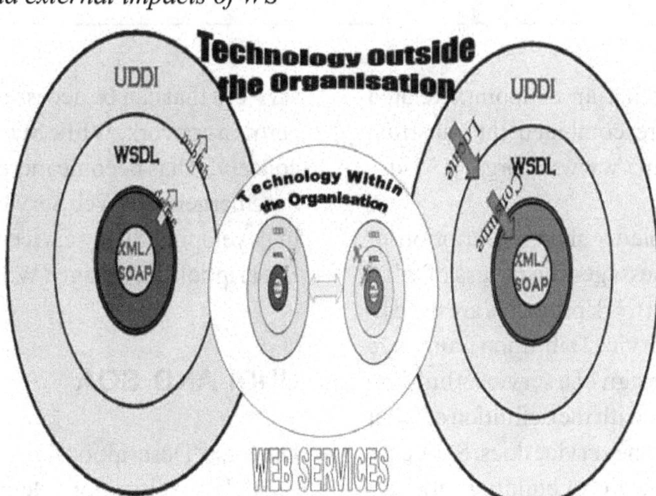

Exhibit A.

```
<collection>
  <description>Examples of code</description>
  <code id="VB">
    <title>Visual Basic code example</title>
    <codeExample>
      Private Sub Form1_Paint()
        Print "Hello World!"
      End Sub
    </codeExample>
  </code>
  <code id="Java">
    <title>Java code example</title>
    <codeExample>
      public class Hello
      {
        public static void main(String[] args)
        {
          System.out.println("Hello, World!");
        }
      }
    </codeExample>
  </code>
  <code id="COBOL">
    <title>COBOL code example</title>
    <codeExample>
       IDENTIFICATION DIVISION.
       PROGRAM-ID. Hello-World.
      *
       ENVIRONMENT DIVISION.
      *
       DATA DIVISION.
      *
       PROCEDURE DIVISION.
       PARA-1.
           DISPLAY "Hello, world!".
      *
           STOP RUN.
    </codeExample>
  </code>
</collection>
```

message format to define an endpoint. Related concrete endpoints are combined into abstract endpoints services (http://www.w3.org/TR/wsdl). See Exhibit B.

WSDL is extensible to allow description of endpoints and their messages regardless of what message formats or network protocols are used to communicate. Web Service Definition Language SOA starts with the design of a service. Building software services start with the definition of what the service is and what the service does. SOA provides a standardised means of building software services that can be accessed, shared, and reused across a network. While SOA is a well-established concept, it has become increasingly popular with the emergence of Web Services. The starting point in developing SOA services is the Web Services Description Language (WSDL).

UDDI AND SOA

Universal Description, Discovery and Integration (UDDI) specifications define a registry service

Exhibit B.


```
<businessEntity
  businessKey="uddi:4589150-5F12-9K45-H048-337910DA52F94">
  <name>ExampleCode Pty Ltd</name>
  <description>For all your example code needs</description>
  <contacts>
    <phone>612-9055-0047</phone>
    <email>info@examplecode.com</email>
  </contacts>
  <businessServices>
    <businessService
      serviceKey="uddi:8181F24-1A42-7850-3664-36599DA515K04"
      businessKey="uddi:35894A5-8745-95FD-0571-9161K577D2604">
      <name>ExampleCode Server</name>
      <description>ExampleCode.com's example code server</description>
      <bindingTemplates>
        <bindingTemplate
          bindingKey="uddi:2549842-F148-9758-24G7-2584D8789A5F5"
          serviceKey="uddi:8181F24-1A42-7850-3664-36599DA515K04">
          <accessPoint URLType="http">
            http://www.examplecode.com/code
          </accessPoint>
          <tModelInstanceDetails>
            <tModelInstanceInfo
              tModelKey="uddi:5791FG2-3460-4G97-2771-1495GJ443925"/>
            </tModelInstanceInfo>
          </tModelInstanceDetails>
        </bindingTemplate>
      </bindingTemplates>
    </businessService>
  </businessServices>
</businessEntity>
```


for Web services and for other electronic and non-electronic services. A UDDI registry service is a Web service that manages information about service providers, service implementations, and service metadata. Service providers can use UDDI to advertise the services they offer. Service consumers can use UDDI to discover services that suit their requirements and to obtain the service metadata needed to consume those services (http://www.uddi.org/faqs.html).

Universal Description, Discovery, and Integration (UDDI) discover the prospective requester from the directory that is also an integral part of an organization. This specification allows for the creation of standardised service description registries both within and outside of organization boundaries. UDDI provides the potential for Web services to be registered in a central location, from where they can be discovered by service requestors. Hence SOA services should be accessed, shared, and reused across a network. The UDDI directory provides the channels of access across the network.

THE USE OF SOA IN COLLABORATIVE ORGANIZATIONS

One of the key challenges in modern day business is the pressing need to integrate their wide and varied software systems and applications. Furthermore, large organizations such as banks and insurance companies have vast amount of data that is embedded in their legacy systems. They have a need to expose those data and the corresponding applications in a 'unified' view to the customer on the Internet - resulting in what is known as 'business integration'. However, as a result of this integration, and technical ability of applications to transact over the Internet, businesses are now readily able to offer and consume 'services' across the Internet. Currently, there is a limited of literature on modelling and managing the challenges emanating from collaboration between varied businesses and applications.

Based on Pasley (2005), service interoperability is paramount. Although researchers have proposed various middleware technologies to achieve SOA, Web services standards better satisfy the universal interoperability needs. In order for multiple organizations to collaborate many challenges were identified as such: technological, methodological and social factors resulting rational interactions between businesses. The good architecture takes place when the services of different applications have the capability to communicate. The previous statement leads us to the concept of Service Oriented Application departing beyond the boundary of standard communications framework.

According to Erl (2004) an SOA is a design model with a deeply rooted concept of encapsulating application logic within services that interact via a common communication protocol. When Web Services are used to establish this communication framework, they basically represent a web-based implementation of Service Oriented Architecture. Business process integration is part of enterprise integration solutions, which is why coordination services for business activities are utilised exclusively for the management of long running business activities.

Based on Chung (2005), Web Services integration enables a dynamic e-business model that fosters collaboration with heterogeneous business services and opens the door for new business opportunities. A service-oriented architecture (SOA) is an application framework that takes everyday business applications and breaks them down into individual business functions and processes, called services.

Figure 2 will clearly explain how Service Oriented Architecture will impact the requirements of collaborative Organizations.

The above Figure 2 shows the importance of SOA in developing the applications of Collaborative Organizations. The technology and the architectural aspects of this integration based on collaboration have also been demonstrated. The requirements of collaborations as far as the multiple organizations are the required technology, required methodology, social threats, how to implement the integration, how to architect the integration and investigate the structural changes to the organization after the integration.

Figure 2. The role oF SOA in collaborative organizations

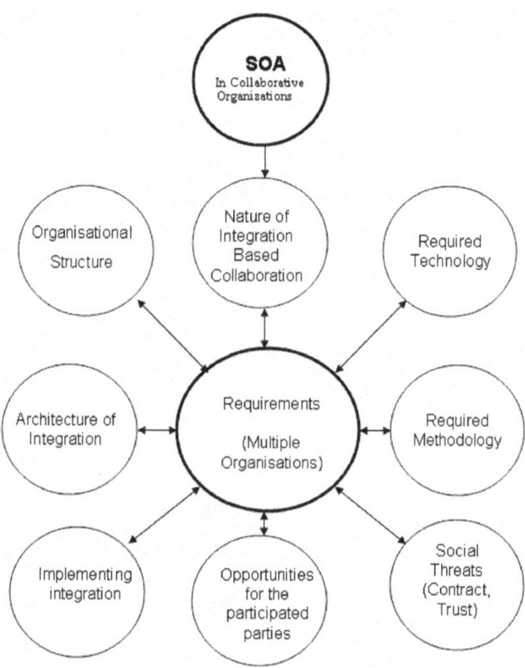

ADAPTING MOBILE AND WEB SERVICES TECHNOLOGIES

The interoperation amongst multiple organizations needs a technology to support the collaboration across their business process especially when the participated organization are not necessarily known to each other, and have never collaborated previously.

According to Barry (2003) the main driving forces for adopting Web Services are classified as interoperable network applications, emerging industry-wide standards, easier exchange of data, reduced developing time, reduced maintain costs, availability of external services and availability of training and tools.

The main restraining forces are also classified as different semantics in data source, semantic translation effect on operation systems for up-to-moment data request, standards evolving not fixed and mergers and acquisition.

Based on our survey, we asked 60 different organizations in the Sydney metropolitan area to inform us about their ideas about the adoption of the Web Services from technical, methodological and social issues. The following Figures present the result of the survey which was already approved by the Ethics committees. The 43% of the organization amounting 26, were medium sized and 57% amounting 34, were large sized organizations. According to the ABS report, the organizations with the number of 10-200 employees are classified as medium size and the organization with the number of more than 200 employees are classified as the large size organizations (Trevin, 2001). Figure 3 illustrate the demographic of the organization based on their organizational size.

Figure 3. Percentage and size of the organizations

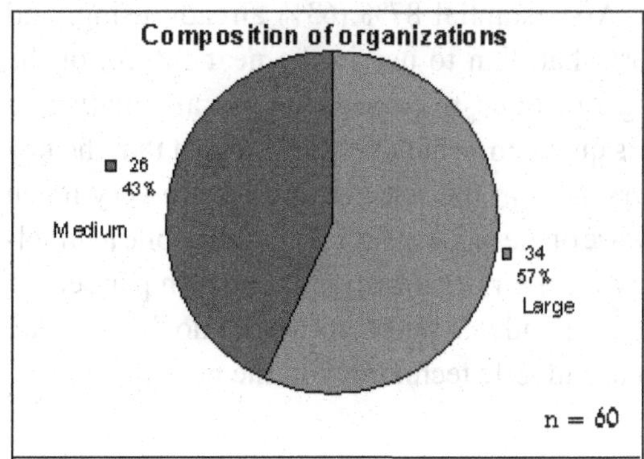

The organizations span across different industries, as listed in table below.

The Organization Category

This section is related to the category of the participated organization. The study identifies the importance of the organization's category as to reach different industries in order to evaluate the general technological adaptation in different organization. Table 1 demonstrate the organizational categories in which responded to the distributed survey.

The majority of the participants are from the Information Technology sector of the industry. The Government departments, education and banking are following in order. The study is able to proceed hence the distribution of the questionnaire has been correctly allocated and the study can evaluate the result achieved based on the different category of the organizations.

The Position of the Participant in the Organization

This part is related to the position of the individuals in the organization who has actually responded to the questions. This section is also very important since the research can understand the role of the respondent and their decision making power to change the technology of the organization. The positions of the respondent are presented in Table 2.

The participants who held the general management positions in their organizations formed the 21.7% while marketing manager and senior management holds 13.3% of the respondents. The remaining of 48.3% of the respondents holds the key role positions in their organizations. These people are the decision makers in the organizations.

Table 1. The category of the organizations

Organizations Categories	Number	Percentage
Information Technology	20	33.3%
Government Departments	14	23.3%
Education and Training	7	11.7%
Banking, Finance and Insurance	7	11.7%
Professional Services (Legal and Accounting)	5	8.3%
Retailing	3	5%
Health and Community Services	2	3.3%
Utility Services and Equipment	1	1.7%
Manufacturing and Processing	1	1.7%
Total	60	100%

Table 2. The position of the respondent in the organization

Position	Number	Percentage
General Management	13	21.7%
Marketing Manager	8	13.3%
Senior Management	8	13.3%
Systems Analyst/Programmer	8	13.3%
IT/MIS Manager	6	10%
Technical Support	6	10%
Executive Manager	5	8.3%
Sales Officer	4	6.7%
Customer Care	2	3.3%
Total	60	100%

MOBILE TECHNOLOGY INFORMATION

This section of the chapter demonstrates the result of the survey in regards to the respondents general thought about mobility in business.

Importance of the Mobility in the Organization

This section is evaluating the use of mobile technology (use of mobile devices) in the daily activities of the business. The query further investigates whether the organizations are already using mobile technology, or are planning to use it in the near future. The responses are detailed in Figure 4.

A substantial 87% (63% already using, and 23% that plan to use in the near future) of the organizations responded in the affirmative to this question, which verifies the fact that the key personnel in the selected sample are very much aware of the value of mobility and mobile technology for their organizations. Thirteen per cent of the respondents said that they do not have a plan to use mobile technology in the near future.

Figure 4. The use of mobile technology in the organizations

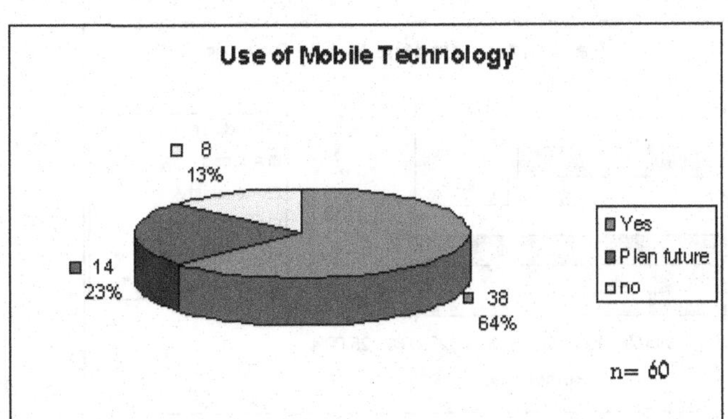

Figure 5. Type of mobile devices in organizations

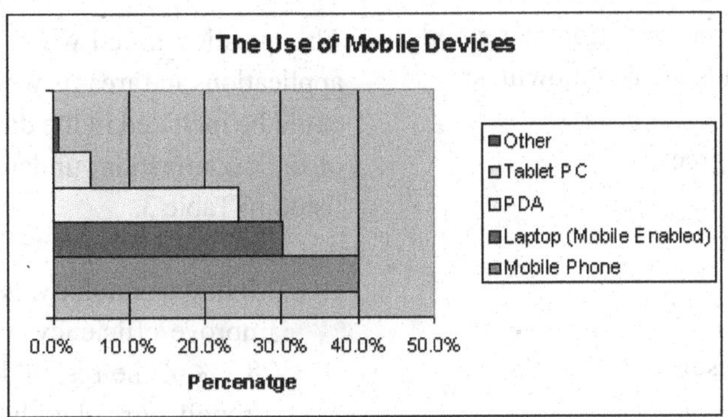

Used Mobile Devices in the Organization

The question is to identify what kind of the devices are in use in order to gain an insight into the current use of mobile technology in the organizations. The responses for this question are listed in Figure 5.

The main issue to consider in this section is that the organizations can use different devices in order to proceed with their daily business activities. The survey identified that 40% of the organizations are currently using mobile devices while 30% of the respondent use mobile enabled laptops. The Figure 6 clearly demonstrates that organizations have realised that they need to take advantage of mobile technologies.

The Scenario in Which Mobile Devices are Used

The respondents were queried about the use of these devices in their business activities. In this section of the research is identifying the reason for the use of mobile devices in order to identify the use of this technology in the collaborative environment. The Figure 6 depicts the typical reasons for the mobile devices in the daily business activates.

Figure 6 presents the result by stating that the majority of participants believe that the use of mobility has increased the performance of their business activities enabling them to have greater access to the employee, as well as being accessible by their customers. The use of mobile

Figure 6. Typical reason for the use of mobile devices

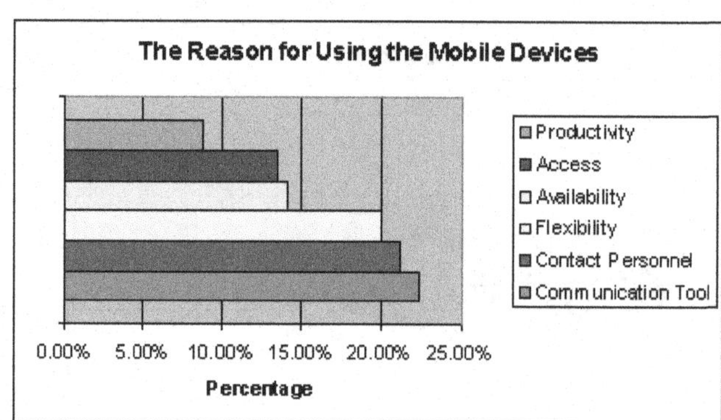

devices has created flexibility, availability and better access.

Questions 7, 8, 9, 12, 21, 22 and 23 have been designed to rate the answers on different method of evaluation. The legends are as followings:

VSA – Very Strongly Agree
SA – Strongly Agree
Ag - Agree
DA – Disagree
SD - Strongly Disagree
VSD – Very Strongly Disagree

Based on these ratings, the following results are extracted from the survey of organizations. In the followings the letter P stands for the Point as it was presented in the survey called Point number.

Current Application of Mobile Technology

The question asked whether there are any new applications and areas in which mobile technology could be included in the daily business activities of the organization, under four propositions, as listed in Table 3.

1. Mobile technology as a special technology improve efficiency in customer meetings. 78.7% of the respondents either agreed or strongly agreed with this proposition.
2. Mobile technology has been used as a special tool to advertise in a captured market. 70.4% of the respondents agreed with this proposition.

Table 3. New applications/areas for use of mobile technology

New Applications	TOTAL	VSA	SA	AG	DA	SD	VSD
1- Special Technology-Improve Efficiencies	47	6	15	16	8	1	1
PERCENTAGE	**100**	**13**	**32**	**34**	**17**	**2**	**2**
2-Advertise in Captured Markets	44	2	9	20	8	2	3
PERCENTAGE	**100**	**5**	**20**	**45**	**18**	**5**	**7**
3-Contacting Office (Any where/Any time)	47	13	15	12	3	1	3
PERCENTAGE	**100**	**28**	**32**	**26**	**6**	**2**	**6**
4-Track Goods in Transit	51	8	12	16	8	3	4
PERCENTAGE	**100**	**16**	**24**	**31**	**16**	**6**	**8**

3. Mobile technology as a tool has enabled people to contact with the office for employees engaged in official travel. 63.8% agreed to this proposition.
4. Mobile technology has enabled the business to track goods in transit. About 70.5% of the responses agreed with this proposition.

The result achieved states that the mobile technology is a major technology which could improve their business activities. Therefore, this technology could also facilitate this research to enter the new proposed collaborative environment.

Advantages of Mobile Technology

The question establishes the advantage of using mobile technology in organizations. Whilst the question queried the availability of applications of mobile technologies that can be included in the organization, the objective of next question is to re-emphasise this question in an alternate way, by probing the advantages of using mobile technology, rather than directly asking about new applications. The results of this question are listed in Table 4.

1. Mobile technology as a special technology is very cost efficient. 72.7% of the respondents either agreed or strongly agreed with this proposition.
2. Mobile technology has been connecting people while out of the office. 93.8% of the respondents agreed with this proposition.
3. Mobile technology has been improving the business productivity. 71% of the respondents agreed with this proposition.
4. Mobile technology has enabled employees to be more flexible hence they can work disregard of their location and time. 72.3% agreed to this proposition.
5. Mobile technology has created better access method for the customer to contact the organization. 85.4 % of the responses agreed with this proposition.

Advantage of Mobile Technology for the Business

The question asked about other factors that would enhance the demand in introducing or using mobile technology in the organization. Four propositions were presented to the respondents

Table 4. Main advantages of mobile technology for oganizations

Mobile Advantages		TOTAL	VSA	SA	AG	DA	SD	VSD
1- Cost Saving		44	8	8	16	10	1	1
	PERCENTAGE	**100**	**18**	**18**	**36**	**23**	**2**	**2**
2-Connect Employees		48	21	15	9	3	0	0
	PERCENTAGE	**100**	**44**	**31**	**19**	**6**	**0**	**0**
3- Improve Productivity		55	13	26	10	6	0	0
	PERCENTAGE	**100**	**24**	**47**	**18**	**11**	**0**	**0**
4-Flexibility of Employees		47	7	10	17	12	1	0
	PERCENTAGE	**100**	**15**	**21**	**36**	**26**	**2**	**0**
5- Better Access for Customers		48	10	13	18	6	0	1
	PERCENTAGE	**100**	**21**	**27**	**38**	**13**	**0**	**2**

Table 5. Factors influencing the use of mobile technology in an organization

Factors Influencing Mobility	TOTAL	VSA	SA	AG	DA	SD	VSD
1- Mobility Demand by Employees	52	7	12	20	13	0	0
PERCENTAGE	100	13	23	38	25	0	0
2- Mobility Demand by Customers	50	4	12	21	12	0	1
PERCENTAGE	100	8	24	42	24	0	2
3- Mobility Demand by Supply Chain	48	3	12	17	12	3	1
PERCENTAGE	100	6	25	35	25	6	2
4- Mobility Demand by Social-Psych Factor	47	4	8	19	14	1	1
PERCENTAGE	100	9	17	40	30	2	2

to choose from. Table 5 lists the results for the question.

1. Employees demand and show interest in using the mobile technology. 75% of the respondents either agreed or strongly agreed with this proposition.
2. Customer demand and show interest in using the mobile technology. 74% of the respondents either agreed or strongly agreed with this proposition.
3. Supply chain sector is more interested and show interest in using the mobile technology. 66.7% of the respondents either agreed or strongly agreed with this proposition.
4. Social-Psychological factors are influencing the people to use the mobile technology. 66% of the respondents either agreed or strongly agreed with this proposition.

Improvement Caused by Mobile Technology

The question investigated the perceived value of mobile technology in the daily activities of the organization. This section allows the respondents to select more than one choice. The survey results are listed in Figure 7.

The most important benefit of using the mobile devices as predicted has been classified as the availability to be contactable at any time, and anywhere. A fact revealed by this question is that cost savings are not the main driver for organizations to use mobile technology.

Problem/Difficulties of Mobile Technology

The question investigated the anticipated problems, difficulties and complaints the respondents may have when using the existing mobile gadgets. The results are listed in Figure 8.

The results state that the most important difficulty is the small screen while the limited applications, battery life span and complicity of mobile devices are classified as the remaining problem of mobile devices.

Disadvantages of Mobile Technology

The question investigated the disadvantages of using mobile technologies, as perceived by the respondents. The results are listed in Table 6.

1. Queried whether the cost of establishment of mobile applications is a concern for the organization. 74% of the respondents either agreed or strongly agreed with this proposition.

Figure 7. Mobile technology advantages to business activities

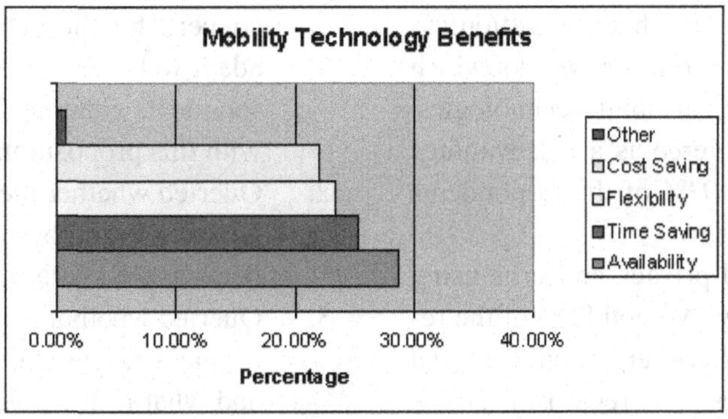

Figure 8. Problems faced by organizations using the mobile gadgets

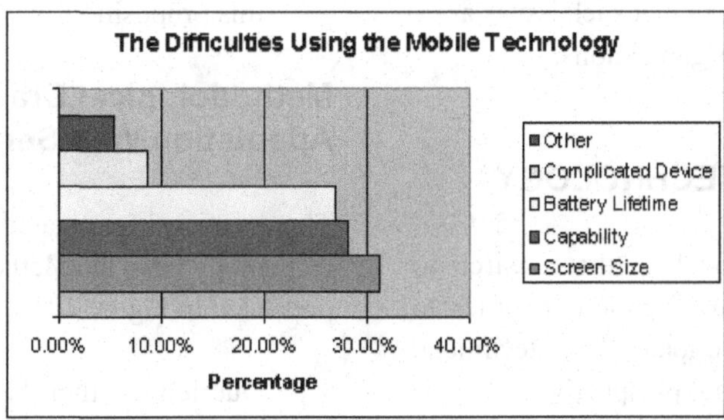

Table 6. The Recognised disadvantages of mobile technology

Disadvantages of Mobile Technology	TOTAL	VSA	SA	AG	DA	SD	VSD
1- Establishment Cost of Applications	56	6	15	20	11	2	2
PERCENTAGE	**100**	**11**	**27**	**36**	**20**	**4**	**4**
2-Recruitment Cost of Mobility	54	5	16	24	6	2	1
PERCENTAGE	**100**	**9**	**30**	**44**	**11**	**4**	**2**
3- Technical Drawback	57	12	16	25	2	2	0
PERCENTAGE	**100**	**21**	**28**	**44**	**4**	**4**	**0**
4-Legal and Privacy Issues	56	9	12	24	9	1	1
PERCENTAGE	**100**	**16**	**21**	**43**	**16**	**2**	**2**
5- Training and Adaptation Issues	55	5	24	14	9	1	2
PERCENTAGE	**100**	**9**	**44**	**25**	**16**	**2**	**4**

2. Queried the recurring cost of using mobile technology as a major tool. 83% of the respondents agreed with this proposition.
3. Queried whether technical drawbacks, which are inherent in current mobile technologies, are a factor considered as a disadvantage by organizations. 93% of the respondents agreed with this view.
4. Queried legal and privacy concerns using mobile technology. Around 80% of the respondents showed concern about the legal and privacy issues with regard to mobile technology.
5. Queried with adoption and training issues in an organization with regard to mobile technology. 78% of respondents in the selected sample agreed that such issues are a concern for their organizations.

WEB SERVICES TECHNOLOGY

The following questions help the research to evaluate the participant's opinion in order to adapt Web Services technology from technical, methodological and social prospective.

Technical Drawbacks of Adaptation Web Services

The question investigated the adaptation to WS technology from the technical perspective presented in Figure 9.

1. Queried whether the unfamiliar concept of the Web Services technology is the great concern for the organizations in order to adapt web Services. About 70% of the respondents either agreed or strongly agreed with this proposition.
2. Queried whether the limitation of the Web Services is important. 65% of the respondents agreed with this proposition.
3. Queried whether the ambiguity of the Web Services is the major concern (What it is and what it does). 70% of the respondents agreed with this view.
4. Queried whether the participants understand how WS could facilitate collaboration. Almost 80% of the participants agreed with this proposition.

Methodological Drawbacks of Adaptation Web Services

The question investigated the adaptation to WS technology from the Methodological perspective presented in Figure 10.

1. Queried whether the impact on WS on existing business process is the main concern while adapting the WS. About 64.9% of the respondents either agreed or strongly agreed with this proposition.
2. Queried whether the training of the employees is the main concern. 61.5% of the respondents agreed with this proposition.

Figure 9. The technical issues adapting the Web services

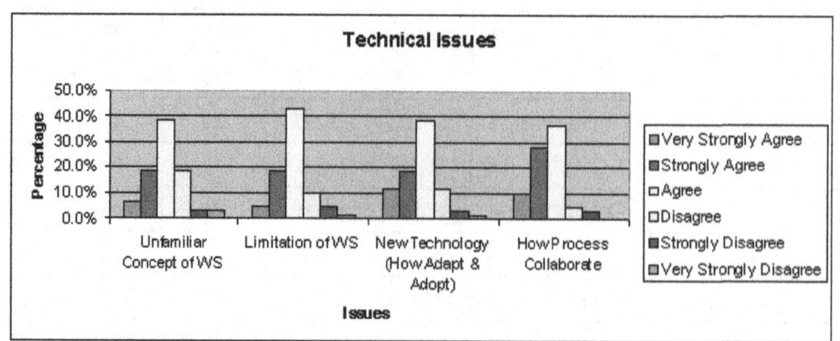

Figure 10. The methodological issues adapting the Web services

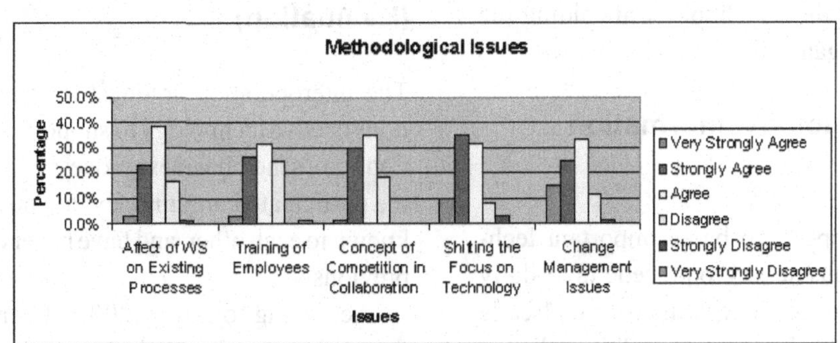

3. The concept of the competition while collaborating (how can you collaborate with your competitor). 86.6% of the respondents agreed with this view.
4. The focus will shift to technology rather than process. Almost 80% of the participants agreed with this proposition.
5. How to manage the change when adapting the WS technology. Almost 75% agreed with the proposition.

Social Drawbacks of Adaptation Web Services

The question investigated the adaptation to WS technology from the social perspective presented in Figure 11.

1. Evaluate the adaptation rate by customer and the employees. About 60% of the respondents either agreed or strongly agreed with this proposition.
2. How the competitor react to change. 75% of the respondents agreed with this proposition.
3. How the technology provide support in order to trust the competitor. Almost 75% of the respondents agreed with this view.
4. What happens to the organizations already in line of collaboration? Almost 65% of the participants agreed with this proposition.
5. The legal issues involved in collaboration (Government and the internal policies). Almost 65% of the participant agreed with the proposition.

ANALYSES OF THE DATA

This section describes the further analyses the overall assessment of the survey in regards to

Figure 11. The social issues adapting the Web services

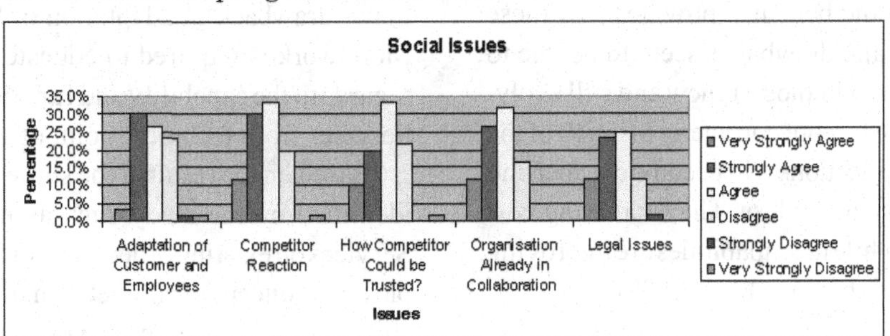

the adaptation of Mobile and Web Services technology as far as these technology are aiding the collaborative organizations.

Mobile Technology Information (Evaluation)

The mobility appears to be an important technology for the businesses to precede their daily activities. 63% of the organizations are already using their mobile devices to run their ordinary activities while 23% has stated that they are planning to adapt it in the near future. The total of 87% of the organizations recognises the importance of the mobile technology while currently the majority of these people mainly use their mobile phones and mobile enabled laptops.

The respondents defined that mobility is a great communication tool, make it easier to find and locate personnel, create more flexibility and increases the general productivity. The major advantage of mobile technology is providing availability to people disregards of their location and time. The study revealed that the accessibility is one of the greatest advantage of the collaborative organizations therefore the advantage of the mobility (Anywhere – Anytime) could provide benefit to collaborative organizations.

The survey has also investigated the current and potential application of mobility, advantages and disadvantages of mobility and the improvements caused by mobility to provide a better understanding of this technology.

Interestingly, the survey identified the cost of mobility is not classified as a big disadvantage in comparison to the benefit it provides. All these disadvantages and drawbacks seem to be due to the fact that the technology is new and still evolving. When there is more commercialisation of the technology, applications will become cheaper and recurring costs will be less. The decreasing cost of technology while the capabilities are improving rapidly is highlighted in (Roth, 1998).

Web Services Technology (Evaluation)

The interoperation amongst multiple organizations needs a technology to support the collaboration across their business process especially when the participated organization are not necessarily known to each other, and have never collaborated previously.

According to Barry (2003) the main driving forces for adopting Web Services are classified as interoperable network applications, emerging industry-wide standards, easier exchange of data, reduced developing time, reduced maintain costs, availability of external services and availability of training and tools.

The main restraining forces are also classified as different semantics in data source, semantic translation effect on operation systems for up-to-moment data request, standards evolving not fixed and mergers and acquisition.

Based on our survey, all the issues identified by the research such as unfamiliarity concepts of Web Services, limitation of Web Services, how to adapt the new technology and how the processes collaborate are classified as the major concerns of the organization in order to adopt Web Services. Only the minority of 10% of the participants very strongly agree to understanding how Web Services could help the collaboration while close to 30% of the participants had the same concern with ticking the strongly agree box. The research has concluded that the organization knowledge in regard to the technical issues of WS is very limited. This lack of knowledge could be classified as the major drawback in adaptation of Web Services. More work is required to educate enterprises in regards to the capability and functionality of Web Services from technical point of view.

Based on the result of the survey, all the issues identified by the study such as impact of Web Services on existing processes, training of the employees, concept of competition in collaboration, shifting the focus of technology and the concept of change management has been classified as important concepts. Almost 40% of the participants agree with these issues while close to 30% strongly agree. Close to 20% of the respondents classify the concepts of change management as their greatest concern for adopting WS technology for their organization. However, about 20% and 30% of these organizations disagree that the affect of WS on existing business processes and training the employees as a great importance. There is no doubt that the methodological issues play an important role in adopting Web Services technology.

Based on the survey, the customer/ competitor reaction and the impact on the organizations that already in collaboration are classified by the participants as a strongly agree point. Almost similar number is attracting the very strongly agree comments however up to 35% of all participants classify all the issues identified by the study as the major drawback for adaptation of WS by organizations.

The research concludes that technical, methodological and social factors identified by this study are to impose the adaptation and adoption of new technology by organizations. The business opportunities resulting from WS have seen these technologies being rapidly adopted across the world. For example, an IDC Report in 2003 revealed that 30% of Australian organizations are already using web services – although a large number of these organization's applications are behind the corporate firewall. Another survey conducted by CSC found 105 of Australia's largest organizations are already using web services or planning to do so (Mackenzie, 2003).

In general, the issues of incompatible technology, competition, licensing agreement (legal issues) and mistrust are also classified as additional major concern while adopting the new technology to be discussed later in the thesis.

The research concludes that technical, methodological and social factors identified by this study are to impose the adoption of new technology by organizations. In general, the issues of incompatible technology, competition, licensing agreement (legal issues) and mistrust are also classified as additional major concern while adopting the new technology.

CONCLUSION AND DIRECTION

Service Oriented Architecture and Web Services were introduced in this chapter extending the mentioned architecture and technologies that support the Collaborative Business Process Engineering. The technical, methodological and social factors in order to adopt Web Services technologies by organizations were also investigated. This chapter has also described a survey carried out in the Sydney metropolitan area in large and medium-sized organisations, in order to assess the organisations' concerns, readiness for and adaptability to emerging technologies of Mobile and Web Services technologies. The final result of the survey has revealed (in fact within the selected sample) that the key personnel of the organisations agree with the major concerns identified by the study and queried in the survey. The above 60% rate has been the result achieved for every individual question. The chapter has presented pictorial illustrations of the achieved results and the analyses provided of the collected data are also discussed.

REFERENCES

http://www.ebizq.net/hot_topics/soa/features/5857.html?&pp=1.Downloaded: 12/10/2006

Alag, H. (2006). *Business Process Mobility.* In B. Unhelkar (Ed.), *Handbook Resources of Mobile Business.* Hershey, PA, USA: IGI Global. USA.

Barry, D. K. (2003). *Web Services and Service-Oriented Architecture. The savvy Manager's*

Guide. USA: Morgan Kaufmann Publishers. ISBN: 1-55860-906-7

Chase, N. (2006, February 14*). Introducing the open Group Architecture Framework, Understanding TOGAf and IT Architecture in today's World.* http://www-128.ibm.com/developerworks/ibm/library/ar-togaf1/ Accessed: 3/04/2007

Chen, X., Wenteng, C., Turner, S. J., & Wang, Y. (2006). SOAr-DSGrid: Service-Oriented Architecture for Distributed Simulation on the Grid. *Proceedings of the 20th Workshop on Principles of Advanced and Distributed Simulation.* ISBN ~ ISSN:1087-4097 , 0-7695-2587-3

Chung, J. Y. (2005). An Industry View on Service-Oriented Architecture and Web Services. *Proceedings of the 2005 IEEE International Workshop on Service-Oriented System Engineering (SOSE'05)* 0-7695-2438-9/05 © 2005 IEEE.

Curbera, F., Khalaf, R., Mukhi, N., Tai, S., & Weerawarana, S. (2003, October). The Next Step in Web Services. *Communications of the ACM, 46*(10).

Erl, T. (2004). *Service-Oriented Architecture. A Field Guide to Integrating XML and Web Services.* Pearson Education, Inc. ISBN: 0-13-142898-5

Falcone, F., & Garito, M. (2006). *Mobile Strategy Roadmap.* In B. Unhelkar (Ed.), *Handbook Resources of Mobile Business.* Herhsey, PA USA: Idea Group. ISBN: 1591408172

Finkelsteing, C. (2006). *Enterprise Architecture for Integration. Rapid Delivery Methods and Technology.* British Library Catalogue in Publication Data. ISBN: 1-58053-713-8

Godbole, N. (2006). *Relating Mobile Computing to Mobile Commerce.* In B. Unhelkar (Ed.), *Handbook Resources of Mobile Business.* Herhsey, PA USA: Idea Group.. ISBN: 1591408172

Ghanbary, A. (2006). Collaborative Business Process Engineering across Multiple Organizations. A Doctoral Consortium. *Proceedings of ACIS 2006.* Australia: Adelaide.

Jostad, I., Dustdar, S., & Thanh, D. V. (2005). A Service Oriented Architecture Framework for Collaborative Services. *Proceedings of the 14th IEEE International Workshops on Enabling Technologies: Infrastructure for Collaborative Enterprise.* ISBN ~ ISSN:1524-4547 , 0-7695-2362-5

Harrison, A., & Taylor, J. I. (2005). WSPeer - An Interface to Web Service Hosting and Invocation. *Proceedings of the 19th IEEE International Parallel and Distributed Processing Symposium (IPDPS'05).* ISBN: 1530-2075/05

Miller, J., & Mukerji, J. (2003). *Model Driven Architecture (MDA) Guide Version 1.0.1.* http://www.omg.org/docs/omg/03-06-01.pdf. Downloaded: 5/10/06

Pasley, J. (2005, May/June). How BPEL and SOA are changing Web services development. *Internet Computing, IEEE, 9*(3), 60-67. Digital Object Identifier 10.1109/MIC.2005.56

The open Group Integration Consortium. http://www.integrationconsortium.org/docs/W054final.pdf. Downloaded: 5/10/2006.

The ACM Digital Library. http://delivery.acm.org/10.1145/610000/606273/p54-lee.html?key1=606273&key2=4006199511&coll=GUIDE&dl=portal,ACM&CFID=11111111&CFTOKEN=2222222#lead-in. Downloaded: 5/10/2006.

Unhelkar, B., & Deshpande, Y. (2004). Evolving from Web Engineering to Web Services: A Comparative study in the context of Business Utilization of the Internet. *Proceedings of ADCOM 2004, 12th International Conference on Advanced Computing and Communications*, Ahmedabad, India, 15-18 December

UDDI.org. http://www.uddi.org/faqs.html. Downloaded: 12/10/2006

W3Consortium. http://www.w3.org/TR/wsdl. Downloaded; 12/10/2006

W3Consortium. http://www.w3.org/XML/. Downloaded: 12/10/2006

This work was previously published in Handbook of Research in Mobile Business: Technical, Methodological and Social Perspectives, Second Edition, edited by B. Unhelkar, pp. 499-517, copyright 2009 by Information Science Reference (an imprint of IGI Global).

Chapter XIV
Modeling and Specification of Collaborative Business Processes with an MDA Approach and a UML Profile

Pablo David Villarreal
CDIDI - Universidad Tecnológica Nacional, Argentina

Enrique Salomone
INGAR-CONICET, Argentina

Omar Chiotti
Universidad Tecnologica Nacional & INGAR-CONICET, Argentina

ABSTRACT

This chapter describes the application of MDA (model driven architecture) and UML for the modeling and specification of collaborative business processes, with the purpose of enabling enterprises to establish business-to-business collaborations. The proposed MDA approach provides the components and techniques required for the development of collaborative processes from their conceptual modeling to the specifications of these processes and the partners' interfaces in a B2B standard. As part of this MDA approach, a UML profile is provided that extends the semantics of UML2 to support the analysis and design of collaborative processes. This UML profile is based on the use of interaction protocols to model collaborative processes. The application of this UML profile in a case study is presented. Also, an overview is provided about the automatic generation of B2B specifications from conceptual models of collaborative processes. In particular, the generation of B2B specifications based on ebXML is described.

Copyright © 2009, IGI Global, distributing in print or electronic forms without written permission of IGI Global is prohibited.

INTRODUCTION

To compete in the current global markets, enterprises are focusing on setting up business-to-business (B2B) collaborative relationships with their partners in order to improve their performance, as well as the global performance of the supply chain (Liu & Kumar, 2003). A B2B collaboration implies the integration of enterprises in two levels: a business level and a technological level. In order to accomplish inter-enterprise integration at both levels, one of the main challenges is the modeling and specification of *collaborative business processes*. Through these processes, enterprises undertake to jointly carry out decisions to achieve common goals, coordinate their actions, and exchange information.

On the one hand, the definition of interenterprise integration at business level requires the conceptual modeling of collaborative processes. Business engineers and system designers have to rely on a language that allows them to model these processes without considering the technology used to implement them. Moreover, such modeling language has to support the particular requirements of the B2B collaborations: enterprise autonomy, decentralization, global view of the collaboration, peer-to-peer interactions, and the use of suitable abstractions to model communicative actions and negotiations among partners.

On the other hand, collaborative process models defined at business level have to be translated into specifications of collaborative processes and systems' interfaces based on a B2B standard so that partners can execute these processes. Currently, however, the development of collaborative processes, from the conceptual modeling up to the specifications in a B2B standard, is costly, time consuming, and complex. In addition, collaborative process models must be consistent with the specifications generated at the technological level. Hence, an approach is required to allow business engineers to focus on the business level, and automatically generate the technological solutions required to carry out a B2B collaboration from the conceptual models of collaborative processes, in order to maintain the consistency between both levels.

The objective of this chapter is to show how the MDA (model driven architecture) initiative (OMG, 2003) can be applied to the development of collaborative processes in order to address the aforementioned issues. Through an MDA approach, collaborative process models play an important role. Hence, business engineers can focus mainly on the design of collaborative process models to define partners' business integration and the behavior of the B2B collaborations. Then, they can transform these models to automatically generate the XML code of the specifications of the collaborative processes and the partners' interfaces in a B2B standard. In this way, an MDA approach intends to reduce the inherent complexity and costs which partners have to incur during the development of collaborative processes and B2B systems, and to ensure that a business solution is consistent with their respective technological solutions.

In addition, this chapter describes how to extend the semantics of UML2 for supporting the conceptual modeling of collaborative processes. A UML profile for collaborative processes is presented that has the aim of supporting the particular requirements of B2B collaborations. These requirements are met through the use of interaction protocols to model collaborative processes. Interactions protocols are based on speech act theory (Searle, 1975) and hence, by means of this UML profile, business engineers can define, in a richer way, communicative actions and negotiations between partners in collaborative processes.

This chapter is organized in the following way. The first section introduces the main concepts of B2B collaborations, then it describes the requirements for both the conceptual modeling of collaborative processes and the automatic generation of B2B specifications, and finally it discusses limitations of current proposals. The second section describes the MDA approach for the development of collaborative processes. The third section describes the UML Profile for Collaborative Business Processes Based on Interaction Protocols (UP-ColBPIP). The fourth section provides an overview of the automatic generation of the specifications of collaborative processes and partners' interfaces from UP-ColBPIP models. In particular, the transformation of UP-ColBPIP models into ebXML specifications is described. Finally, the fifth section outlines future trends, and the last section presents conclusions.

BACKGROUND

A B2B collaboration implies integration of enterprises at two levels: a business level and a technological level. The *business level* refers to the problem domain, that is, business engineers' view of the B2B collaboration. At this level, integration is addressed through the application of a collaborative business model. Examples of these models for the supply chain management are vendor managed inventory (VMI) (CompTIA EIDX, 2004); collaborative forecasting, planning and replenishment (CPFR) (VICS, 2002); and the Partner-to-Partner Collaborative Model (Villarreal, Caliusco, Zucchini, Arredondo, Zanel, Galli, & Chiotti, 2003a). A collaborative model defines the generic rules and parameters to be considered in inter-enterprise collaboration. However, the concrete behavior of the collaboration is formalized in *collaborative business processes* that define the roles performed by partners and how they coordinate their actions and exchange information. Therefore at this level, enterprises have to focus mainly on the definition of these processes, according to the features of the collaborative model agreed by enterprises.

An important requirement at business level is the definition of collaborative processes without considering the technology used to implement them. This is due to the fact that the people involved at this level are not acquainted with or are not interested in dealing with the technical details of the implementation. Furthermore, the modeling of these processes should not be driven by a specific technology (Baghdadi, 2004). The technology should be decided later.

The *technological level* refers to the solution domain, that is, system architects and developers' view on the solution. At this level, integration is addressed through the implementation of a B2B information system. This type of system is composed of autonomous, heterogeneous, and distributed components that are deployed by each enterprise to jointly execute collaborative processes with other partners. Interoperability between these components is a key issue. It can be achieved by using a B2B standard that provides the languages to specify the so-called B2B protocols (Bernauer, Kappel, & Kramler, 2003; Bussler, 2001). Two important interoperability aspects are supported by these protocols: the specification of the collaborative processes and the specification of partners' interfaces that compose the B2B information system, both based on executable languages.

In this way, technology-independent collaborative processes should be modeled at business level, and then specified at the technological level through B2B protocols. Both definitions must have a mutual correspondence in order to make sure that the technological solution is consistent and supports the collaborative processes agreed by the partners. In addition, for the purpose of taking advantage of new market opportunities, enterprises need to reduce cost, time, and complexity in the generation of technological solutions. To address such issues, several authors (Baghdadi, 2004; Bernauer et al., 2003) have recognized the convenience of providing approaches for the design of collaborative processes, regardless of the idiosyncrasies of particular B2B standards; and the automatic generation of B2B specifications based on a B2B standard from those processes.

To achieve the above requirements, model-driven development (MDD) has been identified as an appropriate software development philosophy to be exploited in a method for the development of collaborative processes (Villarreal, Salomone, & Chiotti, 2005). Two premises of MDD are (Selic, 2003) models play an important role, since they are the main development products instead of the programs; the code has to be generated in an automatic way from these models. Therefore, by applying an MDD approach, business engineers and system developers can build and transform collaborative process models in order to generate the XML code of the B2B specifications.

In addition, the OMG's MDA initiative (OMG, 2003) proposes a conceptual framework, along with a set of standards to build model-driven development methods. A key MDA standard is UML. The use of standards provides a significant importance because it allows communication of the best design practices, enables and encourages reuse, facilitates interoperability among complementary tools, and encourages specialization (Selic, 2003).

One principle of MDA is that the development of information systems can be organized around a set of models by imposing a series of transformations between models, organized into an architectural framework of layers and transformations. The components of MDA are platform independent models (PIMs), platform specific models (PSMs), transformations from PIMs into PSMs, and transformations from PSMs into source code (Figure 1). A platform makes reference to the technology that supports the system being built. In this way, the development process consists of: defining the PIMs; selecting the platform and executing the transformations that generate PSMs; and finally, generating the code from the selected PSM.

In order to define an MDA approach for the development of collaborative processes, two main tasks have to be supported :

- Conceptual modeling of collaborative processes to support the analysis and design of these processes without considering the technological issues.
- Automatic generation of B2B specifications from models of collaborative processes.

The requirements to support the above tasks are now discussed and analyzed.

Requirements for the Conceptual Modeling of Collaborative Processes

The traditional approach to model business processes has been the use of workflow modeling languages. However, as it has been previously discussed in several works (Bussler, 2001; Chen & Hsu, 2001) , the use of workflows to manage collaborative processes is not appropriate. This is due to the particular characteristics of the B2B collaborations that impose several requirements (Villarreal, Salomone, & Chiotti, 2003b). Therefore, to support such requirements in the conceptual modeling of collaborative business processes, a suitable modeling language is required.

Figure 1. Development process based on MDA

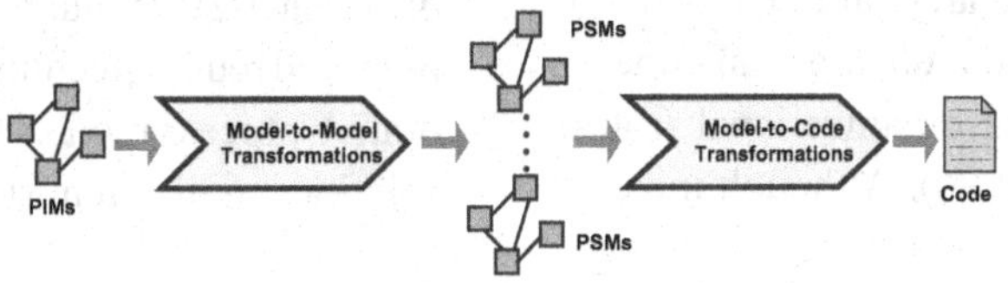

A first requirement is to represent the global view of the interactions between the partners. Public behavior and responsibilities of each partner, in terms of sending and receiving messages, should be explicitly defined in a collaborative process model.

Second, in B2B collaborations, enterprises behave as autonomous entities that collaborate while they hide their internal activities and decisions. This autonomy should be preserved in collaborative process models; that is, internal activities each partner performs for processing the received information or producing the information to be sent should not be defined.

Third, the decentralized management of collaborative processes can be achieved through peer-to-peer (P2P) interactions between the partners (Chen & Hsu, 2001), where each of them manages the role it performs in a B2B collaboration. Therefore, P2P interactions should be also expressed in a collaborative process model. This is correlated with the global-view requirement since this view allows describing P2P interactions.

Fourth, in the supply chain management through B2B collaborations, enterprises carry out joint decision making in order to agree on common demand forecasts, production plans, order plans, and so forth. Therefore, a modeling language for collaborative processes should provide appropriate primitives that enable representing complex negotiations in these processes.

Fifth, as it is discussed later, the definition of B2B interactions in collaborative processes cannot be restricted to the mere information exchange. It is also necessary to support communicative actions and the creation of commitments in the interactions between the parties.

Finally, there are different perspectives that a business process model has to support: functional (actions or activities), behavioral (control flow), informational (exchanged documents), operational (applications), and organizational (roles) (Jablosnky & Bussler, 1996). Although most of them are appropriate in collaborative process models, the operational perspective should not be defined by them, because the knowledge of the private applications that a partner uses to support collaborative processes reduces the enterprise autonomy.

Requirements for the Automatic Generation of B2B Specifications

As it was described previously, collaborative processes are implemented through B2B protocols that contain the specifications of these processes, and the corresponding partners' interfaces. Currently, there are two main technologies proposed for the specification of B2B protocols (Bernauer et al., 2003): standards based on Web services composition, such as BPEL (Business Process Execution Language) (BEA, IBM, Microsoft, SAP, & Siebel, 2003) and Web Services Choreography Description Language (WS-CDL) (W3C, 2004); and standards based on business transactions, such as ebXML (electronic business XML) (OASIS, 1999) and RosettaNet (1999).

On the one hand, standards based on business transactions and standards based on Web services composition are not compatible, and thus enterprises have to decide which ones to use. Furthermore, B2B standards are in constant evolution: new ones are proximate to appear, and there are different versions of them. As a consequence, the automatic generation of B2B specifications requires a particular transformation procedure for each standard and version.

On the other hand, an enterprise should be able to collaborate with several partners using different B2B standards (Medjahed, Benatallah, Bouguettaya, Ngu, & Ahmed, 2003). Moreover, a partner may require implementing the same collaborative processes with several partners using different B2B standards. This requirement can be solved reusing technology-independent collaborative process models to generate technological solutions in different standards.

Limitation of the Current Proposals

Several works have been proposed to support the modeling and specification of business processes in B2B settings. Some of them are MDD approaches, proposed to generate technological solutions based on Web services composition (Baïna, Benatallah, Cassati, & Toumani, 2004; Koehler, Hauser, Kapoor, Wu, & Kumaran, 2003). They focus on the modeling and automatic code generation of business or conversation protocols based on BPEL. This type of protocol refers to the message exchange between a composite Web service and a client of the Web service, without defining the internal business logic of the service. A conversation protocol defines the order in which a partner sends messages to and receives messages from its partners. Therefore, they focus on the modeling and specification of the behavior of collaborative processes, but from the point of view of only one partner. As a result, these approaches do not fulfill the requirement of representing the global view of the interactions between the partners. Also, they only consider as implementation technology the use of a Web services composition standard.

Gardner (2003) proposes an MDD approach, and provides a UML profile for modeling of business processes based on BPEL. Therefore, in this approach the definition of technology-independent process models is not supported, and it is also focused on a specific standard. In addition, BPEL only supports collaborative processes defined as conversation protocols.

Hofreiter and Huemer (2004a) propose the generation of ebXML BPSS (business process specification schema) (UN/CEFACT & OASIS, 2003) specifications from conceptual models of collaborative processes. The modeling language used to support the analysis and design of collaborative processes is that provided by UN/CEFACT modeling methodology (UMM). Such language was defined as a UML profile. Although UMM claims independence of the technology, the main conceptual elements are those used in BPSS, because the BPSS metamodel is a subset of the UMM metamodel. Hence, although the transformation of UMM into BPSS is simple and almost direct, this language influences the adoption of one standard. Moreover, UMM encourages defining collaborative processes in a hierarchical way, first defining business collaborations and then defining business transactions. This hierarchical approach does not enable representing the interactions and partners' responsibilities within a collaborative process in a high abstraction level. They are defined within business transactions, but not in the business collaboration realizing the collaborative process.

In addition, the interaction patterns proposed by UMM to define business transactions do not support complex negotiations. As an example, the *commercial (offer-acceptation)* pattern describes a negotiation with an offer that can be only accepted or rejected. However, in complex negotiations, there may exist different options and counter-proposals. In this way, the different stages of a negotiation into a business collaboration cannot be identified without additional effort. This effort results in a higher complexity to model negotiations in collaborative processes.

Hofreiter and Huemer (2004b) also propose the transformation of collaborative processes defined with UMM into BPEL specifications. However, this approach does not consider the application of an MDD or MDA approach to support the development of collaborative processes.

Table 1 synthesizes the strengths and limitations of these approaches. In brief, although the benefits of MDA for the domain of collaborative processes and B2B specifications are clear, currently, it has not been completely exploited in this domain. First, there is a lack of technology-independent modeling languages that support the identified requirements for the conceptual modeling of collaborative processes: in particular, the requirements of global view of the interactions, support for negotiations, and support for the definition of communicative aspects. Second, some

Table 1. Strengths and limitations of the current approaches

Current approaches	Strengths	Limitations
MDD approach for Web services composition Baïna et al., 2004)	• A MDD approach to generate technological solutions based on Web services composition • Processes are modeled by using extended state machines	• No support to model the global view of interactions • Focus only on a web services composition standard • Use of MDA and UML is not considered • No support for negotiations and communicative actions
MDD approach for Web services composition (Koehler et al., 2003)	• A MDD approach to generate technological solutions based on Web services composition • Explicit separation of the business view and the technological view • Use of UML Activity Diagrams to model processes	• MDA is not considered • No support to model the global view of the collaborative processes • Focus only on a web services composition standard • No support for negotiations and communicative actions.
UML Profile for BPEL (Gardner, 2003)	• Use of MDA and a UML Profile (it essentially uses activity diagrams to model BPEL processes)	• No support to model the global view of interactions • A technology-independent UML Profile is not considered • No support for negotiations and communicative actions.
UMM (Hofreiter and Huemer , 2004a),Hofreiter and Huemer , 2004b)	• Provide a UML Profile to model business collaborations • Support the global view of the interactions • Support to define commitments in the interactions between the partners	• Focus mainly onebXML. • Hierarchical definition of the collaborative processes do not highlight the interactions and the partners' responsibilities in a high abstraction level • Stages of a negotiation into a business collaboration cannot be identified without to exploit the business transactions • MDA is not considered • No support to model transformations.

of the described approaches are not based on a conceptual framework such as MDA and therefore, neither the use of standards such as UML nor the use of model transformation mechanisms to generate code is considered. Finally, most of the above approaches consider only one type of implementation technology, such as the use of Web services composition standards.

An MDA Approach for Collaborative Business Processes

In order to exploit the benefits of the model-driven development for the collaborative process domain, an MDA approach, which aims at enterprises at the different stages of the development of collaborative processes, is proposed.

In MDA, the concept of system does not only refer to the software, but can also refer to an enterprise, a set of enterprises, parts of different systems, and so forth. In the MDA approach proposed in this chapter, the system to be built includes the specifications of the collaborative processes, and the partners' interfaces of the B2B information system, both based on a B2B standard.

In addition, MDA provides the guidelines and the general components that a model-driven development method has to contain, but it does not provide the concrete techniques to be used in each domain. Although UML can be considered as a generic standard modeling language that can also be used to model organizational aspects, it is important to use languages and techniques that are more suitable and closer to the application domain.

Therefore, with the purpose of providing an MDA approach for collaborative processes, the components to be taken into account, along with the languages and techniques proposed to build these components, are described (Figure 2):

Figure 2. MDA approach for collaborative processes

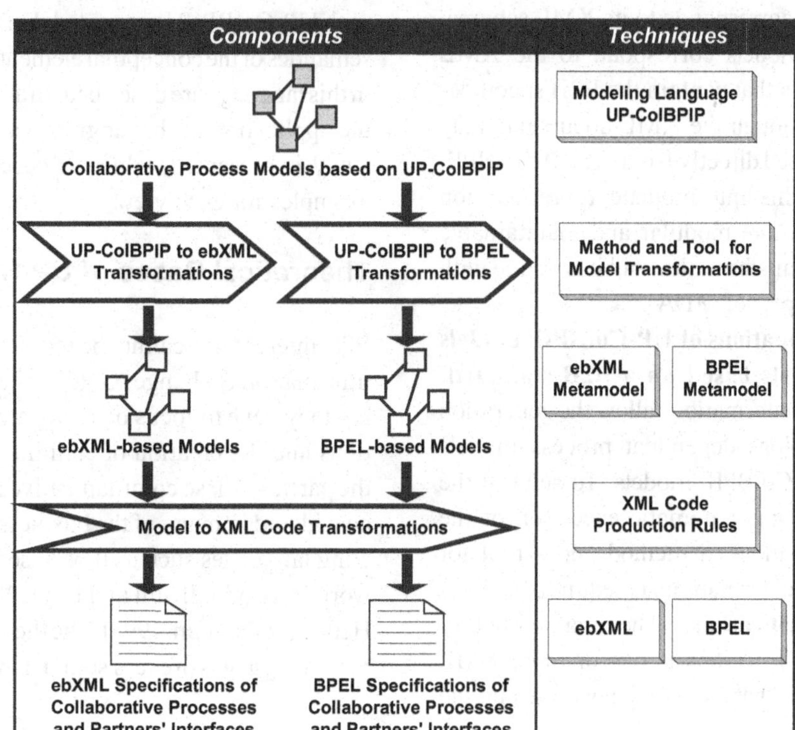

- **Collaborative business process models based on UP-ColBPIP:** These are the technology-independent collaborative process models and, hence, the main development products. For the building of these models, the *UML Profile for Collaborative Business Processes Based on Interaction Protocols (UP-ColBPIP)* is proposed, which is described later.
- **The collaborative business process models based on a B2B standard:** These are the collaborative process models specific to the technology. This MDA approach focuses on the generation of two types of technological solutions that can be derived from UP-ColBPIP models: solutions based on the ebXML standard; or solutions based on Web services composition standards, such as BPEL and WS-CDL. For building these models, it is necessary to define their corresponding metamodels. They can be derived from the XML schemas provided by the languages of the B2B standards. In this way, the metamodel of a B2B standard language corresponds to its XML schema, and the models correspond to the XML documents that contain the B2B specifications. Although the XML documents may be generated directly from the UP-ColBPIP models, this intermediate representation allows a more modular and maintainable process transformation and it is in line with the principles of MDA.
- **Transformations of UP-ColBPIP models into models based on a B2B standard:** These transformations allow the generation of technology-dependent process models from UP-ColBPIP models. To support the definition and automatic execution of the transformations, a method and a tool for model transformations is required.
- **B2B specifications:** The final output of the transformations is one or more XML documents that contain the process and the partners' interfaces specifications based on a B2B standard. The transformation of technology-dependent models into the corresponding specifications is almost direct. This transformation is supported by XML production rules that convert a UML class model into an XML version.

In this way, by applying this MDA approach, enterprises have a robust and systematic method to develop collaborative processes.

The UML Profile for Collaborative Business Processes Based on Interaction Protocols

This section describes the *UML Profile for Collaborative Business Processes Based on Interaction Protocols (UP-ColBPIP)* proposed for modeling collaborative processes. First, the theoretical bases of this language are discussed, along with the objectives of using interaction protocols to model collaborative processes. Then, a description of the different views that can be modeled with UP-ColBPIP is provided. For each view, the semantics of the conceptual elements incorporated in this language are described. In addition, to show the application of the language, a complete case study is presented, which is described through examples for each view.

Theoretical Bases of UP-ColBPIP

B2B interactions cannot be restricted to the mere information exchange (Goldkuhl & Lind, 2004), but they have to focus on the communicative actions and the creation of commitments between the parties. These communicative aspects are not considered in many of the business process modeling languages such as those used for modeling workflows (GoldKuhl and Lind, 2004; Weigand, Heuvel, & Dignum, 1998). The theoretical bases of these languages are less sound and rigid because they have to rely on the intuitive understanding of their axiomatic notions, such as the concept of activity or task (Dietz, 2002). The consequence of this is the ambiguity in the definition of the activities, because two business engineers can have different interpretations of the same model.

The communicative aspects of B2B interactions can be captured by applying the principles of the language/action perspective (LAP) theory (GoldKuhl & Lind, 2004). The main premise of LAP is that communication is a type of action that creates commitments between the parties. LAP emphasizes what the parties do, how the language is used to create a common understanding, and how the activities are coordinated through the language. Its theoretical foundations are built on speech acts theory (Searle, 1975). A speech act is the speaker's expression of a propositional attitude (utterance) toward some proposition. In other words, a speech act represents the intention of the speaker with respect to some propositional content. An argument of the speech act theory is that different intentions (request, propose, accept, and so on) can be applied to the same content. For example *request (order)* and *propose(order)* have the same propositional content, but clearly express different intentions from the speaker.

Through the use of speech acts, the language is used to create a common understanding between the parties because the semantics of speech acts are known and understood by parties. This is important in B2B collaborations in which partners collaborate to establish commitments and achieve common goals. If such understanding cannot be established, it will be very difficult to achieve the collaboration.

There are several approaches based on LAP for modeling business processes: action workflow (Medina-Mora, Winograd, Flores, & Flores, 1992), DEMO (Dietz, 1999) and layer patterns approaches (Lind & Goldkuhl, 2001; Weigand et al., 1998). These approaches emphasize the use of communication patterns that group a set of interactions based on speech acts. The patterns are generic and predefined. Business processes are defined through the composition of these patterns. Moreover, in some approaches, a pattern represents a specific concept, that is, a business transaction (Dietz, 1999; Lind & Goldkuhl, 2001).

In this way, with these approaches, business engineers have to focus on the modeling of processes using concepts such as generic patterns or business transactions, instead of focusing on the most appropriate speech acts to describe the interactions. Although the speech act is the atomic concept, it is not the main concept used to model processes. Therefore, the use of speech acts to define processes is left in a second place. This leads to a loss of descriptive power in business process models viewed as communicative processes. Furthermore, predefined communication patterns are less flexible for the design; there are situations that cannot be contemplated by these patterns. This has been identified as one of the main weaknesses of these approaches (GoldKuhl & Lind, 2004).

These difficulties can be overcome if speech acts are considered not only as the atomic concept, but also as the main concept used to describe interactions between the parties at a high level. Thus, business engineers may focus on the interactions and the creation of commitments between the parties using speech acts as the first-class construction blocks of the processes.

To fulfill this requirement, the UML profile proposed in this chapter incorporates the concept of *interaction protocol* to represent the behavior of collaborative processes. Interaction protocols are based on the application of speech acts, and have been used in the area of multiagent systems for representing interactions between software agents (Bauer, Müller, & Odel, 2001). Since the properties of software agents (such as autonomy, heterogeneity, decentralization, social interactions) are also desirable for enterprises involved in B2B collaborations, the use of interaction protocols to define B2B interactions arises as a very promising approach to be explored (Villarreal et al., 2003b; Villarreal, Salomone, & Chiotti, 2003c).

In the context of B2B collaborations, an interaction protocol describes a high-level communication pattern through an admissible sequence of business messages between enterprises playing different roles (Villarreal et al., 2003b). A business message is an interaction between two parts that is based on a speech act to represent the intention associated to a business document that a partner is communicating to another partner.

The main objective of modeling collaborative processes through interaction protocols is to fulfill the identified requirements for the conceptual modeling of these processes.

- **Enterprise autonomy:** In contrast to activity-oriented process models, interaction protocols focus on the message exchange between enterprises. Activities each partner performs for processing the information to be received or producing the information to be sent are not defined in the interaction protocols. They are kept hidden to the remaining partners.
- **Global view of the interactions, decentralization, and peer-to-peer interactions:** Through the modeling of interaction protocols, the focus is on the representation of the global view of the interactions between the partners. The message choreography describes peer-to-peer interactions and partners' responsibilities in the roles they play. It also shows the decentralized feature of the interactions.
- **Support for negotiations:** Through the use of business messages based on speech acts, interaction protocols also provide an intentional perspective to process models. Decisions and commitments made by the partners can be known from the speech acts. This enables the definition of complex negotiations in collaborative processes.
- **Support for modeling the communicative aspects of B2B collaborations:** The communicative aspects of B2B collaborations can be represented by modeling interaction protocols because they are based on the use of speech acts. In addition, messages based on speech acts are used at a high level, and are the first-class construction blocks. In this way, business engineers have to focus on the semantics of each message selecting the most appropriate speech act.

Description of the Modeling Language UP-ColBPIP

The modeling language UP-ColBPIP has been defined as a UML profile that extends the semantics of UML2 to model collaborative processes. A UML profile is defined using the extension mechanisms provided by UML: stereotypes, tagged values, and constraints. *Stereotypes* define new conceptual elements as extensions of UML metaclasses. *Tagged values* define attributes of the stereotypes. *Constraints* may be defined on the stereotypes or the UML metaclasses to restrict the way in which the original concepts of UML or the stereotypes can be used. One of the purposes behind UP-ColBPIP is to provide the best possible correspondence with UML, so that its graphical notation is intuitive for a business process designer who has worked with UML. Therefore, the semantics of the conceptual elements (stereotypes) of UP-ColBPIP is similar, or there is a correspondence with the semantics of the extended UML2 elements. Appendix A contains a summary of the UP-ColBPIP stereotypes and the UML metaclasses they extend. They can be used to implement this UML profile in any UML case tool that supports it.

UP-ColBPIP encourages a top-down approach to model collaborative processes because it supports the modeling of four views: *B2B collaboration view*, *collaborative processes view*, *interaction protocols view* and *business interfaces view*.

Each view is a refinement of the previous one.

Following, the conceptual elements of UP-ColBPIP that support the modeling of the above views are described. Furthermore, the application of UP-ColBPIP is illustrated through a case study of a B2B collaboration between two manufacturer enterprises. The purpose of this B2B collaboration is that partners carry out a collaborative replenishment based on a vendor-managed inventory (VMI) collaborative model. In this model, the supplier determines when to ship materials and how much to ship for replenishing the customer's inventory. Calculation of the replenishment may be based on a forecast, or only on consumption data. Particularly, the B2B collaboration is defined according to the forecast-based VMI model proposed by EIDX (EIDX, 2004), a consortium of enterprises of the electronics industry.

Defining the B2B Collaboration View

This view captures the participants and their communication relationships in order to provide an overview of the B2B collaboration. To support this view, UP-ColBPIP extends the semantics of the UML collaborations. Therefore, a *B2B collaboration* is defined in a UML composite structure diagram and is represented by the stereotype <<B2B Collaboration>>. A B2B collaboration represents a set of cooperating *trading partners* performing a specific *role*. Communication between the partners is represented by a *B2B relationship* that is represented by a connector with the stereotype <<B2B Relationship>>. Trading partners own *public business interfaces* (*ports* in UML) that allow them to engage in a B2B relationship to interact with another partner and fulfill a specific role. Furthermore, the name of the *collaborative agreement* is associated to the B2B collaboration.

As an example, Figure 3 shows the B2B collaboration of the collaborative replenishment based on a VMI model of the case study. This B2B collaboration indicates *Manufacturer B* performs the role *Customer,* and *Manufacturer A* performs the role *Supplier. Manufacturer A* contains the public business interface *InterfaceWithCustomer,* and *Manufacturer B* contains the public business interface *InterfaceWithSupplier.* Partners communicate through these interfaces. The name of the collaborative agreement is associated to the B2B collaboration.

Furthermore, the B2B collaboration view describes the parameters of the *collaborative agreement* and the hierarchy of common *business goals* that partners have agreed. To represent it, UP-ColBPIP extends the semantics of the UML classes and objects. A *collaborative agreement* defines the parameters (attributes) that govern the B2B collaboration, which are defined in a class with the stereotype <<Collaborative Agreement>>. The collaborative agreement has also an

Figure 3. A composite structure diagram describing a B2B collaboration

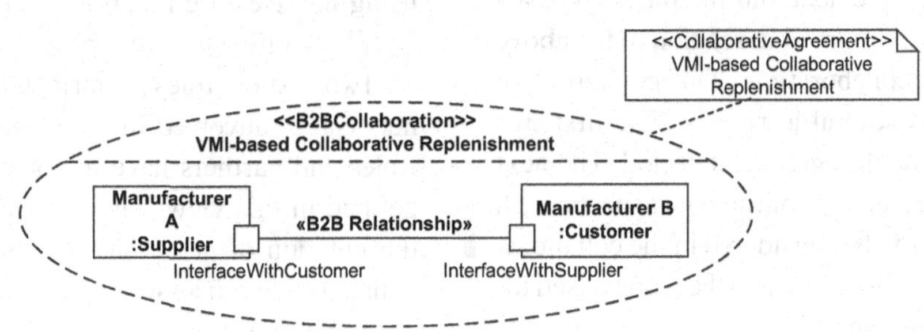

associated hierarchy of common *business goals* that indicates the requirements to be fulfilled in the B2B collaboration. A business goal represents a common objective to be achieved by the partners. Through the definition of common business goals, partners can later evaluate the collaboration performance.

Business goals are defined based on the goal patterns proposed in Eriksson and Penker (2000) to model organizational goals. A business goal can have several subgoals, and there can be one root business goal. Subgoals have to be fulfilled for the achievement of their upper goal. The name of a goal should be defined in terms of a desire state about some information shared by partners, or in terms of optimization such as improve sales, reduce inventory, and so forth. Two types of predefined business goals are included in the profile: *quantitative goal* and *qualitative goal.* Quantitative goals are defined on the basis of performance measurements (such as key performance indicators) about some information shared by the partners. This type of goal is described by a current value (if known), a target value, the measurement unit being used, the computation method (metric), and the update frequency of the defined metric. Qualitative goals are informally described, and they rely on human judgment rather than a specific value. Business goals are defined in a class diagram as instances of the *QuantitativeGoal* or the *QuanlitativeGoal* classes that are stereotyped <<Business Goal>>. Goals and their subgoals are associated by the use of dependency relationships.

Figure 4 shows the class diagram with the collaborative agreement and the business goals that partners have agreed in relation to the above defined B2B collaboration. The collaborative agreement has several attributes. The first two attributes define the agreement period. The next three attributes refer to commercial aspects, such as the products to be considered in the collaboration, the price of products, and the money used for the commercial transactions. The other attributes define the parameters to be used for the inventory management.

The hierarchy of business goals indicates that the root goal defines the main purpose of a VMI model: *decrease inventory average levels.* To achieve this goal, four subgoals have to be fulfilled. All the goals have been defined as quantitative goals with their corresponding attributes. For example, the main goal indicates that the current inventory average level is "2,500 units," the target value to be achieved is "1,500 units," the measurement unit is "product units," the metric is "the sum of the inventory average values of each product," and the update frequency of the metric is "2 months."

Defining the Collaborative Business Processes View

This view is concerned with the identification of the collaborative processes that are required to achieve the business goals defined in the previous view. To support this view, UP-ColBPIP extends the semantics of the UML use cases. In UML, a use case is used to capture the system's requirements, that is, what a system is supposed to do. In UP-ColBPIP, a *collaborative process* is used to capture the actions that partners will perform and the business documents they will exchange as part of the B2B collaboration. In this way, a collaborative process is defined as an informal specification of a set of actions performed by trading partners to achieve a goal. In UML use cases diagrams, collaborative processes are defined using the use case notation with the stereotype <<collaborative business process>>.

Two or more roles performed by trading partners can be involved in a collaborative process. Roles and partners have to correspond to those defined in this view. They are represented with the notation of *actor* and are associated to the collaborative processes.

A business goal can be only achieved through the execution of collaborative processes.

Figure 4. Class diagram describing the collaborative agreement and the business goals

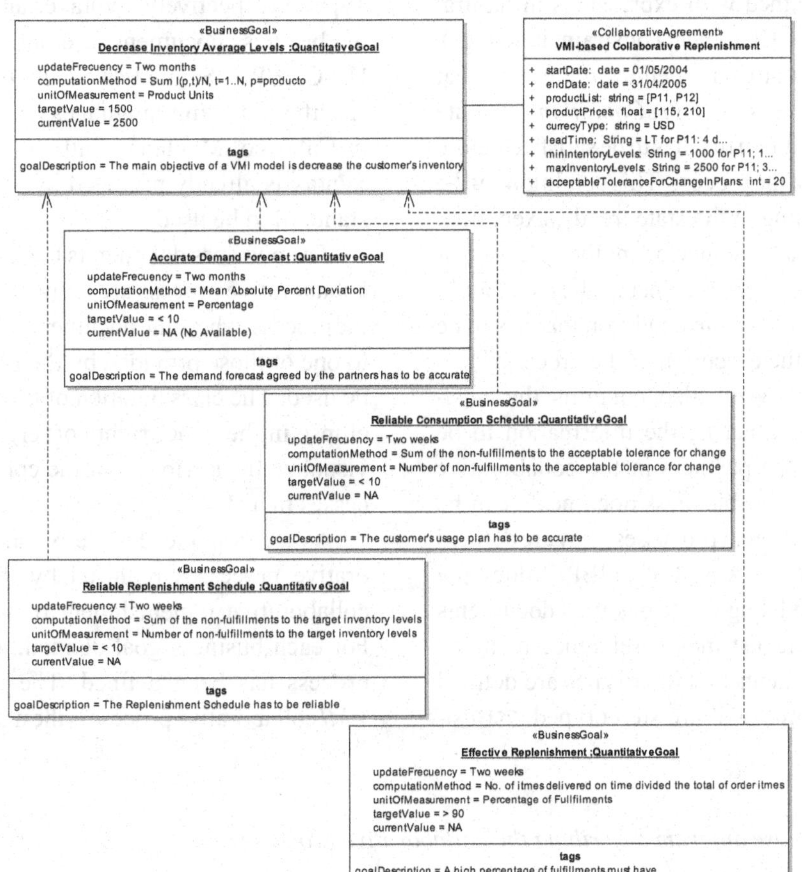

Hence, the dependency relationship stereotyped <<Achieves>> indicates the allocation of a business goal to a collaborative process. Through business goals, the performance of collaborative processes can be also evaluated later.

A collaborative process can be composed of *subprocesses* to indicate that a process contains the behavior provided by other processes. To represent it, the *include* relationship of UML is extended with the stereotyped <<subprocess>>. In addition, a collaborative process can be also composed of exception processes. An *exception process* is a specific type of collaborative process that is used to manage a predefined exception that can occur in a collaborative process. The exception process indicates how the collaborative process can be finished or corrected in case the exception occurs. The place where an exception can occur in a collaborative process is indicated through exception points defined within the process.

The stereotyped <<exception>> represents the relationship between an exception process and a collaborative process. This stereotype extends the semantics of the *extend* relationship of UML. The place where the exception can occur in the behavior of a collaborative process and the condition to be evaluated for enacting the exception process is indicated with a comment associated to the relationship exception.

A collaborative process has several attributes that can be defined with expressions in natural language or in OCL (object constraint language). The *startEvent* attribute defines the events that trigger the process. The *preCondition* attribute defines the condition that has to be satisfied before the execution of the process. This condition can be defined according to the state (ready, executing, or finished) of an instance of another process, or the state of a business document. The *postCondition* attribute defines the condition that has to be satisfied after the execution of the process.

Finally, this view also contains the *business documents*, that is, the information to be exchanged by the partners in the collaborative processes. Because business documents can be exchanged in different processes, they are defined in an independent way. UP-ColBPIP does not support the modeling of the business documents structure, but it just makes reference to them. Business documents and their types are defined in class diagrams, and are stereotyped <<BusinessDocument>> and <<BusinessDocumentType>> respectively. Syntaxes and semantics of the business documents are out of the scope of UP-ColBPIP. Semantics should be defined with specific modeling languages, such as proposed in Caliusco, Maidana, Galli, & Chiotti (2004). Syntax is already provided by the content B2B standard to be used.

The business documents to be exchanged in a collaborative process are defined as attributes of the process, where the document type corresponds to one of those provided by the B2B standard to be used. The class notation of use cases (with an ellipse in the upper-right corner) can be used to visualize the attributes of the collaborative processes in a class diagram.

As an example, Figure 5 shows the collaborative processes required by the VMI-based collaborative replenishment of the case study. For each business goal defined, a collaborative process has been defined. The *forecast-based VMI* collaborative process is the main process and

Figure 5. Use case diagram describing the collaborative processes

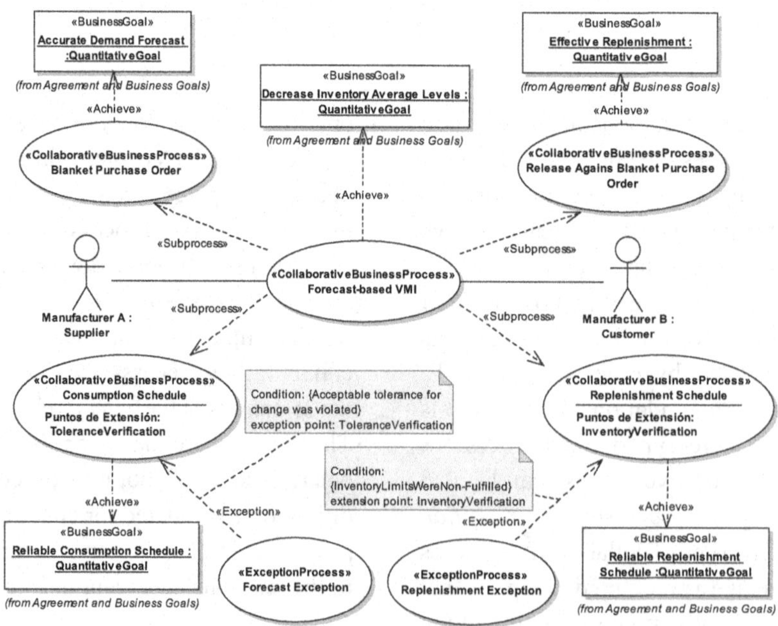

hence, it has allocated the main goal. According to the hierarchy of business goal, the following collaborative processes have been defined: *blanket purchase* order, *consumption schedule*, *release against blanket purchase order* and *replenishment schedule* processes. They are the subprocess of the *forecast-based VMI* process. Each collaborative process has an associated business goal to fulfill.

Furthermore, two exception processes have been defined. In the *consumption schedule* collaborative process, its *SupplierVerification* exception point indicates that an exception can occur when the supplier verifies the customer's consumption plan. If this exception occurs, it is managed by the *ForecastException* process, as the *exception* relationship indicates. The comment on this relationship describes the condition to be satisfied for executing this exception process, and also makes reference to the exception point on which the condition is verified. In a similar way, another exception process is associated to the *ReplenishmentSchedule* process.

Figure 6 shows the attributes of the collaborative process *consumption schedule*. The attribute *startEvent* indicates this process is initiated when the client generates a consumption schedule. The *precondition* indicates that before the execution of this process, the *blanket purchase order (BPO)* business document must be agreed. The *postCondition* indicates this process has to finish with a consumption schedule that fulfills the change tolerances defined in the agreement. Finally, two business documents will be exchanged in this process: the consumption schedule to be sent by the customer, and the schedule response to be sent by the supplier.

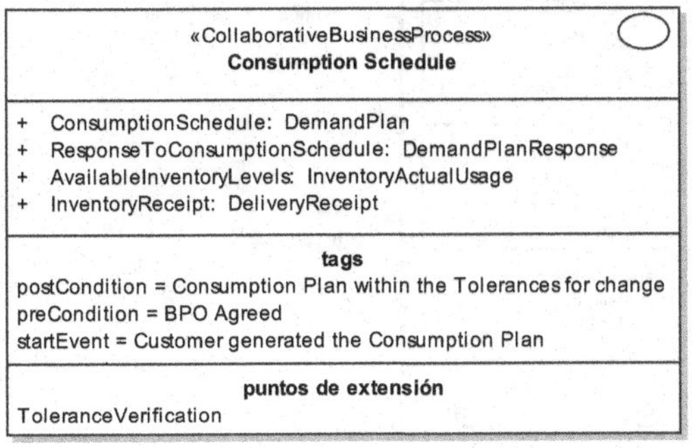

Figure 6. Class diagram describing the attributes of the collaborative processes

«CollaborativeBusinessProcess»
Consumption Schedule

\+ ConsumptionSchedule: DemandPlan
\+ ResponseToConsumptionSchedule: DemandPlanResponse
\+ AvailableInventoryLevels: InventoryActualUsage
\+ InventoryReceipt: DeliveryReceipt

tags
postCondition = Consumption Plan within the Tolerances for change
preCondition = BPO Agreed
startEvent = Customer generated the Consumption Plan

puntos de extensión
ToleranceVerification

Defining the Interaction Protocols View

This view focuses on the definition of the formal behavior of the collaborative processes that are realized through interaction protocols. UP-ColBPIP extends the semantics of the UML interactions to support the modeling of interaction protocols. Therefore, interaction protocols can be visualized in UML2 interaction diagrams: sequence diagram, communication diagram, interaction overview diagram and timing diagram. The former is the best known, and provides a more expressive concrete syntax for interaction protocols. The sequence diagrams describing interaction protocols are stereotyped <<protocol>>.

The behavior semantics of an interaction protocol, that is, the choreography of messages, is defined by the ordered sequence of the following elements: business messages, control flow segments, interaction paths, protocol references, and terminations.

Following, the main conceptual elements used to define interaction protocols are described. Figure 7 shows the notations for the elements of an interaction protocol through a typical protocol that can be used when a partner asks another one to carry out some action or produce some information for the former. In this example, a partner playing the role of supplier is requesting a demand forecast to another partner playing the role of customer.

Trading Partner and Role

The trading partners participating in an interaction protocol and the role they fulfill are represented in *lifelines* (see notation in Figure 7).

Business Message, Speech Acts, and Business Documents

A business message defines an interaction or communication between two roles: a sender and a receiver. A business message contains a speech act and a business document (see notation in Figure 7). The semantics of a business message is defined by its associated speech act. A business message expresses the sender has done an action that generates the communication of a speech act representing the sender's intention with respect to the exchanged business document. Also, the message indicates the sender's expectation, and the receptor then acts according to the semantics of the speech act.

As an example (Figure 7), in the message "request(DemandForecast)," the speech act "request" indicates the supplier's intention of requesting a demand forecast from the customer. It also implies the customer cannot respond with any speech act but a suitable speech act, such as agree, or refuse, indicating the reasons of the acceptance or refusal in its associated business document. Hence, the speech act to use for describing a business message depends on its semantics. To define messages of the protocols, we have used the speech acts provided by FIPA ACL library. The semantics of these speech acts can be found in FIPA (2002).

A business message also represents a one-way asynchronous communication. This feature is essential in B2B interactions because the sender's internal control must not be subordinated to the receptor's response. A business message is managed by the receptor just as a signal that has to be interpreted to activate the internal behaviors of the receptor. In addition, a business message may require the sending of acknowledgments by the receiver toward the sender. A *receipt acknowledgement* indicates that the receptor has to send an acknowledgment if the message has been received. A *read acknowledgement* indicates the receptor has to send an acknowledgment if the message has been validated and understood.

Figure 7. Notations for the elements of the interaction protocols

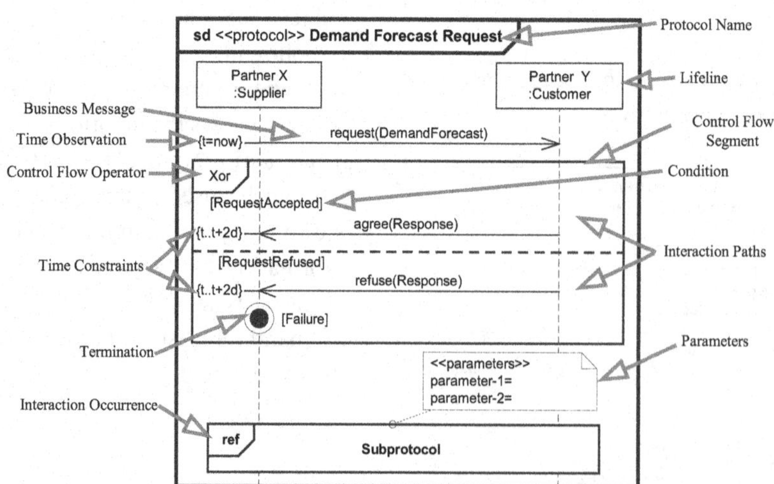

To represent business messages, the semantics of the messages used in the UML interactions is extended. In UML, the *signature* of a *message* can refer to a signal or an operation. However, in our modeling domain, trading partners cannot invoke private behaviors of other trading partners, but they can only manage asynchronous reception signals used to internally activate their behaviors. Therefore, the *signature* of a *BusinessMessage* must only refer to a *signal*, and not to an *operation*. In addition, since the signature of a business message refers to the associated speech act, the stereotype *SpeechAct* extends the semantics of the UML signals.

The acknowledgments of a business message can be added as its tagged values. If these attributes are true, the acknowledgments have to be done.

Finally, a business message can have a condition to indicate when the message can be sent. The condition on a message is indicated before its signature with the following syntaxes: "[<condition expression>]:". Furthermore, a business message may be sent several times. In this case, the acknowledgments must be returned each time the message is sent. The repetition of a message is indicated before its condition or signature. The symbol "*" indicates the message can be sent while the condition is satisfied. Or else, the repetition of a message can be indicated with a natural number.

Control Flow Segment

It is used to represent complex message sequences in the choreography of an interaction protocol. It contains a control flow operator and one or more interaction paths. An interaction path (interaction operand in UML) can contain any element of a protocol: messages, terminations, interaction occurrences, and nested control flow segments. The stereotype *control flow segment* extends the semantics of the *combined fragment* of UML interactions in order to provide well-known control flow operators for defining collaborative processes. It is represented as a box with a rounded rectangle in the upper-left corner that contains a *control flow operator.* The interaction paths are divided by a dashed horizontal line (see notation in Figure 7).

The semantics of a control flow segment depends on the control flow operator being used. The operators provided by UP-ColBPIP are Xor, Or, And, If, Loop, Transaction, Exception, Stop, and Cancel. The *And* operator represents the execution of parallel (concurrent) interaction paths in any order. The execution of the messages of the different paths can be interleaved, but the message sequence in each path must be fulfilled. The *Xor* operator represents that in a set of alternative paths, only one can be executed in case its condition is evaluated to true. The *Or* operator represents two or more paths that can be executed, and at least one of them must be executed. Also, all paths can be executed in case its condition is evaluated to true. The *If* operator represents a path that is executed when its condition is true, or nothing is executed. This can also have an *else* path that is executed when the condition of the first path is false. The *Loop* operator represents a path that can be executed while its condition is satisfied. Two types of *Loop* segments can be defined: a loop "For" with the condition "(1,n)," where the segment path must be executed at least once; and a loop "While" with the condition "(0,n)," where the path can be executed zero or *n* times. The *Transaction* operator represents that the messages and paths of the segment have to be done atomically, and the messages cannot be interleaved with messages of other paths. If a failure occurs in this type of segment, the messages executed and the assumed commitments are discharged. The *Exception* operator represents the path to be followed as a consequence of an exception (defined in the condition of the path) that can occur in the specific point of the protocol where the segment is defined. The *Stop* operator is similar to the *Exception,* but is used to require the abrupt termination of the protocol. The *Cancel* operator represents the paths to be followed to manage an exception. Unlike *Stop* and *Exception* operators, the exception to be managed can occur in any point of the interaction protocol. Hence, a segment with this operator has to be defined at the end of the protocol. This type of segment can be used to define the paths to be followed in case of time exceptions, acknowledgment exceptions, and so forth.

Conditions and Time Constraints

Conditions represent logical expressions that constrain the execution of a message or a path into a control flow segment. They can be defined in natural language or using OCL expressions. Time constraints are used to define deadlines on messages or protocols. A time constraint can be defined using relative or absolute dates. It defines a duration representing the deadline for the execution of a message or protocol. Conditions and time constraints are already provided by UML (see Figure 7 for the notations of these elements).

Interaction Occurrence

This UML element is used to represent that another interaction protocol is being invoked, which is referred to as the nested or subprotocol. Its notation is a rectangle with a pentagon with the keyword *ref* (see notation in Figure 7). When the roles of a protocol and its nested protocol are different, the correspondence between the roles has to be defined as parameters associated to the interaction occurrence.

Terminations

Terminations represent the end of a protocol (see notation in Figure 7). Two termination types can be defined: *success* and *failure*. The former implies the protocol has ended in a successful way. A failure indicates the protocol has not ended as it was expected. This only indicates the protocol did not follow the expected business logic. The semantics of the element *stop* of UML is extended to represent *success* and *failure* terminations.

Protocol Template

It represents a reusable pattern of interaction used to define interaction protocols. It has the same features of an interaction protocol. The difference lies in the fact that a protocol template is not a directly usable protocol, but a parameterized protocol. A sequence diagram with the stereotype <<template>> defines a protocol template. To create a protocol based on a template, each protocol parameter is assigned a value. The parameters are the roles and messages' business documents defined in the protocol template. These parameters are not bounded with any business documents and roles defined in the B2B collaboration. Parameters have to be bound to the specific business documents and roles of a B2B collaboration when a protocol is defined. Instantiations of parameters are indicated with a comment stereotyped <<parameters>> linked to the sequence diagram.

Examples of Interactions Protocols Defined for the Case Study

Following, some of the interaction protocols, which realize the collaborative processes of the case study defined in the collaborative processes view, are described.

Figure 8 shows the sequence diagram corresponding to the protocol *Blanket Purchase Order*. This represents a negotiation process between a *customer* and a *supplier* for agreeing on a *Blanket Purchase Order (BPO)*, that is, an order forecast for the agreement period against which multiple short-term releases will be generated to satisfy the customer's requirements. The BPO business document contains total quantity, conditions, and pricing terms on items.

Figure 8. Sequence diagram of the protocol blanket purchase order

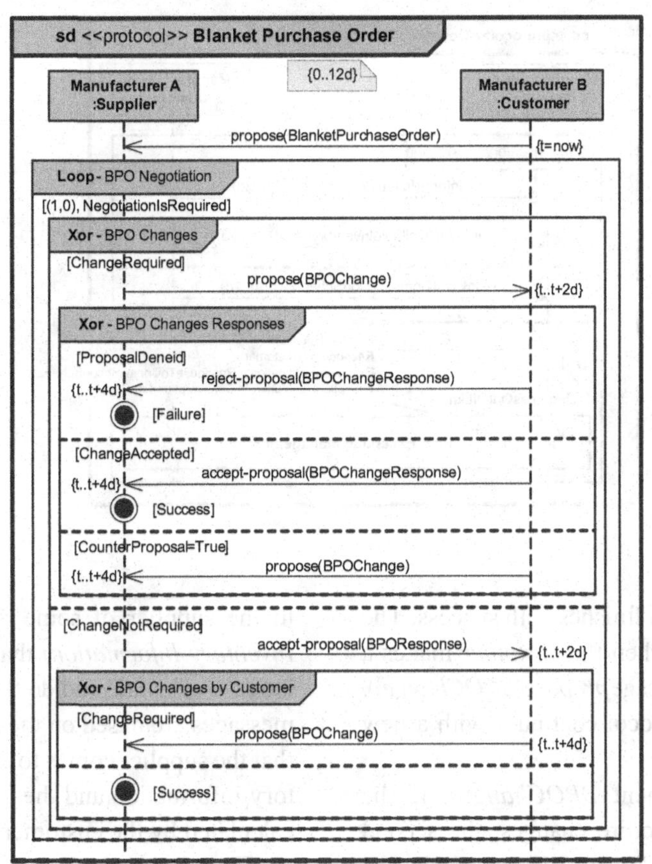

The protocol starts with the *customer*, who based on the results of its internal process of materials requirements planning, sends a business message proposing a BPO, as it is indicated by the speech act *propose* and the business document *BPO* associated to the first message. Then, several negotiation cycles can occur. This is represented by the segment *BPO Negotiation*, which is executed at least once and while the condition *NegotiationIsRequired* is true, that is, while the partners are still interested in following the negotiation. In this loop, the *supplier* internally evaluates the *BPO,* and one of two paths can occur. This is specified by the control flow segment *BPOChanges* with the *Xor* operator.

If changes to the *BPO* are required by the supplier, the first path is executed. The supplier proposes changes to the *BPO* making a counter-proposal (message *propose(BPOChanges)*). Then, the customer evaluates the proposed changes, and it can respond in three different ways as it is indicated by the segment *BPOChangeResponses*. One alternative is when the *customer* rejects the changes to the BPO because it does not agree with the *supplier's* proposal. The message with the speech act *reject-proposal* indicates it. Its associated business document contains the reasons for the rejection. In this case, the protocol finishes with a failure. Another alternative is when the *customer* accepts the *supplier's* proposal, as it is indicated by the speech act *accept-proposal.* In

Figure 9. Sequence diagram of the protocol consumption schedule

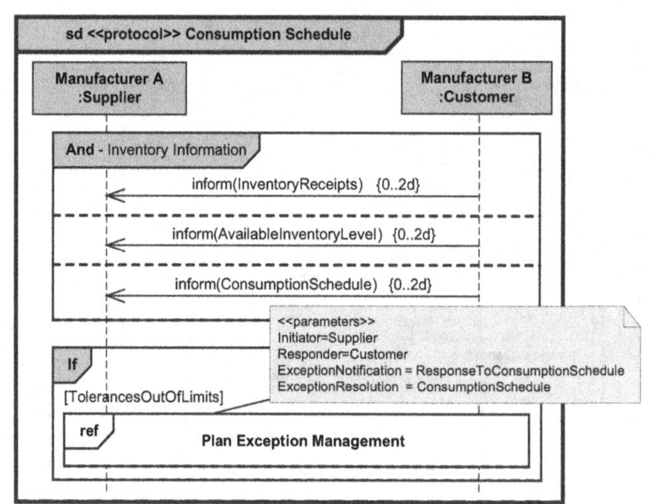

this case, the protocol finishes with success. The third alternative is when the *customer* makes a counterproposal (message *propose(BPOChange)*). In this case, the protocol continues with a new negotiation cycle.

Within the segment *BPOChanges,* if the *supplier* does not require changes, the second path (segment *BPOChanges*) is executed. The *supplier* responds with an *accept-proposal* that represents its acceptance to the BPO proposed by the *customer.* In addition, if the *customer* wants to initiate changes (segment *BPO Changes By Customer*), it makes a counterproposal sending the *propose(BPOChanget)* message. In this case, the protocol continues with a new negotiation cycle, according with the loop segment. Else, the protocol finishes with success.

In this protocol, several cycles of negotiation can occur. However, the duration constraint {0..12d} on the protocol determines that it cannot be executed for more than 12 days. In addition, deadlines are defined on the messages of this protocol through time constraints.

Figure 9 shows the sequence diagram of the protocol *Consumption Schedule.* The objective of this protocol is to make customer notifies to the supplier of some information (segment *Inventory Information*) that will be used by the latter to calculate and do the replenishment. The messages are based on the speech act *inform,* so that the supplier comes to know about the inventory information and the consumption schedule calculated by the customer.

Then, based on the acceptable tolerances for the consumption plan defined in the agreement, if the supplier detects exceptions on the consumption plan, the *Plan Exception Management* protocol is invoked. It realizes the exception process *Forecast Exception* defined in the analysis stage. In order to realize this protocol, and because it was defined as a protocol template, the corresponding values are assigned to the required parameters, as it is indicated in the comment associated to the interaction occurrence referencing to this protocol.

Figure 10 shows the protocol template *Plan Exception Management,* which can be reused to define different protocols that manage exceptions in any type of plan or schedule. This protocol starts with the initiator requesting a change on some information to resolve an exception. Then, the responder sends an *agree* message that represents the commitment of the responder to resolve the

Figure 10. Sequence diagram of the protocol plan exception management

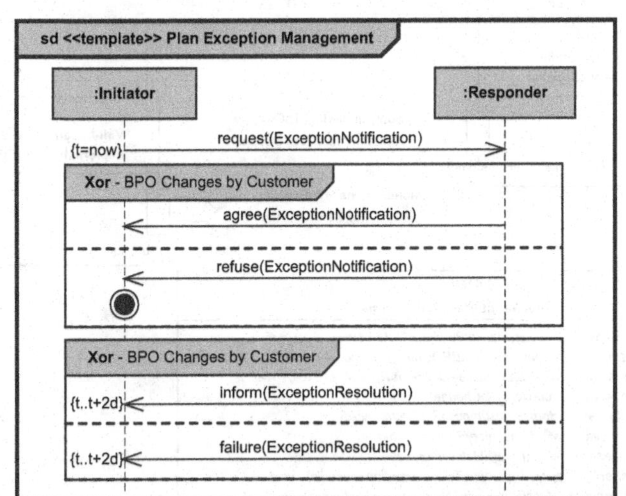

exception in the future; or the responder refuses the requested changes and the protocol finishes. Once the responder made the changes and resolved the exceptions, it informs the initiator of the results.

Defining the Business Interfaces View

This view offers a static view of the collaboration through the business interfaces of the roles performed by the partners. The business interfaces contain the required business services to support the exchange of messages in the interaction protocols defined in this view.

A *business interface* extends the semantics of the UML *interfaces* to declare the public responsibilities and obligations of a role to interact with another one. A role can have a set of *provided* and *required interfaces* that have to be contained in one of its *public business interfaces*. A provided interface gives a view of the messages that a role expects to receive, according to the protocols in which it interacts with another role. A required interface gives a view of the business messages that a role can send to another role.

A business interface is composed of *business services* that manage the asynchronous reception of the business messages. Therefore, business services extend the semantics of the UML receptions. The name of a business service corresponds to the speech act of the message to receive, and it also contains as a parameter the business document transported by the message.

The provided and required business interfaces of the roles are derived from the protocols in which they are involved. The business services are derived from the business messages of these protocols. The notation of the business interfaces and business services is that used in UML for interfaces and operations. Also, the notation of the provided and required business interfaces is that used in UML for the provided and required interfaces of a port.

Figure 11 shows the class diagram describing the business interfaces of the roles *customer* and *supplier*. As an example, the business interface *SupplierInterfaceToCustomer* indicates the business services provided by the supplier to interact with the customer in the protocols defined in this view. It is the provided interface of the supplier and the required interface of the customer. The

Figure 11. Class diagram describing the business interfaces view

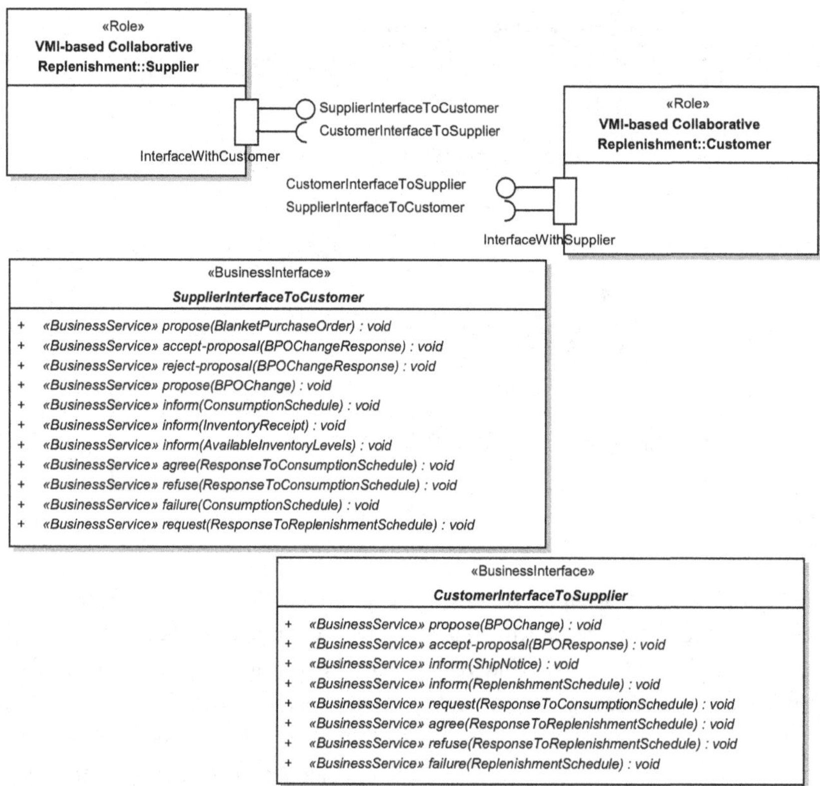

business services of this interface were defined from the business messages that the supplier can receive in the above protocols.

Generation of Technological Solutions from UP-ColBPIP Models

This section describes how UP-ColBPIP models can be used to generate technological solutions that enable the execution of these processes. Not all concepts used in UP-ColBPIP will have a correspondence with concepts used in the technological level. The main views of a UP-ColBPIP model to be considered to generate B2B specifications are the interaction protocols and business interfaces views. Specifications of the processes can be derived from the former, and specifications of the interfaces required by the partners can be derived from the latter.

In particular, the main mappings to generate specifications in the ebXML standard from UP-ColBPIP models are described. Then, an overview of the implementation of the transformations is provided.

Generating ebXML Specifications from UP-ColBPIP Models

The ebXML standard consists of a set of languages for enabling B2B interactions through the exchange of XML-based messages. Two languages are relevant for generating B2B specifications in the proposed MDA approach: Business Process Specification Schema (BPSS) (UN/CEFACT and

OASIS, 1999), and collaboration-protocol profile and agreement (CPPA) (OASIS, 2002). BPSS is used to specify collaborative processes, and CPPA is used to specify the partners' interfaces.

BPSS uses the concept of binary collaboration to represent a collaborative process. A binary collaboration consists of two roles that interact through business transactions by exchanging business documents. It defines a choreography in terms of business states, which can be business activities or control flow elements as fork, join, decision, transition, start, success, and failure. A business activity can be either a collaboration activity or a business transaction activity. The former represents the execution of a binary collaboration within another binary collaboration. The latter represents the execution of a business transaction, which consists of a requesting activity and the responding activity executing one or two business document flows. It may also support one or more business signals.

Table 2 presents the main mappings of UP-ColBPIP elements into BPSS elements. Some aspects of these mappings are now described in order to provide a better understanding of this transformation.

An interaction protocol realizing a collaborative process having two roles is transformed into a binary collaboration. Fragments of interaction protocols are mapped into business states of the generated binary collaboration. In particular, a business message is transformed into a business transaction activity. The *fromRole* and the *toRole* attributes of a business transaction activity are derived from the roles involved in the message. A business transaction activity only represents the order of the business message into the choreography. Interaction between the roles is defined by the business transaction associated to the business transaction activity that realizes the message. Therefore, for representing business messages based on speech acts, business transactions are derived from the speech acts and defined only with the requesting activity that indicates the speech act. The responding activity is not generated. This represents the asynchronous feature of the business messages. The requesting activity is defined with a document envelope referencing the business document to be sent, according to the business document associated to the business message. In addition, if the business message has a time constraint, the *timeToPerform* attribute is generated in the business transaction activity.

To transform the interaction protocol's choreography of business messages into a binary collaboration's choreography of business states,

Table 2. Mapping of UP-ColBPIP elements to BPSS elements

UP-ColBPIP Elements	BPSS Elements
B2B Collaboration	Process Specification
Business Document	Business Document
Interaction Protocol	Binary Collaboration
Partner Role	Role
Fragments	Business States
Business Message	Business Transaction Activity
Speech Act	Business Transaction
Interaction Ocurrence	Collaboration Activity
Success	Success
Failure	Failure
Control Flow Segment	Binary Collaboration

control flow segments (CFSs) are transformed into subbinary collaborations. In the binary collaboration realizing the interaction protocol, a collaboration activity is added with a reference to the new binary collaboration created from the CFS. The reasons for this decision are BPSS does not support complex control flows, such as loops; operators of CFSs have not a direct counterpart in BPSS; CFSs can contain sub-CFSs, hence, their mapping into binary collaborations reduces the complexity in the binary collaboration realizing the interaction protocol.

The mapping of a CFS into a binary collaboration is performed according to the operator contained in the CFS. Table 3 summarizes this mapping. As an example, a CFS with an XOR operator is mapped to a binary collaboration having a fork state with an "XOR" value in its attribute *type,* and a join state with the attribute *waitForAll* settled in false. A CFS with a *Loop* operator is mapped to a binary collaboration having a decision as the first business state if it is a "Loop (0,n)," or else the decision state is defined before the completion states.

More details about the generation of BPSS specifications and an example for that can be found in (Villarreal et al., 2005).

With respect to CPPA, it supports the specification of the interface of a partner in a Collaboration Protocol Profile (CPP). A CPP specifies the way a partner will interact with another one performing the binary collaborations defined in a BPSS specification. The main elements to be derived are the *CollaborationRole* that specifies the BPSS file and the role a partner plays; the *ServiceBinding* that specifies the incoming (element *CanReceive*) and outgoing (element *CanSend*) messages of the role according to the requesting and responding activities of business transactions; and the business signals of a business transaction. *CanReceive* and *CanSend* elements are derived from the provided and required interfaces of the role that a partner performs in the source UP-ColBPIP model. The remaining elements of a CPP specification cannot be generated from UP-ColBPIP because they correspond to the technical details, such as the transport protocol to be used.

Implementation of Transformations

The transformation of UP-ColBPIP models into ebXML specifications was implemented using a model transformation tool prototype proposed in Villarreal (2005). This tool enables the definition

Table 3. Mapping of a control flow segment into a binary collaboration

ControlFlow segment	Binary Collaboration with the following business states		
operator	**Fork.type**	**Join.waitForAll**	**Decision**
Xor	XOR	False	--
Or	OR	False	--
And	OR	True	--
If	--	--	Defined after a start states
Loop (0,n)	--	--	Defined after a start states
Loop (1,n)	--	--	Defined before the completion states
Transaction	A binary collaboration is generated without these states		
Stop	Idem to above. A failure state is included in the BC realizing the IP		
Exception	A binary collaboration is generated without these states		
Cancel	Cannot be mapped in a direct way into a BC		

of model transformations for generating specifications based on different B2B standards from UP-ColBPIP models. Briefly, this tool implements a model transformation language that supports the declarative definition of transformation rules and their composition in rule modules that consist of a hierarchy of rules. For each mapping between elements of the source and target languages, a transformation rule is defined. Transformation rules consist of input and output patterns defined according to the metamodels of the source language and the target language. These patterns are specified in an imperative way using Java code. With this tool, a model transformation to translate UP-ColBPIP models into ebXML specifications has been defined, according to the mappings described in the previous section.

Then, this model transformation can be executed for generating the XML code of the B2B specifications. In this case, the tool uses a transformation engine that takes as an input a UP-ColBPIP model in an XMI format and generates ebXML (BPSS and CPPA) models. Then, it generates the XML documents (corresponding to the ebXML specifications) from the ebXML models through the production rules of XML code incorporated within the tool. In order to manipulate UP-ColBPIP models and import them in an XML format, the tool uses the APIs of the implementation of the UML2 metamodel based on the eclipse modeling framework (EMF) (Eclipse, 2004). Also, for manipulating ebXML models, EMF was also used to generate the API that allows the manipulation of these models.

Future Trends

The benefits of using an MDA approach and a UML profile can be enhanced if they are not only considered to generate technological solutions, but they are also used to verify models. Verification of models means using a tool and formal techniques to analyze the models for the presence of desirable properties and the absence of undesirable ones (Selic, 2003). In the context of B2B collaborations, the verification of collaborative processes is very important to assure the right behavior of the inter-enterprise collaboration. Therefore, the verification of functional requirements of these processes, such as the absence of "deadlooks" and "livelocks," should be done.

Currently, there are proposals for the verification of process' specifications based on a specific standard, such as BPEL (Ferrara, 2004). This implies that the verification is done after the technological solution is generated. However, since an MDA approach encourages the use of models as the main development products, the verification of collaborative processes should be done at the earlier stages of the development, when business engineers make the most important decisions. To support it, it is necessary to verify technology-independent process models, such as those based on UP-ColBPIP. Therefore, future work consists of the formalization of UP-ColBPIP models of collaborative processes and the transformation of these models into formal models, in order to enhance the proposed MDA approach.

On the other hand, Web services are having more and more interest in supporting the execution of collaborative processes. In addition, currently, vendor support is stronger for Web services than ebXML. Therefore, specifications based on Web services composition standards, such as BPEL and WS-CDL, should be also generated from conceptual models of collaborative processes based on UP-ColBPIP. The most important aspect to consider is that some languages, such as BPEL, support the definition of collaborative processes using abstract conversation protocols. This means the choreography is defined considering the view of only one role. Hence, from UP-ColBPIP models, the abstract conversation protocol required by each partner has to be generated. This is possible because interaction protocols show the global view as well as the view of each role.

To generate collaborative process specifications that focus on the global view, the use of the new standard WS-CDL is more appropriate because it supports this requirement. In the same way, it has been demonstrated that ebXML specifications and BPEL specifications can be generated from UP-ColBPIP models (Villarreal, 2005). Our ongoing work is about the generation of WS-CDL specifications from these models.

CONCLUSION

This chapter has described the application of MDA and UML for the domain of collaborative business processes. An MDA approach and a UML profile have been proposed in order to support the modeling of collaborative processes and the automatic generation of technological solutions (B2B specifications) based on B2B standards.

The components and techniques required by the MDA approach for collaborative processes have been described. The main benefits of this MDA approach are

- Increase of the abstraction level in the design of B2B collaborations, because the main development products are the technology-independent collaborative process models. This means business engineers and system designers can design collaborative process models by using the proposed UML profile in order to define the business aspects of the B2B collaboration (e.g., responsibilities and common business goals of the partners, communicative aspects of the interactions), instead of dealing with technical details. In this way, this MDA approach encourages partners to focus mainly on the business aspects, and provides the guidelines and techniques required for deciding and generating technological solutions.
- Reduction of development time and costs, because technological solutions (B2B specifications) are automatically generated from the conceptual models of collaborative processes defined at business level. This automatic generation of the B2B specifications is enabled by applying the model transformations corresponding to the B2B standard to be used.
- The generated technological solutions are consistent with the processes defined at business level. This allows partners to be sure that the generated B2B specifications really support the collaborative processes and eventually, the business goals agreed by the partners at business level. This consistency between the business solutions and the technological solutions is achieved by applying transformations to the collaborative process models for generating their corresponding B2B specifications.
- Independence of the collaborative process models from the B2B standards, which increases the reuse of these models. A collaborative process defined with the UML profile proposed is independent of the B2B standards. To generate the B2B specifications with different B2B standards, it is necessary to define a particular transformation for each case. The MDA approach enables a partner to use a same collaborative process model in several B2B collaborations with different partners, and for each B2B collaboration to generate the process and interfaces' specifications in a different B2B standard.

In order to exploit these benefits, an important requirement is the use of a suitable modeling language. The proposed UML profile is a solution towards that direction. UP-ColBPIP provides the appropriate conceptual elements for modeling technology-independent collaborative processes. It supports the definition of different views of the B2B collaboration and collaborative processes. In this way, UP-ColBPIP encourages a top-down process design from the definition of the business goals to be fulfilled in the B2B collaboration, and the identification of the collaborative processes for achieving those goals, up to the modeling of the interaction protocols that realize these processes and the definition of the partners' business interfaces.

The main theoretical base of UP-ColBPIP is the use of the interaction protocol concept to model the behavior of the collaborative processes, along with the application of the speech act theory. On the one hand, the main purpose of using interaction protocols is to fulfill the identified requirements for the conceptual modeling of collaborative processes. On the other hand, UP-ColBPIP can be considered as a communication-oriented process modeling language. Through the modeling of interaction protocols, business engineers can focus not only on information exchange, but also on the communicative aspects of collaborative processes, allowing for a better understanding of B2B collaborations. Business messages based on speech acts allow representing the intentions of partners when they exchange information in collaborative processes. By means of speech acts, parties can create, modify, cancel, or fulfill commitments. In addition, the use of speech acts simplifies the design of collaborative processes. Designers can use intuitive concepts closer to the natural language and social interactions between human beings. However, for a common understanding of collaborative processes, the semantics of the speech acts must be known and understood in the same way by all the parties. Therefore, the use of a library of well-defined speech acts is important. In this chapter, the FIPA ACL library has been used. However, other standard or proprietary libraries may be used.

Through the use of this UML profile based on UML2, business engineers can apply well-known notations for modeling collaborative processes. Moreover, the use of this UML profile allows extending the semantics of UML for the domain of collaborative processes, providing a more suitable vocabulary for this domain than the original UML; and reusing the existing UML case tools to model collaborative processes.

Finally, this chapter has provided an overview of the aspects required for the automatic generation of technological solutions. Particularly, the mappings of UP-ColBPIP elements into the ebXML standard elements have been described. The main ebXML elements can be derived from UP-ColBPIP models. This indicates that UP-ColBPIP do not only provide the conceptual elements required to model collaborative processes in a high-abstraction level, but also to derive executable specifications based on a B2B standard. In addition, although in this chapter we focused on ebXML solutions according to the components and techniques defined in the MDA approach, from UP-ColBPIP models it is also possible to generate solutions based on Web services composition standards such as BPEL or WS-CDL.

REFERENCES

Baghdadi, Y. (2004). ABBA: An architecture for deploying business-to-business electronic commerce applications. *Electronic Commerce Research and Applications, 3,* 190-212.

Baïna, K, Benatallah, B., Cassati, F., & Toumani, F. (2004). Model-driven Web service development. In A. Persson & J. Stirna (Ed.), *CAiSE'04, LNCS* (Vol. 3084, pp. 290-306).

Bauer, B., Müller, J. P., & Odel, J. (2001). Agent UML: A formalism for specifying multiagent software systems. *Int. Journal of Software Engineering and Knowledge Engineering, 11(3),* 1-24.

BEA, IBM, Microsoft, SAP, & Siebel (2003). *Business process execution language for Web services (BPEL).* Retrieved June 1, 2003, from: http://www-106.ibm.com/developerworks/library/ws-bpel/

Bernauer, M., Kappel, G., & Kramler, G. (2003). Comparing WSDL-based and ebXML-based approaches for B2B protocol specification. In *Proceedings of Int. Conference on Service-Oriented Computing 2003, LNCS, Vol. 2910* (pp. 225-240).

Bussler, C. (2001). The role of B2B engines in B2B integration architectures. *ACM SIGMOD Record, Special Issue on Data Management Issues in E-Commerce, 31(1).*

Caliusco, M. L., Maidana, C., Galli, M. R., & Chiotti, O. (2004). Contextual ontology definition metamodel. In *Proceedings of the IV Iberoamerican Conference on Software Engineering and Knowledge Engineering* (pp. 261-275).

Chen, Q., & Hsu, M. (2001) Interenterprise collaborative business process management. In *Proceedings of the 17th International Conference on Data Engineering (ICDE).*

CompTIA Electronics Industry Data Exchange (EIDX). (2004). *Replenishment scenario 4 - forecast-based supplier-managed inventory (SMI), V. 1.0.* Retrieved May 2004, from http://www.comptia.org/sections/eidx/business_process/replenishment/replmodl4.asp

Dietz, J. L. (1999). Understanding and modelling business processes with DEMO. In *Proceedings of Conceptual Modeling - ER '99, LNCS* (Vol. 1728, pp. 188-202).

Dietz, J. L. G. (2002). The atoms, molecules, and matter of the organizations. In *Proceedings of the 7th International Workshop on the Language Action Perspective on Communication Modeling (LAP 2002).*

Eclipse. (2004). *Eclipse modeling framework.* Retrieved August 2004, from http://www.eclipse.org/emf/

Eriksson, H., & Penker, M. (2000) *Business modeling with UML: Business patterns at work.* New York: John Wiley & Sons.

Ferrara, A. (2004). Web services: A process algebra approach. In *The Proceedings of the 2nd International Conference on Service Oriented Computing (ICSOC 2004).* ACM.

FIPA (Foundation for Intelligent Physical Agents). (2002). *FIPA Communicative Act Library Specification.* Retrieved September 2003, from http://www.fipa.org/specs/fipa00037/.

Gardner, T. (2003). UML modelling of automated business processes with a mapping to BPEL4WS. In *First European Workshop on Object Orientation and Web Services (EOOWS).*

Goldkuhl, G., & Lind, M. (2004). Developing e-Iiteractions — A framework for business capabilities and exchanges. In *Proceedings of the 12th European Conference on Information Systems (ECIS-2004).*

Hofreiter, B., & Huemer, C. (2004a). ebXML business processes — Defined both in UMM and BPSS. In *Proceedings of the 1st GI-Workshop XML Interchange Formats for Business Process Management* (pp. 81-102).

Hofreiter, B., & Huemer, C. (2004b). Transforming UMM business collaboration models to BPEL. In *International Workshop on Modeling InterOrganizational Systems (MIOS).*

Jablonski, S., & Bussler, C. (1996). *Workflow management: Modeling concepts, architecture and implementation.* London: International Thompson Computer Press.

Koehler, J., Hauser, R., Kapoor, S., Wu, F., & Kumaran, S. (2003). A model-driven transformation method. In *Seventh International Enterprise Distributed Object Computing (EDOC 2003).*

Lind, M., & Goldkuhl, G. (2001). Generic layered patterns for business modelling. In *Proceedings of the Sixth International Workshop on the Language-Action Perspective on Communication Modelling (LAP 2001)* (pp. 21-22).

Liu, E., & Kumar, A. (2003). Leveraging information sharing to increase supply chain configurability. In *Proceedings of The Twenty-Fourth International Conference on Information Systems.*

Medina-Mora, R., Winograd, T., Flores, R., & Flores, F. (1992) The action workflow approach to workflow management technology. In *Proceedings of the 4th Conference on Computer Supported Cooperative Work.*

Medjahed, B., Benatallah, B., Bouguettaya, A., Ngu, A. H. H., & Ahmed, K.E. (2003). Business-to-business interactions: Issues and enabling technologies. *The VLDB Journal, 12(1)*, 2041-2046.

OASIS (1999). *Electronic business using eXchange markup language (ebXML).* Retrieved 2001, from http://www.ebxml.org

OASIS ebXML CPP/A Technical Committee (1999). *Collaboration-protocol profile and agreement specification, Versión 2.0.* Retrieved from http://www.ebxml.org/specs/

Object Management Group. (2003). *Model-driven architecture (MDA) guide, Versión 1.0.1.* Retrieved May 20, 2004, from http://www.omg.org/mda

RosettaNet Consortium. (1999) *RossetaNet.* Retrieved May 2001, from http://www.rosettanet.org/RosettaNet/Rooms/DisplayPages/LayoutInitial

Searle, J. R. (1975). A taxonomy of illocutionary acts. In K. Gunderson (Eds.), *Language, mind and knowledge.* Minneapolis, MA: University of Minnesota.

Selic, B. (2003). The pragmatics of model-driven development. *IEEE Software, 20(5)*,19-25.

UN/CEFACT, & OASIS (2003). *ebXML business specification schema, Version 1.10.* Retrieved March 2004, from http://www.untmg.org/downloads/General/approved/

Villarreal, P. (2005). *Modeling and specification of collaborative business processes.* PhD Thesis. Santa Fe, Argentina: CERIDE.

Villarreal, P., Caliusco, M., Zucchini, D., Arredondo, F., Zanel, C., Galli, M. R., & Chiotti, O. (2003a). Integrated production planning and control in a collaborative partner-to-partner relationship. In S. Sharma & J. Gupta (Eds.), *Managing e-business in the 21st century* (pp. 91-110). Victoria, Australia: Heidelberg Press.

Villarreal, P., Salomone, E., & Chiotti, O. (2003b). Managing public business processes in B2B relationships using B2B interaction protocols. *XXIX Conferencia Latinoamérica de Informática (CLEI 2003).*

Villarreal, P., Salomone, E., & Chiotti, O. (2003c). B2B relationships: Defining public business processes using interaction protocols. *Journal of the Chilean Society of Computer Science, Special Issue on the Best Papers of the JCC 2003, 4*(1). Retrieved November 2003, from http://www.dcc.uchile.cl/~mmarin/revista-sccc/sccc-web/volumen4-1.html

Villarreal, P., Salomone, E, & Chiotti, O. (2005). Applying model-driven development to collaborative business processes. In *Proceedings Iberoamerican Workshop on Requirement Engineering and Sowftare Environments (IDEAS'05).*

Voluntary Interindustry Commerce Standard (VICS). (2002). *Collaborative planning, forecasting, and replenishment - Voluntary guidelines, V 2.0.* Retrieved May 2004, from http://www.vics.org/committees/cpfr/voluntary_v2/

Weigand, H., Heuvel, W., & Dignum, F. (1998) Modelling electronic commerce transactions - A layered approach. In *Proceedings of the Third International Workshop on the Language Action Perspective (LAP'98).*

World Wide Web Consortium (W3C). (2004). *Web services choreography description language Version 1.0.* Retrieved May 2005, from http://www.w3.org/TR/2004/WD-ws-cdl-10-20041217/

APPENDIX A: SUMMARY OF THE UP-COLBPIP STEREOTYPES AND THE UML METACLASS THEY EXTEND

UP-ColBPIP stereotype	UML metaclass	Parent
B2BCollaboration	Collaborations::Collaboration	
TradingPartner	StructuredClasses::Class	
PartnerRole	StructuredClasses::Class InternalStructures::Property UseCases::Actor	
B2BRelationship	InternalStructures::Connector	
PublicBusinessInterface	Ports::Port	
CollaborativeAgreement	Kernel::Comment; Kernel::Class	
BusinessGoal	Class	
CollaborativeBusiness Process	UseCases::UseCase	
ExceptionProcess		CollaborativeBusinessProcess
Subprocess	UseCases::Include	
Exception	UseCases::Extend	
ExceptionPoint	UseCases::ExtensionPoint	
Achieves	Dependencies::Dependency	
InteractionProtocol	BasicInteractions::Interaction	
ProtocolTemplate		InteractionProtocol
BusinessMessage	BasicInteractions::Message	
ControlFlowSegment	Fragments::CombinedFragment	
ControlFlowOperators	Kernel::Enumeration	
SpeechAct	Communication::Signal	
BusinessDocument	Kernel::Class	
Failure	Stop	
Success	Stop	
ProtocolParameters	Kernel::Comment	
BusinessInterface	Interfaces::Interface	
BusinessService	Communications::Reception	

This work was previously published in Enterprise Modeling and Computing with UML, edited by P. Rittgen, pp. 13-44, copyright 2007 by IGI Publishing (an imprint of IGI Global).

Chapter XV
A Fundamental SOA Approach to Rebuilding Enterprise Architecture for a Local Government after a Disaster

Zachary B. Wheeler
SDDM Technology, USA

ABSTRACT

As a result of Hurricane Katrina, the destruction of property, assets, documentation, and human life in the Gulf Port has introduced a myriad of challenging issues. These issues involve human, social, government, and technological concerns. This chapter does not address the many immediate human and social concerns brought forth from a natural disaster or major terrorist attack (NDMTA); this chapter addresses a small but significant problem of re-establishing or laying the groundwork for an enterprise architecture for local government during the response phase of the disaster. Specifically, it addresses constructing a high-level data model and fundamental SOA, utilizing the remaining local assets, XML (extensible markup language), and Web services.

INTRODUCTION

Disaster preparedness, response, and recovery received a lot of attention immediately after the terrorist attacks of 9/11 and eventually faded from the forefront of attention after the invasion of Iraq and the global war on terrorism. However, recent natural disasters such as the Indonesian Tsunami in 2004 and the devastating Hurricane Katrina in Louisiana have refocused attention on these three prominent areas. Specifically, the lack of preparedness, inadequate response, and slow recovery has burdened local, state, and federal governments as well as citizens.

The presented enterprise approach and implementation process covers an area that is void in

Copyright © 2009, IGI Global, distributing in print or electronic forms without written permission of IGI Global is prohibited.

the disaster preparedness and response phase; however, it is applicable in each phase: preparedness, response, and recovery. It is recommended that the presented approach be included as part of the disaster preparedness phase, implemented in the response phase, and eventually expanded in the recovery phase. The approach is unique because the enterprise implementation takes place during the actual response phase of the disaster and utilization of the fundamental SOA leads to further expansion during and after the recovery phase.

The approach introduced in this chapter takes advantage of the Zachman framework system model perspective by utilizing Web services on a local level and introducing a practical but efficient method for populating the initial data model. A series of basic assumptions are introduced based on information regarding the recent Gulf Port, Hurricane Andrew, Indonesian Tsunami, and 9/11 disaster events. These assumptions are based on the physical, environmental, and technological conditions immediately after disaster strikes. The assumptions are there will be limited or nonexistent landline and wireless communication, a lack of ability to use generators for power source, limited or nonexistent Internet and intranet, major IT system destruction, and the incapacitation of local government services.

This chapter addresses the problem of reestablishing or laying the groundwork for an enterprise architecture for local government during the response phase of the disaster. Specifically, it addresses constructing a high-level data model and fundamental SOA by utilizing the remaining local assets, XML, and Web services.

BACKGROUND

The fundamental role of local government is to protect the people, provide basic human services, and assist in strengthening communities. This is typically accomplished by establishing various local agencies and departments. These departments are structured to provide essential services for the community. For instance, the fire department role is to help citizens in immediate danger due to fire, gas, or chemical hazard. The role of the health department is to establish policy, programs, and standards regarding health and health related issues. An additional role of the health department is to assist citizens in obtaining basic health care services. Each established department or agency has a role in assisting the community and its residents by providing relevant services. In a typical municipality, each agency has a database of information relating to the citizens and the services provided to the citizen by the agency. For instance, the police department maintains a database of criminals, criminal activity, and citizen complaints. The Department of Human Services maintains a database of child immunization records. In short, each agency maintains a database and application system to enter data, process data, and execute business rules. However, in the wake of an NDMTA, these systems along with other IT assets are destroyed or rendered useless. For instance, Hurricane Katrina destroyed most of New Orleans including property, buildings, human life, landline and mobile communications, Internet services, intranet services, and essentially incapacitated local government. In the terror attacks of 9/11, the same asset destruction was prevalent within a specified geographic area. Hurricane Andrew wreaked havoc among Florida communities and followed the same line of asset destruction and local government incapacitation as Hurricane Katrina. In each of these cases, major response and rebuilding were needed to help reestablish public safety, government, and services to the remaining citizens. This approach suggests that reestablishing a basic framework for IT services can be facilitated during the response phase of a disaster. In that regard, the proposed approach is unique in that the role of rebuilding typically takes place during the recovery phase (University of Florida, 1998).

The extended Zachman Framework system model perspective will be utilized to establish high-level data elements for the model. The utilization of Web services will be used to lay down a basic framework for a fundamental service oriented architecture that can be extended to an enterprise level once essential government services have been restored. In addition, a data collection process is provided for initial population of the primary data elements from the remaining survivors.

The System Model and Zachman

In the initial framework provided by Zachman (1987), he identifies five different perspectives of an enterprise architecture, three views of the enterprise, and introduces the six questions pertaining to an enterprise. The six questions are what, how, where, who, when, and why.

Zachman provides a clear and concise identification of the various views of an enterprise and shows how each view is proper and correct. In 1992, the Zachman framework was extended by Zachman and Sowa (1992). In addition to answering the final three questions, they introduce the conceptual graph to represent the ISA and replace the "model of the information system" with the more generic system model reference for row 3 or the designer perspective. Hence, the various perspectives identified by Zachman are scope, enterprise model, system model, technology model, and components. Our perspective will cover the system model or designer perspective. In the conclusion, the what, how, and where questions of the ISA will be answered.

MAIN THRUST OF THE CHAPTER

Basis for a Conceptual Data Model

The ISA system model perspective represents the system analyst role in information technology. The system analyst is responsible for determining the data elements and functions that represent the business entities and processes. Zachman suggests introducing all of the entities; however, the construction of all data elements, processes, and functions for a local government would be beyond the scope of this chapter, therefore, a high-level perspective for core data elements utilized during the response phase will be presented.

Primary Data Elements

One of the main priorities of local government is to provide services to the citizens of the community. Regardless of the service provided, most government agencies interact with its residents and maintain some form of database of citizen information. In a disaster area, the citizens of the community are the disaster survivors. From a data acquisition perspective, we can obtain valu-

Table 1. Zachman's enterprise questions

Zachman's Six Enterprise Questions	
What?	What entities are involved?
How?	How they are processed?
Where?	Where they are located?
Who?	Who works with the system?
When?	When events occur?
Why?	Why these activities are taking place?

Table 2. Person entity details

PERSON	
Unique_Id	Not Null
Unique_ID_Type	Not Null
First_Name	Not Null
Middle_Name	
Last_Name	Not Null
Name_Suffix (i.e. Jr, Sr, etc....)	
Date_of_Birth	Not Null
Sex	Not Null
Status(Living,Deceased)	Not Null
Phone(Optional)	
Address_Id	

Table 3. Address entity details

ADDRESS	
Address_Id	Not Null
Street_Number	Not Null
Prefix	
Street_Name	Not Null
Street_Type	Not Null
PostDir	
City	Not Null
State	Not Null
Zip	
Current_Address (Y,N)	Not Null

able information from the survivors and with this information begin to develop a conceptual data model for the emerging enterprise. Typically, the conceptual data model does not show actual data details of the entities. Instead, the conceptual data model provides a high-level entity view using the entity relationship diagram (ERD) (Rob & Coronel, 2002). Entity details will be provided in tabular format for clarity; however, the ERD will only show the entities and the defined relationships. Utilizing the following assumptions, we can define each remaining citizen as unique:

- Every entity has a name (names are not unique).
- Every entity has or had an associated address (address is not unique).
- Every entity has a sex (unique).
- Every entity will have an identifying unique number (ID card, green card, federal employee identification number, social security card, or driver's license).

Note: Newborns or infants will be given a temporary generic unique id if they do not have a SSN.

Table 4. Essential local government agencies

Essential Department/Agencies	
Police Department	for maintaining order and protecting the people from physical harm
Department of Health	for maintaining control and administering of basic health services including disease and disease outbreak
Emergency Medical Services	for assisting in medical data collection and medical services
Department of Pubic Works	for cleaning and clearing of debris, corpses and other related health hazards
Fire Department	for maintaining fire, gas, and chemical controls and basic rescue operations

Table 5. Police entity object relating to person

POLICE	
Unique_Id	Not Null
Unique_Id_Type	Not Null
Arrested(Y,N)	Not Null
Officer_Id	Not Null
Comments	
Crime_Id	Not Null

If we further assume that each remaining survivor (citizen) has an associated address then we can define the following address entity.

We are working under the assumption that local assets and asset information have been destroyed, which includes the destruction of roads, streets, bridges, highways, and previously existing addresses. Thus, when the data collection process begins, during the response phase, local officials, or management can glean a geographic representation of survivors and establish a basic address information repository. During the recovery phase, old and new street, road, bridge, highway and address information will be added to the system thus creating a complete address reference or even an address database. For instance, an entity that contains parcel information (square, suffix, and lot) and an instance that contains ownership information (owner name, owner address, etc…) will be needed, however, during the response phase, only the address entity defined above is necessary. The person and address entities are termed primary data elements.

Secondary Data Elements: Extending the Core Elements

In the event of NMDATA, there must be a continuation of basic essential services for the remaining citizens. These essential services required during a disaster, according to Davis (1998), are public safety, public works, and health services. This position is further bolstered by our knowledge of the recent events in the Gulf Port and the establishment of the following five essential services for that particular region.

Based on the five essential departments, five basic data elements can be identified. These essential data elements are termed secondary data elements. Although there are more possible data elements than presented here, an expanded view of potential secondary elements is provided for clarity.

Now that the primary and secondary elements have been identified, we have enough high-level data elements to begin the construction of our

Table 6. Health services entity object relating to person

HEALTH	
Unique_Id	Not Null
Unique_Id_Type	Not Null
Temperature	Not Null
Eyes(Normal,Dialated)	Not Null
Blood_Pressure_Systollic	Not Null
Blood_Pressure_Diastollic	Not Null
Heart_Rate	Not Null
Recommendations	
Comments	
Treatment	
Medicine_Prescribed	
Disease_Id	

Table 7. EMS entity object relating to person

EMS	
Unique_Id	Not Null
Unique_Id_Type	Not Null
Service_Provided_Id	Not Null
EMS_ID	Not Null
Comments	
Service_Provided_Id	Not Null

Table 8. Public works entity object relating to person and address

PUBLIC WORKS	
Work_Order_Id	Not Null
Unique_Id	
Unique_Id_Type	
Address_Id	
Comments	

Table 9. Fire department entity object relating to person and address

FIRE	
Call_Id	Not Null
Response_Unit_Id	Not Null
Address_Id	Not Null
Unique_Id	
Unique_Id_Type	
Comments	

conceptual data model. In the overall enterprise, entities can be identified and added as service agencies are added or new requirements are determined.

WEB SERVICES

The construction of our enterprise architecture, from a technology perspective, relies on the utilization of the data model, Web services, and SOA. In our approach, we take advantage of three different definitions of a Web service while saliently maintaining that a Web service, based on the Web services architecture, is considered a software system (Guruge 2004).

- **Definition 1:** Web services are modular, self-contained "applications" or application logic developed per a set of open standards (Guruge, 2004).
- **Definition 2:** Web services are extensible markup language (XML) application mapped to programs, objects, or databases or to comprehensive business functions (Newcomer, 2002)
- **Definition 3:** A Web service is a particular implementation of a protocol (SOAP), Web services description language (WSDL), and universal description discovery and integration (UDDI) (Fermantle, 2002) where
    - SOAP
    - Uses a RPC or a request-response mechanism based on HTTP.
    - Utilizes an XML message format that contains an address, possible header, and body.
    - Contains one or more elements.
        - The elements are defined using common interoperable data formats (integers, strings, and doubles).
        - The parameters are maybe encoded as child elements of a common parent whose name indicates the operation and whose namespace indicates the service.
    - Can be sent over a common transport typically-HTTP.

WSDL

- Offers the ability to describe the inputs and outputs of a Web service.
- Allows a Web service to publish the interface of a service, thus if a client sends a SOAP message in format A to the service, it will receive a reply in format B. The WSDL has two basic strengths:
    - It enforces the separation between the interface and implementation.
    - WSDL is inherently extensible.

UDDI

- A discovery mechanism used to discover available services.

Although a Web service is a particular implementation of a protocol (SOAP), Web services description language (WSDL) and UDDI, the Web service is composed of one or more independent services. A service represents a particular function of the system and has a well-defined, formal interface called its service contract that:

- Defines what the service does and
- Separates the services externally accessible interface from the services technical implementation (Newcomer 2002).

For instance, a Web service can contain a service that performs the function of adding data, another service that performs the function of retrieving data, and another service that performs the function of generating reports for management. A service can be either an atomic (simple) or a composite (complex) service. An atomic service does not rely on other services and are usually associated with straightforward business transactions or with executing data queries and data updates (Newcomer, 2002). A composite service uses other services, has a well-defined service contract, is registered in the service registry, can be looked up via the service registry, and can be invoked like any other service provider (Newcomer, 2002). Regardless of the service type (atomic or composite), the services are required to satisfy the following basic requirements (Fermantle, 2002):

- **Technology neutral:** Each service is non-technology dependent and can be invoked through the standardized lowest common denominator technologies.
- **Loosely coupled:** Each service has a life of its own, each service remains independent of all other services, and each service does not have knowledge about other services.
- **Support location transparency:** Services should have their definition and location information stored in a repository such as UDDI and is accessible by a variety of clients that can locate and invoke the services irrespective of their location.

The Basic Services

During the response phase and part of the recovery phase, several assumptions are made, such as limited landlines, limited mobile communications, and limited Internet and intranet services. The main objective, however, is to form a basic framework using Zachman's framework (system model perspective), Web services, and service-oriented architecture. By maintaining our focus on basic services for the Web service, a foundation is created for extending our Web services to a service oriented architecture later in the recovery phase.

If we utilize the best practice approach of Krafzig, Banke, and Slama (2004), we can identify two crucial basic service types: simple data-centric services and logic-centric services. A data-centric service is used to handle data manipulation, data storage, and data retrieval (Krafizig, Banke, & Slama 2004). We can easily incorporate logic-centric services at a later date to handle business processing and application logic. In a data centric service, an entity can be encapsulated into a service (Krafizig et al., 2004). This encapsulation acts as data layer and all services developed in the future will have to access these services to access and manipulate the data. In this chapter, the primary data elements are wrapped into services and then a composite service is created that utilizes the simple services of person and address. An example is presented in the following screen shot for clarity.

The PersonAddress Composite service will be used in the initial data collection process for the disaster survivors. The SOAP XML message format representation for the PersonAddress_Composite service is provided for clarity.


```
POST /Primary_Core_Service/Service1.asmx HTTP/1.1
Host: localhost
Content-Type: text/xml; charset=utf-8
Content-Length: length
SOAPAction: "http://tempuri.org/Primary_Core_Service/Service1/PersonAddress_Composite"

<?xml version="1.0" encoding="utf-8"?>
<soap:Envelope xmlns:xsi="http://www.w3.org/2001/XMLSchema-instance" xmlns:xsd="http://www.w3.org/2001/XMLSchema" xmlns:soap="http://schemas.xmlsoap.org/soap/envelope/">
 <soap:Body>
 <PersonAddress_Composite xmlns="http://tempuri.org/Primary_Core_Service/Service1">
   <Person>
    <Person>
     <Person_ID>string</Person_ID>
     <Person_Id_Type>string</Person_Id_Type>
     <First_Name>string</First_Name>
     <Middle_Name>string</Middle_Name>
     <Last_Name>string</Last_Name>
```

```
      <Name_Suffix>string</Name_Suffix>
      <Date_Of_Birth>string</Date_Of_Birth>
      <Persons_Sex>string</Persons_Sex>
      <Living_Status>string</Living_Status>
      <Phone>string</Phone>
     </Person>
     <Address>
      <Address_Id>int</Address_Id>
      <Street_Number>string</Street_Number>
      <Predir>string</Predir>
      <Street_Name>string</Street_Name>
      <Postdir>string</Postdir>
      <Suite_Apt>string</Suite_Apt>
      <City>string</City>
      <State>string</State>
      <Zip>string</Zip>
      <Current_Address>string</Current_Address>
     </Address>
    </Person>
   </PersonAddress_Composite>
  </soap:Body>
 </soap:Envelope>
 HTTP/1.1 200 OK
 Content-Type: text/xml; charset=utf-8
 Content-Length: length

 <?xml version="1.0" encoding="utf-8"?>
 <soap:Envelope xmlns:xsi="http://www.w3.org/2001/XMLSchema-instance" xmlns:xsd="http://www.w3.org/2001/XMLSchema" xmlns:soap="http://schemas.xmlsoap.org/soap/envelope/">
  <soap:Body>
   <PersonAddress_CompositeResponse xmlns="http://tempuri.org/Primary_Core_Service/Service1">
    <PersonAddress_CompositeResult>string</PersonAddress_CompositeResult>
   </PersonAddress_CompositeResponse>
  </soap:Body>
 </soap:Envelope>
```

Individual person and address services were necessary for the initial data population and to make data available to entities and agencies as they are developed. For instance, the police may spot a crime taking place at a particular address thus they must be able to retrieve or add that address to the database thereby identifying the crime location. In another instance, the DMV will require basic person and address data for license issuance, fines, and motor vehicle infractions. The creation of individual and composites services, using data centric services, for each of the essential agencies can be generated for immediate data collection and tracking purposes. Later in the recovery phase, logic centric services can be integrated to provide business rule processing. In the example, below the services are extended to include the Department of Health.

The SOAP message format for the Health Service and PersonHealth_Service is provided below for clarity

```
POST /Primary_Core_Service/Service1.asmx HTTP/1.1
Host: localhost
Content-Type: text/xml; charset=utf-8
Content-Length: length
SOAPAction: "http://tempuri.org/Primary_Core_Service/Service1/Health_Service"

<?xml version="1.0" encoding="utf-8"?>
<soap:Envelope xmlns:xsi="http://www.w3.org/2001/XMLSchema-instance" xmlns:xsd="http://www.w3.org/2001/XMLSchema" xmlns:soap="http://schemas.xmlsoap.org/soap/envelope/">
 <soap:Body>
  <Health_Service xmlns="http://tempuri.org/Primary_Core_Service/Service1">
   <Health>
    <Health_Id>int</Health_Id>
    <Person_Id>string</Person_Id>
    <Person_Id_Type>string</Person_Id_Type>
    <Persons_Temperature>double</Persons_Temperature>
    <Persons_BP_Systollic>double</Persons_BP_Systollic>
    <Persons_BP_Disstollic>double</Persons_BP_Disstollic>
    <Eyes>string</Eyes>
```

```
        <Persons_Heart_Rate>int</Persons_Heart_Rate>
        <Recommendations>string</Recommendations>
      <Treatment>string</Treatment>
      <Comments>string</Comments>
        <MedicinePrescribed>string</MedicinePrescribed>
      <Disease_Id>int</Disease_Id>
     </Health>
    </Health_Service>
   </soap:Body>
  </soap:Envelope>
  HTTP/1.1 200 OK
  Content-Type: text/xml; charset=utf-8
  Content-Length: length

  <?xml version="1.0" encoding="utf-8"?>
  <soap:Envelope xmlns:xsi="http://www.w3.org/2001/XMLSchema-instance" xmlns:xsd="http://www.w3.org/2001/XMLSchema" xmlns:soap="http://schemas.xmlsoap.org/soap/envelope/">
   <soap:Body>
    <Health_ServiceResponse xmlns="http://tempuri.org/Primary_Core_Service/Service1">
     <Health_ServiceResult>
      <Health_Id>int</Health_Id>
      <Person_Id>string</Person_Id>
      <Person_Id_Type>string</Person_Id_Type>
      <Persons_Temperature>double</Persons_Temperature>
       <Persons_BP_Systollic>double</Persons_BP_Systollic>
       <Persons_BP_Disstollic>double</Persons_BP_Disstollic>
      <Eyes>string</Eyes>
        <Persons_Heart_Rate>int</Persons_Heart_Rate>
        <Recommendations>string</Recommendations>
      <Treatment>string</Treatment>
      <Comments>string</Comments>
        <MedicinePrescribed>string</MedicinePrescribed>
      <Disease_Id>int</Disease_Id>
     </Health_ServiceResult>
    </Health_ServiceResponse>
   </soap:Body>
  </soap:Envelope>
```

Composite Person_Health Service

```
POST /Primary_Core_Service/Service1.asmx HTTP/1.1
Host: localhost
Content-Type: text/xml; charset=utf-8
Content-Length: length
SOAPAction: "http://tempuri.org/Primary_Core_Service/Service1/PersonHealth_Service"

<?xml version="1.0" encoding="utf-8"?>
<soap:Envelope xmlns:xsi="http://www.w3.org/2001/XMLSchema-instance" xmlns:xsd="http://www.w3.org/2001/XMLSchema" xmlns:soap="http://schemas.xmlsoap.org/soap/envelope/">
 <soap:Body>
  <PersonHealth_Service xmlns="http://tempuri.org/Primary_Core_Service/Service1">
   <PersonHealth>
    <Person>
     <Person_ID>string</Person_ID>
     <Person_Id_Type>string</Person_Id_Type>
     <First_Name>string</First_Name>
     <Middle_Name>string</Middle_Name>
     <Last_Name>string</Last_Name>
     <Name_Suffix>string</Name_Suffix>
     <Date_Of_Birth>string</Date_Of_Birth>
     <Persons_Sex>string</Persons_Sex>
     <Living_Status>string</Living_Status>
     <Phone>string</Phone>
    </Person>
    <Health>
     <Health_Id>int</Health_Id>
     <Person_Id>string</Person_Id>
     <Person_Id_Type>string</Person_Id_Type>
    <Persons_Temperature>double</Persons_Temperature>
     <Persons_BP_Systollic>double</Persons_BP_Systollic>
```

```
<Persons_BP_Disstollic>double</Persons_BP_Disstollic>
<Eyes>string</Eyes>
<Persons_Heart_Rate>int</Persons_Heart_Rate>
<Recommendations>string</Recommendations>
<Treatment>string</Treatment>
<Comments>string</Comments>
<MedicinePrescribed>string</MedicinePrescribed>
<Disease_Id>int</Disease_Id>
</Health>
</PersonHealth>
</PersonHealth_Service>
</soap:Body>
</soap:Envelope>
HTTP/1.1 200 OK
Content-Type: text/xml; charset=utf-8
Content-Length: length

<?xml version="1.0" encoding="utf-8"?>
<soap:Envelope xmlns:xsi="http://www.w3.org/2001/XMLSchema-instance" xmlns:xsd="http://www.w3.org/2001/XMLSchema" xmlns:soap="http://schemas.xmlsoap.org/soap/envelope/">
<soap:Body>
<PersonHealth_ServiceResponse xmlns="http://tempuri.org/Primary_Core_Service/Service1">
<PersonHealth_ServiceResult>string</PersonHealth_ServiceResult>
</PersonHealth_ServiceResponse>
</soap:Body>
</soap:Envelope>
```

DEFINITION OF SOA WITH WEB SERVICES

SOA is a design model with a deeply rooted concept of encapsulation application logic with services that interact via a common communications protocol. When Web services are used to establish this communications framework, they basically represent a Web based implementation of an SOA (Krafizig et al., 2004).

We can begin to visualize the development and basis of a service-oriented architecture for our enterprise. Our services can be put into action during the response phase of the disaster. This may appear implausible based on our assumptions; however, in the next section we discuss the implementation and data collection process.

IMPLEMENTATION AND DATA COLLECTION

Implementation

In our approach, a single Web service is created, the primary data entities (persons, address, personaddress), one essential agency health services (health, personhealth), and the basic data centric services are created.

The Web service is implemented on a single or multiple servers capable of operating as a Web server for IIS or Linux. We define this as a local or single instance installation. Based on assumptions with regards to limited Internet and intranet capabilities, local instance installation is necessary. If mobile units are used as mechanisms for data collection or multiple servers are setup at different data collection points then data reconciliation can take place at the end of the day. The Web services approach is crucial because of the ability to easily implement and extend the Web services across the Internet or intranet once landline and wireless services become readily available and reliable.

Data Collection

In our approach, data collection is crucial. Based on our assumptions, local assets have been lost or destroyed and city residents have been dispersed or congregated into localized specified areas (i.e., convention center, stadium, etc.). On the surface, data collection from disaster survivors can appear to be a daunting task as survivors may initially feel hysteria, shock, and confusion. However, SDDM technology has observed and identified three stages during which primary data collection can and should be accomplished.

The three stages identified for data collection are food relief, medical relief, and post evacuation. A structured and orderly method of dispensing food and medical supplies to survivors will allow designated staff to capture primary data about disaster survivors using a local installation. For brevity and clarity, we outline a data collection process based on two of the three stages.

Proposed Structured Data Collection Process

In order to maximize data collection and minimize staff efforts SDDM technology proposes the following structured approach.

Food and Medical Relief

- Survivor enters food dispensing station.
- Survivor provides primary data (see primary data) to staff.
- Staff enters primary data into data collection device.
- Staff saves data.
- (Optional) staff issues identification card with photo (data is barcode scanned).
- Staff instructs survivor to food dispensing station.
- Survivor obtains care package.
- Staff walks survivor to medical treatment station.
- Medical staff retrieves primary data from server.
- (Optional) medical swipes id thus retrieving data.
- Medical staff collects and records basic vital signs.
- Medical staff provides basic medical care (if needed).
- Survivor exits process.

SERVICE-ORIENTED ARCHITECTURE

In our approach, we have not explicitly defined the application front-end because the application front-end can be a Web application utilizing the local installation of the Web server or it can be a windows application and still utilize the Web services on the local server. The only requirement with regards for the application front-end is that it must be user interactive for data collection purposes.

For local installation, we do not need a services repository (Krafizig et al., 2004), however, for the extension of the services to the enterprise a services repository will be needed for identifying the location of services and identifying their functions. The service bus for this approach may rely on the technology implementation, for instance enterprise Java Bean, .NET, or IBM MQseries. We make these statements to show that our approach adheres to the definition of a services-oriented architecture given by Krafiz (2004).

Definition of Service-Oriented Architecture

A service-oriented architecture (SOA) is a software architecture that is based on the key concepts of an application front-end, service, service repository, and service bus.

In fact, Krafzig et al. identifies three expansion stages of SOA: fundamental SOA, network SOA, and process-enabled SOA. Based on our assumptions, we take full advantage of the characteristics of a Fundamental SOA (Krafizig et al., 2004) identified by Krafzig, and imply the extension to a full SOA at later stages during the disasters recovery period and beyond.

CHARACTERISTICS OF A FUNDAMENTAL SOA

- A fundamental SOA consists of two layers: the basic layer and the enterprise layer.
- Enables two or more applications to share business logic and live data.
- Provides a strong platform for large enterprise application landscapes.

Enables the enterprise to start small on the technical side and focus on other critical success factors.

WEB SERVICE TRANSACTIONS (LOCALLY)

The ability to apply all or nothing data commit process is paramount in our SOA both on a local and wide area network (WAN) scenario. This all or nothing data commit process is called a transaction. The ability to model and implement transactions is a frustrating and difficult task with regards to services. According to Newcomer, the difficulty lies in the loosely coupled interfaces of services (Newcomer & Lomow, 2004).

On a local level, the two-phase commit transaction process is ideal as the services are relatively close to each other (Newcomer et al., 2004) (they exist on the same server) and a single uniform data repository is used for the initial data collection. Data collection can take place on local servers during the response and certain parts of the recovery phases and data reconciliation, replication or integration accomplished at specified time frames throughout theses two phases. However, with the expansion of our SOA during the recovery and rebuilding phase service transactions will play an important role.

SOA Expansion and Web Service Transactions (Distributed)

As resources and services expand, the fundamental SOA will expand to include other services, business process and data repositories and the reliance on local data stores and Web servers will decrease significantly. A more dispersed and hopefully more robust enterprise will develop while continuing to build on our basic services for the primary agencies. In short, a distributed government and information technology environment will evolve that will require distributed transactions process and distributed transaction systems (DTS). Although there are several distributed transactions system specifications and models to choose from:

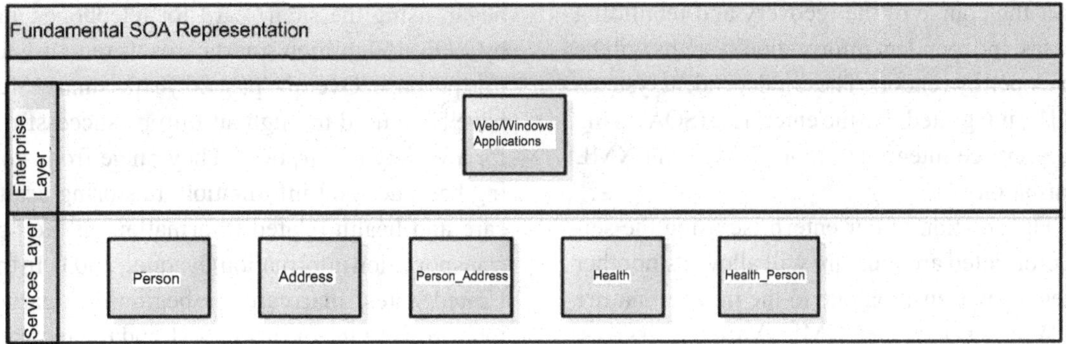

- WS-composite application framework.
- WS-transactions

The WS—transaction specification developed by BEA, IBM, and Microsoft are recommended for our approach. The WS-transaction specification, based on a WS-coordination (WS-C), has the ability to utilize the two-phase commit process defined for our local data collection process. In fact, the WS-transaction is composed of a family of specifications (Newcomer et al., 2004)

- **WS-AtomicTransactions (WS-AT):** A two-phase commit protocol for Web services interoperability.
- **WS-BusinessActivity (WS-BA):** An open nested protocol for long running business processes.
- **WS-Coordination (WS-C):** A pluggable coordination framework supporting WS-AT and WS-BA.

For a more detailed explanation of the implementation of the WS-transaction, we defer to Newcomers et al.'s Understanding SOA with Web services (2004).

SOA Expansion and Other Information Systems

The fundamental SOA by design is expandable to be inclusive of other services, business processes, and data repositories while utilizing the services developed for the response and recovery phase. Over the course of the recovery and rebuilding phases, independent information systems will be developed by vendors. These independent systems will be integrated into the enterprise (SOA) using Web service integration tools, XML, and XML translation.

The creation of our enterprise using the service-oriented architecture will allow a smoother integration transition due to the inherent nature of Web services and XML. Various services, interfaces, data wrappers, application wrappers, and application programming interfaces (API's) can be developed to extract and utilize data and business processes within the framework.

FUTURE TRENDS AND RESEARCH

SDDM technology is in the process of researching Web service security, citizen privacy issues, and the implementation of smart card technology. The maturity of the Web and Web services over the past three years have produced several security specifications worth researching and implementing to provide for tighter and stronger security protocols. In addition, citizen privacy issues will play a major role with the introduction and implementation of smart card technology. Smart card technology will facilitate data collection and data integrity across the municipality. A brief description of this technology is presented for clarity.

Integrating Smart Card and Smart Card Technology

Once the primary data has been collected, the survivor data can be recorded onto a smart card (SC). Smart card technology has been around since 1968 when German inventors Jurgen Dethloff and Helmut Grotrupp applied for the first ICC related patents with similar applications in Japan in 1970 and France 1974 (Litronic, 2003) In 1984, the French Postal and Telecommunications began using the smart card for telephones and by 1996, 150 million smart cards were in use for this purpose. Over the past 20 years, smart cards have been used throughout Europe successfully for a variety of purposes. They range from storing bank account information, to storing health care and health related information, as well as transportation information (Jacquot, 2003). In the United States, smart cards are beginning to garner interest since the events of 9/11 and the increase in identity theft. Current U.S. applications for the smart card are identity security authentication, personal identification, and transportation services. For thoroughness, a brief description of smart cards and smart card technology is provided. The majority of the background information was taken directly from the U.S. Government Smart Card Handbook (GSA Card Handbook, 2004).

What is a Smart Card?

A smart card is a simple plastic card that resembles a credit card in size. It is considered a smart card because a small microprocessor and memory is embedded inside the card. A smart is card is used for storing. In addition to storing data a smart card can also store applications and perform mostly basic and a few complex calculations. The U.S. Government Smart Card Handbook provides an excellent description of a smart card and we will use that description as our basis for the definition of a smart card.

Definition: Smart Card: A smart card is a credit card-sized device that contains one or more integrated circuits (ICs) and also may employ one or more of the following machine-readable technologies: magnetic stripe, bar code (linear or two-dimensional), contactless radio frequency transmitters, biometric information, encryption and authentication, or photo identification. The integrated circuit chip (ICC) embedded in the smart card can act as a microcontroller or computer. Data are stored in the chip's memory and can be accessed to complete various processing applications. The memory also contains the microcontroller chip operating system (COS), communications software, and can also contain encryption algorithms to make the application software and data unreadable.

Although smart cards remain relatively the same, they do not perform the same functions. In fact, the function of the smart card is based on two factors: the chip type and the interface used to communicate with the card reader. In short, there are three chip types: memory only, wired logic, and microcontroller.

- **Memory-only integrated circuit chip cards (including serial protected memory chip cards):** Memory-only cards are "electronic magnetic stripes" and provide little more security than a magnetic stripe card. Two advantages they have over magnetic stripe cards are: (a) they have a higher data capacity (up to 16 kilobits (Kbits) compared with 80 bytes per track), and (b) the read/write device is much less expensive. The memory-only chip cards do not contain logic or perform calculations; they simply store data. Serial-protected memory chip cards have a security feature not found in the memory-only chip card; they can contain a hardwired memory that cannot be overwritten.
- **Wired logic integrated circuit chip cards:** A wired logic chip card contains a logic-based state machine that provides encryption and authenticated access to the memory and its contents. Wired logic cards provide a static file system supporting multiple applications, with optional encrypted access to memory contents. Their file systems and command set can only be changed by redesigning the logic of the IC (integrated circuit).
- **Secure microcontroller integrated circuit chip cards:** Microcontroller cards contain a microcontroller, an operating system, and read/write memory that can be updated many times. The secure microcontroller chip card contains and executes logic and calculations and stores data in accordance with its operating system. The microcontroller card is like a miniature PC one can carry in a wallet. All it needs to operate is power and a communication terminal.

Smart Card Interfaces

There are two primary types of chip card interfaces—contact and contactless. The terms "contact" and "contactless" describe the means by which electrical power is supplied to the integrated circuit chip (ICC) and by which data is transferred from the ICC to an interface (or card acceptance) device (reader). Cards may offer both contact and contactless interfaces by using two separate chips (sometimes called hybrid cards) or by using a dual-interface chip (sometimes called "combi" cards).

Contact Smart Card

- **Contact smart cards:** A contact smart card requires insertion into a smart card reader with a direct connection to a conductive micromodule on the surface of the card.
- **Contactless smart card.**

If the smart card does not have a contact pad then the connection between the reader and the card is done via radio frequency (RF). Contactless smart cards can exchange data without having to make contact with the reader using radio frequency (RF). Hence, contactless smart card communication can take within a perimeter of 10 centimeters or 3.94 inches.

Combo Smart Card

A combo or hybrid card can have both contact and contactless communication with the card reader.

The memory only card could be used for both human and non-human asset data capture during the response phase; however, since we have developed a framework for the future enterprise and we view the survivor data as dynamic and consistently changing due to the addition of agencies and services. Thus, we recommend the contact multi-application cards for issuance to the survivors. A multi-application card has the advantage of having multiple applications on a single card and each application can be managed by a different agency. Thus, when the department of motor vehicles comes online with services the citizen can simply show the card to motor vehicle staff (MVS), MVS will read the primary data off of the card (name, dob, address, etc.…), initiate the immediate process, update the DMV entity(s) utilizing data centric and logic centric services and finally update the smart card with DMV data. Thus we have shown how two separate and distinct agencies (DOH, DMV) with different functions and data requirements are linked by a survivors primary data and how information can be added, updated, retrieved and shared using a smart card. A high-level overview is provided in the following diagram.

With regard to public safety assets, although the maintenance of data will change over time, it will remain static for most of the lifetime of the asset. Integrating smart cards during the response phase will produce immediate returns for emergency workers and government. For instance, the ability to determine and track food rationing (based on food dispensation), the ability to immediately view a survivors vital signs, and possible treatments and the ability to identify public and public safety assets (i.e., street lights, catch basins, down power lines, roadways, alleys, etc).

Smart Card Authentication/ Authorization

A natural question that arises with the utilization or implementation of smart card technology with our approach is the issue of authentication and authorization. To be fair, authentication has received the most interest. We define authentication and authorization utilizing Wikipedia dictionary (Wikipedia Dictionary):

- **Authenticaion** is the act of establishing or confirming something (or someone) as

Initial high-level Web services infrastructure

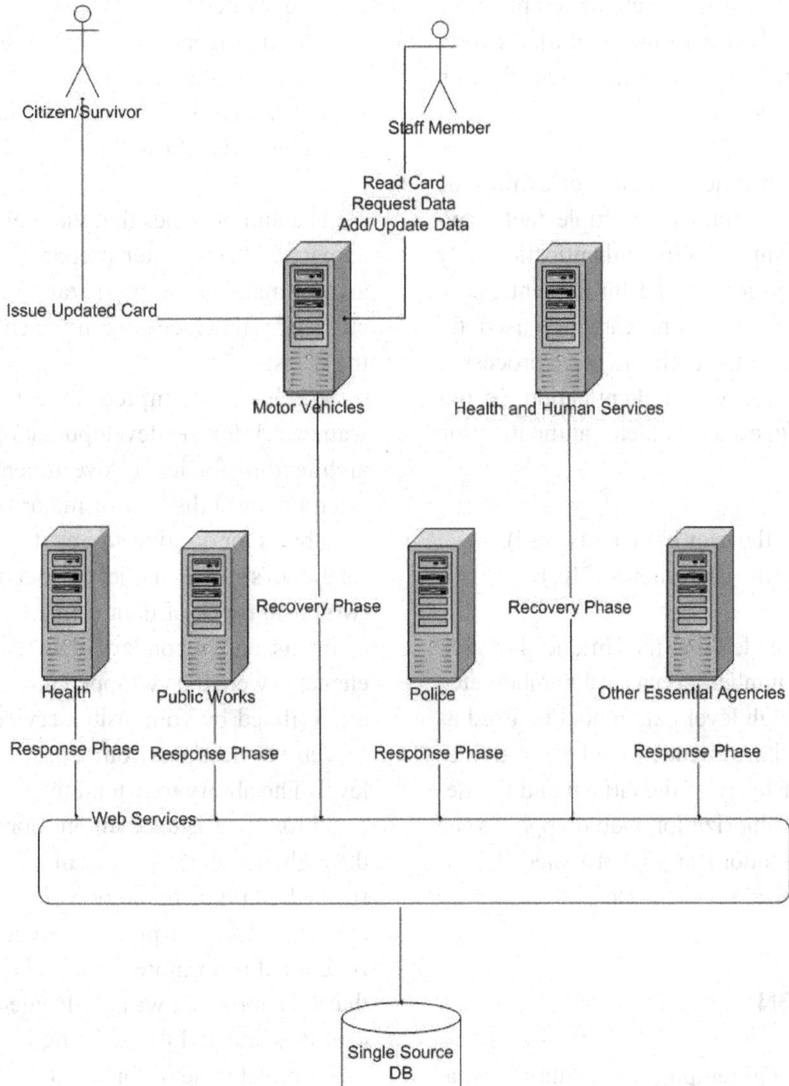

authentic, that is, that claims made by or about the thing is true. Authenticaion of an object may mean confirming it provenance. Authentication of a person often consists of verifying their identity.

- **Authorization** is the process of verifying that a known person has the authority to perform a certain operation.

With regards to authentication, there exists three basic types or categories which are:

- Something the user **is** (e.g., fingerprint or retinal pattern, DNA sequence (there are assorted definitions of what is sufficient), voice pattern (again several definitions), signature recognition, or other biometric identifier.

- Something the user **has** (e.g., ID card, security token, software token, or cell phone).
- Something the user **knows** (e.g., a password, a pass phrase, or a personal identification number (PIN)).

The three authentication categories provide a basis for single factor or multiple factor authentication. In single factor authentication only one of the categories is used for authentication purposes. If more than one category used for authentication then the authentication process is called: multiple-factored authentication. In our approach we suggest a two factor authentication process using:

- Something the user has (smart card).
- Something the user knows (PIN).

It is recommended that the Unique ID (SSN, drivers license number, green card number, etc.) defined in our high level data model be used as the PIN. Thus, the authentication level provides a uniform consistency of the citizen and the defined levels of authorization would apply to the particular (application) service provided (DMV, emergency medical services, etc.).

CONCLUSION

This chapter strongly emphasizes an implementation approach that rests on the Zachman system model perspective. This approach was formulated after the visual confusion of the aftermath of Hurricane Katrina and the lack of preparedness thereof. It is important to note in the conclusion that this approach be considered in the preparedness phase as to circumvent or assist in answering organizational and logistical challenges at the local, state, and federal government level. Natural questions will arise, for instance:

- Where will the back bone of the enterprise be located?
- Which agencies and business processes are next to come online?
- Who will be in control of the fundamental enterprise (SOA)?

The author hopes that viewing this approach as part of the disaster preparedness phase will answer many of the organizational and logistical challenges that face government during and after the disaster.

We have attempted to establish a basic framework for the development of an enterprise architecture for local government immediately after a natural disaster or major terrorist attack. As a basis for our development, we have applied Zachman's system model perspective and defined two basic types of data elements: primary data elements and secondary data elements. These elements were then wrapped into simple services and utilized by composite services to establish a Web services environment on a local server level. The ability to extend the local server level to a broader audience among local government through the Internet or intranet is obvious. In the future SDDM technology will continue to refine the concepts and explore the areas of process and functionality in more detail. The expectation is that this approach will be deemed practical and useful as a model for assisting local government to gain valuable information from survivors, assist survivors in medical need, and eventually provide the basis for a an enterprise utilizing a service-oriented architecture in the rebuilding of local government.

REFERENCES

Davis, T. (1998). *The role of government in a disaster.* The Disaster Handbook 1998 National Edition Institute of Food and Agricultural Sciences. Chapter 3, Section 3.7: University of Florida.

Erl, T. (2004). *Service-oriented architecture: a field guide to integrating XML and Web services.* Upper Saddle River, NJ: Prentice Hall.

Fermantle, P. (2002). Enterprise services: Examining the emerging field of Web services and how it is integrated into existing enterprise infrastructures. *Communications of the ACM, 45*(10), October.

GSA., U.G.S.A., (2004). *Government Smart Card Handbook.*

Guruge. A. (2004). *Web services theory and practice.* Burlington, MA: Elsevier Digital Press.

Jacquot, J. N. (2003). Application Note 104: Smart Cards. Exfo Photonic White Paper.

Krafzig, D., Banke, K., & Slama, D. (2004). *Enterprise SOA: Service-oriented architecture best practices* (The Coad Series). Upper Saddle River, NJ: Prentice Hall.

Litronic, S. (2003). *Introduction to smart cards: A White Paper.* Retrieved September 2005, from www.litronic.com

Newcomer, E. (2002). *Understanding Web services XML, WSDL, SOAP, and UDDI.* Indianapolis, IN: Addison Wesley.

Newcomer, E., & Lomow, G. (2004). *Understanding SOA with Web services.* Indianapolis, IN: Addison Wesley.

Rob, P., & Coronel, C. (2002). *Database systems: Design, implementation, & management.* Boston: Course Technology.

Wikipedia, Defining Authentication and Authorization, from http://en.wikipedia.org/wiki/authentication

Zachman, J. A. (1987). A framework for information systems architecture. *IBM Systems Journal, 26*(3).

Zachman, J. A., & Sowa, J. F. (1992). Extending and formalizing the framework for information systems architecture. *IBM Systems Journal, 31*(3).

This work was previously published in the Handbook of Enterprise Systems Architecture in Practice, edited by P. Saha, pp. 400-418, copyright 2007 by Information Science Reference (an imprint of IGI Global).

Chapter XVI
Towards Theory Development for Emergent E-Business Innovations:
Using Convergent Interviewing to Explore the Adoption of XBRL in Australia

Indrit Troshani
The University of Adelaide, Australia

Sally Rao Hill
The University of Adelaide, Australia

ABSTRACT

The eXtensible Business Reporting Language (XBRL) is an emerging XML-based standard which has the potential to significantly improve the efficiency and effectiveness of intra- and inter-organisational information supply chains in e-business. In this chapter, we present the case for using convergent interviews as an appropriate and efficient method for modelling factors impacting the adoption of emerging and under-researched innovations, such as XBRL. Using this method, we identify environmental, organisational, and innovation-related factors as they apply to XBRL adoption and diffusion. Contentious factors, such as the role of government organisations, XBRL education and training, and the readiness of XBRL as an innovation, and its supporting software solutions are also examined in detail. Taken together, these discussions constitute an important step towards theory development for emergent e-business innovations. Practical adoptions strategies and their implications are also discussed.

Copyright © 2009, IGI Global, distributing in print or electronic forms without written permission of IGI Global is prohibited.

INTRODUCTION

The aim of financial reporting is to communicate useful, relevant, and reliable information timely to both internal and external stakeholders of an organization. However, current reporting practices require the exchange of financial information in a variety of non-interchangeable formats including traditional print, portable document format (PDF), spreadsheets or Web pages formatted using HTML (Doolin & Troshani, 2004). Because further processing and analysis financial of information has to be carried out manually, current reporting practices are time-consuming, labor-intensive, and error-prone (Bovee *et al.*, 2005; DiPiazza & Eccles, 2002). Further, in their current form financial reports are opaque, in that, they provide limited help to external stakeholders to verify whether management has presented a relevant and reliable view of the organisation's performance and position (Bergeron, 2003; Hodge, Kennedy, & Maines, 2004; Roohani, 2003).

Based on XML, eXtensible Business Reporting Language (XBRL) is an open standard innovation which can be used to improve the process of the production, consumption and exchange of financial information among disparate computer platforms, software applications, and accounting standards (Locke & Lowe, 2007; Willis, 2005; Hannon, 2003; Hannon & Gold, 2005; Hasegawa *et al.*, 2003; Jones & Willis, 2003; Weber, 2003; Willis, Tesniere, & Jones, 2003). Particularly, XBRL enhances the efficiency and the effectiveness of the current practices used for generating and exchanging financial reports (Kull *et al.*, 2007; DiPiazza & Eccles, 2002). Thus, XBRL facilitates intra- and inter-organizational information supply chains via digital networks, and in the process, it enhances e-business collaboration and integration. Some argue that the efficiency of the entire information supply chain will be considerably enhanced when XBRL is adopted (Garbellotto, 2006a, 2006b, 2006c; Garbellotto, 2007a; Boyd, 2004a, 2004b), and it is expected to lead to "wondrous new financial reporting capabilities" (Abdolmohammadi et al. 2002, p. 25). Further, XBRL facilitates continuous auditing, thereby maximizing the transparency with which financial information is reported while also facilitating the enforcement of corporate disclosure and accountability legislation (Bovee *et al.*, 2005; Pinsker, 2003; Rezaee, Elam, & Sharbatoghilie, 2001; Roohani, 2003).

As a derivative of XML, XBRL takes advantage of the 'tag' notion which associates contextual information with data points in financial statements. For example, with XBRL, the relationship between a value and the appropriate tag is established as follows: <payroll currency="US Dollars">15000</payroll>. Similar relationships are established between other tags and their respective values for specific financial statements such as annual reports, cash flow statements, and tax returns. When formatted with XBRL tags, financial statements are called XBRL instance documents and can be easily processed by XBRL-enabled software tools. The tags themselves are based on accounting standards and regulatory reporting regimes and are defined in XBRL taxonomies (Pinsker, 2003; Richards & Tibbits, 2002; Bovee *et al.*, 2005). These are developed for specific countries, accounting jurisdictions, and even specific organizations (Deshmukh, 2004; Wallace, 2001). Sometimes, multiple instance documents produced using different taxonomies need to be processed by the same software tool. Capabilities of this nature are enabled by the XBRL specification, which constitutes the technology platform determining how XBRL works. The specification is central to the operation of XBRL (Willis, Tesniere, & Jones, 2003).

XBRL can benefit a wide range of heterogeneous stakeholders. These include individual organizations, accounting firms, investors and stock analysts, stock exchanges and regulatory authorities (Bergeron, 2003; Deshmukh, 2004; Jones & Willis, 2003; Phenix, 2004). Further, as XBRL is an open standard innovation it requires an international body, such as XBRL International to synchronize the efforts of its various stakeholders and oversee the development of its specification. In addition, XBRL International coordinates the efforts of the local jurisdictions which are based on countries, regions and internationally recognized business reporting regimes (Doolin & Troshani, 2004). For example, currently, local jurisdictions which are manged by local consortia, have been established in several countries such as Australia, Canada, UK, The Netherlands, Ireland, Japan, Sweden, and New Zealand.

Also, because XBRL is complex, software tool support is a necessity (Garbellotto, 2007b). These tools are developed by software developers and distributed by vendors. Therefore, there are a variety of stakeholders in the community that can potentially achieve many benefits in their business information supply chains if XBRL were to be successfully implemented. Consequently, XBRL is a network innovation.

The basic concepts surrounding XBRL and its stakeholders are summarized in Figure 1 which has been adopted from the work of Doolin and Troshani (2004). Further information concerning the technical aspects of XBRL, including an XBRL tutorial and illustrating examples can be found in (Deshmukh, 2004; KPMG, 2005).

The adoption of complex network innovations, such as XBRL, is an emerging phenomenon and it constitutes an under-researched area in e-business development and integration research. There is agreement in the literature that theory development in this area is lacking (Reimers & Li, 2005; Zhao, Xia, & Shaw, 2005; Gerst & Bunduchi, 2005; Chang & Jarvenpaa, 2005). In this article, we aim to show how the relatively new qualitative methodology of convergent interviewing can

Figure 1. Summary of basic XBRL concepts. Source (Doolin and Troshani, 2004)

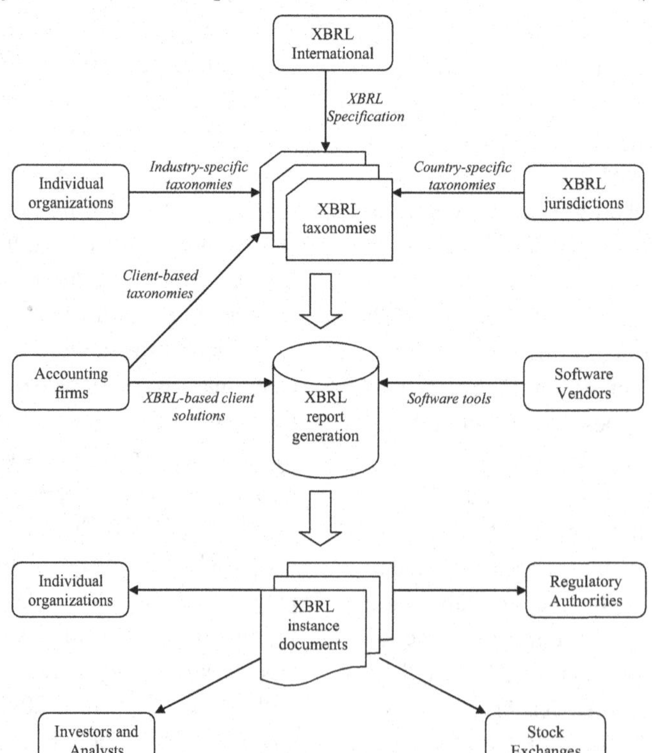

contribute to theory development in this under-researched area.

Essentially, we describe, justify, and apply convergent interviewing as a useful inductive, qualitative method to investigate under-researched areas, and illustrate its use with a research project investigating into the drivers and inhibitors of XBRL adoption in the Australian setting. We believe that our contribution is the first reported, comprehensive treatment of the use of convergent interviewing in XBRL adoption and diffusion research. This chapter is organised as follows. Firstly, extant XBRL research is reviewed followed by an analysis of the convergent interviewing method. Then the research objectives of the illustrative research project are identified before its findings are discussed, concluding remarks made, and future research directions identified.

REVIEW OF EXTANT XBRL RESEARCH

With its espoused benefits, XBRL has caught worldwide attention. Although some argue that the benefits of XBRL have been overstated and 'hyped' by enthusiastic participants (Locke & Lowe, 2007), more than 40 large XBRL projects have been initiated across Europe, Asia, Australia and the U.S., with the U.S. Securities and Exchange Commission (SEC) US$32 million commitment for the XBRL enablement of its EDGAR[i] system being amongst the most prominent (Kull *et al.*, 2007; Hannon, 2006c).

Generally, extant published work has mainly been descriptive in nature focusing on the espoused benefits of using XBRL for financial reporting as well as on the technical mechanisms by way of which XBRL works (Abdolmohammadi, Harris, & Smith, 2002; Bergeron, 2003; Boyd, 2004b; Deshmukh, 2004; DiPiazza & Eccles, 2002; Doolin & Troshani, 2004; Jones & Willis, 2003; Garbellotto, 2006a; Devonish-Mills, 2007; N. J. Hannon, 2006a, 2006b; N. J. Hannon & Gold, 2005).

Although limited and at embryonic stages, empirical XBRL studies, are starting to emerge in the literature. Some have developed proof-of-concept applications and have tested them in experimental settings in attempts to demonstrate that the benefits that XBRL purports to provide can, in fact, become available in practice (Bovee *et al.*, 2005; Hodge, Kennedy, & Maines, 2004). For example, XBRL-enhanced prototype applications based on search-facilitating technologies were found to contribute significantly in helping both professional and non-professional financial statement users extract financial information from complex financial statements, such as balance sheets, income statements, and statements of cash flows. These applications where also found to be effective in helping users integrate the extracted information relatively easily when making investment decisions whilst also enhancing the transparency of firms' financial statement information and the managers' choices for reporting such information (Bovee *et al.*, 2005; Hodge, Kennedy, & Maines, 2004).

Other studies have examined the early phases of XBRL development in the U.S., Australia and Europe by examining XBRL as a network innovation and its impact on a range of heterogeneous institutional stakeholders (Chang & Jarvenpaa, 2005; Doolin & Troshani, 2007; Troshani & Doolin, 2007; Locke & Lowe, 2007). For example, Chang and Jarvenpaa (2005) focus on the change dynamics of institutional stakeholders when developing and adopting XBRL as a standard. Troshani and Doolin (2007) use stakeholder and social network theories as guiding frameworks to examine the impact of stakeholder salience and their instrumental and normative interactions in the diffusion of XBRL across institutional networks. Doolin and Troshani (2007) employ the technology-organization-environment model with an emphasis on the interaction of contextual factors that affect the organizational adoption of XBRL. Locke and Lowe (2007) examine the impact of the governance structure of the XBRL consortium (i.e. XBRL International) on the development of XBRL. Specifically, they find that the paid membership requirement for stakeholders to participate within the consortium and the focus on transacting business at related physical conferences and meetings are particularly critical and have an impact on the development and acceptance of XBRL by a wide range of stakeholders. Yet, another category of XBRL studies have been conceptual and have mainly focused on providing arguments how the complex nature of XBRL unfolds a plethora of avenues for further e-business research which have also been identified, elaborated and justified (Baldwin, Brown, & Trinkle, 2006; Doolin & Troshani, 2004; Debreceny *et al.*, 2005).

Yet, limited research has been found in the literature addressing drivers and inhibitors of XBRL adoption. XBRL is a unique complex network innovation (Bergeron, 2003) which suggests that existing theories may not be readily applicable to its adoption. There is much instability in innovation research which "confounds and dilutes [existing] research outcomes" (Wolfe, 1994, p.409). This is attributed to different characteristics of innovations, including compatibility and relative advantage, and their interactions which have the potential to determine innovation adoption and diffusion patterns (Wolfe, 1994).

Further, other innovation adoption theories, such as the Technology Acceptance Model (TAM) which have received significant attention may not be appropriate for XBRL adoption because they only predict the attitude of individuals towards a particular technology and, therefore, their intention to use it based on their perception of that technology's usefulness and ease of use (Davis, 1989; Subramanian, 1994). XBRL is a grammar rather than a software or a 'computer program (Locke & Lowe, 2007) which is used as a universal language for formatting underlying business data. Because, XBRL is transparent to individual users, our focus is on its organisational adoption rather than on its adoption by individual users.

THE QUALITATIVE THEORY-BUILDING METHODOLOGY OF CONVERGENT INTERVIEWING

This section describes and justifies the choice of convergent interviewing in our research project. Convergent interviewing is an in-depth interview technique with a structured data analysis process - a technique used to collect, analyse and interpret qualitative information about a person's knowledge, opinions, experiences, attitudes and beliefs by using a number of interviews which converge on important issues (Dick, 1990; Nair & Riege, 1995). That is, the process in itself is very structured but the content of each interview only gradually becomes more structured to allow flexible exploration of the subject matter without determining the answers (Nair & Riege, 1995). In this process, more is learned about the issues involved (Dick, 1990).

Essentially, convergent interviewing is a series of in-depth interviews with experts that allow the researcher to refine the questions after *each* interview, to converge on the issues in a topic area. In each interview after the first one, the researchers ask questions about issues raised in previous interviews, to find agreements between the interviewees, or disagreements between them with explanations for those disagreements. That is, probe questions about important information are developed after each interview, so that agreements and disagreements among the interviewees are examined in the next interview. The interviews stop when stability is reached, that is, when agreement among interviewees is achieved and disagreement among them is explained (by their different industry backgrounds, for example), on *all* the issues (Nair & Riege, 1995).

In early stages of theory building, not much is known about the topic area and convergent interviewing is a suitable method to reduce uncertainty about the research topic (King, 1996). Essentially, we argue that convergent interviewing was appropriate to be used in our research because it provides:

- A way of quickly converging on key issues in an emerging area,
- An efficient mechanism for data analysis after each interview, and
- A way of deciding when to stop collecting data.

The following section discusses the strengths and limitations of convergent interviewing for theory building.

STRENGTHS AND LIMITATIONS OF THE CONVERGENT INTERVIEWING TECHNIQUE

Convergent interviewing offers three main strengths. Firstly, convergent interviewing is useful for the exploration of areas lacking an established theoretical base, as was the case for this research. Specifically, convergent interviewing constitutes "a series of tasks which lead to the progressive reduction of uncertainty" (Phillips and Pugh, 1987, p. 72). That is, the flexibility provided by the convergent interviewing method allows for the refinement of both research process and content issues throughout the course of the interviews, resulting in "successive approximations" (Dick, 1990, p. 3) which in turn allow for the consolidation of the existing body of knowledge and a more precisely defined research problem (Dick, 1990). Secondly, it provides a flexible, efficient and structured instrument to allow all issues related to the research problem to be identified and explored. This flexibility of convergent interviewing allows researchers to use a funnelling process in which they control the flow of the type of information being sought while continuously narrowing down broad research issues into more focused ones (Dick, 1990).

Finally, with convergent interviewing, the subjectivity inherent in qualitative data is largely overcome by the interviewer attempting to always explain answers after each interview, that is, to 'disprove the emerging explanations of the data' (Dick, 1990, p. 11). That is, subjective data is refined through the use of convergence and discrepancy which adds objective methods to the refining of subjective data (Dick, 1990).

Despite these strengths, there are limitations associated with the convergent interviewing technique. Firstly, convergent interviewing may allow potential interviewer bias to occur (Dick, 1990), like most qualitative methods. To guard against this bias, the *interviewers* need to be not only skilful and experienced, but also have sufficient knowledge about the subject matter and be able to maintain data quality when recording and analysing the data obtained from the interviews (Aaker & Day, 1990). For example, in this research, the researchers had previous qualitative research training, and had begun to review the literature about the separate, broader literature of innovation adoption and diffusion.

Secondly, the convergent interviewing method requires the *interviewee* to be knowledgeable about the research subject matter and so be able to contribute meaningful information to the exploratory research. Using the snowballing technique (Aaker & Day, 1990), the researchers were able to access experts who could provide their information and experience about the research topic. After each interview, the interviewee was sufficiently familiar with the aims of the research to refer the researchers to other experts. It is advisable to ask each interviewee for *more* than one other expert, at the end of an interview, to reduce the chances of a snowballing research project being locked into a mindset of one network. For example, probe an interviewee for experts from other industries or for experts that the interviewee has rarely or not met. Finally, convergent interviewing may affect the validity of the research because it is not sufficient on its own (Gummesson, 2000) to provide results that can be generalised to the wider population, like most qualitative research (Marshall & Rossman, 1995; Maykut & Morehouse, 1994).

On balance, however, the strengths of convergent interviewing largely outweigh its limitations.

ESTABLISHING THE VALIDITY AND RELIABILITY OF THE CONVERGENT INTERVIEWING RESEARCH

This section examines the issues of achieving validity and reliability in convergent interviews in this research. Validity and reliability in qualitative research can be achieved through forms of cross-checking. These in-built checks and controls for qualitative research can be summarised under four tests of the research design, being construct validity, internal validity, external validity and reliability (Yin, 1994). Table 1 outlines research tests for validity and reliability of this research.

Construct validity refers to the formation of suitable operational measures for the concepts being investigated (Emory & Cooper, 1991). Our convergent interviewing achieved construct validity through three tactics. Firstly, triangulation of interview questions was established in the research design stage through two or more carefully worded questions that looked at innovation adoption constructs from different angles. Secondly, the convergent interview method contained an in-built negative case analysis where, in each interview and before the next, the technique explicitly requires that the interviewer attempts to disprove emerging explanations interpreted in the data (Dick, 1990). Finally, the flexibility of the mode allowed the interviewer to re-evaluate and re-design both the content and process of the interview program, thus establishing content validity.

Internal validity refers to causal relationships and the validity of the influence of one variable on other variables (Patton, 1990; Zikmund, 2000). Internal validity in the convergent interviews in this research was achieved through purposeful sample selection on the basis of "information richness" (Patton, 1990, p. 181).

External validity is concerned with the ability of the research findings to be generalised beyond the immediate study (Emory & Cooper, 1991; Sekaran, 2000). In this research, some external validity was achieved through theoretical replication in the interviewee selection. That is, experts from various categories of the XBRL community were selected to ensure that a cross-section of opinions was provided. However, given the current levels of XBRL adoption in Australia, we anticipated that attempts to achieve external

Table 1. Tests for validity and reliability of qualitative research such as convergent interviewing

Test	Research design	Phase of research
Construct validity	• data collected from multiple sources (convergent interviews) provide multiple measures of the same phenomenon • establishment of triangulation of interview questions • in-built negative case analysis • flexibility of the proposed theoretical framework	research design and data analysis research design and data analysis data analysis research design and data collection
Internal validity	• sample selection for information richness	research design
External validity	• sample selection for theoretical replication	research design
Reliability	• interview guide developed for the collection of data • structured process for administration and interpretation of convergent interviews • use of a steering committee	data collection and analysis data collection research design data collection and analysis

Source: developed from (Yin, 1994) and (Healy & Perry, 2000)

validity through quantitative research would have been significantly hindered by low statistical power effects (Baroudi & Orlikowski, 1989; XBRLAustralia, 2004).

Reliability refers to how consistently a technique measures the concepts it is supposed to measure, enabling other researchers to repeat the study and attain similar findings (Sekaran, 2000). The qualitative studies of this research secured reliability through the use of four tactics. Firstly, reliability was attained through the structured process of convergent interviews. Secondly, reliability was achieved through organising a structured process for recording, writing and interpreting data.

Thirdly, the other procedure recommended by Dick (1990) in which at least two interviewers conduct the interviews and that they work individually but in parallel with each other, was adopted in this research when a co-researcher was available. In addition, research reliability was also achieved through comparison of this research's findings with those of other, albeit few, researchers in the literature. The use of a steering committee to assist in the design and administration of the interview program is another way that reliability can be achieved (Guba & Lincoln, 1994). If a number of the members of the committee agree about a phenomenon, then their collective judgment is relatively objective. Thus, with two researchers conducting the interviews and three analysing them, reliability was addressed as best it could be.

FINDINGS FROM THE CONVERGENT INTERVIEWS ON THE XBRL PROJECT

Before illustrating the outcomes resulting from the application of the convergent interviewing method above to the XBRL phenomenon, we provide additional details concerning the research project on XBRL adoption in Australia. Some preliminary issues for this research project were identified in the literature about innovation adoption and diffusion before the interviews took place.

Environmental and organizational context factors as well as technology or innovation-related ones play a significant role (Al-Qirim, 2003; Elliot, 2002; Wolfe, 1994) in organisational innovation adoption as shown in Table 2. The environmental context constitutes the arena where adopting organizations conduct their business, and includes the industry, competitors, regulations, and relationships with the government (Cragg, Mehrtens, & Mills, 2001; Kalakota & Robinson, 2001; Tidd, Bessant, & Pavitt, 2001). The organizational context includes characteristics such as quality of human resources, availability of financial resources, and managerial structures (Basu *et al.*, 2002; Fillis, Johannson, & Wagner, 2004; Warren, 2004). Innovation related factors focus on how technology characteristics influence adoption (Frambach, 1993; Gilbert, Balestrini, & Littleboy, 2004; Parasuraman, 2000; Rogers, 1995; Russell & Hoag, 2004; Tornatzky & Fleischer, 1990).

Research objectives. In brief, the literature suggests that organisational innovation adoption depends on environmental characteristics, organizational resources, innovation characteristics and readiness, and the process by which the innovation is communicated. However, there have been limited empirical attempts to examine the adoption of XBRL in Australia. Indeed, most of what is known about the organisational innovation adoption process seems to be anecdotal, experiential, *ad hoc* and descriptive. Based on the literature above, the following objectives were identified for this research:

1. What, if any, are the drivers of XBRL adoption in Australia?
2. What, if any, are the inhibitors of XBRL adoption in Australia?

Table 2. Summary of environmental, organizational and innovation factors

Environmental Context Factors	Organizational Context Factors	Innovation Factors
External pressures Culture Legal issues Government Industry associations Successful adoptions	Human capital and employee education Management attitudes Resources	Perceived relative advantage and benefits Perceived costs Compatibility Trialability Observability Complexity Associated costs

Source: (Troshani & Doolin, 2005)

Innovation adoption literature suggests that adoption is a mixture of push and pull influences (Warren, 2004) from innovation suppliers and users (Markus, 1987, 1990). Thus, the suppliers of the XBRL innovation such as XBRL International, the local consortia, and software developers and vendors, and the organizational users were included in the convergent interview sample. All 27 organizational members of XBRL Australia Ltd. were approached via the XBRL-AU user group and by phone calls. Only 11 key informant representatives of these organizations agreed to be interviewed. To maintain anonymity, only the categories of these organizations have been identified in Table 3.

The penultimate outcome of convergent interviewing process is a list of issues or themes progressively raised and investigated in the interviews. Table 4 contains the list of the themes that arose from our interviews about our research objectives. The table shows how the number of issues involved in the topic area increased as each interviewee in turn added their insights to what had been said before, until the final interview added no new issues. Agreements between interviewees are shown, as are disagreements that could be explained. The disagreements are explained next.

Mandating XBRL production and consumption. Most interviewees suggested that XBRL community members with legislative powers, such as the Australian Stock Exchange (ASX) or the Australian Taxation Office (ATO), should mandate the use of XBRL. While two interviewees agree with the strategy in principle, they are sceptical about the success of its application in practice.

First, XBRL adoption would mean that many employees in adopting organisations would suddenly become redundant. XBRL evangelists recognise this implication (Bergeron, 2003), but they argue that employees can be redeployed to more value-adding functions. With XBRL for instance, accountants save significant time in creating reports for their clients, but they can use the saved time to provide high-level consultation services which have "the potential to increase the quality and frequency of customer interactions" (Bergeron, 2003, p. 41). Second, making XBRL compulsory may be a labour-intensive and complex undertaking as it requires amendments to relevant legislation which is an intricate endeavour. Third, before XBRL can be made compulsory, guarantees are required that its adoption will not cause problems. For instance, it is not clear how XBRL instance documents can be assured. While some argue that digital certificate technology can be applied to ensure XBRL instance documents are not tampered with (Pyman, 2004), we have been unable to find any evidence of this in the literature.

XBRL education and training. Most of the interviewees were of the opinion that providing high-level education and training concerning XBRL to employees would constitute a driver for the adoption of XBRL in Australia. The rationale for this is shown in the following statement:

Table 3. Categories of organizations and number of interviews

Organization Category	Number of Interviewees	Interviewees
Large accounting firms	4	B, D, F, I
Software Developers and Vendors	3	E, H, J
Regulatory Agencies	1	A
Local XBRL Consortium (XBRL Australia Ltd.)	1	C
Academics[ii] (Tertiary Accounting Education)	2	G, K
Total Interviews	**11**	

"It's easier to use a[n XBRL enabled software] tool when you understand the fundamental technology underneath it because you know what it can and can't do when you try to push it" (Local XBRL Consortium Interviewee)

However, two interviewees disagreed with this view suggesting that XBRL education and training should be demand-driven and, therefore, carried out when adoption becomes more widespread. Currently, XBRL is not a dominating standard. Therefore, it is likely that XBRL education and training may lose its relevance, if it is replaced by competing standards.

Instability of XBRL specification. Some interviewees view the progression of XBRL through its previous versions as lack of stability. In addition, the different versions of the specification were not compatible. These views indicate that specification instability is a major inhibitor to adoption because it not only adversely affects the useability of XBRL driven software tools, but it also affects the observability and the trialability of XBRL results (Rogers, 1995). Consequently, this affects the ability of XBRL enthusiasts to make a case for XBRL in their organisations. As a result some supporters have withdrawn funding and further support. The other interviewees, however, consider XBRL progression as an incremental evolution which is normal for all innovations. Further, incremental development constitutes an opportunity for all members of the XBRL community to provide input into XBRL development, which is likely to result in a solid and widely accepted standard.

DISCUSSION

The findings in Table 4 from the convergent interviews provided evidence that there are more inhibitors than drivers in XBRL adoption in Australia. The current status of XBRL adoption in Australia is a manifestation of the "chicken and egg syndrome" or a "catch 22 situation" between software developers/vendors and innovation adopters on the one hand as well as producers and consumers of reports on the other. This idea constitutes the general sense of all interviews and is encapsulated in the following statement:

"I think the software providers are very unkeen to invest in developing their software to be XBRL-enabled when their clients aren't demanding it. Because their clients would only demand it if the regulators were saying we need it [regulatory filings] in this [XBRL], but on the other hand you can probably see that the regulators are probably sitting back and waiting too." (Large accounting firm interviewee)

The software developers/vendors presented factors supporting their argument for the need to wait before addressing the Australian market

Table 4. Summary of issues raised in convergent interviews

	Interviewees										
	A	B	C	D	E	F	G	H	I	J	K
Environmental factors											
Lacks of effective, flexible and responsive local adoption strategy	*	√	√	√	√	√	*	√	√	*	√
A "wait-and-see" business culture contributes to slow adoption	√	√	√	√	√	√	√	√	√	√	√
Global pressures can have a positive impact	√	√	√	*	*	*	√	*	√	√	√
Limited local XBRL success stories and champions	√	√	√	√	√	√	√	√	√	√	√
XBRL adoption adversely affected by other pressing priorities that potential adopters face	√	√	√	*	√	√	√	√	*	*	√
Relatively small market and potential adopter size	√	√	*	*	*	*	√	√	*	√	√
Mandating XBRL production and consumption	√	√	×	√	√	√	√	√	*	×	√
Organizational Context Factors											
Employees need to be educated with XBRL advantages	*	×	√	*	√	√	√	√	√	×	√
XBRL adoption has been adversely affected by the limited time, expertise, and funding resources	√	*	√	*	√	√	√	√	√	√	√
Unwillingness to invest as the payback of XBRL investment is blurry	√	*	*	√	√	√	*	*	*	*	*
Innovation Factors											
Limited software tools and support	√	√	√	√	√	√	√	√	√	√	√
Lack of standardization in the way XBRL instance documents are produced and consumed	√	*	*	*	√	√	√	√	√	√	√
Instability of XBRL Specification	√	√	×	*	√	*	*	×	√	×	*
Complexity of XBRL	√	*	√	*	√	*	√	√	√	√	√
Lack of awareness about XBRL and its advantages	√	√	√	√	√	√	*	√	*	*	√

Notes: √= interviewee is in conformity with the statement
×=interviewee is in disconformity with the statement
** = question had not been raised*
Source: analysis of field data

aggressively. These factors include, market size and size of potential adopters, cultural factors, lack of global XBRL adoption pressure, other adoption priorities, lack of managerial support resulting in limited resources and the instability of XBRL specification. The local accounting industry has been under pressure from the Australian Financial Reporting Council (AFRC) to adopt the International Accounting Standards.

The viewpoint of XBRL adopters is slightly different. Generally, they stressed on factors such as lack of a local adoption strategy, lack of widespread awareness of XBRL benefits, and other adoption priorities as major factors justifying the slow XBRL uptake. However, all informants were consistent in arguing that they cannot build up demand for XBRL-enabled solutions, unless these become available allowing them to experience the XBRL benefits.

The "wait-and-see game" is occurring within the XBRL users themselves, namely, between the potential producers and consumers of XBRL reports. This is manifested as follows: the producers do not produce XBRL-based reports unless required by the consumers; and consumers do not require XBRL-based reports unless producers can make them available.

Most informants forwarded the idea that consumers with legislative powers, including regulatory government bodies, such as the Australian Securities and Investment Commission (ASIC), the Australian Tax Office (ATO), the Australian Bureau of Statistics (ABS) are the only ones who can break these deadlocks. Accordingly, these bodies should mandate XBRL reporting by enforcing it as law. This action would not only start mass XBRL adoption, but also boost it significantly. While making XBRL adoption mandatory has not occurred in Australia, there are indications that government organizations such as the ABS are currently making infrastructure investments to support XBRL as part of a federal government initiative called Standard Business Reporting (SBR) which is aimed at minimizing reporting burden for businesses (Gedda, 2007; Ewing, 2007). It is unclear at this stage whether the ABS or other regulators in Australia intend to follow the U.S. SEC model whereby XBRL submissions were first made voluntary (Hannon, 2006c), and now, in a recent announcement SEC appears to be moving closer to mandating XBRL by requiring (at least) all large companies to use XBRL tags when preparing their financial reports (Barlas, 2007).

IMPLICATIONS

Qualitative evidence suggests that a critical mass of both adopters and suppliers at the present time is lacking. While this continues to be the case, XBRL may not have a prosperous future in Australia. With XBRL, it is probably practical for adoption to start with pairs of producers and consumers (Grant, 2004). Aggressive awareness campaigns featuring successful champions are likely to start bandwagon effects enticing partners who are linked via information flow requirements identify stronger reasons for adopting XBRL. As XBRL becomes more ubiquitous, it also becomes increasingly valuable. This is likely to pool further management support and necessary resources. Also, non-adopters are now likely to face the dangers associated with non-adoption, and therefore, have stronger incentives towards making decisions favoring XBRL. This is likely to spiral until the number of adopters in the XBRL community reaches a critical mass in order for its adoption to spread further.

Some likely implications warrant serious attention if the strategy of mandating XBRL is undertaken. First, if regulatory bodies and other adopters were to move their entire operation to XBRL, many of their employees would suddenly become redundant. Second, regulatory bodies can force adoption for their specific needs, which is likely to narrow down the focus of XBRL, and therefore, be a limiting factor to its widespread adoption. Third, making XBRL mandatory may be a labor-intensive and complex undertaking as it requires specific procedures to be followed. This includes ensuring that XBRL will not cause problems to adopters. It also requires amending the relevant legislation accordingly. All this, combined with a democratic-styled economy and the Australian character which is "very suspicious of authority" would make mandating XBRL adoption time consuming and a highly intricate endeavor.

Although probably difficult to implement, the idea of mandating XBRL may sound promising for the future of XBRL in Australia. However, the counter argument should also be considered. For XBRL to become the standard language for financial reporting, it should be a desired standard rather than an imposed one. Therefore, having to mandate XBRL as a standard before the XBRL community demands it, may suggest that its use in Australia is premature. It is possible that the Australian market may not be ready for XBRL yet. Potential adopting organizations may not be ready to adopt because of lack of motivation which may be underpinned by limited awareness about XBRL benefits, functionality and related costs. And yet, these are important as they determine an organization's readiness to adopt an innovation (Parasuraman, 2000).

CONCLUSION AND FUTURE RESEARCH

In summary, there is little research about the organisational adoption and diffusion of the XBRL innovation. Using the existing limited literature and the empirical findings from our convergent interviews, we adopted the environment-organisation-innovation model to the context of an emerging e-business technology. One contribution of our chapter is it has confirmed the usefulness of this model in researching specific instances of e-business technologies, such as XBRL, thereby making important inroads into theory development in this area.

However, the major contributions of this chapter are its comprehensive analysis of the convergent interviewing method and the illustration of its application in the convergence of environmental, organizational, and innovation-related drivers and inhibitors influencing the adoption of XBRL in Australia. In brief, we argue that convergent interviewing is appropriate to be applied in under-researched areas where there are few experts. This is because it provides a way of quickly converging on key issues in the area, an efficient mechanism for data analysis after each interview, and a way of deciding when to stop collecting data. In conclusion, convergent interviews could become a useful qualitative research method to explore new issues concerning the phenomena of organisational adoption and diffusion of emerging innovations such as XBRL. In addition, these may have practical implications for the adoption strategies of the local XBRL consortium in Australia.

As also suggested in the interviews, there is lack of standardization in the way XBRL instance documents are produced and consumed. Related e-business research suggests that lack of standards can determine the success or failure of e-business initiatives (Reimers & Li, 2005). Given the heterogeneity and the multitude of XBRL stakeholders, their representation in standardization processes can be problematic because these stakeholders have different and sometimes even conflicting agendas. Therefore, we argue that further research is required for investigating the social processes that characterize the emergence of complex network e-business innovation standards such as XBRL. Such research becomes particularly relevant in 2008 when the U.S. SEC's XBRL-enabled EDGAR system is expected to come on stream (Kull *et al.*, 2007). Various accounting jurisdictions that are still behind in terms of XBRL adoption may now have to be quick in both assessing how the XBRL-enabled EDGAR might impact their capital markets and finding ways to respond to the U.S. XBRL standard setting agenda. As theory development is currently lacking in this area (Zhao, Xia, & Shaw, 2005; Gogan, 2005; Gerst & Bunduchi, 2005; Reimers & Li, 2005; Chang & Jarvenpaa, 2005) we recommend adopting convergent interviewing as a useful exploratory and investigative method.

ACKNOWLEDGMENT

This research project presented in this paper has been funded by the School of Commerce, University of Adelaide, South Australia. The authors would also like to acknowledge the participation of Professor Bill Doolin (Auckland University of Technology) in the formulation and data collection phases of this research project.

REFERENCES

Aaker, D. A., & Day, G. S. (1990). *Marketing Research* (4th ed.). New York: Wiley.

Abdolmohammadi, M., Harris, J., & Smith, K. (2002). Goverment financial reporting on the Internet: the potential revolutionary effects of XBRL. *Journal of Goverment Financial Management, 51*(2), 24-26, 28-31.

Al-Qirim, N. A. Y. (2003). E-commerce in the aerial mapping industry: A New Zealand Case Study. *Journal of Systems & Information Technology, 7*(1), 67-92.

Baldwin, A. A., Brown, C. E., & Trinkle, B. S. (2006). XBRL: An impacts framework and research challenge. *Journal of Emerging Technologies in Accounting, 3*(1), 97-116.

Barlas, S. (2007). SEC moves closer to mandating XBRL. *Strategic Finance, 88*(5), 14-17.

Baroudi, J. J., & Orlikowski, W. J. (1989). The problem of statistical power in MIS research. *MIS Quarterly, 13*(1), 86-106.

Basu, V., Hartono, E., Lederer, A. L., & Sethi, V. (2002). The impact of organisational commitment, senior management involvement, and team involvement on strategic information systems planning. *Information & Management, 39*(6), 513-524.

Bergeron, B. (2003). *Essentials of XBRL: Financial Reporting in the 21st Century.* Hoboken, New Jersey: John Wiley & Sons, Inc.

Bovee, M., Kogan, A., Nelson, K., Srivastava, R. P., & Vasarhelyi, M. A. (2005). Financial reporting and auditing agent with net knowledge (FRAANK) and eXtensible Business Reporting Language (XBRL). *Journal of Information Systems, 19*(1), 19-41.

Boyd, G. (2004a). *Introduction to XBRL Consortium.* Paper presented at the 9th International XBRL Conference, Auckland, New Zealand.

Boyd, G. (2004b). *XBRL Overview.* Paper presented at the 9th International XBRL Conference, Auckland, New Zealand.

Chang, C., & Jarvenpaa, S. (2005). Pace of information systems standards development and implementation: the case of XBRL. *Electronic Markets: The International Journal, 15*(4), 365-377.

Cragg, P., Mehrtens, J., & Mills, A. (2001). A model of Internet adoption by SMEs. *Information & Management, 39*, 165-176.

Davis, F. D. (1989). Perceived usefulness, perceived ease of use, and user acceptance in information technology. *MIS Quarterly, 13*(3), 319-339.

Debreceny, R. S., Chandra, A., Cheh, J. J., Guithues-Amrhein, D., Hannon, N. J., Hutshison, P. D., Janvrin, D., Jones, R. A., Lamberton, B., Lymer, A., Mascha, M., Nehmer, R., Roohani, S., Srivastava, R. P., Travelsi, S., Tribunella, T., Trites, G., & Vasarhelyi, M. A. (2005). Financial reporting in XBRL on the SEC's EDGAR system: A critique and evaluation. *Journal of Information Systems, 19*(2), 191-210.

Deshmukh, A. (2004). XBRL. *Communications of the Association for Information Systems, 13*, 196-219.

Devonish-Mills, L. (2007). Updates on XBRL and SOX. *Strategic Finance, 99*(9), 14-16.

Dick, B. (1990). *Convergent Interviewing.* Brisbane: Interchange.

DiPiazza, S. A. J., & Eccles, R. G. (2002). *Building Public Trust: The Future of Corporate Reporting.* New York: John Wiley & Sons, Inc.

Doolin, B., & Troshani, I. (2004). XBRL: A research note. *Qualitative Research in Accounting & Management, 1*(2), 93-104.

Doolin, B., & Troshani, I. (2007). Organizational adoption of XBRL. *Electronic Markets: The International Journal, 17*(3), 199-209.

Elliot, S. (2002). Research model and theoretical implications. In S. Elliot (Ed.), *Electronic Commerce B2C Strategies and Models* (pp. 291-326). Brisbane: John Wiley & Sons, Ltd.

Emory, C. W., & Cooper, D. R. (1991). *Business Research Methods*. Homewood: Irwin.

Ewing, I. (2007). *SBR & The national statistical system*. Paper presented at the SBR/XBRL International Conference, Brisbane, 27-28 November.

Fillis, I., Johannson, U., & Wagner, B. (2004). Factors impacting on E-business adoption and development in the smaller firm. *International Journal of Entrepreneurial Behaviour & Research, 10*(3), 178-191.

Frambach, R. T. (1993). An integrated model of organizational adoption and diffusion of innovations. *European Journal of Marketing, 27*(5), 22-41.

Garbellotto, G. (2006a). Broaden your view on XBRL's representational capabilities. *Strategic Finance, 88*(4), 59-61.

Garbellotto, G. (2006b). XBRL is to XML as lemonade is to lemons. *Strategic Finance, 88*(6), 59-61.

Garbellotto, G. (2006c). Exposing enterprise data: XBRL GL, Web services, and Google, Part 1. *Strategic Finance, 88*(2), 59-61.

Garbellotto, G. (2007a). 14th XBRL International Conference: An internal perspective. *Strategic Finance, 88*(7), 57-58.

Garbellotto, G. (2007b). It's time for GL-enabled software. *Strategic Finance, 88*(8), 55-56.

Gedda, R. (2007). ABS moves on business reporting standard. Retrieved 19 December, 2007, from http://www.computerworld.com.au/index.php?id=1395576549&eid=-6787

Gerst, M., & Bunduchi, R. (2005). Shaping IT standardization in the automotive industry - The role of power in driving portal standardization. *Electronic Markets: The International Journal, 15*(4), 335-343.

Gilbert, D., Balestrini, P., & Littleboy, D. (2004). Barriers and benefits in the adoption of E-government. *The International Journal of Public Sector Management, 17*(4), 286-301.

Gogan, J. L. (2005). Punctuation and path dependence: Examining a vertical IT standard-setting process. *Electronic Markets: The International Journal, 15*(4), 344-354.

Grant, A. E. (2004). Sharpening the videoconference target. Retrieved 26 January, 2004, from http://www.tfi.com/pubs/ntq/articles/view/98Q2_A1.html

Guba, E. G., & Lincoln, Y. S. (1994). Competing paradigms in qualitative research. In N. Denzin, K. & Y. S. Lincoln (Eds.), *Handbook of Qualitative Research*. London: Sage Publications.

Gummesson, E. (2000). *Qualitative Methods in Management Research* (2nd ed.). Thousand Oaks: Sage.

Hannon, N. (2003). XBRL for general ledger, the journal taxonomy. *Strategic Finance, 85*(2), 63, 67.

Hannon, N. (2006c). Why the SEC is bullish on XBRL. *Strategic Finance, 87*(7), 59-61.

Hannon, N. J. (2006a). Does XBRL cost too much? *Strategic Finance, 87*(10), 59-60.

Hannon, N. J. (2006b). In search of ROI for XBRL. *Strategic Finance, 87*(9), 59-60.

Hannon, N. J., & Gold, R. J. (2005). XBRL revisited. *Journal of Accountancy Online, February*.

Hasegawa, M., Sakata, T., Sambuichi, N., & Hannon, N. (2003). Breathing new life into old systems. *Strategic Finance, 85*(9), 46-51.

Healy, M., & Perry, C. (2000). Comprehensive criteria to judge validity and reliability of qualitative research within the realism paradigm. *Qualitative Market Research: An International Journal, 3*(3), 118-126.

Hodge, F. D., Kennedy, J. J., & Maines, L. A. (2004). Does search-facilitating technology improve the transparency of financial reporting? *The Accounting Review, 79*(3), 687-703.

Jones, A., & Willis, M. (2003). The challenge for XBRL: Business reporting for the investor. *Balance Sheet, 11*(3), 29-37.

Kalakota, R., & Robinson, M. (2001). *E-business 2.0: Road-map for Success.* Harlow: Addison-Wesley.

King, E. (1996). The use of self in qualitative research. In J. Richardson (Ed.), *Handbook of Qualitative Research Methods for Psychology and Social Sciences.* Leicester: BPS Books.

KPMG. (2005). Step-by-step XBRL 2.0 Tutorial. Retrieved 21 February, 2005, from http://www.kpmg.com/xbrl/kkb.asp

Kull, J. L., Miller, L. E., St. Clair, J. A., & Savage, M. (2007). Interactive data - XBRL: a revolutionary idea. *Journal of Government Financial Management, 56*(2), 10-14.

Locke, J., & Lowe, A. (2007). XBRL: An (open) source of enlightenment or disillusion? *European Accounting Review, 16*(3), 585-623.

Markus, M. L. (1987). Toward a critical mass theory of interactive media: Universal access, interdependence, and diffusion. *Communication Research, 14*(5), 491-511.

Markus, M. L. (1990). Toward a "critical mass" theory of interactive media. In J. Fulk & C. W. Steinfield (Eds.), *Organization and Communication Technology.* Newbury Park, CA: Sage.

Marshall, C., & Rossman, G. B. (1995). *Designing Qualitative Research* (2nd ed.). Newbury Park: Sage Publications.

Maykut, P., & Morehouse, R. (1994). *Beginning Qualitative Research: A Philosophical and Practical Guide*: Burgess Science Press.

Nair, G. S., & Riege, A. M. (1995). *Using convergent interviewing to develop the research problem of a postgraduate thesis.* Paper presented at the Marketing Education and Researchers International Conference, Gold Coast, Queensland.

Parasuraman, A. (2000). Technology readiness index (TRI): A multiple-item scale to measure readiness to embrace new technologies. *Journal of Service Research, 2*(4), 307-320.

Patton, M. Q. (1990). *Qualitative Evaluation and Research Methods* (2nd ed.). London: Sage Publications.

Phenix, P. (2004). *XBRL: Exchanges & Regulators.* Paper presented at the 9th International XBRL Conference, Auckland New Zealand.

Pinsker, R. (2003). XBRL awareness in auditing: a sleeping giant? *Managerial Auditing Journal, 18*(9), 732-736.

Pyman, T. (2004). XBRL ready or not. *Charter,* 54-55.

Reimers, K., & Li, M. (2005). Antecedents of a transaction cost theory of vertical IS standardization processes. *Electronic Markets: The International Journal, 15*(4), 301-312.

Rezaee, Z., Elam, R., & Sharbatoghilie, A. (2001). Continuous auditing: The audit of the future. *Managerial Auditing Journal, 16*(3), 150-158.

Richards, J., & Tibbits, H. (2002). *Understanding XBRL* (CPA Workshop Presentation Notes). New South Wales: CPA Australia, NSW Branch.

Rogers, E. M. (1995). *Diffusion of Innovations* (4th ed.). New York, NY: The Free Press.

Roohani, S. J. (2003). *Trust and Data Assurances in Capital Markets: The Role of Technology Solutions.* Smithfield, RI: Bryant College & Pricewaterhouse Coopers.

Russell, D. M., & Hoag, A. M. (2004). People and information technology in the supply chain: Social and organizational influences on adoption. *International Journal of Physical Distribution & Logistics Management, 34*(2), 102-122.

Sekaran, U. (2000). *Research Methods for Business: A Skill Building Approach*. New York: John Wiley and Sons.

Subramanian, G. H. (1994). A replication of perceived usefulness and perceived ease of use measurement. *Decision Sciences, 25*(5/6), 863-874.

Tidd, J., Bessant, J., & Pavitt, K. (2001). *Managing Innovation: Integrating Technological, Market and Organizational Change*. Chichester: John Wiley & Sons Ltd.

Tornatzky, L. G., & Fleischer, M. (1990). *Processes of Technological Innovation*. Lexington, Massachusetts: Lexington Books.

Troshani, I., & Doolin, B. (2005). Drivers and inhibitors impacting technology adoption: A qualitative investigation into the Australian experience with XBRL. In D. R. Vogel, P. Walden, J. Gricar & G. Lenart (Eds.), *Proceedings of the 18th Bled eCommerce Conference: eIntegration in Action*. June 6-8, 2005, Bled, Slovenia: Moderna Organizacija.

Troshani, I., & Doolin, B. (2007). Innovation diffusion: A stakeholder and social network view. *European Journal of Innovation Management, 10*(2), 176-200.

Wallace, A. (2001). The new language of financial reporting. *Balance Sheet, 9*(2), 29-32.

Warren, M. (2004). Farmers online: Drivers and impediments in adoption of Internet in UK agricultural businesses. *Journal of Small Business and Enterprise Development, 11*(3), 371-381.

Weber, R. (2003). XML, XBRL, and the future of business and business reporting. In S. J. Roohani (Ed.), *Trust and Data Assurances in Capital Markets: The Role of Technology Solutions*. Smithfield, RI: Bryant College.

Willis, M. (2005). XBRL and data standardization: Transforming the way CPAs work. *Journal of Accountancy, 199*(3), 80-81.

Willis, M., Tesniere, B., & Jones, A. (2003). *Corporate Communications for the 21st Century* (White Paper): PricewaterhouseCoopers.

Wolfe, R. A. (1994). Organisational innovation: Review, critique, and suggested research directions. *Journal of Management Studies, 31*(3), 405-431.

XBRLAustralia. (2004). XBRL Australia members. Retrieved 7 April, 2005, from http://www.xbrl.org.au/members/

Yin, R. K. (1994). *Case Study Research: Design and Methods*. Beverley Hills: Sage.

Zhao, K., Xia, M., & Shaw, M. J. (2005). Vertical E-business standards and standards developing organisations: A conceptual framework. *Electronic Markets: The International Journal, 15*(4), 289-300.

Zikmund, W. G. (2000). *Business Research Methods* (6th ed.). Chicago: The Dryden Press.

ENDNOTES

i EDGAR, the Electronic Data Gathering, Analysis, and Retrieval system performs automated collection, validation, indexing, acceptance and forwarding of submissions by companies, both foreign and domestic and others who are required by law to file forms with the U. S. Securities and Exchange Commission (SEC). See http://www.sec.gov/edgar.shtml for further information.

ii The interviewed academics had both been involved in teaching XBRL in tertiary institutions in Australia and also they are members of XBRL Australia Ltd.

This work was previously published in Emergent Strategies for E-Business Processes, Services and Implications: Advancing Corporate Framework, edited by I. Lee, pp. 205-222, copyright 2009 by Information Science Reference (an imprint of IGI Global).

Afterword

With recent advances in network technologies and infrastructure, there is increasing demand for ubiquitous access to networked services. New challenges arise in the study of services engineering, an emerging research area devoted to the software engineering of service-oriented applications. An environment which demands ubiquitous and just-in-time capabilities (or services) which can be discovered and used transparently among dynamic communities of providers and consumers who may or may not have had previous interaction. It is clearly a vision that has only begun to realize its potential and one which depends upon many of the same underlying concerns addressed in distributed computing including architecting, managing and evolving capabilities. However, the XML services computing paradigm is specifically tailored for today's increasingly cross-organizational, cross-jurisdictional and cross-domain enterprise. Moreover, the XML services computing environment depends upon the enterprise network as the platform. The many recent advances in XML services computing technologies and infrastructure has opened the enterprise to increasing demands for interoperable ubiquitous access to networked services that can support an endless array of enterprise business processes. Architecting and deploying Web services-based systems for such an enterprise necessitates full understanding of the business processes and explicit modelling of the internal and external environment so that the constraints can be incorporated in the overall architecture of the enterprise.

In summary, this book crystallizes the emerging XML data technologies and trends into positive efforts to focus on the most promising solutions in services computing. The 16 chapters in this book provide clear proof that XML data technologies are playing an ever increasing important and critical role in supporting business service processes. The chapters also further research new best practices and directions in XML services.

Patrick C. K. Hung
University of Ontario Institute of Technology, Canada
E-mail: patrick.hung@uoit.ca

Copyright © 2009, IGI Global, distributing in print or electronic forms without written permission of IGI Global is prohibited.

Compilation of References

Aaker, D. A., & Day, G. S. (1990). *Marketing Research* (4th ed.). New York: Wiley.

Abdolmohammadi, M., Harris, J., & Smith, K. (2002). Goverment financial reporting on the Internet: the potential revolutionary effects of XBRL. *Journal of Goverment Financial Management, 51*(2), 24-26, 28-31.

Abiteboul, S., Bonifati , A., Cobena , G., Manolescu , I., & Milo, T. (2003). Dynamic XML Documents with Distribution and Replication. In *ACM SIGMOD International Conference on Management of Data* (pp. 527-538). ACM Press.

Aditya, B., & Bhalotia, G., & Sudarshan, S. (2002). *BANKS: Browsing and Keyword Searching in Relational Databases.* The 28th Very Large Data Bases (VLDB) conference, Hong Kong, China.

Agrawal, R., & Srikant, R. (1998). Fast algorithms for mining association rules. In *Readings in database systems* (3rd ed., pp. 580-592). San Francisco: Morgan Kaufmann Publishers Inc.

Agrawal, R., Imielinski, T., & Swami, A. N. (1993). Mining association rules between sets of items in large databases. *Proceedings of the ACM International Conference on Management of Data (SIGMOD 1993)* (pp. 207-216).

Agrawal, S., & Chaudhuri S., & Das, G. (2002). *DBXplorer: a System for Keyword-Based Search Over Relational Databases.* The 18th International Conference on Data Engineering (ICDE), San Jose, California

Aguiléra, V., Cluet, S., Veltri, P., Vodislav, D., & Wattez, F. (2000). Querying XML Documents in Xyleme. In *Proc. of the ACM-SIGIR 2000 Workshop on XML and Information Retrieval.* Athens, Greece.

Aho, A. V., Sethi, R., & Ullman, J. D. (1988). *Compilers: Principles, techniques and tools.* New York: Addison-Wesley.

Ahonen, H. (1997). Disambiguation of SGML Content Models. In C. Nicholas & D. Wood (Eds.), PODP 1996: *Proceedings of the workshop on principles of document processing* (pp. 27-37), Palo Alto, USA, Berlin: Springer-Verlag.

Alag, H. (2006). *Business Process Mobility.* In B. Unhelkar (Ed.), *Handbook Resources of Mobile Business.* Hershey, PA, USA: IGI Global. USA.

Copyright © 2009, IGI Global, distributing in print or electronic forms without written permission of IGI Global is prohibited.

Al-Jadir, L., & El-Moukaddem, F. (2003). Once Upon a Time a DTD Evolved Into Another DTD. In Springer (Ed.), *Proceedings of the international conference on object-oriented information systems* (pp. 3-17), Geneva, Switzerland,proceedings. Berlin: Springer-Verlag.

Alonso, G., Casati, F., Kuno, H., & Machiraju, V. (2004). *Web Services – Concepts, Architectures and Applications.* Berlin, Germany: Springer Verlag.

Al-Qirim, N. A. Y. (2003). E-commerce in the aerial mapping industry: A New Zealand Case Study. *Journal of Systems & Information Technology, 7*(1), 67-92.

Amer-Yahia, S., & Cartmola E., & Deutsch, A. (2006). *Flexible and Efficient XML Search with Complex Full-Text Predicates.* ACM SIGMOD International Conference on Management of Data, Chicago, Illinois.

Andrews, T., Curbera, F., Dholakia, H., Goland, Y., Klein, J., Leymann, F., Liu, K., Roller, D., Smith, D., Thatte, S., Trickovic, I., & Weerawarana, S. (2003). *Specification: Business Process Execution Language for Web Services, Version 1.1.* Available at http://www-106.ibm.com/developerworks/library/ws-bpel/.

Andrews, T., Curbera, F., Dholakia, H., Goland, Y., Klein, J., Leymann, F., Liu, K., Roller, D., Smith, D., Thatte, S., Trickovic, I., & Weerawarana, S. (2002). *Specification: Business Process Execution Language for Web Services (BPEL).* Retrieved October, 2006, from http://www-106.ibm.com/developerworks/library/ws-bpel/

Angluin, D. (1987). Learning Regular Sets From Queries and Counterexamples. *Information and Computation, 75*(2), 87-106.

Antoniou, G., & Harmelen, F. V. (2004). *A semantic web primer.* Cambridge, UK: The MIT Press.

Apostolico, A., & Galil, Z. (Eds.) (1997). *Pattern matching algorithms.* Oxford, UK: Oxford University Press.

Ashrafi, M. Z., Taniar, D. & Smith, K. A. (2004b). ODAM: An optimized distributed association rule mining algorithm. *IEEE Distributed Systems Online, 5*(3).

Ashrafi, M. Z., Taniar, D., & Smith, K. (2005). An efficient compression technique for frequent itemset generation in association rule mining. In *Proceedings of International Conference in Advances in Knowledge Discovery and Data Mining (PAKDD 2005)* (LNCS 3518, pp. 125-135). Heidelberg, Germany: Springer-Verlag.

Ashrafi, M. Z., Taniar, D., & Smith, K. A. (2004a). A new approach of eliminating redundant association rules. In *Database and expert systems applications* (LNCS 3180, pp. 465-474). Heidelberg, Germany: Springer-Verlag.

Ba, C., Carrero, M., Halfeld Ferrari, M., & Musicante, M. (2005). PEWS: A New Language for Building Web Service Interfaces. *Journal of Universal Computer Science, 5*(11), 1215-1233.

Baader, F., Calvanese, D., McGuinness, D.L., Nardi, D., & Patel-Schneider, P.F.(Eds.). (2003). *The description logic handbook.* Cambridge University Press.

Baghdadi, Y. (2004). ABBA: An architecture for deploying business-to-business electronic commerce applications. *Electronic Commerce Research and Applications, 3,* 190-212.

Baïna, K, Benatallah, B., Cassati, F., & Toumani, F. (2004). Model-driven Web service development. In A. Persson & J. Stirna (Ed.), *CAiSE'04, LNCS* (Vol. 3084, pp. 290-306).

Baldwin, A. A., Brown, C. E., & Trinkle, B. S. (2006). XBRL: An impacts framework and research challenge. *Journal of Emerging Technologies in Accounting, 3*(1), 97-116.

Balmin, A., & Hristidis, V., & Papakonstantinon Y. (2004). *ObjectRank: Authority-Based Keyword Search in Databases.* The 30th Very Large Data Bases (VLDB) conference, Toronto, Canada.

Balmin, A., & Hristidis, V., & Papakonstantinon Y., & Koudas, N. (2003). *A System for Keyword Proximity Search on XML Databases.* The 29th Very Large Data Bases (VLDB) conference, Berlin, Germany.

Balmin, A., & Hristidis, V., & Papakonstantinon, Y. (2003). *Keyword Proximity Search on XML Graphs.* The 19th International Conference on Data Engineering (ICDE), Bangalore, India.

Barbosa, D., & Mendelzon, A., & Keenleyside, J., & Lyons, K. (2002). *ToXgene: a template-based data generator for XML.* The Fifth International Workshop on the Web and Databases (WebDB), Madison, Wisconsin. The code downloaded from: http://www.cs.toronto.edu/tox/toxgene/downloads.html

Barbosa, D., Mignet, L., & Veltri, P. (2005). Studying the XML web: Gathering statistics from an XML sample. In *Proceeding of World Wide Web Conference 2005*, (pp. 413-438).

Barlas, S. (2007). SEC moves closer to mandating XBRL. *Strategic Finance, 88*(5), 14-17.

Baroudi, J. J., & Orlikowski, W. J. (1989). The problem of statistical power in MIS research. *MIS Quarterly, 13*(1), 86-106.

Barry, D. K. (2003). *Web Services and Service-Oriented Architecture. The savvy Manager's Guide.* USA: Morgan Kaufmann Publishers. ISBN: 1-55860-906-7

Basu, V., Hartono, E., Lederer, A. L., & Sethi, V. (2002). The impact of organisational commitment, senior management involvement, and team involvement on strategic information systems planning. *Information & Management, 39*(6), 513-524.

Bauer, B., Müller, J. P., & Odel, J. (2001). Agent UML: A formalism for specifying multiagent software systems. *Int. Journal of Software Engineering and Knowledge Engineering, 11(3)*, 1-24.

BEA, IBM, Microsoft, SAP, & Siebel (2003). *Business process execution language for Web services (BPEL).* Retrieved June 1, 2003, from: http://www-106.ibm.com/developerworks/library/ws-bpel/

Benkő, T., Lukácsy, G., Fokt, A., Szeredi, P., Kilián, I., & Krauth, P. (2003). Information Integration through Reasoning on Meta-data. *Proceeding of the workshop, AI moves to IA", IJCAI 2003*, Acapulco, Mexico, (pp. 65-77).

Bergeron, B. (2003). *Essentials of XBRL: Financial Reporting in the 21st Century.* Hoboken, New Jersey: John Wiley & Sons, Inc.

Bernauer, M., Kappel, G., & Kramler, G. (2003). Comparing WSDL-based and ebXML-based approaches for B2B protocol specification. In *Proceedings of Int. Conference on Service-Oriented Computing 2003, LNCS, Vol. 2910* (pp. 225-240).

Bernstein, P. A., Hadzilacos, V., & Goodman, N. (1987). *Concurrency Control and Recovery in Database Systems.* Addison-Wesley.

Biswas, D. (2004). Compensation in the World of Web Services Composition. In *International Workshop on Semantic Web Services and Web Process Composition* (pp. 69-80). Lecture Notes in Computer Science, vol. 3387, Springer-Verlag.

Biswas, D. (2008). Active XML Replication and Recovery. In *International Conference on Complex, Intelligent and Software Intensive Systems* (pp. 263-269). IEEE CS Press.

Biswas, D., & Genest, B. (2008). Minimal Observability for Transactional Hierarchical Services. In *International Conference on Software Engineering and Knowledge Engineering* (pp. 531-536).

Biswas, D., & Vidyasankar, K. (2005). Spheres of Visibility. In *European Conference on Web Services* (pp. 2-13). IEEE CS Press.

Biswas, D., Gazagnaire, T., & Genest, B. (2008). Small Logs for Transactional Services: Distinction is much more accurate than (Positive) Discrimination. In *High Assurance Systems Engineering Symposium* (pp. 97-106). IEEE CS Press.

Björk, S., Holmquist, L.E., Redström, J., Bretan, I., Danielsson, R., Karlgren, J., & Franzén, K., (1999). WEST: a Web browser for small terminals. *Proceedings of the 12th annual ACM symposium on User interface software and technology* (pp.187-196). Asheville, North Carolina, United States.

Botev, C., & Shao, F., & Guo, L. (2003). *XRANK: Ranked Keyword Search over XML Documents.* GMOD International Conference on Management of Data, San Diego, California.

Bouchou, B., & Duarte, D. (2007). Assisting XML schema evolution that preserves validity. In SBBD 2007: *XXII Brazilian Symposium on Databases* (pp. 270-284). João Pessoa, Brazil, proceedings. Porto Alegre: Brazilian Computer Society.

Bouchou, B., Cheriat, A., Halfeld Ferrari, M., & Savary, A. (2006). XML document correction: Incremental approach activated by schema validation. In IDEAS 2006: *10th International Database Engineering and Applications Symposium* (pp. 228-238), Dehli, India, proceedings. Piscataway, USA: IEEE Computer Society.

Bouchou, B., Duarte, D., Halfeld Ferrari, M., Laurent, D., & Musicante, M. A. (2004). Schema evolution for XML: A Consistency-Preserving Approach. In MFCS'04: *29th Mathematical Foundations of Computer Science* (pp. 876-888). Prague, Czech Republic, proceedings. Berlin: Springer-Verlag.

Bovee, M., Kogan, A., Nelson, K., Srivastava, R. P., & Vasarhelyi, M. A. (2005). Financial reporting and auditing agent with net knowledge (FRAANK) and eXtensible Business Reporting Language (XBRL). *Journal of Information Systems, 19*(1), 19-41.

Boyd, G. (2004). *Introduction to XBRL Consortium.* Paper presented at the 9th International XBRL Conference, Auckland, New Zealand.

Boyd, G. (2004). *XBRL Overview.* Paper presented at the 9th International XBRL Conference, Auckland, New Zealand.

Braga, D., Campi, A., & Ceri, S. (2003). Discovering interesting information in XML with association rules. *Proceedings of 2003 ACM Symposium on Applied Computing (SAC'03)* (pp. 450-454).

Braga, D., Campi, A., Ceri, S., Klemettinen, M., & Lanzi, P. L. (2002). A tool for extracting XML association rules. *Proceedings of the 14th International Conference on Tools with Artificial Intelligence (ICTAI '02)* (p. 57).

Braga, D., Campi, A., Klemettinen, M., & Lanzi, P. L. (2002). Mining association rules from XML data. In *Proceedings of International Conference on Data Warehousing and Knowledge Discovery (DaWak 2002)* (LNCS 2454, pp. 21-30). Heidelberg, Germany: Springer-Verlag.

Brickley, D. (2005). The Friend of a Friend (FOAF) Project Web site. Retrieved from http://www.foaf-project.org/

Brüggeman-Klein, A., & Wood, D. (1992). Deterministic Regular Languages. STACS 1992: *9th Annual Symposium on Theoretical Aspects of Computer Science.* Cachan, France, proceedings. Berlin: Springer-Verlag.

Bry, F., & Schaffert, S. (2002). Towards a Declarative Query and Transformation Language for XML and Semistructured Data: Simulation Unification. *In Proceedings Intl. Conference on Logic Programming. LNCS 2401,* (pp. 255-270). Heidelberg, Gerrnany: Springer-Verlag.

Buchner, A. G., Baumgarten, M., Mulvenna, M. D., Bohm, R., & Anand, S. S. (2000). Data mining and XML: Current and future issues. *Proceedings of 1st International Conference on Web Information System Engineering (WISE 2000)* (pp. 127-131).

Bussler, C. (2001). The role of B2B engines in B2B integration architectures. *ACM SIGMOD Record, Special Issue on Data Management Issues in E-Commerce, 31(1).*

Caliusco, M. L., Maidana, C., Galli, M. R., & Chiotti, O. (2004). Contextual ontology definition metamodel. In *Proceedings of the IV Iberoamerican Conference on Software Engineering and Knowledge Engineering* (pp. 261-275).

Calvanese, D., De Giacomo, G., Lenzerini, M., Nardi, D., & Rosati, R. (1998). *Description Logic Framework for Information Integration, Principles of Knowledge Representation and Reasoning,* (pp. 2-13).

Cardelli, L., & Mitchell, J.C. (1991). Operations on records. *Mathematical Structures in Computer Science, 1,* 3–48.

Caron, P., & Ziadi, D. (2000). Characterization of Glushkov Automata. *Theoretical Computer Science, 233*(1-2), 75-90.

Carpenter, B. (1992). *The logic of typed feature structures.* Cambridge University Press.

Chamberlin, D., & Fankhauser, P., & Florescu, D., & Robie, J. (2006). XML Query Use Cases. *W3C Working Draft 2006*. Retrieved from: http://www.w3.org/TR/2006/WD-xquery-use-cases-20060608/

Chandra, S., & Ellis, C.S. (1999). JPEG Compression Metric as a Quality Aware Image Transcoding. *Second Usenix Symposium on Internet Technologies and Systems* (USITS '99). (pp. 81–92) Boulder, CO.

Chandra, S., Ellis, C., & Vahdat, A. (2000). Application-Level Differentiated Multimedia Web Services Using Quality Aware Transcoding, *IEEE Journal on Selected Areas in Communications*, *18*(12), 2265–2544.

Chang, C., & Jarvenpaa, S. (2005). Pace of information systems standards development and implementation: the case of XBRL. *Electronic Markets: The International Journal, 15*(4), 365-377.

Chang, C.Y., & Chen, M.S. (2002). Exploring Aggregate Effect with Weighted Transcoding Graphs for Efficient Cache Replacement in Transcoding Proxies. *Proceedings of the 18th IEEE International Conference on Data Engineering (ICDE-O)* (pp. 383—392). San Jose, CA, USA.

Chase, N. (2006, February 14*). Introducing the open Group Architecture Framework, Understanding TOGAf and IT Architecture in today's World.* http://www-128.ibm.com/developerworks/ibm/library/ar-togaf1/ Accessed: 3/04/2007

Chawathe, S. S., Rajaraman, A., Garcia-Molina, H., & Widom, J. (1996). Change Detection in Hierarchically Structured Information. In *SIGMOD'96: ACM SIGMOD international conference on management of data* (pp. 493-504), Montreal, Canada, proceedings. New York: ACM Press.

Chawathe, S.S. (1999). Comparing Hierarchical Data in External Memory. In *Proc. of 25th Int. Conference on Very Large Data Bases (VLDB'99),* September 7-10, 1999, Edinburgh, Scotland, UK, (pp. 90–101). Morgan Kaufmann.

Chawathe, S.S., & Garcia-Molina, H. (1997). Meaningful Change Detection in Structured Data. In *Proc. of ACM SIGMOD Int. Conference on Management of Data,* May 13-15, 1997, Tucson, Arizona, USA, (pp. 26–37). ACM Press.

Chawathe, S.S., Abiteboul, S., & Widom, J. (1998). Representing and Querying Changes in Semistructured Data. In *Proc. of the 4th Int. Conference on Data Engineering (ICDE'98),* February 23-27, 1998, Orlando, Florida, USA, (pp. 4–13). IEEE Computer Society.

Chawathe, S.S., Abiteboul, S., & Widom, J. (1999). Managing Historical Semistructured Data. *Theory and Practice of Object Systems, 5*(3), 143–162.

Chawathe, S.S., Rajaraman, A., Garcia-Molina, H., & Widom, J. (1996). Change Detection in Hierarchically Structured Information. In *Proc. of the ACM SIGMOD Int. Conference on Management of Data*, Montreal, Quebec, Canada, June 4-6, 1996, (pp. 493–504). ACM Press.

Chawathe, Y. (2003). Scattercast: an adaptable broadcast distribution framework. *Journal Multimedia Systems, 9*(1), 104-118.

Chen, J., DeWitt, D.J., Tian, F., & Wang, Y. (2000). NiagaraCQ: A Scalable Continuous Query System for Internet Databases. In *Proc. of the ACM SIGMOD Int. Conference on Management of Data*, May 16-18, 2000, Dallas, Texas, USA, (pp. 379–390). ACM.

Chen, L., Browmick, S. S., & Chia, L. T. (2004). Mining association rules from structural deltas of historical XML documents. In *Proceedings of International Conference in Advances in Knowledge Discovery and Data Mining (PAKDD 2004)* (LNCS 3056, pp. 452-457). Heidelberg, Germany: Springer-Verlag.

Chen, N. (2008). A Quick Development Framework Based on Process/Data Relationship Model. In J. Zhou (Ed.), *Proceedings of the 2008 International Conference on Computer Science and Information Technology.* (pp. 597-600). Washington, DC, USA: IEEE Computer Society.

Chen, Q., & Hsu, M. (2001) Interenterprise collaborative business process management. In *Proceedings of the 17th International Conference on Data Engineering (ICDE).*

Chen, X., Wenteng, C., Turner, S. J., & Wang, Y. (2006). SOAr-DSGrid: Service-Oriented Architecture for Distributed Simulation on the Grid. *Proceedings of the 20th Workshop on Principles of Advanced and Distributed Simulation.* ISBN ~ ISSN:1087-4097 , 0-7695-2587-3

Cheney, J. (2001). Compressing XML with multiplexed hierarchical PPM models. In *Data Compression Conference*, Snowbird (pp. 163-172).

Chien, S.-Y., Tsotras, V.J., & Zaniolo, C. (2000). *A Comparative Study of Version Management Schemes for XML Documents.* Technical Report TR51, TimeCenter.

Chien, S.-Y., Tsotras, V.J., & Zaniolo, C. (2001). XML Document Versioning. *SIGMOD Record, 30*(3), 46–53.

Chung, J. Y. (2005). An Industry View on Service-Oriented Architecture and Web Services. *Proceedings of the 2005 IEEE International Workshop on Service-Oriented System Engineering (SOSE'05)* 0-7695-2438-9/05 © 2005 IEEE.

Clark, J., & Murata, M. (2001). *Definitive specification for RELAX NG using the XML syntax.* Retrieved December 20, 2006, from http://www.relaxng.org/spec-20011203.html

Clark, T., & Warmer, J. (2002). *Object Modeling with the OCL: The rationale behind the Object Constraint Language.* Springer.

Clifton, N. (2003). *Data Access Patterns: Database Interactions in Object-Oriented Applications.* USA: Addison-Wesley Professional Press.

Cobena, G., Abiteboul, S., & Marian, A. (2002). Detecting Changes in XML Documents. In *Proc. of the 18th Int. Conference on Data Engineering (ICDE'02)*, 26 February - 1 March 2002, San Jose, CA, USA, (pp. 41–52). IEEE Computer Society.

Cobena, G., Abiteboul, S., & Marian, A. (2005). *XyDiff tools: Detecting changes in XML documents.* Retrieved February 2006, from http://www.rocq.inria.fr/gemo

Cohen, E., Kaplan, H., & Milo, T. (2002). Labeling Dynamic XML Trees. In *Proc. of the 21st ACM SIGACT-SIGMOD-SIGART Symposium on Principles of Database Systems*, June 3-5, Madison, Wisconsin, USA, (pp. 271–281). ACM.

Cohen, S., & Kanza, Y. (2005). *Interconnection Semantics for Keyword Search in XML.* The ACM 14th Conference on Information and Knowledge Management (CIKM), Bremen, Germany.

Cohen, S., & Mamou, J., & Sagiv, Y. (2003). *XSEarch: A Semantic Search Engine for XML.* The 29th Very Large Data Bases (VLDB) conference, Berlin, Germany.

CompTIA Electronics Industry Data Exchange (EIDX). (2004). *Replenishment scenario 4 - forecast-based supplier-managed inventory (SMI), V. 1.0.* Retrieved May 2004, from http://www.comptia.org/sections/eidx/business_process/replenishment/replmodl4.asp

Coox, S. V. (2003). Axiomatization of the Evolution of XML Database Schema. Programming and Computing Software, *29*(3), 140-146.

Costello, R., & Schneider, J. C. (2000). Challenge of XML Schemas - Schema Evolution. *The XML schemas: best practices.* Retrieved September, 2002, from http://www.xfront.org/EvolvableSchemas.html

Cragg, P., Mehrtens, J., & Mills, A. (2001). A model of Internet adoption by SMEs. *Information & Management, 39*, 165-176.

Curbera, F., & Epstein, D.A. (1999). Fast difference and update of XML documents. In *XTech.* San Jose, CA, USA.

Curbera, F., Ferguson, D.F., Nally, M., & Stockton, M.L. (2005). Toward a programming model for service-oriented computing. In *Proceedings of International Conference on Service Oriented Computing,* (pp. 33-47).

Curbera, F., Khalaf, R., Mukhi, N., Tai, S., & Weerawarana, S. (2003, October). The Next Step in Web Services. *Communications of the ACM, 46*(10).

da Luz, R. da, Halfeld Ferrari, M., & Musicante, M. A. (2007). Regular Expression Transformations to Extend Regular languages (with Application to a Datalog XML Schema Validator). *Journal of algorithms, 62*(3-4), 148-167.

Daconta, M.C., Obrst, L.J., & Smith, K.T. (2003). *The Semantic Web – a Guide to the Future of XML, Web Services, and Knowledge Management.* Indianapolis, USA: Wiley & Sons.

Daly, O., & Taniar, D. (2004). Exception rules mining based on negative association rules. In *Computational science and applications* (LNCS 3046, pp. 543-552). Heidelberg, Germany: Springer-Verlag.

Dantsin, E., & Voronkov, A. (1999). A nondeterministic polynomial-time unification algorithm for bags, sets and trees. In Proceedings of *the Second International Conference on Foundations of Software Science and Computation Structure 1999,* (pp. 180-196).

David, L., Jun, P., Kincho, H. L., & Gio, W. (2004). Efficient Integration of Web Services with Distributed Data Flow and Active Mediation. In M. Janssen (Ed.), *ACM International Conference Proceeding Series: Vol. 60. Proceedings of the 6th international conference on Electronic commerce.* (pp. 11-20). New York, NY: ACM.

Davis, F. D. (1989). Perceived usefulness, perceived ease of use, and user acceptance in information technology. *MIS Quarterly, 13*(3), 319-339.

Davis, T. (1998). *The role of government in a disaster.* The Disaster Handbook 1998 National Edition Institute of Food and Agricultural Sciences. Chapter 3, Section 3.7: University of Florida.

Debreceny, R. S., Chandra, A., Cheh, J. J., Guithues-Amrhein, D., Hannon, N. J., Hutshison, P. D., Janvrin, D., Jones, R. A., Lamberton, B., Lymer, A., Mascha, M., Nehmer, R., Roohani, S., Srivastava, R. P., Travelsi, S., Tribunella, T., Trites, G., & Vasarhelyi, M. A. (2005). Financial reporting in XBRL on the SEC's EDGAR system: A critique and evaluation. *Journal of Information Systems, 19*(2), 191-210.

Dekeyser, S., Hidders, J., and Paredaens, J. (2003). A Transactional Model for XML Databases. *World Wide Web, 7*(1), 29-57. Kluwer Academic.

Denny M. (2002). Ontology Building: A Survey of Editing Tools. *O'Reilly XML.COM.* Retrieved from: http://www.xml.com/2002/11/06/Ontology_Editor_Survey.html

Deshmukh, A. (2004). XBRL. *Communications of the Association for Information Systems, 13,* 196-219.

Deutsch, A., Sui, L., & Vianu, V. (2004). Specification and verification of data-driven web services. In *Proceedings of Symposium in Principles of Database 2004,* (pp. 71–82).

Devonish-Mills, L. (2007). Updates on XBRL and SOX. *Strategic Finance, 99*(9), 14-16.

Dick, B. (1990). *Convergent Interviewing.* Brisbane: Interchange.

Dietz, J. L. (1999). Understanding and modelling business processes with DEMO. In *Proceedings of Conceptual Modeling - ER '99, LNCS* (Vol. 1728, pp. 188-202).

Dietz, J. L. G. (2002). The atoms, molecules, and matter of the organizations. In *Proceedings of the 7th International Workshop on the Language Action Perspective on Communication Modeling (LAP 2002).*

Ding, O., Ricords, K., & Lumpkin, J. (2003). Deriving general association rules from XML data. *Proceedings of the ACIS 4th International Conference on Software Engineering, Artificial Intelligence, Networking and Parallel/Distributed Computing (SNPD'03)* (pp. 348-352).

DiPiazza, S. A. J., & Eccles, R. G. (2002). *Building Public Trust: The Future of Corporate Reporting.* New York: John Wiley & Sons, Inc.

Doolin, B., & Troshani, I. (2004). XBRL: A research note. *Qualitative Research in Accounting & Management, 1*(2), 93-104.

Doolin, B., & Troshani, I. (2007). Organizational adoption of XBRL. *Electronic Markets: The International Journal, 17*(3), 199-209.

Duarte, D. (2005). *Une méthode pour l'évolution de schémas XML préservant la validité des documents.* Unpublished doctoral dissertation, University of Tours, Tours - France.

Dupont, P. (1996). Incremental Regular Inference. In ICGI 1998: *Third International Colloquium on Grammatical Inference* (pp. 222-237), Montpellier, France, proceedings. Berlin: Springer-Verlag.

Eclipse. (2004). *Eclipse modeling framework*. Retrieved August 2004, from http://www.eclipse.org/emf/

El-Khatib, K., & Bochmann, G. v. (2003, December). *Profiles in Content Adaptation*. Technical report. University of Ottawa, Canada.

El-Khatib, K., Zhang, Z. E., Hadibi, N. & Bochmann, G. v. (2004). Personal and Service Mobility in Ubiquitous Computing Environments. *Journal of Wireless communications and Mobile Computing, 4*(6), 595-607.

Elliot, S. (2002). Research model and theoretical implications. In S. Elliot (Ed.), *Electronic Commerce B2C Strategies and Models* (pp. 291-326). Brisbane: John Wiley & Sons, Ltd.

Emory, C. W., & Cooper, D. R. (1991). *Business Research Methods*. Homewood: Irwin.

Eriksson, H., & Penker, M. (2000) *Business modeling with UML: Business patterns at work*. New York: John Wiley & Sons.

Erl, T. (2004). *Service-Oriented Architecture. A Field Guide to Integrating XML and Web Services*. Pearson Education, Inc. ISBN: 0-13-142898-5

Erl, T. (2004). *Service-oriented architecture: a field guide to integrating XML and Web services*. Upper Saddle River, NJ: Prentice Hall.

Ewing, I. (2007). *SBR & The national statistical system*. Paper presented at the SBR/XBRL International Conference, Brisbane, 27-28 November.

Falcone, F., & Garito, M. (2006). *Mobile Strategy Roadmap*. In B. Unhelkar (Ed.), *Handbook Resources of Mobile Business*. Herhsey, PA USA: Idea Group. ISBN: 1591408172

Feng, L., Dillon, T., Wiegand, H., & Chang, E. (2003). An XML-enabled association rules framework. In *Proceedings of International Conference on Database and Expert Systems Applications (DEXA 2003)* (LNCS 2736, pp. 88-97). Heidelberg, Germany: Springer-Verlag.

Fermantle, P. (2002). Enterprise services: Examining the emerging field of Web services and how it is integrated into existing enterprise infrastructures. *Communications of the ACM, 45*(10), October.

Ferrara, A. (2004). Web services: A process algebra approach. In *The Proceedings of the 2nd International Conference on Service Oriented Computing (ICSOC 2004)*. ACM.

Fillis, I., Johannson, U., & Wagner, B. (2004). Factors impacting on E-business adoption and development in the smaller firm. *International Journal of Entrepreneurial Behaviour & Research, 10*(3), 178-191.

Finkelsteing, C. (2006). *Enterprise Architecture for Integration. Rapid Delivery Methods and Technology*. British Library Catalogue in Publication Data. ISBN: 1-58053-713-8

FIPA (Foundation for Intelligent Physical Agents). (2002). *FIPA Communicative Act Library Specification*. Retrieved September 2003, from http://www.fipa.org/specs/fipa00037/.

Fisher, B., Agelidis, G., Dill, J., Tan, P., Collaud, G., & Jones, C. (1997). CZWeb: Fish-Eye Views for Visualizing the World-Wide Web. In *Proceeding of the 7th Int. Conf. on Human-Computer Interaction (HCI International '97)* (pp. 719-722). Elsevier, Amsterdam.

Floyd, R., & Housel, B. (1998). Mobile Web Access Using eNetwork Web Express. *IEEE Personal Communications, 5*(5), 47–52.

Fowler, M., & Scott, K. (1998). *UML Distilled: Applying the Standrad Object Modeling Language*. Addison-Wesley.

Fox, A., Gribble, S.D., & Chawathe, Y. (1998). Adapting to Network and Client Variation Using Infrastructural Proxies: Lessons and Perspectives. (1998). *IEEE Personal Communications, 5*(4) 10–19. Springer Berlin/Heidelberg.

Fox, A., Gribble, S.D., Chawathe, Y., Brewer, E.A., & Gauthier, P. (1997). Cluster-Based Scalable Network Services. In *Proceeding of the 16th ACM Symp. On Operating Systems Principles* (pp. 78–91). Saint-Malo, France.

Frambach, R. T. (1993). An integrated model of organizational adoption and diffusion of innovations. *European Journal of Marketing, 27*(5), 22-41.

Ganek, A. G., & Corbi, T. A. (2003). The dawning of the autonomic computing era. *IBM Systems J., 42*(1), 5-18.

Garbellotto, G. (2006). Broaden your view on XBRL's representational capabilities. *Strategic Finance, 88*(4), 59-61.

Garbellotto, G. (2006). XBRL is to XML as lemonade is to lemons. *Strategic Finance, 88*(6), 59-61.

Garbellotto, G. (2006). Exposing enterprise data: XBRL GL, Web services, and Google, Part 1. *Strategic Finance, 88*(2), 59-61.

Garbellotto, G. (2007). 14th XBRL International Conference: An internal perspective. *Strategic Finance, 88*(7), 57-58.

Garbellotto, G. (2007). It's time for GL-enabled software. *Strategic Finance, 88*(8), 55-56.

Garcia-Molina, H., Papakonstantinou, Y., Quass, D., Rajaraman, A., Sagiv, Y., Ullman, Y. D., Vassalos, V., & Widom, J. (1997). The TSIMMIS approach to mediation: Data models and languages. *Journal of Intelligent Information Systems, 8(2)*, 117-132.

Garcia-Molina, H.,Ullman, J.D., & Widom, J.D. (2005). *Database systems: the complete book*. Prentice-Hall.

Gardner, T. (2003). UML modelling of automated business processes with a mapping to BPEL4WS. In *First European Workshop on Object Orientation and Web Services (EOOWS).*

Garey, M.R., & Johnson, D.S. (1979). *Computers and intractability*. San Francisco: W.H. Freeman.

Garofalakis, M. N., Rastogi, R., Seshadri, S., & Shim, K. (1999). Data mining and the Web: Past, present and future. *Proceedings of the 2nd Workshop on Web Information and Data Management (WIDM 1999)* (pp. 43-47).

Gedda, R. (2007). ABS moves on business reporting standard. Retrieved 19 December, 2007, from http://www.computerworld.com.au/index.php?id=1395576549&eid=-6787

Gerst, M., & Bunduchi, R. (2005). Shaping IT standardization in the automotive industry - The role of power in driving portal standardization. *Electronic Markets: The International Journal, 15*(4), 335-343.

Ghanbary, A. (2006). Collaborative Business Process Engineering across Multiple Organizations. A Doctoral Consortium. *Proceedings of ACIS 2006*. Australia: Adelaide.

Ghelli, G., Re, C., & Simeon, J. (2006). XQuery!: An XML query language with side effects. In *International Workshop on Database Technologies for Handling XML Information on the Web* (pp. 178-191). Lecture Notes in Computer Science, vol. 4254, Springer-Verlag.

Gilbert, D., Balestrini, P., & Littleboy, D. (2004). Barriers and benefits in the adoption of E-government. *The International Journal of Public Sector Management, 17*(4), 286-301.

Girardot, M., & Sundaresan, N. (2000, May). Millau: An encoding format for efficient representation and exchange of XML over the Web. In *Ninth International World Wide Web Conference*, Amsterdam (pp. 747-765).

Godbole, N. (2006). *Relating Mobile Computing to Mobile Commerce*. In B. Unhelkar (Ed.), *Handbook Resources of Mobile Business*. Herhsey, PA USA: Idea Group.. ISBN: 1591408172

Gogan, J. L. (2005). Punctuation and path dependence: Examining a vertical IT standard-setting process. *Electronic Markets: The International Journal, 15*(4), 344-354.

Goldkuhl, G., & Lind, M. (2004). Developing e-Iteractions — A framework for business capabilities and exchanges. In *Proceedings of the 12th European Conference on Information Systems (ECIS-2004).*

Graham, P. (1995). *ANSI common LISP*. Prentice-Hall.

Grant, A. E. (2004). Sharpening the videoconference target. Retrieved 26 January, 2004, from http://www.tfi.com/pubs/ntq/articles/view/98Q2_A1.html

Gray, J.N. (1998). *Notes on Database Operating Systems* (RJ 2188). IBM Research Lab, California, USA.

Grigorova, V. (2006). Semantic Description of Web Services and Possibilities of BPEL4WS. *Information Theories and Application, 13*, 183-187.

GSA., U.G.S.A., (2004). *Government Smart Card Handbook.*

Guba, E. G., & Lincoln, Y. S. (1994). Competing paradigms in qualitative research. In N. Denzin, K. & Y. S. Lincoln (Eds.), *Handbook of Qualitative Research.* London: Sage Publications.

Guerrini, G., Mesiti, M., & Rossi, D. (2005). Impact of XML Schema Evolution on Valid Documents. *In WIDM'05: 7th annual ACM international workshop on web information and data management,* (pp. 39-44), Bremen, Germany, proceedings. New York, USA: ACM Press.

Gummesson, E. (2000). *Qualitative Methods in Management Research* (2nd ed.). Thousand Oaks: Sage.

Guruge. A. (2004). *Web services theory and practice.* Burlington, MA: Elsevier Digital Press.

Guttman, E., Perkins, C., Veizades, J., & Day, M. (1999). Service Location Protocol. Version 2. http://ietf.org/rfc/rfc2608.txt.

Hafid, A., & Bochmann, G.v., (1996). Quality of Service Negotiation in News-on-Demand Systems: an Implementation. In *Proceedings of the Third International Workshop on Protocols for Multimedia Systems* (pp. 299-315). Springer Berlin/Heidelberg.

Haller, A., Cimpian, E., Mocan, A., Oren, E., & Bussler, C. (2005). WSMX - a semantic service-oriented architecture. *In Proceedings Intl. Conference on Web Services ICWS 200 5,* (pp. 321-328).

Han, R., Bhagwat, P., LaMaire, R., Mummert, T., Perret, V., & Rubas, J. (1998). Dynamic adaptation in an image trans-coding proxy for mobile WWW browsing. *IEEE Personal Communication, 5*(6).

Hannon, N. (2003). XBRL for general ledger, the journal taxonomy. *Strategic Finance, 85*(2), 63, 67.

Hannon, N. (2006). Why the SEC is bullish on XBRL. *Strategic Finance, 87*(7), 59-61.

Hannon, N. J. (2006). Does XBRL cost too much? *Strategic Finance, 87*(10), 59-60.

Hannon, N. J. (2006). In search of ROI for XBRL. *Strategic Finance, 87*(9), 59-60.

Hannon, N. J., & Gold, R. J. (2005). XBRL revisited. *Journal of Accountancy Online, February.*

Harrison, A., & Taylor, J. I. (2005). WSPeer - An Interface to Web Service Hosting and Invocation. *Proceedings of the 19th IEEE International Parallel and Distributed Processing Symposium (IPDPS'05).* ISBN: 1530-2075/05

Hasegawa, M., Sakata, T., Sambuichi, N., & Hannon, N. (2003). Breathing new life into old systems. *Strategic Finance, 85*(9), 46-51.

Healy, M., & Perry, C. (2000). Comprehensive criteria to judge validity and reliability of qualitative research within the realism paradigm. *Qualitative Market Research: An International Journal, 3*(3), 118-126.

Hewlett-Packard Development Company (2005). Jena Semantic Web Framework Web site. Retrieve from http://jena.sourceforge.net/

Hjelm, J. (2001). *Creating the semantic web with RDF: Professional developer's guide.* New York: Wiley.

Hodge, F. D., Kennedy, J. J., & Maines, L. A. (2004). Does search-facilitating technology improve the transparency of financial reporting? *The Accounting Review, 79*(3), 687-703.

Hofreiter, B., & Huemer, C. (2004). ebXML business processes — Defined both in UMM and BPSS. In *Proceedings of the 1st GI-Workshop XML Interchange Formats for Business Process Management* (pp. 81-102).

Hofreiter, B., & Huemer, C. (2004). Transforming UMM business collaboration models to BPEL. In *International Workshop on Modeling InterOrganizational Systems (MIOS).*

Horrocks, I. (2002). Reasoning with Expressive Description Logics: Theory and Practice. In *Proceeding of the 18th International Conference on Automated Deduction (CADE 2002)* (pp. 1-15).

Hristidis, V., & Papakonstantinou, Y. (2002). *DISCOVER: Keyword search in Relational Databases.* The 28th Very Large Data Bases (VLDB) conference, Hong Kong, China.

http://www.ebizq.net/hot_topics/soa/features/5857.html?&pp=1.Downloaded: 12/10/2006

Huffman, D. A. (1952). A method for the construction of minimum-redundancy codes. *Proceedings of the Institute of Radio Engineers, 40*(9), 1098-1101.

INEX (2004). *Initiative for the Evaluation of XML Retrieval.* Retrieved from: http://inex.is.informatik.uni-duisburg.de:2004/

Ivica, C., & Magnus, L. (2002). Challenges of component-based development. *Journal of Systems and Software, 61*(3), 201-212.

Jablonski, S., & Bussler, C. (1996). *Workflow management: Modeling concepts, architecture and implementation.* London: International Thompson Computer Press.

Jacob, J., Sachde, A., & Chakravarthy, S. (2005). CX-DIFF: a change detection algorithm for XML content and change visualization for WebVigiL. *Data & Knowledge Engineering, 52*(2), 209–230.

Jacquot, J. N. (2003). Application Note 104: Smart Cards. Exfo Photonic White Paper.

Jagadish, H. V., & Patel, J. M. (2006). TIMBER. *University of Michigan.* Retrieved from: http://www.eecs.umich.edu/db/timber/

Jea, K.-F, Chen, S.-Y, & Wang, S.-H (2002). Concurrency Control in XML Document Databases: XPath Locking Protocol. In *International Conference on Parallel and Distributed Systems* (pp. 551-556). IEEE CS Press.

Jhingran, A.D., Mattos, D., & Pirahesh, N.H. (2002). Information Integration: A research agenda. *IBMSystem Journal,* 41(4) , 55-62.

JINI network technology (TM) (1998). Http: //java.sun.com/product/JINI

Jones, A., & Willis, M. (2003). The challenge for XBRL: Business reporting for the investor. *Balance Sheet, 11*(3), 29-37.

Jostad, I., Dustdar, S., & Thanh, D. V. (2005). A Service Oriented Architecture Framework for Collaborative Services. *Proceedings of the 14th IEEE International Workshops on Enabling Technologies: Infrastructure for Collaborative Enterprise.* ISBN ~ ISSN:1524-4547, 0-7695-2362-5

Juneja, G. (2005). XML Validation Benchmark. *Sarvega.* Retrieved from: http://www.sarvega.com

Kalakota, R., & Robinson, M. (2001). *E-business 2.0: Road-map for Success.* Harlow: Addison-Wesley.

Kangasharju, J., Tarkoma, S., & Lindholm, T. (2005, November). Xebu: A binary format with schema-based optimizations for XML data. In *Proceedings of the International Conference on Web Information Systems Engineering,* New York (pp. 528-535).

Kapur, D., & Narendran, P. (1992). Complexity of unification problems with associative-commutative operators. *Journal of Automatic Reasoning, 9*(2), 122-140.

Karastoyanova, D., Wetzstein, B., van Lessen, T., Wutke, D., Nitzsche, J., & Leymann, F. (2007). Semantic Service Bus: Architecture and Implementation of a Next Generation Middleware. *In Proceedings of the Second International Workshop on Service Engineering SEIW 2007,* (pp. 347-354).

Katchabaw, M., Lutfiyya, H., & Bauer, M. (1998). *Driving resource management with application-level quality of service specifications,* (pp. 83-91) ACM Press.

Katz, H. (2005). XQEngine version 0.69. *Fatdog Software.* Retrieved from http://www.fatdog.com/. The engine downloaded from: http://sourceforge.net/projects/xqengine

King, E. (1996). The use of self in qualitative research. In J. Richardson (Ed.), *Handbook of Qualitative Research Methods for Psychology and Social Sciences.* Leicester: BPS Books.

Klein, M. (2001). XML, RDF, and relatives. *IEEE Intelligent Systems, 16*(2), 26-28.

Knublauch, H., & Musen, M., & Rector, A. (2002). *Editing Description Logic Ontologies with the Protégé OWL Plugin.* Technical discussion for logicians, Stanford University, CA.

Koehler, J., Hauser, R., Kapoor, S., Wu, F., & Kumaran, S. (2003). A model-driven transformation method. In *Seventh International Enterprise Distributed Object Computing (EDOC 2003).*

KPMG. (2005). Step-by-step XBRL 2.0 Tutorial. Retrieved 21 February, 2005, from http://www.kpmg.com/xbrl/kkb.asp

Krafzig, D., Banke, K., & Slama, D. (2004). *Enterprise SOA: Service-oriented architecture best practices* (The Coad Series). Upper Saddle River, NJ: Prentice Hall.

Kuikka, E., Leinonen, P., & Penttonen, M. (2000). An Approach to Document Structure Transformations. In M.-C. G. Yulin Feng & D. Notkin (Eds.), *Conference on software: Theory and practice* (pp. 906-913), Beijin, China, proceedings. Dordrecht, Netherlands: Kluwer.

Kull, J. L., Miller, L. E., St. Clair, J. A., & Savage, M. (2007). Interactive data - XBRL: a revolutionary idea. *Journal of Government Financial Management, 56*(2), 10-14.

Kung, H.T., and Robinson, J.T. (1981). On Optimistic Methods for Concurrency Control. *Transactions on Database Systems, 6*(2), 213-226. ACM Press.

La Fontaine, R. (2001). A Delta Format for XML: Identifying changes in XML and representing the changes in XML. In *XML Europe.* Berlin, Germany.

Laurent, M., Denilson, B., & Pierangelo, V. (2003). The XML Web: A first study. *Proceedings of the International WWW Conference* (pp. 500-510).

Lei Z., & Georganas N.D. (2001). Context-based Media Adaptation in Pervasive Computing. On *Proceeding Can.Conf. on Electr. and Comp. Engg.* (pp. 913-918). Toronto, Canada.

Lenzerini, M. (2002). Data integration: A theoretical perspective. *In Proceedings Principles of Database Systems Conference PODS'02,* (pp. 233-246).

Levenshtein, V. I. (1966). Binary codes capable of correcting deletions, insertions, and reversals. *Cybernetics and Control Theory 10,* (pp. 707–710).

Li, S-H., Huang, S-M., Yen, D. C., & Chang, C-C. (2006). Migrating Legacy Information Systems to Web Services Architecture. *Journal of Database Management, 18*(4), 1-25.

Li, Y., & Yu, C., & Jagadish, H. (2004). *Schema-Free XQuery.* The 30th Very Large Data Bases (VLDB) conference, Toronto, Canada.

Liefke, H., & Suciu, D. (2000). XMill: An efficient compressor for XML data. In *Proceedings of the 2000 ACM SIGMOD International Conference on Management of Data,* Dallas, TX (pp. 153-164).

Lind, M., & Goldkuhl, G. (2001). Generic layered patterns for business modelling. In *Proceedings of the Sixth International Workshop on the Language-Action Perspective on Communication Modelling (LAP 2001)* (pp. 21-22).

Litronic, S. (2003). *Introduction to smart cards: A White Paper.* Retrieved September 2005, from www.litronic.com

Liu, E., & Kumar, A. (2003). Leveraging information sharing to increase supply chain configurability. In *Proceedings of The Twenty-Fourth International Conference on Information Systems.*

Locke, J., & Lowe, A. (2007). XBRL: An (open) source of enlightenment or disillusion? *European Accounting Review, 16*(3), 585-623.

Lukácsy, G., Benkő, T., & Szeredi, P. (2007). Towards Automatic Semantic integration. In *3rd International Conference of Interoperability for Enterprise Software and Applications (I-ESA 2007).*

Lum, W.Y., & Lau, F.C.M. (2002) On Balancing Between Trans-coding Overhead and Spatial Consumption in

Content Adaptation. *Mobicom 2002*, (pp. 239 - 250). Atlanta, USA.

Maheshwari, P., Tang, H., & Liang, R. (2004). Enhancing web services with message-oriented middleware. In *Proceedings of IEEE International Conference on Web Services 2004*, (pp. 524–531).

Marian, A., Abiteboul, S., Cobena, G., & Mignet, L. (2001). Change-Centric Management of Versions in an XML Warehouse. In *Proc. of 27th Int. Conference on Very Large Data Bases (VLDB'01)*, September 11-14, 2001, Roma, Italy, (pp. 581–590). Morgan Kaufmann.

Markus, M. L. (1987). Toward a critical mass theory of interactive media: Universal access, interdependence, and diffusion. *Communication Research, 14*(5), 491-511.

Markus, M. L. (1990). Toward a "critical mass" theory of interactive media. In J. Fulk & C. W. Steinfield (Eds.), *Organization and Communication Technology*. Newbury Park, CA: Sage.

Marshall, C., & Rossman, G. B. (1995). *Designing Qualitative Research* (2nd ed.). Newbury Park: Sage Publications.

Martelli, A., & Montanari, U.(1982). An effcient unification algorithm. *ACM Transactions on Programming Languages*, *4*(2), 258– 282.

Martin F. (2002). *Patterns of Enterprise Application Architecture.* Addison-Wesley Professional Press: USA.

Masek, W.J., & Paterson, M. (1980). A Faster Algorithm Computing String Edit Distances. *Journal of Computer and System Sciences, 20*(1), 18–31.

Maykut, P., & Morehouse, R. (1994). *Beginning Qualitative Research: A Philosophical and Practical Guide*: Burgess Science Press.

McBride, B. (2001). Jena: Implementing the RDF Model and Syntax Specification. In *Proceedings of the 2nd International Workshop on the Semantic Web*, Hong Kong, China.

Medina-Mora, R., Winograd, T., Flores, R., & Flores, F. (1992) The action workflow approach to workflow management technology. In *Proceedings of the 4th Conference on Computer Supported Cooperative Work.*

Medjahed, B., Benatallah, B., Bouguettaya, A., Ngu, A. H. H., & Ahmed, K.E. (2003). Business-to-business interactions: Issues and enabling technologies. *The VLDB Journal, 12(1)*, 2041-2046.

Mei, H., Cheng, F., Feng, Y., & Yang, J. (2003). ABC: An Architecture Based, Component Oriented Approach to Software Development. *Journal of Software, 14(4)*, 721-732.

Miller, J., & Mukerji, J. (2003). *Model Driven Architecture (MDA) Guide Version 1.0.1.* http://www.omg.org/docs/omg/03-06-01.pdf. Downloaded: 5/10/06

Mohan, R., Smith, J.R., & Li, C.S. (1999). Adapting Multimedia Internet Content for Universal Access. *IEEE Trans. on Multimedia, 1*(1), 104-114.

Moss, T.E.B. (1981). *Nested Transactions: An Approach to Reliable Distributed Computing.* Unpublished doctoral dissertation, MIT Laboratory for Computer Science, USA.

MPEG-21 (2001): International Standards Organisation. Information technology – multimedia framework (MPEG-21) – part 1: Vision, technologies and strategy. ISO/IEC 21000-1. Accessed on Jan 10, 2007.

MPEG-7. http://www.chiariglione.org/mpeg/standards/mpeg-7/mpeg-7.htm. Accessed on Jan 10, 2007.

Murata, M., Lee, D., & Mani, M. (2001, August). Taxonomy of XML schema languages using formal language theory. In *Proceedings of Extreme Markup Languages*, Montreal, Canada (pp. 153-166).

Myers, E.W. (1986). An O(ND) Difference Algorithm and Its Variations. *Algorithmica, 1*(2), 251–266.

Nair, G. S., & Riege, A. M. (1995). *Using convergent interviewing to develop the research problem of a postgraduate thesis.* Paper presented at the Marketing Education and Researchers International Conference, Gold Coast, Queensland.

Narayanan, S., & McIlraith, S.A. (2002). Simulation, verification and automated composition of web services. In *Proceedings of World Wide Web Conference 2002,* (pp. 77–88).

Nayak, R. (2005). Discovering knowledge from XML documents. In J. Wong (Ed.), *Encyclopedia of data warehousing and mining* (pp. 372-376). Hershey, PA: Idea Group Reference.

Nayak, R., Witt, R., & Tonev, A. (2002). Data mining and XML documents. *Proceedings of the 2002 International Conference on Internet Computing* (pp. 660-666).

Newcomer, E. (2002). *Understanding Web services XML, WSDL, SOAP, and UDDI.* Indianapolis, IN: Addison Wesley.

Newcomer, E., & Lomow, G. (2004). *Understanding SOA with Web services.* Indianapolis, IN: Addison Wesley.

Ng, C.W., Tan, P.Y., & Cheng, H. (2001). *Quality of Service Extension to IRML.* IETF INTERNET-DRAFT, 'draft-ng-opes-irmlqos-00.txt'.

Nguyen, B., Abiteboul, S., Cobena, G., & Preda, M. (2001). Monitoring XML Data on the Web. In *SIGMOD Conference.* Santa Barbara, CA, USA.

Niedermeier, U., Heuer, J., Hutter, A., Stechele, W., & Kaup, A. (2002, August). An MPEG-7 tool for compression and streaming of XML data. In *Proceedings of the IEEE International Conference on Multimedia and Expo*, Lausanne, Switzerland (pp. 521-524).

OASIS (1999). *Electronic business using eXchange markup language (ebXML).* Retrieved 2001, from http://www.ebxml.org

OASIS ebXML CPP/A Technical Committee (1999). *Collaboration-protocol profile and agreement specification, Versión 2.0.* Retrieved from http://www.ebxml.org/specs/

Oberle, D., Staab, S., Studer, R., & Volz, R. (2005). Supporting application development in the semantic web. *ACM Transactions on Internet Technology, 5*(2), 328-358.

Object Management Group. (2003). *Model-driven architecture (MDA) guide, Versión 1.0.1.* Retrieved May 20, 2004, from http://www.omg.org/mda

Orriens, B., Yang, J., & Papazoglou, M. (2003). A Framework for Business Rule Driven Web Service Composition. Jeusfeld, M.A. & Pastor, O. (Eds.), *In Proceedings ER'2003 Workshops, LNCS 2814,* (pp. 52-64). Heidelberg, Germany: Springer-Verlag.

Osamu, T. (Ed.). (2003). *Exploring WebSphere Studio Application Developer Integration Edition V5, IBM RedBook SG24-6200-00.* USA: IBM.

Parasuraman, A. (2000). Technology readiness index (TRI): A multiple-item scale to measure readiness to embrace new technologies. *Journal of Service Research, 2*(4), 307-320.

Parekh, R., & Honavar, V. (2001). Learning DFA From Simple Examples. *Machine learning, 44*(1-2), 9-35.

Pasley, J. (2005, May/June). How BPEL and SOA are changing Web services development. *Internet Computing, IEEE, 9*(3), 60-67. Digital Object Identifier 10.1109/MIC.2005.56

Passin, T. B. (2004). *Explorer's guide to the semantic web.* Greenwich, CT: Manning Publications.

Paterson, M.S., & Wegman, M.N.(1978). Linear unification. *Journal of Computer and System Sciences, 16*(1), 181-186.

Patton, M. Q. (1990). *Qualitative Evaluation and Research Methods* (2nd ed.). London: Sage Publications.

Payne, T. and Lassila, O. (2004). Semantic Web Services. *IEEE Intelligent Systems*, 19(4), 14-15.

Peltier, M., Bezivin, J, & Guillaume, G. (2001). MTRANS: A general framework, based on XSLT, for model transformations. *In Proceedings of the Workshop on Transformations in UML WTUML'01.* Retrieved 21 July 2008 from: http://citeseer.ist.psu.edu/581336.html

Phenix, P. (2004). *XBRL: Exchanges & Regulators.* Paper presented at the 9th International XBRL Conference, Auckland New Zealand.

Pinsker, R. (2003). XBRL awareness in auditing: a sleeping giant? *Managerial Auditing Journal, 18*(9), 732-736.

Pires, P.F., Mattoso, M.L.Q., and Benevides, M.R.F. (2003). Building Reliable Web Services Compositions. In *Web, Web-Services, and Database Systems* (pp. 59-72). Lecture Notes in Computer Science, vol. 2593, Springer-Verlag.

Poellabauer, C., Abbasi, H., & Schwan, K. (2002). Cooperative run-time management of adaptive applications and distributed resources. In *Proceeding of the Tenth ACM Internationalconference on Multimedia,* (pp. 402-411) ACM Press.

Powers, S. (2003). *Practical RDF.* Sebastopol, CA: O'Reilly.

Pu, C., & Leff, A. (1992). Autonomous Transaction Execution with Epsilon-serializability. In *RIDE Workshop on Transaction and Query Processing* (pp. 2 -11).

Pu, K.Q., Hristidis,V., & Koudas, N.(2006). Syntactic rule based approach to web service composition. In Proceedings of *International Conference on Data Engineering 2006,* (pp. 31–43).

Pyman, T. (2004). XBRL ready or not. *Charter,* 54-55.

R'emy, D. (1989). Type checking records and variants in a natural extension of ML. In *Proceedings of Symposium on Principles of Programming Languages 1989,* (pp. 77–88).

R'emy, D. (1994). Type inference for records in a natural extension of ML. In Proceedings of *Theoretical Aspects of Computer Software 1994,* (pp. 67-95).

RDF Core Working Group. *Resource description framework.* Available at http://www.w3.org/RDF

Reimers, K., & Li, M. (2005). Antecedents of a transaction cost theory of vertical IS standardization processes. *Electronic Markets: The International Journal, 15*(4), 301-312.

Reynaud, C., Sirot, J.P., & Vodislav, D. (2001). Semantic Integration of XML Heterogeneous Data Sources. *In Proceedings IDEAS Conference 2001,* (pp. 199–208).

Rezaee, Z., Elam, R., & Sharbatoghilie, A. (2001). Continuous auditing: The audit of the future. *Managerial Auditing Journal, 16*(3), 150-158.

Richards, A., Rogers, G., Witana, V., & Antoniades, M. (1998). Mapping user level QoS from a single parameter. In *Second IFIP/IEEE International Conference on Management of Multimedia Networks and Services.* (pp. 14-20). Versailles, France.

Richards, J., & Tibbits, H. (2002). *Understanding XBRL* (CPA Workshop Presentation Notes). New South Wales: CPA Australia, NSW Branch.

Rob, P., & Coronel, C. (2002). *Database systems: Design, implementation, & management.* Boston: Course Technology.

Roddick, J., Al-Jadir, L., Bertossi, L., Dumas, M., Estrella, F., Gregersen, H., et al. (2000). Evolution and Change in Data Management - Issues and Directions. *SIGMOD Record, 29*(1), 21-25.

Rogers, E. M. (1995). *Diffusion of Innovations* (4th ed.). New York, NY: The Free Press.

Roohani, S. J. (2003). *Trust and Data Assurances in Capital Markets: The Role of Technology Solutions.* Smithfield, RI: Bryant College & Pricewaterhouse Coopers.

Rosenberg, F., & Dustdar, S. (2005). Business Rules Integration in BPEL - A Service-Oriented Approach. *In Proceedings 7th International IEEE Conference on E-Commerce Technology,* (pp. 476- 479).

RosettaNet Consortium. (1999) *RossetaNet.* Retrieved May 2001, from http://www.rosettanet.org/RosettaNet/Rooms/DisplayPages/LayoutInitial

Rougemont, M. d. (2003). The Correction of XML Data. In ISIP 2003: *The first franco-japanese workshop on information, search, integration and personalization* (pp. 1-17), Sapporo, Japan. Hokkaido, Japan: Hokkaido University Press.

Rouvellou, I., Degenaro, L., Rasmus, K., Ehnebuske, D., & McKee, B. (2000). Extending business objects with business rules. *In Proceedings 33rd Intl. Conference on Technology of Object-Oriented Languages*, (pp. 238-249).

RSS-DEV Working Group (2000). Resource Description Framework Site Summary (RSS) 1.0 Web site. Retrieved from http://web.resource.org/rss/1.0/

Russell, D. M., & Hoag, A. M. (2004). People and information technology in the supply chain: Social and organizational influences on adoption. *International Journal of Physical Distribution & Logistics Management, 34*(2), 102-122.

Rusu, L. I., Rahayu, W., & Taniar, D. (2005). Maintaining versions of dynamic XML documents. In *Proceedings of the 6th International Conference on Web Information System Engineering (WISE 2005)* (LNCS 3806, pp. 536-543). Heidelberg, Germany: Springer-Verlag.

Rusu, L. I., Rahayu, W., & Taniar, D. (2005). A methodology for building XML data warehouses. *International Journal of Data Warehousing and Mining, 1*(2), 67-92.

Sandoz, P., Triglia, A., & Pericas-Geertsen, S. (2004). *Fast infoset.* Retrieved December 20, 2006, from http://java.sun.com/developer/technicalArticles/xml/fastinfoset

Sankoff, D., & Kruskal, J. (1983). *Time warps, String Edits, and Macromolecules.* Addison-Wesley, Reading, Massachussets.

Sayood, K. (2000). *Introduction to data compression* (2nd ed.). San Francisco: Morgan Kaufmann Publishers.

Schaffert, S. (2004). *Xcerpt: A Rule-Based Query and Transformation Language for the Web.* PhD Thesis, University of Munich.

Schmidt, A. R., & Waas, F., & Kersten, M. L., & Florescu, D., & Manolescu, I., & Carey, M. J., & Busse, R. (2002). The XML Benchmark Project. *Technical Report INS-R0103, CWI.* Retrieved from: http://www.xml-benchmark.org/. The benchmark downloaded from http://monetdb.cwi.nl/xml/downloads.html

Searle, J. R. (1975). A taxonomy of illocutionary acts. In K. Gunderson (Eds.), *Language, mind and knowledge.* Minneapolis, MA: University of Minnesota.

Segoufin, L., & Vianu, V. (2002). Validating streaming XML documents. In *Proceedings of the 21st ACM SIGMOD-SIGACT-SIGART Symposium on Principles of Database Systems*, New York (pp. 53-64).

Sekaran, U. (2000). *Research Methods for Business: A Skill Building Approach.* New York: John Wiley and Sons.

Selic, B. (2003). The pragmatics of model-driven development. *IEEE Software, 20(5)*,19-25.

Selkow, S.M. (1977). The Tree-to-Tree Editing Problem. *Information Processing Letters, 6*(6), 184–186.

Seltsikas, P., & Currie, W.L. (2002). Evaluating the application service provider (ASP) business model: the challenge of integration. *In Proceedings 35th Annual Hawaii International Conference 2002.* 2801 – 2809.

Shasha, D., & Zhang, K. (1990). Fast Algorithms for the Unit Cost Editing Distance Between Trees. *Journal of Algorithms, 11*(4), 581–621.

Smith, J. R., Mohan, R., & Li, C.-S. (1999). Scalable Multimedia Delivery for Pervasive Computing. *ACM Multimedia*, (pp. 131 – 140). Orlando, Florida, United States.

Stal, M. (2002). Web Services: Beyond Component-based Computing. *Communications of the ACM, 45(10)*, 71-76.

Stern, A., & Davis, J. (2004). Extending the Web services model to IT services. *In Proceedings IEEE International Conference on Web Services*, (pp. 824-825).

Storer, J., & Szymanski, T. (1982). Data compression via textural substitution. *Journal of the ACM, 29*(4), 928-951.

Su, H., Kramer, D., Chen, L., Claypool, K. T., & Rundensteiner, E. A. (2001). XEM: Managing the Evolution of XML Documents. In RIDE 2001: *Eleventh International Workshop on Research Issues in Data Engineering: Document Management for Data Intensive Business and Scientific Applications* (pp. 103-110). Heidelberg, Germany, proceedings. Piscataway, USA: IEEE Computer Society.

Su, H., Kuno, H., & Rundensteiner, E. A. (2001). Automating the Transformation of XML Documents. *In WIDM'01: 3rd annual ACM international workshop on web information and data management,* (pp. 68-75), Atlanta, USA, proceedings. New York, USA: ACM Press.

Subramanian, G. H. (1994). A replication of perceived usefulness and perceived ease of use measurement. *Decision Sciences, 25*(5/6), 863-874.

Sun Microsystems, Inc. (2005). Java 2 Platform, Standard Edition (J2SE) Web site. Retrieved from URL http://java.sun.com/j2se/

Szyperski, C. (2002). *Component Software: Beyond Object-Oriented Programming – 2nd Ed.* New York, USA: Addison-Wesley.

Taha, K., & Elmasri, R. (2007). *OOXSearch: A Search Engine for Answering Loosely Structured XML Queries Using OO Programming.* The 24th British National Conference on Databases (BNCOD), Glasgow, Scotland.

Tai, K. C. (1979). The Tree-to-Tree Correction Problem. *Journal of the ACM, 26*(3), 422–433.

Tartanoglu, F., Issarny, V., Romanovsky, A., & Levy, N. (2003). Coordinated Forward Error Recovery for Composite Web Services. In *22nd Symposium on Reliable Distributed Systems* (pp. 167-176). IEEE CS Press.

The ACM Digital Library. http://delivery.acm.org/10.1145/610000/606273/p54-lee.html?key1=606273&key2=4006199511&coll=GUIDE&dl=portal,ACM&CFID=11111111&CFTOKEN=2222222#lead-in. Downloaded: 5/10/2006.

The Internet Society (2005). Uniform Resource Identifier (URI) Generic Syntax. Retrieved from http://www.gbiv.com/protocols/uri/rfc/rfc3986.html

The open Group Integration Consortium. http://www.integrationconsortium.org/docs/W054final.pdf. Downloaded: 5/10/2006.

Tidd, J., Bessant, J., & Pavitt, K. (2001). *Managing Innovation: Integrating Technological, Market and Organizational Change.* Chichester: John Wiley & Sons Ltd.

Tjioe, H. C., & Taniar, D. (2005). Mining association rules in data warehouses. *International Journal of Data Warehousing and Mining, 1*(3), 28-62.

Tolani, P., & Haritsa, J. R. (2002, February). XGRIND: A query-friendly XML compressor. In *Proceedings of the International Conference on Data Engineering*, San Jose, CA (pp. 225-234).

Toman, V. (2004, June). Syntactical compression of XML data. In *Proceedings of the International Conference on Advanced Information Systems Engineering,* Riga, Latvia.

Tornatzky, L. G., & Fleischer, M. (1990). *Processes of Technological Innovation.* Lexington, Massachusetts: Lexington Books.

Troshani, I., & Doolin, B. (2005). Drivers and inhibitors impacting technology adoption: A qualitative investigation into the Australian experience with XBRL. In D. R. Vogel, P. Walden, J. Gricar & G. Lenart (Eds.), *Proceedings of the 18th Bled eCommerce Conference: eIntegration in Action.* June 6-8, 2005, Bled, Slovenia: Moderna Organizacija.

Troshani, I., & Doolin, B. (2007). Innovation diffusion: A stakeholder and social network view. *European Journal of Innovation Management, 10*(2), 176-200.

Turker, C., Haller, K., Schuler, C., & Schek, H.-J (2005). How can we support Grid Transactions? Towards Peer-to-Peer Transaction Processing. In *Biennial Conference on Innovative Data Systems Research* (pp. 174 -185).

UDDI.org. http://www.uddi.org/faqs.html. Downloaded: 12/10/2006

Ullman, J. (1997). *Elements of ML programming.* Prentice-Hall.

UN/CEFACT, & OASIS (2003). *ebXML business specification schema, Version 1.10.* Retrieved March 2004, from http://www.untmg.org/downloads/General/approved/

Unhelkar, B., & Deshpande, Y. (2004). Evolving from Web Engineering to Web Services: A Comparative study in the context of Business Utilization of the Internet. *Proceedings of ADCOM 2004, 12th International Con-*

ference on Advanced Computing and Communications, Ahmedabad, India, 15-18 December

Varga, L.Z., Hajnal, A., & Werner, Z. (2004). An Agent Based Approach for Migrating Web Services to Semantic Web Services. *Lecture Notes in Computer Science Vol. 3192*, Springer-Verlag GmbH, Heidelberg, Germany. In C. Bussler & D. Fensel (Eds.), *Artificial Intelligence: Methodology, Systems, and Applications 11th International Conference, AIMSA 2004*, Varna, Bulgaria, September 2-4, 2004, Proceedings, (pp. 371-380). ISBN-3-540-22959-0.

Varga, L.Z., Hajnal, Á., & Werner, Z. (2005). The WSDL2Agent Tool. In R. Unland, M. Klusch, & M. Calisti (Eds.), Software Agent-Based Applications, Platforms and Development Kits. Whitestein Series in Software Agent Technologies, (pp. 197-223). Viaduktstrasse 42, CH-4051 Basel, Switzerland, Springer Group, ISBN 3-7643-7347-4, 2005.

Vasiliu, L., Harand, S., & Cimpian, E. (2004). The DIP Project: Enabling Systems & Solutions For Processing Digital Content With Semantic Web Services. *EWIMT 2004 European Workshop on the Integration of Knowledge, Semantics and Digital Media Technology.*

Vidyasankar, K., & Vossen, G. (2004). Multi-level Model for Web Service Composition. In *International Conference on Web Services* (pp. 462-471). IEEE CS Press.

Villarreal, P. (2005). *Modeling and specification of collaborative business processes*. PhD Thesis. Santa Fe, Argentina: CERIDE.

Villarreal, P., Caliusco, M., Zucchini, D., Arredondo, F., Zanel, C., Galli, M. R., & Chiotti, O. (2003). Integrated production planning and control in a collaborative partner-to-partner relationship. In S. Sharma & J. Gupta (Eds.), *Managing e-business in the 21st century* (pp. 91-110). Victoria, Australia: Heidelberg Press.

Villarreal, P., Salomone, E, & Chiotti, O. (2005). Applying model-driven development to collaborative business processes. In *Proceedings Iberoamerican Workshop on Requirement Engineering and Sowftare Environments (IDEAS'05).*

Villarreal, P., Salomone, E., & Chiotti, O. (2003b). Managing public business processes in B2B relationships using B2B interaction protocols. *XXIX Conferencia Latinoamérica de Informática (CLEI 2003).*

Villarreal, P., Salomone, E., & Chiotti, O. (2003c). B2B relationships: Defining public business processes using interaction protocols. *Journal of the Chilean Society of Computer Science, Special Issue on the Best Papers of the JCC 2003, 4*(1). Retrieved November 2003, from http://www.dcc.uchile.cl/~mmarin/revista-sccc/sccc-web/volumen4-1.html

Voluntary Interindustry Commerce Standard (VICS). (2002). *Collaborative planning, forecasting, and replenishment - Voluntary guidelines, V 2.0.* Retrieved May 2004, from http://www.vics.org/committees/cpfr/voluntary_v2/

W3C – the World Wide Web Consortium. (2004). *The Semantic Web Initiative.* Retrieved March 9, 2008 from http://www.w3.org/2001/sw

W3C. Document type definition. Available (http://www.w3.org/TR/html4/sgml/dtd.html)

W3Consortium. http://www.w3.org/TR/wsdl. Downloaded; 12/10/2006

W3Consortium. http://www.w3.org/XML/. Downloaded: 12/10/2006

W3Schools (n.d.a). Extensible Markup Language (XML) Tutorial Web site. Retrieved from http://www.w3schools.com/xml/

W3Schools (n.d.b). Resource Description Framework (RDF) Tutorial Web site. Retrieved from http://www.w3schools.com/rdf/

Wagner, R.A., & Fischer, M.J. (1974). The String-to-String Correction Problem. *Journal of the ACM, 21*(1), 168–173.

Wallace, A. (2001). The new language of financial reporting. *Balance Sheet, 9*(2), 29-32.

Wan, J. W., & Dobbie, G. (2003). Extracting association rules from XML documents using XQuery. *Proceedings* of the 5th ACM International Workshop on Web Information and Data Management (WIDM'03)* (pp. 94-97).

Wan, J. W., & Dobbie, G. (2004). Mining association rules from XML data using XQuery. *Proceedings of International Conference on Research and Practice in Information Technology (CRPIT 2004)* (pp. 169-174).

Wand, M. (1987). Complete type inference for simple objects. In Proceedings of *IEEE Symposium on Logic in Computer Science 1987,* (pp. 37–44).

Wang, J. T.-L., Zhang, K., Jeong, K., & Shasha, D. (1994). A System for Approximate Tree Matching. *Knowledge and data engineering, 6*(4), 559-571.

Wang, Y., DeWitt, D. J., & Cai, J. Y. (2003). X-Diff: An effective change detection algorithm for XML documents. *Proceedings of the 19th International Conference on Data Engineering (ICDE 2003)* (pp. 519-530).

Wang, Y., DeWitt, D.J., & Cai, J. (2003). X-Diff: An Effective Change Detection Algorithm for XML Documents. In *Proc. of the 19th Int. Conference on Data Engineering,* March 5-8, 2003, Bangalore, India, (pp. 519–530).

Warren, M. (2004). Farmers online: Drivers and impediments in adoption of Internet in UK agricultural businesses. *Journal of Small Business and Enterprise Development, 11*(3), 371-381.

Weber, R. (2003). XML, XBRL, and the future of business and business reporting. In S. J. Roohani (Ed.), *Trust and Data Assurances in Capital Markets: The Role of Technology Solutions.* Smithfield, RI: Bryant College.

Weigand, H., Heuvel, W., & Dignum, F. (1998) Modelling electronic commerce transactions - A layered approach. In *Proceedings of the Third International Workshop on the Language Action Perspective (LAP'98).*

Werner, C., Buschmann, C., & Fischer, S. (2005). WSDL-driven SOAP compression. *International Journal of Web Services Research, 2*(1), 18-35.

Werner, C., Buschmann, C., Jäcker, T., & Fischer, S. (2006). Bandwidth and latency considerations for efficient SOAP messaging. *International Journal of Web Services Research, 3*(1), 49-67.

Widom, J. (1995). Research problems in data warehousing. *In Proceedings of 4th International Conference on Information and Knowledge Management,* (pp. 25-30).

Wiederhold, G. (1992). Mediators in the architecture of future information systems. *IEEE Computer, 25,* 38-49.

Wikipedia, Defining Authentication and Authorization, from http://en.wikipedia.org/wiki/authentication

Willis, M. (2005). XBRL and data standardization: Transforming the way CPAs work. *Journal of Accountancy, 199*(3), 80-81.

Willis, M., Tesniere, B., & Jones, A. (2003). *Corporate Communications for the 21st Century* (White Paper): PricewaterhouseCoopers.

WML: Wireless Markup Language (2001). *Wireless Markup Language (WML) 2.0 Document Type Definition.*

Wolfe, R. A. (1994). Organisational innovation: Review, critique, and suggested research directions. *Journal of Management Studies, 31*(3), 405-431.

World Wide Web Consortium (W3C) (2004). Resource Description Framework (RDF) Official Web site. Retrieved from URL http://www.w3.org/RDF/

World Wide Web Consortium (W3C) (2004). Resource Description Framework (RDF) Validation Service. Retrieved from http://www.w3.org/RDF/Validator/

World Wide Web Consortium (W3C) (2005). Extensible Markup Language (XML) Official Web site. Retrieved from http://www.w3.org/XML/

World Wide Web Consortium (W3C) (2005). World Wide Web Consortium (W3C). Retrieved from http://www.w3.org/

World Wide Web Consortium (W3C). (2004). *Web services choreography description language Version 1.0.* Retrieved May 2005, from http://www.w3.org/TR/2004/WD-ws-cdl-10-20041217/

World Wide Web Consortium (W3C). (2005). *Charter of the efficient XML interchange working group.* Retrieved December 20, 2006, from http://www.w3.org/2005/09/exi-charter-final.html

World Wide Web Consortium (W3C). (2005). *Working group note: XML binary characterization.* Retrieved December 20, 2006, from http://www.w3.org/TR/xbc-characterization

World Wide Web Consortium (W3C). (2007). *Working draft: Efficient XML interchange (EXI) format 1.0.* Retrieved January 22, 2008, from http://www.w3.org/TR/2007/WD-exi-20071219

World Wide Web Consortium (W3C). (n.d.). Retrieved February 2006, from http://www.w3c.org

WSDL: Web Service Description Language (2002). http://www.w3.org/TR/wsdl.

Wu, C. T. (2004). *An introduction to object-oriented programming with Java* (3rd ed.). New York: McGraw-Hill.

Wu, D., Hou, Y.T., & Zhang, Y. (2001). Scalable Video Coding and Transport over Broad-band Wireless Networks. *Proceeding of the IEEE, 89*(1), 6-20.

Wu, S., Manber, U., Myers, G., & Miller, W. (1990). An O(NP) Sequence Comparison Algorithm. *Information Processing Letters, 35*(6), 317–323.

Xalan. (2005). *The Apache Software Foundation: Apache XML project.* Retrieved December 2005, from http://xml.apache.org/xalan-j/

XBRLAustralia. (2004). XBRL Australia members. Retrieved 7 April, 2005, from http://www.xbrl.org.au/members/

XQuery. (2005). Retrieved February 2006, from http://www.w3.org/TR/2005/WD-xquery-20050915/

Xu, X., & Papakonstantinou, Y. (2005). *Efficient Keyword Search for Smallest LCAs in XML Databases.* SIGMOD International Conference on Management of Data, Baltimore, Maryland.

Yang, W. (1991). Identifying Syntactic differences Between Two Programs. *Software - Practice and Experience, 21*(7), 739–755.

Yin, R. K. (1994). *Case Study Research: Design and Methods.* Beverley Hills: Sage.

Zachman, J. A. (1987). A framework for information systems architecture. *IBM Systems Journal, 26*(3).

Zachman, J. A., & Sowa, J. F. (1992). Extending and formalizing the framework for information systems architecture. *IBM Systems Journal, 31*(3).

Zhang, K. (1996). A Constrained Edit Distance Between Unordered Labeled Trees. *Algorithmica, 15*(3), 205–222.

Zhang, K., Statman, R., & Shasha, D. (1992). On the Editing Distance Between Unordered Labelled Trees. *Information processing letters, 42*(3), 133-139.

Zhang, K., Wang, J.T.L., & Shasha, D. (1995). On the Editing Distance between Undirected Acyclic Graphs and Related Problems. In *Proc. of the 6th Annual Symposium on Combinatorial Pattern Matching,* (pp. 395–407).

Zhang, S., Dyreson, C.E., & Snodgrass, R.T. (2004). Schema-Less, Semantics-Based Change Detection for XML Documents. In *WISE 2004, Proc. of the 5th Int. Conference on Web Information Systems Engineering*, Brisbane, Australia, November 22-24, vol. 3306 of Lecture Notes in Computer Science, (pp. 279–290). Springer.

Zhang, Z., & Yang, H. (2004). Incubating Services in Legacy Systems for Architectural Migration. *In Proceedings 11th Asia-Pacific Software Engineering Conference APSEC'04*, (pp. 196-203).

Zhao, K., Xia, M., & Shaw, M. J. (2005). Vertical E-business standards and standards developing organisations: A conceptual framework. *Electronic Markets: The International Journal, 15*(4), 289-300.

Zhao, Q., Bhowmick, S. S., & Mandria, S. (2004). Discovering pattern-based dynamic structures from versions of unordered XML documents. In *Proceedings of International Conference on Data Warehousing and Knowledge Discovery (DaWaK 2004)* (LNCS 3181, pp. 77-86). Heidelberg, Germany: Springer-Verlag.

Zhao, Q., Bhowmick, S. S., Mohania, M., & Kambayashi, Y. (2004). Discovering frequently changing structures from historical structural deltas of unordered XML.

Proceedings of ACM International Conference on Information and Knowledge Management (CIKM'04) (pp. 188-197). Heidelberg, Germany: Springer Berlin.

Zhu, F., Turner, M., Kotsiopoulos, I., Bennett, K., Russell, M., Budgen, D., Brereton, P., Keane, J., Layzell, P., Rigby, M., & Xu, J. (2004). Dynamic Data Integration Using Web Services. *In Proceedings 2nd International Conference on Web Services ICWS'2004*, (pp. 262-269).

Zhu, Y. (2007). *Declarative Rule-based Integration and Mediation for XML Data in Web Service-based Software Architectures.* M.Sc. Thesis. Dublin City University.

Zikmund, W. G. (2000). *Business Research Methods* (6th ed.). Chicago: The Dryden Press.

About the Contributors

Patrick Hung is an associate professor and IT Director at the Faculty of Business and Information Technology in UOIT and an Adjunct Faculty Member at the Department of Electrical and Computer Engineering in University of Waterloo. Patrick is currently collaborating with Boeing Phantom Works (Seattle, USA) and Bell Canada on security- and privacy-related research projects, and he has filed two US patent applications on "Mobile Network Dynamic Workflow Exception Handling System." Patrick is also cooperating on Web services composition research projects with Southeast University in China. Recently he is working on a mobile healthcare project with the Hong Kong Red Cross with the Chinese University of Hong Kong. He is an executive committee member of the IEEE Computer Society's Technical Steering Committee for Services Computing, a steering member of EDOC "Enterprise Computing," and an associate editor/editorial board member/guest editor in several international journals such as the *IEEE Transactions on Services Computing (TSC), International Journal of Web Services Research (JWSR)* and *International journal of Business Process and Integration Management (IJBPIM).* He has been published more than 100 research and technical articles in international journals, conferences and workshops.

* * *

Talel Abdessalem is an associate professor at the Computer Science and Networks Department of Telecom ParisTech since 1998. He received a PhD degree in computer science from the University of Paris-Dauphine in 1997, and a master degree from the University of Paris II. His research interests cover several aspects of the web and database fields: data modeling, query languages, optimization, XML, data streams, spatio-temporal data, and uncertainty handling. He published many papers and supervised PhD students on these subjects. One of his actual research interests is data sharing in web communities, change detection and distributed access control.

Debmalya Biswas is currently a PhD student at IRISA/INRIA, France. He works for the Active XML project which explores interesting interdependencies between data and processes in a distributed environment. He has worked for Infosys Technologies Limited and Oracle Corporation developing software from August 2000 to August 2003. He received his MSc (computer science) degree from Memorial University of Newfoundland, Canada in 2005. His research interests include transactional and security related aspects of distributed systems, mainly Web Services and P2P systems.

Copyright © 2009, IGI Global, distributing in print or electronic forms without written permission of IGI Global is prohibited.

Gregor v. Bochmann is professor at the School of Information Technology and Engineering at the University of Ottawa since January 1998, after 25 years at the University of Montreal. He is a fellow of the IEEE and ACM and a member of the Royal Society of Canada. He did research on programming languages, compiler design, communication protocols, and software engineering and had many research projects in collaboration with industry. His present work is the area of software requirements engineering for distributed systems, quality of service and security management for distributed web-based applications, and control procedures for optical networks.

Béatrice Bouchou is an associate professor of Computer Science at Université François Rabelais Tours - LI, Campus Blois, in France, since 1999. Since 2007, she is the head of the professional undergraduate studies in Quality and Security in Information Systems (Licence professionnelle QSSI). She has got her PhD degree from Université de Franche-Comté (France) in 1995. Her main current research topics concern XML database theory: structural constraints and tree automata, updates, integrity constraints, XML design (application to natural language programming (NLP) resource specification).

Ning Chen is associated professor of computer software and theory, Xi'an polytechnic university in Xi'an. He received BS (1992) and MS (1996) degrees in microelectronics from Xi'an JiaoTong University, China. He received the PhD degree in computer software and theory from Xi'an JiaoTong University in 2006. Since 2007, he has been a faculty member of Xi'an polytechnic university. His research interests include software process modeling, process and workflow management, patterns and frameworks, requirements engineering, automated software specification, component-based software engineering, automated software design and synthesis. He received top prize for progress in electronic industry (970203) from ShaanXi Electronic Bureau in 1997.

Gregory Cobena is R&D Project Manager. He graduated from Ecole Polytechnique in 1998 and from Telecom ParisTech in 2000. He worked at INRIA from 2000 to 2003 with Serge Abiteboul and received a PhD in computer science and databases. The PhD thesis was about change-management for semi-structured data and in particular Web data. Until 2004 he worked in IT company "Xyleme" on a 'content mart' solution based on XML technologies. He was in charge of crucial R&D projects such as high-availability. He is currently responsible of Front-Office projects for financial derivatives in software company "Sophis".

Denio Duarte is an associate professor of Computer Science at the University of Chapecó (*Unochapecó*) and participates as an associate researcher of the Unochapecó Information Systems and Network Group. He received a PhD (2005) in computer science from the *Université François Rabelais Tours, in France*; and the master in Computer Science from *Universidade Federal do Paraná* (UFPR), *Curitiba*, PR, Brazil, in 2001. He is an active member of different research projects founded by the Brazilian agency FAPESC. His main research interests include tree language applied to XML, XML schema evolution, semi-structured databases and software engineering.

Abdulmotaleb El Saddik is university research chair and professor, SITE, University of Ottawa and recipient of the Professional of the Year Award (2008), the Friedrich Wilhelm-Bessel Research Award from Germany's Alexander von Humboldt Foundation (2007) the Premier's Research Excellence Award (PREA 2004), and the National Capital Institute of Telecommunications (NCIT) New Professorship

Incentive Award (2004). He is the director of the Multimedia Communications Research Laboratory (MCRLab). He is a Theme co-Leader in the LORNET NSERC Research Network. He is associate editor of the *ACM Transactions on Multimedia Computing, Communications and Applications (ACM TOMCCAP)* and *IEEE Transactions on Computational Intelligence and AI in Games* (IEEE TCIAIG) and Guest Editor for several IEEE Transactions and journals. Dr. El Saddik has been serving on several technical program committees of numerous IEEE and ACM events. He has been the general chair and/or technical program chair of more than 18 international conferences on collaborative hapto-audio-visual environments, multimedia communications and instrumentation and measurement. He is leading researcher in haptics, service-oriented architectures, collaborative environments and ambient interactive media and communications. He has authored and co-authored two

Khalil El-Khatib was an assistant professor at the University of Western Ontario prior to joining the Faculty of Business and Information Technology, University of Ontario Institute of Technology, in July 2006. He received a bachelor degree in computer science from the American University of Beirut (AUB) in 1992, a master degree in computer science from McGill University in 96, and a PhD degree from the University of Ottawa in 2005. Between the years of 1992 and 1994, he worked as a research assistant in the computer science Dept. at AUB. In 1996, he joined the High Capacity Division at Nortel Networks as a software designer. From Feb. 2002, he worked of research officer in the Network Computing Group (lately renamed the Information Security Group) at the National Research Council of Canada for two years, and continued to be affiliated with the group for another two years. His research interest includes security and privacy issues for the Internet and for mobile wireless ad hoc networks (MANET), ubiquitous computing environments, QoS for multimedia applications, personal and service mobility, IP telephony, feature interaction for VoIP, and Parallel Discrete Event Simulation.

Ramez Elmasri is professor of Computer Science and Engineering at The University of Texas at Arlington, USA since 1990. He completed his MS and PhD degrees in computer science at Stanford University –California, USA - in 1980. He has over 150 referred publications in journals and conference proceedings. He is the co-author of the textbook Fundamentals of Database Systems (5th edition, Addison-Wesley, 2007). Prof. Elmasri was an Assistant Professor from 1982 to 1987 and an Associate Professor from 1987 to 1990 at The University of Houston, Houston, Texas. He was a *Consultant* for the following companies: *Bell Communications Research*, Morristown, New Jersey (1990); *Bell Communications Research*, Piscataway, New Jersey (1989); *Rome Air Development Center*, Rome, New York (1987); *Honeywell Inc.*, Computer Sciences Center, Golden Valley, Minnesota (1982-1987). His research interests are in database systems, XML, network management information systems, web modeling and ontologies, e-commerce, temporal databases, conceptual modeling, object-oriented databases, distributed object computing, operating systems, systems integration, database models and languages, DBMS system implementation, indexing techniques, software engineering environments.

Mírian Halfeld Ferrari is an associate professor of Computer Science at *Université François Rabelais Tours- LI, Campus Blois,* France, since 1998. In 2007, Mírian obtained her HDR *(Habilitation à diriger des recherches)* degree from *Université François Rabelais Tours.* She received her PhD degree from *Université Paris-Sud* (XI) - LRI in 1996. Since 2007, she is the head of undergraduate studies in Computer Science (*Licence Informatique*). Her main current research topics are theoretical and dynamic aspects of XML databases, tree languages, tree automata and their applications on XML and web services.

Ákos Hajnal was born in Budapest, 1972. He was graduated at Budapest Technical University in 1996; studied electrical engineering. Since then he has been working at Computer and Automation Research Institute of the Hungarian Academy of Sciences (MTA SZTAKI), as research fellow. From 1997 to 2000 he was a Ph.D. student at Eötvös Lóránd University of Sciences, Budapest; he is currently working on his PhD thesis.

Tamás Kifor is a research assistant in the Computer and Automation Research Institute of the Hungarian Academy of Sciences (MTA SZTAKI). He also got a position from IT Consult-PRO (ITC), an IT shareholder group, to start the mobile devices unit of the company in 2006. He graduated in Maths and Computer Sciences from University of Debrecen. His work is focused on autonomous software agents, distributed systems and mobile developments especially in healthcare and library systems.

IL-GON KIM is currently working for KISA (Korea Information Security Agency) as a researcher since 2007 and evaluates security products such as web-application firewalls, IDS, IPS, secure OS based on Common Criteria (CC). He was a post-doc researcher in the DISTRIBCOMM group at INRIA Rennes during November 2005 ~ November 2006. In the Active XML project, he analyzed its security aspect potentially caused by embedded service calls in AXML document, by applying model checking. He was also a research professor of Computer Science and Engineering of Korea University during March 2005 ~ November 2005. He received MSc and PhD degrees from Korea University. His research interests include common criteria, security engineering, network security, security protocol, web services, formal methods, process algebra.

Gergely Lukácsy got his MSc in computer science at The Budapest University of Technology and Economics. He wrote his PhD on semantic technologies and their relation to logic programming. Currently he is a senior lecturer in the Department of Computer Science and Information Theory. He is a co-author of the Hungarian textbook entitled "Theory and Practice of Semantic Web" and the corresponding university course. His research interests are in semantic integration, semantic web and logic programming.

Martin Musicante received his PhD at Universidade Federal de Pernambuco, Brazil in 1996. He is an associate professor at Universidade Federal do Rio Grande do Norte-UFRN (Natal, Brazil), where he acts as head of undergraduate studies in Computer Science. He is part of the graduate program in Computer Science UFRN. He is also a guest researcher at LI - Université François Rabelais Tours, Campus Blois, since 2002. Martin Musicante's main current research topics are XML database theory and Web Services.

Claus Pahl is a senior lecturer at Dublin City University's School of Computing, where he is the leader of the Software and Systems Engineering group. Claus has graduated from the Technical University of Braunschweig and has obtained a PhD from the University of Dortmund. He has published more than 140 papers in various journals, books, conference, and workshop proceedings. He is on the editorial board five journals and is a regular reviewer for journals and conferences in the area of Web and software technologies and their applications. He is the principal investigator of several basic and applied research projects in Web software engineering. Claus' research interests cover a broad spectrum from service- and component technologies in software engineering to infrastructure and development technologies for Web applications.

Ken Pu has received his PhD in computer science from University of Toronto, and is now an assistant professor at Faculty of Science, University of Ontario Institute of Technology. His research area is in database and information systems. His past work includes applications of formal methods to analysis of query quality and correctness, spatio-temporal index structures and visualization of OLAP data. His working research interest is in the area of management and mining of streamed and semi-structured databases and dynamic information-centric processes.

Kamal Taha is a PhD candidate and an instructor in the Department of Computer Science and Engineering at the University of Texas at Arlington. He has nine referred publications that have appeared (or are forthcoming) in conferences and workshops proceedings, in addition to a book chapter. Kamal worked as Engineering Specialist for *Seagate Technology* (a leading computer disc drive manufacturer in the USA) from 1995 to 2005. His research interests include XML keyword and loosely structured querying, distributed XML processing and caching, recommendation systems, and personalized search.

Laszlo Zsolt Varga is a senior scientific associate and head of the System Development Department at MTA SZTAKI. He was visiting researcher in CERN and in the Department of Electronic Engineering at Queen Mary & Westfield College, University of London where his research focused on basic and applied research into the development of multi-agent systems. His current research interests include agent, grid and web computing for semantic interoperability in scientific and business applications. He has PhD in informatics from the Electronic Engineering and Informatics Faculty of the Technical University of Budapest. He is steering committee member of the Artificial Intelligence Special Interest Group of the John von Neumann Computing Society.

Yaoling Zhu is a postgraduate research student at the School of Computing at Dublin City University. Yaoling is a graduate in Computer Science from the Zhengzhou Institute of Engineering, China. Yaoling has extensive experience in the software sector, working for several years as a senior software engineer for multinational companies such as Oracle, where he has been working on e-business outsourcing and Web service technologies in Oracle's European Development and Technology Centre. Yaoling's research focuses on data integration problems in Web-based software systems.

Index

Copyright © 2009, IGI Global, distributing in print or electronic forms without written permission of IGI Global is prohibited.

D

E

F

G

H

I

S

T

U

V

W

X

Z